ALSO BY

Cecil Woodham-Smith

THE REASON WHY

FLORENCE NIGHTINGALE

THE GREAT HUNGER

QUEEN VICTORIA

QUEEN VICTORIA

QUEEN VICTORIA

From her birth to the death of the Prince Consort

CECIL WOODHAM-SMITH

Alfred A. Knopf

New York   1972

THIS IS A BORZOI BOOK
PUBLISHED BY ALFRED A. KNOPF, INC.

Library of Congress Cataloging in Publication Data

Woodham-Smith, Cecil Blanche (Fitz Gerald)
    Queen Victoria.

  1. Victoria, Queen of Great Britain, 1819-1901.
  2. Great Britain—History—Victoria, 1837-1901.
DA554.W8 1972   942.081'092'4 [B]   72-2235
ISBN 0-394-48245-X

Manufactured in the United States of America

FIRST AMERICAN EDITION

To the Memory of

G. I. W–S

Contents

Illustrations

Acknowledgments

My first thanks are due to Her Majesty the Queen, who graciously allowed me access to the Royal Archives at Windsor Castle. I am deeply grateful to the Earl Mountbatten of Burma, K.G., P.C., G.C.B., G.C.V.O., F.R.S., who encouraged me by showing interest in the book from the earliest moment and I owe thanks to the Trustees of the Broadlands Archives who gave me permission to use the Palmerston Papers recently removed from the Archives at Broadlands. I should like to thank Miss Felicity Ranger, Registrar for the National Registry of Archives, for her assistance in making use of them.

I am indebted to Mr R. Mackworth Young, C.V.O., the Royal Librarian, for his advice and for the careful attention he gave the text. Miss Jane Langton, M.V.O., Registrar of the Royal Archives at Windsor, has been a tower of strength. I owe more than I can express to her patience and erudition. I am much obliged to Mr Oliver Millar, C.V.O., for his kind and generous help with the illustrations, and to Mr Hugh Murray Baillie of the Royal Commission on Historical Manuscripts for reading the text and advising me on the difficult subject of German principalities. I am grateful to the Master of Balliol College, Oxford, the librarian and staff for enabling me to obtain permission to use the Conroy Papers and for their assistance while I was consulting them.

I am once again especially indebted to Mr Kenneth Timings and the staff of the Public Record Office for their interest and patience, and for drawing my attention to references and papers I would otherwise have missed. I am under a great obligation to Sir Philip Magnus-Allcroft, who has given me permission to quote his admirable account of the destruction of Queen Victoria's Diary and assisted me by writing, on my behalf, to Mrs Prance, owner of the important Gibbs Papers, which she allowed me to use. I must also express my thanks for information kindly provided by Major-General H. D. W. Sitwell, C.B., M.C., F.S.A., Keeper of the Jewel House, Tower of London; Mr W. Keith Neal and Mr R. Scaltiel, both of the Worshipful Company of Gunmakers; Miss E. Yemm, assistant archivist, Devon Record Office; Mrs D. Gibbens, honorary curator of the Sidmouth Museum, and Mr Orson G. Crane, manager of the Royal Glen

Hotel, Sidmouth. Finally, I owe an overwhelming debt of gratitude to my friend and publisher, Mr Roger Machell. The present volume was written in circumstances of difficulty for me personally; without his encouragement it would never have been begun; without his continued encouragement and support it would never have been finished.

I have refrained from adding names of all those who have helped me but I hope that the staff of the Manuscript Department of the British Museum, the staff of the London Library, Mrs Geoffrey de Bellaigue of the Windsor Archives and Miss Carolyn Merion, my research assistant, will accept my thanks.

QUEEN VICTORIA

Chapter One

By 1819, the year of Queen Victoria's birth, the British Empire was within sight of the heights of power and of wealth from which it was, briefly, to dominate the world.

The final defeat of Napoleon at Waterloo in 1815 had left Britain the leading country in Europe. The great powers of the eighteenth century had been wrecked by the Napoleonic wars, France lay exhausted, bled white, Germany was an uneasy federation of antagonistic states, Austria's predominance was increasingly challenged by Prussia, Spain was barely a third-rate power. In the North, it is true, was the colossus of Russia, but Russia as yet stood apart from Europe, almost another continent. At this moment Britain, small though she was, uninvaded, undefeated, mistress of the seas, 'that right little, tight little island,' in the words of a contemporary song,* held the ascendancy in Europe.

Outside Europe, the Roman Empire itself had not surpassed the extent of the territories and the magnitude of the riches which the British Empire was rapidly acquiring. One of the great periods of world exploration and exploitation was in progress, and because Britain had not been exhausted by the Napoleonic wars and was mistress of the seas, the explorers who opened up unknown territories, and the traders who followed in search of profits, were most frequently British. In Asia, in Africa, in North and South America and Australia, the inhabitants of the most fertile and productive regions were submitting to British authority; year after year fresh areas on the map of the globe were tinted crimson

---

* The song 'The Tight Little Island' was written and composed by Thomas John Dibdin (son of Charles Dibdin, author of the well-known song, 'Tom Bowling') during the Napoleonic wars. The first stanza runs:

> Daddy Neptune one day to Freedom did say
> If ever I live upon dry land
> The spot I should hit on would be little Britain,
> Says Freedom, 'Why that's my own Island!'
> *Chorus*
> Oh! what a snug little Island
> A right little tight little Island,
> All the Globe round none can be found
> So happy as this little Island.

as new provinces and protectorates were added to the Empire until the whole world seemed to have turned British red.

In Great Britain itself, a native wealth of coal and iron combined with long freedom from war on British soil had made possible industrial development on a scale undreamed of. Over immense areas of what had once been country-side the smoke from factory chimneys, the glare of furnaces, the clatter of textile mills, spelt money. Raw materials from countries not yet industrially developed poured into Britain to be manufactured, and—a further source of profit—were transported in British ships. Britannia ruled the waves and carried the goods of the world.

The affluence of the British mercantile and middle classes astonished strangers. The British aristocracy, enriched by the presence of mines, mills and factories on their inherited acres, lived in splendour as great as, if not greater than European princes, and while in Europe, during the past hundred years, war and revolution had taken a heavy toll of the possessions of kings, British sovereigns had enjoyed their revenues and their palaces in security and peace.

Certainly there was discontent, savage discontent—industrial discontent, rural discontent and in Ireland recurrent famines and armed rebellion.

Behind British affluence and prosperity lay a nightmare of poverty, filth and misery. A population leaping upwards in one of the great population explosions of history, industries rapidly expanding, great fortunes being made and a total lack of any protective legislation resulted in living and working conditions which shocked even contemporary Europe. Children of five years old, for instance, were worked fourteen hours a day in factories and mills. But a vast pool of cheap labour was created, and to the low cost of labour the British industralist owed much of his success.

And yet, not only were prosperous British citizens proud and complacent but British workers, in spite of conditions in mine, factory and field, were equally filled with national pride.

A high degree of pride and of complacence was justified. Britain had survived twenty-two years of deadly peril. Trafalgar and Waterloo had been fought and won: Napoleon, Britain's most dangerous enemy, was a prisoner in exile on St Helena: the ninety-nine years of the Pax Britannica had begun.

British belief in the superiority of the British nation knew no bounds. It was an article of faith that one Englishman could beat six Frenchmen, more than six of any other foreign nation, and it was an almost religious conviction that the British possessed a sense of justice and fair play to be found nowhere else. An Englishman stood up for the weak, faced disaster without losing his head, kept his word and never kicked a man when he was down.

2

From the highest to the lowest, the British loved their country with passion. Prince George, son of the Duke of Cambridge, spoke for the nation when he wrote 'The fact is however one likes seeing foreign countries . . . still upon returning to England one feels that everything here is so very superior to what one has seen that one is doubly proud of being an Englishman and of belonging to a nation that has such a country to live in.'[1]

The English throne was the greatest prize in Europe, and, until very recently, the succession to the throne had seemed secure.

True the reigning sovereign, George III, lived shut away in Windsor Castle, victim of a disease (porphyria) not then identified or understood which affected his brain, but he had already produced a family of fifteen children, of whom seven sons and five daughters survived. His eldest son George Prince of Wales, later George IV, who acted as Regent during his father's illness, was married and had a daughter, Princess Charlotte, who would in due course succeed him on the throne.

The Prince's marriage had been disastrous. Undertaken to obtain money to pay his debts, it had ended—after only twelve months and some resounding scandals—in separation. The sole child of the marriage, Princess Charlotte, was however of unquestionable legitimacy, and, handsome and high spirited, she was the darling and hope of the nation.

In 1816 Princess Charlotte married Prince Leopold of Saxe-Coburg. The people of England hailed the marriage with delight. Prince Leopold was intelligent and handsome. It was, said Mr Wilberforce in the House of Commons, not an arranged marriage but 'a marriage of the heart' and for this reason 'the Princess Charlotte and the excellent man of her choice were so much endeared to the nation'.[2] A new age, it was confidently believed, would dawn when Princess Charlotte with her consort sat on the throne.

But after eighteen months of happiness she died, on 6th November 1817, at the age of 21, in giving birth to a stillborn son after a labour of more than fifty hours.

Violent demonstrations of popular grief followed. Never had the nation mourned as it mourned for poor young Charlotte; but more than extremity of grief was involved: issues of the gravest national importance were raised by Charlotte's death.

'. . . The great and general question which everyone asked himself and asked his neighbour' said the Prime Minister, Lord Liverpool, in the House of Lords 'was how will this event operate on the succession to the Crown? . . .' It had hardly been realised, so great had been the national satisfaction in Princess Charlotte, that of the twelve living descendants of George III, the youngest of the seven princes was now 43 years of age,

3

none of the five princesses was under forty and not one had a legitimate child to inherit the throne.

*

The British nation prefers to have a sovereign at the head of the state; indeed the devotion of the British nation to the monarchical system has long been the envy of European rulers. But—the British sovereign must abide by the laws and limitations imposed by British custom and reign as a constitutional monarch. British sovereigns who have attempted to reign as absolute monarchs have found themselves forced to vacate the throne.

It was difficult to contemplate any of the sons of George III as a constitutional sovereign without grave misgivings. The Regent and his brothers were notorious for debts, scandals and discreditable private lives. Thomas Creevey M.P., a shrewd political observer, reported he had been told that 'the profligacy and unpopularity of all the Princes . . . will produce a storm'. Queen Victoria referred to them later as 'my disreputable uncles'. The Duke of Wellington declared they were 'the damnedest millstone about the necks of any Government that can be imagined'.[3] Though all, with the possible exception of the Duke of Clarence, who was inclined to eccentricity, were of more than average intelligence, their upbringing had done nothing to fit them for their position in life. They had been brought up with severity. Princess Augusta, daughter of George III, recalled seeing her two eldest brothers held by their arms like dogs and flogged with a long whip. But they had never been taught the value of money, and the Royal Marriages Act, which declared the marriage of a member of the Royal Family void unless contracted with the consent of the sovereign, freed them from normal responsibility. Lord Melbourne told Queen Victoria 'I don't wonder at their running wild, all very handsome young men; though that Marriage Act may have been a very good thing in many ways, still it sent them like so many wild beasts into society, making love wherever they went and then saying they were very sorry they couldn't marry . . . whereas in general that is a check on a man, that he feels if he is too much about a girl he must marry her, but they were, as it were, quite invincible.' Lord Melbourne added 'They would have married right and left directly, if they could. . . .'[4]

The popularity of Princess Charlotte had owed much to contrast with her uncles, but now Charlotte was dead, and it appeared that the nation, after the Prince Regent should have had his reign, would be ruled by Royal Duke after Royal Duke, unless one managed to produce legitimate offspring.

It was most unlikely that the Prince Regent himself would ever have another child. He was 55 and still married; though he had separated from

4

his wife, Queen Caroline, Princess Charlotte's mother, twenty years before, they had never been divorced. Once a beautiful and captivating youth, excesses in eating and drinking had made him grossly fat. Young women had ceased to interest him, and even if he succeeded in obtaining a divorce and re-married, it was improbable that an heir would result. The succession lay in the hands of the six Royal Dukes, of whom three were already married and three were not.

The first married duke, the Duke of York, was 54, a year younger than the Prince Regent, and had been the husband of the Princess Royal of Prussia, to whom he was conspicuously unfaithful, for twenty-five years. She was an eccentric lady who disliked going to bed, and if she did, remained there only for an hour or two. Her custom was to lie fully dressed on a couch, sometimes in one room, sometimes in another, while a lady in waiting read aloud to her all night. She lived surrounded by troops of dogs, forty at least, besides monkeys and parrots, on whom she lavished her affections. She had no children. In 1809 the Duke of York had been involved in a peculiarly unsavoury scandal. Following a Parliamentary enquiry it had been proved that one of his mistresses had sold army promotions and commissions, with, it was alleged, the knowledge and connivance of the Duke. In consequence he was suspended, for a period, from his appointment as Commander-in-Chief. It cast a startling light on the relations of the royal brothers that the prime mover in the Duke of York's exposure was openly stated to be the Duke of Kent, his younger brother, who considered that he himself should be Commander-in-Chief. However, Greville, the celebrated diarist, who had excellent opportunities of observation as he was Clerk to the Privy Council, distinguished the Duke of York from the other Royal Dukes as being the only one who had the feelings of an English gentleman.[5]

The second married duke, the Duke of Cumberland, the furiously Protestant Grand Master of the Orange lodges, was 46 and had become the third husband of the Princess of Solms-Braunfels in 1815. A disagreeable reactionary, with the appearance of an ogre, due in fact to the effects of a severe facial wound honourably received at the Battle of Tournai in 1794, he was detested and feared by the people of England and believed guilty of frightful crimes, not excluding murder, and of incest with one of his sisters. Considerable scandal also attached to his wife, who was rumoured to have expedited the death of one of her former husbands and who had given mortal offence to King George III and Queen Charlotte. After her first husband, Prince Louis of Prussia, died, she accepted an offer of marriage from the Duke of Cambridge, younger brother of the Duke of Cumberland, only to throw him over without warning and secretly marry the Prince of Solms-Braunfels. '. . . This fatal event has certainly made me very miserable' wrote the Duke of Cambridge to his

5

father.[5] His parents were furious, and, when the Princess, widowed for the second time, married the Duke of Cumberland, Queen Charlotte refused to receive her, nor would Parliament grant the Duke of Cumberland the increased income customary on marriage. The Duke and Duchess of Cumberland had no living children, though early in 1817 a daughter had been born dead.

The third married duke, the Duke of Sussex, aged 44, had been married twice, first to Lady Augusta Murray and after her death to Lady Cecilia Buggin, born Lady Cecilia Gore, widow of Sir George Buggin, well-known in the City of London. Neither match, however, had received the consent of the sovereign, and therefore by the provisions of the Royal Marriages Act, both were void and the Duke's son and daughter by Lady Augusta Murray were not in the line of succession to the throne.

Of the three unmarried dukes, the eldest, the Duke of Clarence, was 52. He had served in the Navy, and been Nelson's friend and best man at Nelson's wedding. For nearly twenty years he lived in quiet domesticity with the well-known comedy actress, Mrs Jordan, by whom he had ten much loved illegitimate children, but in 1811 he abruptly left her. The explanation, she wrote, was '*money*, money ... or the want of it'.[7] In common with five out of the six Royal Dukes, the Duke of Clarence was overwhelmed with debts. He proceeded to try and improve his finances by marrying an heiress, proposing first to five rich English women and then to two foreign princesses, one the sister of the Tsar of Russia. Refused by all seven ladies, he returned to the house in Bushey where he had lived with Mrs Jordan, and settled down there with his ten children. Five years later, having lost her voice and her popularity, Mrs Jordan died in reduced circumstances in lodgings outside Paris.

The death of Princess Charlotte brought the Duke of Clarence new importance. After the Prince Regent and the Duke of York, both childless and unlikely to found a family, he would succeed to the throne, and, judging by the size of his illegitimate family, it seemed possible that, if he married, he might, even now, provide for the succession.

The youngest of the unmarried dukes, the Duke of Cambridge, was 43, and the only Royal Duke not heavily in debt. It was, however, pointed out in the House of Commons that the Duke of Cambridge had practised economy in circumstances which made economy easy. In London he had had a 'table', food and wine provided for himself and his friends at St James's Palace: in Hanover he had a town house, a country house, a shooting lodge, the use of the stables and servants and an income of about £18,000 a year, worth double its purchasing power in England. He had never kept a mistress and the only proposal of marriage he was known to have made was to the lady who was now Duchess of Cumberland. Henry Brougham, known to his contemporaries as 'that devil Brougham' on account of his biting wit, power of invective and recklessness of statement, commented that 'viewing, as he did, economy not only as meritorious but as a virtue (and if not a virtue the most rigid moralist would allow it to be the parent of many virtues) he should offer to his Royal Highness the tribute of his admiration'.[8] The Duke spent many hours practising his violin, sang, took an interest in science, gave entertainments which were greatly appreciated in Hanover, and invested large sums in the funds. He wore a blond wig, was not ungenerous, lent money on occasion to his brothers, but was apt to talk too much.

One more Royal Duke remained, Edward, Duke of Kent, fourth son of George III, unmarried, but accompanied by a middle-aged mistress with whom he had lived for twenty-seven years, and destined to become the father of Queen Victoria.

In 1817 the Duke of Kent was fifty, a tall, heavy, stately man, 'of soldier-like bearing' conveying a formidable impression of strength and obstinacy, with a high colour, a fleshy arrogant face, prominent eyes and a bald head with a fringe of hair and whiskers dyed black. In spite of his bald head, however, he 'might still be considered a handsome man'.[9] His career had been in the Army and as a military commander he was despotic and harsh, a notorious disciplinarian, merciless to his troops. Yet he had some redeeming qualities: he was humane to animals, opposing for instance the cruel practice, then fashionable, of docking horses' tails; he was fond of young people and was liked by them. It was less sympathetic that although ready with protestations of friendship and promises he was not to be relied on. '. . . damme! d'ye know what his sisters call him?' said the Duke of Wellington. 'By God! they call him *Joseph* Surface!'[10] (the arch hypocrite in Sheridan's play *The School for Scandal*). Liberal principles were in the minority among the upper classes in England, but the Duke of Kent professed himself to be a Liberal and had Radical friends, infuriating his Tory brothers with all of whom he was 'on most unfriendly terms'.

He was, with the exception of the Prince Regent, the most intelligent of the six brothers. The Duke of Wellington observed that he never knew any man with more natural eloquence in conversation than the Duke of Kent, 'always choosing the best topics for each particular person, and expressing them in the happiest language'. He excelled in after-dinner speeches—'all the brothers tried . . . but he alone greatly succeeded'[11]— and in drawing up statements. He united a pedantic love of detail with a love of interfering and setting right, and 'maintained an active and very extensive correspondence, which three or four private secretaries were scarcely able to master. . . . His name was never uttered without a sigh by the functionaries of every public office.' Greville, who disliked the

7

Duke of Kent, declared he was 'the greatest rascal that ever went unhung', 'far the worst of the family', and asserted that when Queen Victoria came to the throne people were watching for 'the bad blood to come out'.[12] But the Duke's mistress, Madame de St Laurent, remained with him for twenty-seven years; his wife, Queen Victoria's mother, loved him; he was Princess Charlotte's 'favourite and beloved uncle', and for more than twenty-five years Maria Fitzherbert, the beautiful, devout Catholic widow, with whom the Prince Regent had fallen in love and whom he had illegally married, was his friend. Addressing her as 'my ever dearest Mrs Fitzherbert' he confided his difficulties and grievances to her in frequent long letters.[13]

He was not, and he never had been, happy. From the beginning of his life he was consumed by a sense of grievance. First, in his estimation, he was unfairly treated by his parents. The truth was they did not like him. 'George III always had his eyes marvellously open to the Duke's faults; and Queen Charlotte, who never would see the Regent's errors, nor admit as excessive the lavish expenditure of that costly personage, regarded Edward's wants as "monstrous"—and himself as a paragon of "imprudence and extravagance".'[14] Born Prince Edward Augustus he was raised to the dignity of Duke of Kent, with a Parliamentary grant of £12,000 a year, when he was 28. This was in itself a grievance, since his brothers the Dukes of York and Clarence had received their grants and dukedoms at 23 and 24 respectively. The Duke of Kent calculated that the delay had deprived him of at least £60,000.

Debts proved his curse. He began to borrow at 17, when he was sent to Hanover to be given a German military training. His parents did not, he considered, give him sufficient money to live in a style befitting a Prince of the Blood Royal of England, so he was forced into borrowing and had continued to borrow ever since.

In his personal habits he was a strictly moderate man, rising at 5 a.m., eating sparingly, frowning on gambling, and drinking little. He detested drunkenness, and his officers were required to smell the breath of the non-commissioned officers, and the non-commissioned officers the breath of the men, before the regiment came on parade. In action he was courageous and distinguished himself for bravery in the West Indian campaign against the French, though here too he had a grievance, '. . . the wish entertained then in certain quarters was that I might *fall*' he wrote mysteriously. He had a taste for music, his band of wind instruments accompanied him everywhere, and he appreciated the points of a good horse.[15]

But his virtues brought him no reward. He received neither the military promotion nor the income which he considered his due; on the contrary, reprimands and writs were his daily lot. Child of misfortune as he felt himself to be, circumstances conspired to increase his financial embarrassments. He was involved, for instance, in heavy losses over his 'outfits'. At this period the word 'outfit' covered any articles and equipment bought for a special purpose. An ambassador going to a post in a foreign city took an outfit with him, officers of the Army proceeding abroad acquired an outfit, when one of the Royal Family married it was usual for Parliament to vote a sum for an outfit, as well as an income. Plate, glass, linen, china, furniture and furnishings, wine, books might all be included. As a result of friction arising from excessive severity to his troops while the Duke was in command at Gibraltar he was sent to Canada, and during his Canadian service he lost his outfits no less than six times. Three were captured by the enemy, England then being at war with France; one, packed on sledges for transport during the Canadian winter, cracked through the ice and vanished into the depths of Lake Champlain before the Duke's eyes; two were wrecked. A particularly fine outfit which had cost the Duke between £11,000 and £15,000 and included 5,000 books, went to the bottom, with all hands, off the North American coast. The Duke reckoned that his personal loss on his outfits was well above £25,000.[16]

As he grew older his character hardened. He had been trained in the German school of savage and pedantic military discipline, and to be commanded by the Duke of Kent was, as the Duke of Wellington remarked, 'fraught with petty vexations'. For example, officers found themselves compelled to be attended by their hairdresser at 4 a.m. in order to appear on morning parade with every curl placed exactly as the Duke laid down, while the troops, endlessly polishing and pipe-claying, drilled to exhaustion and mercilessly punished, were 'unable to endure the discipline to which the regiment was subjected'.[17] Wherever the Duke of Kent was in command there were floggings, punishments, executions and, as the men grew desperate, desertions and mutinies.

In 1803 the Duke's military career abruptly ended. Appointed for the second time to command at Gibraltar, where the garrison admittedly was out of hand, he restored order with such frightful severity that a serious mutiny broke out. Saying farewell to Canada to which he had been sent in exile in 1791 owing to the 'bestial severity' of his discipline and leaving eleven soldiers behind him in barracks awaiting their execution under sentences of death, the Duke, accompanied by Madame de St Laurent, landed at Gibraltar in May 1802 and a reign of terror followed.[18] The barrack square resounded with 'fearful blood-curdling cries of men being flogged by the Duke of Kent's orders, 100 lashes being the punishment for trifling defaults in dress'. Sentences of 400, 500 and 700 lashes were given: three Spaniards were hanged for stealing £500 of goods. A private soldier named La Rose, unable to bear the severity, deserted. The Duke of Kent assisted in tracking the man down, signed the sentence imposing 999 lashes, the maximum allowed under the Mutiny Act, and witnessed its execution. This episode was followed by the flogging to death of Serjeant Benjamin Charles Armstrong and an enquiry on 5th March 1803 into the Duke's conduct. Fury against him was such that a conspiracy to assassinate him involved almost the whole rank and file of the Army. In consequence the Duke was informed that he would receive no further active military employment. He was, however, promoted Field Marshal in 1804.

The next fourteen years were spent by the Duke in England struggling with his debts, though he purchased a house for Madame de St Laurent in Knightsbridge and a country house, Castle Hill, near what was then the rural village of Ealing, on which he spent £50,000. 'His pecuniary difficulties goaded him to the very quick' and his heart, he wrote in 1815, was 'half-broken'. He appealed to his brother the Prince Regent, wrote to the Prime Minister, drew up a number of schemes to borrow a substantial sum of money, pay off his debts and repay the borrowed sum by instalments.[19] Mr Joseph Hume, the well-known Radical, was invited to examine the Duke's affairs and the Duke drew up a statement dealing with the possibility of approaching some millionaire, perhaps Sir Francis Baring who was noted for his liberality, who would deal with his financial difficulties on a non-commercial basis and lend him money in consideration of his rank. The same idea had also occurred to the Duke of Clarence. All schemes were unsuccessful and by the spring of 1816 it was clear that the Duke of Kent would have to resort to drastic remedies. In March he paid a visit to Brussels, then famous for its low cost of living, and took the lease from an Admiral Donnelly of a furnished house, standing in its own grounds, with a stable yard, a fine flower garden and plenty of fruit on the walls, which with white-washing, painting, carpeting and installing a number of stoves might, he thought, be made comfortable. A meeting of his creditors was held and a committee formed to whom the Duke handed over his income of £27,000 a year. The committee allowed him £11,000 a year for living expenses, the remaining £16,000 a year to be applied to paying off his debts. The Duke expected to live abroad for a number of years.

To provide ready money the solvent Duke of Cambridge raised a bond with Mr Thomas Coutts on his brother's behalf for £4,200, and on 19th August 1816, preceded by Madame de St Laurent, the Duke of Kent left England for Brussels.[20] It was in Brussels in November 1817 that he received the news of Princess Charlotte's death.

On 11th December 1817, the Duke of Kent asked Mr Creevey, the wit and politician who was also economising in Brussels, to come and see him: a remarkable conversation took place. The subject was the Duke's marriage. He would have to marry, said the Duke. Now that Princess Charlotte was dead, marriage was being forced on him for the sake of the succession, though God only knew the sacrifice he would make in separating from Madame de St Laurent, with whom he had lived in all climates and all difficulties for twenty-seven years. What would be Mr Creevey's feelings, asked the Duke, if he was forced to separate from Mrs Creevey? Unfortunately, a few days before at breakfast he had tossed over to Madame de St Laurent a copy of the *Morning Chronicle* newspaper, in which she had read a demand for his immediate marriage for the sake of the succession. She had been most painfully affected, had all but fallen into a fit and the Duke had 'entertained serious apprehensions for her safety'. He went on to remark that if Madame de St Laurent was to return to live amongst her friends, 'it must be in such a state of independence as to command their respect'. As for himself he wanted very little, though a few servants and a carriage would be necessary. He added that when he married, suppose he did marry, he would be ready to accept the same settlement as the Duke of York had received in 1792, an additional £25,000 a year, and would make no claim on account of the fall in the value of money since that date. The Duke then remarked that Mr Creevey had possibly heard the names of the Princess of Baden and the Princess of Saxe-Coburg mentioned as possible brides: the Princess of Saxe-Coburg would probably be the better connection, since she was the sister of Prince Leopold of Saxe-Coburg, husband of the late Princess Charlotte, who was extremely popular in England. However, before any steps were taken, the Government and the nation must do justice to Madame de St Laurent.[21]

In fact the Duke of Kent had been looking out for a suitable wife for nearly two years before Princess Charlotte's death. He was being forced into marriage, as his elder brother the Prince of Wales had been forced into his disastrous marriage with Caroline of Brunswick, by the pressure of his debts. A marriage approved under the Royal Marriages Act would bring him an increased income from Parliament, money for an 'outfit' and, perhaps, a sum towards clearing his indebtedness.

Early in 1816 the Duke had suggested to the Russian Ambassador in London that Princess Katherine Amelia of Baden might be a suitable match for him. She was extremely well connected, twin sister of the Queen of Bavaria, sister of the Tsarina of Russia, of the ex-Queen of Sweden and of the Grand Duchess of Hesse. The Duke borrowed a thousand guineas from the Tsar[22] for the expenses of a journey of inspection (the Russian Ambassador noted that as soon as the Duke received the thousand guineas he asked for a bearskin as well) and on 12th September 1816 left Brussels in his travelling 'baroutsch'. Madame de St Laurent was conveniently visiting her sister in Paris.

The introduction took place on 18th September at Darmstadt and was a failure. '. . . that odious Princess Amelia of Baden' wrote the Duke to Mrs Fitzherbert. He had seen 'the old maiden' and though she was well connected, 'from her being the only one of the six sisters left on hand at the age of 41 and the eldest too, you may judge how little desirable she is . . .'.[23]

There was, however, as the Duke had mentioned to Mr Creevey, another possibility, the lady whom he described as the Princess of Saxe-Coburg, sister of Prince Leopold, who was in fact the Dowager Princess of Leiningen, Princess Victoire,[24] a young widow with two children, thirty years of age, inclined to plumpness but with a good figure, fine brown eyes and hair and a fresh complexion. '. . . most lively' wrote one of her sisters-in-law, 'with not at all a *handsome* but *a very pretty countenance*'. A friend who had known her from childhood pronounced her 'altogether most charming and attractive. Nature had endowed her with warm feelings and she was naturally truthful, affectionate and friendly, unselfish, full of sympathy, and generous.'[25]

She had not had an easy life. At just 17 she had been married to a widower twenty-three years older than herself, whose first wife* had been her mother's sister and who openly declared he would never have contemplated marrying again if his only son had not died as well as his wife.

The marriage was solemnised in 1803, Prince Charles succeeding to the principality of Leiningen in 1805. He was gloomy and morose in character, tormented by gout and given to brooding angrily over lands and rights which had been taken from him by Napoleon. Most of his time was spent at his hunting lodge in the forest, Wald Leiningen, while his young wife was left at his residence of Amorbach, near Darmstadt, 'in quiet solitude' with her lady-in-waiting, Baroness Spaeth. The administration of the household, as well as of the principality, was tightly controlled by Prince Charles, who permitted 'no slightest participation' by his young wife. The relationship between the Prince and Princess of Leiningen, wrote an observer at the court, was 'the authority of the uncle and the reverence of the niece'.[26]

In July 1814, however, Prince Charles died, leaving his wife Regent of Leiningen and guardian of their two children, Prince Charles, now nearly 12 years of age, and Princess Feodora, aged ten.

The young Dowager Princess needed an adviser. She was untrained in business, lacked self-confidence, was over-anxious and had been

* The first wife of Charles Emich of Leiningen was born Henrietta Reuss zu Ebersdorf. Her sister Augusta married Francis Duke of Saxe-Coburg and Saalfeld. Princess Henrietta died in 1801 and Charles Emich of Leiningen married secondly in 1803 Augusta Duchess of Saxe-Coburg's youngest daughter Princess Victoire, who was therefore his first wife's niece.

brought up to accept the decisions of others. To add to her difficulties her late husband's advisers began to quarrel violently amongst themselves.

One of them was Captain 'von' Schindler. The son of an official at the Court of the Counts of Reuss—the family of the Prince of Leiningen's first wife—young Schindler had attracted the Prince's attention, been taken under his protection and eventually entered the Austrian service, rising to the rank of captain. The Prince of Leiningen appointed him Master of the Horse and though a commoner, Schindler proceeded to assume the prefix of nobility 'von'. He had had very little education, but understood the art of pleasing, especially of pleasing women, and was an accomplished courtier. After the Prince's death he advanced rapidly, was appointed Master of the Household as well as Master of the Horse, and in a short time was taking a leading part in the government of Leiningen, holding a little court of flatterers, being addressed as 'Excellency', and acting as co-Regent with the Dowager Princess.

However, the Princess's life was about to change. Since her brother Prince Leopold's marriage in 1816, she had struck up an enthusiastic friendship, by correspondence, with his wife Princess Charlotte, who had a special reason for feeling affection and gratitude towards her uncle the Duke of Kent. She had fallen in love with Prince Leopold, who was remarkably good-looking, when he came to London in 1814 but for nearly two years her father, the Prince Regent, had refused to consider the match, and between 1814 and 1816 the letters between them, 'all this delicate correspondence', passed through the Duke of Kent's hands. 'Otherwise' wrote Leopold 'it would have been impossible as she was really treated as a sort of prisoner.' The Duke of Kent was 'the chief promoter of the marriage'.[27]

Since the Duke was looking for a wife, who could be a better bride for Princess Charlotte's favourite uncle than her charming sister-in-law, the young widowed Dowager Princess of Leiningen?* During his journey to Germany, Princess Charlotte arranged for the Duke to visit Amorbach and gave him a letter, 'not of introduction but of recommendation', which he was himself to place in the Dowager Princess's hands.

The Duke arrived at Amorbach, stayed a day or two, was entertained one evening by a 'concert of wind instruments' which, he wrote, was 'perfect', admired the Dowager Princess and forthwith plunged into a proposal of marriage. In an immensely long letter[28] he confessed that the object of his visit to Amorbach was to make the acquaintance of the Dowager Princess. After referring to his close friendship with Princess Charlotte and Prince Leopold, he came to the point: the Dowager Princess had so many graces, such charming manners and accomplishments

* See Appendix 1.

exactly to his taste, that he would regard it as the greatest good fortune that could befall him if she would share his lot. His brother, the Prince Regent, he assured her, desired him to marry and he sketched out their future life; the winters, for the next three or four years, in fact until he had paid off his debts, would be spent at Brussels where he had taken an excellent house, the summers at Amorbach, paying *short* visits to England. With the aid of the Princess's accomplishments, the pleasure of her delicious band and some good horses, the days could never be too long. He was ready, however, to accept any other arrangement the Princess preferred and 'from the day when I shall have the happiness of possessing you I shall cherish your dear children as my own'. Begging the Princess to pardon his temerity, he asked for two lines in reply immediately.

He was rejected.[29]

The Duke had a powerful enemy in Schindler, and Schindler was against the match. One look would have told him that the Duke was the last man to tolerate either Schindler himself or his pretensions. The objections Schindler raised were nevertheless powerful; it was 'sheer stupidity' he declared, for the Dowager Princess after 'such sad experiences during her first marriage', to give up her 'enviable independence'. She would sacrifice about £5,000 a year to marry another elderly man, older than the Prince of Leiningen had been when she married him, 'whom she hardly knows by sight'. The Duchess of Kent was born in 1786, so in 1803 when she married the Prince of Leiningen and he was 23 years older than she, he was 40 and she was 17. The Duke of Kent was born in 1767, so when she married him in 1817 he was 50 and she was 31. The Duke had, however, made an extremely favourable impression on the Dowager Princess. The real obstacle was the guardianship of her children.[30] Fatherless children of the princely houses of Germany, of which Leiningen was one, were placed under the authority of the Court of Wards, composed of sovereigns presided over by the Grand Duke of Baden. The agnates, the relatives of the children on the male side, had rights of supervision and control, and in the case of the Leiningen children the situation was complicated. Charles, son of the Dowager Princess, was the only representative of the legitimate line. The agnates were descended from an illegitimate branch, which had wrongfully contrived to assume the name and pretensions of Leiningen. If the Princess re-married she feared the agnates would dispute her guardianship in the Court of Wards and contrive to have it taken away from her, especially if she left Amorbach for any length of time.

The Duke did not despair. He was 'pleased and flattered' to hear from Prince Leopold that he had made a good impression. Perhaps, he told the Prince, he had been too precipitate in proposing. As for taking the Princess away, he found Amorbach and its neighbourhood 'delicious' and there could be no question, at the moment, of an establishment in England, since from his income of £27,000 a year, he was paying out £16,000 to liquidate his debts.[31]

Princess Charlotte and Prince Leopold continued to press the Dowager Princess to consent and by the New Year of 1817 she was telling Princess Charlotte that while she was certain the Duke of Kent possessed every quality to make a woman happy, and that she would find in this union all the happiness she wished, there still were 'obstacles'.[32] An affectionate correspondence between the sisters-in-law continued; Princess Charlotte became pregnant, was overjoyed, though there were, reported Lady Holland, 'some strange awkward symptoms',[33] and received good advice from her sister-in-law. On 6th November 1817 the calamity occurred and she died.

The marriage of the Duke of Kent now assumed dynastic importance. That of the Duke of Cambridge was already being arranged. With remarkable promptitude he had sent off his proposals to Augusta Princess of Hesse-Cassel before Princess Charlotte had been dead ten days. 'The succession stakes' had started and Prince Leopold urged the Duke of Kent to insist on an answer, adding that, distraught with grief though he was, he had himself sent a letter to his sister.[34]

At this juncture a strong partisan of the Duke of Kent returned to Amorbach. Polyxene von Tubeuf,* a handsome young woman in her middle twenties and a favourite of the Dowager Princess, came back from a long visit to Dantzig and took up arms for the Duke. '. . . Should the Princess renounce not only her conjugal happiness but also a connection to the first of all Royal Courts? Never!' she exclaimed. Detesting Schlinder, she 'employed from now on every weapon of her mind and eloquence to show up the cunning selfish foe in his true light, and, when she succeeded in this, to urge the still hesitating mind, still fighting the inner battle between conflicting duties, into a decision. "How could you" quoth she in the heat of her ardour "reject such an honourable proposal. . . . Did you not confess that the fine figure of the Duke, his refined and tactful and noble behaviour has left a deep impression on you? Follow the voice of your heart!". . .'

* Born on 23rd April 1792, daughter of Baron von Tubeuf, a 'Forstmeister' (Ranger) in the service of the Prince of Leiningen, Freiin Polyxene von Tubeuf became an intimate friend of the young Dowager Princess, who entrusted her with the education of her daughter. Polyxene married George Wagner, tutor to Charles Prince of Leiningen with whom he remained as Counsellor until the Prince's death in 1856. George Wagner himself died on 15th October 1869. He and Polyxene had a daughter, named Victoire, and a son, Eduard. Their seven grandchildren received an annuity from Queen Victoria until their majority. As a young man Prince Leopold, later King of the Belgians, seems to have had an admiration for Polyxene but the romance ended when Prince Leopold joined the Russian army in October 1810 and went to London in the suite of the Tsar. Polyxene herself died on 7th September 1848.[35]

Early in 1818 the admonishments of Polyxene von Tubeuf received powerful support from the Prince Regent. It was intimated unofficially that the Prince Regent approved the proposed marriage of the Duke of Kent, and intended, as soon as a formal announcement was made, to write round to the sovereigns composing the Court of Wards, informing them that Prince Charles of Leiningen and his sister Princess Feodora were under the Prince Regent's protection. Before the power of 'the first of all Royal Courts' opposition melted. Though the official announcement by the Grand Duke of Baden that the Dowager Princess would retain her guardianship after re-marriage was not made until the spring, on 25th January 1818 the Princess wrote to the Duke 'Monseigneur . . . my hand is yours'. Since she need not desert her children, and since the Duke had consented to spend a part of each year in Germany, she had no further objections to make. She was as flattered as she was honoured by his proposal and hoped he would find happiness with a woman he had only glimpsed once and whose qualities and faults he did not know. She reminded him that Charlotte, for whom she had never ceased to weep, had wished for the marriage.[36]

The Duke replied in a tender letter '. . . I want you to know, my very dear Princess, that I am nothing more than a soldier, 50 years old and after 32 years of service not very fitted to captivate the heart of a young and charming Princess, who is 19 years younger'. He would, he vowed, make her the first object of his life and in the care he would take of her, his tenderness and affection, she might be able to forget the difference in age.[37]

On 29th May 1818 at half past nine in the evening the Duke of Kent and the Dowager Princess of Leiningen were married, according to the rites of the Lutheran Church, in the Hall of the Giants in the Schloss Ehrenburg, Coburg. The Duke had borrowed £3,000 from Thomas Coutts for the expenses of his marriage and honeymoon and was expecting a substantial extra allowance, and an 'outfit' of at least £12,000 for furnishing a suitable establishment, to be granted him by Parliament.

The ceremony was impressive,[38] the magnificent hall brightly lit, the guests richly dressed. The Duke as he stood waiting for his bride 'looked very well in his English Field Marshal's uniform'; the Princess was 'charming' in a dress of the pale silk lace called 'blonde', adorned with orange blossoms and white roses. Both bride and groom were seen to be deeply moved during the ceremony, though the Princess's mother, the Dowager Duchess of Coburg, had been surprised to find her daughter so 'unperturbed' at the prospect of becoming the wife of a man she had only seen once. 'May she' wrote the Dowager Duchess in her diary '. . . find in this second marriage a happiness which she never found in the first.' After a salute of guns and a state banquet the Dowager Duchess conducted the newly married couple to their apartment. Calling on them at breakfast time next morning, she 'found the pair sitting together in friendly intimacy'. From the first their relationship was, as it remained, harmonious, even the Duke of Cumberland admitting 'Edward was most happy with her'.

Four days later bride and bridegroom left for England, where a second marriage was to be celebrated in accordance with the rites of the Church of England.

Madame de St Laurent, the mistress with whom the Duke had lived for more than twenty-seven years, departed for Paris and was henceforward known as the Comtesse de Montgenet, a courtesy title granted by Louis XVIII.

Although the sister with whom Madame de St Laurent now proposed to live was known as the Comtesse de Jansac, there are circumstances which make it improbable that the family were of aristocratic descent.

Until recently it was a favourite theory that Madame de St Laurent was a French Canadian widow, member of an aristocratic Catholic family, whom the Duke met when he was sent to Canada in 1792. In Canada it has also been widely believed that the Duke of Kent and Madame de St Laurent were married and had children, and to this day in Quebec and in London persons alleged to be their descendants are pointed out as being the rightful sovereigns of Great Britain.

Exhaustive research into Madame de St Laurent's career has recently been carried out by a Canadian writer.[39] The volume, which traces her birth to Besançon, derives, as far as local information is concerned, from 'material at the Bibliothèque Municipale at Besançon'. Madame de St Laurent is identified as the daughter of a civil engineer called Jean Montgenet and his wife Claudine (née Pussot). She was mistress to two members of the French aristocracy before joining the Duke of Kent at Gibraltar (her second French protector having lost his fortune through the revolution). She was not married to the Duke, and had no children by him. In any event their marriage could not have conformed with the provisions of the Royal Marriages Act and received the consent of the reigning sovereign.

The Duke of Kent told Mr Creevey in 1817 that Madame de St Laurent was 'of very good family and has never been an actress, and I am the first and only person who ever lived with her'.[40] He met her in 1790 when he was still Prince Edward (his dukedom was conferred in 1799), and she was then described as 'the charming Mdlle de St Laurent', a 'jeune personne' engaged not only to sing with Prince Edward's band but to live with him. The terms were plain. A Monsieur Fontiny, acting as Prince Edward's agent in the matter, had been instructed to find the Prince a young person who would not only be an ornament to the Prince's concerts, but also his 'amie' and at the same time as she shared his bed ('qu'elle partagera mon lit'), do the honours of his house and receive whoever the Prince chose to invite. These terms were accepted by Mdlle de St Laurent before she had even seen the Prince.[41]

Unquestionably the Duke would have liked to marry Madame de St Laurent and their long connection displays the mutual consideration and domesticity which characterise a successful marriage. They were the same age and long after the charms of youth had passed the Duke continued to be deeply attached to Madame de St Laurent. A contemporary pamphlet describes 'The Duke's affection for his old French lady, whom he lamented he could not marry.'[42] Twenty-four years after they first lived together, the Duke would not leave her to go out to dinner when she was unwell. 'If on Sunday or Monday I should feel more easy about quitting her, for a few hours,' he wrote to Sir William Beechey in 1814 'I will then without fail apprise you.'[43] He told a friend they 'had never for a moment been separated during the preceding twenty-eight years'.

After the Duke married the Princess of Leiningen, though he did not see Madame de St Laurent, they wrote to each other and his solicitude for her was anxious. Writing from Amorbach to ask his friend the Baron de Mallet and his wife to call 'on our excellent friend the Comtesse de Montgenet', who was in Paris at the Hotel de St Aldegonde, 116 Rue de Grenelle, Faubourg St Germain, he begged the de Mallets to 'bear in mind, that her nerves are *still* in a *very critical* state, and to avoid, if possible, therefore, *any* allusion to the Duchess'. An old friend had called on the Comtesse, praised the Duchess and spoken in such terms of her relationship with the Duke that the Comtesse's feelings were 'hurt a good deal and those I am particularly anxious to spare, for, although an intimacy now of eight months with the Duchess has attached me *sincerely* to *her*, in every point that regards the Countess de Montgenet we must *never* lose sight that our unexpected separation arose from the imperative duty I owed to obey the call of my family and my Country to marry, and *not* from the least diminution in an attachment which had stood the test of twenty-eight years and which, but for *that* circumstance, would unquestionably have kept up the connexion, until it became the lot of one or other of us to be removed from this world'.[44]

The Duke's affection for the Duchess was genuine. After again describing, this time to Lord Buchan,[45] the pain with which he had parted from Madame de St Laurent, he wrote 'but after saying this it is a duty I owe to the amiable partner whom I have taken for life, and of whose estimable character I perceive your lordship is *fully aware*, to add that I never can be sufficiently grateful to Providence, for having permitted me to draw such a prize, and I trust my conduct to her will prove that I appreciate the boon. . . .'

At 4 p.m. on the afternoon of Monday, 13th July 1818, the Duke and Duchess of Kent were married at the Palace of Kew, in a double wedding with the Duke of Clarence, who married Princess Adelaide, aged 25, eldest daughter of George Frederick Charles Duke of Saxe Meiningen. In the case of the Duke of Clarence no previous marriage had taken place. The ceremony took place at Kew instead of at the 'Queen's House' (now Buckingham Palace) because Queen Charlotte, mother of the two dukes and Consort of George III, was too ill to make the journey to London. The formidable little old Queen, mother of fifteen children, was failing, was subject to 'spasms', and died four months later. She had recently suffered a severe attack following the news that the Duchess of Cambridge, wife of her favourite son, had been seen to meet and embrace the Duchess of Cumberland, of whom she violently disapproved, and whom she refused to receive: '. . . she was in such a rage that the spasm was brought on, and she was very near dying'.[46]

A temporary altar was set up in the drawing-room at Kew. The Archbishop of Canterbury and the Bishop of London officiated, the Prince Regent gave away the two brides and a wedding banquet followed. After a few days at Claremont with Prince Leopold, the Duke and Duchess returned to the Duke's apartment in Kensington Palace.

It was already apparent that the Duke and Duchess had better return to Amorbach. The £3,000 which Mr Coutts had lent for the Duke's marriage expenses was inadequate. Under the marriage contract, £1,500 was due to the Duchess. In addition, £500 had to go to Madame de St Laurent ('. . . you must be aware' wrote the Duke to Mr Coutts '*that* is a point that can suffer no delay') leaving only £1,000, far more than which the Duke had spent on wedding presents alone. He had given the Duchess jewellery from Burchardt, two saddle horses, his own miniature and a pianoforte at a cost of £1,670.1.2 and paid for a riding habit which cost £12.0.6 and music costing £30.3.0. He had bought the Duchess perfumery to the value of £75 and paid for the wedding dress of blonde silk lace which cost £97.6.0. The Duchess was fond of hats—she generally chose to have her portrait painted wearing a hat—and several sums were paid to milliners, the largest amounting to £108.10.0; others were for £26.16.3, £26.5.0 and £14.7.0. Brussels lace accounted for two items of £100 and £18. Presents given by the Duke on marriage to personages at Coburg and Amorbach, including £42 for 'small jewellery', amounted to £1,220.11.0. The Prince Regent's servants were given £20 'for attention to the Duchess', and the widow of a postilion, killed while driving one of the Duke's carriages between Sittingbourne and Rochester, received £31.[47]

Marriage plunged the Duke still further into debt and the behaviour of the House of Commons with regard to increasing his allowance on marriage had been a severe disappointment. In November 1817 the Duke had mentioned a figure of £25,000 a year to Mr Creevey; he also expected £12,000 for an 'outfit'. In fact £6,000 a year and nothing for an 'outfit' was all the Duke was able to obtain, and the House of Commons had shown itself to be in a bad temper. Mr Brougham objected to the idea that one of the younger princes had only to be named to receive £6,000 annually. Lord Althorp said that it might be desirable for some of the Royal Family to marry, but it was not desirable that the country should be called on to enable all of them to marry. Sir Charles Monck considered that no other member of the Royal Family should come to the House and ask for an additional allowance till all hope of increase from the marriage of the Duke of Clarence had ceased.[48] 'By God' said the Duke of Wellington on these scenes being reported to him '. . . they [the Royal Dukes] have insulted—*personally* insulted—two-thirds of the gentlemen of England, and how can it be wondered at that they take their revenge upon them when they get them in the House of Commons? It is their only opportunity, and I think, by God! they are quite right to use it.'[49]

The Duke of Kent had hoped something might result from a 'full discussion' with Mr Joseph Hume, the noted Radical, one of the committee who administered his income on behalf of his creditors. The Duke considered that having regard to the heavy expenses he had been forced to incur in connection with his marriage and the inadequate funds provided, he was entitled to some financial concession. Mr Hume unfortunately was abroad. The Prince Regent disliked the Duke intensely and having given the Duchess away at her wedding and entertained the pair at Carlton House, would do no more. His mother, Queen Charlotte, 'a person' remarked the Duke 'of the greatest possible firmness of mind', pressed him to leave the country immediately. A careful old lady, she was afraid she would be asked to lend him money from her privy purse.

Early in September the Duke and Duchess were on their way back to Amorbach.

On 11th September they visited the Duke of Wellington at Valenciennes. Three years after Waterloo there was still an allied army of occupation in the Low Countries under the supreme command of the Duke, and that night there was a dinner and ball. The Duchess of Kent 'waltzed a little, and the Duke put his hand on her cheek to feel if she was not too hot', a 'display of tenderness' which was observed with amusement.[50] At this moment, however, the Duke and Duchess were probably entertaining the first hopes that she was pregnant. Eight months later Princess Victoria was born.

By the middle of November the pregnancy of the Duchess was certain and on 18th November 1818, in one of his immense letters, the Duke through Sir Benjamin Bloomfield, the Prince Regent's private secretary and privy seal, officially informed the Prince Regent of her expectations.

The situation called for tact. The Prince Regent's separation from his wife, Princess Caroline, had now lasted for twenty years. The strain of their long bitter scandalous quarrel and the death of his only child Princess Charlotte, though he had been unable to love the daughter of the wife he detested, had brought him to a state of morbid sensibility on the subject of the succession.

The Duke of Kent's letter was calculated to produce irritation. Though the Duke always disclaimed ambitions and never failed to point out that any child of his must come after the children of his three elder brothers, he was inwardly certain that his child would succeed to the throne. 'My brothers' he often said 'are not so strong as I am; I have led a regular life, I shall outlive them all; the crown will come to me and my children.'[51] Gossip said that he was also influenced by the prophecy of a gipsy at Gibraltar that he would have a daughter who would become a great Queen.[52]

In this spirit, swelling with importance, he wrote to Sir Benjamin, enclosing a few lines for the Prince Regent, who, as he was aware, did not like to be bored with long letters, stating that the Duchess would be confined in May 'in consequence of which we shall feel it our duty to set out for England early in April . . . it is incumbent upon us to adopt such measures, as will enable the child to be born at home'.[53] He relied on the Prince Regent, 'the goodness of his heart and his liberality, to give us such assistance, and grant us such indulgence, as may be in his power for our comfort, upon an occasion which will necessarily bear hard upon our limited income. . . .' The Duke then set out precisely what he required under five heads: '*First* pecuniary assistance to perform the journey. . . . *Secondly* the yatcht [*sic*] to cross over, *Thirdly* the loan of the Princess of Wales's late apartments (in Kensington Palace) for the period of the Duchess's confinement; *Fourthly* an arrangement for our Table during that time, upon a very limited scale, from the Board of Green Cloth; *Fifthly* should the Physician recommend (which at present he does) that the Duchess should have a few weeks sea bathing . . . after her confinement, the same indulgence the Prince Regent granted the Princess of Hesse Homburg of occupying some one of the Houses of the suite at Brighton or one of those of his Majesty at Weymouth. . . .' Details were particularised, the extent of the Table to be provided by the Board of Green Cloth, only the Duke, Duchess and personal attendants, no 'company', otherwise it would evidently be an enormous expense to bring over cooks, house stewards, table deckers, etc. The journeys to and from Amorbach would each cost at least £1,200; short stages must be travelled to save the Duchess from fatigue through the 'brutal driving of the Postilions' who 'rattle the carriage' over stony roads. Without such 'comforts', the Duke and Duchess's last journey from England to Amorbach had cost £750. On the subject of the loan of the Princess of Wales's apartments, which adjoined his own, the Duke pointed out that he had been promised the rooms before 'the sudden order given by the King [George III], for fitting up an apartment for the Princess of Wales' and carefully detailed the alterations he wished made, certain doors to be closed, a communication to be made to the kitchen to enable the dinner to be carried under cover, certain other doors to be opened, rooms papered.

The Duke appeared to feel no shadow of doubt that what he asked would be given. The importance of the child to be born filled his mind and was, he assumed, as evident to the rest of the world. But the Prince Regent delayed his answer and it was not until 17th December that he sent, through Sir Benjamin Bloomfield, a crushing reply.[54] There was no money to pay for the Duke of Kent's proposals. '. . . His Royal Highness commanded me to obtain accurate information as to the ability of the different Departments to meet this increase of expenditure. . . . It is . . . with the deepest regret that His Royal Highness, in consequence of the report of the State Officers, commands me to acquaint you that their funds are inadequate to meet the slightest increase without incurring debt, and, as there remained no other expedient, in this state of things, than appealing to Lord Liverpool [the Prime Minister], I accordingly did so, and this morning his Lordship has distinctly declared his inability to contribute in the least possible sum to the proposal of your Royal Highness, and as a grant from Parliament furnishes the only source from which a supply could be obtained, His Lordship is persuaded that your Royal Highness would not willingly expose yourself to a fresh discussion upon this subject. . . .'

As a final blow the Duke of Kent was reminded that his Duchess was not alone in expecting a baby. The Duke and Duchess of Clarence had obediently gone to Hanover, much against the will of the Duke of Cambridge, Regent of Hanover, who objected to having the cost of their maintenance thrust on him,[55] and the Duchess of Clarence was at that moment making preparations for her confinement there. In addition, the Duchess of Cambridge was herself expecting a baby in Hanover. The Prince Regent 'could not resist' recommending that the Duke of Kent should 'adopt the same measure, by which, not only great expenditure would be avoided, but, what is of higher Importance, Her Royal Highness relieved from the Dangers and fatigues of a long journey at [this] moment. . . .' In a letter to Mr Putnam, one of his committee, the Duke of Kent wrote that he was told that if in spite of the Prince Regent's refusal to assist him he still came to England, '*I must not expect to meet with a cordial reception*'.[56]

For the moment, however, being 'totally deprived of all pecuniary means', he had no choice but to 'submit to the mandate, harsh though it was' and remain at Amorbach. 'I see no other prospect' he wrote to General Wetherall, an old friend who was Comptroller of his Household, on 19th December 1818, 'but that of my *necessarily* remaining *here* for the *whole* of the next *five* years'. By then his debts should be paid off. Nevertheless, he went on, Schindler was getting him a pair of peculiarly fine black mares for 100 guineas, he was also replacing the Duchess's oldest pair of carriage horses and proposed to pay by instalments; would General Wetherall arrange with Coutts?[57]

The Duke had had some addition to his income. He had prevailed on his committee to allow him to draw an extra £2,000 a year at the expense of his creditors, which was to be retrospective to April 1818, and he had the extra annual income of £6,000 voted him by Parliament. He was, however, giving the Duchess a generous allowance, £3,000 a year pin money.

Since August 1818 he had had an Engineer Surveyor and Architect from England, Captain W. B. Hulme, at Amorbach and when he arrived with the Duchess at the end of October he began to make improvements there, especially to the stables.[58]

Amorbach had originally been an abbey, ecclesiastical property, seized by Napoleon and given to the Prince of Leiningen in 1801, in exchange for the lands taken from him on the left bank of the Rhine. It had no stables fit to house the fine horses the Duke loved.

Princess Feodora was at home, the Duke was at his best with young people and she became attached to him. As for the Duchess herself, as the Duke's sister, Princess Augusta, wrote 'She quite adored poor Edward; and they were truly blessed in each other.'[59] On New Year's Eve, 31st December 1818, in spite of the fact that they were under the same roof, the Duke wrote the Duchess a fond letter.

'Thursday evening 31st December 1818. This evening will put an end, dear well beloved Victoire, to the year 1818, which saw the birth of my happiness by giving you to me as my guardian angel. I hope that you will always recall this year with the same pleasure as I do, and that each time a new anniversary comes round, you will be as contented with your fate, as you make me hope you are today . . . all my efforts are directed to one end, the preservation of your dear health and the birth of a child who will resemble you, and if Heaven will give me these two blessings I shall be consoled for all my misfortunes and disappointments, with which my life has been marked.

'I would have wished to be at least able to say all this to you in pretty verses but you know that I am an old soldier who has not this talent, and so you must take the good will for the deed and in accepting this little almanack you will remember that it comes from your very deeply attached husband, for whom you represent all happiness and all consolation. On that I tell you in the language of my country, *God bless you, love me as I love you*. . . .'[60]

As the Duchess's pregnancy advanced the Duke repeatedly pointed out the unsuitability of Amorbach for a confinement.[61] The ventilation of the residence was so bad that when Princess Feodora was born the Duchess had had to be moved to a part of the old convent, now no longer available because it was occupied by Government officials. Amorbach was isolated, it was fifty English miles from the nearest large town where additional medical help might be obtained at the time of the birth.

His letters brought no result and by January 1819 financial difficulties had again become so acute that it was necessary to appeal again to the Duke of Cambridge, and for a substantial sum, £8,500. Debts were outstanding in every direction, amongst smaller sums £300 sterling had been borrowed from 'Mr de Schindler', presumably the Master of the Household at Amorbach. The Duke of Kent's plan, which he described as 'so necessary for my comfort', was that his committee should be the guarantor to the Duke of Cambridge and pay the interest on his £8,500. Detailing the money required the Duke estimated £1,139.11.0 for the cost of the Duchess's 'accouchement'. He wrote with some irritation of the 'enormous expenses' he had been put to within the last nine months, and trusted that the 'great exertions' now being made to obtain a sum to cover them would at least be crowned with success.[62] There is no evidence that he ceased to improve the stables.

However reluctant the Prince Regent may have been to recognise the fact, the infant to be born to the Duchess was a person of the utmost importance. Though the Duke of Kent was merely the fourth son, the Prince Regent and the Duke of York hardly counted dynastically any longer and only the possible offspring of the Duke of Clarence stood between the coming infant and the throne. The Duke's friends urged him to return to England. Mr Joseph Hume wrote that to bring the Duchess over for her confinement was 'the greatest and most important duty your Country looks for from you . . . the time may come when legitimacy may be challenged, and challenged with effect, from the circumstance of the birth taking place on foreign soil . . . to have a Son and heir born abroad a foreigner, will be thought by the nation to arise from the wish of the Duchess to remain in her own country'.[63] Alderman Wood, an influential member of the Duke of Kent's committee, detested by the Prince Regent for having been one of the principal supporters of his estranged wife, wrote to urge the Duke at all costs to ensure that the birth took place on

English soil. The Duke replied that he heartily agreed, the difficulty was that he was 'totally deprived of all pecuniary means'.

The importance of a birth in England was considered so great by Alderman Wood that he joined with Lord Darnley, also a member of the Duke's committee, to sign a bond for £10,000 'to make the removal and settlement in England possible'.[64] The news reached the Duke at Amorbach on 14th March 1819. He was overjoyed. The news had, he wrote, 'taken an enormous weight off my mind, for, as an *Englishman*, I felt it my first duty to my *Country*, to my family and to my *Child*, to make every possible sacrifice to ensure the Infant being born, *ipso facto*, on British ground'.[65]

At the same time two other friends, Lord Dundas and Earl Fitzwilliam, raised £2,500 each and placed £5,000 in the hands of General Wetherall for the Duke, Lord Dundas writing that he was 'truly sorry that my exertions have not succeeded to the full extent of what Your Royal Highness seemed to wish'.[66]

The Duke now had £15,000 at least and on 15th March 1819 wrote to Sir Benjamin Bloomfield with some triumph.[67] He had been 'induced' to proceed with the Duchess to England for the Duchess's confinement. He would arrive at Calais on 18th April, and asked the Prince Regent to grant the accommodation of the Royal yacht to cross to Dover next morning. Some modest extra accommodation at Kensington Palace would be 'an act of kindness', but he requested Sir Benjamin to assure the Prince Regent that it was far from his intention to trouble the Prince with applications for assistance 'of *any* sort'.

A postscript to the letter contained, for the first time, the name of Conroy. Captain Conroy of the Royal Artillery, wrote the Duke, had charge of matters of detail relating to his arrival in England and Sir Benjamin was requested to let him know the Prince Regent's decision on these two matters.

Captain Conroy was an Irishman, ambitious, handsome and unscrupulous, destined to be the evil genius of the Duchess of Kent. Schindler had been significant. Within a year the Duchess was once more to be left alone, and as she had turned to Schindler so she would turn to Conroy, but with more fatal results. At this point, however, Captain Conroy was the Duke of Kent's equerry, remunerated at the rate of £60 a month.[68]

On this occasion the Prince Regent granted his brother's requests: the yacht and the apartment at Kensington Palace were put at the Duke and Duchess's disposal.[69] Although the Prince Regent had no choice but to agree, since the Duke of Kent was paying his own expenses, he took the opportunity to express his very great regret that the Duke should have thought it expedient for the Duchess to undertake a journey at this advanced period. The journey was formidable, about four hundred and twenty-seven miles, over the primitive roads of the period, ending in a sea passage noted for rough weather, and the Duchess had now reached the eighth month of her pregnancy. However, the eighth month was considered safer than the seventh, when the Duke in his original proposal on 18th November had proposed bringing the Duchess to England.

The Duchess embarked on the journey 'with joyful anticipation'. In March her mother, the Dowager Duchess of Coburg, was staying at Amorbach, and found the Duchess looking very well and 'thoroughly happy in her new married life' though the Dowager Duchess confessed that the journey to England 'somewhat alarms me in her present condition'. However, when the Dowager Duchess left Amorbach on 24th March she wrote '. . . I carried with me the comforting certainty that she is really happy and contented, and that Kent makes an excellent husband'.[70]

On 28th March 1819 the Duke and Duchess set out. The cavalcade[71] was imposing. The Duke drove the Duchess himself in a cane phaeton, drawn by their own horses. The advantages of a phaeton were superior springing and more effective control of the horses, consequently the Duchess would be less shaken. In fact, in her condition, the phaeton was too short for comfort, but she would not admit she was uncomfortable for fear of hurting the Duke's feelings. The Duchess's landau followed with little Princess Feodora's women and the English maids, then the Duke's travelling 'birouche' with the Duchess's lady-in-waiting, Baroness Spaeth, and a female obstetrician, Madame Siebold, who had qualified as a physician and surgeon at the University of Göttingen, 'like a man', in whom the Duchess's mother had great faith. These three vehicles were followed by the Duchess's 'dormeuse' or large post chaise, which accompanied her the whole way, empty in case of rain, the post chaise with little Princess Feodora and her governess, the cabriolet with two cooks, the caravan with the plate in charge of an English manservant, Thomas Kingsthorn, a low phaeton built at Brussels especially for the Duchess's condition in which a coachman drove the second pair of horses, a gig in which the Duke's valet Mathieu travelled with the Duchess's footman, a second gig in which Mr Choveaux, an assistant clerk, travelled with a helper, and finally Dr Wilson's curricle. Dr Wilson was an ex-naval doctor, late of H.M. frigate *Hussar*, who had become the Duke's personal physician and 'managed the Duchess to perfection' from the beginning of her pregnancy. The Duchess also brought her own bedstead and bedding.

The plan was to travel 25 miles a day, but as considerable space was required to accommodate the party at an inn, sometimes it was necessary to go considerably further, sometimes to stop short. No more than three consecutive days were spent travelling without taking a day's rest. Fortunately the weather was fine.

The Duke's anxiety for the Comtesse de Montgenet did not diminish, and when the party reached Frankfort he wrote a hurried letter to the Baron de Mallet.[72] He had to continue his journey to England immediately and had only time to thank the Baron and his wife for their kind attentions to the 'dear Countess'. 'In your next pray state to me, your opinion of her health, her looks and her spirits *very particularly*, for I fear what she recently read in the papers, has had again a very sensible effect on her nerves, which I gather, from the contents of her last letter, written, although with her usual affection, yet evidently under great agitation.'

On 5th April 1819 the party reached Cologne. The journey was being a triumphant success. 'It seems' wrote the Duke to Mr Putnam, one of his committee, 'as if Providence absolutely prospered our undertaking for . . . we had the finest weather under Heaven and not an accident of any sort has happened. . . . I am happy to say that on the whole the Duchess is even *less* fatigued of an evening on her journey than she used to be when resting quietly at home.'[73]

Meanwhile in Hanover on 26th March the Duchess of Cambridge had given birth to a healthy son, and on 27th March a daughter, who only lived seven hours, was born to the Duchess of Clarence. The Clarences' misfortune increased the importance of the child to be born to the Duchess of Kent. In England there is no Salic law, which permits only a male to inherit the throne; the essential for the succession was not that a male heir should be born to the Duke of Kent, but that the baby should be healthy. A princess, daughter of the Duke of Kent, the fourth son, would ascend the throne before the son of the Duke of Cambridge, the seventh.

The progress of the cavalcade across Europe continued to be prosperous and on 18th April, according to plan, Calais was reached. The yacht was waiting, but the wind was unfavourable and the party was windbound until the 24th. Writing to his old friend General Knollys, the Duke was again anxious about the Comtesse de Montgenet: 'I appreciate your kind attempts and those of your son, to see my old friend and Companion, but I perceive clearly, what the Duke of Orleans has long told me, that her nerves are not in a state to see those who had known her in the happy times of our intimacy, indeed, I know that last summer, one fell casually in her way, and it occasioned her a shock, she did not recover for weeks.'[74]

On 24th April the wind came round, the Channel was crossed and the Duke, safely on English soil, wrote to the Dowager Duchess of Coburg from Dover.[75] It was 'with very great joy' that he made his report on his 'beloved little Victoria'. They had had a very short crossing less than three hours from Calais but 'fairly rough'. The Duchess was 'certainly very sick'; the Duke gave intimate particulars of her sickness, but there were no harmful symptoms and both Dr Wilson and Madame Siebold said everything was as satisfactory as possible. 'All has ended well' finished the Duke.

The apartment in Kensington Palace which the Duke and Duchess of Kent were to occupy for the period of the Duchess's confinement had stood empty for nearly five years, since the Princess of Wales, the Regent's estranged wife, had left England in 1814. An order[76] had been issued that it was to be put in order and ready by 18th April, the day the Duke and Duchess should arrive at Calais, but as late as 10th April nothing had been done because the Lord Chamberlain's Office had not received Treasury permission to spend £674.4.0, a moderate sum considering the length of time the apartment had been vacant. It must be especially allowed as 'an extra charge, it being quite impossible to defray the expense out of the limited allowance for the ordinary services of the Lord Chamberlain's Office'.[77]

Before the Duke started for England General Wetherall had warned him that Mr John Nash, the Regent's architect in charge of the fabric at Kensington, was uneasy about the state of the apartment. The Duke replied he was convinced that any application he might make would prove useless, all his applications had proved useless from some time past, he was to be 'kept down'. A further letter received at Brussels on his way to England informed him that a large part of the apartment had been 'stripped' of both fixtures and furniture.[78]

In May the Duke purchased furniture 'on private account' from Elliot and Francis, 104 New Bond Street, spending over £2,000, and bought, or had moved in, from his other houses 'several thousand pounds worth of glasses' (mirrors), dealing mainly with Mr Baily of Mount Street.[79]

The situation of the apartment was charming; the windows, including those of the Duchess's bedroom, looked out on fine trees, great sweeps of lawn and grass glades. Kensington was in the country and Kensington Palace a country house. '. . . all the arrangement of the apartment is such as I believe it ought to be to be most complete and most healthy' wrote the Duke 'with the advantage of being as quiet as possible, near the town and a view over the most magnificent Park, with the most beautiful piece of water that it is possible to see'.[80] The suite of large reception rooms, each with three tall windows, was pillared, the saloon opened into a private garden. All the upholstered furniture in the Duchess's bedroom and dressing-room was newly covered in white dimity, a cotton fabric woven with a stripe. The curtains at her windows and the cushions on her window seats were white. The hangings of the four-posters (the Duke and Duchess slept in two, each 3 ft. 10 in. wide) were white glazed cambric and each had a pair of bed steps. In the centre of the room was an Etruscan lamp. 'The New north room or Nursery' contained a 'cribb bedstead of mahogany' with furniture of white glazed cambric waiting for the coming baby. The window curtains were white, made of glazed cambric with inner curtains of white muslin, and cost the considerable sum of £100, while those in the Duchess's bedroom cost £90. The nursery had an opaque lamp and a child's wardrobe of mahogany four feet high. The Duchess had a 'bedchair to place over the bolster' and a bed table for her convalescence, costing together nearly £55. Twelve 'stool back' chairs in the drawing-room were re-covered in yellow satin, the dining-room had new red curtains and carpet, and a Grecian lamp. In addition to his expenditure with Elliot and Francis of over £2,000, the Duke had his library fitted up with 'book cases in 52 parts', a writing desk and 'booksteps'.

In 1820 Messrs Elliot and Francis valued all the Duke's furniture in the apartment at £6,000.[81]

The work of repairing the apartment in Kensington Palace and making good the damage caused by years of standing empty, proceeded only slowly. The room where the Duchess was to be confined, which seems to have been the Duke's dressing-room, since Elliot and Francis supplied 'white glazed furniture to His Royal Highness's bed for the Duchess's lying in',[82] was only completed, with carpets down, curtains hung and furniture in place, on 22nd May. Next day, 23rd May, General Wetherall complained to Colonel Stephenson, Auditor to the Treasury, that the window sashes 'constantly' let in the rain.[83] They had been condemned years ago and ought to have been replaced. There was no time for repairs. At 10.30 p.m. on the evening of 23rd May the Duke sent an urgent note to General Wetherall—the Duchess's labour had begun.[84] H.M.'s ministers (Privy Councillors) had been sent for and the sooner General Wetherall came the better, to assist in receiving them. 'My time of course' wrote the Duke 'will be exclusively taken up with the Duchess.'

There were present, not in the room itself but waiting in an adjoining room, the Duke of Wellington, the Archbishop of Canterbury, the Bishop of London, the Marquess of Lansdowne, Earl Bathurst, the Rt Hon. George Canning, the Rt Hon. Nicholas Vansittart, Chancellor of the Exchequer, the Duke of Sussex and Lieut.-General F. A. Wetherall.[85]

After a labour of six and a quarter hours, at 4.15 a.m. on Monday, 24th May 1819, the Duchess was safely delivered of a healthy child, 'a pretty little Princess, as plump as a partridge'.[86] It was a typical English early summer morning, chilly—the temperature never rose above 51 degrees all day—and with a light rain falling. There had been a dramatic change in the weather, and a heat wave between 26th April and 18th May, during which Keats composed the *Ode to a Nightingale*, described by Robert

Gittings as 'filled with the garden setting of fruit, flowers, undergrowth, green lawns and birdsong',[87] had been succeeded by cool weather.*

The joy of the Duke, who had remained with the Duchess throughout, at the safety of his wife and the arrival of a vigorous healthy infant, was almost uncontrollable. The same evening he sent off by courier a long letter to his mother-in-law, the Dowager Duchess of Coburg.[88] The little girl 'is truly a model of strength and beauty combined. . . . Thank God the dear mother and the child are doing marvellously well. . . . It is absolutely impossible for me to do justice to the patience and sweetness with which she behaved . . . for you will easily believe that I did not leave her from the beginning to the end, and it would be just as difficult to express whether the excellent Mademoiselle Siebold has shone most by her care or by her talents for it is not possible to show more activity, more zeal and more knowledge than she has done.'

*

A number of legends and misconceptions have gathered round the birth of Queen Victoria. One legend is that the birth was difficult and in the words of Miss Agnes Strickland's book, *Victoria from Birth to Bridal*, published in 1840 '. . . lengthened suffering and great danger to Her Royal Mother preceded the happy moment when the hope of Great Britain first saw the light'. But, when Miss Strickland was sent a copy of Queen Victoria's comments on this and other statements in her book '. . . the well-intentioned authoress . . .' writes Prince Albert 'promptly had the whole edition recalled and destroyed'. Beside Miss Strickland's account of her birth the Queen wrote 'Not true'.[89]

This is confirmed by a letter[90] written to the Duchess of Kent by her mother, the Dowager Duchess of Coburg, on 31st May 1819 after receiving news of the birth: 'My God how glad I am to hear of you. . . .I cannot find words to express my delight that everything went so smoothly. . . . I cannot write much or reasonably to you, dear mouse, for I am much too happy . . . to God be praise and thanks eternally that everything went on smoothly. . . .'

Another legend is that a well-known Welsh doctor, Doctor David Daniel Davis, who practised in London and was one of the foremost obstetricians of his day, was in fact responsible for bringing Queen Victoria into the world. According to this story, the birth is said to have been so difficult that Madame Siebold gave up hope of saving mother or child; Dr Davis intervened, safely delivered the Princess Victoria and saved the lives of both. Dr Davis was one of the doctors in attendance on

* The 24th May was the fourth wettest day of the month, cloudy, with an east wind. There was no rain on the 25th or 26th. (Records of the Meteorological Office, London Road, Bracknell, Berkshire.)

the Duchess of Kent during the birth, but there is no evidence that he took an active part. The Duke of Kent in his letter to the Duchess's mother does not mention him, but praises Madame Siebold, and three months later, on 26th August, Madame Siebold acted as midwife at the birth of Prince Albert, son of the Duchess of Kent's brother, the reigning Duke of Coburg, and future husband of Queen Victoria.[91] It is unlikely if she had failed at the Princess Victoria's birth that she would have been asked by the Coburg family to officiate again. Twenty-four years later she still had a flourishing practice among Continental royalties.[92]

The most probable explanation of Dr Daniel Davis's presence is that Madame Siebold was a foreigner and a German, both unpopular at the time, and it was thought wiser to have a well-known British obstetrician at hand as well as a foreign expert.

Chapter Two

The Prince Regent, observed Prince Leopold, hated the Duke of Kent 'most sincerely',[1] and the possibility of a child of the Duke of Kent's sitting on the throne which should be occupied by a child of his own was gall and wormwood to him.

Nor was the Duchess of Kent regarded with affection by any member of the English Royal Family, with the possible exception of the two dutiful daughters of George III, the Princesses Augusta and Mary. The Duchess of Kent was felt to be too German, too fond of Germany, too closely surrounded by German relatives and retainers. Not a clever woman, she found extreme difficulty in learning English and adapting herself to English customs. She had not made a good impression and the general wish of her new Royal relatives was that she should go back to Germany as soon as possible, not failing to take the Duke with her.

The Duke of Kent, however, had no intention of leaving England. His advisers implored him to be careful how he conducted himself, and to expect nothing from the Prince Regent; but his daughter's destiny—and in that his faith never wavered—required that she should be brought up as an English child, in England.

*

Indeed the Duke's faith in Victoria's destiny never wavered and an on-looker of unquestionable reliability described him as showing the infant Princess 'constantly to his companions and intimate friends with the words "Take care of her for she will be Queen of England" '. The onlooker—to be seen sometimes in London, sometimes at other European courts—was a quiet, unobtrusive, youngish man, never unfortunately in very good health, one Dr Christian Stockmar.[2] He was a Coburger of Swedish descent, and had been a physician until, in 1816, at the age of 29 he became private secretary to Prince Leopold and accompanied him to England when he married Princess Charlotte. On the fatal morning of Princess Charlotte's death it was into Stockmar's arms that Prince Leopold collapsed, begging Stockmar to give a promise never to leave him. Stockmar gave the promise and from that moment his life and remarkable talents were dedicated to the service of Prince Leopold and the House of Coburg.

He occupied no official position of importance but was known to be Prince Leopold's right-hand man and private agent. Possessing unparalleled discretion, tact and sagacity, without ambition for his own advancement and with unrivalled opportunities for observation, he became the receiver of Royal confidences, the Keeper of Royal Secrets at the English and German courts.

In gloomier moments the Duke remarked that the child was too healthy to please some members of his family who regarded her as an intruder. She was remarkably strong: 'The little one is rather a pocket Hercules, than a pocket Venus' the Duke wrote to his intimate friend the Duke of Orleans. He regarded the infant Princess's vigour as a just reward for the moderation and rectitude of his life. 'My health remains unimpaired, as I have a right to expect from the life I have ever led' he told Mrs Fitzherbert.[3] To the Prince Regent, dosing himself into a stupor with laudanum to relieve the pain of his swollen, inflamed legs, grossly fat, saddled with a wife he loathed, whose only child was in her grave, the spectacle of the Duke of Kent arrogating to himself the role of father to the heir to the throne was insupportable.

The Duke always denied that he felt any disappointment because the baby was a girl. 'For my own part,' he wrote to his friend Baron de Mallet, 'I have no choice between Boy and Girl and I shall always feel grateful for whichever of the two is bestowed upon us, so long as the Mother's health is preserved. . . .'[4]

He was a doting father, supervising and regulating, as was his habit, the details of nursery management. The Duchess did not engage the customary wet nurse but fed her baby herself. 'Everybody is most astonished' she told her mother, but she adored her baby so much she could not bear to think of some other woman performing this function. The Duke closely observed 'the process of maternal nutriment' and reported to the Duchess's mother in the same ample detail in which he had previously reported the Duchess's seasickness. The interesting fact was also mentioned twice in *The Times*. The Duchess's temperament made her a nervous mother. On 22nd June 1819 she wrote to her mother, 'Today the little mouse has been in the open air for the first time, she was so unmanageable that I nearly cried. To my shame I must confess that I am over anxious in a childish way with the little one, as if she were my first child . . . she drives me at times into real desperation.'[5]

In his triumph and satisfaction the Duke did not forget the Comtesse de Montgenet. '. . . You have done quite right in not naming to the Countess, when you saw her on the 31st ultimo, anything of this circumstance (the birth of the Princess]' he wrote to Baron de Mallet 'and till *she* speaks of it to *you*, I am sure you and Mrs Mallet will have the kindness carefully to avoid the subject. I rejoice . . . that she is quite recovered from

33

her indisposition of which she made mention to me in her last letter. . . .
I trust when she gets into her New House, as it will carry with it no
painful recollections . . . it will be the means of restoring her gaiety and
good spirits, or if not that at least to serenity and tranquillity, for, until I
am satisfied on *that* head, I never can enjoy my own domestic happiness.'

The Duke had periods of depression. The Duchess of Clarence had
lost one child but would almost certainly have another, she was only 26
and the Duke of Clarence, elder brother of the Duke of Kent, was the
father of ten illegitimate children. Moreover the hostility of the Prince
Regent was impossible to ignore. Early in June the Duke wrote des-
pondently to the Duke of Orleans: '. . . As far as the position of my
little girl is concerned I cannot allow myself to forget that . . . the brother
before me [the Duke of Clarence] will *in all human probability yet have a
family.*' The Duke of Kent was doubtful if the Prince Regent had formally announced the birth of the little Princess to the courts of Europe
through his ambassadors, as he ought, since she was in the direct line of
succession to the throne and entitled to formal honours.

'. . . The plan' wrote the Duke of Kent 'is evidently to *keep me down.*'
Soon the Princess would be christened; the godfathers, he believed,
would be the Prince Regent and the Emperor Alexander I of Russia, the
godmothers the Duke's sister, the Queen of Württemberg, eldest daughter
of George III, and the Dowager Duchess of Coburg, mother of the
Duchess of Kent. The Duke wished the infant Princess to be named
Victoire Georgina Alexandrina Charlotte Augusta, '. . . and I hope to
hold to it' he wrote.

On Friday 21st June the Prince Regent abruptly communicated his
decisions on the christening to his brother. It was to take place almost at
once, on Monday 24th June, at 3 p.m., and was to be private. Only the
Duke and Duchess of York, Princess Augusta, the Duke and Duchess of
Gloucester, Prince Leopold and Princess Sophia were to be invited. There
would be no dressing up, no uniforms glittering with gold, the Duke of
Kent was to be given no chance to make a grand occasion of the ceremony:
'as His Royal Highness [the Prince Regent] considers the Ceremony as
Private, the dress best suited to the Occasion will be Frocks' (plain skirted
coats). No foreign dignitaries would arrive in pomp to add splendour to
the occasion; the Prince Regent proposed to stand in person, the Emperor
of Russia would be represented by the Duke of York, the remaining
godparents by other members of the Royal Family. The Archbishop of
Canterbury would be instructed by the proper authority, and the
Chamberlain's office would attend to the font etc. No opportunity was
to be given for the Duke of Kent to organise or interfere. As to the names,
'the Prince Regent will explain himself to your Royal Highness, previous
to the Ceremony'.[6]

No more was heard from the Prince Regent until the evening before the christening. The list of names had been submitted to him when he was asked to stand as godfather, and it was assumed he approved it, but on Sunday evening he sent a message to the Duke of Kent that the name of Georgina was not to be used 'as He did not chuse to place the name before the Emperor of Russia's, and He could not allow it to follow'. With regard to the other names, the Prince Regent repeated that he would speak to the Duke at the ceremony.[7] He had in fact, however, already approached Prince Leopold asking him to prevent the name Charlotte being given.

The christening[8] took place in the Cupola Room at Kensington Palace. The 'gold' font,* part of the regalia of the Kingdom, was brought from the Jewel House in the Tower of London and the walls were hung with crimson velvet draperies from the Chapel Royal, St James's.

At 3 p.m. the modest company assembled. The Prince Regent did not speak to the Duke of Kent. The service began, with the Archbishop of Canterbury and the Bishop of London officiating, and then, 'just as The Child was about to be baptised' wrote the Duchess of Kent 'His Late Majesty [the Prince Regent] forbad the names of Charlotte and Augusta being given, deeply wounding the Duke's feelings and mine thereby.' It was embarrasingly plain that the Prince Regent would not allow his niece to bear any of the traditional names of the English Royal Family.

The Archbishop enquired from the Prince Regent by what name he might baptise the child. The Prince Regent replied 'Alexandrina'. The Duke of Kent requested that another name should be added and 'urged' Elizabeth. The Prince Regent refused, adding 'brusquely', 'Give her the mother's name also then, but it cannot precede that of the Emperor.'

The infant princess was then baptised 'Alexandrina Victoria', the Archbishop subsequently registering her baptism at the Chapel Royal, St James's.

During her earliest years the Princess was sometimes called 'Drina', but Victoria was the name her mother, and later she herself, preferred. As a baby her mother called her Vickelchen; at four years of age, she traced

* The 'gold' font is in fact silver gilt, and the London date mark is that of 1660, when much of the Royal and State silver melted down during the Cromwellian period was being replaced. Charles II ordered this magnificent piece, which consists of a font and cover, richly chased with cherubs and foliage and adorned with figures, 37 inches high overall and weighing about 718 ounces Troy. The first officially recorded use of the 'gold' font was for the christening, in 1688, of Prince James Francis Edward, son of James II, later known as the 'Old Pretender', and nearly all the children of George III were christened in it. There is no official record that the font was used at the christening of Princess Victoria, but the weight of contemporary evidence is so great that the use of the 'gold' font is accepted as an historical fact. The absence of official record may be explained by the fact that the Prince Regent probably required the Duke of Kent to pay for the expenses of cleaning and transport. The 'gold' font is on view, with the regalia, in the Jewel House at Her Majesty's Tower of London.

her signature, over dots, as Victoria. On her accession to the throne she was proclaimed as Victoria, and the use of 'Drina' disappeared.

That evening the Duke and Duchess of Kent gave a dinner party in their apartment in Kensington Palace, to celebrate the christening. The Prince Regent was not present.

Before the Duke had returned to England, his trustee and well-wisher, Mr Joseph Hume, gave him a stern warning against 'munificent and princely plans'.[9] The Duke ought to live quietly in Kensington Palace on £4,000 or so a year, keep four horses instead of twenty, three carriages instead of ten, and cease to solicit loans. He must pay off his debts not by fresh borrowings but by economy and must realise he would never obtain anything from the Prince Regent.

His income had been increased, since on marriage his trustees allowed him an extra £2,000 a year, and Parliament had voted him an annual £6,000. But he had already exceeded this income. By how much Mr Hume was mercifully unaware, but he did know that the Duke had applied to his trustees for sums totalling £18,000 to pay off 'extra claims'. He implored the Duke to practise economy, be modest and extricate himself from his difficulties by his own means.

The Duke was annoyed and wrote to General Wetherall about Mr Hume's limited outlook. Captain Conroy, the Duke's equerry, read Mr Hume's letter 'with sentiments of indignation'.[10] At the same time the moment had arrived when it was impossible for the Duke to raise a substantial sum of money, and a substantial sum was what he urgently required.

The one piece of solid property the Duke of Kent still possessed—it had cost altogether about £120,000—was his country house, Castle Hill at Ealing, but he had failed to sell it. Possibly the mechanical devices he had installed, waterfalls and fountains concealed in closets, cages of artificial singing birds, musical clocks with dancing figures, and a drive illuminated with red and blue lights, did not appeal to the prosperous family men who usually purchase roomy country houses.

It was now suggested that Castle Hill might be sold by lottery. The permission of the sovereign—which the Prince Regent would certainly have refused—was not necessary, but Parliamentary consent would have to be obtained. On 2nd July 1819 a motion was brought forward in the House of Commons by the Duke of Kent's trustee Alderman Wood to enable the Duke to sell the house by means of a lottery.

Lord Castlereagh, leader of the House of Commons, dispelled any hopes the Duke might entertain. He flatly refused. 'If the present motion were agreed to he knew not where the practice of lotteries for the disposition of private property could stop.' The motion was therefore withdrawn.[11]

In the following month, August, the Duke's prestige received a serious blow. At a reception given by the Spanish Ambassador, the Prince Regent publicly broke with him, insulting the Duke by turning his back on him and refusing to speak to him, though he greeted the Duchess.

With the Duke and Duchess of Kent out of favour, the members of the Royal Family, wrote Prince Leopold, 'were all looking to the Clarence family', and 'the little girl', as they called the infant Princess Victoria, was 'a real thorn in their side'.

*

In the same month, in the Duchess of Kent's native land, Coburg, an event took place destined to be of overwhelming importance in the life of the little Princess. On 26th August 1819, almost exactly three months after the birth of the Princess Victoria, Madame Siebold again brought a baby into the world, this time a boy. He was the second son of the young Duchess Luise, wife of the Duke of Saxe-Coburg and Saalfeld, brother of the Duchess of Kent.

Sitting by the bedside of the young Duchess, the Dowager Duchess of Coburg wrote[12] that all had gone 'quite easily and quickly', and she had found 'the little mother a little limp' but gay. She was 19 and only fourteen months had passed since the birth of her elder son. The new baby arrived at The Rosenau, a summer residence about four miles from the city of Coburg. 'The stillness of the House, which is broken only by the splashing of the water is quite too pleasant' wrote the Dowager Duchess. Last year Ernest, the first son, had been born in the castle at Coburg, and 'nobody takes into account the uproar in the Castle, the racket of the children, the rumbling of the carts . . .' Yesterday, 'Siebold was woken at 3 and at 6 the little one shrieked his way into the world, and looked about him with a pair of great black eyes [in fact they were blue], as lively as a squirrel. Tomorrow we christen the baby, he bears the name of Albert.' His names in full were Francis Charles Augustus Albert Emmanuel. Albert, however, was the name he used. His elder brother Ernest, wrote the Dowager Duchess, 'runs like a weasel (at fourteen months), is teething and is as wicked as a little dragon . . . he is not pretty yet, apart from his wonderful, beautiful, black eyes. How pretty the little Mayflower will be, when I manage to see her in a year! Siebold cannot say often enough what a lovely little darling she is.'

The plan of a marriage between the two first cousins existed from the moment of Prince Albert's birth. In the nursery he was repeatedly told by his nurse that his destiny was to marry the little English Mayflower; his grandmother, the Dowager Duchess of Coburg, called him 'the pendant to the pretty cousin'. Marriage to Princess Victoria was to be his vocation and he accepted it, never considering anything else.

Unhappily for Albert, his father and mother were unsuited to each other, so unsuited that tragedy was inevitable. But, in August 1819, the young Duchess was absorbed in her beautiful baby, who closely resembled her; 'Albert est superbe' she wrote 'd'un beauté extraordinaire'.

*

Meanwhile across the Channel in England the infant Princess Victoria, at ten weeks old, had been successfully vaccinated.[13] 'A subject free from disease and the child of healthy parents', the six-weeks-old infant of Colonel Eliot M.P., was in the course of undergoing vaccination and was brought to Kensington Palace on 2nd August 1819. Vaccine lymph was taken from the vesicle, the cavity filled with pus resulting from the insertion of the vaccine on the arm of Colonel Eliot's child, and inserted into two places on the Princess's left arm and one on her right. By the 26th day after vaccination the 'encrustations', scabs, had dropped off leaving 'a small radiated and rather depressed cicatrix'. The vaccination had been successful and the infant Princess suffered no 'eruptions or any other derangement of the system'. Princess Victoria was vaccinated again both in 1827 and in 1835, on each occasion because the marks of previous vaccinations were 'less evident' than the doctors desired to see them. In 1827 there was some irritation on the right arm, but otherwise she suffered no discomfort.

Princess Victoria's abounding health was not a recommendation to her royal relatives. As the Duke of Kent said, she was too healthy to please some members of his family. When the Prince Regent set the example and snubbed the Kents, his family, who feared and fawned upon him, followed suit. On 10th September 1819 Princess Mary, Duchess of Gloucester, gave the Regent a mocking description of a visit the Kent family paid to Windsor.[14] 'The Kents passed two nights at Windsor with bag and baggage, I mean by that besides the baby she brought her daughter and Mdlle de Spate [Baroness Spaeth] and they all *retired* to *rest* both evenings at 9 o'clock. The Duke and Dss of Kent, baby, nurse, the Pss Feodore and Mdlle de Spate *all* wished them good night at the same time & *actually went to bed* to the very great *amusement* of the whole society at Windsor'.

*

The Duke's finances did not improve; by the end of August General Wetherall had been unable to raise even £10,000 and another period of enforced economy was approaching.

Early in September the Duke composed a memorandum[15] to be submitted to his committee, stating the income he required to live as he was living at present, based on his experience of spending six months in England. He calculated he needed £16,000 a year, to include the annual visit he was bound to make to Leiningen. It was an optimistic estimate, only £2,000 a year more than he was receiving at present, and the Duke did not include the furniture, the horses and carriages, the mirrors, the clothes and the presents for the Duchess which he was buying, nor did he take any account of his additional debts. Before leaving Amorbach he had told General Wetherall he already owed about £2,000 to the bankers there. But, optimistic though the estimate was, his committee thought it too high. The Duke could not afford to live in London, he must leave and economise in the country.

The sea coast of Devonshire was the suggestion the Duke favoured. Appearances would be preserved since, before Princess Victoria's birth, the Duke had announced his intention of taking the Duchess to benefit by sea air after her confinement.

Towards the end of October the Duke, with Captain Conroy in attendance, went down to Devonshire to find a house. On 25th October he wrote from the Bishop's Palace at Salisbury to his 'beloved and very dear wife'. Bishop Fisher was an old friend; for a period during the Duke's boyhood he had been his tutor and Captain Conroy had married his niece. Owing to his assiduous attentions to royalty Bishop Fisher had earned the nickname of 'Kingfisher'. The Duke found the cold 'excessive more like the month of January than that of October'; however, 'the good Bishop received me with open arms and made me take some excellent soup which warmed me excellently'. The Duke sent off a letter daily to his 'beloved little Victoire'[16] and on the 27th after inspecting houses at Torquay, Teignmouth and Dawlish, none of which were suitable, he wrote that he was going to try Sidmouth and then come home.

Sidmouth proved satisfactory and Alderman Wood took a house for them, a large 'cottage orné' known as Woolbrook Cottage.

'We have a plan to leave here in three weeks for Devonshire' the Duke told his brother-in-law, the Duke of Coburg, on 19th November 1819, 'where the winter is much less severe and where my dear Victoire can take advantage of luke warm sea baths which will do her rheumatism good, which, though not alarming, is disagreeable.' Most seaside resorts at that period had a bath-house where baths of warmed sea water could be taken under cover all the year round.

'Our little one at six months is as advanced as children generally are at eight' he wrote proudly. The infant Princess had been weaned, and 'does not appear to thrive the less for the change', he informed a member of his committee in the course of a letter otherwise about money matters.[17]

On 2nd November 1819 the Duke celebrated his birthday. He was 52. A family festival took place. A letter written by the Duchess was presented to her father by the little Princess, now nearly six months old, dressed in a white frock with bows of red and green ribbon (a piece has been preserved at Windsor) and wearing a Scotch bonnet. Princess Feodora sang some verses composed for the occasion, verses of congratulation were presented and Prince Charles of Leiningen, now at school in Geneva, wrote a letter in English to please 'my dear father', promised a drawing and sent 'filial congratulations'.[18]

Ultimately, the Duke and his family did not leave London for Sidmouth until nearly Christmas. The Duke was making a desperate effort to raise the substantial sum of money which would deliver him from his creditors.[19] £30,000 was his target, though he also considered £45,000 and wrote out a scheme to borrow £50,000 at 5 per cent to be repaid through a sinking fund in nine years. He approached Mr Thomas Coutts, and asked him to advance £30,000 as a private loan, but Mr Coutts was totally unable to accommodate the Duke from his own fortune, though Mrs Coutts had pressed him. Bosanquet and Co., bankers, Lombard Street, also declined his Royal Highness's proposal to advance £30,000 for a year or more, in the present state of commercial affairs. The Duke's main asset was still Castle Hill and though the lottery had failed Mr Karslake, the Duke's solicitor, estimated that Castle Hill, if broken up, might fetch about £35,000. The furniture auctioned off in lots should fetch £15,000, the mansion house sold as building material and the land sold in building lots should fetch £20,000. But December was not the month to sell; he had consulted several auctioneers and the Duke was advised to wait until May.

It was suggested that perhaps Castle Hill might be sold by tontine. Each member of a tontine takes a share, in this case 100 guineas, and the last surviving shareholder becomes owner of the property. The sale of three hundred, four hundred, or perhaps five hundred, shares would bring in the sum the Duke needed. But a tontine took time to organise and the Duke could not afford to stay in London. He was, as always, on excellent terms with his committee who, he wrote, 'evinced every disposition to do all in their power to make me comfortable', so, leaving the organisation of the tontine in the hands of 'two or three active members of the committee', the Duke and his family set out for Sidmouth.

On 21st December they reached Salisbury; after staying for a day or two at the episcopal palace, they arrived at Sidmouth about two in the afternoon of Christmas Day 'in the midst of a tremendous snow storm' wrote the Duke. '. . . all well except that the water had already begun to play the very deuce with my bowels. . . .' A severe gastric attack followed, and though the Duke wrote on 31st December 'I am now completely recovered', the attack had weakened him.[20]

Woolbrook Cottage was charmingly situated, standing in the pretty little valley called Woolbrook Glen only about 150 yards from the sea, but the winter of 1819–20 was exceptional, with glacial cold, storms of rain and fierce gales. 'There has not been for many years a season more disastrous for shipping' reported *The Times* on 23rd December 1819.[21] The whole Kent family, including the infant Princess, caught colds, and the Duchess, always over-anxious, was terrified a few days after their arrival by an alarming accident.

About four in the afternoon of 28th December 1819, the Duchess was sitting in the drawing-room with the infant Princess, when, to her terror, a shot shattered the window. She was '*most* exceedingly' alarmed. The culprit turned out to be an apprentice boy named Hook, who was in the road, firing at birds and using an unnecessarily heavy type of shot, swan shot. After this agitating incident the Duke and Duchess of Kent showed themselves at their best. Within half an hour Captain Conroy wrote on the Duke's behalf to a Mr George Cornish, probably the local magistrate, asking him to 'adopt some measures for the prevention of such an occurrence. But, their Royal Highnesses desire me most particularly to request that the Boy may not be punished, they only interfere to prevent the thing happening again.'[22]

Unfortunately, owing to the exceptional winter, the climate of Sidmouth was not turning out as the Duke expected. Though the days were often sunny, the air was sharp and the nights bitter. '. . . rather Canadian' wrote the Duke. The Duchess spent a great deal of time with the infant Princess, worked hard at her English lessons, went for walks on the sea shore with Princess Feodora, collecting 'pretty interesting Marine Plants', and took sea-water baths. The Duke's principal occupation was writing letters. Captain Conroy was in attendance, living in separate lodgings; General Wetherall and Dr Wilson were also lodged separately.

The Duke was beginning to think of going back to Amorbach, and on 6th January 1820 he wrote to Admiral Donnelly, whose house he had occupied in Brussels, asking him to enquire for some little black Friesian mares, 'in consequence of my having to forward four carriages to Amorbach in the spring'. He added '. . . our little Girl now between seven and eight months old looks like a child of a year, and has cut her two first teeth without the slightest inconvenience. . . .'[23]

On this letter is written, 'The last letter His Royal Highness ever wrote'.

The Duchess kept up an intimate correspondence with her old friend and confidante Polyxene von Tubeuf,[24] and on 7th January wrote she was depressed, 'Vickelchen' had a sore throat and was 'restless'. The Duke had also caught a cold, but insisted on going out and walked some distance with Captain Conroy, 'looking after the horses'. He came back chilled through, with wet feet, and next day his cold was violent. The weather now turned to bitter cold and though the Duke attempted to walk outside with the Duchess, they were forced to come in. On Sunday his cold was still worse, but he had asked people in for the evening and would not cancel the party. During the night he was feverish and next morning the Duchess kept him in bed and sent for Dr Wilson, who pronounced him seriously indisposed. 'Your poor friend is terribly cast down and in need of your encouraging sympathy' wrote the Duchess to Polyxene von Tubeuf, '. . . my dear husband is not well'. The Duke's bedroom was 'small and inconceivably cold', his 'indisposition' worried her greatly, 'also I have been troubled by a number of unpleasant business letters from Amorbach'. The Duke's 'indisposition' rapidly turned into a serious illness. 'May God protect him and spare my dearest husband to me' the Duchess wrote next day. '. . . I am nursing my beloved one to the best of my abilities. . . . The Doctor is going to apply leeches to the chest. Feodora has also unfortunately caught a chill . . . the cold is almost unbearable. . . . Vickelchen' the Duchess added 'is well again and a greater darling than ever, but she is beginning to show symptoms of wanting to get her own little way. . . .'

On Wednesday, 12th January, the Duchess had the Duke's bed moved to another room, somewhat larger and warmer; but in the evening he became delirious, with high fever, pain in his chest and vomiting. He was bled, in the belief that blood-letting would reduce the fever, and when the next day, Thursday, brought no improvement, was bled again. The Duchess, now terrified, sent a messenger to London begging Sir David Dundas, one of the most able and experienced of the royal physicians, who had known the Duke from childhood, to come immediately. Dr Wilson urged the Duchess to rest, but she would not leave the Duke, except to spend a few minutes with the infant Princess. Every dose of medicine he took throughout his illness was administered by her hand. The Duke did not allow his daughter to be brought into the sick-room, but spoke of her constantly; 'she was his joy' wrote the Duchess.

A battle now began between the magnificent constitution of the Duke and the medical treatment of the period. On Saturday evening Dr Wilson applied a blister to the Duke's chest. 'Oh! how they do torment him, and, as far as I can see to no purpose' wrote the Duchess to Polyxene. The Duke was kept lying down 'in a recumbent position, very distressing for him, but Dr Wilson was positive'. The Duchess was in despair at the impossibility of keeping the house warm. The infant Princess, she wrote, 'had caught another cold'. She was 'anxiously awaiting the arrival of Sir David Dundas' who should arrive on Monday, and the Duke's condition was deteriorating.

On Sunday evening the Duke was in a high fever, restless and wandering, and Dr Wilson decided he must be 'cupped'. This painful operation was a method of bleeding. A cut was made in the patient's flesh, over it was placed a heated cup, usually holding four ounces; as the cup cooled a vacuum was created and blood was drawn out. The Duke was cupped, not only all over his body, but on his head, which, it was thought, would relieve his headache. 'For four hours they must have tormented him' wrote the Duchess to Polyxene 'and it made me nearly sick. As finally the cupping seemed of little use, they had recourse again to bleeding. I could hardly bear to watch the proceedings, but, whatever I may have felt I hardly left him for a moment.'

On Monday afternoon the doctor from London arrived, but not Sir David Dundas. The old King, George III, was very ill and Sir David could not leave him. In his place Dr William Maton was sent. He was a physician of eminence, had been physician to the late Queen Charlotte and was in the confidence of the Royal Family, but his arrival left the Duchess 'sadly depressed'. Dr Maton spoke little French, and, as the Duchess had made only poor progress in learning English, they could not talk together.

Unhappily for the Duke, the physician from London, Dr Maton, was a believer in bleeding. He considered, he remarked afterwards, that in the course of his illness the Duke had not been sufficiently bled. There had been taken from him 120 fluid ounces, 6 pints of blood, but, especially in the early stages, 'he would have borne more depletion'.

On Wednesday, 19th January, he ordered the Duke to be cupped again, 'which upset me dreadfully' wrote the Duchess to Polyxene 'as my poor dear Edward has had already to endure so much. I cannot think it can be good for the patient to lose so much blood, when he is already so weak . . . the whole morning he was tormented with this dreadful cupping and I was beside myself. . . .' In the evening the doctor decided bleeding was again necessary. When the Duke was told, he wept.

He now had a high fever, a racking cough, hiccups, an 'unendurable' pain in his side, and was wandering in his mind. Nevertheless next day, for the sixth time, he was cupped and bled; 'even if he should become weaker, the *only* remedy for relieving the inflammation was bleeding' wrote the Duchess. 'Oh! dearest Polyxene it is too dreadful . . . there is hardly a spot on his dear body which has not been touched by cupping, blisters, or bleeding. He was terribly exhausted yesterday after all that had been done to him by those cruel doctors. . . . Dear little Vickelchen was not at all well yesterday; she had a heavy cold and had to be given an emetic, but today she is better again.'

On Thursday it was thought wise to send messengers to Prince Leopold and other relations, informing them in the Duchess's name of the Duke's dangerous illness. The messenger with the 'horrifying news'[25] found Prince Leopold shooting at Lord Craven's in Berkshire; and the Prince set out at once for Sidmouth, accompanied by Stockmar, 'in bitter cold and damp weather I shall not easily forget'.

General Wetherall, the Duke's Comptroller, wrote to Sir Benjamin

Bloomfield in order that the Prince Regent might be officially informed, and in reply the Regent sent a letter expressing his 'anxious solicitude' for his brother's restoration to health, which 'imparted to the Duke the most heartfelt satisfaction'.[26]

General Wetherall was anxious that his will should be signed. Stockmar, who arrived with Prince Leopold on 22nd January, was an old friend and a qualified and skilful doctor, though, on the grounds of being a foreigner, he had declined to take charge of Princess Charlotte. At about five o'clock on Saturday afternoon the Duchess led Stockmar into the sick-room. While she waited 'in heart rending anguish' Stockmar took the Duke's pulse. The Duke was 'half delirious' and Stockmar told the Duchess, for whom he had had an affection since her childhood, that 'human help could no longer avail'; with such a pulse it was doubtful if the Duke would survive the night. As to signing the will the question was whether the Duke could be roused to sufficient consciousness 'for the signature to have legal force'. When, however, General Wetherall was brought in, the voice and presence of his old friend had 'a wonderfully stimulating effect' on the Duke. He came to himself, enquired about various matters and persons, spoke of his wife and his child and had his will read over to him twice. Then, gathering all his strength, he managed to sign clearly and legibly, looking attentively at each letter as he formed it, asked if the signature was clear and legible, and, being assured that it was, fell back on his pillows, exhausted.

Next morning, Sunday, 23rd January 1820, as the clocks were striking ten, the Duke died.[27] The Duchess was kneeling beside the bed and holding his hand in hers.

The death of the Duke of Kent shocked and astonished the world. 'He was the strongest of the strong' wrote Mr Croker, the Tory politician, 'never before ill in his life, and now to die of a cold, when half the kingdom had colds with impunity. . . .'[28]

'Think, my dearest Lady Harcourt' wrote the Duke's sister, Princess Augusta, from Windsor Castle 'that yesterday *five* weeks, he was here on His way to Sidmouth; so happy with his excellent good little Wife and his lovely Child . . . when I think of His poor Miserable Wife and His innocent Fatherless Child, it really breaks my Heart. . . .'[29]

The Duchess of Kent deeply mourned the Duke. They had suited each other and he had been, wrote Stockmar, 'a chivalrous husband'. She had leaned on him, and he had cherished her, with borrowed money, it is true, but the Duchess had not understood that. '. . . I am hopelessly lost without dearest Edward, who thought of everything and always shielded me' she wrote, and again, 'He was my adored partner in life, whatever shall I do without his strong support?'

The situation of the Duchess and her infant daughter was now extremely precarious. The Duchess was penniless, the Duke had left nothing but debts and the will he had exerted himself to sign was worthless because no funds existed to execute its provisions. The Duchess did not have enough money to leave Woolbrook Cottage for London.

'I know not what would have become of you and your Mama, if I had not then existed' wrote Prince Leopold later to Queen Victoria. 'You, poor little soul, about 9 months old!! [in fact Princess Victoria became eight months old the day after her father's death] the state of affairs of your poor Father so bad that there was no means for the journey back to Kensington, [and] on the highest quarter, the *greatest animosity* and the wish to drive the Duchess to the continent. . . .'[30]

*

Though Prince Leopold became devoted to the little Princess, he had painful feelings to overcome first. The sight of the baby, 'that little blooming face', brought back heartrending memories of Charlotte and his dead baby son. For the first days of her life he could not bring himself to look at his infant niece, and even when the Duchess had persuaded him to see her, he shrank from looking at her again. He attended the christening, but, wrote the Duchess, it was a great sacrifice made out of love for her. But when Fate threw the all but friendless infant into his arms, 'from that moment his love and care for his dear niece never ceased'.[31] He transferred to her something of what he had felt for Charlotte; she might be Queen as Charlotte would have been Queen, she represented England as Charlotte had represented England, and the two became united in his mind.

The day after the Duke's death, surgeons, embalmers and undertakers invaded the limited space of Woolbrook Cottage. A post-mortem had to be carried out and the Duke's lying in state arranged in what was described as a 'spacious room, hung with black cloth and lighted with thirty wax candles', from which the light of day was 'entirely excluded'. The Duke's immense coffin, 7 ft 5½ in. long, weighing over a ton, was raised on trestles, and 'covered with a rich velvet pall, turned up at each end to show the splendid material. . . . At the head of the coffin was raised a superb plume of feathers, and three smaller plumes were placed at each side, also right and left were three large wax tapers in solid silver candle-sticks, standing five feet high. . . .'[32] A crowd was expected to file past, and Prince Leopold 'implored' his sister to 'leave this place as soon as possible'.[33] The Duke's coffin would not start on its last journey to Windsor until 7th February.

On 23rd January Prince Leopold, the Duchess and the little Princess left 'melancholy Sidmouth' for ever. The Duchess, who during the Duke's illness had not taken off her clothes for five consecutive nights, 'utterly

45

broke down' as she drove away from 'the place where his remains still lay'.

But as she drove away the Duchess did not know where she was to go. Though the Prince Regent had sent a kind message to his brother when the Duke of Kent was on his deathbed, it was not certain if he would allow the Duchess and the infant Princess to return to Kensington Palace, and at Prince Leopold's own house, Claremont, there was an epidemic of measles.

Prince Leopold begged Princess Mary, Duchess of Gloucester, at the moment the Regent's favourite sister, to intercede and persuade him to allow the Duchess to return to the Duke's apartments at Kensington.

On the day the Duchess left Sidmouth, Princess Mary wrote to her brother, in the fulsome style adopted when addressing him by 'the sisterhood'.

In her letter—which incidentally disposes of the notion that under-lining of words was a practice originated by Queen Victoria—she implored the Regent to consider the situation of the 'poor unfortunate' Duchess of Kent and to allow her to return to Kensington. '. . . *She* very properly feels a *delicacy* in returning to the apartments at Kensington without your *leave* and *full permission*. She has therefore called upon me . . . to lay her at your *feet* (as She is unequal to writing herself) & to say that in every respect *her situation* is most melancholy for Edward had nothing in the world but debts & now there are all his old servants without a penny piece to provide for them. She knows what your goodness of heart is & she is sure you *will* do what you can for them. . . .' The Duchess of Kent, with her brother and child, Princess Mary wrote, was leaving Sidmouth immediately and would sleep at Salisbury on Wednesday or Thursday night 'according as *her own* health will stand the fatigue of travelling & the child (who has got a cold), perhaps you would kindly have some *letter* wrote to her or the P. of Coburg that might find them at Salisbury, which I am *sure will contain nothing* but *comfort and kindness* from you & in her heavy affliction will be the *greatest consolation to her* . . . she wants all poor Edward's family can give her at this *moment* & who can do it so well and so *effectually* as *yourself*. . . . I am *gratified* at being called upon to deliver such a *message* because I feel it will be received by the most affectionate and kindest of Brothers. . . .'

As his brother, the Duke of Kent, was not yet buried, the Prince Regent could not decently turn out his penniless widow and her infant. A letter was written giving permission to return to Kensington and sent off by Princess Mary to catch the Duchess at Hertford Bridge. '. . . It was *most* particularly kind of you to allow such a letter to be written' wrote the Princess to the Prince Regent. '. . . as it prevented any misunder-standing & proved your *excellent* and most *affect. of hearts*, which I *wish* all the world *knew* only one quarter as well as I do, as *then* you would be valued as *you ought to be.*'[34]

On 29th January 1820, little after four weeks since their arrival at Sidmouth, the Duchess and the little Princess came back to Kensington Palace to be greeted by the news that the old King George III was dead. The Prince Regent would now ascend the throne as George IV: he had been Regent since 1811.

On 30th January the Duchess wrote to Polyxene 'Here I am again and sitting at the same table I have so often written to you from in the Highdays of my happiness. . . .' The carriages on the journey had been very bad 'and poor little Vickelchen got very upset by the frightful jolting'. The Duchess of Clarence had called the very afternoon the Duchess of Kent arrived and every day afterwards. 'Dearest William [the Duke of Clarence]' wrote Princess Augusta 'is so good hearted, that He has desired Adelaide to go to Kensington every day, as she is a Comfort to the poor Widow; and her sweet, gentle mind is of great use to the Duchess of Kent . . . they can read the same *Prayers* and *talk the same Mother Tongue* together'.[35]

The Duke of Sussex, who had come down to Sidmouth during the Duke of Kent's illness, called and the Dukes of York and Clarence paid visits, but towards them the Duchess of Kent was resentful. The Duke of York had been 'so unkind and had so deeply hurt my beloved husband' —the Duchess thought he 'seemed rather embarrassed in his manner'— while the Duke of Clarence was 'rather offhand'. They were much pleased with 'little Vickelchen', but the Duchess did not forget they had not been reconciled with their brother before his death.

When the Duke of Kent's coffin started on its way to Windsor, she 'sat in my solitude here, eating my heart out'. She had wished to be present at the funeral service in St George's Chapel, Windsor, but etiquette forbade. 'I am sick at heart and very lonely, for I was never parted from Edward since our marriage. I have just been putting dear, sweet, little Vickelchen to bed. God has indeed been good in letting me have such a treasure. . . .' she wrote to Polyxene von Tubeuf. She was feeling unwell and her head was often so confused she could hardly think. 'I have been so spoilt in having everything done for me that I am hopelessly lost without dearest Edward.'

Nevertheless in spite of the bleakness of the Duchess's future outlook, her want of money and the wounding indifference of the English Court towards herself and her child, Prince Leopold told her she must live in England. He never ceased to impress on her the importance of the destiny which might be in store for her infant daughter, and though she was greatly attached to her son Charles, now aged 16, on her brother's advice she resigned the Leiningen Regency and prepared to settle permanently in England.

The Duchess's financial position, however, was desperate. In the event of the Duke's death, Parliament had directed that the £6,000 a year settled on the Duke on his marriage should revert to her, but, as Prince Leopold wrote '. . . no Royal Duchess with Children can live on £6,000 a year', especially as in the case of the Duchess of Kent 'she had not a spoon or napkin of her own, as everything belonged to the creditors'.[36] Very curious figures were produced by the late Duke's friends. General Wetherall, his staunch supporter, put his assets at £89,000,[37] but in fact every asset was mortgaged or pledged and on 2nd February 1820 Princess Mary wrote[38] to her brother George IV to tell him 'of the deplorable *reduced* state the unfortunate Dss. of Kent is left in—and some little immediate assistance I plead is necessary'.

The King would not give his sister-in-law a sixpence. Though the Duchess was allowed to retain the Duke's apartments at Kensington Palace, she was 'left without Furniture, Plate, Linen, Wines, Horses, Carriages, or in fact any one of the Materials of an Establishment, and these she was obliged to purchase at an expence of twelve thousand pounds. . . . Half that sum it was necessary to borrow at interest, guaranteed by Prince Leopold, and the debt operated as a most serious drawback upon Her Royal Highness's means. . . .'[39]

The Duke of Kent had held the Rangership of the Home Park, Hampton Court, an appointment of value. In addition to the use and occupation of the Great Lodge, its privileges and emoluments included a supply of venison, certain rights of pasturage and the profits of the herbage of the Park—the grass and hay—worth £800 a year. The Duchess of Kent hoped the Rangership might be continued to her, since it was not unusual for a rangership to be held by a woman (later Queen Adelaide was Ranger of Bushey Park), but George IV conferred it on Lady Bloomfield, the wife of his Private Secretary.

George IV was determined to drive the Duchess and the infant Princess back to Amorbach. 'It was wonderful' wrote Prince Leopold, in a reminiscence[40] when King of the Belgians, 'how George IV was bent on this idea; and in those days the wish and will of the head of the state was still a very serious concern and the people very subservient to it'.

Amorbach, however, was in no condition to receive the Duchess. At the moment the residence was uninhabitable. The Duke's alterations had been extensive; the principal staircase had been taken down and re-modelled, rooms re-designed, and a temple was in course of erection on an island in the canal, with a picturesque bridge and a sloping walk leading to the mansion. About £3,500 was already owing, to which sum must be added the cost of completing the alterations before the house could be lived in. No bills had been paid since November 1819, the servants' wages were owing for the quarter ending 31st December 1819 and Captain Hulme, the architect and engineer whom the Duke had brought out from England, had not received his salary.[41]

Prince Leopold financed the Duchess. When the House of Commons met on 3rd July 1820 to vote the continuation of the parliamentary allowances which had been made to the sons and daughters of the late King George III, the Royal Dukes and the Princesses, 'to place those illustrious personages in the same situation in which they stood previously to the demise of the Crown', the leader of the Commons, Lord Castlereagh, stated '. . . the Duchess of Kent and the infant Princess might also be thought to have claims on the justice of Parliament; but he should not then propose any vote to them . . . as the Prince Leopold with great liberality, had taken upon himself the charge of the support and education of the infant Princess. . . .'[42]

Prince Leopold made the Duchess an allowance of £3,000 a year from his own income; he was receiving £50,000 annually from the British Government, settled on him when he married Princess Charlotte; £1,000 of this income was to be spent on a seaside or country holiday, as the Duchess had no residence out of London.

Unfortunately in the Duchess's nervous condition she found her brother Prince Leopold irritating. He was given to deliberation, and had a tendency to pomposity and an insistence on careful weighing of pros and cons which had led his father-in-law, George IV, to christen him 'le Marquis Peu à Peu'. 'Good Leopold' wrote the Duchess[43] 'is rather slow in the uptake and in making decisions.'

She had, however, another and more sympathetic adviser. Captain John Conroy, the late Duke's Equerry, had a capacity for making light of difficulties which the Duchess found soothing. He had been what the Duke termed 'my very intelligent factotum'[44] since the Duke's marriage, had helped in nursing the Duke at Sidmouth, and now remained with the Duchess. He was acting, she wrote, 'as a dear devoted friend of my Edward and does not desert his widow, doing all he can by dealing with my affairs. . . . His energy and capability are wonderful.' Her present position was 'not of the pleasantest' but Conroy was doing all he could to arrange matters as well as possible. He was 'invaluable, I don't know what I should do without him'. The Duchess was, as Stockmar had discerned, optimistic and she wrote that she did not share 'Leopold's black views' as to the future.

With characteristic generosity, almost immediately after the Duke of Kent's death the Duchess communicated with Madame de St Laurent, now Comtesse de Montgenet. In a letter to Mr Coutts, on 3rd February 1820, Louis Philippe Duke of Orleans wrote that he realised the Duke's intentions of providing for the Comtesse de Montgenet were 'impracticable', but the Comtesse had documents 'which appear to establish a clear right on her part to receive £4,000 out of the £30,000 for which the late Duke had insured his life for the security of his creditors . . . the Duchess of Kent having been so good, so generous & I may say so admirable, as to manifest to Mme. de Montgenet (since the Duke's death) the interest which she takes in her fate and her good wishes for Mme. de Montgenet's future welfare, I have informed Prince Leopold of the intentions of our friend (the Duke of Kent) towards Mme. de M. . . .'[45]

The Duke's estate, however, was hopelessly insolvent, and on 16th March 1820[46] the Duchess of Kent renounced all interest in it on behalf of herself and her daughter, in order that the estate might be administered solely for the benefit of the creditors.

Events now brought the question of the succession into the foreground again. Immediately after succeeding to the throne in January 1820 George IV fell desperately ill with pleurisy; 'as near death as any man but poor Kent ever was before—150 ounces of blood let have saved his *precious* life' wrote Creevey.[47] Had the King died, only the childless Duke of York and the childless Duke of Clarence would have stood between Princess Victoria and the throne. On 6th August 1820 the Duchess of York died and George IV urged the Duke of York to marry again. He refused '. . . my mind is quite made up to do no such thing, and so I have given the King to understand' he told Lord Lauderdale. He had in fact at the age of 57 fallen youthfully and blissfully in love with the Duchess of Rutland.

Towards the end of August the Countess Granville was invited to Cleveland House for 'a royal morning'. Lady Granville was the daughter of the Duke of Devonshire and wife of Earl Granville, who was twice British Ambassador at Paris. She met the Duchess of Clarence, whom she thought 'ugly but with a good tournure and manner'. The good tournure was surprising as the Duchess was five months pregnant. The Duchess of Kent Lady Granville thought 'very pleasing indeed and raving of her baby "C'est mon Bonheur, mes délices, mon existence. C'est l'image du feu roi." ' The infant Princess was not present, but Lady Granville wrote 'Think of the baby. They say it is le Roi George [*sic*] in petticoats. . . .'[48]

On 10th December 1820 the Duchess of Clarence gave birth to a live daughter, born six weeks too soon, but 'doing well'. Princess Victoria was no longer the eventual heiress to the throne. George IV and the Royal Family were delighted; the 'thorn in their side',[49] the prospect of the child of the Duke and Duchess of Kent on the throne, was removed. George IV had refused to allow a family name to be given to the infant Victoria, but the little Clarence Princess was christened Elizabeth Georgina in addition to her mother's name of Adelaide.

'We are all on the kick and go', wrote Conroy. 'Our little woman's nose has been put out of joint.'[50]

Meanwhile the Duchess of Kent was getting further and further into debt. Her income was barely adequate, royal persons were expected to keep up some state, and if the Duchess had had a sense of the value of money she could not have lived happily with the Duke of Kent. Her habits were simple enough but she had Conroy looking after her finances, and Conroy's dealings with money proved later to be unsatisfactory.[51]

In February 1821 Lord Liverpool, the Prime Minister, spoke to George IV of the necessity for making some provision for the fatherless infant Princess. 'The royal answer' wrote Prince Leopold 'was that he would be d—d if he consented to it, that *her* Uncle was rich enough to take care of her.' George IV in common with the nation resented continuing to pay Prince Leopold his annual allowance of £50,000 a year. In February 1821 Prince Leopold told Lord Liverpool he would be most happy to undertake the care of the little Princess 'but remember it was not I who grasped at the management of the Princess, but that the Princess is by the King in this manner confided to me, and H.Maj. thereby delegates to me a power which belongs to him'.

Less than a month later, on 4th March 1821, the infant Princess Elizabeth unexpectedly died at St James's Palace from an 'entanglement of the bowels', a condition for which, at that period, it was impossible to operate. 'For God's sake come down to me' wrote George IV from Brighton to his confidential adviser, Sir William Knighton '. . . the melancholy tidings of the almost sudden death of my poor little niece has just reached me & has overset me beyond all I can express to you. . . .'[52]

Once again the little Princess Victoria was restored to the position of heiress to the throne, though there was still a hope that the Duchess of Clarence, who was only 29 years of age, having given birth to one living child might give birth to another. George IV did not make any acknowledgment of the position of Princess Victoria, nor did he offer the Duchess any financial help, so that, in April 1821, it was necessary for the Duchess to borrow £6,000 from Thomas Coutts, on a bond signed by the Duchess of Kent and the Duke's two executors, General Wetherall and Captain Conroy.[53]

The Duchess keenly felt and keenly resented the dislike which both George IV and his brother the Duke of Clarence, the next heir to the throne, openly displayed towards her. After the death of the Duke of Kent, she declared she stood, with her daughter, 'friendless and alone, in a country that was not her own'.[54] It was a serious drawback that she found English almost impossible to learn. The Duchess of Kent was 'very pleasing',[55] affectionate and gay, but foreigners were, as always, unpopular in England, and, at the moment, Germans were the most unpopular of all. 'Why should we have Germans to rule over us?' burst out

Lady Jersey, at a party in December 1820.[56] Lady Jersey's countenance, commented Lady Granville, was so stern that it affected her beauty.

In August 1821 royal relationships shifted again. Queen Caroline, the wife from whom George IV had been separated since 1796, died unexpectedly. Her conduct had been deplorable, but her humiliations were cruel and after she had been ignominiously turned from the door of Westminster Abbey on the day of George IV's coronation, though constitutionally Queen of England, she fell ill. '. . . I am going to die' she remarked 'but it does not signify' and she did die, during the night of 7th August 1821.

After twenty-five years George IV was free and it was reported that in spite of his years—he was 59—and his infirmities, he was determined to marry again. 'His mind is clearly made up, according to Lauderdale [Lord Lauderdale was an intimate friend of the Royal Family], to have another wife' wrote Creevey 'and all his family are of that opinion. He goes straight for Hanover and Vienna after his Irish trip, so probably he will pick up something before his return at Xmas. . . .'[57]

The little Princess Victoria had now passed her second birthday, in appearance a typical English child with a beautiful fair skin and large blue eyes, easy to amuse, inclined to be obstinate and self-willed. She was becoming conscious of the world around her, faces were beginning to sort themselves out, incidents registered themselves in her recollection. A face she welcomed with delight belonged to the enchantingly pretty Princess Feodora, her half-sister and senior by twelve years, daughter of the Duchess of Kent by her first husband, the Prince of Leiningen. In spite of the difference in age the two girls grew up devoted to each other. Princess Feodora was the closest friend Queen Victoria ever had, either as Princess or Queen, and, outside her children, probably the only woman in her life she truly loved.

In 1872, nearly fifty years later, Queen Victoria wrote down some recollections of her early childhood.[58] Her first memory was of crawling on a yellow carpet in a room in Kensington Palace and being told that if she cried and was naughty her 'Uncle Sussex', who lived next door, would hear her and punish her. 'For which reason' writes the Queen 'I always screamed when I saw him!' At an early age she had 'a great horror of *Bishops* on account of their wigs and *aprons*'. This was overcome in the case of Bishop Fisher of Salisbury, the old friend of her father and mother, 'by his kneeling down and letting me play with his badge of Chancellor of the Order of the Garter'. The visits paid to Claremont, Prince Leopold's house near Esher, were her greatest treat. She loved, she wrote, 'to be under the roof of that beloved Uncle', to be allowed to listen to music in the hall when there were dinner parties and to go and visit Mrs Louis— 'dear old Louis! the . . . devoted Dresser and friend of Princess Charlotte

... who was with her when she died'. Mrs Louis 'doted' on the little Princess Victoria who was 'too much an Idol in the House'. Up to her fifth year, wrote Queen Victoria, she was 'very much indulged by everyone and set pretty well *all* at defiance. Old Baroness de Spaeth, the devoted Lady of my Mother, my Nurse Mrs Brock, dear old Mrs Louis—*all* worshipped the poor little fatherless child. . . .' Spaeth's devotion, wrote Princess Feodora, sometimes showed itself foolishly; 'with you it was a kind of idolatry when she used to go on her knees before you when you were a child. . . .'[59] 'Naturally very passionate', the little Princess was 'always most contrite afterwards' and was taught to beg her maid's pardon for any naughtiness or rudeness.[60] She was not fond of learning and stubbornly refused to learn her letters until she was five years old. Another childish recollection was of a donkey she used to ride, her nurse Mrs Brock and Princess Feodora walking beside her. Mrs Brock always admonished Princess Victoria, as the gentlemen touched their hats to her, 'Bow your head, Princess'.[61] The donkey was a gift from her uncle the Duke of York. He 'was very kind to me' wrote the Queen. 'I remember him well—tall, rather large, very kind, but extremely shy. He always gave me beautiful presents.'[62] Once he had a Punch and Judy show for her at a friend's villa at Brompton. George IV almost ignored his niece as a small child; she remembered being taken to Carlton House by her mother only once, to see the King. He was about to give a large dinner party.

On 3rd December 1819, before Princess Victoria was a year old, a formidable personality had arrived at Kensington Palace. Louise Lehzen[63] was the daughter of a Lutheran clergyman in the small village of Lagenhagen in Hanover and came to be Princess Feodora's governess. The engagement had been made by the Duke of Kent through Dr Kuper, the reader at the German Lutheran Chapel at St James's Palace.* Dr Kuper was told that when Princess Victoria's nurse left her, it was the Duke's intention that Fräulein Lehzen should become the little Princess's governess. 'Lehzen', as she came always to be called, was 35 years of age, dark, good-looking, pronounced by Charles Greville to be 'a clever agreeable woman'[64] and with the highest recommendations; she had been governess to three daughters in the aristocratic von Marenholtz

---

* Known first as the Queen's Chapel and often mentioned by Pepys, the chapel, which stands in what is now Marlborough Gate facing St James's Palace, was designed by Inigo Jones and built for the use of Queen Henrietta Maria as a Roman Catholic Chapel. Later Queen Catherine of Braganza worshipped there. King William III handed it over to the French and Dutch Protestant congregations in London in 1700, and from 1781 it was occupied by the German Lutherans. Princess Victoria's half-sister, Princess Feodora, was confirmed there in 1823 and married there in 1828 to the Prince of Hohenlohe-Langenburg. (From *St James's Palace*, by the Rev. Edgar Sheppard, Sub-Dean of H.M. Chapels Royal; Longmans Green & Co., London, 1894. Vol. II, p. 245.)

family. She possessed strength of character, powers of attraction and a capacity for devotion.

She found, she writes, Princess Victoria to be 'a splendid baby', and Princess Feodora at 12 years old already 'very prepossessing'. She was at Sidmouth during the Duke's fatal illness and when back at Kensington Palace, with Princess Feodora, shared all Princess Victoria's walks and drives for five easy and pleasant years. From a very early age, while her nurse, Mrs Brock, was dressing Princess Victoria, Lehzen used to read little stories aloud to her, not as an indulgence but in order that she might not get into the habit of chattering to servants. In 1824, when Princess Victoria was five years old and Mrs Brock was leaving, the Duchess of Kent and Prince Leopold asked Lehzen to take charge of the little Princess. 'After a short silence' writes Lehzen 'I said that I had often thought of the great difficulties which such a person might have to encounter in educating a Princess, destined perhaps to ascend a throne and perhaps not; but if Her Royal Highness and Prince Leopold put that confidence in me, I had but one favour to ask, namely ... should the Duchess see strangers, where the Princess's presence was required I ought to attend Her. ... I added, that in the room where I was to live with the Princess in Kensington Palace I was to see no one but those the Duchess chose to send, *never* my own acquaintances. ... I never kept a journal as it would not have been a prudent thing. ...'[65]

The little Princess Victoria was not an easy child to manage. She was a Hanoverian, with a Hanoverian temper, given to Hanoverian fury at contradiction. There were outbursts of rage, shrieks and stamping of angry feet when the Princess could not have her own way. Once in a fit of temper she threw a pair of scissors at Lehzen.[66] But Lehzen brought about a transformation, without physical punishment. She had known the little Princess since babyhood, she loved her and won her heart. The Princess was a noticeably affectionate child, and Lehzen devoted herself entirely to her charge. 'She never for the 13 years she was governess to Pss. Victoria, *once left her*' wrote Queen Victoria in her reminiscences '... and knew how to amuse and play with the Princess so as to gain her warmest affections. The Princess was her only object and her only thought. She was very strict and the Pss. had great respect and even awe of her, but with that the greatest affection. ...'[67] For her part Lehzen found Princess Victoria 'a delightful child' and recalled how she used to ask 'May I tell a story?'

Visits to Prince Leopold at Claremont remained glimpses of paradise, 'the brightest epoch of my otherwise rather melancholy childhood' wrote the Queen. Both the Princesses disliked their life at Kensington Palace, though both loved Lehzen. For Princess Victoria '... the return to Kensington ... was generally a day of tears', and Princess Feodora 'always left Claremont with tears for Kensington'.[68] They were brought up always under their mother's eye. Princess Victoria never had a room she could call her own until she was nearly grown up and slept in a little bed in her mother's room until she came to the throne. A familiar sound in childhood was the tick, tick of a large tortoiseshell repeater watch which had belonged to the Duke of Kent. 'We lived in a very simple plain manner' writes the Queen 'breakfast was at half past eight, luncheon at half past one, dinner at seven—to which I came generally (when it was no regular large dinner party)—eating my bread and milk out of a small silver basin. Tea was only allowed as a great treat in later years.'

Later Princess Feodora told Queen Victoria 'when I look back upon those years which ought to have been the happiest in my life . . . I cannot help pitying myself. Not to have enjoyed the pleasures of youth is nothing, but to have been deprived of all intercourse and not one cheerful thought in that dismal existence of ours, was very hard. My only happy time was going or driving out with you and Lehzen; then I could speak and look as I liked.'

The qualities of friendliness, affection, generosity and truthfulness which Stockmar praised in the Duchess of Kent had, for the moment, disappeared. Always apt to submit herself to masculine direction and without much faculty of criticism, the Duchess had unfortunately found, what her brother Prince Leopold described as a 'Mephistopheles'[69] in Captain Conroy, now Comptroller of her household.

Captain John Conroy was an Irishman, with limitless ambitions, good looks and charm. His family* came from Co. Roscommon in Connaught, wildest, most primitive and most remote of the Irish provinces—James I used to tell rebellious courtiers to go to Hell or Connaught—and only a comparatively short time had elapsed since the Conroys emerged from the Connaught wilds. The spelling of the name had only recently been fixed, earlier Conroys appear as O'Malconnaire's or O'Maolconrys; and though Captain John Conroy's great-grandfather had anglicised his name to Conry, he bore a native Irish first name, Feafeara. The Conroys had immense family pride and a pedigree among the Conroy papers, six to seven feet in length, traces the family descent in a direct line from Niallus Magnus, Niall of the Nine Hostages, Monarch of Ireland in A.D. 400.

John Conroy's father, John Ponsonby Conroy, turned his back on Ireland and went to live at Maizey Castle, Caernarvonshire, where on 21st October 1786 his eldest son was born and christened John.

Young John chose the Army as his profession and in 1803, at the age of 17, obtained a commission in the Royal Artillery and was posted to a company serving in Ireland. He did well, became Adjutant of the Western

* See Appendix 2.

55

District and was described by his commanding officer as 'an excellent pen and ink man, possessing great knowledge of horses'. In 1805 he was offered a transfer to the Horse Artillery, socially a more desirable regiment which he accepted, continuing to serve in Ireland.

In December 1808, when he was 22, like his father and grandfather before him he made an advantageous marriage, marrying Elizabeth Fisher, only child of Major General Fisher, Commanding Engineer in Ireland and niece of the Right Reverend John Fisher, Bishop of Salisbury, Chancellor of the Order of the Garter and formerly tutor to the sons of the English Royal Family. Major General Fisher, who was described by the Duke of Kent as one of his oldest friends, had served in Canada at the same time as the Duke, and his daughter Elizabeth, who was 17 at the date of her marriage, was born at Government House, Quebec, in 1791.

A few months after his marriage, in the spring of 1809, Captain John Conroy was selected by Major General Fisher to act as Major of Brigade to the Engineer Department in Ireland, and in 1812, when Major General Fisher became Commanding Engineer in the Portsmouth Division, he appointed Captain Conroy to be his aide-de-camp. At the end of 1812 Captain Conroy returned briefly to Dublin to wind up matters of business and accounts relating to the period of Major General Fisher's appointment as Commanding Engineer Ireland, 'which he did to the entire satisfaction of the government', the sum involved amounting to nearly £300,000.[70]

Captain John Conroy's career held out good prospects of success when, in September 1814, Major General Fisher died. No longer backed by his father-in-law's influence, Captain Conroy had to make a fresh start. He was appointed Headquarters Adjutant, but he was looking for opportunities not offered by the everyday round of regimental duties, nor was he anxious for active service. The Peninsular and Waterloo campaigns were fought between 1808 and 1815, but he took no part in either. He had become friendly with the Duke of Kent, through his wife's connections, and the Duke did his best to advance him, writing to Sir George Beechwith[71] who required a military secretary that Captain Conroy 'son-in-law of our late mutual friend M General Fisher is in every respect a treasure ... as well from experience and practice, as from talent and a great habit of application'. However, neither this nor any other application on Captain Conroy's behalf was successful and in 1817 when the Duke was forming an establishment before his marriage, Captain Conroy entered the Duke's household as Military Equerry. After his marriage the Duke of Kent continued to exert himself on Captain Conroy's behalf, writing from Amorbach in December 1818 to the Duke of Wellington,[72] who was on the eve of being appointed Major General of the Ordnance, to recommend Captain Conroy as 'an officer *particularly* deserving of your notice'.

Perhaps the Duke of Wellington would place Captain Conroy 'in some position of confidence about his person?' But this application, too, was unsuccessful, and Captain Conroy was still in the Duke's household when the Duke died in 1820.

John Conroy was, with some justification, a disappointed man. His abilities, of which he had the highest opinion, were in fact considerable, yet he had achieved almost nothing. He already had six children, four sons and two daughters, to support and provide for out of a small income. His wife, who had seemed an advantageous match, was beginning to fail in health, and was of no assistance to him. Her mental powers were described as 'below the average' and she was 'a perfect cypher'.

Fate had not used him kindly. But, with the death of the Duke of Kent, opportunity, on a scale undreamed of, opened before him. As counsellor director, indeed master, of the Duchess of Kent, he could be master of the future Queen of England and, in due course, of her kingdom. Power, riches, position would be his, all his ambition craved would be within his grasp, and he decided to make the Duchess of Kent his career.

He intended to gain domination over Princess Victoria. The probability that she might come to the throne was strengthening daily. No other Clarence infant had appeared after the death of little Princess Elizabeth in 1821. The Duke of York had adhered to his resolution not to re-marry, George IV had not re-married, he was a bad life, as was the next heir to the throne, the Duke of Clarence. Though Royal Persons came of age at 18, it seemed likely that Princess Victoria would succeed before she was of age. In that case there would be a regency; the Duchess of Kent would almost certainly be appointed Regent, and controlling the Duchess of Kent would be John Conroy. He was ambitious, he wanted a country estate, he wanted to be a peer, he wanted money. He had established his domination over the Duchess of Kent but to secure his position he must also establish his domination over the round-headed, fair-haired, blue-eyed little girl, with a reputation for obstinacy, who would one day sit on the throne. In a fatal moment he decided he must break her will.

In May 1825 'without any application or representation on her part' the Duchess of Kent was informed that the Government intended to propose a grant of £4,000 annually for the 'better support and maintenance' of Princess Victoria; at the same time a grant of £6,000 annually was to be proposed for the maintenance of Prince George of Cumberland, son of the unpopular Duke of Cumberland. The Duchess of Kent refused the £4,000. '. . . She could not consent to accept a lower figure for the Princess than that assigned to a member of the family who was further removed from the throne' and 'would rather continue with the very reduced allowance which she received than be a party to an arrangement which Her Royal Highness considered derogatory. . . .'[73] When the proposal came before Parliament the grant to the Duchess for her daughter was raised to £6,000 annually, and the reception of the proposal, in the House of Commons especially, demonstrated the position held by the little Princess Victoria in the nation's affections. After the Duke of Cumberland had been roundly abused and assured that every man, woman and child in the country had a dislike for him, though he got his grant nevertheless, Princess Victoria was described by Mr Brougham as 'the heiress presumptive to the British throne'. 'All parties' said Mr Secretary Canning 'agreed in the propriety of the grant, and if the government had anything to answer for on this point, it was for having so long delayed bringing it before the House. . . .' In the House of Lords, the Earl of Darnley paid a tribute to the Duchess of Kent as 'an example of prudence and of excellent conduct'.[74]

The grant of £6,000 a year and the praise, the first the Duchess of Kent had received, were a foretaste of the benefits which would flow from the little Princess. The Duchess of Kent had been harshly treated, she had endured humiliations, eaten the bread of dependence, but now her hour of triumph was coming. As mother of the heiress presumptive to the throne, and later, very likely, as Regent ruling the country for the young Queen, she was about to become a person of national importance and prestige.

Prince Leopold advised she should make changes in her establishment suitable to altered circumstances, now that the position of the little Princess as heiress presumptive was acknowledged.[75] He was, he wished her to know before she made plans, proposing to continue the allowance of £3,000 annually. The Duchess demurred before she accepted. She did not want her brother Prince Leopold to be able to interfere; she wanted to keep the little Princess entirely under her influence, as Conroy advised, but the £3,000 a year was needed. She had debts amounting to £9,000, debts not created by any want of economy but because she had to buy everything on the Duke's death and was allowed no 'outfit'. She proposed to put aside £2,000 a year to pay off her debts. Three extra servants were needed in her household and the others ought to be paid in a manner suited to her station; bills should also be regularly discharged, which was not the case at present, and she wished to relieve her son, the Prince of Leiningen, who was embarrassed financially, of the maintenance of his sister, Princess Feodora. Conroy wrote a long letter on her behalf to Prince Leopold in which she detailed her new plans.[76] The horizon was brightening indeed, but all plans, all hopes, all schemes, the coming power, and the coming glory hung on the little girl, now six years old, who embodied in her person the majesty and might of what was, at the moment, the greatest Empire in the world.

In the summer of 1825 (though the Queen, in her recollections written in 1872,[77] places the illness in the autumn of 1826), fate gave a warning how slight that thread was. Staying at Claremont the little Princess became seriously ill with something 'which assumed the appearance of dysentery.' An epidemic of dysentery had broken out in the neighbouring town of Esher in which several children died, including the daughter of the local doctor who 'lost his head'. Mr Blagden, who was especially skilful in the treatment of children, was summoned from London and after some days of acute anxiety the little Princess recovered. She remembered 'being very cross and screaming dreadfully at having to wear, for a time, flannel next my skin'. On 18th September 1825 the Duchess was able to assure George IV that Princess Victoria 'is better now'.[78] George IV had by now accepted his niece as the heiress presumptive to the throne and was showing interest not only in her, but in her half-sister as well. Princess Feodora was now 17 and, writes Queen Victoria, 'was very lovely . . . and had charming manners about which the King was extremely particular'.[79] In her letter of 18th September the Duchess of Kent thanked him for a letter about her elder daughter '. . . at this moment to receive so very kind, so affectionate a letter from you about Feodora has been a great comfort to me. . . . Feodora would be quite unhappy, if I did not lay her duty at your Majesty's feet, she is quite overwhelmed with your graciousness. . . .'

In 1826 ('I think' writes the Queen[80]) George IV asked Princess Victoria, Princess Feodora and the Duchess of Kent to Windsor. They stayed at Cumberland Lodge; the Royal Lodge was occupied only by the King himself and the Conyngham family. Lady Conyngham was the last of his mistresses, the best-natured but also the most rapacious. 'When we arrived at the Royal Lodge' writes Queen Victoria 'the King took me by the hand, saying "Give me your little paw". He was large and gouty but with a wonderful dignity and charm of manner. He wore the wig which was so much worn in those days.' He gave the Princess a miniature of himself set in diamonds, a replica of the miniature worn by his sisters the Royal Princesses as an order on a blue ribbon on the left shoulder. Lady Conyngham pinned it on, and the little Princess felt very proud. Next day the Princess with the Duchess and Lehzen went for a drive to Virginia Water 'and met the King in his phaeton, in which he was driving the Duchess of Gloucester—and he said "Pop her in", and I was lifted in and placed between him and Aunt Gloucester who held me round the waist. (Mamma was much frightened.) I was greatly pleased, and remember that I looked with great respect at the scarlet liveries etc. (the Royal Family had crimson and green liveries and only the King scarlet and blue in those days).' The party then went on Virginia Water in a large barge and fished, while a band played on another barge floating near them. 'There were numbers of great people there . . . the King paid great attention to my Sister, and some people fancied he might marry her!'

The influence possessed by Lady Conyngham over the King and his state of mental and physical health make it unlikely that George IV ever seriously contemplated a marriage with the lovely young Princess Feodora. In any case very different plans were being made for her. On 14th July 1826 Conroy wrote to the Duchess about the urgency of marrying her off.[81] The Prince of Schönburg, the Austrian Minister, was interested, but the possibility of the Princess coming to London as the wife of a minister would be, Conroy thought, most *disadvantageous* both to the Duchess and to Princess Victoria. The Duke of Nassau had paid attention and would be a very splendid match, but Conroy favoured a marriage with Prince Hohenlohe Langenburg, a connection of the Duchess of Clarence: '. . . in that marriage' wrote Conroy 'I think the Princess would find that character, that dignity of conduct which would tend to preserve her own happiness, and that if her life was unmarked by anything very splendid it would be free from the disquietudes that would attend either of the other two'. However, in case the Hohenlohe Langenburg match did not materialise the Duchess should temporise with the Prince of Schönburg; 'Much as I dislike this prospect it is *better than none*—and I must unequivocally state to you, that it is not only essential to the interest and happiness of the Pss. Feodora that she should marry *soon*, but it is necessary for yours and the Pss. Victoria's interest that it should take place —the influence you ought to have over her [Princess Victoria] will be endangered if she sees an older sister not so alive to it as she should be— and recollect, once your authority is lost over the Princess V you will never regain it. . . .'

To the public, her future subjects, the seven-year-old Princess Victoria appeared the very picture of a happy unspoilt child. Lord Albemarle, at that time a young man of 27, in waiting on the Duke of Sussex, wrote in his recollections[82] 'One of my occupations of a morning, while waiting for the Duke, was to watch from the window the movements of a bright pretty little girl, seven years of age. It was amusing to see how impartially she divided the contents of the watering pot between the flowers and her own little feet.' She wore 'a large straw hat, and a suit of white cotton; a coloured fichu round the neck was the only ornament she wore. The young lady I am describing was Princess Victoria. . . .'

Leigh Hunt 'with a peculiar kind of personal pleasure' met the little Princess in Kensington Gardens coming up a cross path from the Bayswater Gate holding another little girl by the hand. A large footman followed behind them, looking like 'a gigantic fairy'.[83]

Leigh Hunt was a critic of the Royal Dukes and had served two years in prison for a bitter and contemptuous article which legally libelled the Prince Regent, but he was ready to be enchanted by the little Princess.

Simple as her upbringing was, Princess Victoria's status and importance were being consciously, and indeed dramatically, built up, not without a view to increasing the prestige and importance of her mother, and her mother's adviser.

In 1827 it was asserted that Lehzen, who had had the Princess under her charge for nearly three years, was not a fit person to eat at the same table as the heiress to the throne because she had no noble rank. Conroy approached Princess Sophia, the King's sister, who lived in Kensington Palace and with whom he had struck up so intimate a friendship that she was described as his 'chère amie'; she had also made Conroy her Comptroller and he had charge of her money.[84] Princess Sophia was an unbalanced character, warped by a tragic youth. The old King George III, her father, had kept all his daughters with oriental strictness. '. . . There they were' wrote Greville 'secluded from the world, mixing with few people, their passions boiling over. . . .'[85] Princess Sophia had fallen in love and given birth in secret to an illegitimate child.

At Conroy's instigation she approached George IV who, as King of Hanover, not only raised Lehzen to the rank of Hanoverian Baroness, but created Conroy himself a Knight Commander of the Hanoverian Order, so that he became Sir John Conroy.[86]

Towards the end of 1827 Princess Feodora's betrothal to Prince Ernest Christian Charles of Hohenlohe Langenburg was announced. It was the marriage Conroy had recommended to the Duchess as being most likely to render the Princess harmless and get her out of the way. Prince Ernest was handsome, intelligent, 32 years of age, and Greville considered the Duchess of Kent was under a great obligation to the Duchess of Clarence for having 'made' the marriage.[87] But from a worldly point of view the match was not a good one. The Hohenlohe Langenburgs were poor. Like the Leiningens, they were mediatised princes who had been brought to the verge of ruin by the Napoleonic wars, and Princess Feodora was tormented by money difficulties all her married life. Though devoted to Prince Ernest, her beauty, intelligence and charm, combined with her close connection with the powerful English Court, fitted her for a more brilliant existence than the economy, the dullness and isolation of life at Schloss Langenburg, an immense building, sparsely furnished and celebrated for the icy cold of its corridors 'like caves'. On 18th February 1828 the marriage took place. George IV directed it should be held in private and he himself would give the bride away. However, four days before the ceremony he discovered he had not regained sufficient strength after an attack of gout to be able to stand on his legs and did not appear.[88] Princess Victoria was a bridesmaid and wore a lace dress. '. . . dearest little girl as you were' wrote Princess Feodora 'dressed in white going round with the basket presenting the favours'.[89]

Princess Feodora did not marry for love but to get away from life at Kensington Palace. '. . . I escaped some years of imprisonment, which you, my poor dear Sister, had to endure after I was married' she wrote to Queen Victoria in 1843.[90] '. . . Often have I praised God that he sent my dearest Ernest, for I might have married I don't know whom—merely to get away. There was that odious Prince Schönburg who wanted to marry me; if Mamma had wished it, I think I should have done it without liking him in the least. . . .'

The first days of the honeymoon were spent at Claremont, then on 26th February 1828 Princess Feodora crossed the Channel and disappeared for the moment from Princess Victoria's life.

The little Princess was left alone. The Duchess of Kent and Sir John Conroy had her to themselves, to mould, as they imagined, into the person they wished her to be. It was assumed that Lehzen, being 'entirely dependent' on the Duchess of Kent, would do as she was told.

On the part of the Duchess there was no wish to be unkind. She always adored Victoria, but she never understood her. The Duchess was a duck who had hatched a swan. Her unreasoning, self-doubting, emotional nature—always asking for advice, said her brother Prince Leopold— made it possible for Conroy to impose his schemes on her; the loyalty which was perhaps her most admirable trait led her to support him through thick and thin.

Conroy, devoured by ambition, was determined to gain his ends and not particular how he did so.

The result was what came to be known as 'the Kensington System'.

Chapter Three

The aim of the 'Kensington System' was to bring up the little Princess to be utterly dependent on her mother. Through Conroy's influence over the Duchess of Kent, an influence, wrote King Leopold, which might once have been called witchcraft, he would then in effect be King of England. It happens that the methods adopted to produce this result have been recorded in detail. In 1841, when the Princess had become Queen and Conroy had left the Court, Charles Prince of Leiningen, Queen Victoria's half-brother, became uneasy about his own position. He was anxious to explain how it came about that for many years he had been Conroy's friend and supporter and he dictated a long memorandum to Prince Albert's librarian, Dr Praetorius, entitled 'A complete History of the Policy followed at Kensington, under Sir John Conroy's guidance'.[1]

When Prince Charles first came to England in 1824 he found Conroy 'a companion as pleasant as he was extremely charming', and accepted Conroy's assurances that he was bound to the Duchess of Kent and the little Princess Victoria by ties of 'unlimited affection'. Conroy was fond of relating how the Duke of Kent, on his deathbed, had entrusted the Duchess and the baby Princess into his care and alleged that he gave his services to the Duchess for nothing. However, beside an account of this alleged episode the Queen has written 'Untrue'. The Duchess herself 'repeatedly' told Prince Charles that Conroy had 'done more'; he had pledged part of his property to guarantee her debts and it was understood that 'at a later date', that is, when Princess Victoria came to the throne, he and his family would be rewarded. Conroy declared to Prince Charles that his first aim was 'to give the Princess Victoria an upbringing which would enable her in the future to be equal to her high position', his second 'to win her so high a place in the hearts of her future subjects, even before her accession, that she would assume the sceptre with a popularity never yet attained and rule with *commensurate* power'.

These laudable intentions occupied only a couple of paragraphs, and Conroy went on to his third aim 'to assure a pleasant and honourable future for the Duchess of Kent as well'. The Duchess of Kent's future, dealt with in detail, occupied almost the whole remainder of the long memorandum.

Conroy eagerly anticipated a regency. George IV's health was failing; the Duke of York died in 1827. Next in succession was the Duke of Clarence, already over 60, and, since Princess Victoria was barely ten years old when the Kensington system was devised, and would not be 18 (when at that time Royal Persons came of age) until 1837, it was therefore very probable that the Princess would come to the throne while still a minor and a regency would be inevitable. The Duchess of Kent must gain a strong position 'so that . . . the nation should *have* to assign her the Regency'. She must achieve two objects: first her daughter must be completely dependent on her; 'every effort must be made to keep the education of the daughter completely in the hands of her mother and to prevent all interference . . . *nothing* and *no one* should be able to tear the daughter away from her'. Second, 'in order to be sure of winning and retaining this strong position . . . the Duchess of Kent should win for herself the esteem and approbation of the *entire* nation'. In other words 'she must acquire popularity and a wide following'. She must also have 'an unswerving resolution both in public and in private to carry out the measures necessary for achieving her object'.

'A hundred times' records Prince Charles 'Sir John Conroy explained the foregoing to me as the *only aim*, the only motive, the basis of all actions, of the whole system followed at Kensington for many years.'

To make the Princess completely dependent on her mother she was to be isolated within the Kensington circle, no risk must be taken of anyone from outside winning the Princess's affections and undermining her mother's authority. 'Regulations', as Prince Charles calls them, to produce this result were laid down and enforced.

Lehzen owed her appointment to Conroy's Kensington policy. She was not chosen on account of her success as governess to Princess Feodora 'but' says Prince Charles 'principally on account of the difficulty and danger of bestowing this post on any English woman, who would necessarily have a political connexion and influential friends'. It was also considered that 'the Baroness being *entirely dependent* upon the Duchess of Kent would also conform in all matters entirely with the latter's will'. In this expectation Conroy and the Duchess of Kent were disappointed.

The first and most necessary step, Conroy told Prince Charles, was to separate the little Princess from the English Royal Family, the uncles and aunts, who were her most powerful relatives. Conroy declared that a desire was 'continually cherished' among them to remove the Princess from her mother's authority and treat the Duchess as 'a children's nurse'. This was true. The Duke of Wellington told Charles Greville that George IV, who disliked the Duchess of Kent, 'was always talking of taking her child from her', which, said Greville, 'he inevitably would have done but for the Duke. . . .'² (of Wellington). Conroy also alleged that the hostility felt towards the Duke of Kent by his brothers and sisters had been transferred to his widow and child, with the one exception of Princess Sophia, who lived next door to the Duchess of Kent in Kensington Palace and was intimate with her, dining three or four nights a week, and spending most evenings in the Duchess's apartment. Princess Sophia, said Prince Charles, 'stood in close-linked friendship with Sir John Conroy'. She 'was considered by him to be very favourably disposed towards the Kensington system and was used by him whenever necessary and in various ways, for the carrying out of his plan. . . .' He called her his 'spy', and frequently, when the Duchess of Kent complained about Princess Sophia, who was so difficult in temperament as to be unbalanced, Sir John Conroy counselled indulgence or toleration, because Princess Sophia was 'indispensable'.

As Princess Sophia's unofficial Comptroller, financially Conroy stood very close to her indeed; he was, wrote his son, Edward Conroy, 'Princess Sophia's heir de facto . . . she gave him nearly all her large income', and in 1826 had financed his purchase of an estate in Montgomeryshire for £18,000.[3]

The Duke of Sussex, who occupied apartments adjoining the Duchess of Kent's in Kensington Palace, was also considered by Conroy to be friendly 'in part'. Conroy, says Prince Charles, flattered himself he was leading the Duke 'by the nose'.

A second reason, Conroy asserted, for separating the Princess from her father's family was their moral standard. It was essential the nation should be clearly shown that Princess Victoria was being brought up on high moral principles, very 'different . . . from those of the English Royal family, against whom so many public accusations of misconduct persisted', therefore no friendship must exist.

For the same reason, a 'regulation' of the Kensington System separated Princess Victoria from her mother's family, the Coburgs. The Duchess's brother, Ernest I, Duke of Saxe-Coburg and Saalfeld, was rivalling the English Royal Dukes in extravagance and dissipation, and his beautiful young Duchess, Luise, mother of Prince Albert, was not blameless. 'In Coburg the very sparrows on the roof twittered stories of the amours both of Duke and Duchess'[4] and in 1824 the marriage ended in the flight of the Duchess and, eventually, divorce. Meanwhile, states Prince Charles, '. . . many derogatory rumours and publications about them were in circulation' and it was thought that 'their future dissemination or reproduction in England could have become dangerous to the Duchess of Kent particularly as regards public opinion'.

Prince Leopold and Stockmar both agreed with Conroy that the Coburgs had better be 'kept away'.

Prince Leopold himself should have been the insurmountable obstacle in Conroy's path. Brother of the Duchess of Kent, he was her 'natural counsellor', and the natural protector of his niece the little Princess. But from 1829 onwards Prince Leopold withdrew for some years from his sister's affairs.[5] He has been blamed. Prince Albert told Queen Victoria later 'Mama here would never have fallen into the hands of Conroy, if Uncle Leopold had taken the trouble to guide her'.

But, from the first days of her widowhood, the Duchess of Kent had refused to be guided by her brother, though she accepted £3,000 a year from him. She was irritated by Prince Leopold's caution and deliberation and turned to Conroy. Conroy meanwhile, under an appearance of respect and admiration for Prince Leopold, set to work to poison the Duchess's mind against her brother. He declared that he wanted to 'serve under Prince Leopold's banner', but the Prince was 'pursuing his own ends rather than following the advantage of the Duchess of Kent and Princess Victoria'. He told the Duchess that, unknown to her, Prince Leopold was working to secure the Regency for himself, 'concerning which Conroy had held the documents in his own hands', and complained to Prince Charles that by neglecting her Prince Leopold *compelled* the Duchess to walk alone'.

It is unlikely that at this period Prince Leopold appreciated what was taking place at Kensington Palace. Although he was aware the Duchess of Kent was easily influenced, he did not realise the hold Conroy had obtained over her. He himself was anxious and preoccupied about his own affairs, he had reached a crisis in his life and the question of his future was urgent.

He could not be content to spend the rest of his life as a private gentleman in England, 'in effect' he wrote 'a pensioner of the English government'. He had not forgotten Princess Charlotte, he never did forget her, but he was ambitious, his talents were exceptional and his life in England was not entirely pleasant. His father-in-law, George IV, disliked him, and his continuing to draw the allowance of £50,000 a year which Parliament had voted him on his marriage was a subject of unkind comment. His rather pompous and formal manners were not popular in English society and malicious persons nicknamed him 'Prince Humbug'.

During the first years of anxiety over his future, much of Prince Leopold's attention was absorbed by a love affair with a German actress, Karoline Bauer, who bore a startling resemblance to Princess Charlotte, so startling that, Karoline asserts, the Duke of Wellington had been taken aback by it. Prince Leopold saw her performing on the Berlin stage in 1826 and her likeness to Princess Charlotte struck him with the force of an explosion, his habitual caution and reserve were swept away and he fell immediately and violently in love with her. The situation was complicated by her being Stockmar's first cousin. However, arrangements were made, and after Stockmar had warned her that Prince Leopold was economical and she must not expect a life of splendour, Karoline left the Berlin stage and, with her mother, was brought to England and established in a villa in Regent's Park. Here, according to Karoline's highly unreliable memoirs,[6] she lived amid splendours of pink silk, blossoming flowers, aviaries of brightly coloured birds, cooing doves and marble baths. But Karoline resembled Princess Charlotte only physically, and while Prince Leopold found satisfaction in gazing at her, he wanted little else. Every afternoon he called at the villa and occupied himself in 'drizzling', an amusement invented at the court of Marie Antoinette consisting of a little box and a device by means of which the gold and silver threads were extracted from old epaulettes, tassels and bullion lace. The precious metal thus extracted was weighed and sold, and with the proceeds of his winter's work, Prince Leopold bought and presented a silver soup tureen to Princess Victoria. While he 'drizzled' Karoline read aloud from an improving moral tale. She spoke no English and was never taken out by Prince Leopold for fear they should be seen together and cause scandal. When he went to Claremont she went too, but was put in a dark gloomy cottage shrouded by tall trees, where he called every afternoon and 'drizzling' and reading aloud went on as usual. Karoline grew to detest Prince Leopold and pours savage mockery on his habits of economy, his black wig, the cork soles he wore in his boots, the two little gold clamps he placed between his back teeth at night to preserve the enamel, in case he ground his teeth while asleep. After about a year, unable to support her dismal existence, she alleges that she and her mother ran away, but, quite possibly, she was bought off by Prince Leopold.

It happened that during the next few years changes took place in the kaleidoscope of European politics which resulted in Prince Leopold being offered two thrones in quick succession, first the throne of Greece, then that of Belgium, and in the complications and excitements of negotiating for a crown Kensington and its problems took, for the moment, second place.[7] In any case, he wrote, from Princess Victoria's point of view he could be of more use to her if he gained influence in Europe than in his present unsatisfactory position.

The offer of the throne of Greece came in 1829, after Greece had freed herself from Turkish domination in the Greek War of Independence. Prince Leopold was drawn to Greece. But the English government was hostile. George IV considered Leopold 'not qualified for this peculiar situation'; there were difficulties over settling the new frontier and in May 1830 Leopold withdrew.

For the rest of his life he had regrets. Greece, he told Stockmar, 'would have satisfied his phantasy', the poetic longings and dreams he prided himself on possessing; but in England, little Princess Victoria welcomed his withdrawal with rapture. 'The Queen well remembers her joy when this took place, as she adored her Uncle and was in despair at the thought of his departure for Greece'[8] she wrote.

Six months later, in November 1830, by what Stockmar called 'a freak of fate' Prince Leopold received overtures inviting him to become the King of the Belgians. The prospect was not entirely attractive. Catholic and pro-French, Belgium had recently risen in a successful rebellion against its ruler the Protestant King of Holland, and had elected a Catholic King, the Duc de Nemours, son of Louis Philippe, King of the French. But Louis Philippe had secured his throne only a few months before, as the result of yet another rebellion, and did not venture to antagonise Protestant England, the most formidable power in Europe. On his son's behalf he prudently declined, and in April 1831 the throne of Belgium was officially offered to Prince Leopold, a Protestant, who, after negotiation, accepted. Much, however, remained to be done and no bed of roses awaited the Prince. Though Belgium, in the heart of Europe, offered a better field for his talents than distant primitive Greece, he would have to establish himself on his throne; in parts of the country fighting was still in progress, and Catholic interests and sentiment would have to be successfully conciliated.

On the day he left London for Brussels, 16th July 1831, Prince Leopold renounced the £50,000 a year voted him on his marriage to Princess Charlotte. The sum received by the Treasury, however, was not of the size expected. Prince Leopold deducted the cost of the upkeep of Claremont, horses and carriages for use in England, pensions to English servants, donations to English charities and institutions and subscriptions to English clubs, the whole totalling about £20,000 a year.[9]

*

Meanwhile in Kensington Palace, the little Princess was being subjected to the Kensington System. She was never allowed to be alone day or night, she slept in her mother's room, there were frequent differences of opinion as to whether the light should be lit or not lit, and, when she had been put to bed, Lehzen sat in the room until the Duchess came to retire. She was never permitted to see anyone, young or old, unless a third person was present, and until she was nearly grown up, never walked downstairs without someone holding her hand. Dolls played an important part in her life, but not the usual role of a make-believe family of which the Princess was the mother; the Princess did not care for babies and thought any child under six months was ugly. Her dolls were her friends, substitutes for the girl companions she was never allowed to have.[10] With the exception of Victoire Conroy, whom she did not like, and an occasional girl visitor the Princess passed long hours alone with her dolls. They were adult dolls, not the child dolls small children usually play with, dressed by the Princess with the help of Lehzen, as the Princess scrupulously acknowledged. They mainly represent characters from plays and operas seen by the Princess. They lived in a box and she kept a list of 132 of them mentioning the name of each and the character it was intended to represent. The dolls themselves had no magnificence, they were quite ordinary, from three to nine inches high with the 'Dutch doll' type of face, easy to pack away. The Princess found an outlet for her imagination and affection in dressing and playing with her dolls and they continued to be a favourite amusement until she was nearly 14.

But though she was isolated it was an important part of the Kensington policy that she should be known to her future subjects, and it was made easy to catch glimpses of her walking, playing, or riding her donkey, from the public paths which ran through Kensington Gardens.

Charles Knight, author of *Passages of a Working Life*, saw the Princess breakfasting out of doors with her mother on the lawn before Kensington Palace as he walked down the Broad Walk and heartily approved. 'What a beautiful characteristic it seemed to me of the training of this royal girl, that she should not have been taught to shrink from the public eye, that she . . . should enjoy the freedom and simplicity of a child's nature; that she should not be restrained when she starts up from the breakfast-table and runs to gather a flower in the adjoining pasture; that her merry laugh should be as fearless as the notes of the thrush in the groves around her. I passed on and blessed her. . . .'[11]

Lehzen and the Duchess of Kent between them taught the little Princess excellent manners. Socially the behaviour of the Duchess was impeccable and the delightful manners of her elder daughter, Princess Feodora, to whom Lehzen had also been governess, were admired by the greatest authority on deportment in Europe, King George IV. On 3rd May 1828, when Princess Victoria was almost nine, Mrs Arbuthnot, the friend and confidante of the Duke of Wellington, met her at Kensington Palace. The little Princess Victoria, she wrote, 'is the most charming child I ever saw. She is a fine, beautifully made, handsome creature, quite playful & childish playing with her dolls and in high spirits, but civil and well bred & Princess like to the greatest degree.' Mrs Arbuthnot added 'The Duchess of Kent is a very sensible person and educates her remarkably well.'

The Duchess of Kent was taking her place with success in society. Very distant were the days when she had sat ignored in Kensington Palace, visited out of kindness by the Duchess of Clarence; grand entertainments were now given in the Duchess's apartments. Princess Lieven, wife of the Russian Ambassador, famous for her political influence, went on 8th December 1829 to a 'brilliant dinner' given by the Duchess of Kent. Six princesses were present, two princes and three ambassadors. It was, wrote Princess Lieven, 'a long and most royal dinner'.[12]

The impression Conroy wished the Duchess of Kent to create was being created; the little Princess seemed a happy child, and, viewed from outside, the Kensington System appeared a success. But within the Palace were squabbles, unhappiness and intrigue. Conroy had made himself a dictator at Kensington. He ordered every detail of life, even choosing the little Princess's tutors. He decided what policy the Duchess should adopt and what actions she should take and his plans were then sanctioned by the Duchess; not always without difficulty.

Prince Charles records that the Duchess was brought to agree with Conroy's plans 'often after lengthy discussion and many disputes'. Conroy insisted the Duchess should report details of every incident which happened in her life and in the Princess's, '*everything* down to the smallest and most insignificant detail. . . . The Duchess became gradually accustomed to this as well.' With the passage of time Conroy's hold over the Duchess strengthened; he had now indulged and consoled her since the death of the Duke nearly ten years before, and 'he knew' says Prince Charles 'how to act to impress a generous and affectionate heart with the *immensity* of his *service* and *sacrifice*'.

*

The precise nature of the relationship between the Duchess of Kent and Conroy is not certain, but a similar relationship, probably platonic, had existed with Schindler at Amorbach before she married the Duke of Kent. The Duchess and Conroy were the same age, 44, both handsome, both gifted with vitality. When Charles Greville asked the Duke of Wellington if the Duchess of Kent and Conroy were lovers, the Duke replied that he 'supposed so'. On a later occasion the Duke observed that the 'hatred' of Conroy displayed by the young Queen was the result of having witnessed 'familiarities' between her mother and Conroy.[13] Whatever the truth may have been, the treatment to which she was subjected during the years of the Kensington System, including 'personal affronts' from Conroy of which she complained 'vehemently' to her half-brother Prince Charles, provided ample grounds for dislike.

Conroy was no diplomat, nor was he clever or sensitive; he had a quick temper, and opposition made him angry. If Conroy had been more intelligent, instead of trying to force his will on the little Princess he would have made every effort to gain her affection. She was an affectionate child and she was lonely.

In the autumn of 1829, when the Princess was ten years old, a domestic upheaval agitated the little world of Kensington Palace. The Duchess of Kent dismissed her middle-aged lady-in-waiting, Baroness Spaeth, who had been with her for twenty-five years, and allowed it to be known that she intended to send away Lehzen as well. Lehzen and Spaeth had become intimate friends.

A memorandum survives, evidently one of many, written to Conroy on 14th October 1829 by Princess Sophia, his 'spy'.[14] It reports a conversation with the Duchess of Clarence, soon to be Queen Adelaide, on the removal of Spaeth and Lehzen. Names are childishly disguised, for instance the Duke and Duchess of Clarence are 'the Aquatics' presumably on account of the Duke's naval service, the Duchess of Kent is V (her name was Victoria), the little Princess Victoria is 'the child'.

'Mrs Aquatic' (the Duchess of Clarence) told Princess Sophia she was sure that being sent away would kill Spaeth. She had already, she said, told Spaeth how sorry she was not to see her more often in V's room. 'She [Spaeth] said she must submit . . . and as long as she could see "the child" she would endure any privation' and, Princess Sophia reminded Conroy, 'you know she was forbid going out with or walking with the child for the last year'. The Duchess of Clarence went on to send a warning to the Duchess of Kent. V [the Duchess of Kent] should be more careful, if she dismissed Spaeth it would make 'a great noise'; for instance, when Berkeley Paget, one of the gentlemen-in-waiting and the nephew of Lord Anglesey, was told Spaeth was going 'he burst into tears and said "Going! Impossible & oh! who has done this? It is not the Duchess of Kent, she is so good, so kind. Oh! how cruel after so many years of faithful service to send her away. . . ." '

To dismiss Lehzen was 'impossible', the Duchess of Clarence said bluntly, another Lehzen could not be found. Princess Sophia reported to Conroy with pride that she had instantly answered that a second was not wanted.

Numerous reasons were advanced to justify the removal of Baroness Spaeth. It was necessary, Conroy considered, to surround the Duchess of Kent with English ladies of high rank, and Spaeth was a German; she talked too much, received too many visitors, had manners which were unsuitable for England, and spoiled Princess Victoria by too much adulation. Finally she frequently expressed 'adverse opinions' of the Kensington System.

But these in themselves were not adequate reasons for dismissing her. Spaeth had held an intimate position in the Duchess of Kent's service for twenty-five years. She had been with the Duchess during her first marriage and widowhood and during the courtship of the Duke of Kent and her marriage to him. Spaeth had accompanied the Duchess when, at the end of her pregnancy, she travelled across Europe to England in order that her child might be born on English soil; Spaeth had sat beside the Duchess, and been seasick, in the open boat which landed them in a storm at Dover; she had been in Kensington Palace when the Princess Victoria was born, and had watched with the Duchess at Sidmouth through the Duke's last night on earth.

The real reason why the Duchess of Kent so summarily dismissed Spaeth was, in the opinion of the Duke of Wellington, to be found in the Duchess's relations with Conroy. The Duke told Greville[15] that Princess Victoria 'witnessed some familiarities between them [her mother and Conroy]. What She had seen She repeated to the Baroness Spaeth, and Spaeth not only did not hold her tongue, but (he [the Duke] thinks) remonstrated with the Duchess herself on the subject. The consequence was that they got rid of Spaeth, and they would have got rid of Lehzen too if they had been able; but Lehzen, who knew very well what was going on, was prudent enough not to commit herself, and She was besides powerfully protected by George 4th and William 4th so that they did not dare to attempt to expel her.' Spaeth found a refuge with Princess Feodora with whom, as lady-in-waiting, she remained for many years.

It was inevitable that gossip should be rife. Conroy was an adventurer, he and the Duchess were living in the publicity of a court, every whisper was overheard, every gesture watched and noted. Early in the New Year, on 12th January 1830, the Duchess of Clarence wrote a letter of warning directly to the Duchess of Kent.[16] It was 'the general wish' that she should not allow Conroy 'too much influence over you, but keep him in his place'. 'He . . . has never lived before in court circles or in society, so naturally he offends sometimes against the traditional ways, for he does not know them. . . . In the family it is noticed that you are cutting yourself off more and more from them with your child. . . . This they attribute to Conroy, whether rightly or wrongly I cannot judge; they believe he tries to remove everything that might obstruct his influence, so that he may exercise his power alone, and alone, too, one day reap the fruits of his influence. He cannot be blamed for cherishing dreams of future greatness and wanting to achieve a brilliant position for his family; no one can take this amiss in him, but everyone recognises these aspirations, towards which his every action is directed. . . . It is well known who Sir J. C. is; he cannot make himself higher or lower than he is, nor does he need to, as a man of merit; only he must not be allowed to forbid access to you to all but his family, who in any case are not of so high a rank that they alone should be the entourage and the companions of the future Queen of England.'

The Duchess of Clarence's letter was a bitter pill to swallow, even more bitter for Conroy than the Duchess of Kent, and violent hostility was henceforward shown to both the Duke and Duchess of Clarence, who were shortly to ascend the throne as King William IV and Queen Adelaide.

*

Princess Victoria was now nearly 11 years old, and Conroy and the Duchess of Kent decided a favourable moment had come to remind influential persons of her existence, at the same time taking the opportunity of drawing attention to the maternal devotion and model life of the Duchess. Some such testimony was necessary if the misgivings expressed by the Duchess of Clarence were widely shared.

On 1st March 1830 the Duchess opened the campaign with an immensely long letter[17] to the Bishops of London and Lincoln, asking them to test the result of the Princess Victoria's education by personal examination. The Duchess wished to know 'Has the course hitherto pursued in her education been the best; if not where has it been erroneous? . . . The Princess is not aware of the Station she is likely to fill—she is aware of its duties, and that a Sovereign should live for others—So that when Her innocent mind receives the impression of Her future Fate, she receives it with a mind formed to be sensible of what is expected from her.' Reminding the Bishops of her pathetic situation the Duchess wrote 'By the death of her revered father, when She was but 8 months old Her sole care and charge devolved to me. Stranger as I then was, I became deeply impressed with the absolute necessity of bringing her up entirely in this country, that every feeling should be that of her native land and proving thereby my devotion to duty by rejecting all those feelings of home and kindred that divided my heart.'

The Duchess did not mention that it was only with considerable difficulty that she had been persuaded to stay in England by her brother, Prince Leopold, at a cost to him of £3,000 a year.

The Princess's education had begun when she was 'approaching five' but as she admitted 'I was not fond of learning as a little child—and baffled every attempt to teach me my letters up to 5 years old—when I consented to learn them by their being written down before me.'

It did not begin in earnest until 1827, when she was eight years old. The Reverend George Davys, a liberal evangelical clergyman, Fellow of Christ's College, Cambridge, and Vicar of Willoughby-on-the-Wolds, Leicestershire, was appointed her Principal Master, on the advice of the Vicar of Kensington, and came to live in Kensington Palace, where he remained until the accession of the Queen in 1837. Mr Davys, who became Dean of Chester in 1831, and was finally advanced to be Bishop of Peterborough in 1839, was the author of numerous tracts, published by the Society for Promoting Christian Knowledge, with such titles as 'A village conversation on the Catechism of the Church of England'. He grew greatly attached to the little Princess and told the Duchess in March 1830 he was afraid of giving an opinion about the Princess's capacities 'because my feelings towards the Princess may prevent me from being an impartial judge'.[18]

The Princess worked to a regular timetable. She did lessons from 9.30 a.m. until 11.30 a.m., then played, went for a walk and had dinner at 1 p.m. From 3 p.m. until 5 p.m. she did more lessons, including drawing, and from 5 to 6 she learned poetry by heart, English, French and German. On Wednesday afternoon she learned her catechism and received religious instruction from Mr Davys. On Thursday she had a dancing lesson, which she loved, and on Friday morning a music lesson from Mr Sale, the organist at St Margaret's Westminster, who also taught her singing. She had a soprano voice, not powerful but remarkably sweet and true. On Saturday she worked shorter hours, went over the lessons she had learned during the week until 11 a.m. and was then free until a German lesson at 3; from 4 to 5 p.m. she wrote letters and from 5 to 6 p.m. had French Repetition. The Duchess of Kent in her letter to the Bishops stated that she herself 'almost always . . . attended every lesson or a part', but when Miss Agnes Strickland wrote the biography *From Birth to Bridal* in the year of the Queen's marriage and repeated the Duchess of Kent's statement, Queen Victoria wrote on the margin 'Not'.

The Princess was emphatically brought up 'in the Church of England as by law established', and by the time she was 11 she could repeat her catechism and appeared to understand the principal doctrines of the Church of England. A large part of her lesson time was devoted to modern languages. She had a French tutor, M. Grandineau, who reported on 3rd March 1830 that she could carry on a conversation in French, her grammar was excellent and her accent would, he thought, eventually be perfect, but she did not write as well as she spoke. He 'humbly begs' that a little more time should be given to French, at the same time assuring the Duchess that 'the Princess is much more advanced than most children of her age'.[19]

The Princess's German tutor, the Rev. Henry Barez, a Lutheran clergyman, reported that the Princess 'has acquired a correct German pronunciation, particularly remarkable for its softness and distinctness'.[20] A German grammar, suitable for her age, had been specially written for her, which she studied constantly, and she could translate 'Mary and her Cat' into German. She knew most German words in common use, about 1,500, and understood the leading rules of the German language, but had not yet begun to study German schrift.

The extent to which the German language was spoken and used by the young Princess has been a matter of argument. In Miss Strickland's *Birth to Bridal* the author says: 'If she had a favour to ask, or a request to prefer, she soon found it was most agreeable to the maternal ear when lisped in the Teutonic accents of the Duchess of Kent's dear father-land, therefore many caressing phrases were addressed by the little Princess to her Royal Mother in German.' However, when a copy of the book was submitted to the Queen she wrote in the margin beside this paragraph 'Not true. Never spoke German until 1839, not allowed to. Not true her Mother stimulated her to speak German', and on a later page the Queen wrote 'did *not* speak German with fluency'. Certainly after the Queen's betrothal to Prince Albert of Saxe-Coburg, when she was writing her first love letters to him, she apologises for breaking into English when writing in German because her German is not good enough to express her meaning.[21] The truth seems to be that the Princess studied German as she studied Italian and French, as a lesson, but did not use it as a second mother tongue.

The Princess's writing master, Mr Steward, also taught her arithmetic, for which he considered she had a particular talent; she worked out sums correctly and understood his explanations of the rules. Writing was not so satisfactory; the Princess must imitate the writing examples. She had begun Latin, under Mr Davys, using *An introduction to the Latin Tongue as printed for the use of Eton School*, and was reading translated extracts from Cicero, but she did not take to Latin and 'was not so far advanced'.

In geography, and history, also studied under Mr Davys, the Princess was 'better informed than most young persons of the same age'. She read poetry aloud 'extremely well', and had a talent for drawing. Mr Richard Westall, the well-known R.A. who both drew and painted her portrait, was her drawing master.

Lehzen read aloud to the Princess while she was dressing and while her hair was being brushed, but the books she read were educational and informative, no works of fiction were allowed.

The Princess Victoria's besetting sin was inattention, termed 'absence of mind'. However, Mr Davys was able to report to the Duchess in 1830 that in the course of the past year 'that absence of mind which your Royal Highness had, for some time, so much lamented in the Princess, has been in a great measure corrected, by the improving understanding of her Highness'.[22]

To sum up, the examination of the Princess which took place in the first week in March 1830 was a triumphant success.[23] The Bishops of London and Lincoln expressed themselves 'completely satisfied'. 'In answering a great variety of questions proposed to Her the Princess displayed an accurate knowledge of the most important features of Scripture, History and of the leading truths and precepts of the Christian religion as taught by the Church of England; as well as an acquaintance with the Chronology and principal facts of English history, remarkable in so young a person. To questions of Geography, the use of the Globes, Arithmetic and Latin Grammar, the answers which the Princess returned were equally satisfactory; and Her pronunciation both of English and Latin is singularly correct and pleasing. Due attention appears to have been paid

75

to the acquisition of modern languages; and, although it was less within the scope of our enquiry, we cannot help observing that the pencil drawings of the Princess are executed with the freedom and correctness of an older child.'

On 10th March 1830 the Bishop of London asked for an interview[24] in order that he might clear up a point on which he was in doubt. Did the Princess know what was likely to be her future situation in the country and would her further education be planned to put her in possession of this knowledge? The Duchess told him she had not yet made up her mind to tell the Princess she would be Queen, hoping she would 'come to the knowledge by accident, in pursuing her education'.

On the very next day, however, 11th March 1830—by accident according to the Duchess of Kent, by arrangement according to Lehzen[25]—the little Princess discovered her destiny.

It must be remembered that Lehzen's account was written and sent to Queen Victoria in 1867, thirty-seven years after the scene described had taken place. Lehzen's sense of drama embellished her recollection and some of the Princess Victoria's remarks, supposedly uttered by a child of 11, are not convincing.

After the examination was over, on the same day, Lehzen 'spoke [*sic*] to the Duchess of Kent . . . that now, for the first time, Your Majesty ought to know Your Place in the succession. Her Highness agreed with me and I put the chronological table into the historical book. When Mr Davys was gone, Princess Victoria opened, as usual, the book again and seeing the additional paper said: "I never saw that before"; "It was not thought necessary you should, Princess" I answered.—"I see I am nearer to the Throne than I thought". "So it is Madam" I said. After some moments the Princess resumed "Now—many a child would boast but they don't know the difficulty; there is much splendour, but there is more responsibility!"—the Princess having held up the fore finger of her right hand, while she spoke, gave me that little hand saying "I will be good! I understand now, why you urged me so much to learn, even Latin, my cousins Augusta and Mary never did; but you told me, Latin is the foundation of the English grammar and of all the elegant expressions; and I learned it as you wished it, but I understand all better now!"; and the Princess gave me again her hand repeating: "I will be good" .'

In the margin at this point Queen Victoria has written 'I cried much on learning it and ever deplored this contingency'.

'I then said' continues Lehzen ' "but your Aunt Adelaide is still young and may have Children and of course they would ascend the Throne after their father William IV and not you, Princess".'

In the margin at this point the Queen has written 'I always hoped she would have children'; and Lehzen reports 'The Princess answered "And if it was so I should never feel disappointed, for I know by the love Aunt Adelaide bears me, how fond she is of children." ' A further note in Prince Albert's handwriting adds 'The Queen perfectly recollects this circumstance & says the discovery made her very unhappy.'

On 13th March the Duchess of Kent told the Bishops of London and Lincoln that the Princess now knew her destiny: 'what accident has done, I feel no art could have done half so well. . . . I cannot sufficiently express the happiness I feel . . . we have everything to hope from this child.' The Bishops were not aware, however, of the full extent and nature of the benefits from Princess Victoria hoped for by the Duchess and Conroy.

A few days after the Bishops' favourable report had been received, on 27th March 1830, the Duchess used it to bring herself to the notice of the Archbishop of Canterbury, Archbishop Howley, spiritual head of the Church of England and the greatest ecclesiastical dignitary in the Kingdom, who took precedence of all other subjects after the Royal Family. She asked for an interview. 'I feel anxious to have some very confidential conversation with you, relative to a subject very near my heart, the education of the Princess.' She had hesitated to trouble him earlier on account of his eminence and had consulted the Bishops of Lincoln and London. She made much of the support she had derived in her responsibility for 'this singularly situated and precious Child' from the approval of Parliament bestowed on her in 1825. 'I could hardly have supposed that my retired and unobtrusive life would have allowed of my conduct to be known' she wrote modestly. She sent the Archbishop all the papers and the Bishops' report relating to the Princess's education by 'my confidential servant Sir John Conroy', and an interview took place on 2nd April 1830 which was most successful, the Archbishop subsequently retaining the papers at Lambeth as being of national importance.[26]

The campaign to draw attention to the little Princess and her mother could not have been better timed. King George IV's health was rapidly deteriorating. He was probably, like his father George III, the victim of one of the group of diseases called porphyrias, not then diagnosed or understood,[27] which range from merely an excessive sensitivity of the skin to the sun, to recurrent attacks of agonising pain, accompanied by difficulty in breathing, mental derangement and sometimes fits. The porphyrias are as old as history and derive their name from the symptom common to all types, the passing of dark red urine 'the colour of burgundy'. Porphyrias are to be found in every part of the world and among persons of every race, whether men, women or children. The disease is hereditary; Mary Queen of Scots brought it into the English Royal Family. There is no evidence whatsoever to suggest that Queen Victoria suffered from porphyria or passed it on to any of her children. The character of George IV, with its extraordinary contradictions, his intelligence, good taste, kindness and charm on the one hand, and storms of unreasonable rage, treachery, lying and delusions on the other, should be considered in the light of this terrible disease. Since 1828 he had experienced acute pain in his bladder and took large and frequent doses of laudanum to dull his suffering with a fatal effect on his general health. However, in 1829 he recovered sufficiently to resume normal life and in May even gave a children's ball in honour of the little Queen of Portugal who was visiting London. Greville relates that when the King spoke of inviting Princess Victoria, Lady Maria Conyngham tactlessly said 'Oh do, it will be so nice to see the *two little Queens* dancing together.' At which the King was 'beyond measure provoked'.[28]

By the spring of 1830 his condition was pitiable. Stupefied by laudanum, he was frequently unable to transact business, his legs were so swollen he could walk only with crutches, he was going blind and had already lost the sight of one eye, his heart was affected and he had difficulty in breathing. It had become impossible for him to lie down, his nights were spent sitting up, in an armchair, leaning forward over a table and resting his head on his hands. He died in the early morning of 26th June 1830.

The Duke and Duchess of Clarence now succeeded to the throne as King William IV and Queen Adelaide.

The new King was 65 years of age, excitable and eccentric. However, his service in the Navy and friendship with Nelson assured him considerable popularity, and he began his reign well, presiding at his first Council looking 'like a respectable old Admiral'. The Duke of Wellington, then Prime Minister, was pleasantly surprised to find him easier to do business with than George IV and his first acts won public approval. He opened a public passage from Waterloo Place into the Park and sent away all George IV's French cooks. He had, however, no conception of the dignity expected from a King; he loved to ramble about the streets alone, had to be rescued from an over-friendly mob, after being kissed by a street-walker, issued informal invitations, and offered 'lifts' to his friends in the royal equipages. But his good nature and simplicity, especially after the difficulties of dealing with George IV, were 'very striking', and Greville[29] voiced the general opinion in summing him up as 'a kind hearted, well meaning, not stupid, burlesque, bustling old fellow, and if he doesn't go mad may make a very decent King, but he exhibits oddities'.

Queen Adelaide was a woman of character and piety. Her disposition was sweet, her manners excellent, she possessed extraordinary patience. It was unfortunate that her qualities of patience, sweetness and humility contrived to recall a German governess. Her features were good but her complexion 'horrid', and she had little pretension to beauty. Nevertheless she had inspired a romantic passion in the breast of her Chamberlain, Lord Howe, who already possessed a beautiful wife, sister of the Lord Cardigan who later led the Charge of the Light Brigade, at the battle of Balaclava in 1854. Only 26 at the time of her marriage to the 54-year-old Duke of Clarence, she had conducted herself in a difficult situation with dignity and won her husband's devotion and respect. She had freely received his illegitimate children and borne with their tempers, follies and disrespect. She had managed her husband with tact and protected him from exposure. She loved children and had endured the loss of both her daughters and the premature ending of several pregnancies without becoming bitter. When she lost her second little Princess in 1821 she wrote to the Duchess of Kent 'My children are dead, but yours lives and She is mine too!'

From Princess Victoria's babyhood, 'Aunt Adelaide' was a favourite and the first letter ever received by the Princess, at the age of two, is an affectionate note from 'Aunt Adelaide' to 'my dear little Heart' written in May 1821, only two months after the death of her own baby daughter.[30]

Both William IV and Queen Adelaide accepted the little Princess as their heiress and successor without resentment and wished to lavish affection on her and to be generous to her. Their good intentions were defeated by Conroy and the Duchess of Kent.

The next day after George IV had expired, Conroy and the Duchess sent a long letter,[31] written by Conroy and signed by the Duchess, to the Duke of Wellington to be submitted to the new King. The Duchess asserted that the death of King George IV made Princess Victoria 'more than Heiress Presumptive' to the throne, and demanded 'that the offices of Regent and Custos [Guardian] are proposed to be vested fully, and without any interference whatsoever, in Her Mother'. As to the regency, if she consulted her own inclinations she would decline being Regent, but her judgment 'imperatively' told her that it would be contrary to the interest of the Princess if she should hesitate to bear that heavy burden should the Princess succeed before she was of age.

The Princess's position was now 'totally different' and the Duchess wished a lady of rank, suggesting the Duchess of Northumberland, to be the Princess's official governess. There already existed what the Duchess described as a 'sub-governess', Baroness Lehzen, ennobled in Hanover by King George IV. The Duchess did not wish for a Bishop to be permanently attached to the Princess's Household but 'once or twice a year the Archbishop of Canterbury, the Lord President of His Majesty's Privy Council, the Bishops of London and Lincoln and the Lord Chief Justice of the Kings Bench, should examine the Princess with regard to her studies'.

The Duchess then demanded that she herself should be treated as Dowager Princess of Wales, and given an income suitable to that rank. It was to the interest of the Princess, she wrote, that no grant should be made directly to her. Until she was of age, or was Queen, her mother would pay everything for her. Finally the Duchess spoke of her present financial position: '. . . the hour is come—when I feel that my singular situation, even for the past, should be looked to.' The entertainments at Kensington Palace had cost money and the Duchess was deeper in debt.

The Duke of Wellington was horrified. He had not considered it expedient, he wrote on 30th June,[32] to lay the letter before the King, or even to communicate it to his colleagues. 'I earnestly advise and entreat your Royal Highness to allow me to consider it as a Private and Confidential Communication; or rather as never having been written.' The affairs of the Duchess of Kent and her 'August Daughter' must shortly come before Parliament and it was much better for the Duchess that a settlement should be considered in the regular course by the King and his ministers than that such a claim should be put forward by her. This letter made Conroy and the Duchess angry and a sharp reply went to the Duke by return. The Duchess was determined to have the Regency. '. . . Irksome as it must ever be to my feelings, to be Regent, in case of the Princess being a minor Queen, I feel I *owe it in my conscience, to Her.* . . . It is for her benefit, I should wish to have that office. . . . If I am not to express my wishes and feelings, I daresay it will occur to your Grace that I am not likely to be asked for them—and by expressing them, I give you an opportunity of forwarding matters essential to the good of the Princess. . . .' The Duke replied immediately, assuring the Duchess that there is 'no Party, nor no Individual of an influence in the Country who can entertain the idea of injuring the interests of your Royal Highness and the Princess'; being as explicit as he dared he finished 'and I entreat your Royal Highness not to allow any Person to persuade you to the contrary'. At this the Duchess 'took great offence', would not speak to the Duke, or see him, and when he wished to explain the draft of the Regency Bill to her, told him to communicate with Sir John Conroy.[33]

On 6th July the Regency question was raised in the House of Commons, in a manner which cannot fail to have irritated William IV and pained Queen Adelaide. Mr Robert Grant, member for Fortrose, Inverness, Nairn and Forres in Scotland, moved an address to the King on the expediency of making provision against the dangers which would arise when the demise of the Crown occurred. There was the possibility that the King would leave behind him 'an infant of tender age, or, it might even be a posthumous child . . . suppose that in the case of the demise of the crown the nation was expecting a posthumous issue—the Privy

I   PRINCESS VICTORIA, AGED 4
from the portrait by S. P. Denning

2   PRINCESS CHARLOTTE AND PRINCE LEOPOLD
AT THE OPERA
from the drawing by Dawe

Blood Royal

3   THE DUKE OF CUMBERLAND
(*subsequently King of Hanover*)
from 'Blood Royal' by Rowlandson

4   THE DUKE OF KENT, 1802
(with Gibraltar in the background)
from the portrait by Eridge

5   THE DUCHESS OF KENT, 1829
from the miniature by William Charles Ross

6 WOOLBROOK GLEN, SIDMOUTH
(*where the Duke of Kent died, 1820*)

7 BARONESS LEHZEN
from the miniature by Koepke

8   PRINCESS FEODORA, 1828
from the miniature by William Charles Ross

9   QUEEN ADELAIDE
from the miniature by William Charles Ross

Council was ordered to assemble and proclaim the Sovereign, whom would they have to proclaim? They must preface their proclamation by taking the Oath of Allegiance. To whom must they take it?' There was a second contingency, that the succession would fall on the niece of the King who was 'a child of very tender years'. Then would arise the question, who should be Regent? Were they to adopt the doctrine that the next heir in blood had 'a strict and indefeasible right to be Regent . . . if the next heir was a King on an alien throne?' The King on the alien throne (the Duke of Cumberland, who on the death of William IV would ascend the throne of Hanover) represented the crux of the Regency question. Princess Victoria could not succeed to the Hanoverian throne because Hanover was subject to the Salic law under which the succession passed to males only. Further, should Princess Victoria die, the Duke of Cumberland would succeed to the throne of England as well. The notion of the Duke of Cumberland as Regent and Guardian of the little Princess, his extraordinary unpopularity, the suspicion with which he was regarded, the horrible crimes unjustly associated with his name, filled the nation with dread. It was already believed by many people that he was plotting against Princess Victoria's life* and the appointment of a Regent other than the Duke of Cumberland seemed a matter of urgency.

When Parliament re-assembled in November the Duchess of Kent was appointed sole Regent 'not fettered by any Council but left to administer the Government by means of the responsible Ministers of the Crown'. 'It would be quite impossible' said the Lord Chancellor, Lord Lyndhurst, in the House of Lords on 15th November 1830 'that we should recommend any other individual for that high Office than the Illustrious Princess, the mother of her Royal Highness the Princess Victoria. The manner in which her Royal Highness the Duchess of Kent has hitherto discharged her duty in the education of her illustrious off-spring—and I speak upon this subject not from vague report, but from accurate information—gives us the best ground to hope most favourably of her Royal Highness's future conduct. . . . It is the recommendation of His Majesty's Ministers that, in the event of the demise of the Crown . . . her Royal Highness the Duchess of Kent should be appointed sole Regent.'[34]

Lord Lyndhurst did not intend, he said, to provide for a child being born to Queen Adelaide, 'Whenever there is reasonable probability of the speedy occurrence of this event, it will be competent to the Legislature to provide for it.'

In fact at the end of the following year Queen Adelaide's hopes of an heir were again disappointed. On Friday 16th December 1831 she wrote in her diary that she had been unwell: 'I had flattered myself with hopes

* See Appendix 3.

which have unfortunately not been realised, and although I hardly dared hope, yet the proof of the contrary hurt me very much.'[33] As late as 1835, Princess Lieven, wife of the Russian Ambassador, reported that Queen Adelaide was pregnant.[36]

At the news of the Regency Conroy and the Duchess of Kent were jubilant. The Duchess declared that the day of her appointment as Regent was her first happy day since she lost the Duke of Kent. Meanwhile Sir John Conroy busied himself in drawing up a memorandum[37] defining the powers which could be exercised by the Sovereign over the heir presumptive to the throne. Attempts at interference by King William IV were expected and the Duchess of Kent and Conroy wished to be prepared with their legal rights.

*

In the unhappy story of disagreement between the Duchess of Kent and William IV which followed, both sides were to blame. Both were obstinate, both demanded impossibilities; the Duchess had an evil genius in Conroy, William IV's lack of self-control led him into statements and acts which were unforgivable. The little Princess Victoria remained apart, doing her lessons, arranging her dolls.

At the end of July 1830 the Duke of Wellington was succeeded as Prime Minister by Earl Grey, who in December asked the Duchess of Kent for an audience. This took place on 24th December. Sir John Conroy was present and wrote a lengthy memorandum.[38] Lord Grey came, as he said, in consequence of the King's having asked him if the Duke of Wellington, on relinquishing his post as Prime Minister, had left behind him any paper relating to the financial position of the Duchess of Kent. No such paper had been left by the Duke, and Lord Grey told the Duchess that it had been arranged between the King and his ministers that £6,000 additional income for her should be proposed to Parliament. The Duchess said that it was a delicate matter for her to say anything on.

It must, actually, have been a considerable disappointment, since earlier the Duke of Wellington had mentioned to Lord Ellenborough a figure of £20,000 a year additional income.

Lord Grey then passed to his second point. The King wished some lady of rank to be named, as had been the case with Princess Charlotte, to be in attendance on Princess Victoria. The Duchess of Kent replied that she had thought of this and was not unprepared, she had already been in communication with the Duchess of Northumberland, but felt that the appointment should be delayed until after Parliament had settled her allowance.

Lord Grey's third point was a bombshell. The King wished Princess Victoria's name to be changed to an English one. To this request, approaching an insult, since the Princess bore the name of her mother, the Duchess made a dignified reply: '. . . the name was dear to the Princess— but she was so educated, as to do whatever would suit the feelings of the country. The names had not been of the Duchess's selection but were forced on her.' Her Royal Highness then requested Earl Grey to communicate with her in writing so that she might have time to consider what she should do.

The sequel was curious. The Duchess did not write for more than a month; then, on 28th January 1831,[39] after giving an account of the behaviour of the late King George IV at the Princess's christening, and of the manner in which the Princess came to be christened by her names of Alexandrina Victoria, she consented: '. . . I cannot conceal from the King, that it would grieve me to see my child lay aside the name of Victoria, which she alone uses, as being mine, and, as I mentioned verbally to your Lordship, She has also a great attachment to that name. But, I must look upon this question, as I have taught myself to look upon many others—and be ready to do that which is most suitable to Her Station and the feelings of the Country.

'I therefore freely admit that the two foreign names She bears are not suited to our national feeling, and that they should be laid aside.'

Lord Grey told the Duchess that the change might take place either by Act of Parliament or at the Princess's confirmation; the Duchess asked that an Act of Parliament might be used and passed as soon as possible, so that the Princess and the country might get used to the change. The Princess could then be confirmed in her new name. As to what the new name should be, it was the Duchess's most anxious wish that Alexandrina should be omitted and Charlotte, the name both of the Duke of Kent's mother and of Princess Charlotte, substituted. The name Victoria was to remain though it would not be used, but its retention would 'gratify all the feelings my child and I share from bearing alike that same name'. To this suggestion the King gave his entire approbation, and as a reward for acquiescence informed the Duchess that 'in *adverting to . . . the financial situation of your Royal Highness from the period of the Duke of Kent's death* . . . it will be His Majesty's earnest desire to promote such an arrangement as may best contribute to your Royal Highness's dignity and comfort. . . .'[40]

However, by 23rd April the Duchess was wavering and wrote[41] to Lord Grey that though she herself had disclosed nothing the change was being talked about and had even been mentioned in the newspapers. The nation was not anxious for the change of name, people had become accustomed to Victoria, it was a high-sounding name, and the name Alexandrina was never used. Among those who did want a change some preferred Elizabeth to Charlotte. Did the King know there was very strong religious feeling against the change, baptism being a sacrament? Perhaps the King should consult the Archbishops and Bishops.

On 8th June Dr Howley, Archbishop of Canterbury, informed[42] the Duchess that no Archbishop or Bishop could at confirmation change a name given at baptism. However, as giving a name had no valid connection with the sacrament of baptism, it might be legally possible to make such a change by Act of Parliament.

By 25th June the Duchess had reversed her first decision and wrote to Earl Grey '. . . it will be *quite contrary* to the Princess's and my feelings, if the King persists in changing Her name—and I trust His Majesty may be advised to abandon the intention: I see nothing now, on mature reflection, in its favour but many grave reasons against it. . . .'

Lord Grey in reply 'can not conceal from your Royal Highness my apprehension that it may greatly disappoint His Majesty after the full assent given by your Royal Highness . . . in your letter of January 28th'. William IV was furiously annoyed. A true Hanoverian, he could not endure to be thwarted and wrote angrily to Lord Grey on 26th June deploring '. . . the introduction to the Throne of these United Kingdoms of a name which is not English, had never been known heretofore as a Christian name in this country, is not even German but of French origin. . . . His Majesty would not object to the name of Elizabeth . . . his sole aim being that the name of the future Sovereign of this country should be *English*', and with a parting thrust at Conroy he finished, 'His Majesty cannot but regret that Her Royal Highness should have suffered impressions to be made upon her Mind by Representations which do not, in His Judgment, rest upon sufficient foundation.'[43]

The Duchess on this occasion was justly incensed, but further disagreements followed in which she was to blame.

William IV, having accepted the little Princess as heiress presumptive, had wished her to take a part in Court functions, and on 26th July 1830, dressed in deep mourning for the death of King George IV, with a long Court train and a veil reaching to the ground, she walked behind Queen Adelaide at a chapter of the Order of the Garter held at St James's Palace, and stood to the left of the throne during the investiture of the King of Württemberg. The Duchess and Conroy saw danger. The little Princess would be separated from her mother and lead an independent existence, so the Duchess 'contrived' to make the Princess's attendances at Court 'as few as possible', thus both irritating and wounding the King. On 24th February 1831 the Princess attended a Drawing-room, her first, in honour of Queen Adelaide's birthday, but William IV, who watched her closely, complained that the Princess looked at him 'stonily'.[44] Relations between the Duchess of Kent and the King now reached a state of perpetual friction, the Duchess, primed by Conroy, pressing forward at every opportunity to increase the importance of herself and her daughter; William IV, wounded and frustrated in his kind intentions, becoming more and more irritated.

In August 1831 the Duchess of Kent submitted a long high-flown memorandum[45] to the Prime Minister, Lord Grey, embellished with historical precedents and drawn up by Conroy, asserting the claim of the Princess Victoria to be styled 'Royal' Highness. She had been so styled in the Regency Bill, but styled Highness only when the King sent a message to Parliament on the Duchess of Kent's increased allowance. However, claims and assertions were cut short by Lord Grey informing the Duchess of Kent that the omission of 'Royal' in the Princess's title was an error 'solely due' to the mistake of a clerk who had been entrusted with copying the King's message. The mistake had already been corrected in the Parliamentary resolutions and would be corrected in all official documents.

A more serious clash took place a few weeks later. The coronation of King William IV and Queen Adelaide was to take place on 8th September 1831, and the King, possibly to punish the Duchess of Kent for her recent attempt to make a difficulty over the Princess's 'Royal' rights, announced that, though heiress presumptive, Princess Victoria was not to walk immediately behind him in the procession through Westminster Abbey, but to come after his brothers, the Royal Dukes. The Duchess of Kent insisted that as heiress presumptive the Princess had a right to follow immediately after the Sovereign. The King refused to give way, upon which the Duchess declined either to attend the coronation herself or to allow the Princess to be present, making excuses that the expense would be too great (she was by no means satisfied with the £6,000 annual increase in her income), and that she feared the strain on the Princess's health. The Princess was bitterly disappointed. 'Nothing could console me' she wrote 'not even my dolls' and she wept 'copious' tears.[46]

Friction between the Duchess and the King was further aggravated by political differences. King William IV and Queen Adelaide were fanatical Tories; the Duchess, like the Duke of Kent, was a Whig and in 1831 more than questions of political doctrine were involved. This was the year of the Reform Bill, a period of political agitation unparalleled in the history of the country, when England hung on the verge of revolution. The Reform Bill itself abolished 'rotten boroughs, places like Old Sarum, once of importance, which had almost or entirely ceased to exist but, owing to their ancient rights, still returned members to Parliament, while the great new manufacturing towns were all but unrepresented. The Reform Bill was a surprisingly moderate measure of common justice, and has since been criticised mainly on the ground that it did not go far enough, but it was greeted by the Tories, headed by William IV, with furious and hysterical opposition. Revolution was declared certain, the British constitution would be overthrown and the passing of the Bill followed by the worst excesses of the French Revolution. William IV felt the crown tottering on his head.

As a Whig, the Duchess of Kent gathered Whigs and Reformers round her at Kensington. Her position, and the position of the little Princess as heiress to the throne, made her an asset in the present political struggle, and she found that the antagonism of her Whig advisers to King William IV and Queen Adelaide was sympathetic. Queen Adelaide had cast aside propriety and become a violent anti-Reformer, more violent even than the King, losing the last shreds of her moderate popularity in the process.

The chief, and most formidable of the Duchess of Kent's Whig advisers, John George Lambton, is better known by the title conferred on him in 1828, of Lord Durham. He was a man of outstanding intellectual capacities, but of overbearing and violent temper, great vanity and poor health. For many years he had been identified with the cause of Reform, had brought forward without success a motion for reforming Parliament as early as 1821, and together with Lord John Russell had drafted the Reform Bill of 1831, under the supervision of Lord Grey who was his father-in-law. His historical importance, however, rests on the famous Durham 'Report on the affairs of British North America' submitted in January 1839, after he had resigned as High Commissioner and Governor General of the provinces now called Canada.

Another prominent member of the Whig clique at Kensington was George James Agar Ellis, Lord Dover, a man with a cultivated taste and a liberal mind who in 1823 was largely responsible for the foundation of the National Gallery, now in Trafalgar Square. Lord Howe, Queen Adelaide's devoted Chamberlain, considered that Lord Durham and Lord Dover were responsible for the Duchess of Kent's behaviour towards William IV and Queen Adelaide. 'Conroy alone however well inclined to be impertinent would not dare.'[47]

Princess Victoria was becoming an object of curiosity to her future subjects, who, for the most part, had nothing but praise for the Princess herself, her manners and education. Lady Wharncliffe,[48] dining at Kensington Palace, was 'delighted with our little future Queen. She is very much grown though short for her age, has a nice countenance and distingué figure, tho' not very good; and her manner the most perfect mixture of childishness and civility I ever saw. She is born a Princess without the *least* appearance of art or affectation. Her Mother's conduct is the most sensible thing I ever saw . . . the way in which she brings the child *gradually* forward quite perfect. When she went to bed we all stood up and after kissing *Aunt* Sophia, she curtsied, first to one side, and then

86

the other, to all the Ladies, and then walked off with her governess. She is really very accomplished by *taste*, being very fond both of music and drawing, but fondest of all of her *dolls*. In short I look to her to save us from Democracy, for it is impossible she should not be popular when she is older and more seen.'

Charles Greville, however, who a few years later became one of the young Queen's devoted admirers, was not much impressed by the 12-year-old Princess. 'A short vulgar looking child'[49] was his verdict after seeing her at her first Drawing-room.

In the following year, 1832, changes took place in the life of the Princess. She was now 13 and the Duchess, accompanied by Conroy, began to take her on 'journeys' in the provinces, so that she might become acquainted with the country she was to rule and with some of her principal future subjects. In the course of the 'journeys' visits were paid to great country houses.

The 'journeys' were conducted with ceremony, there were guards of honour from the local yeomanry, welcoming bands, decorations and floral arches were erected, flowers strewn, addresses presented. William IV, who found the Duchess's journeys almost unbearably irritating, dubbed them 'Royal Progresses'.

In the same year, in July 1832, the Princess began to keep a diary in a small leather-bound volume given her by the Duchess of Kent, and continued the practice all her life.

*

A diarist of the first rank has been lost to the world in Queen Victoria. To begin with she showed only average promise, her powers of expression were limited and her comments ordinary; in spite of the praise lavished on her education by the Bishops, she was not a well-educated nor an advanced child. Her Journal was read, both by Lehzen and her mother. Consequently she wrote passages designed to be read by them, especially by Lehzen. But later, supervision ended and she wrote for herself alone, and she possessed to a remarkable degree the diarist's equipment. Her observation was acute and she had 'total recall', the ability to recollect everything that had been said or done during a visit, an interview or a conversation. Her style of writing, far from literary, was admirably vivid; characters leap alive from her pages. She was honest, the leading characteristic of her nature; she did not write to justify herself, or to explain, but poured out with vehemence, enthusiasm, passion, sometimes with violence, but never with rancour, everything she had done, observed and experienced during the course of the day. She had the diarist's capacity to record and could write an entry of 2,500 words at the end of a long day. Ultimately Queen Victoria's Journal filled more than 122 volumes, a record of persons, events and emotions without parallel in European history.

Unhappily, Queen Victoria's Journal no longer exists. Her youngest daughter, Princess Beatrice, was appointed by the Queen to be her literary executor. Some years after the Queen's death the Princess, actuated by sincere motives of filial piety, decided that Queen Victoria's Journal was not suitable for general reading, and destroyed almost all of it. Only the early closely supervised years were spared. After January 1837, the year in which the Queen came to the throne, her Journal perished. In the middle of a volume half the pages have been wrenched out and the volumes that follow no longer exist.*

*

The first volume of the Queen's Journal is dated 31st July 1832 and inscribed 'This Book Mamma gave me that I might write the journal of my journey to Wales in it. Victoria.' The Journal at this point is written in pencil inked over by an adult hand.[50]

The party included Conroy and his daughter, Victoire, intended to be Princess Victoria's friend. She is, however, barely mentioned. But the Princess's cousins, two sons of the Duchess of Kent's sister Sophie, Hugo and Alfonso Mensdorff, who had been staying at Kensington, were greatly missed. In the Princess's youth it is noticeable how much she yearned for the society of young people, for 'mirth', jokes, dancing, games —but not with the young Conroys. She writes of the young Mensdorffs 'they were so merry and kind in the house'.

The royal party went to North Wales through the Midlands, and the Princess was astonished and horrified by a coal-mining district. 'The men, women, children, country and houses are all black . . . the grass is quite blasted and black. Just now I saw an extraordinary building flaming with fire. The country continues black, engines flaming, coals, in abundance, everywhere, smoking and burning coal heaps, intermingled with wretched huts and carts and little ragged children.'[51]

The 'journey' was accompanied by celebrations which greatly annoyed William IV. Welshpool was decorated 'with arches, flowers, branches, flags, ribbons &c., &c.'; as the royal carriage drove up to Powis Castle cannon fired and a band played. The next week at Caernarvon, the Corporation was waiting accompanied by 'an immense crowd', a salute was fired and the Duchess was presented with an address. At Conway children walked two and two before the royal party strewing flowers in their path. Arches of flowers were erected up the steps to the Castle, a salute was fired from the ramparts and the Duchess received another address. At the Menai Bridge a male choir sang 'God Save the King' unaccompanied, in

*See Appendix 4.

the Welsh fashion. Lord Anglesey lent the Duchess his house, Plas Newydd in Anglesey, where the Princess greatly enjoyed herself—'*dear* Plas Newydd' she wrote. She sailed in the *Emerald*, the tender to the royal yacht, *The Royal George*, and galloped her little horse at top speed over the fields—'Rosa went an enormous rate, she literally *flew*.'

The Princess was not well during the journey; she mentions feeling sick, being unable to come down to dinner, having backache, waking up at 4 a.m. and being sick, waking at 7 a.m. and being sick again. All the party were indisposed, Lehzen was unwell and could not come out in the *Emerald*, the Duchess of Kent had to lie on her bed all one day, the Conroy family was 'very unwell' and Lady Catherine Jenkinson, appointed the Duchess of Kent's lady-in-waiting in 1830, was too ill to come out to a luncheon at which medals were presented by the Princess to Bards and Poets. From Plas Newydd the royal party went on to Eaton Hall, the immense house (now demolished) owned by Lord Grosvenor, and visited Chester, where on 17th October the Princess opened the Victoria Bridge over the River Dee. Three days were spent in splendour with the Duke of Devonshire at Chatsworth, and a magnificent luncheon was given by Lord Shrewsbury at Alton Towers at which everything was served on 'splendid gold plate'. The Princess had taken a liking to Lady Catherine Jenkinson, who was 20 or 21, and a visit was paid to Lady Catherine's father, the Earl of Liverpool, brother of the late Prime Minister, at Pitchford in Lancashire. Lord Liverpool was noted for his kindliness and the Princess 'at once formed for him an almost filial affection' destined to be of importance.[52]

The Princess and the Duchess travelled in a style calculated to attract attention. 'Our carriage is drawn by grey horses,' wrote the Princess 'the post boys have pink silk jackets, with black hats, and the horses have pink silk reins with bunches of artificial flowers.' Flowers were everywhere, the Princess mentions arches of flowers, wreaths of dahlias (it was autumn), bouquets of flowers fastened to poles, her name done in flowers and ribbons. A troop of local yeomanry escorted their carriage, one troop taking over from another as they passed into a fresh neighbourhood. At Oxford, where they were 'most WARMLY and ENTHUSIASTIC-ALLY received', Lord Churchill at the head of a troop of yeomanry himself escorted the royal party through the city to the Sheldonian Theatre, where the Duchess received an address and Conroy the honorary degree of Doctor of Civil Law and the freedom of the City of Oxford. The party then went to luncheon with the Vice-Chancellor. The 'journey' ended on Friday, 9th November 1832, and Christmas was spent in company with the Conroy family at Kensington Palace.

William IV found the Duchess's 'journey' 'disgusting' and not less disgusting because it was a success. The Duchess was already arrogating to herself the position that she and her daughter would occupy at his death, while she opposed and irritated him in every possible way. A sore point was the Duchess's behaviour to William IV's ten illegitimate children by Mrs Jordan, whose existence she refused to acknowledge. Queen Adelaide freely received them, but the Duchess of Kent told the Duchess of Northumberland '. . . I never did, neither will I ever, associate Victoria in any way with the illegitimate members of the Royal family; with the King they die. Did I not keep this line, how would it be possible to teach Victoria the difference between vice and virtue?' It was impossible to avoid being in the same house with one of the ten since William IV invited them to stay constantly both at Windsor and St James's. It was, however, the Duchess's practice when one of them came into a room where she was sitting to rise and withdraw.[53]

Even the political situation in the country increased William IV's anger with the Duchess. In May 1832 the Reform Bill became law. In 1831 Reform riots of appalling violence had broken out; in the autumn of 1831, in Bristol, a considerable part of the city was destroyed, troops were ordered out, fired on the crowd and many persons were killed. Sensible men realised that the mass of the people was determined to have Reform and, though King William IV was thought about to lose his mind, he was forced to give way. The Reform Bill passed, and the Whig clique at Kensington triumphed.

Appearances, however, were preserved. At the end of April 1833 the Duchess gave a large dinner for the King. Queen Adelaide found herself unwell and unable to come, but royal and other dukes, marquesses and marchionesses, earls and countesses abounded. Princess Victoria appeared with Lehzen in the saloon after dinner, the band of the Grenadier Guards played and the Princess stayed up until 11 p.m. On 24th May 1833 the Princess wrote 'I am today fourteen years old! How *very old*',[34] and the King gave a Juvenile Ball at St James's Palace in her honour, which she opened by dancing with her cousin, Prince George of Cambridge.

Beneath the surface, however, friction continued, so bitterly that the possibility of a formal breach between Kensington and the Court at St James's was discussed. There were squabbles about invitations that had been refused, about Sir John Conroy's uniform, about the retinue of the Duchess of Kent, about rank and about salutes.

The Duchess of Kent had taken to visiting the Isle of Wight for sea air. The Princess was fond of sailing, she had been given a 'little schooner' of her own and the *Emerald* was at their disposal. But as the Duchess with the Princess sailed about the Solent there was a 'continual popping in the shape of salutes to H.R.H.'[55]

William IV signified his pleasure that the salutes should cease; Lord Grey, the Prime Minister, was consulted and advised that negotiation should be attempted. It was suggested to the Duchess that, as she was sailing for her own amusement when she went to the Isle of Wight, she might send word that she would waive the right to be saluted whenever she appeared. She refused. Sir James Kempt, Master General of the Ordnance, reported Conroy had said 'that as H.R.H.'s *confidential* adviser he could not recommend her to give way on this point'. Since the Duchess insisted on her right to be saluted, the only solution was to alter the regulations. On 3rd July 1833 the King summoned a Council and by an Order in Council made a change; in future the Royal Standard would be saluted only when the King or the Queen was on board.

*

The character of the child who was growing up in the midst of constant disputes and antagonisms was nevertheless eagerly affectionate, with a disposition to admire enthusiastically, little disposition to criticise and a longing for young society.

When the Princes Alexander and Ernst Württemberg, the Duchess's nephews, sons of her sister Princess Antoinette, the wife of Prince Alexander of Würtemberg, came to stay in June 1833 Princess Victoria wrote 'They are both *extremely tall*, Alexander is *very handsome* and Ernst has a *very kind expression*. They are both *extremely amiable*.' When they left about a month later, she was '*very very* sorry that they are going . . . we shall miss them at *breakfast*, at *luncheon*, at *dinner*, *riding*, *sailing*, *driving*, *walking*, in *fact everywhere*'.[56]

Victoire Conroy was constantly with her, for instance on the 13th, 14th, 15th, 16th, 17th and 18th of May, but the Princess lavished no endearments or ecstasies on her. Her presence was noted, nothing more. A great deal of devotion was bestowed on animals, especially 'dear sweet little Dash', a spaniel originally given to the Duchess of Kent by Conroy, Rosa the Princess's little horse and various birds, including a parakeet and a canary. The Princess treated 'dear Dashy' as a doll, dressing him 'in a scarlet coat and blue trousers'. Naturally fearless, she loved to ride as fast as she was allowed and her Journal is sprinkled with notes that 'dear little Rosa went beautifully'.

The Duchess of Kent gave many parties in 1833. During May she had dinners on the 1st, 6th, 8th, 15th, 29th and in June on the 3rd, 7th, 12th, 17th, 19th, 20th.[57] From July until October there was another 'journey', this time to the south coast.

On 2nd August 1833 the Princess was involved in what might have been a serious accident. As the *Emerald*, which had sails only, was being towed up to Plymouth by a steam ship, with the Duchess and the Princess on board, she ran foul of a hulk and broke her mast. After a moment of horror-struck suspense, the mast caught in the rigging and did not fall.

The Princess's anxiety was all for Dash. 'Sweet Dash was under Saunders'* arm the whole time, but he never let him drop in all the danger.'[58]

After Plymouth the Princess visited Portsmouth where she went over the *Victory* and sailed to the Eddystone lighthouse, then paid a brief visit to Torquay, where she was welcomed by a procession of young girls, with a child carrying a crown in their midst, and the Duchess received an address. After Torquay the royal party visited Exeter and inspected the cathedral, spent two nights at Weymouth, where the town was illuminated in their honour, then drove on in an open carriage escorted by the Dorsetshire Yeomanry through enthusiastic crowds to stay at Lord Ilchester's seat, Melbury.

On this tour the royal party made their headquarters at Norris Castle in the Isle of Wight, while the Conroy family was established close by at Osborne Lodge, later the site of Queen Victoria's own house.[59] On 22nd August the Duchess gave a large 'rout' and evening party, for the local gentry. The Princess wrote in her Journal 'The whole Conroy family came'.

The Princess did not enjoy 'journeys'. The travelling exhausted her and she dreaded the round of public engagements. At this point in her life her health was not good; she mentions being 'bilious', feeling sick, being 'prostrated' by headaches, having 'sore eyes', backache and frequent colds. Her Uncle Leopold advised her to be careful how much she ate; she was a Hanoverian and the Hanoverians were noted for large appetites and a tendency to plumpness. He wrote that he had heard 'a certain little princess . . . eats a little too *much*, and almost always a little *too fast*'. He begged her not to eat too much at luncheon, or, if she did, to eat less at dinner. He had been told she did not like to take exercise, she must 'force herself to do so'. Her height caused concern and her Uncle Leopold made no secret of his anxiety to see her grow. His remarks would have induced painful inferiority in a less unselfconscious and honest nature. He wrote he had heard she was 'growing very much' and hoped she would 'persist in so laudable a measure', in another letter he had 'not been able to ascertain that you really have grown taller lately, I must recommend it strongly'. On receiving a present of her portrait he remarked that the Princess 'shines more by her virtues than by her tallness'.[60]

A note written for James Linton the artist† on 3rd August 1882 gives

* Joseph Saunders was a non-commissioned officer with the rank of Master of which the modern equivalent is navigating officer. He commanded the *Emerald* tender from 9th June 1831 and disappears from the Navy List 1839-40. (PRO Adm 6/162 and Index 9191.)

† James Linton was knighted in 1885. In 1882 he was painting a picture of the Duke of Albany's wedding and had asked for the heights of those figuring in it. The note giving the Queen's height as 'about 5 feet 3 inches' is in Sir Henry Ponsonby's writing and may have been the Queen's own estimate. (RA PP 1/3/53.)

the Queen's height as 5 feet 3 inches. This estimate is hardly likely; 5 feet 3 inches is a normal height, many women never considered conspicuously short are no taller, but the Queen is constantly described as 'the little Queen'. She was probably about 5 feet in height.

In the early spring of 1834 the Princess was laid up with an 'indisposition' which kept her confined to her room for nearly a month. She did not fail to mention in her Journal 'how *very anxious my dear* Mama was throughout my indisposition, and how *unceasing* dear Lehzen was in her attentions to me',[61] thus presenting both readers of her Journal with a tribute each. 1834 was a quieter year than 1833. There was no 'journey', the Duchess did not give so many dinners though there was a large evening party in May for which she borrowed Princess Sophia's garden next door, the gardens were hung with lamps, the flower garden was illuminated and the effect was 'very pretty'. The band of the Scots Fusiliers played and Princess Victoria received the guests with her mother, staying up until 1 a.m.

The great event of the year was the visit of Princess Feodora with her husband Ernest Prince of Hohenlohe-Langenburg and her two eldest children: 'my *dearest* sister Feodora whom I had not seen for *6 years*' wrote the Princess.[62] Feodora arrived on 5th June and the Princess and her half-sister had the delightful experience of resuming an intimacy unchanged by the passage of time. Older than Princess Victoria by eleven years, Princess Feodora's affection was protective and maternal. 'I was delighted to see a little letter directed to me from your darling hands' she wrote in 1828 soon after her marriage. 'How I should like to kiss them and your whole little person. I long very often after you, my sweet Victoria. . . .'[63] Feo never wrote often enough to satisfy her sister, but her letters nearly always came once a fortnight and discussed at length, with tenderness and sympathy, Victoria's dolls, the tame otter, parakeets and guinea-pigs kept by Prince Ernest, Feo's husband, Victoria's fondness for flowers and sea shells, and Victoria's courage when having a tooth pulled out.

During the visit of June 1834 the sisters slipped back into their old ways. They went driving with Lehzen in a phaeton as they had six years before, often taking two of Feo's children with them. 'They are *dear sweet* children, not at all shy, and so good, they never hurt or spoil anything' wrote Princess Victoria in her Journal. She spent many hours alone with Feo and the children in the rooms Feo had been given at Kensington; they were 'so merry' together. Princess Victoria loved romping. Even after she had become Queen she enjoyed romping with Lord Ashley's children in the corridors of Windsor Castle.

Princess Feodora was in the habit of giving her sister frank advice. Victoria must not open her mouth when having her likeness taken; years before when they drove out every day with Lehzen, Princess

Feodora used to notice Victoria always had her mouth open. Victoria had a bad habit of taking too much salt with her meat. 'I am certain it is very bad for you, pray think of your old sister when you look at the salt cellar with the intention of mixing so much of its contents with your knife in the gravy, you have a peculiar quick and expert way of doing it, sometimes in absence [of mind] I observed. You dearest love! every action and habit of yours is present to my mind, which loves to dwell on you.'[64]

On 11th June Princess Victoria and the Duchess of Kent went to stay at Windsor Castle, where Princess Feodora and her husband had already arrived, and on Thursday 13th June Princess Victoria went for the first time to the races at Ascot. She enjoyed herself immensely, was rapturously received by the crowd and made a bet with her good-natured uncle, King William IV, by which to her surprise and delight she won a beautiful little dark chestnut mare named Taglioni, after the famous danseuse.

But on 25th July 1834 Princess Victoria wrote in her Journal 'It was my last drive with dearest, dear Feodora'; next day the visit ended and Feodora went away.

'. . . the separation was indeed *dreadful*' wrote Princess Victoria. 'I *clasped* her in my *arms*, and *kissed* her and *cried* as if my *heart* would break, so did she *dearest* Sister. We then tore ourselves from each other in the *deepest grief*. . . . When I came home I was in such a state of grief that I knew not what to do with myself. I sobbed and cried most violently the whole morning. . . . My dearest best sister was friend, sister, companion all to me, we agreed so well together in all our feelings and amusements. . . . I love no one better than her.'[65]

Princess Feodora was deeply moved. 'I must tell you that the thought often tormented me that we two should be strangers to each other; for you were such a child when I left England. . . . I loved you dearly as a sweet child and little sister—but now I can love you as a sister and friend, for the accordance of heart and mind attaches me much more than the feelings of relationship alone. I am much older than you, my dearest sister, but while I was with you I could enter into all your opinions and, you will not be angry with me for saying it, your little whims and faults, in which I have often found my own of former days.'[66]

'Sad, dull evenings' began again for the Princess when her sister had gone.

Some degree of emotional tension was inseparable from the age of the Princess. She was 15, but the situation at Kensington both affected her spirits and contributed to the poor health from which she suffered at this period. Kensington Palace was the scene of a perpetual struggle to dominate the Princess, between Conroy and the Duchess on the one hand and Lehzen and the Princess on the other.

A long letter survives, written by Stockmar on 4th July 1834 in response to an appeal from the Duchess of Kent.[67] The Duchess had begged Stockmar, who was on a visit to London, to try and improve the situation at Kensington, by talking to the persons concerned. He told her the task was impossible.

'How can my words help when nobody wishes to change and nobody wants to give in? The main difficulty lies, in my opinion, neither in the personality of your Royal Highness, nor in that of the Baroness [Lehzen], it seems to me to lie much more in the Princess herself and Sir John Conroy. The latter seems to me to be an excellent business man and absolutely devoted to your Royal Highness. But how can I overlook that he is vain, ambitious, most sensitive and most hot tempered?' Baron Stockmar then reveals that the Duchess and Conroy were already at this stage planning to make Conroy the Princess's adviser when she came to the throne. But Stockmar points out that since Conroy's characteristics had already made him enemies in his present situation, 'will they not become more dangerous in a new and much more difficult position . . .? Will he of his own accord find the way back to that place which he should never have left and which he only left in the hope of fulfilling those dreams which the Regency Bill awoke in his imagination? I doubt it. And how does one see his future position as adviser to the Princess? . . . Is it at all in the power of the Princess to nominate him Private Secretary, even if her responsible advisers should advise against such an appointment? Would he have the self-control, modesty and flexibility for such a delicate position?' Even supposing he gained a very influential position and the Princess had full confidence in him, how long would his influence last? 'Not longer than until the Princess marries. Would a dignified, able, determined Prince suffer such an exclusive influence? Not for an hour! And could one allow the Princess to marry an incompetent husband? Would she accept one?'

Stockmar went on to deal with the character of the Princess. The Princess differed in her views, sentiments and opinions from Sir John Conroy but it was wrong to look for the explanation solely in the influence of Baroness Lehzen. 'I rather think' wrote Stockmar 'that the real reasons for those differences are to be found in the innate personality of the Princess, in the inner circumstances at Kensington and in the behaviour of Sir John towards the Princess'. The Princess, in the last few years, had evidently had different opinions on many things from those of her mother, but 'there is no reason to think that the seeds which have produced these differences have been implanted from elsewhere, they have been within the Princess herself. Your Royal Highness must not forget that the Princess must have known from her earliest youth that she is a Princess. Wherever she looked in the house, she encountered Sir John as the sole regulator of the whole machine. As soon as she felt

95

something unpleasant in the house . . . she recognised the main cause of it in the person of Sir John. Such impressions go deepest at a youthful age. . . . With every day the Princess grew up . . . she became resentful of what must have looked to her as an exercise of undue control over herself. . . . Your Royal Highness yourself has agreed with me that Sir John's personal behaviour towards the Princess has been apt only too often to worsen this state of affairs.'

With many expressions of courtesy and devotion Stockmar reminded the Duchess of the accusations which had been made against his master the King of the Belgians of 'tampering' with the Princess. He did not wish to run the risk of that charge being brought against him. *'To tamper means intrigue, I don't know any other word for it.'* He ended his letter with a plea: 'May Your Royal Highness not do anything that could *produce coldness and distance between you and the Princess,* neither *now nor in the future.'* He had, he added with a note of warning, kept 'an exact copy of this letter'.

On 4th November 1834 the Duchess took the Princess to St Leonards-on-Sea for an autumn holiday. In addition to the usual decorations of flowers and flags, six fishermen in blue jackets, red caps and white aprons, preceded by a band, presented the royal party with a basket of fish, ornamented with flowers. The Princess was delighted.[68] 'It was indeed a most splendid reception' she wrote.

Though the house was comfortable and the Princess enjoyed the absence of fog and the sunsets and sunrises over the sea she was not well, felt sick and had pains in her back. The whole Conroy family had come down to St Leonards and several members lunched or dined with the Duchess every day. 'The usual party' writes the Princess.

Soon after their arrival the royal party was involved in another accident. The Duchess of Kent and the Princess, accompanied by Lehzen, Lady Flora Hastings, her new lady-in-waiting, and the Princess's dog Dash, were driving in a landau with a postilion and two horses. One horse became entangled in the traces and fell dragging the other with him. As the horses were on the ground, kicking and struggling, there was a danger that the landau would be overturned and perhaps broken up, but two gentlemen who were passing contrived, at some risk, to sit on the first horse's head while the traces were cut and the occupants of the landau scrambled out, the Princess with Dash in her arms. Meanwhile the second horse struggled to its feet and galloped off down the road, while the Duchess and her party took refuge behind a wall.[69] For his services on this occasion one of the gentlemen, Mr Peckham Mickelthwaite, was created a baronet after the Princess became Queen.

During the past year a small but significant change had taken place in the Princess's routine. When she went out with Lehzen they no longer walked or drove alone; Lady Flora Hastings, who had become the Duchess of Kent's lady-in-waiting in 1834, was almost always with them. Lady Flora, who was 28, was the eldest child of the first Marquess of Hastings, clever (a volume of her poems and translations was published after her death) and possessed of a sharp wit.

The Duchess of Kent had engaged her for the express purpose of giving Princess Victoria suitable companionship, but had done so without consulting the Princess and against Stockmar's advice. Stockmar told the Duchess[70] that it was time the Princess had her own ladies and nominated them herself. The Duchess ought to prove to the Princess 'by deed' that she no longer intended to treat her 'as a mere child, but as a grown up daughter and friend'. In Stockmar's opinion the Princess was afraid that if she herself named anyone there would be fresh 'misunderstandings' with her mother; he urged the Duchess to 'take the initiative' as soon as possible and invite the Princess to name the ladies she wished to have. If the Princess named any lady to whom the Duchess had 'real, considerable, reasons' for objecting, 'may it please you to tell them quietly to the Princess and permit the Princess to utter her point of view, so that the whole matter may be settled in a quiet and cordial manner'.

But it did not suit the policy being pursued at Kensington for the Princess to be surrounded by friends. There was no consultation with the Princess before Lady Flora was appointed, and in the struggle at Kensington Palace, Lady Flora joined Conroy's party and formed a friendship with him which did not pass unremarked.

The introduction of Lady Flora heralded a new campaign to drive out Lehzen, who was 'treated with contempt and incredible harshness', so brutally that on 6th March 1835 the Duchess of Northumberland, Princess Victoria's official governess, wrote to Princess Feodora suggesting she should ask King Leopold, who was Princess Feodora's uncle as well as Princess Victoria's, to intervene on Lehzen's behalf. Princess Feodora replied in agitation that the letter '. . . made me tremble when I read it. . . . Dear Duchess we must do everything to preserve Baroness L[ehzen]. The King [William IV] is the person to uphold her and say she *must* and *shall* remain with the Princess . . . for what sort of person may be put near her, to further the plans of that man. As the Queen [Adelaide] knows of it I am sure she will do all in her power to protect poor L, but I think it is only the King, as head of the family, that can speak a decisive word in this business. . . . How very good it would be if your Grace could communicate with B.L. [Baroness Lehzen] and advise her what to do at such a moment, but I know, but too well, how difficult, almost impossible that is at the Palace. . . . In you, dear Madam, I place my whole confidence, and intreat you to watch over our beloved Princess, and, if necessary, tell the King what he *ought* to do.'[71]

At the moment, however, Conroy and the Duchess of Kent were engaged in scheming to get rid of the Duchess of Northumberland. She had been a disappointment. The intention had been that her appointment should be a 'nominal one' and Conroy had been 'overjoyed' when she accepted. Kensington needed 'the lustre of her name', but the Duchess insisted on taking 'an active part'. Both she and the Duke were highly esteemed by William IV and Queen Adelaide. The Duchess wished to attend Princess Victoria's lessons, so that she might be able to report from personal knowledge, 'when asked by High Authority as to Her Royal Highness's progress'. She asked questions about the amount of recreation the Princess enjoyed, she concerned herself with the Princess's further education and submitted lists of books for her to read. Conroy soon came to consider the Duchess of Northumberland 'extremely hostile to the system at Kensington' and also to himself.

He therefore wrote a letter[72] for the Duchess of Kent, to be placed before William IV. The Princess 'has entered her seventeenth year and is on the eve of confirmation' and the Duchess of Kent proposed to make alterations in her establishment and the system of her education. The Princess was to become her mother's companion and the appointment of the Duchess of Northumberland, made in order that the Princess might have some lady of rank to attend on her on public occasions, 'is one, as its name "Governess" implies, which ceases with the Princess's present age. The Baroness Lehzen, who has been the Princess's nursery and schoolroom Instructress, as well as attendant, naturally ceases also.' The Princess was to have a Lady of the Bedchamber and the Lady of the Bedchamber was to be Lady Flora Hastings.

Before the letter could be delivered Conroy's hot temper betrayed him. William IV discovered that 'Kensington' had treated the Duchess, the valued friend of the King and Queen and one of the greatest ladies in England, with discourtesy. William IV had sent a communication relating to Princess Victoria's coming confirmation through the Duchess of Northumberland to the Duchess of Kent, who had received it 'in a manner . . . very little suited to Her Grace's station in society', and, instead of returning an answer through the Duchess of Northumberland as etiquette required, had sent the reply over her head, to be conveyed to the King through the Archbishop of Canterbury.

William IV boiled with indignation and very soon another squabble between 'Kensington' and the Court was in progress.[73] In an angry letter the Archbishop of Canterbury was informed, 'The King is anxious to convince the Duchess of Northumberland of his determination not to countenance any proceeding inconsistent with the high estimation in which he holds the Duchess of Northumberland and the exemplary course she has invariably pursued. His Majesty conceives that he owes it to Her Grace (and indeed to himself) to require that his Communication should be acknowledged thro' the Channel to which His Majesty thought fit to entrust it, and his Majesty trusts your Grace will ensure this to be understood by the Duchess of Kent.'

The Archbishop of Canterbury accordingly informed the Duchess of Kent that His Majesty, having commissioned the Duchess of Northumberland to ascertain Her Royal Highness's wishes on the subject of her daughter the Princess Victoria's confirmation, 'expects an answer to be returned through the same channel'. The Duchess of Kent refused; she would not communicate with the King through the Duchess of Northumberland; the King refused to communicate through anyone else and Sir Herbert Taylor, William IV's secretary, wrote to the Archbishop on 17th July 1835 '. . . Thus the matter stands and I fear it may have the effect of delaying the Confirmation of the Princess Victoria'.

William IV, however, was too angry to let the matter rest and took the unprecedented step of writing a letter in his own hand to the Bishop of London, bearing the sign manual, the King's signature, 'forbidding the Bishop, as Dean of the Chapels Royal, to allow the Princess Victoria, the Duchess of Kent's daughter, to be confirmed in any of them'.

The Duchess of Kent could no longer resist; she blamed the Archbishop of Canterbury, but gave way and sent a communication to the King through the Duchess of Northumberland. On 30th July 1835 Princess Victoria was confirmed by the Archbishop of Canterbury, assisted by her tutor Dr Davys, Dean of Chester since 1831, in the Chapel Royal, St James's. King William IV led in the Princess, Queen Adelaide and a gathering of the Princess's royal relatives attended, Lady Flora Hastings and Lehzen were both present. Conroy also came into the Chapel but as soon as William IV saw him he was ordered out, a public affront which Conroy bitterly resented and never forgave.

The Princess wore a white lace dress, and a white crepe bonnet with a wreath of roses round it. The bonnet was removed for the ceremony. The Archbishop of Canterbury, Dr Howley, was not an eloquent man, but the address he delivered to the Princess on this occasion, dealing with her future responsibilities, affected her so much that she was 'drowned in tears and frightened to death'.[74]

The Princess was, however, under an emotional strain quite sufficient to account for tears. More than usually observant, she cannot fail to have been aware of the renewal of the campaign to send Lehzen away, and, on the day of her confirmation, as soon as the ceremony was over, the Duchess handed her a long letter[75] in which, after enlarging on her maternal devotion and many sacrifices, she told the Princess that her manner to Lehzen must change. The Princess had now reached the period of her life 'that brings changes with it'; the Duchess herself had written a letter to Lehzen telling her that in future there must be a difference and she wished the Princess to do the same. The Princess should write to Lehzen 'recollecting with every grateful sentiment her attentions to you in the years that are past' but intimating that in future Lehzen would be treated with dignity: dignity and friendly manners 'are quite compatible'. The Duchess went on to introduce a new idea: 'Until you are at the age of either eighteen or twenty-one years . . . you are still confided to the guidance of your affectionate mother and friend.' But royal persons come of age at eighteen. Was Princess Victoria to be treated differently and for what reason?

The importance of Lehzen in the Princess's life was overwhelming. She represented security. She had been at Kensington Palace as long as the Princess could remember, and she had remained. Everyone else had been lost to the Princess. The Princess had loved her half-sister Feo, and she had gone away; her childish love for her mother, the Duchess of Kent, had been changed to distrust through the Duchess's relations with Conroy; even Spaeth, 'poor old Spaeth', who loved her unwisely but well, had been removed. The companions of her own age selected for her were Victoire and Jane Conroy, whom she despised. Only Lehzen was always there.

In the winter of 1834, when she was unwell, she wrote in her Journal 'At 8 Mama, Lady Flora, Lady Conroy, Jane and Victoire came into my room. Lehzen of course being with me.'[76]

Yet, in the affection, the adoring affection, the Princess cherished for Lehzen, there was a tinge of fear. She was 'greatly in awe' of Lehzen, who was 'very strict'.[77] Lehzen was a woman of formidable character and in the numerous expressions of love for Lehzen, gratitude to Lehzen, longing for Lehzen, which are scattered through the Princess's Journal there is a hint of propitiation. Lehzen, after all, read the Journal, and passages were written to please her. But, without Lehzen, without Lehzen's strength, Lehzen's support, Lehzen's not unimportant influence in high places, it is doubtful if Princess Victoria would have survived the 'Kensington System'. She was little more than a child and except for Lehzen she was alone. Without Lehzen's shrewd advice it is unlikely that she would have conducted herself in her most difficult situation with such skill and when, like a butterfly from a chrysalis, the young Queen burst on the world, it was Lehzen, more than any other person, who was responsible for the astonishing result.

*

The Sunday after the confirmation of the Princess, on 2nd August 1835, she noted in her Journal[78] that she took the Sacrament for the first time according to the rites of the Church of England, after morning service in the Chapel Royal, St James's. The group who knelt with her consisted of the Duchess of Kent, Sir John Conroy, Lady Flora Hastings and '*dear Lehzen*'.

Three days later, on 5th August 1835, the Duchess and her household again left London, and after spending two nights at Buxted Park, Sussex, with Lord Liverpool, went on to Tunbridge Wells.

The Princess still felt 'very poorly', had constant backache and in Tunbridge Wells spent a considerable amount of time in her bedroom, lying on a couch, while Lehzen read to her. On 17th August the Princess wrote in her Journal 'Lehzen being always in the house I do not always mention her. She always breakfasts, lunches, dines and goes out with us everywhere. Lady Flora is also staying in the house.'[79]

The Conroy family had come with the Duchess to Tunbridge Wells and Conroys lunched and dined daily, but the Princess no longer allows the Conroy daughters the intimacy of Christian names. Victoire and Jane have become 'the two Miss Conroys'.

Sir John Conroy had arranged a 'journey' for the autumn of more than usual splendour 'which bore some resemblance to a triumphal procession'.[80] It was to begin on 3rd September 1835, and cover the north midlands and east of England with visits to the mansions of Wentworth, Belvoir Castle, Burghley, Holkham and Euston Hall.

At the last moment the Princess protested. She did not want to go. She could not face it. A scene followed with the Duchess of Kent, who again wrote her a long letter.[81] The Princess should 'give up the idea that you have that I am angry, when I try to convince you, that you have formed an erroneous view of a subject. . . . You may imagine that I feel very much disappointed and grieved, that the journey we are to commence to-morrow is not only disagreeable to you, but that it makes you even unhappy; that the fatigue of it will make you ill, that you dislike it. . . . You will not see, that it is of the greatest consequence that you should be seen, that you should know your country, and be acquainted with, and be known by all classes. If the King was another man, and if he *really* loved you he would, instead of wishing to stop our Journey, which he tried every way to do, but which his Ministers told him he could not do, as it would do him harm; as his jealousy is too well known . . . even press me to them. I must tell you dearest Love, if your conversation with me could be known, that you had not the energy to undertake the journey, or that your views were not enlarged enough to grasp the benefits arising from it, then you would fall in the estimation of the people of this country. . . . Can you be dead to the calls your position demands? Impossible! Reflect—before it is too late. . . . Turn your thoughts and views to your future station, its duties, and the claims that exist on you.'

The 'journey' therefore proceeded as arranged, the Princess writing in her Journal[82] on the first day 'I felt very tired, had a headache and pain in my back'. Even before York was reached in less than a week, the Princess, wrote Lehzen, was 'so markedly unwell, in body and soul, that it seems almost a marvel that she did not succumb there'.[83] During the celebrations at York where a music festival was taking place the Princess heard Handel's *Messiah*, sung in York Minster, and disliked it. 'I must say with the exception of a few Choruses and one or two songs' she wrote in her Journal 'it is very heavy and tiresome. . . . I am not at all fond of Handel's music, I like the present Italian school such as Rossini, Bellini, Donizetti &c., *much better*.'

The success of the journey, however, was tremendous. The crowds were 'vast' and enthusiastic, the royal carriage was drawn through Lynn by the inhabitants, at Worksop the entire population escorted the carriage on foot, there were more decorations, more bands, more addresses than ever. At Stamford an address was read to the Duchess by the Marquess of Exeter and it was noted that 'Conroy handed the answer, just as the Prime Minister does to the King'. At Burghley House the Princess opened a ball of 300 guests with the Marquess of Exeter as her partner, but had a 'dreadful headache' and went to bed after the first dance. Throughout the journey she was 'greatly fatigued', 'well nigh dead by the heat and fatigue', 'cannot eat', '*forced* a cup of cocoa down without eating anything' and suffered from backache. She complained that 'when one arrives at any nobleman's seat, one must instantly dress for dinner and consequently I could never rest properly'.

On Friday, 25th September 1835, the Duchess and her household returned to Kensington Palace and on 28th September set off again for an autumn holiday at Ramsgate.

Princess Victoria's spirits rose: her uncle the King of the Belgians was coming to Ramsgate, with his young wife, whom the Princess had never met, to stay informally for almost a week.

King Leopold had succeeded in establishing his position in Belgium, and had gone far to conciliate pro-French Catholic opinion by marrying Princess Louise, daughter of Louis Philippe, King of the French. Born in 1812, Princess Louise was only seven years older than Princess Victoria and four years younger than Princess Feodora. She had been married at twenty. King Leopold described her as being very like Princess Feodora, but thinner; Princess Feodora found her 'very amiable and good' with 'a very elegant little figure, thin certainly, a beautiful foot . . .'.[84] She was always very well dressed and danced excellently.

Since the Princess had ceased to be a small child her uncle King Leopold had been writing her serious letters of good advice, and, as surviving letters indicate, he also received confidential reports on the welfare of the Princess and the situation at Kensington Palace from Lehzen.

Unfortunately, in a disastrous fire at the Belgian Royal Palace at Laeken near Brussels in 1890,[85] the Belgian Royal Archives were all but totally destroyed and only those memoranda and letters are in existence which, for some reason, had been sent out of Belgium.

King Leopold's relationship to the future Queen of England and the influence he might in due course exercise over her, and be known by other governments to exercise over her, were political assets of the highest importance to him. He had remained in the background partly because he was establishing his position in Belgium, partly because it was his nature to proceed secretively and with caution and partly because he had been overwhelmed with private sorrow. Once again he had lost his first-born child; a son, Prince Louis Philippe, born to Queen Louise in July 1833, died in May 1834. A second son, Prince Leopold, had, however, been born in April of the present year, 1835.

The burden of her Uncle Leopold's advice to her was the responsibility of being a Queen.[86] 'Our times as I have frequently told you are hard times for Royalty' he wrote. She must fit herself for her high station by self-examination, by not allowing her mind to be taken up by trifles or 'frivolous amusements'. He endeavoured to form her political judgment by sending her books, memoranda and extracts showing the mistakes made by other monarchs. Replying to a letter from King Leopold enclosing an extract showing the political mistakes made by Queen Anne, the Princess displayed signs of impatience: 'I am much obliged to you, dear Uncle, for the extract about Queen Anne, but must beg you, as you have sent me to show what a Queen *ought not* to be, that you will send me what a Queen *ought to be*.' King Leopold commented '. . . a very clever sharp little letter'.

In the autumn of 1835 King Leopold, aware of the situation in the Duchess of Kent's household, judged the moment had come to talk matters over with his niece in a personal interview, and introduce her to her new aunt, Queen Louise. He chose to visit Ramsgate instead of risking the intrigues and formalities of London, crossing from Ostend and staying about a week at the Albion Hotel.

On Tuesday, 29th September 1835, Ramsgate was festive with flags and arches of flowers and an 'immense concourse' of people watched as the vessel with the King and Queen of the Belgians steamed into Rams-gate Harbour to the sound of loud cheers and the firing of guns from the pier.[87] The Princess, with Lehzen, Lady Flora and Lady Conroy, watched 'with beating hearts' from a window of the Albion Hotel. After '1/4 of an hour of anxious suspense', King Leopold appeared with Queen Louise on his arm. The Princess was ecstatic. 'What a happiness it was for me to throw myself in the arms of that *dearest* of Uncles, who has always been to me like a father, and whom I love so *very dearly*' she wrote in her Journal. 'I had not seen him for 4 years and 2 months.' Queen Louise made an instant conquest. 'She is delightful, and was so affectionate to me directly . . . she drew my arm within hers and said so kindly "You must be quite at ease with me, you must consider me like a sort of elder sister." ' Twice during the next few days Queen Louise came informally and sat with the Princess in her room. 'She really is quite *delightful*, I love her *most dearly*.' On Sunday, 4th October, the Princess went to church and was shocked by the sermon. 'Oh! gracious me!' she wrote in her Journal. 'In all my life I never heard such a sermon. It was all against the Roman Catholic religion. It was a most impious, unchristian-like and shocking affair. I was quite shocked and ashamed.'

The same afternoon the purpose of the visit was fulfilled. King Leopold came up to her room and talked to her from five until a quarter to six. 'He gave me very valuable and important advice. We talked over many important and serious matters. I look up to him as a Father, with complete confidence, love and affection. He is the best and kindest adviser I have. He has always treated me as his child and I love him most dearly for it.'[88]

Two days later he came again. 'I have such *great* love for him and such *great* confidence in him. I had a very *important* and *useful* conversation with him. He gave me *very good* and *valuable advice*' wrote the Princess.

Meanwhile the visit proceeded from delight to delight. The Princess admired Queen, now Aunt, Louise's clothes and the way she arranged her hair, and Aunt Louise sent her hairdresser to arrange the Princess's hair in the same way, with side curls, the kind known in French as 'anglaises'. Aunt Louise gave the Princess little presents from her own things, cravats, ribbons, a cap, a tippet. She interested herself in the Princess's drawings and played draughts with her after dinner. The Princess noted with approval that neither Uncle Leopold, nor the Duc de Nemours, Aunt Louise's handsome brother, stayed drinking with the gentlemen in the dining-room after dinner but came immediately to the drawing-room.

Unfortunately the Princess was not at all well during her uncle and aunt's visit, and three times Dr Clark had to be called in. Dr (later Sir James) Clark had been physician to King Leopold, at whose suggestion he had been appointed physician to the Duchess of Kent in 1834 and in April of the present year put in charge of Princess Victoria's health.

The Princess complained of her usual symptoms, inability to eat, nausea, pains in her back and in addition feelings of stiffness. She was, however, buoyed up by the excitement and pleasure of the visit, and

Lehzen wrote that she *alone*, who knew the powers of self-control possessed by the Princess, realised what her real state was. On Wednesday, 7th October 1835, the day King Leopold and Queen Louise sailed for Belgium, the Princess felt 'very poorly' but managed to get to Dover and on board their steamer to bid them farewell. But when she was in the carriage to return to Ramsgate, she collapsed and was '*very* ill'.

In a report to King Leopold Lehzen related what followed.[89] Conroy and the Duchess made light of the Princess's illness, and at first Dr Clark under Conroy's influence did the same. Conroy habitually represented the Princess as being stupid (an opinion with which her half-brother Prince Charles of Leiningen did not agree), fanciful and spoilt, a creature of 'whims' in which she was encouraged by Lehzen. The Princess's aversion from Conroy, her dislike of 'journeys', her frequent feelings of illness, were all described as 'whims', sometimes 'childish whims'. Conroy's intention was to create doubt as to whether the Princess possessed sufficient capacity to govern, so that even when she attained her majority and even if she had succeeded to the throne the Regency would be prolonged.

On the 7th October, on the way back from Dover when the horses were changed, the Duchess of Kent, alarmed by the Princess's condition, asked 'Where is Doctor Clark?' Conroy then came up with a bottle of medicine and an unsealed letter from Dr Clark and told her 'Gone to London with Van der Weyer'. Sylvain Van der Weyer, the Belgian Ambassador in London, was one of King Leopold's trusted advisers. Conroy had encouraged Dr Clark to go to London without asking the Duchess's consent: Lehzen thought Conroy had planned this to discredit Dr Clark with whom he had recently had some differences. The Princess herself, while demanding that Dr Clark should be sent for, believed that the cause of her feeling so ill might be the grief she felt at parting from her aunt and uncle. She went upstairs and lay on her bed, feeling 'so ill'.[90] Dr Clark did not come until Friday, when Lehzen saw him in the presence of the Duchess of Kent who directed her to describe the Princess's symptoms. But as she was beginning the Duchess ordered her to be silent, Dr Clark was going to see the Princess and leave written instructions for her treatment. After he had seen the Princess, Lehzen, who was not present, was told that he had said the Princess was suffering from an indisposition which would pass in two or three days. The Duchess added 'Dr Clark says that if all you report were true, they would be the most alarming symptoms, but I know it to be nothing but Victoria's whims and your imagination.' Dr Clark left Ramsgate the same day.

During that day and the following night the Princess became worse, with a mounting fever and a pulse of over 130. Each day Lehzen was questioned by the Duchess about the Princess's condition and each day was told she was exaggerating. Dr Clark was not to come again until Tuesday, but on Sunday the Princess demanded that an express message should be sent asking him to come at once. The Duchess told Lehzen 'How can you think I should do such a thing? What a noise that would make in town; in short we differ so much about this indisposition that we had better not speak of it at all.'

Tuesday came but no Dr Clark, who sent a letter saying that since he had heard nothing to the contrary he assumed the Princess had now recovered. The Duchess became anxious; though she would not admit the fact to Lehzen, she had been increasingly worried for the last three days and, on Wednesday, after the Princess had passed 'a long fearful day' and a bad night, could no longer conceal her terror. Dr Clark was urgently summoned, but sent word he could not arrive until very late that night. At six in the evening the Princess became delirious and it was decided medical advice must be obtained at once. Mr Plenderleath, a Ramsgate doctor with an excellent reputation, was called in. Lehzen was told to inform Conroy and noted that 'even *he* was visibly upset', though he insisted that to summon a local doctor was politically dangerous, to which Lehzen replied that she 'would not gamble with the life of the Princess for any political considerations'.

Mr Plenderleath came and looked grave, but the Princess became no worse during the night and in the morning Dr Clark appeared. He had seen Conroy on arrival and was inclined to be 'touchy' but '. . . when he saw the Princess and examined her thoroughly' wrote Lehzen 'the scales fell from his eyes. Now the real worth of this excellent doctor and good man became apparent; his treatment of the Princess was exemplary, and with great courage, he also succeeded in restoring to her the necessary *peace of mind.*' The emotional strain of her situation must always be taken into account in considering the Princess's health as a young girl.

The Princess was kept in her room for nearly five weeks. Dr Clark stayed in Ramsgate and she was nursed by Lehzen. '*Dear good* Lehzen' wrote the Princess early in November,[91] when she was able to resume her Journal, 'takes such care of me, and is so unceasing in her attentions to me that I shall never be able to repay her sufficiently for it but by my love and gratitude. I never can sufficiently repay her for all she has *borne* and done for me. She is the *most affectionate, devoted, attached* and *disinterested* friend I have and I love her most *dearly.* . . . I feel that I gain strength every day.'

The illness from which the Princess suffered has been variously diagnosed. Dr Clark called it a 'bilious fever'. Sir Sidney Lee, who was well acquainted with the Royal Family and wrote the entry for Queen Victoria in the *Dictionary of National Biography*, later expanded into the first serious biography of the Queen, describes it as 'an attack of typhoid fever'.[92] However, he places it wrongly, in spring, instead of autumn, 1835. The Prince Consort, in a note on papers of 1835, wrote in his own hand 'A dangerous illness at Ramsgate during the months of October and November'.[93] Conroy, when he had recovered from his fright at the possibility of losing the Princess, told Charles Prince of Leiningen that the illness at Ramsgate was 'a mere indisposition'.

From contemporary accounts, modern doctors are inclined to think that the Princess Victoria suffered from tonsillitis, septic tonsils. The operation of tonsillectomy to remove infected tonsils was then unknown. For years she was being poisoned by her tonsils resulting in the indigestion, nausea, headaches, exhaustion and frequent colds from which she suffered. But being strong and possessing an excellent constitution when she grew older she was able to combat the infection and throw it off.

On 3rd November 1835 Princess Victoria wrote to King Leopold 'I am much better and getting stronger, but am still confined to my room. . . . I am grown *very* thin and also a little taller and Dr Clark says I shall grow quite tall after this. I should be glad if it was the case, if it was only to please you, dear Uncle.'[94]

A week later the Princess was able to go downstairs and meet 'Lady Flora, Lady Conroy, the 2 Miss Conroys and Sir J. C.' and to go into raptures over two boxes of dresses and hats sent her from Paris by Queen Louise, who had not a high opinion of the Duchess of Kent's taste in clothes. Three dresses besides bonnets arrived 'made by Mdlle. Palmyre the 1st Marchande des Modes in Paris'. In addition a large box contained special hairpins for curls, but the Princess had lost her hair so 'frightfully' through her illness that she feared she was 'literally now getting bald, the comb tray was full every morning with my hair; as a last and desperate refuge [*sic*] Lehzen . . . cut off half and even more of back hair, once so thick that she could hardly take it in her hand'.[95]

Dr Clark had been made anxious by the state of the Princess's general health and he proceeded in a long memorandum to prescribe a new routine for her, which meant a new life. The Duchess must move from the ground-floor apartment she occupied at Kensington to the next floor. Plans for putting this floor in repair and redecorating the rooms had been drawn up in 1832, but never carried out because the King refused his permission.

The doctor recommended that the Princess should have frequent exercise in the open air, 'indeed Her Royal Highness should be as much in the open air, and in a *healthy bracing* air as possible'.[96] He considered the air of Kensington relaxing. The Princess should not study for long at a time and frequent walks, even while in the house, were essential to improve her circulation. The Princess since her illness suffered from cold feet, which Lehzen rubbed every evening, sometimes for an hour at a time. It would be beneficial if the Princess wrote from time to time at a standing desk, to give her change of position. Her rooms must be well ventilated and in dry weather the windows always opened when the Princess was out of her rooms. She should take a warm bath every fourth or fifth day. He advised the use of *Indian clubs* to improve the figure and promote good circulation and finally laid stress on the importance of 'perfect and deliberate mastication' to the satisfactory state of the digestive organs. 'I venture to urge the steady adoption of these measures with an earnestness which arises from a conviction of their necessity to secure the Princess's future health.'

Dr Clark's simple commonsense measures were successful, Princess Victoria's general health began to improve, and whatever was the true nature of the illness from which she had just suffered, tonsillitis, bilious fever, typhoid, or perhaps collapse from strain, no further attack occurred.

By 12th January 1836 the Princess had completely recovered and the Duchess with her household left Ramsgate for Kensington Palace. The Princess had regrets on leaving 'in spite of my illness and various other reasons of dullness; Uncle and Aunt's visit being one of the principal causes', but she was looking forward to being in London 'to see all the new plays, operas, etc'.[97] However, more important events than plays and operas awaited her. She was entering her eighteenth year; new and stirring prospects opened before her, but new pressures as well were applied.

Chapter Four

At a little before 2 p.m. on 13th January 1836, the Duchess and the Princess drove up to Kensington Palace, and went upstairs 'up *two* staircases', wrote the Princess, to their new apartments.[1] This was surprising because the Duchess had been forbidden to occupy these apartments by King William IV. In 1832 she had asked Sir Jeffry Wyatville, the architect responsible for the restoration and re-modelling of Windsor Castle for King George IV, to prepare plans for new apartments in Kensington Palace for the Princess and herself. Sir Jeffry's plans were more ambitious than the modest apartments the Duchess and the Princess had hitherto occupied on the lower floors of Kensington Palace, 'dreadfully dull, dark and gloomy', as the Princess described them in a letter to Princess Feodora. Rooms suitable for entertaining were included, in need of re-plastering but large, pillared and with fine carvings. The grand staircase, designed and painted by William Kent for George I, was to be cleaned and restored, and the King's Gallery, built by William III, divided to make three fine rooms. The view from the apartments was excellent, almost every window looked out over lawns, trees and flowers. Sir Jeffry also had plans for improving the approach and entrance to the Palace.

King William IV refused to agree and, after two interviews, in which Sir Jeffry vainly begged the King to consent, he wrote on the plans 'The King says "No" '.[2] Yet, three years later, the Duchess was moving in. All the alterations King William IV had refused had been made, with the exception of the improved approach and entrance, and additional rooms had been added. Apartments in palaces built during the seventeenth century were not self-contained, and the Duchess was able to appropriate two 'remarkably fine' rooms from the neighbouring apartments of the Duke of Sussex; she also continued to occupy several rooms in her old apartments on a lower floor.

At the moment Kensington Palace was not highly regarded, its beauties had gone out of fashion. Princess Victoria repeatedly writes of it as 'our poor old Palace', and it was infested by domestic pests. In a letter to her half-brother, Charles Prince of Leiningen, the Princess refers to 'our Kensington friends, the black beetles',[3] and in 1899 Sir Arthur Bigge (later Lord

Stamfordham), Queen Victoria's private secretary, wrote '. . . the fact is, during the occupancy of the Palace by the Duchess of Kent, the State Apartments and the Denmark Wing* were almost in a state of ruin'.[4] Ruinous or not, Kensington Palace was, as it remains, one of the most beautiful buildings in the kingdom. After Princess Victoria's alarming illness at Ramsgate Dr Clark had urged she should have airy living quarters; she was also heiress presumptive to the throne of the United Kingdom and the regal, if slightly dilapidated, splendours of the new apartments were more suitable to her position and her health than the more modest rooms below.

Subsequently King William IV declared that all the work on the apartments had been carried out by the Duchess unknown to him,[5] and it is true that in the vast ramifications of the Royal Establishment much might be done without the King's knowledge, especially as the approach and entrance to the Palace were not touched.

Princess Victoria was delighted with the apartments, '. . . our new sleeping and sitting apartments . . . are very lofty and handsome' she wrote. '. . . our bedroom is very large and lofty and is very nicely furnished . . . the old gallery is partitioned into 3 large, lofty, fine and cheerful rooms. One only of these . . . is ready furnished; it is my sitting room, and is *very* prettily furnished indeed.'

She went downstairs to pay a visit to their old apartments and visited her former bedroom, where Lehzen was now sleeping, and her former sitting-room. Though she felt some nostalgic regrets she commented '. . . our new rooms are much more airy and roomy'. The first week she was busy running up and down stairs, carrying her books, dolls, china and ornaments to their new home, getting rid of '2 ugly oil paintings of my father and mother' and hanging a print of Hayter's portrait of herself and the Duchess in their place.

On 25th January 1836 lessons began again. Mr Davys, who had been created Dean of Chester in 1831, now came every morning and the Princess studied more advanced subjects, including anatomy, and read Blackstone's *Commentaries on English Law* in the original four volumes, '*not* the extracts'. She read the English newspapers every day with Lehzen to keep up with current affairs, and wrote a letter in French every week, making a draft first, to Aunt Louise, the Queen of the Belgians. She read French and English classical authors aloud with Lehzen, each reading in turn, reading French in the original, '*never* in translation'. In English history Clarendon's *History of the Rebellion*, the Civil War of the time of Charles I, proved too dry and had to be given up.[6]

Three or four times a week the Princess was taken for a long walk in

* So called because it had been occupied by Prince George of Denmark, husband of Queen Anne.

the bracing air of Hampstead. Her health improved and continued to improve, thanks, wrote her Uncle Leopold, to his exertions. It was through his 'expostulations and entreaties at Ramsgate that his sister, the Duchess of Kent, had been persuaded to adopt the doctor's recommendations of fresh air and exercise' with such delightful results. It was he, King Leopold, who, while at Ramsgate, had realised the lonely, unhappy life the young Princess was leading, surrounded by the squabbles and intrigues of her mother's little court. A sense of protection and support was needed by her, and in a letter written on 7th January 1836 King Leopold promised that his wife Queen Louise, 'Aunt Louise', would write every week on Tuesday and that he himself would write on Friday, all his 'dear bought' political experience was to be placed at the Princess's disposal and in one of his first letters he gave her a detailed description of the Belgian system of government.[7]

The Princess led a tedious life. Almost daily she wrote in her Journal that the 'usual party', Princess Sophia, Lady Conroy, Sir John Conroy and other members of the Conroy family, had dined at Kensington Palace. Occasionally she was taken to pay calls, and on 13th February 1836 visited Lady Milton, daughter-in-law of the Lord Fitzwilliam who had been Viceroy of Ireland, to see her new baby; but Princess Victoria did not like small babies. The child, a little girl, 'is today five weeks old' wrote the Princess in her Journal 'and is for that age considered a very pretty child, but I for *my* part think all children till six months old very ugly'.[8] Her chief pleasure was to go to the theatre or opera and she usually visited one, or both, at least once a fortnight. Occasionally she dined formally with her uncle and aunt, King William IV and Queen Adelaide; very occasionally she attended a drawing-room at St James's Palace. When she was taken for long walks on Hampstead Heath, as Dr Clark had prescribed, the companions provided for her were 'the two Miss Conroys' and Lady Flora Hastings, thirteen years her senior. She was, of course, accompanied by Lehzen. The Duchess of Kent stubbornly refused to follow Stockmar's advice and allow the Princess to choose some young girl companions for herself.

It was a dull existence for a girl of nearly 17, especially a girl endowed with the energy and vitality of Princess Victoria, and her lively interest in young men. She was bored. 'I am very fond of *pleasant* society' she wrote to King Leopold 'and we have been for the last 3 months immured within our old Palace. I longed sadly for some gaiety.'[9] She enjoyed the prettiness of other girls; when she went to a party she had an endearing habit of making a list of the prettiest girls in the room. She enjoyed the good looks of young men, she especially loved gay conversation, music, jokes, dancing, laughter—what she described as 'mirth'.

By restricting this eager young creature to a life of dullness, the Duchess of Kent, and Conroy, did not seem to be aware that they were running a risk. Princess Victoria was, after all, a warm-blooded Hanoverian, she was also the greatest matrimonial prize in Europe, and she might have become entangled in a clandestine attachment, as Princess Charlotte had become entangled with Charles Hesse.* Princess Victoria was never left alone, but nor had Princess Charlotte been left alone. The difference was Lehzen; Princess Charlotte had no Lehzen to be a devoted watchdog, but Lehzen might become ill, or, as Conroy wished, be sent away.

How eagerly Princess Victoria reached out to life was evident when her Uncle Ferdinand, Duke of Saxe-Coburg, and his two sons Ferdinand and Augustus came to Kensington for a visit in March 1836. The choice of German Princes for the inspection of Princess Victoria was eccentric; Prince Alexander, eldest of the first two, the Württemberg Princes, had been a well-known profligate; Prince Ferdinand, eldest of the two Coburg Princes, tall and attractive, though he spoke through his nose, was already married.

In February 1836 he had married the little Queen of Portugal, Dona Maria da Gloria, by proxy and he was now on his way to Portugal to meet his bride, whom he had never seen, and consummate the marriage. He was nervous. The little Queen of Portugal was a month older than Princess Victoria; when, as children, they had met in London, Princess Victoria had liked Dona Maria, finding her 'warm hearted, honest and affectionate'.

Though the Portuguese marriage was a brilliant match for Prince Ferdinand, Dona Maria was the ruler of a Catholic nation. The marriage had been negotiated by King Leopold, and was one of the series of alliances known as 'the Coburg marriages'. King Leopold himself, though he remained a Lutheran Protestant to the end of his life and was buried according to the rites of the Lutheran Church, had, as has already been seen, married the devoutly Catholic daughter of Louis Philippe King of the French, a marriage which went far to soften the hostility of pro-French

---

* When Princess Charlotte was 18 years old she was driving in an open carriage in Windsor Park, with her governess Lady de Clifford, when, presumably by chance, they met a young man known to Lady de Clifford, Captain Charles Hesse of the 18th Light Dragoons. He was handsome, reputed to be the illegitimate son of the Duke of York, and Lady de Clifford indiscreetly introduced him to the Princess and allowed him to ride beside the open carriage. Captain Hesse contrived to meet the Princess daily on her drives and rode beside her for six weeks. Notes passed between them, and when his regiment moved to London they continued to meet with the connivance of Princess Charlotte's mother, Princess Caroline of Brunswick, the detested wife of the Prince Regent. Eventually the seriousness and long duration of the affair alarmed Lady de Clifford who confessed everything to the Prince Regent. Princess Charlotte then threw herself on her father's mercy, saying 'God knows what would have become of me, if he had not behaved with so much respect to me', to which the Prince Regent rejoined solemnly 'My dear child, it is Providence that has saved you'.

Belgian Catholics towards him. But in England the Coburg Catholic marriages were regarded with suspicion and the possibility that English royal children might be brought up as Catholics provoked animosity. The fires of Smithfield, in which Queen Mary Tudor had caused many respectable Protestant English tradesmen to be burned, still continued to burn in England.

Duke Ferdinand and King (formerly Prince) Leopold were brothers. There was a family custom that, though all the sons of the reigning Duke of Saxe-Coburg and Gotha (Gotha had been added to Saxe-Coburg in 1826 replacing Saalfeld) were entitled to designate themselves Duke, only the two eldest did so; other sons used the title Prince. Hence Leopold, the third son, was known as Prince Leopold until he became King of the Belgians in 1831. Duke Ferdinand, the second son and King Leopold's elder brother, spent most of his life in a cavalry regiment of the Austrian Army and married the fabulously beautiful and wealthy only child and heiress of the Hungarian Prince Kohary. There was a story that the only condition on which Prince Kohary would consent to his daughter's marriage to a penniless German princeling was that he should change his name to Coburg Kohary, which he did. But when Queen Victoria was consulted later she denied that any addition of Kohary to Coburg had ever been made. 'None of the family ever did it' she wrote 'but the Austrian nobility at one time did, but none of our family ever called him so, and I am sure there was no condition on the subject.'[10]

The festivities to celebrate Prince Ferdinand's union to his Portuguese Catholic bride were to be family rejoicings. On Thursday, 17th March 1836, the day the two Princes, Ferdinand and Augustus, and their father arrived in England, a large dinner party followed by dancing was to be given by King William IV and Queen Adelaide at Windsor Castle, and Duke Ferdinand with his two sons, the Duchess of Kent and Princess Victoria were invited to stay two nights at Windsor Castle. During the following week the Duchess of Kent sent out invitations for two balls at Kensington Palace, one a full dress 'Grand Ball' on Saturday, 19th March, and a fancy dress dance on Monday, 21st March.

On 17th March Duke Ferdinand and his sons did not arrive at Windsor for several hours after they had been expected, owing to bad weather in the English Channel. Agonies of seasickness were endured by foreign Princes determined to reach England. King Leopold's method was to stand on deck, bolt upright, with one hand grasping the rail and his eyes tightly closed to avoid even a sight of the sea. This method proved successful but was almost unbearably fatiguing.

That evening at Windsor, when the dancing was over, the Princess scribbled at length in her Journal 'Ferdinand is taller than Charles,* has

* Charles Prince of Leininge, her half-brother.

a very slight figure, rather fair hair, beautiful dark brown eyes, a fine nose and a very sweet mouth; he has a dear good and clever expression in his face. . . . Augustus is as tall . . . he has very fair hair, small blue eyes, a very pretty nose and likewise a very pretty mouth . . . they are both dear good young men. . . . Ferdinand speaks through his nose and in a slow funny way, which is at first against him, but it very soon wears off. He is very good looking, I think. It is impossible to see or know him without loving him.'[11]

Next day Princess Victoria went for a drive in Queen Adelaide's open carriage, and sat on the back seat with Ferdinand, liking him 'more and more'.

On Saturday the party went back to London. Princess Victoria hoped that the Princes would drive up with her, but they rode beside Queen Adelaide's open carriage because she wished to show them the beauties of Windsor Great Park. However, dinner before the 'grand' ball at Kensington was all enjoyment, though the Princess noted the presence of 'Sir J.C.' She sat between 'dear Ferdinand and dear Augustus, two delightful neighbours. It was a most merry and happy dinner, the merriest we have had for a long long time. When Ferdinand is not in company, he is most funny and childishly merry, which I delight in. . . . We laughed a great deal together.'[12] King William IV and Queen Adelaide attended the ball and the Princess received the guests with her mother.

It is a peculiarity of the Princess's Journal that she so seldom mentions what she, or anyone else, wore and only outside comments tell us how she looked. On this occasion King Leopold was told that both the Princess and the Duchess were 'remarkably elegantly dressed', and he considered his wife, Queen Louise, with her exquisite taste in clothes, was responsible 'at least in part' for the success of their appearance. He had heard of 'a pink gown of uncommon beauty which had been forwarded to a certain Princess', and even Queen Adelaide's appearance had been improved with Queen Louise's aid.[13]

The fancy dress ball on Monday, 21st March, was even more enjoyable, though the Princess does not mention what costume she wore. She danced seven quadrilles before supper, and her delight in her cousins was ecstatic. 'Oh! could they but be always with us! How happy should I be! . . . Oh! when I think how very soon I shall not see that dear dear Ferdinand any more I feel quite wretched! This is the last day we spent together! Oh! I love him so much, he is so excellent.'

The parting took place on 27th March. Princess Victoria and Prince Ferdinand embraced, wept, and, when later she went for a walk, tears were filling her eyes 'half the time'.

However, Prince Augustus, Prince Ferdinand's younger brother, and his father, the Duke Ferdinand, remained at Kensington for another fortnight, and on 31st March 1836 the Princess wrote in her Journal

'Augustus has a very fine hand, it is not at all small, but is very white, soft and very finely formed and very well kept'. Grieving for Prince Ferdinand was over and the Journal of the Princess is henceforward occupied with Prince Augustus. '. . . He is a dear boy and is so extremely good, kind and gentle.' He often came and sat with Princess Victoria in her sitting-room and did little tasks for her, such as helping her seal her letters: '. . . he burnt a cover in sealing it, dear boy, for me, which made us both laugh'.

On 2nd April 1836 Augustus and his father went back to Coburg. 'I miss them *dreadfully*' wrote the Princess in her Journal the same day 'particularly Augustus. . . . Grieved and sad as I was to part from our beloved Ferdinand, whom I love *very dearly*, I did not feel *so* sad by far, as I do now that Uncle Ferdinand and Augustus are gone.'

The Princess was 16, emotional, and it was natural that she should fall a little in love with every young man she met and enjoy giggling over trifles with Prince Augustus. But these were schoolgirl enthusiasms; she had, as yet, no conception of serious feeling, she never mentions marriage, never considers one of the young men she rhapsodises over as a possible consort.

She did regret, with all her heart, the end of the balls, the parties, the 'mirth'. 'Oh how sad I am' she wrote in her Journal 'to think that, that dear pretty ball, and all the parties at which I was so happy with my dear Cousins are over! . . . It seems like a dream that all our joy, happiness and gaiety should thus suddenly be over.'[14]

King Leopold sent her some cold comfort, if she felt Kensington Palace dreary 'after all the bustle and social life which filled it, this, unfortunately, is the picture of life; *all transitory except the thirst for happiness and bliss*, which seems to indicate that in *some future state alone it can be quenched*'.[15]

However, the tedium of Kensington, the continual society of 'the Misses Conroy', the daily walks with Lady Flora as well as Lehzen, the daily lessons with the Dean of Chester on 'dry' subjects was about to be enlivened by a new pleasure. On 19th April 1836, trembling with nervousness, as nervous, apparently, wrote her half-sister Princess Feodora, as her cousin Prince Ferdinand when he was about to be introduced to the bride he had married by proxy but never seen,[16] the Princess had her first singing lesson with Luigi Lablache.

Lablache was one of the foremost, if not the foremost, European singer of his day, and the greatest Leporello, in Mozart's opera *Don Giovanni*, in musical history. He was half Neapolitan and half Irish, famous for acting as well as singing, and he coaxed the Princess. She must not be frightened: ' "Personne a jamais eu peur de moi", which I am sure nobody ever can be who knows him' wrote the Princess.

The lesson was triumphantly successful and Lablache became one of Princess Victoria's heroes. 'He looks far younger off the stage, extremely gentlemanlike' she wrote in her Journal. 'I sung in fear and trembling "Or che in cielo". He praised my voice.' 'Or che in cielo' is the barcarolle from Donizetti's opera *Marino Faliero*, published the previous year, an ambitious choice. The following week the Princess and the Duchess of Kent sang duets together, including two from *Norma*, while Lablache accompanied, after which the Princess sang duets with Lablache to his accompaniment, which she enjoyed greatly, including 'a very pretty little duo from *L'Elisire d'Amore* by Donizetti. I liked my lesson extremely, I only wish I had one every *day* instead of one every *week*.'[17] Lablache made no attempt to train the Princess's voice by imposing the discipline of exercises on her; she sang arias from operas which Lablache transposed and adapted to be within her range, duets with her mother to Lablache's accompaniment and with his criticism, and duets with Lablache himself who helped her over 'the hard bits'. The Princess had a small but true voice with the same sweetness as her speaking voice. Lessons with Lablache became one of her greatest pleasures, she admired him whole-heartedly, his wonderful voice, his talent for acting, his patience, his good humour, his kindness; when she went to the opera to hear him she was 'in raptures' and the 'lessons' continued for more than twenty years, long after she had come to the throne.

She was astonished to find Lablache admired Handel. She had been to a concert of sacred music in aid of the Charing Cross Hospital on 15th April 1836, and found it 'terribly tiresome and long, for there were very few singers and such a deal of old tiresome Handel's music'.

In May 1836, when the Princess was within a week of her seventeenth birthday, the question of her future marriage was not only unsettled, it had hardly been discussed. King William IV was 71, was subject to asthma and severe attacks of gout, and had developed chalk stones in his fingers which made it difficult for him to hold a pen; he was evidently and rapidly ageing.

The idea of a marriage between Princess Victoria and Prince Albert of Saxe-Coburg now, writes Charles Prince of Leiningen, 'cropped up again'.[18] The Duchess was devoted to her nephew, as he was to her; the marriage had been planned by the Coburgs from the moment of his birth and the time had now arrived for the Duchess, backed by her elder brother Ernest, the Duke of Saxe-Coburg and Gotha, by King Leopold and by Stockmar, to come into the open. 'From this time onwards the connection was regarded as the one aim to which all energies should be directed' wrote Prince Charles.

A memorandum by Prince Charles deals with 'the visit of the Duke of Saxe Coburg Gotha and the Princes Ernest and Albert of Saxe Coburg

Gotha in 1836 and its secret history'. At the end of the memorandum Prince Albert has written in his own hand: 'The preceding memorandum was written for me by Prince Leiningen in 1841. I was aware at the time of our visit in 1836 of the difficulties attending it.'

The difficulties were created by the intense antipathy of William IV towards the House of Coburg in general and the Duchess of Kent in particular. He had also a contempt for King Leopold, whose personality he disliked, and who drank water, not wine, at dinner. William IV was determined[19] to marry Princess Victoria to one of the sons of the Prince of Orange, the eldest son of the King of the Netherlands, hereditary ally of England, whose name was synonymous with Protestantism, in contrast with the numerous Catholic connections of the Coburgs.

The relationship between the Prince of Orange and King Leopold was delicate. Princess Charlotte had been betrothed to the Prince of Orange in 1813 and had jilted him to marry Prince Leopold, as he then was. It was also against Holland that the Belgians had recently and successfully revolted and elected Prince Leopold to be their King. The Prince of Orange, who had lived in Belgium and tried to reconcile the Belgians to the Dutch government, therefore detested King Leopold. 'Voilà un homme qui a pris ma femme et mon royaume' he used to say.

King Leopold, on his side, equally detested the Prince of Orange, whom he accused of breaking a truce and other dishonourable behaviour, during the final stages of the fighting in Belgium in 1831, calling him 'our most bitter enemy'.[20] The situation was complicated by the fact that the Belgian high nobility, although good Catholics, nevertheless were staunchly loyal to the house of Orange and boycotted Leopold, whom they regarded as a parvenu revolutionary.

In April 1836 it became known at Kensington that William IV had invited the Prince of Orange and his two sons to visit him 'with the serious intention' of marrying Princess Victoria to one of the sons. 'Great consternation' was felt at Kensington. A visit from Ernest Duke of Saxe-Coburg and Gotha, and his two sons, Princes Ernest and Albert, was already being arranged and the Duchess of Kent wrote an urgent letter telling them to leave at once. On hearing this King William IV flew into a rage and ordered Lord Palmerston, then Foreign Secretary, to inform the Duchess of Kent that she must prevent her brother and his sons coming to England. 'The King particularly insisted that he could not allow the two young Princes to live under the same roof with the Princess Victoria.' This was a cut at the questionable reputation of the Duke of Coburg, which his elder son Ernest showed signs of repeating. The Duchess refused to give way. She could not see, she wrote to Lord Palmerston on 12th May 1836, why any significance should attach to the visit of her brother and her nephews, except the pleasure of seeing them.

She had been instructed to write to Queen Adelaide informing her of the visit and she had duly written; she did not know where she had gone wrong.[21] 'I really cannot . . . look at this visit as of any consequence or as entailing any difficulties, when I consider that it is not until three or four years hence that the Princess will be called upon to change her situation in life. Nor can I see any difference between my brother being accompanied by his sons, to the Prince of Orange having brought his.' With considerable dignity the Duchess of Kent wrote that she had 'felt assured, he [King William IV] would receive these members of my Family with the same civility as he does other distinguished strangers and relations of members of the Royal Family'. In any case the Duke of Coburg and his two sons had already started. The King had to give way, and on 13th May Lord Palmerston wrote to the Duchess that if the Duke of Saxe-Coburg and Gotha could not be put off 'the King says he will receive his Serene Highness with all the attentions due to his high station and to his connections with the Royal Family'.

On the same day Lord Palmerston informed Sir John Conroy that 'the orders to Lord Hill [the Commander-in-Chief] and to the other departments for receiving the Duke of Saxe Coburg with the proper honours wherever H.S.H. may land, were sent from my office today'.

In a private letter Lord Palmerston urged Conroy if possible to arrange that the Duke of Coburg and his sons 'should during their stay here be lodged at an hotel in London, instead of at Kensington Palace; such an arrangement would remove the main objection felt by the King to the visit, that the Princes and Princess Victoria were going to live under the same roof'.[22] This suggestion the Duchess of Kent ignored.

In Belgium King Leopold was furiously angry.[23] 'I am really *astonished* at the conduct of your old Uncle the King' he wrote to Princess Victoria on 13th May 1836. 'This invitation of the Prince of Orange and his sons, this forcing him upon others, is very extraordinary. . . . No later than yesterday I got a half official communication from England, insinuating that it would be *highly desirable* that the visit of your relations *should not take place this year*, qu'en dites vous? The relations of the King and Queen therefore are to come in shoals and rule the land, when *your relations* are to be forbidden. . . . Really and truly I never heard anything like it, and I hope it will a *little rouse your spirit* now that slavery is even abolished in the British Colonies, I do not comprehend *why your lot alone should be to be kept a white little slavey in England* for the pleasure of a Court, who never bought you, as I am not aware of their having gone to any expense on that head, or the King's even having *spent a sixpence for your existence*. . . . I expect my visits to England will also be prohibited. . . . I have not the least doubt that the King, in his passion for the Oranges, will be *excessively rude to your relations*, this however will

118

not signify much, they are *your* guests and not *his*, and will therefore not mind it. . . . God bless you, give me some news by return of messenger.'

The Prince of Orange and his sons had already arrived and on Friday, 13th May 1836, King William IV and Queen Adelaide gave a ball in their honour at St James's Palace. Princess Victoria was present attended by the Duchess of Northumberland, Lady Flora Hastings and Lehzen, but though she loved dancing, she records no enjoyment in her Journal.[24] The principal partners offered her were the Princes William and Alexander of the Netherlands and her first cousin Prince George of Cambridge, whom she did not like at this time. In all she only danced five times.

On 17th May she wrote to King Leopold[25] 'I shall . . . give you an account of the Oranges, whom we have the dissatisfaction of having here. The Prince . . . I think looks put out [and] embarrassed, particularly so with us. The boys are both very plain and have a mixture of Kalmuck and Dutch in their faces, moreover they look heavy, dull and frightened and are not at all prepossessing. So much for the *Oranges*, dear Uncle.'

Meanwhile the two Coburg Princes and their father were making their way down the Rhine towards England and Kensington Palace, 'afraid of nothing but sea sickness'. They left the Rhine steamer and crossed from Rotterdam, meeting Princess Victoria for the first time on 18th May 1836.[26] She found them both 'very amiable, very kind and good, and extremely merry, just as young people ought to be; with all that they are extremely sensible and fond of occupation. Albert is extremely good looking, which Ernest certainly is not, but he has a most good natured, honest and intelligent countenance. . . .' Princess Feodora, Queen Victoria's half-sister, preferred Ernest to Albert.[27] 'I am very fond of them both, Ernest is my favourite, although Albert is much handsomer and cleverer too, but Ernest is so honest and good natured.' Princess Feodora thought her sister would find both 'more manly' than Ferdinand and Augustus Saxe-Coburg. Both Princes were exceptionally fond of music, 'like me' wrote Princess Victoria. 'We took them . . . to hear *Puritani* and . . . they were in perfect ecstasies.' The Princess's attention, however, was largely absorbed by 'a most delightful Lory', a bird resembling a large parrot, which her uncle Duke Ernest had brought her. It was so tame that 'you may put your finger into its beak or do anything with it, without its ever attempting to bite. It has . . . a most beautiful plumage; it is scarlet, blue, brown, yellow and purple.'

'Great doings' in the way of social gaieties were planned for the visit of the two Princes, more strenuous than Albert could support. Since childhood he had been afflicted with an irresistible sleepiness, which set in about half past nine in the evening. If his bedtime was delayed he would fall asleep over his supper, and, as a boy, had been known to slide off his chair and go to sleep tranquilly on the floor. Late nights, social chatter, rich food, were not merely disliked by Prince Albert but made him physically ill and, struggle though he might, he never enjoyed great dinners, balls or any of the amusements of the fashionable world.[28]

During this visit his sufferings were severe. On Friday 20th May, after a 'long and fatiguing levée', there was a large formal dinner at St James's Palace and a 'beautiful concert' at which the Princes had to stand until 2 a.m.[29] Next day the King's birthday was celebrated by an exceptionally large drawing-room at St James's Palace at which about 3,800 people passed before King William IV and Queen Adelaide, followed in the evening by a 'great dinner' and a concert which lasted until 1 a.m. On Monday, 23rd May, the Duchess of Kent gave a large dinner at Kensington Palace. Princess Victoria noticed that Prince Albert was 'not quite well' and he went to bed soon after dinner. Next day, 24th May, was her birthday, she was entering the all-important year, her eighteenth year; on her next birthday, as a royal person she would come of age. The King and Queen gave a state ball in her honour at St James's Palace, but Albert had reached the limit of his endurance. 'Poor dear Albert, who had not been well the day before, looked very pale and felt very poorly' wrote the Princess[30] '. . . after being but a short while in the ball room and having only danced twice, turned as pale as ashes; and we all feared he might faint; he therefore went home.'

Two days later[31] 'I am sorry to say' she told her uncle King Leopold 'we have an invalid in the house in the person of Albert, who, though much better today, has had a smart bilious attack. He was not allowed to leave his room all day yesterday, but by dint of starvation, he is again restored to society, but looks pale and delicate.'

The weekend was quiet, with a 'very pleasant evening on Sunday' spent by the Princess seated on the sofa between her two cousins while they looked over autographs, but on Monday, 30th May, the Duchess gave a 'grand' ball at Kensington Palace. King William IV and Queen Adelaide did not come, but the Prince of Orange with his two sons was present. A newspaper cutting which the Princess added to her Journal (unfortunately with the name of the paper cut off) reported[32] '. . . the suite of reception rooms, the grand saloon and the vestibule were opened for dancing. The sides of the saloon were hung with light and tasteful drapery (tent fashion), the centre of each compartment being formed by a very large pier glass. Both Ball rooms had orchestras fitted up in the angles for Wupperts quadrille bands and both were brilliantly illuminated by cut glass chandeliers. The drawingrooms, which were open en suite, had at one end, in front of a pier glass, a marble bust of his late Royal Highness, the Duke of Kent, and at the other a marble bust of His Majesty, King Leopold . . . the band of the Grenadier Guards was stationed near the grand staircase and performed favourite selections in the course of the evening and also received the Royal Family on their arrival with "God Save the King". Shortly before ten o'clock the company began to arrive at the Palace by the Duke of Sussex's entrance and were ushered through the corridor and up the grand staircase to the drawingroom. The Duke of Wellington was present and it was noticeable that he treated Princess Victoria with particular deference.'

The Princess danced five times before supper, with the Duke of Brunswick, Prince William of the Netherlands, Prince Ernest of Saxe-Coburg and Prince Alexander of the Netherlands. After supper she danced with Prince Albert, and the Duchess of Kent 'valsed' with the Prince and his father. A country dance followed, which Princess Victoria danced with Prince Albert. Unfortunately Prince Albert was still unwell, and, wrote Princess Victoria, 'after I had gone once down [the set], I and my dear partner stopped, but the others kept it up for some time . . . we all stayed up until $\frac{1}{2}$ past 3 and it was broad daylight when we left the room.' She found herself 'all the better for it next day'. Gaiety and late hours agreed with Princess Victoria. 'You are very kind dear Uncle' she wrote to King Leopold next day 'to think of my health and of my not fatiguing myself; I can assure you all this dissipation does me a great deal of good.'[33]

As a result of the evidently differing tastes of the Princess and Prince Albert it was thought wise that Prince Albert should be given a little more experience of the world and social usages. He and his brother were therefore to spend a year in Brussels, to be 'broken in and styled'[34] and to go into society in Florence and Rome during a projected tour of Italy. King Leopold insisted that Prince Albert should have dancing lessons, reporting his progress to the Princess, and that he should cultivate his voice to sing agreeably in the drawing-room. The early nights and philosophical studies which the Prince was eagerly anticipating at the University of Bonn were not to become his sole preoccupation.

The remaining days of the Coburg Princes' visit were less exacting. Princess Victoria played the piano with Prince Albert and 'stayed up until 10 minutes past 10'.[35] They sang duets together and twice Prince Albert shared Princess Victoria's lesson with Lablache. Several times her uncle, Albert's father, called on her in her private sitting-room and had confidential conversations with her. On 8th June 1836 a party of royal persons including Princess Victoria, the Duke of Saxe-Coburg and Gotha and his two sons, went to the Opera to hear Luigi Lablache in *Marino Faliero*. 'Alas!' wrote the Princess in her Journal 'it was the last time we were at the Opera with my dear Uncle and my *dearest, most beloved* cousins, I liked the Opera twice as much with them than alone. Both dear Ernest and dear Albert . . . are so fond of music and so attentive to it and our box looked so full and was so merry.' On 10th July the Princes and their father said farewell. 'At 9 we all breakfasted for the *last* time together! It was our last *happy happy* breakfast with this dear Uncle and these *dearest* beloved Cousins, whom I *do* love so *very, very* dearly, *much more dearly* than any other Cousins in the *world*. Dearly as I love Ferdinand and also good Augustus, I love Ernest and Albert *more* than them, oh yes, MUCH more. Augustus was like a good affectionate child, quite unacquainted with the world, phlegmatic, and talking but very little; but dearest Ernest and dearest Albert are so grown up in their manners . . . and are very clever, naturally clever, particularly Albert. . . . Though I wrote more when Uncle Ferdinand and Augustus went, in my Journal . . . I feel this separation more deeply, though I do not lament as much as I did then, which came from my nerves not being strong then. I can bear more now.'

Before Prince Albert left, Princess Victoria wrote a letter to King Leopold telling him that, in the Prince, she accepted the husband whom her uncle had selected for her. She was not, however, at this time in love with the Prince, nor the Prince with her. Reviewing this period later the Prince wrote 'We stayed from 3–4 weeks at Kensington, Princess Victoria and myself, both at the age of 17, were much pleased with each other, but not a word in allusion to the future passed either between us, or with the Duchess of Kent. It was my first visit to England and was not repeated until October 1839.'[36]

On 7th June 1836 Princess Victoria wrote to King Leopold 'I must thank you my beloved Uncle, for the prospect of great happiness you have contributed [*sic*] to give me, in the person of Dear Albert. Allow me then, my dearest Uncle, to tell you how delighted I am with him, and how much I like him in every way. He possesses every quality that could be desired to make me perfectly happy. He is so sensible, so kind and so good and so amiable too. He has besides the most pleasing and delightful exterior and appearance that you could wish to see.'[37]

In fact, at the age of 17 Prince Albert had not yet attained the remarkable good looks he possessed a few years later. At 17 he was described as 'very stout' and not so tall as Ernest;[38] it was not until three years later that he became the slim, strikingly handsome figure with whom the young Queen fell in love.

The understanding with Albert was to be a protection for the Princess. King Leopold was apprehensive that an unsuitable candidate for her hand might be forced on her. Though Conroy at the moment seemed all in favour of Prince Albert, King Leopold was well aware of his unreliability and the extraordinary power he possessed to sway the Duchess of Kent.

On 1st May 1836, before Prince Albert and his brother arrived, King Leopold had written a confidential letter to Lehzen, instructing her to convey its contents to Princess Victoria.[39] 'I talk to you at length and through you speak to Victoria. . . . For years Victoria has unfortunately been treated as a mere subject for speculation . . . her youth, as well as her future gave ample opportunities for a thousand avaricious schemes. . . . Only two people cared about her for her own sake, that is, you, my dear Lehzen and I . . . and because this was so we were systematically persecuted, for it was particularly feared that the child might grow fond of us, and find in us friends apart. . . . The chief plan has been, since 1828, to drive you away. Had I not stood firm . . . you would have followed Spaeth. . . . Had I not come to England last year, and had I not had the courage, in Ramsgate, to tear apart the whole web of intrigue, Clark would never have learned the true state of affairs, and God knows what would have become of the Princess; that visit was one of the most important factors in her recovery. . . . The Princess's 17th birthday marks an important stage in her life: only one more year and the possibility of a Regency vanishes like an evil cloud. This is the perfect time for us, who are loyal, to take thought for the future of the dear child. An immediate alliance is out of the question; she must reach her 18th birthday, perhaps even more—her health must decide that; but the Princess might perhaps do well, for the sake of composure and peace of mind to find a choice and firmly anchor herself to it.'

Prince Albert was selected by King Leopold and Stockmar for Princess Victoria. It might be objected, wrote King Leopold, that he was too young, but 'his youth was the guarantee for his pure unspoilt nature'. Stockmar considered that his excellent intelligence would 'enable him to give the Princess the political support she will one day so badly need', moreover 'in the whole Almanach de Gotha there is not a single Prince of riper years to whom we could entrust the dear child, without incurring the gravest risk'.

The result of Lehzen's conversation with Princess Victoria was the letter written by the Princess on 7th June 1836. She did not regard the arrangement with Prince Albert as binding her to marriage within a short time, all was in the hazy indeterminate future, indeed she declared later that she did not regard herself as bound to Albert at all; meanwhile she regretted the parties, the gaiety and the dancing, above all the dancing, more than the loss of Albert's society. Once more 'merriment' was over and she was left to sigh in empty rooms, read Blackstone's *Commentaries on English Law* with the Dean of Chester, take walks with Lehzen and Lady Flora and go to bed at half past nine.

She went to the Zoological Gardens to see the giraffes: 'The Giraffes have beautiful large black eyes and are very good-tempered.' She went to the Opera with Lady Flora and 'Miss V. Conroy', a sad change from sitting in a box filled with laughing chattering Princes, 'in all 8!', all day long, she wrote, she 'lounged about in a state of "dolce far niente". Oh!

fà più caldo di jeri! Oh! non è supportabile.' Lessons with Lablache were her outlet, she longed to go to Italy and dreamed of Naples, Lablache being a Neapolitan. 'Oh! could I but once behold *bella Napoli*, with its sunny blue sky and turquoise bay dotted with islands' she wrote in her Journal.[40]

In this frame of mind her eye was caught by Charles Duke of Brunswick* and she devoted much speculation to him.[41] He was always at the Opera, in the same box, and was evidently interested in her. She rather admired the way he and his gentlemen wore their hair; '. . . it is divided all down the head [parted in the middle] and hangs I should say about 2 inches below the ear all round. It may not suit ugly people, that's true, but it certainly becomes these handsome ones.' On another evening she noted the Duke was in his box and had 'taken off his fur'. She met him with his gentleman in Kensington Gardens: 'he is, *I* think, very good looking, for we passed him close, though I was told by a lady who had seen him at Almacks, that he was not so, but I don't think she saw him very close, and perhaps he looks handsomer by daylight and with his hat on. He was very elegantly dressed.' Next day they went to the Opera to hear *Otello*, probably the version by Rossini, and the Duke was in his box. The following day 'as we were driving in the Park we saw the Duke of Brunswick and his friend driving down Oxford Road. The Duke was driving four in hand from the box of a barouche . . . his friend sat next him, and both, but particularly the Duke, looked very wild and odd.' The Duke of Brunswick was in fact the Princess's cousin and a thoroughly unsuitable connection; though his father—brother of the detested and troublesome wife of King George IV—had deserved well of England, having been killed at Waterloo, he himself inherited the family eccentricity.

On 8th August 1836 the Princess had her last lesson of the season with Lablache. 'I shall count weeks and months eagerly till next April, when he said he would be back in London, and when I shall resume my delightful lessons with him' she wrote.[42]

On 10th August, with the Duchess and the household she left 'our poor old Palace' and after staying a few days with Lord Liverpool at Buxted Park went on to Claremont, King Leopold's house in Surrey where the Duchess intended to spend the rest of the summer and the autumn.

At first the Princess enjoyed the change. 'All looks so comfortable and cheerful at dear Claremont' she wrote, but the tensions and intrigues of Kensington were being repeated as the months passed by; it was now only nine months before she would come of age. The situation with Conroy and the Duchess at Kensington made a struggle inevitable. She

---

* Charles Duke of Brunswick had been expelled from his country in 1830 as unfit to rule, and the regency entrusted to his brother William.

heard with relief that King Leopold intended to send Stockmar over to England to be her adviser. 'I have to thank you again in giving me the prospect of having as Counsellor and Friend my old friend Stockmar' she wrote.[43] 'I cannot say how happy this thought makes me & how earnestly I beg you to tell Stockmar my pleasure at this quieting news.'

King Leopold promised that he himself would come over in September.

In the meantime relations between the Duchess of Kent and King William IV had deteriorated further. In April 1836 the King refused to receive the Duchess's daughter-in-law, the wife of Charles Prince of Leiningen, in the 'Closet', the room reserved for the reception by the reigning sovereign of persons of royal blood. The lady in question had been a Countess Kebelsberg, the marriage had been opposed by the Duchess and the Countess could boast no trace of royal blood. But the Duchess was furious.[44] It was manifestly impossible for her to take her son, Prince Charles, with her into the Closet and leave his wife outside, and a stiff note was written informing the Lord Chamberlain that the Prince and Princess of Leiningen would be unable to have the honour of paying their duty at St James's Palace.

Worse followed. Two weeks later, while a drawing-room was actually in progress, the King suddenly ordered the Duchess of Kent's gentlemen to leave the Throne Room.[45] Accordingly Sir John Conroy, together with such respected persons as Sir George Anson, General Hill and Colonel Harcourt, had no choice but to withdraw. Once again the Duchess was furious but the King informed her that only gentlemen of the King's and Queen's households had a right to be in the Throne Room, other members of the Royal Family were entitled to be attended by their ladies only. 'The distinction . . . has long been established, though the rule has been departed from in the instance to which His Majesty was pleased to direct his attention.' This episode was followed by the King's attempt to prevent the Duchess's brother and nephews from visiting Kensington Palace and the Duchess was therefore in no very reasonable frame of mind when the King invited her to bring Princess Victoria to Windsor for Queen Adelaide's birthday celebrations on 13th August, and stay on over 21st August, for the private and public celebrations of his own birthday.[46] The Duchess of Kent had not forgiven Queen Adelaide for remonstrating with her on the subject of her relationship with Conroy, and, ignoring the invitation to Queen Adelaide's birthday, she wrote that her intention was to celebrate her own birthday at Claremont on 17th August, but she would come to Windsor on 20th August and bring the Princess with her. 'This' it was observed 'put the King into a fury, but he made, however, no reply.' What followed on 20th August when the Duchess had arrived at Windsor with the Princess was related to Greville, the diarist, by Lord Adolphus FitzClarence, one of the King's illegitimate sons, who was present.[47] At dinner time that evening the King did not appear; he had gone to London to prorogue Parliament and, presumably, been detained. He had, in fact, on a sudden impulse gone to 'look about' Kensington Palace. 'When He got there' according to Lord Adolphus 'He found that the Duchess of Kent had appropriated to her own use a suite of apartments, seventeen in number . . . for which She had applied last year and which he had refused to let her have. This increased his ill humour, already excessive.'

At about ten o'clock he came into the drawing-room at Windsor 'where the whole party was assembled . . . went up to the Princess Victoria, took hold of both her hands, and expressed his pleasure at seeing her there and his regret that he did not see her oftener. He then turned to the Duchess, made her a low bow' and said he had just come from Kensington, where ' "a most unwarrantable liberty had been taken with one of his Palaces. . . . He found apartments had been taken possession of not only without his consent, but contrary to his commands, and that he neither understood nor would endure conduct so disrespectful to him." This was said loudly, publicly, and in a tone of serious displeasure.'

It is almost incredible that the King, concerned as he always was for the welfare of the Princess, should not have known that, in consequence of her illness at Ramsgate, she had been moved to more airy rooms in the Palace, even if the details of the alterations had been concealed from him. His irritation with the Duchess of Kent was now so intense as to be uncontrollable and the scene in the drawing-room that evening was 'only the muttering of the storm which was to break the next day'.

Although the celebration of the King's birthday on 21st August 1836 was described as 'private', a hundred people were invited to dinner at Windsor. The Duchess of Kent sat on one side of the King, one of his sisters on the other, and Princess Victoria sat opposite. Lord Adolphus FitzClarence 'sat two or three from the Duchess, and heard every word of what passed. . . . ' After dinner the toast 'His Majesty's health and long life to him' was drunk upon which the King 'poured forth the following extraordinary and *foudroyant* tirade: "I trust in God that my life may be spared for nine months longer, after which period, in the event of my death, no Regency would take place. I should then have the satisfaction of leaving the royal authority to the personal exercise of that Young Lady (pointing to the Pss), the Heiress presumptive of the Crown, and not in the hands of a person now near me, who is surrounded by evil advisers and who is herself incompetent to act with propriety in the station in which She would be placed. I have no hesitation in saying that I have been insulted—grossly and continually insulted—by that person, but I am determined to endure no longer a course of behaviour so disrespectful to me. Amongst many other things I have particularly to complain of the manner in which that Young Lady has been kept away from my Court; she has been repeatedly kept from my drawing-rooms, at which She ought always to have been present, but I am fully resolved that this shall not happen again. I would have her know that I am King, and that I am determined to make my authority respected, and for the future I shall insist and command that the Princess do upon all occasions appear at my Court, as it is her duty to do." This awful philippick . . . uttered in a loud voice and excited manner', was followed by consternation. Queen Adelaide 'looked in deep distress, the Princess burst into tears, and the whole company were aghast. The Duchess of Kent said not a word', but, when the ladies retired, a 'terrible scene' took place. The Duchess announced her immediate departure, ordered her carriage and was only with difficulty prevailed on to stay overnight. Next day the King asked Lord Adolphus FitzClarence what had been thought of his speech? Lord Adolphus answered that it was thought that the Duchess of Kent deserved the rebuke, but it ought to have been given her in private and not at a dinner before a hundred people, to which the King replied 'that He did not care where he said it, or before whom, that "By God he had been insulted by her in a measure that was past all endurance, and he would not stand it any longer" '.

Greville commented 'Nothing can be more unaccountable than the Dss. of Kent's behaviour to the King, nothing more reprehensible, but his has always been as injudicious and undignified as possible, and this last sortie was monstrous . . . such a gross and public insult offered to her at his own table, sitting by his side and in the presence of her daughter, admits of no excuse. It was an unparalleled outrage from a man to a woman, from a Host to his guest, and to the last degree unbecoming the station they both of them fill.'

Next day the Duchess hastened back to Claremont.

A calm period followed, no 'journey' was undertaken, no visits were paid to country mansions. On 13th September 1836 King Leopold arrived at Claremont as he had promised and Princess Victoria was in ecstasies.[48] 'I love him so *very very much*; oh! my love for him approaches to a sort of adoration. . . . He is indeed "*il mio secondo padre*", or rather "*solo* padre"! for he is indeed like my real father, as I have none!' He came and sat with her alone for an hour and 'talked over many important things. He is *so* clever, *so* mild, and *so* prudent; he alone can give me good advice on *every* thing.' Queen Louise did not come, she was expecting another baby. 'She is an *Angel*' wrote Princess Victoria in her Journal 'and I do so love her! How *very much* do I regret that she cannot come over and be with us here. . . . I can see dearest Aunt Louise sitting opposite to me . . . with that angelic look and expression so peculiar to her; I can see her at dinner, walking, everywhere.' King Leopold brought a present of dresses from Queen Louise '. . . a most lovely light blue silk dress and a light blue satin bonnet. . . . They are quite *lovely*. They are *so well* made and in *so very* elegant a manner.' Queen Louise had already sent a number of dresses to the Princess, a thick pink silk dress, a silk dress *couleur de poussière* for the morning and a very light figured pink silk for the evening; 'All these dresses' wrote the Princess in her Journal 'are made by Mdlle Palmyre, the *first* dress-maker in Paris.'

King Leopold did his best to impress on the Princess that 'your dear Mama's affection was at all times the same and equally warm', but Conroy dictated the behaviour of the Duchess and the treatment of the Princess by her mother did not bear out his assurances. As King Leopold himself commented later, Conroy's influence over the Duchess was 'so strong that it would once have been called witchcraft'.[49] Between Conroy and King Leopold disputes and scenes occurred. 'I told him at Claremont in 1836' King Leopold wrote subsequently[50] 'that his conduct was madness and must end in his own ruin, and that, although late, there was still time!—but no, he continued in the same way, as the events of 1837 did show.'

When King Leopold went away Princess Victoria was deeply grieved. Her life at her mother's court did not become more satisfactory.[51] 'It is dreadful how quickly this long looked for stay of dearest Uncle has come and is passed. Oh! it is dreadful . . . that one is almost always separated from those one loves dearly and is encumbered with those one dislikes . . .' she wrote; looking forward to a winter with the Conroys. King Leopold crossed the dreaded English Channel in rough weather on 21st September, and was forced below by fatigue where he became 'unwell'. He had been annoyed while in England to find he was not universally welcome.[52] Opposition to his visit had come from the Duke of Cumberland, head since 1807 of the Orange Lodges, an association of violent and bigoted Protestants. 'They want to make me out a *Popish King*' he wrote angrily to Princess Victoria on 14th October 1836.[53] He did not understand the strength of Protestant opinion in England, or the suspicion with which the Coburgs were regarded owing to their Catholic alliances. What had the Coburgs ever done, he asked, to deserve such treatment?

In October the Duchess and her household went for an autumn holiday to Ramsgate, where the Princess had to say goodbye to one of her few friends, Lady Catherine Jenkinson, daughter of Lord Liverpool, who had become Lady of the Bedchamber to the Duchess of Kent in 1830. 'She will be a great loss for our society' wrote the Princess in her Journal 'for, independently of her extraordinary talent for music . . . which was a great delight to me—she is a great friend of my *dearest invaluable* Lehzen, who quite possessed her confidence. . . .'[54] It was unlikely that anyone who was a close friend of Lehzen should remain in the household of the

Duchess. However, the reason given for her retirement was 'her poor health, which is *very delicate*' as the Princess admitted. Lady Catherine later married Colonel Harcourt, but never had any children.

By 5th December the Princess was back at Claremont with the prospect of Christmas with the Conroys before her. At this period the Princess overflowed with suppressed emotions. She was heartbroken to learn that her drawing master, old Mr Richard Westall, had died at the age of 71 in extreme poverty.[55] 'It *grieves* and *pains* me beyond *measure* that I could not ... render his dying moments comfortable and quiet and undisturbed. ...' She interested herself in some poor gipsies, persuading the Duchess to send them soup, blankets, old clothes and 'I trust some money'. A baby boy was born to one of the young women; the Princess noted they were all called Lee or Cooper, well-known gipsy names. 'Had I been my own mistress I would willingly have told them to call the boy Leopold [he was born on 16th December, King Leopold's birthday] but of course I could not' and the baby was named Francis. She was fired by the wrongs of Ireland: 'How ill treated that poor country and nation has been.'[56]

Christmas passed, 1837 began, February succeeded January and the Princess yearned for a little gaiety. 'I do not quite know when we shall leave this place' she wrote to King Leopold from Claremont on 6th February 1837. 'You must be pleased, dear Uncle I think, for we shall have been *six months* in the country next Thursday, as we left town on the 10th of August last, and I am sure you will stand by me having my season fully.[57] [She wished to go to London as soon as the season began, which at that period was in March, and not be kept at Claremont until much of it was over.] You may understand that my *Operatic* and *Terpsichorean* feelings are pretty strong now that the season is returning, and I have been a very good child, not even *wishing* to come to town until now. ...'

However, when about a fortnight later Princess Victoria was back at Kensington Palace, life was not gay. '... We have seen nobody and therefore I can tell you no news' she wrote to King Leopold from Kensington on 22nd February 1837.[58] The Princess had had a cold but cured it by staying in her room and eating nothing but barley soup. By 7th March she was 'as well as well can be, and fit for a great deal of dissipation, which unfortunately I have not had'.[59] The following week the Duchess had a dinner '... which amused me as I am very fond of *pleasant* society [i.e. not the society of the Conroys] and we have been for these last three weeks immured within our old Palace and I longed sadly for some merriment after being so very long in the country. ... After Easter I trust I shall make ample amends for all this solitariness.' Lord Palmerston had been at the dinner 'with whom I had much pleasant and amusing conversation after dinner—you know how agreeable he is'[60] she wrote to King Leopold.

The Princess had been sent back to her lessons and on 27th February the Dean came as usual at 10 a.m. and she had a history lesson followed by French dictation. Visits to the opera and ballet remained the only amusement provided for her. She was being kept close, Conroy and the Duchess did not intend to let her escape from their grasp during this critical period.

In preparation for the coming struggle, towards the end of February 1837 the Duchess sent to Germany for her son Charles Prince of Leiningen, advising him to consult with Stockmar on the family situation before he started. As a child Princess Victoria had been fond of her half-brother, but Lehzen assured King Leopold in one of her confidential reports[61] that the Princess was now 'fully aware of the wickedness of the Prince of Leiningen and his friend S. J. [Sir John]' and also aware that 'they count cowardice among all their good qualities'. Stockmar went to Gotha to see Prince Charles, and, speaking 'frankly, but not incautiously', since he knew everything he said would be passed on to the Duchess and Conroy, he told Prince Charles that though he often found himself in agreement with Conroy, admired his grasp of affairs and thought he deserved to be rewarded for his zeal, Conroy's lack of tact and his temper were such that 'were we to do everything possible to bring Conroy to the most brilliant and influential position, *he would, through his own folly break his neck in no time at all*'.[62] Prince Charles should keep his eyes open, and use his own judgment, however favourably inclined towards Conroy, and 'not regard treachery, lies and fraud as the weapons of success'.

In spite of this warning, however, when Prince Charles, with his wife and children, arrived at Kensington Palace in April 1837 he became Conroy's ally.

During the opening months of 1837 King William IV's health gave no grounds for unusual anxiety. He was feeble, suffered from asthma and was 72, but no crisis was anticipated, and it seemed probable that he would survive for a considerable period. On 3rd March 1837 Lord Palmerston thought him 'looking remarkably well . . . and in very good humour'.[63] He remained well during April and as the birthday of the Princess became imminent Conroy became frantic. Stockmar told King Leopold[64] that Charles Prince of Leiningen and Conroy shared 'the same madness, the same perversity, the same clinging to straws which they make out to be of immense importance'. Conroy stressed the fact that even though the Princess should reach the age of 18, when the Regency would terminate, she would legally still be a minor and subect to control until she was 21.[65] 'God knows' wrote Stockmar to King Leopold 'what schemes are being built on this fact of which everyone who knows the circumstances is aware.' The Princess meanwhile kept her own counsel and Stockmar wrote that neither Conroy nor Prince Charles knew how they stood and 'in constant anxiety and apprehension . . . change their plans as often as they change their clothes'.

King Leopold and Stockmar were agreed that some separation of the Princess and her mother ought to take place when she was officially of age to reign 'at least as far as the ordering of the household was concerned' but 'must be achieved with great discretion. . . . However bad the past was,' wrote Stockmar, 'however much bitterness it has aroused she [Princess Victoria] must be lenient. Everything that political enemies could seize on, such as an unnatural want of filial affection would be such a weapon in the hands of calumny that the Princess would *never* be able *to retrieve her reputation.*' The obvious course was for the Princess, when she was 18, to marry, but here there were difficulties. From evidence in Stockmar's confidential letters to King Leopold it is clear that the development of Princess Victoria had been adversely affected temporarily at least by the circumstances of her upbringing, the nervous strain to which she had been subjected for many years, the self-control, unnatural for her age, she had been forced to exercise and the ill-health due to her septic tonsils. On 3rd April 1837 Stockmar wrote to King Leopold '. . . The physical danger and therefore impossibility of a marriage in the near future must soon be made as clear as possible on the testimony of sensible and conscientious doctors.' Referring to William IV's cherished scheme to marry Princess Victoria to one of the Princes of Orange, whom she found repulsive, Stockmar added 'should a kind of ravishment never the less be attempted, mother and uncle [the Duchess of Kent and King Leopold] would have to declare . . . that force in such matters is neither wise nor practicable'.

On 18th May it was observed that the King received the guests both at the levée and the drawing-room held that day, sitting in a chair.[66] He was not well, and a few days later he was ill. On 22nd May the Princess wrote in her Journal that the King's doctor Sir Henry Halford brought back news that 'the King was in a very odd state and decidedly had the hay fever and in such a manner as to preclude his going to bed. I trust he *may* get over it, but he is 72.'[67]

A legend has arisen that Princess Victoria was kept in ignorance of her uncle's condition and that her accession to the throne came as a surprise to her, but her Journal makes it clear she was aware of every stage in King William IV's illness.

On 23rd May he was better but on 26th May Lord Palmerston wrote 'Our King is in a very precarious state. He will probably rally this bout; but it is not likely he can last long. It is desirable he should wear the crown some time, however, for there would be no advantage in having a totally inexperienced girl of 18, just out of a strict guardianship, to govern an Empire. It would be well for her and for us, that her ascent to the throne should be preceded by some little intercourse with the world.' On 30th May Lord Palmerston wrote 'The King is better and will probably rally this time' and on 2nd June reported 'The King is progressing mending and will recover this time . . . but he is 72 and his constitution, though strong, has received a severe shake.'[68]

Meanwhile, a few weeks earlier, the King had taken a step which brought difficulties with the Duchess of Kent to a head, including the difficulties between Princess Victoria and her mother. On 18th May the King wrote the Princess a letter, which he gave to the Lord Chamberlain, Lord Conyngham, together with a communication bearing the sign manual —to be shown 'to whomever he may find in Attendance'—instructing him to place the letter in Princess Victoria's own hands the next morning.[69] In it the King informed the Princess that it was his intention when she came of age to reign, on 24th May, to apply to Parliament for £10,000 a year to be 'entirely in her power and disposal'. She was to appoint her own Keeper of her Privy Purse 'who would be responsible to her *only*', and she was to form her own establishment if she wished. (The King's original suggestion was a Lady Privy Purse, but the last Lady Privy Purse had been the Duchess of Marlborough in the reign of Queen Anne, not an encouraging precedent.) Lord Melbourne, the Prime Minister, suggested as Keeper of the Privy Purse Sir Benjamin Stephenson who had been Master of the Household at Windsor, but the Duchess regarded this suggestion as an insult. It was well known that Sir Benjamin Stephenson was particularly odious to her, she wrote, which was no doubt why he had been suggested. They had had differences over the decorations of her new apartments at Kensington. Lord Melbourne replied he was ignorant of any differences.

The Duchess was furiously angry. The Regency would end in a few days, which was disastrous enough; now the King was attempting to emancipate the Princess entirely, give her an independent income and even a separate establishment; and she wrote Lord Melbourne a sharp letter. The previous morning, 19th May, the Marquess Conyngham had called at Kensington Palace and told Sir John Conroy he had a letter from the King to place in Princess Victoria's own hands, showing him 'a Paper written by the King . . . to which the Sign Manual was affixed ordering Lord Conyngham to do so'. The Duchess on being informed by Sir John replied that the Princess should receive the letter in her mother's presence, which she did, and, after reading it, handed it to her mother. The Duchess demanded whether she and the Princess Victoria were to consider Lord Melbourne's government responsible 'for all these Proceedings'. Lord Melbourne replied the same day that 'every proposition submitted by the Crown to Parliament must, according to the Constitution have been previously advised by His Majesty's confidential servants, and that for that advice they are necessarily responsible. . . .'

The Duchess answered instantly and in a rage '. . . It is my duty, without any reserve to inform you that, if it is your intention to advise the King to send a message to Parliament, for a grant as described to the Princess, and which the Princess and myself never asked for; and which is to be given . . . in a manner calculated to wound every feeling that belongs to my maternal station,—contrary also to the wishes of my child and which does not correspond with the confidence reposed in me by the country,—I trust that the representatives of it will refuse to vote money for such a purpose. Passed over, wounded on every occasion that circumstances will allow, I still know what is due to my station and to my maternal duties, supported by the tears of my child; who has, of her own free will, told the King that she desires nothing but to be left as heretofore with Her Mother:—conscious that every moment of my life has been devoted to my duties to her and to the country . . . the Princess and myself reject the idea, that on such a subject, we could have a separate feeling. All I have is Hers. . . .'[70]

On 6th June Princess Victoria dictated a memorandum to Lehzen recording the course of events.[71] After receiving the King's letter on 19th May she had proposed to the Duchess that she should answer immediately and ask the King if her tutor, the Dean of Chester, might be named Privy Purse for the present. The Duchess refused. The Princess then asked the Duchess if there might be a private conversation with Lord Melbourne. This was also refused. 'At last on the 20th, as an *answer* must be given, I wrote my answer to the King . . . that answer was the copy of a letter written by my Mother.' The draft letter presented by the Duchess to the Princess bears a note in the Prince Consort's hand. 'Written by the Duchess of Kent on Sir John Conroy's advice.' In it the Princess, after referring to 'my youth and inexperience [which] naturally unfits me to enter into all the details of the subject', continues 'I wish to remain as I am now, in the care of my dear Mother. . . . Upon the subject of money, I should wish that whatever may be necessary to add, may be given to my dear Mother for my use, who always freely does everything I want on pecuniary matters. . . .'

After reading this communication the King said 'Victoria has not written that letter.'[72]

Lord John Russell now proposed to Lord Melbourne that the £10,000 should be split, £6,000 annually being paid to the Duchess and £4,000 to the Princess. The King accepted this proposition, saying he would not insist on a separate establishment or 'raise captious objections' to embarrass his government, and Lord Melbourne was charged to convey the offer to the Duchess of Kent.[73]

Lord Melbourne was apprehensive. He feared, he wrote to the King, that the Duchess of Kent intended to make an appeal to public sympathy which might have 'serious and embarrassing results. It is worth while to make almost any sacrifice in order to avoid open difference and dissension in the Royal Family. It is highly expedient that the Princess should continue to remain at present in the same family with her Mother and under her care. The public feeling and the public interest both require it.'[74]

Writing to Sir Herbert Taylor, the King's confidential secretary, on 22nd May, barely forty-eight hours before the Princess came of age, Lord Melbourne reminded Sir Herbert 'It is always to be remembered that, after her attaining the age of eighteen, the Princess will still be a Minor, like any other Infant, in all respects and for all purposes except succeeding to the throne. . . . It is to be observed how determined her Royal Highness [the Duchess of Kent] is to fix me with the responsibility of what has been done, which shows that she contemplates publicity. . . .'[75] Sir Herbert had a simple explanation: 'The real fact is that the Duchess and King John want money.'

On 24th May the Princess came of age.[76] 'How old! and yet how far am I from being what I should be' she wrote in her Journal. 'I shall from this day take the *firm* resolution to study . . . to keep my attention always well fixed on whatever I am about, and to strive every day to become less trifling and more fit for what, if Heaven wills it, I'm some day to be!' The affection of the people for the Princess was evident. 'The parks and streets were thronged and everything looked like a gala day' she noted. That evening the King gave a state ball in her honour, though he himself was not yet well enough to attend. 'The court yard and the streets were crammed when we went to the Ball' wrote the Princess 'and the anxiety of the people to see poor stupid me was very great, and I must say I am quite touched by it.'

Two incidents at the ball provoked comment.[77] The King directed that the little Princess should sit on his chair of state, which she did, and going to the ball the Duchess of Kent put the Princess in a separate carriage and followed in another. 'The consequence was the Princess arrived first and alone, which had a strange appearance.' It was thought that both in manner and time of staying, which was not even until supper, the Duchess was exceptionally ungracious, while Sir John Conroy had an air of triumph and defiance and seemed happy at the prospect of an explosion 'which those who wish Royalty well, should deprecate and deplore'.

In fact Conroy was in a desperate state. He saw wealth and influence slipping through his fingers. The hope of a Regency was already over; very possibly within a few months, or even less, the Princess would be

Queen and he would revert to being nothing more than the Duchess of Kent's equerry. The only solution was to induce the Princess to bind herself in advance by selecting him for such a position of trust that he would be unassailable. Conroy demanded that the Princess should place him at the head of all her affairs and appoint him to be her confidential Private Secretary. Owing to the long illness of George III and the peculiarities of his successors, the position of the Sovereign's Private Secretary in the British administration had acquired great importance and influence. The Princess refused. Meanwhile the King, who had been reported to be 'mending' on 2nd June, fell ill again, and Conroy became frantic. The Princess steadily resisted all pressure; she was supported by Lehzen, and also by Stockmar, who had arrived in England on 25th May, the day after her birthday. Conroy had previously spoken 'with the greatest respect and friendliness' of Stockmar, but a long conversation now took place from which Conroy returned 'very heated and little satisfied . . . from this time on the friendly relationship between the two gentlemen came to an end'.[78] Stockmar was an old and valued friend of the Duchess of Kent, but speedily discovered she was no longer to be trusted. On 29th May Stockmar asked the Princess to give him 'the most explicit and candid' answer to two questions. First the Duchess of Kent assured him that the revised offer from the King of £6,000 for herself and £4,000 for the Princess, contained in a letter from Lord Melbourne and personally delivered by him, was laid before the Princess immediately after delivery. Was this a fact? Second, the Duchess asserted that the letter rejecting the offer had been written 'with your Royal Highness's full consent and approbation'. Was this also a fact? The Princess replied next day 'Not only have I *never seen* nor heard of this letter, but was never told by my Mother that Lord Melbourne had been here. . . . As I *never* knew anything of Lord Melbourne's letter, I am, of course, also totally ignorant of the answer.' On 6th June the Princess dictated the memorandum[79] already referred to declaring 'I have objected on the 19th of May [the date the King's offer of an additional £10,000 annually was received] as well as always before to allowing Sir John Conroy any interference in my affairs. Whatever he has done, it has been done by order of my Mother, as I requested in *her* name, without making me responsible for any of her actions, as Sir John Conroy is *Her* private secretary and neither *my* Servant, nor Adviser, nor *ever was*.'

In spite of her preoccupations, the Princess was still interested in the Duke Charles of Brunswick. On 1st June at a charity ball she writes 'I saw at a distance, in the crowd, my unfortunate cousin (for so he really is) the Duke of Brunswick; he was in a black or dark blue uniform with silver; his hair hanging wildly about his face, his countenance pale and haggard; I was very sorry I could not see him *de près* for once, that I may really see if he is so ferocious looking, but I must say I think it was well felt in him not to come near.'[80]

The King's condition deteriorated. On 9th June the Princess recorded in her Journal that he was _very_ ill and the news was very bad. She faced the prospect of ascending the throne with calm. She was aware that accession offered her an escape from the frustration and strain of life with her mother and Conroy. Once she was Queen power would be in her hands.

Stockmar came to see her that afternoon and they talked from two in the afternoon until a quarter past three. 'It was a _most_ important conversation' wrote the Princess.[81] Stockmar 'found the Princess fairly cool and collected, and her answers precise, apt and determined. I had, throughout the conversation, the impression that she is extremely jealous of what she considers to be her rights and her future power and is therefore not at all inclined to do anything which would put Conroy into a situation to be able to entrench upon them. Her feelings seem, moreover, to have been deeply wounded by what she calls "his impudent and insulting conduct" towards her. Her affection and esteem for her mother seem likewise to have suffered by Mama having tamely allowed Conroy to insult the Princess in her presence, and by the Princess having been frequently a witness to insults which the poor Duchess tolerated herself in the presence of her daughter. . . . On the 10th, 11th and 12th we in Kensington were constantly playing out some comedy or tragedy. O'Hum [Conroy] continues the system of intimidation with the genius of a madman, and the Duchess carries out all that she is instructed to do with admirable docility and perseverance. . . . The Princess continues to refuse firmly to give her Mama her promise that she will make O'Hum her confidential adviser. Whether she will hold out, Heaven only knows, for they plague her, every hour and every day; old people have often failed me—why should not young ones do so?'[82]

The Princess was in fact reaching the limits of her endurance. For the past three weeks Conroy and the Duchess had daily been launching the most violent attacks on her, in order to make her promise to put Conroy at the head of all her affairs when she came to the throne. Though she had withstood all attacks she was frightened and alone. Lehzen was devoted but in an inferior position and a foreigner; Stockmar was also a foreigner and his confidential connection with King Leopold was resented and suspected. King Leopold himself was a foreigner, and hundreds of miles away. In this situation the Princess turned for advice to Lord Liverpool, for whom she had long cherished 'an almost filial affection' and whose daughter, Lady Catherine Jenkinson, was one of her few friends. She asked him in strict confidence to advise her on her situation with her mother and Conroy, contriving to see him '_alone_' on 15th June.[83] Lord Liverpool told her she must continue to live with her mother and the

Princess replied that she intended to do so. As for Conroy and his scheme to become her private secretary and political adviser, Lord Liverpool had already told him he was totally unsuitable for the office of Private Secretary; when the Princess came to the throne her only political advisers must be the Ministers, in particular Lord Melbourne. The position occupied by Sir Herbert Taylor with King William IV was a peculiar one and would not continue. There was no objection to Lehzen remaining, but she must remain as the Princess's private friend. The Princess then asked Lord Liverpool to see Stockmar who 'would tell him many things I liked not to name' and to ask his own daughter for details of Conroy's offensive conduct towards herself.

News of the King continued to be very bad. On 13th June Lord Palmerston wrote that all hope was given up and on 15th June all the Princess's lessons except with the Dean of Chester were cancelled and she and the Duchess stayed in the Palace, going nowhere and seeing nobody. The battle between the Princess, Conroy and the Duchess nevertheless continued. On 16th June Stockmar was at Kensington Palace and reported '. . . the struggle between the Mama and daughter is still going on. She [the Duchess] is pressed by Conroy to bring matters to extremities and to force her Daughter to do her will by unkindness and severity.' In Stockmar's opinion if what was taking place came out 'the Princess must appear *what she is*, an oppressed Person, and everybody I am sure *would fly to her assistance*'.[84]

Conroy was losing control of himself. In the presence of her son Prince Charles he declared to the Duchess he had been advised that 'if Princess Victoria will not listen to reason, *she must be coerced*'.[85] Prince Charles 'immediately warned the Duchess of Kent very earnestly against any such action', speaking in German, and the matter was not carried further. Conroy afterwards told Prince Charles that the reason why he had abandoned this course was that he did not credit the Duchess of Kent with enough strength of mind for such a step.

On 18th June the Princess wrote in her Journal 'The poor King, they say, can live but a few hours now'[86] and towards seven o'clock on the evening of 19th June 1837 it became evident that the King was rapidly approaching his end. Prince Ernest Hohenlohe, husband of Princess Feodora, who was staying with his cousin Queen Adelaide, saw Princess Victoria at Kensington Palace in the presence of the Duchess of Kent. When she was told the King was dying, she 'turned pale, burst into tears and continued very much affected', leading Prince Ernest to suppose she had been kept in ignorance of the King's state. Lord Conyngham, the Lord Chamberlain, and the Archbishop of Canterbury were directed to prepare to go to Kensington Palace at six o'clock next morning as it was expected the King's death would take place before that hour.

On Tuesday, 20th June, the Princess records in her Journal[87] 'I was awoke at 6 o'clock by Mamma who told me that the Archbishop of Canterbury and Lord Conyngham were here and wished to see me. [The Duchess writes in her Diary that she woke the Princess with a kiss, but the Princess does not mention a kiss.] I got out of bed and went into my sitting room (only in my dressing gown) and *alone*, and saw them. Lord Conyngham (the Lord Chamberlain) then acquainted me that my poor Uncle, the King, was no more, and had expired at 12 minutes past 2 this morning and consequently that *I* am *Queen*.'

Chapter Five

The young Queen revealed herself to be very different from the childish girl the Duchess and Conroy had endeavoured to present to the world. The Duchess barely set eyes on her daughter on the day of her accession. The Queen received the announcement from the Archbishop of Canterbury and the Lord Chamberlain 'alone'. After she had dressed she breakfasted talking to Stockmar, and then wrote two letters, one to King Leopold, one to her much loved half-sister Princess Feodora, signing herself 'your devoted attached sister VR'. At nine she received Lord Melbourne, whom she saw 'of COURSE *quite* ALONE as I shall *always* do all my Ministers'. He kissed her hand, she acquainted him with her intention to retain him and the present Ministry at the head of affairs and he kissed her hand again. At half past eleven she held her first Privy Council in the red saloon. 'I went in of course quite alone.'[1]

Greville, who was present in his official capacity as Clerk to the Privy Council, wrote 'There never was anything like the first impression She produced, or the chorus of praise and admiration which is raised about her manner and behaviour, and certainly not without justice. It was very extraordinary, and something far beyond what was looked for. Her extreme youth and inexperience, and the ignorance of the world concerning her, naturally excited intense curiosity. . . . He [Melbourne] asked her if She would enter the room accompanied by the Great Officers of State, but She said She would come in alone. . . . She bowed to the Lords, took her seat, and then read her speech in a clear, distinct and audible voice, and without any appearance of fear or embarrassment. . . . She went through the whole ceremony (occasionally looking at Melbourne for instruction when She had any doubt what to do, which hardly ever occurred) and with perfect calmness and self-possession, but at the same time with a graceful modesty and propriety particularly interesting and ingratiating. . . .'

Croker, a prejudiced Tory, wrote 'I cannot describe to you with what a mixture of self-possession and feminine delicacy she read the paper. Her voice, which is naturally beautiful, was clear and untroubled; and her eye was bright and calm, neither bold nor downcast, but firm and soft.

There was a blush on her cheek . . . and certainly she *did* look as interesting and handsome as any young lady I ever saw.' 'She not merely filled her chair,' said the Duke of Wellington, 'she filled the room.' That evening she gave a number of audiences 'all in my room and alone', dined 'upstairs alone', and had another conversation with Lord Melbourne which lasted for nearly an hour. 'Each time I see him I feel more confidence in him; I find him very kind in his manner too.'[2] Only after she had seen him did she go to say goodnight to the Duchess of Kent.

Next day the Queen went in state to be formally proclaimed at St James's Palace standing at an open window of the Privy Council Chamber between Lord Melbourne and Lord Lansdowne. As the first cheers rang out she was observed to be affected, she turned pale and her eyes filled with tears. Later in the day the proclamation was repeated at Trafalgar Square, Temple Bar, Wood Street and the Royal Exchange. In all official documents of the first day of her reign the Queen is named as Alexandrina Victoria, but at her own request she was proclaimed Victoria only and henceforward the name Alexandrina disappears.

To Court circles the first week of the new reign made it evident that the Duchess of Kent's influence had waned. 'Poor woman' wrote Lord Holland on 27th June. 'The importance of her actions and opinions are gone by [*sic*]. She will count for little or nothing in the new court.'

The propaganda originating from Conroy about the Queen's childishness and lack of mental power had not prepared the world for her shrewdness, her self-possession, her 'premature good sense'. Curiosity concerning her was intense. Lord Holland* replying to an urgent request for information from Lord Granville, British Ambassador in Paris, wrote on 30th June 'Well, I have been to Court and in spite of a bad night and lameness have been closeted . . . with our Virgin Queen. I am come back quite a courtier & a bit of a lover, for really her manner and demeanour deserve all that is said of them, announce sense, taste, a feeling of good breeding, and her looks, in my judgment, far exceed the most favourable account I heard. Though not a beauty & not a very good figure, she is really in person, in face, & especially in eyes and complexion, a very nice girl & quite such as might tempt.' Lord Holland's enthusiasm did not evaporate. Some weeks later he wrote 'without prejudice or exaggeration, the

* Henry Richard Vassall Fox, third Baron Holland, was the nephew of Charles James Fox by whom, when left an orphan, he was brought up. He eloped with Lady Elizabeth Webster, wife of Sir Godfrey Webster. After resounding scandal she obtained a divorce, married Lord Holland, and subsequently, as mistress of Holland House, became a celebrated hostess. Lord Holland passed his life in high political circles, never held any office of importance but was universally beloved and the recipient of confidences. Sydney Smith wrote 'There never existed in any human being a better heart, or one more purified from the bad passions, more abounding in charity and compassion, and which seemed to be so created as a refuge to the helpless and the oppressed.' He died on 22nd October 1840.

demeanour, feeling and conduct of our little Queen seem to me to be quite extraordinary ... like the rest of the world I am captivated and surprised', while Lord Granville's wife exclaimed 'such a little love of a Queen!'[3]

For the first time in her life the Queen was enjoying the intoxicating experience of personal success. 'I *delight* in this work' she wrote in her Journal.

Charles Greville, who in his post as clerk to the Privy Council had many opportunities of observing her, commented 'Everything is new and delightful to her. She is surrounded with the most exciting and interesting enjoyments; her occupations, her pleasures, her business, her Court, all present an unceasing round of gratifications. With all her prudence and discretion She has great animal spirits, and enters into the magnificent novelties of her position with the zest and curiosity of a child.'

The shadow on the young Queen's happiness was Conroy. Immediately King William IV expired, Conroy hastened to press his claims. In a memorandum dated 20th June 1837 (with a comment written by the Prince Consort: 'The King had died that very morning') the Queen records[4] that she received a paper from Baron Stockmar, containing the claims of Sir John Conroy, which she would take 'the earliest opportunity of putting into Lord Melbourne's hands and would consult with Lord Melbourne and decide upon it as soon as possible'. The paper was given to Lord Melbourne as he came out of the Queen's first Council. Conroy acknowledged to Baron Stockmar that he was 'completely defeated', and considered his public life at an end. 'He had therefore' wrote Stockmar 'come to the conclusion that ... retirement would be the best course for him to take. ... To effect this he had stated his arguments and conditions upon paper; and if the latter were made good he was ready to retire.' In Stockmar's opinion Conroy's retirement was 'the only measure' which could prevent further mischief between the Duchess of Kent and the young Queen, and he hoped that Lord Melbourne would do all in his power to arrive at that end. Conroy's estimate of the rewards he deserved was high. He had, he asserted, entered the Duke and Duchess of Kent's service nineteen years ago and served for eighteen years without a day's respite. He had relinquished the Artillery, in which he would have risen to emolument and rank; he had refused promotion in the Army; he had refused high office in the civil service, to dedicate himself to the Duchess. He had become a marked man, the King had persecuted him and his family, he had spent a fortune in the service. 'My reward for the *Past* I conceive should be—a peerage, the red ribbon [the Grand Cross of the Bath]—and a pension from the Privy Purse of £3,000 a year.' Conroy asserted that Sir Benjamin Bloomfield, private secretary to George IV, and 'only a servant', to whom Conroy, as adviser to the Duchess of Kent, held a superior position, had retired with the red ribbon, an Irish peerage, an embassy and £10,000 a year, having also made near £150,000. As Lord Melbourne read through the paper, it more than once fell from his hands, and he exclaimed aloud, outraged, 'This is really too bad! Have you ever heard such impudence? Why if Bloomfield has done as it is asserted he has, he ought to have been hung for it.' The amount of the pension demanded by Conroy was exorbitant, he could not in conscience advise the Queen to grant it, and the merits of the case and public opinion made it quite impossible to make him a peer or give him the Bath. The most Lord Melbourne could offer was the pension and a baronetcy. Conroy, however, clung 'most tenaciously' to the peerage. Stockmar urged the extreme importance of getting rid of Conroy for the sake of the young Queen's peace of mind and Lord Melbourne, partially, gave way. On 26th June 1837 he gave Conroy a promise, in writing, that if he [Lord Melbourne] should continue to be Her Majesty's adviser, it was his intention when the state of the Irish peerage should authorise a new creation to advise Her Majesty to confer it upon Conroy and added that this promise was made 'with the knowledge, assent and approbation of Her Majesty'. The promise was accepted by Conroy, but did not have the effect Stockmar had expected. Conroy neither went away nor resigned his place in the Duchess's household. On the contrary he told Stockmar 'sneeringly, that he was not bound to fulfil the engagement upon his part before the Queen has fulfilled all she had promised upon hers'.[5]

Meanwhile he continued to exercise his extraordinary power over the Duchess. On 20th June 1837, the day on which the young Queen ascended the throne, the Duchess asked permission to take Conroy and Lady Flora Hastings with her next day, presumably to the proclamation of the Queen's accession at St James's Palace. The Queen refused and the Duchess persisted: 'I assure you if it was only *for me* I would not ask you for it. But it will be observed and remarks will be made which you should certainly avoid the first day. . . .' The Queen, writing hurriedly in pencil, refused again. 'I am sorry I must give you the same answer as last night. It is Lord M's decided opinion. . . .'

At this the Duchess lost her temper. Neither she nor Conroy appears to have understood the strength of the Queen's resentment against against them nor her determination to have no dealings with Conroy ever again. 'You do not know the world' wrote the Duchess. 'S.J. [Sir John] has his faults, he may have made mistakes, but his intentions were always the best. . . . This affair is much tattled and very unhappily. . . . Take care Victoria, you know your Prerogative! take care that Lord Melbourne is not King. . . .'

The Queen, however, did not come to the throne without having carefully considered the course she ought to pursue after her accession;

on the first day of her reign she wrote in her Journal 'It had long been my intention to retain him [Lord Melbourne] . . . at the head of affairs and it [*sic*] could not be in better hands than his. . . . I like him very much and feel confidence in him. He is a very straightforward, honest, clever and good man.'[6]

In 1837 William Lamb, Viscount Melbourne, was 58 years of age. He had possessed dazzling good looks and was still remarkably handsome, his eyes and the set of his head being particularly admired. His social talents were exceptional, his wit odd, entertaining, and unconventional, he frequented the society of women and was attractive to them. His slight air of melancholy was attributed to private misfortunes, since, in spite of brilliance, looks and riches, his life had been disappointing. He had married, against the wishes of his family, the lovely, eccentric, and wilful Lady Caroline Ponsonby, only daughter of Lady Bessborough. Having made herself a public scandal by her unrequited passion for Byron, despite years of patience, forbearance and forgiveness on Melbourne's part, she became so excitable as to be insane. A separation was inevitable and she died in 1828. Their son, Melbourne's only child Augustus, proved feeble-minded and died a year later.

Melbourne had become Prime Minister for the second time in 1834 and was therefore at her accession automatically the Queen's chief and proper adviser. Out of consideration for the Queen, he also non-officially assumed the duties of her Private Secretary.

It was a stroke of good fortune for the Queen that such a man as Melbourne should have been at hand to give her a second education and fill the gaps left by her years of isolation at Kensington. She adored him. His charm, his wit, his 'stores of knowledge', his constant kindness and patience, the entertainment of his company were irresistible, while his manner to the Queen, the discretion and purity of his conduct were admired, respected, and liked by the whole Court. It seemed incredible to his friends that Melbourne, sophisticated Melbourne, should have been able to bring himself to endure life at the young Queen's Court, the nursery atmosphere, the long evenings spent in playing school-room games (the Queen was particularly fond of draughts and in putting together 'dissected pictures', a precursor of jig-saw puzzles), the conversation made up of 'trivial, wearisome and laboured inanities'.

An example of conversation at Court is recorded by Greville 'with accurate fidelity'. It should be noted that Court etiquette forbade the introduction of any topic of conversation except by the Queen herself, and that the young Queen Victoria was shy and dreaded the duty of speaking to each member of her circle of guests, known as 'circling'.

Q. Have you been riding today, Mr Greville?
G. No, Madam, I have not.

Q. It was a fine day.
G. Yes, Ma'am, a very fine day.
Q. It was rather cold though.
G. (like Polonius) It *was* rather cold, Madam.
Q. Your sister, Ly Francis Egerton, rides I think, does not She?
G. She does ride sometimes, Madam.
(A pause, when I took the lead though adhering to the same topic)
G. Has your Majesty been riding today?
Q. (with animation) Oh yes, a very long ride.
G. Has your Majesty got a nice horse?
Q. O, a very nice horse.
—gracious smile and inclination of head on part of Queen, profound bow on mine. . . .

'I have no doubt he [Melbourne] is passionately fond of her' wrote Greville 'as he might be of his daughter if he had one; and the more because he is a man with a capacity for loving without anything to love. It is become his province to educate, instruct and form the most interesting mind and character in the world.'[7]

In all respects but one Melbourne's influence on the young Queen was wholly beneficent. Unfortunately Melbourne had no sympathy with reform or with the struggle of the workers against the appalling poverty and overcrowding of Victorian England. In common with most politicians of his period Melbourne believed in 'laissez faire'—leave things alone and the law of supply and demand will solve all problems—a comforting doctrine which held particular appeal for Melbourne, who above all things hated 'bother'. He was capable of assuring the Queen that endeavours, such as Lord Shaftesbury's, to improve the lot of factory children, infants of five and six who worked twelve to fifteen hours a day in cotton mills and mines, were useless and unnecessary; the reports of their conditions were greatly exaggerated, working kept the children out of mischief and he imagined they did not want to starve.

Nor should it be forgotten that Melbourne was responsible for the notorious case of the Tolpuddle Martyrs. The trades union movement, to which Melbourne was bitterly opposed, was in its infancy and alarm was created when, in 1834, numbers of agricultural labourers began to join. The upper classes in England had never forgotten that the French Revolution began in the country; moreover, in 1830, agricultural labourers in south and south-east England, driven to desperation by starvation wages, 7s. a week, enclosures of common land and the rising cost of food, had committed acts of violence.[8] Ricks and houses were burned, machines broken and in London there was a wave of hysterical alarm.

In 1834, when Lord Melbourne was Home Secretary, the labourers in Tolpuddle, a starving parish near Dorchester in Dorset where wages were seven shillings a week, had previously met together and decided to approach the Tolpuddle masters for an increase to the wage paid by other masters in the district, namely ten shillings a week. An agreement was reached and all the labourers returned to work. But the increase was not paid, only nine shillings a week was given, and after some months this in turn was reduced to eight shillings. Shortly afterwards a labourer who had complained, George Loveless, with two or three others was summoned to see the Chief Magistrate at Dorset County Hall who told them they must work for what their employers thought fit to give them and there was no law to compel masters to give any fixed sum to their servants. Remonstrance that an agreement had been made between labourers and masters was in vain, and shortly afterwards wages were reduced first to seven and then to six shillings a week. On this wage it was impossible for a family to keep alive, without dishonesty, and George Loveless then remembered he had seen accounts of Trade Societies. A Friendly Society was formed among the Tolpuddle labourers and two delegates from a Trade Society paid Tolpuddle a visit and instructed them how they should proceed. On 21st February 1834 placards were posted up threatening any man who should join the 'Union' with seven years' transportation. On 24th February at daybreak, when on his way to work, George Loveless was arrested with several other Tolpuddle labourers, marched by the police constable to Dorchester, where their heads were shorn, they were put in irons and locked in Dorchester jail.*

Lord Melbourne, having approved their committal on 10th March 1834, issued an enquiry to the Law officers of the Crown, the Attorney General and Solicitor General, requesting them to inform him as soon as possible under what statute it would be advisable to proceed against the Dorchester labourers. Various societies, some called 'Regeneration Societies', others 'Trade Unions', were spreading throughout the United Kingdom, having for their object the increase of wages of labourers, the regulation of hours of work and establishing a common fund for supporting all such workmen as struck for work while unemployed. 'At the meetings of these Societies secret Oaths not to divulge or make known the proceedings of the Meeting are administered.'[9]

Several statutes existed. The most severe passed at the time of the naval mutiny at the Nore, 1797 (37 George III, Cap. 123), imposed a sentence of seven years' transportation for the taking of an illegal oath and was known, by the few who recollected it, as the Secret Oaths Act. Further statutes containing various modifications existed and Lord Melbourne would have preferred to use a later statute, in some respects even

* George Loveless, *Victims of Whiggery. Statement of the persecutions experienced by the Dorchester Labourers*, 1837. Facsimile printed 1969 by Progress Bookshops.

more severe, the 'new' Sedition Act of 1817 (57 George III, Cap. 19) which made taking a secret oath treason or a felony punishable by death, but the magistrates preferred to proceed under the Secret Oaths Act of 1797.

On 17th March 1834 the labourers were tried at the Dorchester Assizes before Baron Williams. Evidence was given that a secret oath had been administered at Tolpuddle. The prisoners were blindfolded, knelt down, a book was put into their hands and an oath administered, on which the book was kissed. The proceedings were vague, the language of the oath, the nature of the book not clear. Something was said about the rules of the society and paying one shilling admission and while the men were blinded a voice, thought to be that of Loveless or his brother, said something which was repeated and which ended 'Remember your end'. Among Loveless's belongings had been found a book entitled *Rules for a General Society of Labourers* which forbade the use of any violence or violation of the laws. Counsel for the defence submitted that the rules showed the society was in the nature of a Friendly Society. Baron Williams then sentenced the six labourers to seven years' transportation.[10]

An outburst of indignation at the severity of the sentence followed. In the House of Commons the case was debated on several occasions.* The sentences were described as 'atrocious'. It was doubtful whether the men had understood what they were doing, cruel treatment of their relatives was alleged and the precipitate execution of the sentences condemned. The prisoners had been almost instantly transported. Awkward questions were asked relating to the ultra-Protestant Orange Lodges in Ireland where secret oaths were regularly administered. The Orange leader was the Duke of Cumberland.

Public protest meetings were held; two hundred and fifty thousand persons signed a petition and a procession of thirty thousand headed by a clergyman in full canonicals marched down Whitehall to deliver it at Downing Street. Melbourne 'smiling and unperturbed' watched from a window, and refused to receive it. In his view the object of government, to maintain order and enforce contracts, had been fulfilled.

Lord John Russell, however, was not satisfied. He felt the question of the Orange Lodges and the immunity they enjoyed was difficult to explain. Why were the Dorchester labourers transported and not the Duke of Cumberland? Sir Robert Peel was showing an interest in the case.

Lord Melbourne demurred, he had thought the case was finished, but when he saw Lord John was going to be tiresome and persist he gave way. 'I do not myself care much what is done respecting the Dorchester labourers' he wrote.[12]

The sentences were remitted and after some delay the six were given

* On 26th March and 14th, 16th, 18th, 28th, 30th April 1834.[11]

146

a free passage home, and settled on farms in England. Later four emigrated to Canada. One returned to Tolpuddle, to live, die and be buried there.[13] The tree, now aged and much propped up, under which the six are said to have met prior to their arrest, has become a place of pilgrimage.

*

One of the very few valid criticisms of Queen Victoria is that she was not sufficiently concerned with improvement of the conditions in which a great mass of her subjects passed their lives. She lived through an age of profound social change, but neither public health, nor housing, nor the education of her people, nor their representation, engaged much of her attention. As a young girl she had not been lacking in humane and generous impulses, she had been moved by the poverty of the poor gipsies at Claremont and by the sorrows of Ireland. It is a commonplace of human development that such impulses pass away with adolescence and she had as well a leaning towards absolutism, which made Louis XIV the object of her young admiration. Some part of what was lacking, however, must be attributed to the influence of Melbourne. At an impressionable period, made doubly impressionable by the deprivations of her earlier life, it was unfortunate that she should have come under the influence of a man with so much charm and so little belief in human nature, with such a touching capacity for tenderness allied to dislike of reform, and such want of sympathy with the struggling mass of the workers that he was capable of callousness.

*

On 13th July 1837 the Queen moved from the 'poor old Palace' at Kensington into Buckingham Palace. The Duchess of Kent drove with her and on arrival they walked together round the garden, the Queen was delighted to see that her favourite spaniel, 'dear' Dashy, was 'quite happy' in it. To her mother the Queen's manner was 'irreproachable' but Palace gossip reported she had no real affection for the Duchess, hardly ever saw her and required her mother to send a message or note asking permission before she visited the Queen's apartments. To these messages the Duchess frequently received an answer that the Queen was too busy to see her. On the other hand one of the Queen's first acts at Buckingham Palace was to have a communication made in the wall between her bedroom and Lehzen's room. To the Queen Dowager, her aunt Queen Adelaide, the young Queen showed every consideration. The day she went down to visit the Queen Dowager at Windsor, she told Melbourne, 'to his great surprise', that as the flag on the Round Tower would be at half mast it might be thought necessary to raise it on her arrival and it would be better to send beforehand to tell them not to do so. Melbourne commented that he 'had never thought of the flag, or knew anything about it', but it showed the young Queen's knowledge of forms and her attention to trifles.

The first summer of the new reign passed by with new experiences for the young Queen almost every week. On 14th July in full dress and wearing the blue ribbon and star of the Garter and the Garter round her arm the Queen sat on the throne in the throne room and received addresses, afterwards holding a chapter of the Order; on Monday the 17th she prorogued Parliament, entering the House of Lords preceded by the officers of State, wearing the Parliamentary robe, which she found 'enormously heavy', and with Lord Melbourne, who bore the Sword of State, immediately in front of her. He had coached her in the speech she was to read and stood 'quite close' to her on the left of the throne. 'I feel always a satisfaction to have him near me on such occasions, as he is such an honest, good, kind hearted man and is my *friend*, I know it.' The Duchess of Kent was deeply moved. 'I shall never forget my feelings' wrote the Duchess in her Diary 'when I saw her sit on the Throne! That young girl 18 years old, being the sole sovereign of this great country. . . .'

Heinrich von Bülow, the Prussian envoy in London, wrote to his wife Gabriele that he 'was greatly surprised by the appearance of the little Queen when I caught sight of her in the procession. She was beautifully, tastefully, and becomingly dressed; upon her head she wore a tiara of diamonds, which had the appearance of a crown in front, and added somewhat to her height. Her dress was of white embroidered satin, profusely decorated with jewels, the sleeves were wide and cut open in the latest fashion . . . She walked with firm unhesitating step, held her head high, and bowed very graciously.' Bülow noticed the 'great curiosity' that was felt among the English aristocracy about her, and wrote that 'old Lady Jersey had armed herself with powerful opera glasses which she relentlessly fixed upon the young Queen!'[14]

On Wednesday the 19th the Queen held a levée at which she had her hand kissed 'nearly 3,000 times!' and in the following month, on 15th August, she began to ride again 'for the first time for 2 years'. Naturally fearless, riding was one of her chief pleasures, she liked a horse to be spirited and a little restive to give her 'something to do'. The 17th of August was the Duchess of Kent's birthday, and the Queen showed some softening towards her. 'This day is my poor (for so much has of late occurred which makes me pity her) dear Mother's birthday.' The Duchess was miserable. 'This was neither a happy nor a merry day for me. Everything is so changed' she wrote. Conroy was still at Kensington and Princess Lieven, wife of the Russian Ambassador, was told he bullied the unfortunate Duchess 'incessantly'.

After an evening which the Queen particularly enjoyed, putting dissected pictures together, with the assistance of Lord Melbourne and

Lord Conyngham—'The pleasantest gayest evening I have passed for some time. I sat up until ½ past 11'—the Court migrated to Windsor, where the Duchess of Kent was more miserable than ever. Her apartment was 'very far from the room Victoria now occupies. . . . I am very much out of health. I always ride with Victoria which does not agree with me.'

The Queen was still winning golden opinions. 'Everyone continues to sing the Queen's praises,' wrote Lady Cowper, later to become Lady Palmerston, 'there is but one mind on that question; the closer you come to her, the more you admire her. She herself is very happy, and appears to enjoy her position, but with a becoming modesty. I have never heard anyone speak a single word in dispraise of her, or find fault with her in any way—this is indeed a rare happiness.'[15]

The Queen's requirements were not exacting. She had 'my kind good friend Lord Melbourne . . . I am so fond of him and his conversations do me so much good'. Merry evenings were passed 'all sitting round a table, I drawing, the others working, laughing and talking' while the Duchess played whist which she did every evening. The Queen rode every day. 'It was a most delicious ride and Monarch went *beautifully*; he is the nicest horse I've ever ridden, so full of spirit and so soft.' Sometimes the Queen rode Duchess, 'a nice bay horse, but rather too quiet and not near so pleasant as Monarch'. Frequent visitors came to Windsor Castle including 'my *dearest most beloved* Uncle Leopold and my *dearest most beloved* Aunt Louise'. '. . . It is an inexpressible *happiness* and *joy* to me to have these dearest beloved relations with me and in *my own* house.' Queen Louise brought the young Queen two evening dresses from Paris, one light blue flowered silk, the other moiré with black lace and pink ribbons, and the Queen noted how beautifully Queen Louise herself was dressed. She played two games of draughts against her aunt after dinner, assisted by advice given her by Lord Melbourne, Lord Palmerston and Lord Conyngham. She won both times and stayed up until 11.15.

King Leopold was said to have given his sister, the Duchess of Kent, advice during his visit which had an excellent effect. She no longer appeared so disgruntled as she used, was in better spirits and was rumoured to be intending to get rid of Conroy 'which would be a wise step for her, as well as for everyone else. . . .'[16]

On Friday, 8th September, there was another merry evening: 'We were much amused by Lord Palmerston's efforts to undo a Puzzle, and by his playing at Spillikins with Mme. de Mérode, he is very agreeable and amusing.' The Queen 'played two games of German Tactics with Uncle Leopold (both of which I won) and two of draughts with dearest Aunt Louise'. She began to learn chess, taught by Queen Louise, and played a game against her advised by Lord Palmerston and Sir John Hobhouse, 'who differed totally and got quite excited and serious about it'. As a result the Queen was beaten. On 18th September the visit of King Leopold and Queen Louise came to an end with the usual torrents of grief from the Queen about which Lord Melbourne was 'very feeling'.[17]

On 28th September the Queen held a review of the 1st Regiment of Life Guards, the Grenadier Guards and a detachment of Lancers in Windsor Great Park. She was mounted, wearing the Windsor uniform, dark blue with red collar and cuffs, the Order of the Garter and a military cap. She rode up to where the Sergeant was stationed with the colours, stopped and was saluted by the troops. 'I saluted them by putting my hand to my cap like the officers do, and was much admired for my manner of doing it' she wrote in her Journal. She then cantered along the lines, with the gentlemen all in uniform, the ladies attending in carriages, and returned to her previous position for the march past and evolutions. Her mount Leopold remained steady though bands played in his face, and there was firing and skirmishing. The Queen enjoyed herself immensely. 'The whole went off beautifully' she wrote 'and I felt for the first time like a man, as if I could fight myself at the head of my Troops.'

This was the last function at Windsor. A few days later the Court moved to Brighton for a seaside autumn holiday. 'I am *very sorry* indeed to go!' wrote the Queen in her Journal on 3rd October. 'I passed such a very pleasant time here; the pleasantest summer I EVER passed in *my life*, and I shall never forget this first summer of my Reign. I have had the *great* happiness of having my beloved Uncle and Aunt here with me, I have had very pleasant people and kind friends staying with me, and I have had *delicious* rides which have done me a world of good. Lord Melbourne rode near me the whole time. The more I see of him and the more I know of him, the more I like and appreciate his fine and honest character. I have seen a great deal of him, every day, these last 5 weeks and I have always found him in good humour, kind, good and most agreeable; I have seen him in my Closet for Political Affairs, I have ridden out with him (every day), I have sat near him constantly at and after dinner, and talked about all sorts of things, and have always found him a kind and most excellent and very agreeable man. I am very fond of him. . . .'[18]

The Queen did not like Brighton and thought the Pavilion 'a strange, odd Chinese looking thing, both inside and outside; most rooms low, and I only see a little morsel of the *sea* from one of my sitting room windows. . . .' By 4th November she was back at Buckingham Palace and on 9th November was greeted by extraordinary demonstrations of affection and popularity on her way to the Guildhall for the Lord Mayor's banquet. 'Our young Queen's reception in the City was magnificent,' wrote Lady Cowper[19] to Princess Lieven, 'loyalty, worship, applause . . . all the streets decorated with flags—all the houses scaffolded—*and hardly a soldier anywhere*; this is the sort of thing that is only seen in England. In France, Austria or Russia there would have been rows of soldiers to hold back the people.'

The shadow on the Queen's happiness was still Conroy. Conroy still haunted the Palace, the Duchess still persisted in writing letters and making scenes, trying to induce the Queen to receive Conroy and his family at Court. The Queen noted 'an unhappy scene I had with poor Mama', 'an extraordinary letter I had just got from Mama'. Lord Liverpool was again called in and told Stockmar 'It is a hard and unfair trial of the Queen, whose mind and health should not be exposed to such absurd vexation and torment . . . altho' I should be very sorry to see Mother and Daughter separated, yet anything I am sure is better than the present state of things.' The Queen steadily refused to relent. 'I thought you would not expect me to invite Sir John Conroy' she wrote 'after his conduct towards me for some years past, and still more so after the unaccountable manner in which he behaved towards me, a short while before I came to the Throne. . . . I imagined you would have been *amply* satisfied with what I had done for Sir John Conroy, by giving him a pension of £3,000 a year, which only Ministers receive, and by making him a Baronet . . . I thought you would have expected no more. . . .'[20]

In November the Duchess attempted to take Conroy to attend her to the Guildhall banquet; again the Queen refused permission and again the Duchess persisted. 'When asked before my birthday' wrote the Duchess 'for the names of those I would take with me I gave in his, it was so announced by himself, by my orders. To make now a change would look like the greatest persecution. . . . I appeal to your heart, to your love for me. . . . I conjure you for the sake of your mother to relent in your line of conduct towards Sir John and his family. If you cannot like, at least forgive, and do not exclude and mark him and his family, *more* I do not ask. . . . The Queen should forget what displeased the Princess. Recollect I have the greatest regard for Sir John, I cannot forget what he has done for me and for you, although he had the misfortune to displease *you*. . . .'

The Queen again refused. 'I cannot depart from the line of conduct which I have adopted. . . .' She began, however, to show signs of strain, felt 'poorly', 'fainted', was 'sick and miserable', suffered from 'nausea'.

In November fresh difficulties and complications arose over the payment of the Duchess's debts, now admitted to amount to at least £55,000. The Duchess and Conroy wished the Queen to undertake the payment of £30,000 of the Duchess's debts out of her Privy Purse. By giving this undertaking the Queen would make herself personally responsible, no investigation would take place, and no awkward questions be asked; the

Duchess was then prepared to charge herself with the payment of £25,000 provided her income was 'suitably increased'. The Queen's Ministers refused to allow her to agree, it would be 'irreconcilable with their duty'. However, the Chancellor of the Exchequer, Mr Spring Rice, later Lord Monteagle, sent a message to the Duchess that he was prepared to recommend to Parliament that such of the Duchess's debts as had been incurred during the Queen's minority should be paid by a vote of public money. This solution was rejected by the Duchess as an outrage to her delicacy. 'She feels it due to her Honour and her position as Mother of the Queen to decline negotiating with Her Majesty's servants. . . . Please tell Mr Spring Rice she declines any negotiation with him. Rather than negotiate she will go straight to Parliament and tell her hard story.'[21]

Lord Melbourne refused to be moved by threats. '. . . It is impossible and entirely out of the question that your Majesty should be required to take this debt of £30,000 upon your Privy Purse' he told the Queen. The Duchess was offered an annual addition of £8,000 on the settlement of the Civil List, bringing her income up to £30,000 a year. Upon this offer she 'reconsidered' her previous declaration and a message was sent from the Queen to Parliament on 11th December 1837 asking for the increased income for the Duchess. When Lord Melbourne read the message in the House of Lords there was opposition from Lord Brougham, and Lord Melbourne told the Queen there might be difficulty in the House of Commons. However, the vote passed both houses, Lord Melbourne telling the Queen that 'the vote for Mama had only been carried out of respect and consideration for me'. This Lord Melbourne said 'with tears in his eyes'.[22] The affection of Parliament was further shown in the provision made for the Queen herself; an annuity of £385,000 was granted her, £10,000 more than William IV had received. Of this impressive sum £60,000 was appropriated to the Queen's Privy Purse, £131,260 to the salaries of her household, £172,500 to the expenses of her household, £13,200 to the Royal Bounty. Repairs to the Queen's official residences and the maintenance of the royal yachts were paid for by the Treasury apart from the Civil List revenues, and £8,040 was unappropriated. The Queen resigned all the hereditary revenues of the Crown, but retained the revenues of the Duchies of Lancaster and Cornwall, which, thanks to good management, doubled in a few years, producing more than £60,000 a year. On 23rd December 1837 the Queen went to Parliament in person to express her thanks, and at once began to fulfil her promise to pay off her father's debts.[23] She was careful and methodical about money, in spite of her heredity. When she came to the throne she had assured her Ministers she never got into debt on her allowance of £10 monthly and by next autumn she had paid off nearly £50,000 from her Privy Purse. A year later the whole had been discharged and in October 1839 she received formal thanks from the late Duke's creditors through Sir Henry Wheatley.

Though the Duchess's financial affairs now appeared to be settled, Conroy still remained and no means of getting rid of him appeared to exist. 'I confess to you' Lord Liverpool told Stockmar 'that much as I was prepared for Lord M's careless way of doing things, I did not expect that he would so completely have let himself be duped as he has on this occasion, when he consented to C's [Conroy's] pension Baronetcy and promise of Peerage . . . surely never was such a blunder committed as letting this man have the most unlimited means of intriguing against the Queen's government. . . .' [24]

In January 1838 trouble with the Duchess's finances began again. On 15th January the Queen wrote in her Journal 'Got _such_ a letter from Mama, oh! oh! _such_ a letter', and a few weeks later the Queen was taken aback to hear from the Duchess indicating that the increase in her income had already been swallowed up. 'I showed him [Lord Melbourne] a letter I had got from Mama yesterday, relative to her debts, at which she was much schocked [the Queen's usual spelling at this period] and grieved, I showed him also a list of the number of things I had paid and which money was owing to tradesmen; about my dress etc., etc. which had never been paid. . . . They (Mama and J.C.) ought to remember what incalculable falsehoods they have told about these debts. During the King's life [i.e. King William IV's] they said there were no debts and that it was all calumny of the King's—which is really infamous.'

The Queen confided to Lord Melbourne that being 'plagued' by her mother had a bad effect on her temper, she had great difficulty in not being irritable. Lord Melbourne told her she ought to struggle as much as she could against that feeling: 'I daresay you find you have much more command over yourself now and you can keep that in now very well.' The Queen replied 'I could but I still let out my temper towards my servants which I was very sorry for.'[25]

In addition to personal problems the Queen was working hard at learning the business of government, and at the moment was studying the mass of papers relating to the revolt in Canada which broke out in 1837, when the French and English provinces of Canada both demanded Parliamentary self-government. A large part of the Queen's Journal is devoted to the causes of the revolt, and its progress. Lord Durham, a Radical, erstwhile adviser and friend of the Duchess of Kent, was sent out to restore order. Though he was successful, his methods were so high-handed and he himself so arbitrary and arrogant, that he was recalled and dismissed, an event hailed as a Tory triumph. Before his dismissal, however, he had directed and inspired Charles Buller and Edward Gibbon Wakefield to draw up the famous Durham Report, which declared that self-government with voluntary, patriotic allegiance to the Crown was the only practical link to hold a far-flung territorial Empire together. Henceforward for many years the Durham Report formed the basis of British colonial policy.

Lord Melbourne was not the only tutor of the young Queen. Lord Palmerston, then Foreign Secretary, played an important part in her training.

There was a bond between Palmerston and Melbourne; Lord Palmerston had for many years been in love with Lord Melbourne's sister, Lady Cowper. When she became a widow they married, though both were middle-aged. The Queen enjoyed the society of Lord Palmerston, describing him as 'clever', 'amusing' and 'agreeable'. He was a man most women liked, his nickname was 'Cupid'.

Lord Palmerston taught the Queen formalities,[26] the correct method of writing to other sovereigns, the history of such matters as the regulations governing the acceptance of foreign orders and the etiquette to be observed for diplomatic presentations at drawing-rooms. He had 'atlasses' drawn to help her understand foreign despatches, supplied her with plans and an Almanach de Gotha, advised her on the treatment of notabilities ('treat Prince Orloff with tact'), and cautioned her to bear in mind when sending presents to important foreign personages that usages in other countries varied; Russians, for instance, were not allowed to wear the portrait of a foreign sovereign, otherwise the stock gift from the Queen was a miniature of herself set in diamonds to be worn as a brooch. He also taught the Queen the history of foreign relations, as affecting commerce and commercial treaties. An interview of three hours was occupied in explaining the history of Greece, particularly interesting to the Queen on account of her uncle King Leopold. Another lesson was devoted to Persia.

In the spring of 1838 the attention of the nation began to be fixed on the coronation of the Queen which was to take place on 28th June. The crowning of a young and charming girl of 19, sole sovereign of a great Empire, and enjoying unparalleled popularity among her subjects, was an event to which her ministers determined to do justice. Fifty thousand pounds had been spent on the coronation of her predecessor, William IV, but for the coronation of Queen Victoria £200,000 was voted by Parliament. Westminster Abbey was to be magnificently decorated in crimson and gold, bands were to play festive music in the Parks, a two-day fair on a huge scale with balloon ascents was arranged in Hyde Park, there were to be illuminations, firework displays. Changes in procedure were made to gratify the people. The coronation banquet had been abolished by William IV and it was decided not to revive it; a formal state procession, discontinued since the coronation of George III, was to take its place, at an extra cost of £26,000. Dressed in the coronation robes, wearing a crown and carrying the orb and sceptre, the Queen was to progress through the streets of her capital in the state coach and show herself to her subjects. The maximum number of her people was to have the opportunity of seeing their Queen. 'The great merit of this coronation is that so much has been done for the people,' wrote Greville.

The Crown of England, St Edward's Crown, traditionally placed on the head of the Sovereign at the coronation by the Archbishop of Canterbury, was heavy, weighing over 5 lb. It had been designed for King Charles II, a tall powerful man of over six feet in height, not a slender, tiny princess. Another crown was available among the Regalia known as the Imperial Crown, which had been made for the coronation of George IV and also worn by William IV at his coronation. It was thought to be 'unsuitable' for the new Queen, however, and a brand new 'Crown of State' was fashioned, using the historic jewels from the Imperial Crown, 'according to the Model approved by the Queen', at a cost of £1,000. This crown, somewhat lighter than St Edward's Crown, weighing 2 lb. 13 oz., the Queen would wear both during the coronation and the state procession afterwards.[27]

Magnificently jewelled, the Crown of State has been worn by the Sovereign on ceremonial occasions, such as the state opening of Parliament, ever since. Besides diamonds and pearls it displays the great ruby known as 'the Black Prince's Ruby' given to the Black Prince in the fourteenth century, and worn by Henry V in his helmet crown at Agincourt in 1415; the famous Stuart sapphire, almost as large, taken by James II when he fled from England and re-purchased from Cardinal Henry Benedict, the last of the Stuarts, and in the uppermost cross of the crown what may be the oldest Crown jewel of all, a sapphire said to have been taken from a ring on the finger of Edward the Confessor when his tomb was opened in the twelfth century.

Immediately before the coronation the new crown became the subject of much heart-burning. The Keeper of the Jewel House containing the Regalia at that period received no salary but was dependent for his remuneration on the shillings paid by visitors who came to see the Crown jewels. Interest in the new crown being made for the young Queen was particularly great and the keeper of the Jewel House, Mr Swift, looked forward to a golden harvest. Mr Swift's financial circumstances were not flourishing and he had a large family of infant children to provide for.

His consternation therefore was great, when Rundell, Bridge & Rundell, the celebrated jewellers who had made the new crown, placed it on show in their shop on Ludgate Hill. 'For some days past' wrote Mr Swift to the Lord Chamberlain's office on 22nd June 1838 'Her Majesty's New Crown is visited by *crowds*. . . . The street is daily & all day long lined with carriages . . . even Policemen are stationed at the doors, to keep off the passengers and regulate their entrance. I am sure, by the evidence of my own eyes yesterday and today, the numbers are to be counted each day *by hundreds*. Everyone of these would have come to the Tower *after* the Coronation . . . Now not one of them will visit the Jewel House. There is not one of Mr Bridge's visitors which is not to me a loss of at least one shilling. . . . You will I am sure, my dear Sir, feel for me, under this cruel loss of *all* my hopes & prospects which depended on the New Crown when placed in the Jewel Room. Oppressed with difficulties and distressed as I have been and am, a thing like this destroys all my chance of extrication from them.'

Mr Swift, however, was not successful, Mr Bridge maintaining to the satisfaction of Lord Conyngham, the Lord Chamberlain, that interest in every detail of the coronation, especially in the new Crown of State, was so great that the exhibition in his shop had merely 'whetted' the public appetite for further inspection. Admission to Mr Bridge's establishment had been by complimentary gratuitous ticket, and police protection had been obtained to prevent his doors being forced by the crowd.

As the day of the coronation approached London became packed. 'There never was anything seen like the state of this town,' wrote Greville, 'it is as if the population had been on a sudden quintupled; the uproar, the confusion, the crowd, the noise are indescribable. Horsemen, footmen, carriages squeezed, jammed, intermingled, the pavement blocked up with timbers, hammering and knocking, and falling fragments stunning the ears and threatening the head; not a mob here or there, but the town all mob, thronging, bustling, gaping, and gazing at everything, at anything, or at nothing; the Park one vast encampment, with banners floating on the tops of the tents, and still the roads are covered, the railroads loaded with arriving multitudes.'[28]

Stands had been erected along the whole route of the procession, and four hundred thousand people were said to have spent the night before the coronation in the streets.

On the afternoon of 27th June, at 4.20 p.m. the Queen, in an open carriage, drove to Westminster Abbey, 'crowds in the streets and all *so* friendly' she wrote. She wished to try the thrones she was to use next day. It was fortunate she did; both were too low.

This was the only attempt at anything in the nature of a rehearsal given the Queen for a ceremonial lasting about five hours, an ordeal that even on its physical side would be severe. Dr John Ireland, Dean of Westminster, officially in charge, was too infirm even to attend; he had been Dean of Westminster since 1816, was nearly 78 and had conducted the coronation service for George IV as well as for William IV. His place was taken by the Sub-Dean, Lord John Thynne, who rehearsed with the

Archbishop but no one else. The Bishop of Durham, Dr Maltby, who had an important part to play—at one moment he was in charge of the orb—was, complained the Queen, 'remarkably maladroit and never could tell me what was to take place'. The Queen herself showed presence of mind, seemed, to spectators at least, never to lose her composure and performed her part with 'great grace and completeness', but the other participants, the officiating clergy in particular, 'were always in doubt as to what came next', wrote Benjamin Disraeli, who was present.

On the night before the coronation, the Queen slept badly; she had, she wrote, 'a feeling that something very awful was going to happen tomorrow'.[29] At 4 o'clock on the morning of the coronation, Thursday, 28th June, she was woken by the sound of guns firing in the Park, and 'could not get to sleep again on account of the noise of the people in the streets, bands etc.' At 7 a.m. she got up and looked out at the Green Park which presented a 'curious spectacle', crowds of people up Constitution Hill, soldiers and bands. She made two attempts before she could eat any breakfast. Princess Feodora, who was staying at Buckingham Palace, came into her room and by 9.30 she was dressed, wearing the white satin petticoat ornamented with gold and the red velvet kirtle she had worn to prorogue Parliament, and on her head a circlet of gold set with diamonds. At 10 a.m. accompanied by the Duchess of Sutherland, Mistress of the Robes, and Lord Albemarle, Master of the Horse, the Queen got into the state coach for the first part of her progress up Constitution Hill, along Piccadilly, down St James's Street and across Trafalgar Square to Westminster Abbey. The crowds were immense, larger than the Queen had ever seen, 'many as there were the day I went to the City, it was nothing—nothing, to the multitudes, the millions, of my loyal subjects who were assembled in *every spot* to witness the Procession. Their good-humour and excessive loyalty was beyond everything, and I really cannot say *how* proud I feel to be the Queen of *such* a *Nation*.'

During the period of waiting within the Abbey more licence was permitted than today and popular arrivals were greeted with a murmur of applause, the loudest being for the Duke of Wellington until the arrival of Marshal Soult, the old opponent of the Duke in the Peninsula, special envoy from France, who was greeted by acclamation the whole way down the nave of the Abbey to the choir and had been cheered all along the route. He was moved to tears by the generosity of his reception.

The Queen reached the west door of the Abbey 'amid deafening cheers', a little after 11.30 a.m. and when she had assumed her red Parliamentary robe lined with ermine in the robing room, her eight train-bearers took hold of it and Lord Conyngham, the Lord Chamberlain, picked up the end. The train-bearers, all young unmarried girls, wore white and silver dresses, with silver wreaths trimmed with pink rose buds in their hair.

Their dresses, designed by the Duchess of Richmond, had been the subject of complaints, but the Duchess had her way; she told Lord Melbourne 'One thing I was determined about; that I would have no discussion with their Mammas about it.' Lord Melbourne thought the dresses beautiful, the effect was as if the Queen floated in a silvery cloud.

As soon as the Queen's mantle was arranged the procession began, the Queen's 'very diminutive' childish figure immediately preceded by Lord Melbourne, who carried the Sword of State, which he found 'excessively heavy', led by the other great officers of state bearing the Regalia and the Bishops carrying the Chalice, the Patena and the Bible. When the interior of the Abbey burst on the Queen she paused, caught her breath, clasped her hands and turned pale. The scene was breath-taking, the Abbey gorgeous in crimson and gold, the rows of peeresses blazing with diamonds facing the peers in their robes, the magnificent copes of the Bishops, which had been worn at the coronation of King James I, the altar covered with splendid gold plate.

Slowly, the elaborate antique ceremonial unwound. The boys of Westminster School exercised their historic privilege of shouting 'Vivat Victoria Regina'; the Recognition of the Queen, presented by the Archbishop, as 'the undoubted Queen of this realm' was greeted by a universal cry of 'God Save Queen Victoria' while the Queen turned herself to north, south and west; the Litany was recited and the Queen took the oath to maintain the Protestant religion 'as established by law', afterwards kneeling in prayer while the choir sang 'Veni, Creator, Spiritus'. Retiring to St Edward's Chapel, 'a small dark place behind the altar' wrote the Queen, she took off her robes, divested herself of her circlet of diamonds, and having assumed a linen shift and the super tunica of cloth of gold returned bare-headed to the Abbey where, as she sat in St Edward's Chair, four Knights of the Garter held a canopy of cloth of gold over her head and the Archbishop performed the ceremony of the Anointing. The want of rehearsal was evident. 'Pray tell me what I am to do, for they [the officiating clergy] don't know' the Queen begged Lord John Thynne at one solemn moment. The orb, put into her hand unexpectedly by the Bishop of Durham, proved almost too heavy for her to hold. When the right moment came for the Archbishop to hand her the orb, she had it already, and the Bishop of Durham had 'disappeared'.

The supreme moment was now approaching. The Dalmatic robe of cloth of gold lined with ermine was clasped round the Queen, she received the sceptre and the ring which the Archbishop forced on to the wrong finger, so that she nearly screamed with pain, and, after saying a short prayer for the Queen, the Archbishop received the Crown of State from the acting Dean of Westminster and placed it on her head. At the same instant with a flashing of diamonds all the peers and peeresses put on their coronets, guns fired in the Parks and at the Tower, drums beat, trumpets sounded while the Abbey and the streets outside resounded with shouts of 'God Save the Queen'.

Lord Melbourne, who was standing near the Queen, was, she noted, '*completely* overcome', and she herself was greatly moved.

The Enthronisation and Homage followed, the Archbishop first, followed by the Queen's uncles and the peers in turn. While the peers were doing homage the Lord Chamberlain and his officers flung medals, designed by Pistrucci, among the spectators and an undignified scramble followed, the maids of honour being especially active. The Commons for the first time in history took a part in the ceremony, cheering their sovereign nine times. 'There was another most dear being present at this ceremony' wrote the Queen 'in the box immediately above the Royal Box, and who witnessed all; it was my dearly beloved Lehzen, whose eyes I caught when on the Throne and we exchanged smiles.'

A celebrated incident occurred during the ceremony. Old Lord Rolle, who was 82 years old and infirm, stumbled as he was about to offer his homage; he fell to the bottom of the steps of the throne but was not hurt. As he was about to make the attempt to re-ascend, the Queen, exclaiming 'May I not get up and meet him?' rose from the throne and descended the steps 'to the end' to prevent another fall. The simplicity and kindliness of the Queen evinced in this incident made a great impression. 'Nothing could be more effective' commented Benjamin Disraeli.

At the conclusion of the Homage the Queen left the throne and, taking off the crown and divesting herself of the symbols of temporal sovereignty, received the Sacrament alone. As she knelt at the altar, a ray of sunlight illuminated her bare head, and the Duchess of Kent burst into tears.

The Queen then put on her crown and robes again while the service continued. A pencil note made by the Sub-Dean in his copy of the Order of Service records that, after the *Gloria in Excelsis* was sung, the Bishop of Bath and Wells, it was 'supposed from turning over two pages' at once, informed the Queen that 'the Service was concluded and H.M. retired to the Confessor's Chapel. The Sub-Dean inquired of the Ld. Chamberlain (Conyngham) if H.M. was ill. "No," he said, "all is over." Being told that it was not all over reference was made to H.M. and by her order to the Sub-Dean for advice. He referred the L.Ch. to the Prime Minister (Melbourne) who replied "What does it signify?".'[30] But the Sub-Dean insisted, the Queen was brought back and the service proceeded to its finale; the choir burst into the Hallelujah Chorus while the Queen with her ladies and train bearers and the peers bearing the regalia withdrew—correctly, this time—to St Edward's Chapel, Lord Melbourne remarking it was 'more *unlike* a Chapel than anything he had ever seen; for, what was *called* an *Altar* was covered with sandwiches, bottles of wine, etc'.

The Archbishop now came in and should have delivered the orb, but the Queen had already got it. Lord Melbourne, who seemed completely worn out, drank a glass of wine and the Queen changed her robes once more, assuming her royal robe of purple velvet, and again put on the Crown of State which she admitted hurt her 'a good deal'. She took the orb in her left hand and the sceptre in her right and, the procession having-reformed, 'thus *loaded*' proceeded through the Abbey which resounded with cheers, to the robing-room, where the Duchess of Kent was waiting with two of the Queen's aunts. The ceremony, which had lasted for five hours, was at an end.

A delay of about an hour followed, occupied by the Queen in having her hand bathed in ice-cold water, to remove the ring which the Archbishop had forced on to the wrong finger, 'which I did at last with great pain'.

At about 4.30 p.m. the Queen re-entered the state coach in full panoply, wearing the Crown, attired in robes of purple velvet, carrying the sceptre in her right and the orb in her left hand, and drove back to Buckingham Palace by the same route which she had followed to the Abbey. The crowds, if possible, were larger and the thunders of applause even more enthusiastic. She writes in her diary that she reached Buckingham Palace a little after six 'and I shall ever remember this day as the *proudest* of my life'. Lord Melbourne said 'I must congratulate you on this most brilliant day', adding 'And you did it beautifully—every part of it, with so much taste; it's a thing that you can't give a person advice upon; it must be left to a person.'

Count Sebastiani, the French Ambassador, told the Queen he had no idea 'que les Cérémonies Protestantes fussent aussi belles'; and that he had seen Napoleon's coronation when the Pope officiated and that it had not been so touching 'ni *si imposant*'.

Lord Melbourne was not at all well. He had over-exerted himself at the coronation, found the Sword of State much too heavy, was anxious about the Queen, and took a large dose of laudanum, which disagreed with him, to get through the State Ball next day. Finally he had to go to bed. The Queen was upset. 'This is *most provoking and vexatious*, and makes me *quite cross*' she wrote on 4th July 'for I'm *so* spoilt and accustomed to see this *kind* and I *may* venture to say *even dear* friend . . . *every day* that I'm *quite annoyed* and *put out* when my agreeable daily visit does not take place. . . . And I've a Council today . . . and there I must be, as it were, without the person who makes me feel safe and comfortable.'[31] At this point the Queen recollected that the diary was going to be read by Lehzen and hastened to pay her a compliment as well, 'for when Lehzen cannot be with me, I feel *he* replaces her; but I'm childish, though these feelings are *very* natural'. She had recently flattered Lehzen by giving her a new pet name 'Daisy', 'my adored angel Daisy'.

From this date onwards the Queen never speaks affectionately of Lord Melbourne without handing out a compliment to Lehzen as well; Lehzen had become so jealous and possessive that the Queen was frightened of her.

On 10th July the Queen had a slight rash on her hands which by the 13th covered both hands and neck and 'somewhat astonished' Lord Melbourne who told her 'on no account to scratch it'. Once more the Queen was suffering from nervous strain. Throughout the coronation period the burden imposed on her was heavy. The strain of the coronation ceremony itself was followed by a State Ball, a review in honour of Marshal Soult, the acceptance of a large number of loyal addresses, more than twenty in one day, and speeches of congratulation. The Queen visited the amusements of the people, the fair in Hyde Park, and coronation dinners, performing these duties unsupported and alone.

In addition Conroy was giving trouble. On 9th March 1838 *The Times* had published an article attacking Conroy and casting doubt on the integrity of his management of the Duchess of Kent's affairs. The reference to Conroy was unmistakable—'a certain newly created baronet attached to the Household of the Duchess of Kent when her daughter ascended the throne of these realms'. It was suggested that the Duchess's debts amounted to about £80,000 and that an annuity of £30,000 had recently been granted to her with 'an understanding that a gradual liquidation of the £80,000 should silently take place'. 'Who can so well understand wiping off as he who has chalked on?' enquired *The Times*, and mentioned 'a certain estate in Wales, purchased and paid for not long ago. If any public enquiry should take place whence the money for the payment came who so competent to answer the question as the Baronet?' At this Conroy lodged a criminal information for libel against *The Times*. Determined to prove justification, *The Times* issued a number of subpoenas calling on persons connected with the Duchess of Kent to attend as witnesses and give evidence at the trial. Lehzen, Stockmar, Lord Conyngham, the Lord Chamberlain, Lord Melbourne all received writs and it was rumoured that the Duchess herself would be called. Lord Melbourne remarked she would probably enjoy it. He himself, he told the Queen, could not be examined because he was a member of the Privy Council. He explained to the Queen that the object of *The Times* was not to discredit or attack anyone except Conroy, but to show that *The Times* authorities could prove justification if they were allowed to take evidence from the witnesses. This, however, would not be permitted.

The Queen was disturbed because she had heard through Stockmar that the Duchess of Kent was piling up debts again and borrowing from Coutts Bank. Lord Melbourne said 'If she gets into debt again, she will be in a dreadful scrape' and observed that paying off her debts naturally left her with a smallish income. The Queen said £12,000 a year *ought* to be enough and Lord Melbourne agreed, 'if' he said 'it is well managed but not if *he* makes money by it'.[32]

What seemed a minor unpleasantness was the return of Lady Flora Hastings to the Duchess of Kent's household as lady-in-waiting. The Queen, during the Ramsgate period when, she wrote, 'indescribable torments' were inflicted on her by Conroy and her mother, had learned to dislike and distrust Lady Flora. The Queen told Lord Melbourne that Lady Flora was 'an amazing *spy*, who would repeat everything she heard, and that he better take care of what he said before her'. He said 'I'll take care', and 'we both agreed it was a very disagreeable thing having her in the house'. However, the Queen was powerless, and on 25th April Lady Mary Stopford, sister of Lord Courtown, was replaced 'by that odious Lady Flora'.[33] The Queen told Lord Melbourne that Lady Mary had incurred the displeasure of the Duchess by living on good terms with the Queen's ladies.

The summer of 1838, in spite of the glories of the coronation, did not have the halcyon radiance of the summer of 1837. The first raptures, the carnival of praise and admiration which had followed the Queen's accession were over, and the Queen was losing the flower-like delicacy which had made her girlish looks touching. As early as August 1837 Lord Holland commented that the Queen looked 'more robust'; in November 1838 he thought she looked well but her appearance had not improved. Her complexion was a little rougher and muddier than was becoming, perhaps from constant riding, and 'she has perhaps rather more appearance of a full habit of body than nice & nervous observers of health would quite approve'.[34] She was putting on weight, a tendency she was to struggle against for the rest of her life. Lord Melbourne repeatedly told her she ate too much—over-eating, he said, was a family failing. He considered the sick headaches and fits of irritation from which she suffered could be cured by a strict attention to diet. The Queen loved beer, but she ought not to drink it. He remarked that it was not good to eat when one was not hungry, but only when one was hungry. Upon which the Queen said '*I* should be eating all day', since she was always hungry. Lady Holland wrote to Lord Melbourne from Paris that gossip reported the Queen's new dresses were being made larger, which the Queen admitted was true, but declared the explanation was that she could not bear anything tight. Lord Melbourne told her if she did not want to be fat she ought to walk more, she would soon lose the use of her legs. The Queen retorted that she disliked walking for the sake of walking, it made her feel tired and sick. Lord Melbourne insisted that the only way to prevent getting fat was to take exercise. For the sake of her health she should get out more in the fresh air and be prudent about her diet. On 13th December 1838 the Queen was weighed and 'to my horror' found she weighed 8 stone 13 lb., 'an incredible weight for my size'. Lord M. noticed she was 'rather yellow', and she felt 'cross and low'. Disenchantment had begun. 'This year I did not enjoy pleasure so much' wrote the Queen; she was 'quite changed from what I was last year'. The year as Queen of England had had its effect.[35] Stockmar, who sent daily reports from London to King Leopold, found she had become 'as passionate as a spoilt child, if she feels offended she throws everything overboard without exception'.

Stockmar found the Queen 'had begun to take ill every piece of advice . . . which does not agree with her own opinion, and to see it as unjustified and undeserved criticism. On these occasions I have also found in her an underlying feeling that resembles the wounded pride of a person so highly placed that she says to herself "in normal circumstances these admonitions might be appropriate, but for me they are out of place" . . . and Lehzen encourages her. Just like the nurse who hits the stone that tripped the child up.'[36] The Queen had become estranged from her uncle, King Leopold, whom she found interfering. Since her accession he appeared 'nettled' that she did not ask his advice more often, 'but dear Uncle is given to believe that he must rule the roast [sic] everywhere'. His influence over herself, the Queen noted, was now small. 'Lehzen always tells her she is right,' wrote Stockmar, 'the uncle cannot love the niece as much as he pretends, or he would not reproach and hurt her. . . .'

Lehzen was 'extraordinarily suspicious'. She thought King Leopold wanted to hasten on the marriage with Albert 'so as to be able to rule the niece through the husband'. Queen Victoria and Prince Albert had not met since 1836, and neither was prepossessed in the other's favour at this moment. The Queen sent Stockmar a letter from Prince Albert 'to show how badly he writes'. Stockmar had to admit that 'the letter could not be poorer in content nor less clearly expressed'. She denied to King Leopold that she had ever made anything in the nature of a promise to Albert, '. . . one can never answer beforehand for feelings and I may not have the feeling for him which is requisite to ensure happiness. I may like him as a friend, and as a cousin and as a brother . . . and should this be the case (which is not likely) I am very anxious that it should be understood that I am not guilty of any breach of promise, for I never gave any.'[37] This, however, was hardly accurate. Prince Albert wrote that he heard Victoria had become 'fearfully obstinate',[38] took no interest in nature but liked to stay up dancing all night and sleep half the day.

Estrangement between King Leopold and the young Queen was increased by political events. In 1838 English statesmen became anxious to have the questions between Belgium and Holland settled which had been pending since the separation of the two countries in 1830, when Leopold became King of the Belgians. Settlement could be reached only by the agreement of the four great powers, Austria, Prussia, England and

France, by whom a conference was called in London. To the Queen's dismay and irritation King Leopold announced his intention of coming over. She wrote urgently to Stockmar to stop him '. . . everybody, all Europe wld say he comes for his own affairs and if he fails how awkward his position wld be. . . . Lord Melbourne is excessively anxious that Uncle shld not come at least till the end of Sept. when we should hope matters will be settled perhaps. Lord Palmerston is equally, nay more eager. . . . It is so self evident to me that I can't conceive Uncle's not seeing it. . . .'[39]

The Queen's attitude made King Leopold angry. A state of affairs had come about 'in which they [the Belgian people] seem destined to be *bullied* by *everybody* and *protected* by *nobody*. This feeling is strongest against *England*—which the people expected to see a support and only found a strong determination to decide *everything against them*.'[40]

Lord Melbourne, however, drafted a soothing letter for the Queen, speaking of her great affection for her uncle and the importance of settling the Belgian question, while Stockmar told King Leopold it was essential that he should explain to the Queen his intention to 'keep to a basic text',[41] namely, 'Heaven knows I do not want to criticise you, tutor you, marry you off, rule you—in short I want only your well being. I shall not speak to you again about your marriage until you yourself ask me to. If you have no need whatsoever to talk to me about affairs of state and hear my advice then we can avoid that too. . . .'

The Belgian negotiations continued until 19th April 1839, when Lord Palmerston sent a message to the Queen[42] that a successful solution had at last been reached: 'Treaties between Belgium and Holland . . . have just been signed, so that this long pending matter is at length finally settled.'

In this uneasy atmosphere the Queen found herself confronted with the first major problem of her reign.

On 2nd February 1839 the Queen noted in her Journal that she had informed Lord Melbourne of an 'awkward business' which had arisen in connection with Lady Flora Hastings. After rejoining the Duchess's household in November, Lady Flora had not been in the Palace above two days before Lehzen and the Queen noticed how exceedingly suspicious her figure looked, 'more have since observed this, and we have no doubt that she is—to use the plain words—*with child*!!' Sir James Clark, physician both to the Queen and the Duchess of Kent, 'cannot deny the suspicion' the Queen wrote; 'the horrid cause of all this is the Monster and Demon Incarnate, whose name I forbear to mention [Conroy] . . . Lady Tavistock, accordingly, with Lehzen's concurrence told Lord Melbourne of it . . . he, accordingly replied to me this evening, without—very properly—mentioning names, that the only way is to be quiet and watch it. . . . Clark had told him it had been reported about.'[43]

In spite of the Biblical starkness of the Queen's language—Lady Flora 'is with child'—she was an ignorant young girl. Melbourne talked to her frankly, considering some degree of enlightenment part of her education, but she had no experience and no judgment. In the tragic situation which now unfolded, her long-standing dislike of Lady Flora, dating back to the years of 'torment' at Kensington and the Duchess of Kent's attempt to break up the relationship between her daughter and Lehzen by imposing the constant presence of Lady Flora on them, stifled the normally generous impulses of the Queen's nature. An intimate relationship was also said to exist between Lady Flora and Conroy, and the Queen's hatred for Conroy was pathological—it was a subject on which she was hardly sane. Some months before the change in her figure became noticeable, Lady Flora had travelled back overnight from Scotland, alone in a post-chaise with Conroy. Melbourne indiscreetly told the Queen that the Duchess of Kent was jealous of Lady Flora, commenting that he himself considered Lady Flora the ugliest woman he had ever seen.[44] His advice to the Queen in the present situation was his customary advice, she should do nothing and the matter would settle itself. 'If you remain quite quiet, you'll get through it well' he said.

Worse advice could hardly have been given. Melbourne failed to grasp the dangerous vulnerability to scandal of 'the Court of a young unmarried girl Queen'. The Queen, by no means displeased by Lady Flora's plight, gleefully predicted 'that odious Lady Flora' was about to be shown up in her true colours. Melbourne agreed Lady Flora's character was bad and she was 'odd in her manner' and 'free' in her conversation, but he did not appreciate what popular feeling would be at the association of the Queen with such a sordid and discreditable story nor the possibilities of the case of Lady Flora being used as a political weapon in the hands of the Tories against the Whigs.

Advice to 'keep quite quiet' proved impossible to follow. The Court seethed with gossip, 'it was at first whispered about, and at last swelled into a report and finally into a charge'. With whom the charge originated was not clear. The Queen insisted with childish pride that she herself with Lehzen had first noticed the change in Lady Flora's figure. There was mention by the Conroy party of 'a snake in the grass', i.e. Lehzen, whose antagonism to Lady Flora was known. The names of Lady Portman, a senior member of the ladies of the Queen's bedchamber, Lady Tavistock, daughter-in-law of the Duke of Bedford, and 'ladies of the Palace' were also cited. According to a statement made by Lady Flora herself,[45] she came into waiting on the Duchess of Kent on 10th January 1839, and having been suffering from bilious illnesses since the beginning of December placed herself under the care of Sir James Clark. To Clark's rough manners and discourtesy a large part of what followed must be attributed. 'Unfortunately' wrote Lady Flora 'he either did not pay much attention to my ailments or did not quite understand them, for in spite of his remedies, the bile did not take its departure. However, by dint of walking and porter I gained a little strength and as I did so the swelling subsided to a very remarkable degree.' She had her dresses taken in. From 10th January until 16th February Sir James Clark visited Lady Flora twice a week, and on several occasions examined her over her dress. He then asked to be allowed to examine her without her clothes, which Lady Flora refused. On 16th February, according to Lady Flora's statement, 'Sir James Clark came to me, and asked me if I were privately married, giving as his reason that my figure had excited the remarks of "the ladies of the palace". On my emphatic denial he became excited, urged me to "confess" as "the only thing to save me" and stated his own conviction to agree with that of the "ladies"; it had occurred to him at the first that "no one could look at me and doubt it", and remarks even yet more coarse.'

The same day Lady Portman asked the Duchess of Kent for an audience, which the Duchess declined. Lord Portman, Lady Portman's husband, an amiable and loyal man, devoted to his wife but not distinguished for wisdom, then intervened and on Sunday, 17th February, asked for and obtained an interview with the Duchess of Kent. A document exists in the Royal Archives endorsed 'Draft of what Lady Portman was to say, and did say, to the Duchess of Kent on Sunday, 17th February 1839'.[46] 'That Sir James Clark, having expressed his strong suspicion upon this subject, it is impossible that the honour, either of the Court, or of the Lady can admit of the least doubt or delay in clearing up the matter. . . . That if the suspicion is unfounded, it should be removed as speedily as possible. If well founded the Lady should leave the Palace immediately. That nothing but the opinion of medical men can possibly be satisfactory. That it is quite impossible that the Queen should admit the Lady into her presence until her character is cleared.'

Lady Flora now came to the conclusion that however distasteful she must submit to a medical examination. On being asked to name a second physician Lady Flora named Sir Charles Clarke, an eminent practitioner who was expected shortly at the Palace and who had known her from childhood. As it happened Sir Charles had arrived earlier than expected; he was already in the Palace and the examination took place the same day in the presence of Lady Portman and Lady Flora's own maid, who was dissolved in tears. Sir James Clark was accused of behaving with unnecessary roughness. So humane and experienced an observer as Lord Holland considered that 'the poor young lady' 'on medical examination must have been exposed to dreadful mortification and have submitted to much indelicate enquiry'.[47] The result of the examination was Lady Flora's vindication. The two doctors issued a certificate, dated Buckingham Palace, 17th February 1839, and signed Charles M. Clarke, M.D. Jas. Clark, M.D., which declared 'We have examined with great care the state of Lady Flora Hastings with a view to determine the existence, or non-existence, of pregnancy, and it is our opinion, although there is an enlargement of the stomach, that there are no grounds for suspicion that pregnancy does exist, or ever has existed.'[48] On receiving the report the Duchess of Kent instantly dismissed Sir James Clark from her service.

Consternation followed. 'The Court is plunged in shame and mortification at the exposure' wrote Greville. '. . . The Palace is full of bickerings and heart-burnings, while the whole proceeding is looked upon by society at large as to the last degree disgusting and disgraceful. It is inconceivable how Melbourne can have permitted this disgraceful and mischievous scandal, which cannot fail to lower the Court in the eyes of the world, and from a participation in which discredit the Queen's youth and inexperience can alone exempt her. There may be objections to Melbourne's extraordinary domiciliation in the Palace; but the compensation ought to be found in his good sense and experience preventing the possibility of such transactions and *tracasseries* as these.'[49]

Lady Flora had proved to be a virgin, but Sir Charles Clarke mentioned to Lord Melbourne he had known cases when, nevertheless, pregnancy had taken place. Melbourne repeated this statement to the Queen and the Queen to the Duchess of Kent. Suspicion continued to rest on Lady Flora and when the Queen talked to Lord Melbourne of 'Lady Flora's being ill (she hasn't appeared since Tuesday) and so sick. "Sick?" said Lord M. with a significant laugh.'

Immediately the medical examination had cleared Lady Flora's character, the Queen sent a message by Lady Portman, expressing her regret and offering to see Lady Flora that evening, but Lady Flora was too wretchedly ill to appear, and it was not until a week later that the interview took place. The Duchess of Kent meanwhile looked after Lady Flora personally and treated her 'with all the tenderness of a mother'. On 23rd February 1839 the Queen made peace with her mother, seeing the Duchess twice, and received a promise from her '*all is over*, and is promised to be *forgotten* for *my* sake. . . .' The interview with Lady Flora followed in the Queen's own sitting-room. 'She was dreadfully agitated' wrote the Queen 'and looked very ill, but on my embracing her, taking her by the hand, and expressing great concern at what had happened, and my wish that all should be forgotten,—she expressed herself exceedingly grateful to me, and said, that for Mama's sake she would suppress every wounded feeling, and would forget it etc.'[50] This solution seemed perfectly satisfactory to the Queen, who, since peace and harmony within the Palace were apparently restored, turned back to her latest craze, Van Amburgh the celebrated lion-tamer and his lions, whose portraits were being painted by Landseer.

Lady Flora herself seemed satisfied and even went so far as to thank Lady Portman for her conduct during the affair. Conroy, however, was still hanging about the Palace and he was 'the prime mover in all the subsequent hubbub', inciting Lady Flora and the Duchess of Kent to new outbursts of wrath and throwing fresh fuel on the flames. The Hastings were a family noted for pride and violent temper; Lady Flora herself behaved with duplicity, for while she was pretending general reconciliation and amicability at Buckingham Palace, she was writing to her uncle by marriage, Mr Hamilton FitzGerald, who had married her aunt Lady Charlotte Hastings in 1814, a letter containing the facts and allegations which were to produce a second explosion.

In May 1839 the Queen found herself faced with a much graver crisis. Experienced observers, like the Whig Lord Holland, were of opinion that the Lady Flora Hastings affair was being given publicity as a political weapon by the Tories to discredit the young Queen and her Court. 'The Tories are just now more busy' wrote Lord Holland to Lord Granville in Paris 'in inventing imaginary propaganda and commenting on scandalous tales about the Palace, with a view of lowering the Queen and all about her. They have made poor Lady Flora Hastings the peg on whom to hang all their calumnies. They pretend that she has been, or is, falsely accused at Court of having been with child & the Queen has most harshly forbidden her and her mother's [the Duchess of Kent's] appearance at dinner. . . . I believe there is not the shadow of foundation for the scandal, but it is rather ominous that such stories, true or false, should have begun to be canvassed about the Court of a Virgin Queen. . . .'[51]

The Queen was a devoted Whig, her father had been a Whig, her friends, almost without exception, were Whigs, Lord Melbourne was a Whig, she had no hesitation in declaring openly with what regret and sorrow she anticipated the eventual victory of the Tories. The present position of the Whig party was a source of perpetual anxiety to her. During the past four years, in spite of two considerable accessions of support, the Irish led by O'Connell, and the unconcealed favour of the Queen, the weakness of the Whig party had become almost daily more apparent. They were 'as tottering as the French Government', and on 22nd March 1839 had been defeated by five votes in the House of Lords on a motion to enquire into the state of Ireland. On hearing the news the Queen burst into tears and remained sobbing for some time.

Lord Melbourne, however, did not intend to resign on a defeat in the

House of Lords. In 1836 he had declared that as long as he retained the confidence of the Crown, and of the House of Commons, he would continue to carry on the Queen's government. But, he told the Queen, after the Easter holidays the wishes of the House of Commons must be ascertained by a vote approving or disapproving the policy of the Whig government in Ireland. 'If we lose that question, or carry it by a small majority, we must resign. . . .'[52]

Meanwhile, the long and detailed letter written by Lady Flora Hastings to Mr Hamilton FitzGerald had reached him in Brussels on 13th March 1839, and was being 'extensively circulated' in private.[53] The accusation against the Queen was that she had failed to make any adequate reparation or even adequate apology to Lady Flora for the false charges brought against her, and for the humiliating ordeal to which she had been sub-jected. Moreover the Queen, unlike the Duchess of Kent, had not dis-missed Sir James Clark from her household when the result of Lady Flora's examination became known. On the contrary, he continued to hold his appointment as her personal physician undisturbed. In May 1839, when the position of the Whig government was becoming daily more critical, Mr Hamilton Fitzgerald wrote to *The Times* quoting from Lady Flora's letter and alleging this step was forced on the Hastings family by scandalous falsehoods current about Lady Flora in all the capitals of Europe.

Throughout the session of 1839 Lord Melbourne's government steadily lost its hold on the House of Commons. The government, however, fell unexpectedly on a colonial issue. The sugar planters of Jamaica refused to approve the great measures abolishing slavery and negro apprentice-ship in the British Empire passed by the British Imperial Parliament in 1834–1835. The Whig government proposed to suspend the Constitution of Jamaica for five years and rule by a Governor General and Council. The Tories considered this unnecessary and were supported by a number of Radicals. Defeat, or a majority so narrow as to be unworkable in practice, was inevitable.

On Tuesday, 7th May, the blow fell. Lord Melbourne's government had a majority of only five in the Commons, and Lord Melbourne sent a letter to the Queen saying that, in his opinion, 'the determination of the Cabinet must be that the relative numbers upon this vote . . . leave your Majesty's confidential servants no alternative but to resign their offices into your Majesty's hands.'[54]

The effect on the Queen was catastrophic. 'The state of agony, grief and despair into which this placed me may be easier imagined than de-scribed! *All all* my happiness gone! That happy peaceful life destroyed, that dearest kind Lord Melbourne no more my minister. . . . I sobbed and cried much; could only put on my dressing gown. At 10 m past 12 came Lord Melbourne. . . . It was some minutes before I could muster up courage to go in—and when I did, I really thought my heart would break; he was standing near the window; I took that kind, dear hand of his, and sobbed and grasped his hand in both mine and looked at him and sobbed out, "You will not forsake me"; I held his hand for a little while, unable to leave go; and he gave me such a look of kindness, pity, and affection, and could hardly utter for tears, "Oh! no," in such a touching voice. We then sat down as usual and I strove to calm myself. . . . After a pause he said "You must try and be as collected as you can and act with great firmness and decision. I don't think you'll hear any more of Lady Flora Hastings; that was only kept up for party purposes." . . . I went on crying and feeling as thoroughly wretched as human mortal can be.'[55]

At 3 that afternoon the Queen saw Lord John Russell; she was still unable to control her feelings, crying and sobbing throughout the interview. She wrote three times during the afternoon begging Lord Melbourne to dine or at least to come and see her. He refused to dine, it would not be proper while the negotiations for forming a new government were in progress; he did, however, call during the afternoon and gave her a paper, in which he had written instructions as to what, in his opinion, she should do. She should send for the Duke of Wellington, and if the Duke advised her to send for Sir Robert Peel, she must take his advice. She must make allowance for Sir Robert Peel's 'close stiff manner', and she must be vigilant that all measures and appointments were stated correctly, as, owing to the confidence with which the Queen had honoured Lord Melbourne, preliminaries may have been left too much to Lord Melbourne's discretion. ' "Your Majesty had better express your hope that none of your Majesty's Household, except those who are engaged in politics may be removed. . . . I think you might ask him [Sir Robert Peel] for that." I quite agreed in this . . . I said it was so hard to have people forced on you whom you disliked; Lord M. said "It is very hard, but it can't be helped." I burst into tears and said "You don't know what a dreadful thing it is for me." . . . He looked really *so* kindly at me and seemed much affected.' He then told the Queen that he had better not come to see her again while the negotiations were going on. 'I sobbed much, again held his hand in both mine, and kept holding his hand for some time fast in one of mine, as if I felt in doing so he could not leave me. . . . He then got up, and we shook hands again and he kissed my hand, I crying dreadfully. . . . I wrote once more to him. "The Queen ventures to maintain one thing, wh she thinks *is possible*; wh: is, that if she rode out tomorrow afternoon, she might just get a glimpse of Lord Melbourne in the Park; if he knew where she rode, she wld meet him, as she did Lord Anglesey, & various others,—& it wld be such a comfort; there surely cld be no earthly harm in this; for, I may *meet anyone*; Ld Melbourne may think this childish but the Queen *really* is so *anxious* it might be; & she wld bear thro' all her trials so much better if she cld just see a friends face sometimes." . . . I could eat nothing. Wrote one line to the Duke of Wellington to request him to come. Till nine, I sobbed and cried convulsively . . . and went to bed calmer at 12.'

'On waking *all* this dreadful reality came back most forcibly to my mind and I cried dreadfully.' Lord Melbourne called to see the Queen during the morning. She could write to him now, as under the British Constitution all Ministers retain their offices until their successors are appointed; 'Tell the Baroness [Lehzen] to put it into a cover and send it to me' Lord Melbourne told her and warned her against showing ' "too great dislikes to people, for that's repeated and creates such bitter enemies . . . they'll not touch your ladies," Lord M. added. I said they dared not and I never would allow it.'[56]

On Wednesday morning, 8th May, the Duke of Wellington called on the Queen, who had regained her calmness and self-possession. The interview lasted about twenty minutes. The Duke told her he regretted that his age and deafness prevented him from serving her as he would desire and he advised her to send for Sir Robert Peel, in whom she could place confidence and who was a man of honour and integrity. The Queen spoke of her sorrow at having to part from her Ministers, particularly Lord Melbourne for whom she felt the warmest regard and who had acted almost a parental part towards her. 'The Duke was excessively pleased with her behaviour and with her frankness.' He told the Queen she should write to Sir Robert Peel herself, not send a message, and this she agreed to do. The same afternoon, shortly after 2, Peel went to the Palace, in full dress according to etiquette, and was given the Queen's commands to form a government. 'She received him (though She dislikes him) extremely well, and he was perfectly satisfied.'[57] The Queen thought, however, he seemed 'embarrassed and put out'. 'The Queen talked of her great friendship for, and gratitude to, Lord Melbourne' with which he agreed; she mentioned her Household to which at present he would give no answer, but said nothing should be done without the Queen's knowledge and approbation, 'but he is such a cold, odd man she can't make out what he means'. The Queen's impression was that he was 'not *happy* and sanguine. . . . The Queen don't like his manner after—oh! how different, how dreadfully different, to that frank, open, natural and most kind, warm manner of Lord Melbourne. . . . The Queen was very much collected, civil and high, and betrayed no agitation during these two trying Audiences. But afterwards again *all* gave way.' 'I felt too wretched; the change; the awful incomprehensible change . . . drove me really to distraction, and with the exception of walking up and down the room and . . . writing another letter to Lord M. and my Journal I could do nothing.'

Sir Robert Peel had already been given some excellent advice by his 'truly attached friend' Lady de Grey.* 'Now, dear Peel, the first impression on so young a girl's mind is of immense consequence, accustomed as she has been to the open and affectionate manner of Lord M, who, *entre nous*, treats her as a father, and, with all his faults, feels for her as such. Forgive this. I wish you success from my friendship for you, from my high esteem and admiration of your noble character . . . and I fear that even with such qualities you may not succeed in gaining the Queen's confidence, as I think your bearing too reserved and too cautious.'[58]

The Queen recorded her opinion that Sir Robert Peel was a 'cold, unfeeling, disagreeable man'. Melbourne agreed that Peel had an 'unfortunate manner'. Careful, cautious, appearing to weigh every word and with a singularly chilly smile, 'like the silver plate on a coffin', he was devoid of popular or ingratiating qualities. But, though he might be a man whom it was difficult to like, he was also a man whom it was impossible not to respect. His intelligence was brilliant, he displayed consummate political skill, vigour and power in debate and an unrivalled capacity for administration. He came, however, from the despised manufacturing class, not the landed aristocracy, and in spite of great wealth, excellent taste, and good looks in addition to brains, was the target of sneers which explain his stiffness and coldness.

The 9th of May began in misery, the Queen feeling more wretched even than before—crying and sobbing and being in despair—but during the course of the day she received a letter from Lord Melbourne in which he advised her 'to urge this question of the Household strongly as a matter due to yourself and your own wishes; but if Sir Robert is unable to concede it, it will not do to refuse and to put off the negotiation upon it'.[59] An idea had been put into the Queen's head, and as soon as Sir Robert Peel had left her, a little before 2 p.m. she sat down and scribbled a note to Lord Melbourne. He was to hold himself in readiness 'for what *may* happen in a very few hours'. She had seized on the question of the ladies of her Household. Sir Robert Peel, she declared, 'has behaved very ill, and has insisted on my giving up my Ladies, to which I replied that I never would consent, and I never saw a man so frightened. He said he must go to the Duke of Wellington . . . he was quite perturbed—but this is *infamous*. . . . I was calm but very decided, and I think you would have been pleased to see my composure. . . . Keep yourself in readiness, for you may soon be wanted.'[60]

Sir Robert Peel was in a position of difficulty. He was endeavouring to

* Henrietta Frances (1784–1848), youngest daughter of the first Earl of Enniskillen, married in 1805 Thomas Philip Weddell, third Baron Grantham, afterwards second Earl de Grey (1781–1859).

form a new government with a minority in the House of Commons; this was his reason for desiring the power of changing the Queen's household, which she described as 'dismissing her ladies'. Sir Robert did not wish to present to the world the spectacle of a Court entirely hostile to him, consisting of ladies whose husbands were his strongest political opponents, creating an impression that the confidence of the Queen was bestowed on his enemies and not on himself. Sir Robert Peel had never intended to remove all the Queen's ladies, but only to change those holding certain appointments of importance, for instance the Mistress of the Robes, whose husbands were actively opposed to the government. Moreover, 'so little disposition' existed on the part of Peel to interfere with the Queen's social comforts or in any way to fail in consulting her wishes 'that when She said "You must not expect me to give up the society of Lord Melbourne," He replied that "Nothing could be further from his thoughts ... and that he should always feel perfectly secure in the honour of Lord Melbourne" '. He immediately agreed to the Queen's choice of her old friend Lord Liverpool as Lord Steward, but when he mentioned ' "some modification of the Ladies of her household", She stopped him at once, and declared She would not part with any of them'. Henceforward this became the matter in dispute. It was, as Greville pointed out, something very near a pretext: 'the talent of a clever but rather thoughtless and headstrong girl; and, secretly longing to get back her Old Ministers (if she could by any pretext or expedient), She boldly and stubbornly availed herself of the opening which was presented to her.'[61]

At 10 minutes past 5 Sir Robert Peel returned and said that unless there was '*some* demonstration of my [the Queen's] confidence and if I retained all my Ladies they agreed unanimously they could not go on'. The Queen replied that she felt certain she would not change her mind, but would not do anything in a hurry and would write him her decision either that evening or the next morning; he said meanwhile he would suspend all further proceedings. 'This was *quite* wonderful! The Ladies his only support!! What an admission of weakness! What a blessed and unexpected escape!'

'I wrote to Lord Melbourne ... and begged him to come as soon as possible. . . . At ½ p. 6 came my dear and excellent Lord Melbourne. . . . It was a true and real and unexpected happiness to see him again after so much anxiety. I took and pressed his hand warmly. "You look better," he said. I said I had been so indignant. "Now you can tell me all," said Lord M. when we were seated.'[62]

The Queen explained to Lord Melbourne that though the Duke of Wellington and Sir Robert Peel came together, she had seen them separately and while Sir Robert Peel discussed the question of the Ladies with her in practice, the Duke discussed the question in principle; both found her 'firm and immoveable'. 'When the Duke arrived at the Palace, after the rupture had occurred he said on entering "Well, I am very sorry to find there is a difficulty"—to which she instantly replied with a naïveté so very girlish "O *He* began it and not me".'

The Whig Ministers were now told of the difficulty and Lord John Russell entreated Melbourne to call the Cabinet for a general consultation. Ministers were hastily summoned, some from dinners, Lord Morpeth from the opera, and Lord Melbourne laid before the Cabinet a summary of two letters from the Queen, written in a high tone and war-like spirit, such as Queen Elizabeth employed when addressing her troops on the eve of the Armada; indeed Queen Victoria's letters have curious echoes of the famous Tilbury speech. 'Do not fear that I was not calm and composed. They wanted to deprive me of my ladies, and I suppose they would deprive me next of my dressers and my housemaids; they wished to treat me like a girl, but I will show them that I am Queen of England.'[63] In her Journal the Queen wrote 'The Queen of England will not submit to such trickery'. The Cabinet was swept off its feet. Later the text of what the Queen had written was read in full and it was declared impossible to desert such a Queen and such a woman. A letter was composed for her to sign in which she declined to place the Ladies of her household at Peel's discretion, and on 10th May Peel resigned his commission to form a government into the Queen's hands. The Whigs were back in office, no more firmly entrenched than before and with no more reliable a majority behind them, but the Queen had Lord Melbourne, and his government was to pursue its rickety way for two more years. The crisis had lasted only four days.

The immediate effect of the announcement was universal indignation. 'It is a high trial of our institutions when the caprice of a girl of nineteen can overturn a great Ministerial combination.' 'There is something which shocks one's sense of fitness and propriety in the spectacle of this mere baby of a Queen setting herself in opposition to this great man [the Duke of Wellington], the decus and testamen of her kingdom, invested with all the authority of his experience and sagacity, of his profound loyalty, his devoted patriotism, and to whom her Predecessors had ever been accustomed to look up with unlimited confidence as their surest and wisest Councillor in all times of difficulty and danger.'

'The simple truth in this case is that the Queen could not endure the thought of parting with Melbourne, who is everything to her. Her feelings which are *sexual* though She does not know it, and are probably not very well defined to herself, are of a strength sufficient to bear down all prudential considerations. . . . Nothing else would have emboldened her to resist the advice and opinion of the Duke of Wellington and to oppose so unbendingly her will to his authority.'[64] The Queen, lonely, isolated, supported by Lehzen, but made nervous by Lehzen's jealousy and possessiveness, clung to Lord Melbourne. The romantic childish and innocent admiration of a young inexperienced girl for an older still charming man who is acting as her tutor is a common variety of first love and the young Queen's devotion to Lord Melbourne is a classic example.

Throughout these anxious negotiations the unpleasant undercurrent of the Lady Flora Hastings affair continued. Lord Holland pitied the Queen: 'I cannot but think that Peel has been harsh, cold and un-gentleman-like. . . . The English public are generally generous, even to weakness, to Royalty, Rank, Youth and Women & had it not been for the unlucky business of Lady Flora . . . enthusiasm in favour of the Queen . . . might have been confidently reckoned upon, but many amongst us are afraid there will be little or no sympathy with her or her ladies. What . . . I should say the poor little Lady wants to support her is an active zealous and well organised Press . . . the pens of those who can feel & write should leap from their inkstands to rescue the poor little woman.'[65]

For the Queen the most important consequence of the Lady Flora Hastings affair was that it brought matters between herself and her mother to a climax. The Duchess of Kent took the side of the Hastings family, and identified herself with Lady Flora, while the Queen talked openly to Lord Melbourne of her 'daily growing dislike for Mama'. The Queen declared 'It was too bad to have to endure this for such a *nasty woman*, as I said, and shall and will say, Lady Flora is.' The next day, Tuesday, 16th April, the Queen wrote '. . . that wicked foolish old woman Lady Hastings has had her whole correspondence with Lord Melbourne published in the *Morning Post* . . . in a manner so infamous against my noble excellent Lord Melbourne . . . that I could have and would have wished to have hanged the Editor and the whole Hastings family for their infamy.' Lord Melbourne entreated the Queen to take no notice of the abuse heaped on him, it was done for effect while so much was going on in Parliament. The Queen then said that it would be a very bad thing if the Duchess were to leave her, 'but that really I would do anything if she would; as it was having an Enemy in the house. . . .' The following day the Queen lamented to Lord Melbourne 'how dreadful it was to have the prospect of torment for many years by Mama's living here; and he said it was dreadful, but what could be done? She had declared (some time ago), I said, she would never leave me as long as I was unmarried; "Well then, there's that way of settling it", he said; that was a schocking alternative I said.

However, the next day the Queen was more irritated than ever. Her mother did provoke her so, she told Lord Melbourne, and Lady Flora was 'such a detestable person', it was 'very hard I should have to bear so much for *such* a woman'. If she went away the Queen must tell the Duchess she was never to return, but of this Lord Melbourne could not approve. It would look as if Lady Flora had been calumniated and, that failing, had been sent away.

The Queen then 'mustered up courage, and said that my Uncle's [King Leopold's] great wish—was—that I should marry my Cousin Albert . . . but, that . . . I could decide nothing until I saw him again. . . . "How would that be with the Duchess?" he asked, for that if I was to make such a connection and then he was to go with Mama, that would be dreadful for me. I assured him he need have no fear *whatever* on that score; then he said "Cousins are not very good things" and "Those Coburgs are not popular abroad; the Russians hate them." I then said, who was there else? We enumerated the various Princes, of whom not one, I said would do. For myself, I said, at present *my* feeling was quite against ever marrying. . . . I said Uncle Ernest [the Duke of Saxe-Coburg and Gotha, Prince Albert's father] pressed me much about it. . . . Did he [Lord Melbourne] see the necessity? I did not think so, till this (getting Mama away) and certainly the present state is dreadful, always . . . on the verge of a quarrel. . . . I said, why need I marry at all for 3 or 4 years? . . . I said I dreaded the thought of marrying; that I was so accustomed to have my own way, that I thought it was 10 to 1 I shouldn't agree with anybody. Lord M. said, "Oh! but you would have it still" (my own way). Lord M. asked if Prince Albert wasn't coming; I said, he would come with his elder brother in the autumn.'[66]

The Queen's capacity for enjoyment and her resilience were remarkable. With the continuing affair of Lady Flora Hastings, the Bedchamber crisis and a series of shattering quarrels with her mother, she had had a nerve-racking year. Nevertheless at the State Ball given for the visit of the Grand Duke Alexander of Russia, eldest son of Tsar Nicholas I, to Windsor on 27th May she danced with vigour and enjoyment a number of quadrilles, but not waltzes, neither she nor the Grand Duke owing to their high station being permitted to waltz. The Grand Duke was tall and very strong; after supper she danced a turn in a mazurka with him and he whisked her round in a way she found very pleasant. 'I really am quite in love with the Grand Duke,' she wrote in her Journal, 'he is a dear delightful young man.' They danced a country dance which was a novelty to the Queen, the 'Grossvater', during which the gentlemen leapt over a handkerchief while the ladies ran beneath it. There was a great deal of joking and laughter, 'merriment' such as the Queen delighted in. 'I never enjoyed myself more,' she wrote in her Journal, 'we were all so merry.' She remarked to Lord Melbourne that 'all this excitement did her good'; when the Grand Duke took leave he pressed her hand, she

10　PRINCESS VICTORIA, 1833
from the portrait by Sir George Hayter

11   SIR JOHN CONROY
from the painting by A. Tidey

I 2   LORD MELBOURNE
from the portrait by J. Partridge

13   'SUSANNAH AND THE ELDERS'
The Queen between Lord Melbourne, the Prime Minister,
and Lord John Russell, Home Secretary
and Leader of the House
from the drawing by HB

14   KING WILLIAM IV, 1834
'A Great Actor Rehearsing His Part'
from the drawing by HB

15   LADY FLORA HASTINGS
silhouette by Pearce

16   BARON STOCKMAR
from the painting by Winterhalter

17   THE DUKE OF WELLINGTON
IN CONVERSATION WITH SIR ROBERT PEEL
from the painting by Winterhalter

18   THE PRINCE CONSORT
from the miniature by William Charles Ross

19   THE MARRIAGE OF QUEEN VICTORIA
AND PRINCE ALBERT
10 February 1840
study for the painting of the wedding at the
Chapel Royal, St. James's Palace, by Sir George Hayter

kissed his cheek, upon which he kissed hers 'in a very warm and affection-ate manner'. She commented to Lord Melbourne on having 'so disliked the idea of the Grand Duke's coming' but that now she 'was so *very very* sorry at his going'.[67] The contrast the Queen frequently exhibited between lethargy succeeded by almost frantic enjoyment might have made an experienced observer pause, but Lord Melbourne remarked tranquilly that this was very often the case.

On 1st June 1839 came a piece of electrifying news. Conroy intended to resign his place in the Duchess of Kent's household and to go abroad within a fortnight. He asked for an interview with Lord Melbourne in order that he might notify his intention. Lord Melbourne received this notification with scepticism. He was afraid Conroy might take a tour and then return. The Queen feared the Duchess might take Edward Conroy, Sir John's son, in his father's place. A young man of considerable charm, he had eloped to Gretna Green in 1837 with, and subsequently married, Lady Alicia Parsons, daughter of the second Earl of Rosse. They separated in 1847. Mr Abercromby, Speaker of the House of Commons, after-wards Lord Dunfermline, a man of excellent character and a friend of Conroy (the Duke of Wellington remarked that he could not consider Conroy completely worthless on account of his friendship with Dunferm-line), in a sensible letter warned Conroy against expecting any profitable results from his withdrawal, some post of responsibility, a governorship for instance, for which Conroy hoped. 'Nothing has caused more general regret than the belief that the relations between Her Majesty and Her Mother are not such as could be wished. . . . You cannot be ignorant that it is everywhere boldly asserted, that your remaining in the family of the Duchess of Kent, is the main cause, and even the sole cause of that dissension which is deplored.' If Conroy withdrew and there was a reunion, Abercrombie was sure he would rejoice at the happy result. 'If it fails to produce that effect you will have the satisfaction of proving that what has been so generally asserted is untrue. . . . I have looked at the whole case, as one of the greatest public importance, and as involving the security of the Throne. . . .'[68]

The Duke of Wellington believed that it was he himself alone 'who got Conroy to resign and leave the country; and this he did by cajoling and flattering Conroy himself and representing to him that his conduct in retiring would not only be gratifying to the Duchess's family but be honourable to himself and appreciated by the public; and by honeyed words like these he prevailed on Conroy at last to go.'[69] 'Plenty of butter' was the Duke's description. 'The primary motive of Conroy's retirement was, however, the unanimous opposition which he met with from the Coburg family. . . . They had a common sitting room at the Palace in the Dss's apartments, and they complained that Conroy used insolently to come and sit there and they asked the Duke [of Wellington] if he should not be formally warned off. But the Duke said this could not be; the Duchess was a great Princess, independent, and having an undoubted right to select her own Servants and attendants, with whom no one could with decency interfere; and to prohibit her officer from entering her apartment would be an outrage.' Nevertheless when the Duke was summoned by the Duchess of Kent he spoke 'pretty roundly' to her. She began to explain why she kept Conroy and the Duke said 'I won't hear any reasons, it's quite enough if the Queen disapproves of it.'

On 10th June it became known that Conroy had dismissed all his servants and was going first to Italy and then to Ems, a well-known German resort in the province of Hesse-Nassau not far from Coblenz. Lord Melbourne told the Queen the Duke of Wellington had told him 'That fellow's going' and seemed 'in great joy at it'. The Queen said it was quite indifferent to her; she could not get on with her mother in any case. Lord Melbourne said she used not to think Conroy's going away would do *no* good, but the Queen said she had grown callous and she did not believe his departure would be final.

Reports of Lady Flora's health continued to be bad, and 'after great gulping', the Queen sent to enquire after her. The Queen's dislike of Lady Flora was insurmountable. 'Lord M. said, "But it was quite the right thing to do; first of all, because she is under your roof, and then because it shows feeling; for suppose she was to die, which might happen, you would be open to reproach." '[70] The Queen refused to take Lady Flora's illness seriously and said it was 'only a bilious attack'. The Queen had not yet learnt compassion, there was some excuse for describing her at this stage as 'a heartless child'.

The fact that Lady Flora's condition had not improved, which Lord Melbourne thought very odd and wondered that it didn't excite more curiosity, left the Queen unmoved. She changed the subject and asked Lord Melbourne how he liked her hair in curls.

Four days later the Queen was told by the Duchess that Lady Flora was very ill, 'could keep nothing upon her stomach, and had continued fever; "Then she'll die," said Lord M. . . . she was evidently in a very bad state of health and it was, in his opinion, Clark's mistake in not seeing it was a disease. . . .'[71]

That evening, Sunday, 16th June, the Queen sent for Lord Melbourne and told him there had been 'such a piece of work' before the Ball, the Duchess of Kent had been crying and saying Lady Flora was dying '. . . and that I didn't believe she was so very ill as they said she was. "As you say Ma'am," said Lord M, "it would be very awkward if that woman was to die." '

The Duchess of Kent continued in a 'dreadful' state about Lady Flora,

178

'crying etc.' Dr Chambers had been called in, who told Sir James Clark he thought Lady Flora in very great danger and was anxious she should be moved to some better room. The Queen, however, was unmoved, she wrote in her Journal that a ball she attended that evening 'was *so* gay and pretty and I enjoyed myself excessively'. As the Queen observed of herself, she had very strong personal dislikes.

Nevertheless Lady Flora was now so ill that her sister Lady Sophia Hastings had to be asked by the Queen to stay at Buckingham Palace, an invitation which was refused. The Duchess of Kent was miserable, not only did she miss Conroy's constant visits, but the various members of the Conroy family had made up an important part of her daily life. Jane Conroy was 'delicate', and bundles of notes among the Conroy Papers show that the Duchess, whose kindness of heart was genuine, visited her several times a week.[72] Her sister Victoire, the Duchess of Kent's name-sake and god-daughter, intended to be Princess Victoria's playmate, was helped financially. A further collection of letters proves that the Duchess did all she could to obtain appointments for Conroy's sons. A void was left in the Duchess of Kent's life when the Conroy family departed, and she was tortured by anxiety over the unfortunate Lady Flora, whose state grew steadily worse.

Dr Chambers, who had now succeeded Sir James Clark as the Duchess's physician, gave a bad account of her; she was weaker and could digest nothing. On Tuesday, 25th June, the Queen went to the opera, but next day she did postpone the ball she had intended to give in the evening, an announcement greeted in the social world with relief, and sent word to Lady Flora that she was ready to go to see her that afternoon if Lady Flora wished. Lord Melbourne was 'touched' but owing to Lady Flora being given laudanum, she slept on and then awoke feeling very faint. The visit was therefore to take place next day. Lord Melbourne thought the Queen should put off a 'great' dinner she had intended to give to the Queen Dowager, Queen Adelaide, but saw no objection to small dinners. Dr Chambers thought Lady Flora so ill that the Queen should go and see her at once, while she still lived. The summons for the Queen came while Lord Melbourne was with her. 'I said I would be up again in a minute; and he said "Don't be in a hurry" . . . I went in alone; I found poor Lady Flora stretched on a couch looking as thin as anybody can be who is still alive; literally a skeleton, but the body *very* much swollen like a person who is with child; a searching look in her eyes, a look rather like a person who is dying; her voice like usual, and a good deal of strength in her hands; she was friendly, said she was very comfortable, and was very grateful for all I had done for her, and that she was glad to see me looking well. I said to her, I hoped to see her again when she was better, upon which she grasped my hand as if to say "I shall not see you again".

I then instantly went upstairs and returned to Lord M. who said: "You remained a very short time." '[73]

On Saturday, 29th June, Lady Flora rallied a little and the Queen went to the opera.

On 1st July Lady Flora was still lingering and the Queen remarked to Lord Melbourne that 'it was disagreeable and painful to me to think there was a dying person in the house'. Dr Chambers had said there was no hope.

On Friday, 5th July, at 2 a.m., Lady Flora died: 'the poor thing died without a struggle and only just raised her hands and gave one gasp'.[74]

An outburst against the Queen followed. The *Morning Post* became even more venomous and attacked the Queen daily 'with the most revolting virulence and indecency'. 'There is no doubt that an effect very prejudicial to H.M. has been produced, and the public, the women particularly, have taken up the Cause of Lady Flora with a vehemence which is not the less active because it is senseless.'[75] At Ascot, the fashionable race meeting near Windsor attended by the Queen, she was given a demonstration of her unpopularity. According to custom, she drove up the course in an open carriage accompanied, on this occasion, by Lord Melbourne. As her carriage came opposite Lord Erroll's stand, two ladies identified as Lady Sarah Ingestre (later Countess of Shrewsbury) and the Duchess of Montrose hissed. The Queen's reaction was to wish she could have them both flogged. Denials and counter-accusations followed but the fact was established and was due to the Queen's alleged treatment of Lady Flora Hastings. Lord Ilchester thought the excitement so great that the Queen should go out of town, he feared it would be made very disagreeable for the Queen on the day of the funeral and Lord Liverpool found the excitement such that he feared an insult was meditated on the day of Lady Flora's burial. The Queen herself with her naïve obstinacy, the obstinacy of a young child, told Lord Melbourne that she 'felt *no* remorse, I felt *I* had done nothing to kill her'. The post-mortem disclosed disease of long standing, the liver enlarged to a frightful degree, and by pressing on the lower parts causing the enlargement of the person.[76]

Lord Melbourne was in favour of the Queen sending a carriage to Lady Flora's funeral, in spite of the fact that a demonstration was anticipated and a force of police ordered to be in readiness. It was feared the Queen's carriage might be stoned; however, no disturbance occurred. The Queen now 'very dexterously' appointed Lady Sandwich, wife of a Tory peer, born a Paget, daughter of the Marquess of Anglesey, to fill the vacancy in the Bedchamber caused by the retirement of Lady Breadalbane.[77] Not only did the Queen secure 'one of the favoured Paget race' who were her intimate personal friends, but since the Pagets were Tories she put an end to the exclusively Whig composition of her household. It is a pity some similar solution had not been attempted earlier. Sixty years later the Queen told Sir Arthur Bigge, later Lord Stamfordham 'I was *very* young, only 20 & never should have acted so again—Yes! it was a mistake . . .'[78] Riding in Hyde Park on 17th July with Lord Melbourne, the crowd 'was very great and there was *not one* hiss, and they cheered me as I rode through the Gate into St James's Park. This is a *good* answer' wrote the Queen with her accustomed vigour 'to those fools who say that the public feeling—a few paid Wretches—was displayed on Thursday by hooting at Ministers.'[79]

The Queen, however, was neither well nor happy. The affair of Lady Flora was not allowed to drop by the Hastings family. The Queen had sent £50 to Lady Flora's maid but old Lady Hastings sent it back. Lord Hastings, Lady Flora's brother, challenged Lord Melbourne to a duel on the ground that Lord M. had insulted his mother. The Queen felt low, wretched and cross, from having so much business and so much anxiety. Trouble was brewing over the marriage, illegal under the Royal Marriages Act, of the Duke of Sussex and Lady Cecilia Buggin, widow of a City magnate who wished to be advanced in rank to an equality with the Royal Family and be recognised by the Queen. 'If I was a private in-dividual' the Queen said 'I should leave the country immediately, as I was so disgusted at the perpetual opposition.' She was 'disgusted with everything' and added she 'felt tired of riding'. 'Tired of *riding?*' Lord Melbourne said with astonishment.[80]

On Tuesday, 6th August, the Queen discussed the forthcoming visit of King Leopold and the Coburg Princes Ernest and Albert, which Lord Melbourne agreed was bound to create 'observation'. In fact there had already been a paragraph about it in one of the papers and the Editor of the *Observer* had written to Lord Melbourne asking if he should con-tradict it, but Lord M. said 'I thought it better not.' The Queen reminded him that he had said he did not like the connection, at which he hesitated, but on being urged said 'I don't like it very much'. This did not please the Queen who said much as she loved her country, and was ready to do what was for its good, still she thought her own liking was one of the principal things. 'I think you have a right to expect that' Lord M. said. 'It's a very difficult subject; I don't think a foreign Prince would be popular.' But the Queen wrote 'I said I *couldn't* and wouldn't like to marry a subject, and whatever family he belonged to, Lord M. said, they would be the object of jealousy. "No, I don't think it would do," he added.' The Queen said she 'heard Albert's praises on all sides, and that he was very handsome'.[81]

At the end of August a visit was paid to Windsor by Duke Ferdinand of Saxe-Coburg and Gotha, father of Ferdinand, King of Portugal, and uncle both of Queen Victoria and of Prince Albert. Duke Ferdinand, who was accompanied by several of his children, was one of the uncles who expected the young Queen Victoria to pay his bills; the other was Albert's father, Ernest, Duke of Saxe-Coburg and Gotha. Duke Ferdinand was described by the Queen as the 'stingy one', Duke Ernest as the 'difficult' one.[82]

On Friday, 6th September 1839, the party was joined by King Leopold of the Belgians and Queen Louise, who came over to make final arrangements for the visit of the Coburg Princes, Ernest and Albert, and a general expedition was made to Woolwich to say goodbye to the Ferdinand family. The ship was inspected, presents exchanged, tears shed, marine arrangements admired. As the Queen was about to leave the ship the captain and officers betrayed some anxiety and a desire to help her down the tall side of the vessel. The Queen 'looked up with the greatest spirit, and said quite loud' in her 'silvery' voice, 'No help, thank you! I am used to this', and then descended, as an eyewitness observed, 'like an old boatswain'. She was enthusiastically cheered by the sailors.[83]

Thursday, 10th October, opened with an unexpected incident at Windsor. Stones had been flung through the Queen's dressing-room window and were lying on the floor, two panes having been broken; other stones had been thrown and windows broken in three further rooms, the stones were lying on the floor. No explanation for this apparently meaningless incident was ever forthcoming, nor was the perpetrator discovered. On the way back that day from a walk on the Terrace with Lord Melbourne, one of the Queen's pages came running to her with a letter from King Leopold: Prince Albert and Prince Ernest would arrive that evening.

At 7.30 p.m. the Queen found herself standing at the top of the staircase at Windsor to receive her cousins. The Channel crossing had been bad, and they arrived, as frequently happened, without their baggage. This was a crucial moment of her life, within a short time she must make a decision of immense importance. She knew Albert was good-looking, everyone spoke of his handsomeness, but she was not prepared for the reality. 'It was with some emotion that I beheld Albert—who is *beautiful*' she wrote.[84]

One of the most celebrated romances in history had begun, the Queen had fallen in love.

Chapter Six

During the three years since 1836 Prince Albert had developed into one of the best-looking young men in Europe. 'Albert really is quite charming, and so excessively handsome,' wrote the Queen, 'such beautiful blue eyes, an exquisite nose, and such a pretty mouth with delicate mustachios and slight but very slight whiskers; a beautiful figure, broad in the shoulders and a fine waist; my heart is quite *going*. . . .'[1] Three years ago Prince Albert had been 'much shorter than his brother, already very handsome but very stout', now he had grown tall, slim and graceful. The Queen, whose response to masculine good looks was strong, was swept off her feet. The first evening there was dancing after dinner; the two young princes could not appear at the meal itself because their evening clothes were held up with their baggage, but they came in for the dancing and the Queen watched Prince Albert enraptured. She herself danced one quadrille with him and he 'danced beautifully'; etiquette forbade her to dance more intimate dances, but 'it is quite a pleasure to look at Albert when he gallops and valses, he does it so beautifully, holds himself so well with that beautiful figure of his'.

The Queen took only an hour or two to make up her mind. The second evening after Prince Albert arrived, she sent him a message by Lehzen, through the Prince's equerry, Baron von Alvensleben, to let the Prince know he had 'made a very favourable impression on her'. On 14th October the Prince was informed, 'through the same channel', 'that V. had almost decided to choose me as her future husband and would probably make her declaration personally to me' shortly.[2]

On 13th October the Queen told Lord Melbourne that seeing her cousins had 'a good deal changed my opinion (as to marrying)', though she did not tell him she had already reached a decision. Lord Melbourne remarked she could take a week to make up her mind, adding that Prince Albert was 'certainly a very fine young man, very good-looking'. What was taking place, however, was rather more obvious than the Queen imagined. The same day Lord Melbourne had written to Lord John Russell 'What I mentioned to you the other day is evidently taking the course which I expected. . . . A very strong impression is evidently made

... and I do not know that anything better could be done. He seems a very agreeable young man, he is certainly a very good looking one, and as to character, that, we must always take our chance of. ...'[3] On the evening of the 14th October the Prince pressed the Queen's hand with significant warmth when saying good night.

Next morning, about half past twelve, the Prince was summoned to a private audience. 'I said to him' wrote the Queen 'that I thought he must be aware *why* I wished them to come here, and that it would make me *too happy* if he would consent to what I wished (to marry me); we embraced each other over and over again, and he was *so* kind, *so* affectionate; Oh! to *feel* I was, and am, loved by *such* an Angel as Albert was *too great delight to describe*! he is *perfection*; perfection in every way—in beauty—in everything! I told him I was quite unworthy of him and kissed his dear hand—he said he would be very happy "das Leben mit dir zu zubringen" [to share life with you] and was so kind and seemed so happy, that I really felt it was the happiest brightest moment in my life, which made up for all I had suffered and endured. Oh! *how* I adore and love him, I cannot say!! *how* I will strive to make him feel as little as possible the great sacrifice he has made; I told him it was a great sacrifice,]—which he wouldn't allow. .... I feel the happiest of human beings.'[4]

It was, however, unlikely that the married life of the Queen and the Prince could pass without storms. The Queen had charm and admirable qualities; she was affectionate, loyal and evoked attachments, but she was also emotional, obstinate, determined to have her own way.

Prince Albert's character was difficult and complicated—it could hardly be otherwise. His father, Ernest I, the Duke of Saxe-Coburg and Gotha, ruled over a court notorious for its profligacy and was a spendthrift weighed down by debts. 'Could you keep Papa from continually demanding money from me' wrote Prince Albert to Stockmar,[5] and Queen Victoria complained that her father-in-law expected her to pay his bills and lend him money when he came to England. Nevertheless, in spite of the Duke's dissolute habits and an unattractive physical appearance, genuine affection united the Princes with their father. He was fond of them, he saw them frequently, enjoyed their company and his treatment of them was mild. We read nothing of punishments or the floggings inflicted on the sons of George III.

How is it possible, Stockmar was asked, that with such a father and such a brother, equally unprincipled and thoughtless, such an extreme contrast should exist in the character of Prince Albert? The Prince himself thought he was indebted to the instructions of his tutor Florschütz, but Stockmar[6] considered that the Prince's character derived from his own purity of mind, Florschütz had kept him carefully from the knowledge or the sight of anything vicious; the Prince's brother had the same advantages, but was so lacking in equal natural excellence that the result was widely different. Ernest grew up to ruin not only his character but his health by dissipation and became incapable of having children. Stockmar was most anxious for Prince Albert's early removal from Coburg for he could not have retained his simplicity and purity of character had he been left to pass his life in such company. The Prince would not have become vicious, it was not in his nature, but it must have had some effect. Stockmar added that he himself never saw the Duke of Coburg now; they kept apart. When the Duke of Coburg married the beautiful Luise of Gotha he had been a dissipated man of 30; she was a girl of 16 who had received a romantic education—according to King Leopold her father had allowed her mind to become corrupted by reading Persian poetry.[7] Two sons, Ernest and Albert, were born in two successive years. The Duke then returned to his former habits of dissipation and Duchess Luise was neglected. Prince Albert was the better looking of the two boys, 'beautiful as an angel', with large blue eyes and fair curls; he was also delicate, had digestive troubles, became—as we have seen—easily tired and was subject to attacks of croup. Nevertheless when Prince Albert was four he and his brother were taken by their father from their nursery and their nurse and placed, against the advice of relatives, under the care of a tutor, Herr Florschütz of Coburg.

This was not a sorrow for the Prince, for even as a child he showed 'great dislike to being in the charge of women, and rejoiced instead of sorrowing over the contemplated change'.[8] In Herr Florschütz the little Princes were fortunate; he was gentle, learned, affectionate and patient. Both Princes became devoted to him, in particular Prince Albert, who called him 'Thus' and leaned on his affection as if he had been a woman. In 1839, the year before Prince Albert married, he and his brother were separated from Herr Florschütz and from each other and Prince Albert was sent for a tour in Italy under the supervision of Stockmar. Prince Albert longed for the companionship of Herr Florschütz. He had an abscess on a tooth, 'the most violent toothache I have ever had to bear . . . but nowhere could I find my beloved "Thus" to sob out my pain in his arms. . . . At length last night—New Year's Eve—at the hour when, in Coburg, the postilions ride trumpeting through the town . . . a very large abscess . . . burst.' Prince Albert's domestic attendant was also masculine, his Swiss valet Cart, who looked after him from the time he was a small boy, carried him up and down stairs in his arms when he was too little to walk and remained with him for more than thirty years.

Before Prince Albert was five his parents' marriage ended. The Duchess separated from the Duke of Coburg and never saw her two sons again. After an interval there was a divorce and both the Duke and Duchess re-married, the Duchess dying of cancer, after a long and tragic illness, at the age of 31. Her two sons, Albert in particular, never forgot her. One of his first gifts to Queen Victoria was a little pin his mother had given him. The Coburg family recognised she was not wholly to blame and she was freely mentioned in the family circle with pity and sadness, not with reproach.

After this chequered childhood Prince Albert was marked down for a destiny which, splendid though it was, did not in many respects suit or attract him. He was to marry the heiress presumptive to the throne of England and to this end he was trained from babyhood, as for a profession. In March 1838, when the Prince was 18, King Leopold wrote to Stockmar that he had had 'a long conversation with Albert' (on the subject of his marriage) and 'put the whole case honestly and kindly before him. He looks at the question from its most elevated and honourable point of view; he considers that troubles are inseparable from all human positions, and that therefore if one must be subject to plagues and annoyances it had better be so for some great and worthy object than for trivial and paltry ends.'

In spite of this realistic approach, the Prince had become discouraged. By nature Prince Albert was a student, he was happiest at the University at Bonn (where he studied under Fichte), 'lighting his little green student's lamp punctually every morning at five', working long hours, taking pleasure in walking tours, but he accepted the edict that to please the young Queen he must 'go into society, learn the ways of the world and vitiate my culture with fashionable accomplishments. And I will do it. I will find so much pleasure in a mixture of foppishness, impudence, unceremoniousness, trifling chatter on trivial subjects and will come back ... the true type of elegant man of the world of the nineteenth century.'

Reports on the young Queen did not encourage him. 'V. is said to be incredibly stubborn, and her extreme obstinacy at war with her good nature; she delights in court ceremonies, etiquette and trivial formalities. ... She is said to take not the slightest pleasure in nature, to enjoy sitting up late at night and sleeping late into the day.' [9]

The limit of the Prince's endurance had been reached when later the young Queen told her uncle, King Leopold, that for three or four years she could not think of marriage and wished the matter to be postponed. King Leopold told Stockmar on 12th September 1838 '... I have spoken to Albert ... Albert has now passed eighteen [the Prince was 19 on 26th August 1838] ... if he waits it will be impossible for him to begin any new career and his whole life would be *marred* if the Queen should change her mind.'

When the Prince came to England in October 1839 it was his intention to put an end to the plan. 'I went therefore' he wrote to his intimate student friend, Prince William of Löwenstein 'with the quiet but firm resolution to declare, on my part, that I also, tired of the delay, withdrew entirely from the affair.' If, after waiting several years, the match fell through, 'he would be known to have failed with Queen Victoria: other desirable Princesses would have married elsewhere and he would find himself left 'an object of ridicule'.

The Queen herself wrote[10] later that she could not now 'think without indignation against herself, of her wish to keep the Prince waiting for probably three or four years, at the risk of ruining all his prospects for life, until she might feel inclined to marry! . . . The only excuse the Queen can make for herself is in the fact, that the sudden change from the secluded life at Kensington to the independence of her position as Queen Regnant at the age of eighteen, put all ideas of marriage out of her mind, which she now most bitterly repents. A worse school for a young girl, or one more detrimental to all natural feelings and affections cannot well be imagined than the position of a Queen at eighteen, without experience and without a husband to guide and support her.'

But the Queen fell in love and within a few days had sent for Prince Albert and proposed marriage to him.

'I have obtained the height of my desire' the Prince told Herr Florschütz.

Marrying Queen Victoria was Prince Albert's career, and his first sensation was triumph. He was also 'bewildered' by the suddenness of the Queen's declaration when she offered him 'her hand and heart'. 'The joyous openness of manner in which she told me this' wrote the Prince to his grandmother the Dowager Duchess of Gotha 'quite enchanted me, and I was quite carried away by it. She is really most good and amiable, and I am quite sure that heaven has not given me into evil hands and that we shall be happy together.' He told Prince William of Löwenstein that 'I think I shall be *very* happy, for Victoria possesses all the qualities which make a home happy, and seems to be attached to me with her whole heart.'[11]

On the evening of 15th October, the betrothal day, both Princes wore the 'Windsor Uniform' for the first time, dark blue with red facings and cuffs.

The Queen was in a state of bliss. The Prince sent her the letters to read which he had written to his father, the Duke of Saxe-Coburg and Gotha, to King Leopold and to Stockmar: 'They were *so* beautiful, so full of affection and kindness towards me, as touched me deeply and made me feel *so* happy! I . . . felt so overcome with joy, gratitude and happiness at Albert's love for me, that it made me cry.' The Prince's good looks were an unfailing delight. 'I love and admire him more and more; those eyes of his are bewitching, and so is the whole face.' Running about in Windsor Park with his greyhound, Eos, 'he looked so beautiful with all the colour in his dear lovely face'. When they were alone they kissed 'repeatedly'. 'Oh! when I look in those lovely, lovely, blue eyes, I feel they are those of an angel' wrote the Queen.[12]

Throughout October 1839 'the love and trust between the Prince and the Queen increased'. The Queen had faults, of obstinacy, and of limited outlook, but these became unimportant; her affectionate nature, her warmth and her sincerity endeared her to persons who came into contact with her throughout her life.

For his part, the Prince continued bewildered. He wrote to Stockmar begging him to come to England and help him; he did not understand English customs, none of his party could endure the English climate or digest English food. Baron von Alvensleben, the Prince's equerry, had succumbed to illness and Prince Ernest had been confined to his room for days with a bilious attack and 'a face the colour of an orange'. Lord Alfred Paget, the Marquess of Anglesey's son, one of the numerous Paget family who were favourites with the Queen, said that when German Princes came over to England they ate too much. Prince Albert was moderate but on the night of the proposal he too had had to retire with a severe nose-bleeding. He felt at sea. 'Victoria is so good and kind to me' he told Stockmar 'that I am often puzzled to believe that I should be the object of so much affection ... more or more seriously I cannot write; I am at this moment too much bewildered to do so ... the climax has come upon us with surprise, before we could have expected it.'[13]

Like the insertion of the key piece into a puzzle the betrothal of the Queen to Prince Albert was followed by a general fitting of relationships into place. King Leopold wrote that nothing could have given him greater pleasure than the news: 'I had, when I saw your decision, almost the feeling of old Zacharias, now lettest thou thy servant depart in peace.' For years he had been convinced that the choice of Prince Albert was the best plan for the Queen's happiness—'the maximum of a good arrangement'. The Queen and her uncle were reconciled and resumed warmth and intimacy. The Prince and the Queen lunched with the Duchess of Kent several times a week, accompanied by the Prince's favourite greyhound Eos. '... she is so gentle, and so clever,' wrote the Queen, 'gives her paw, jumps an immense height, eats off a fork etc., and loves Albert so dearly—which is natural.' Softened by happiness, the Queen's relations with her mother, temporarily at all events, improved, and the Prince, who did not share the Queen's Whig prejudices, proposed an 'amnesty' for the Tories.

During their companions' indisposition the Queen and the Prince spent their time alone in the Queen's little blue sitting-room, the Prince sitting beside the Queen. 'I signed some papers and warrants etc.' wrote the Queen 'and he was so kind as to dry them with blotting paper for me. We talked a good deal together, and he clasped me so tenderly in his arms, and kissed me again and again, and called me "vortrefflichste" [matchless] and was so affectionate, so full of love! Oh! what happiness is this! How

I *do adore* him!! I kissed his dear hand. He embraced me again so tenderly.'[14]

Next day the Prince told the Queen that he must leave in about two weeks, as he could not otherwise be in Germany by the end of November and wished to have two months at home before he married. The Queen was 'deeply grieved' and they embraced as if they were to be parted there and then.

The arrangements were made by the Queen with Lord Melbourne: the Prince and his brother would leave England on 14th November and the marriage take place on 10th February 1840, giving the Prince time to recover from the journey back to England. The Prince dreaded saying farewell to his fatherland. 'While I shall be untiring in my efforts and labours for the country to which I shall in future belong . . . I shall never cease to be a true German, a true Coburg and Gotha man' he wrote.

Lord Melbourne thought the announcement would be 'very well received; for I hear there's anxiety now that it should be'. With what Stockmar described as 'characteristic carelessness', Lord Melbourne assured the Queen that the Cabinet did not anticipate any difficulty in passing the Prince's allowance of £50,000 annually through Parliament.[15] The wives of George II and George III had both been voted the same sum, as had Prince Leopold, though only the consort of the heiress presumptive to the throne. Melbourne did not take into account the damage done to the cause of penniless German Princes by King Leopold's subsequent behaviour.

On 1st November the Queen held a review at Windsor, mounted on her charger Leopold and wearing a uniform and cap. For the first time she was accompanied by Prince Albert, an accomplished horseman, 'looking *so* handsome in his uniform on my right'. It was cold, raining and blowing a gale and Albert 'en grande tenue' was frozen wearing the green Coburg uniform and 'tight cazimere pantaloons (nothing under them) and high boots'. The Queen was protected by her cape 'which dearest Albert settled comfortably for me'. Afterwards they lunched with the Duchess of Kent and Albert was reported 'cold but pleased'.

That evening the Queen and the Prince, alone together in the Queen's little sitting-room seated side by side on the sofa, went through the precedents for the marriage of a Queen Regnant. Queen Mary Tudor was the historic example but hardly provided a precedent as she and Philip of Spain were Catholics and married according to the Catholic ritual, Queen Anne and Queen Mary II were both Princesses when they married. It was decided to follow the very full and exact account of the circumstances relating to the marriage of George III and Queen Charlotte in the Chapel Royal on the evening of 8th September 1761.

'He [Prince Albert] was *so* affectionate, *so* kind, *so* dear,' wrote the Queen' 'we kissed each other again and again and he called me [in German] "Darling little one, I love you *so* much" and that we should have a very fortunate life together. Oh! what *too* sweet delightful moments are these!! Oh! how *blessed*, how happy I am to think he is *really* mine; I can scarcely believe myself *so blessed*. I kissed his dear hand and do feel *so* grateful to him; he is such an Angel, such a *very* great Angel! We sit so nicely side by side on that little blue sofa; no two Lovers could ever be happier than we are! . . . He took my hands in his, and said my hands were so little he could hardly believe they *were* hands, as he had hitherto *only* been accustomed to handle hands like Ernest's.'[16]

The Queen was firm in her disapproval of the marriage of Lady Cowper, Lord Melbourne's sister, who after being intimate with Lord Palmerston for years proposed, now she was widowed, to marry him, though both were over fifty. The marriage turned out a success and Lord and Lady Palmerston were happy, but the Queen thought it foolish, disliked it and refused to promise not to say so.

The Queen was capable of rebuking Lord Melbourne himself. She had been a good deal annoyed, she wrote in the summer of 1839, to hear from Lord Normanby that Lord John Russell was coming to town the following Monday in order to change with him. The Cabinet was being reconstructed after the 'Bedchamber crisis'. 'Lord Melbourne *never* told the Queen that this was definitely settled, on the contrary he said it would "remain in our hands" to use Lord Melbourne's own words, and only be settled during the Vacation . . . she thinks and feels he ought to have told her this was *settled* and not let the Queen be the last person to hear what is settled and done in her name. . . .' When the Queen wrote this letter, she was not many months over 20.[17] As her Ministers were to discover, the Queen was insistent on her rights and little escaped her attention.

Absorbed by these personal problems, the Queen paid little attention to the rise of Chartism, a revolutionary democratic agitation among the masses of the population. Lord Melbourne had warned her in 1838 that she could not expect the political life of the country to proceed as smoothly and quietly as it had since her accession, but her betrothal, with its excitements and complications, wiped all other considerations from her mind.

Chartism was, fundamentally, an expression of the disappointment felt by the mass of the nation at the results of the Reform Bill of 1832, which proved to enfranchise the middle classes only, not the workers. Colliers, factory workers, hand-loom weavers were passing through a period of misery and starvation, unprotected by effective legislation, especially in the case of children; while a leading Chartist leader, Feargus O'Connor, was a representative of the most miserable of all workers, the Irish, and a champion of Irish freedom. Discontent broke out into riots in November 1839, one of the most serious being in Newport, Monmouthshire, on 4th November. A crowd estimated at 20,000, of whom 3,000 were believed to be armed with rifles, marched on the town, but with 'great gallantry' the Mayor, Mr T. Phillips, called out the available troops and ordered them to load. The rioters, said to have fired first, were dispersed by the disciplined fire of the troops. For these services Mr Phillips was knighted and received the freedom of the City of London. On 23rd December 1839 Mr Phillips came to Windsor to be knighted and Charles Greville persuaded Lord Normanby that it would be a wise and popular thing and do good to the Queen to keep him there, 'load him with civilities . . . and send him back rejoicing to his province'. Lord Normanby said etiquette would not permit one of Mr Phillips' rank in life to be invited to the royal table. Greville said this was all nonsense; if he was good enough to come to Windsor and be knighted, he was good enough to dine there. He stayed, the Queen was very civil to him and he was delighted.[18]

Mr Phillips' knighthood, however, did not solve the Chartist problem but the Queen, having done as she was asked and exercised her charm on Mr Phillips, took no further interest in the Chartist cause.

On 10th November 1839 the Queen decided to tell the news of her engagement to the Duchess of Kent. After consulting Prince Albert the Queen wrote: 'I then sent for Mama . . . when she came, I said to her, I was going to tell her something which I was sure would please her, namely that I had chosen Albert to be my future husband; she took me in her arms and cried, and said, though I had not asked her, still that she gave her best blessing to it, and seemed delighted. . . . I sent for dearest Albert, whom she embraced and said it made her so happy, that she was *as* anxious for his happiness as for mine. . . .'

Thinking the news over, however, the Duchess became tiresome, as tiresome as she had ever been, the Queen wrote; her mother 'plagued' Prince Albert, declared she had not slept all night, urged that her friend Lord Dunfermline, the ex-Speaker, should be appointed Prince Albert's adviser and said she wished to live with Queen Victoria and Prince Albert at Buckingham Palace after their marriage 'which we agreed *never* would do'.[19]

There was a brighter interlude on Monday afternoon when the Queen, who possessed a natural talent for dancing, was taught to valse by Prince Albert, while Prince Ernest, restored to a normal colour, played the piano. After dinner the Queen valsed with Prince Albert and 'did very well', starting badly but finishing *'brilliantly'*.

The Duchess of Kent meanwhile never ceased to grumble. She felt 'very low', and complained to Prince Albert she was being turned out of the house by her daughter.

Prince Albert was to leave on the morning of Thursday, 14th November; as the days passed the coming separation weighed more and more heavily on the Queen but she did not indulge in the extravagant torrents of grief which had accompanied previous less important partings. She had matured. The Prince said farewell to her in the little blue sitting-room where so many hours of bliss had been spent and gave her a turquoise pin which had belonged to his mother. She had already said goodbye to his gentlemen to whom she gave presents, and the Prince had sent Eos in to say goodbye to her while she was dressing. It would be two months before she and the Prince were alone again, and then he would come as her bridegroom. She leant 'on that dear soft cheek, fresh and pink like a rose'. Prince Albert said he must look once more into her 'beautiful eyes', then it was ten o'clock and time for him to go. The Queen went into her dressing-room, where Ernest and the Duchess of Kent were waiting, embraced Ernest, gave Albert a final kiss at the top of the staircase and watched him get into the carriage and drive away.

She then 'cried much, felt wretched, yet happy to think we should meet so soon again! Oh! how I love him, how intensely, how devotedly, how ardently! . . . Walked, Cried. Wrote a letter to my dearest precious angel'; that night she 'cried in bed for a little while'. Much of the afternoon was spent with Lord Melbourne discussing the problem of the Duchess of Kent's behaviour. The Duchess had written to the Queen complaining vehemently that she had not been told earlier of the Queen's engagement. 'Lord M. said he feared I should have great difficulty in getting her out of the house. "There must be no harshness," said Lord M., "yet firm." ' The Queen pointed out that in the settlement of her mother's finances, the Duchess had agreed to give up £18,000 a year towards paying her debts while she was with the Queen and £10,000 when she was no longer with her, which proved the Duchess knew she could not remain in Buckingham Palace once the Queen married. Nonetheless she went back to her old tactics, plaguing the Queen with letters of complaint; even Prince Albert's valet, she declared, had known the news before she did, which the Queen said was not true, though of course there had been servants' gossip. Lord Melbourne said the Duchess had said to him earlier that she was 'quite a slave in fact, and wasn't mistress of her own house or anything in the house, and now she didn't wish to go which made us laugh etc. . . . I told Lord M. that Mama had said it would be so very painful for her to separate from me; that she was *not* independent, which I told her she was; etc.; that we were so young, and that, in fine I thought she wished to *fix* herself *in* the house.' The feeling in the country was that the Duchess could not live with her once she was married, said the Queen.[20]

The Queen had now written to the Royal Family to tell them of her engagement and was gratified by the cordiality of their good wishes. The Cambridge family called, including Prince George, the Queen's first cousin, son of the old Duke of Cambridge, who was the Queen's uncle. Prince George had grown taller but '*very* ugly, his skin in a shocking state. They were all very kind and civil, George quite different towards me, much less reserved, and evidently happy to be clear of me.'

Prince Albert wrote frequently to the Queen, the first letter was written as soon as he arrived at Calais, and she was again in a heaven of bliss at receiving her first love letters. Bliss, however, alternated with nervous depression when she did not receive a letter from the Prince for several days, and towards the end of November she had no letter for more than a week. She vented her unhappiness on her domestic servants and on the Tory newspapers who were attacking the Whigs. 'Decency, feeling, propriety, everything is forgotten in the feeling of disappointed ambition' she told Prince Albert. '. . . It disgusts me. I rage, as Uncle L. calls it. . . . Oh! if only I could be with you. How far away is February.'

On 28th November a letter from Prince Albert arrived. 'This morning I received your dear, dear letter of the 21st' wrote the Queen in ecstasy. 'How happy do you make me with your love! Oh! my Angel Albert, I am quite enchanted with it! I do not deserve such love! Never, never did I think I could be loved so much.'[21]

By now, the Queen wrote, Prince Albert would have heard that further discussion had taken place on the advisability of his becoming a peer and she would like to repeat a few remarks she had already written to King Leopold. 'The English are very jealous of any foreign interference in the Government of the country and have already in some of the papers (who are friendly to me and to you) expressed a hope that you would not interfere:—now, tho' I know you never would, still, if you were a peer they would all say the Prince meant to play a political part—I am sure you will understand;—but it is much better not to say anything more about it now and to leave the whole affair alone.' The Prince's opinion of an English peerage was that 'It would be almost a step downwards, for as a Duke of Saxony, I feel myself much higher than as Duke of Kent or York. . . .'

Throughout this correspondence the pattern of their future life together was taking shape. Prince Albert was the instructor, the Queen the pupil. She promises to do her utmost to free herself from all her bad habits before he returns, she will copy his handwriting and form her German letters properly, she will take his advice, see her mother and show her the rooms suggested for her. She feels that she is making so many silly mistakes in German that she had better write in English.[22] 'Dearest beloved Albert, I pray daily and nightly that I may become more worthy of you, dearest, dearest Albert. . . . I am always, always seeing your dear angel's face before me and I can hardly believe, that I will be so happy, so very happy, as to become your wife!'

The Queen liked to be guided, though the advice must coincide with her wishes, and because she was fatherless she idealised paternal affection, a longing intensified by her unsatisfactory relationship with her mother. By 21st November she had moved from Windsor to Buckingham Palace; everyone knew of her intended marriage and had been most kind. 'Thank God the secret is out now!' wrote the Queen to the Prince 'it makes me very happy because now I can talk about you so much more, my own dearest Angel!'

The Pagets had been staying, the gay sons and daughters of the celebrated Lord Uxbridge, now Marquess of Anglesey, who had led the cavalry and lost a leg at Waterloo and was a close friend of the Duke of Wellington. The party, but not the Queen, had danced to a galoppe composed by Prince Albert.

On Saturday, 23rd November, the Queen summoned the Privy Council to announce her decision to marry. In a short speech she declared her intention 'to ally myself in marriage with the Prince Albert of Saxe-Coburg and Gotha. Deeply impressed by the solemnity of the engagement, which I am about to contract, I have not come to this decision without mature consideration, nor without feeling a strong assurance that, with the blessing of Almighty God, it will at once secure my domestic felicity and serve the interests of my country.

'I have thought fit to make this resolution known to you at the earliest possible period, in order that you may be fully apprised of a matter so highly important to me and to my kingdom, and which, I persuade myself, will be most acceptable to all my loving subjects.'

The Queen was nervous, so nervous that Greville, present as Clerk to the Privy Council, observed her hand trembled so much that she could hardly hold the paper. Nevertheless, she read the declaration in the 'clear, sonorous sweet-toned' voice which was one of her charms, and did not make a single mistake.[23] She told Lord Melbourne that Prince Albert's picture, which she always wore, seemed to give her courage. The Queen had also to announce her marriage in her speech to Parliament but thought this nothing in comparison with the Privy Council.

However, a series of disagreeable occurrences was to follow.

The Queen's enthusiasm for Prince Albert was by no means shared by her subjects. Little was known of the Prince except that he was German, very young, remarkably good-looking and penniless. Want of money, it was reported, had made it necessary for the Prince to cut short his Italian visit and to return by the cheapest and most direct route which he did not wish to take. When his father, the Duke of Saxe-Coburg and Gotha, had been in London, the Queen found herself expected to lend him money and to do the same for Duke Ferdinand.

The British public and Parliament did not welcome the prospect of another penniless German Prince being provided with a large income out of the national revenue.

In Europe Albert was regarded as having won a prize above his station. The Queen herself, though she felt proposing to Prince Albert was 'a much more nervous thing' than making the declaration to the Privy Council, recognised it would have been impossible for him to propose to the Queen of England. 'He would never have presumed to take such a liberty', she told her aunt, the Duchess of Gloucester. The Queen differentiated between herself as a person, a capacity in which she was humble and unassuming, and her position as Queen of England, in which she was tenacious of every detail of her rights, insistent on her superiority, by virtue of her function, to any other person in the realm, not to be swayed or softened by considerations of affection.

Difficulty arose over the payment to the Prince of the £50,000 annuity which Lord Melbourne had told the Queen would go through without trouble. On 24th January 1840 Lord John Russell proposed a provision of £50,000 a year to be granted by the Queen to Prince Albert out of the Consolidated Fund but made the mistake of estimating the salaries the Prince would have to pay for his household at about £7,000–£8,000 a year.

Mr Joseph Hume, the Radical, enquired what was to become of the rest. 'Did the noble Lord know the dangers of setting a young man down in London with so much money in his pocket? (laughter).' The financial position of the country was not good, people were starving. Mr Hume put forward a motion to reduce the Prince's annuity from £50,000 annually to £21,000. The motion was defeated by 267 on 27th January but was immediately succeeded by a motion advanced by Colonel Sibthorp, a noted Tory, reducing the Prince's annuity from £50,000 to £30,000. Colonel Sibthorp's amendment was supported by Sir Robert Peel and Radicals and Tories united in showing an 'insulting distrust' of the Prince, though Sir Robert Peel qualified his support of the reduction by recommending that if the Prince survived the Queen, was the father of a family and lived permanently in the United Kingdom, his annuity should be raised to £50,000. He also reminded the House that at the time Prince Leopold received £50,000, the universal feeling had been that the grant was too great. Colonel Sibthorp's amendment was then put to the vote, and carried by a majority of 104, and the Prince's annuity was reduced.[24]

Lord Melbourne was forced to accept the decision of the House. It was not merely the Tories whom the Prince had to thank for curtailing his income, he remarked to Stockmar, but the Tories, the Radicals and 'a good many of our own people' the rank and file of Whig members. The feeling of the country had shown itself against £50,000 a year for the Prince and Melbourne had to submit. The Queen declared that everything that happened and the comments in the newspapers made her hate the Tories more and more.

Prince Albert himself took the reduction well. No irritation manifested itself, either at that time or later. 'What pained him most' he said 'was the restriction that would thereby be imposed on him in his endeavours to do good and to assist poor artists and savants.'[25]

A further unpleasantness which provoked the Queen to another access of fury against the 'abominable infamous Tories' arose when a 'great outcry' was made that Prince Albert had 'papistical leanings', because he had not been specifically designated as a Protestant Prince in the Declaration of the Queen's intended marriage to the Privy Council. Numbers of Coburgs had been converted to the Catholic Church, an even larger number had married Catholics, and the English government had always been aware of the situation. When the Prince and his brother arrived at Windsor in October 1839 Lord Melbourne advised that they should without fail attend the Protestant church on Sunday, as 'the others' had gone to mass.

Both King Leopold and Stockmar considered the word 'Protestant' should be included in the Declaration. In Stockmar's opinion the doubts cast on the Prince's Protestantism emanated from the King of Hanover, the Queen's uncle, a violent reactionary Protestant and arch intriguer; but Melbourne did not wish to offend the 'other Coburgs', nor the Irish Catholic members, who were all important at the moment to the Whig majority in the House of Commons.

King Leopold predicted 'interminable growling' in future and Stockmar was consulted 'in great haste' by Lord Palmerston, who wished to know as soon as possible if Prince Albert belonged to any sect, which, though Protestant, held doctrines which would prevent him from taking part in the celebrations of Holy Communion according to the rites of the Church of England. The Prince, he was informed, belonged to no such sect, but to the Lutheran branch of the Protestant Church and could thus take part in Church of England rites.

The Queen was particularly incensed at the suggestion that the Prince was a Catholic like his Coburg cousins. She found it difficult to believe that any one of her subjects was unaware of the penalty under the Act of Settlement which made 'the Sovereign's marriage with a Roman Catholic an ipso facto forfeiture of the Crown'. She supported Lord Melbourne, the Cabinet supported Lord Melbourne for political reasons, and the 'growling' threatened to become serious. The Duke of Wellington then added the adjective 'Protestant' to the word 'Prince' as an amendment to the address in the House of Lords and carried the amendment against the government.[26] There was never serious doubt of the Prince's Protestantism but it was a satisfaction to the country to have the fact distinctly affirmed as a proof that England still retained the character of a Protestant State. The growling died away.

Additional unpleasantness arose over the question of Prince Albert's rank and precedence, a subject of importance to the Queen. It had been urged by King Leopold that the Prince should be created an English peer, '. . . the reason why I do wish it, is that Albert's foreignership should disappear as much as possible. I have, in different circumstances to be sure, suffered greatly from having declined the peerage conditionally, when it was offered me in 1816.'

Neither the Queen nor the Prince agreed. The Prince did not wish to bear any title but his own and the Queen, while sympathising, wished the Prince to be given rank, and therefore precedence, immediately after herself for the whole of his lifetime. By an Act of Parliament the Prince Regent had been empowered to give Prince Leopold, when he married Princess Charlotte, precedence over every person but the Princes of the Blood Royal and the Queen wished Prince Albert's precedence to be settled in the same way, but to be more elevated, with Prince Albert ranking above the Princes of the Blood Royal.

An Act of Parliament was necessary and the consent of the Queen's uncles had to be obtained. After some hesitation the Dukes of Sussex and Cambridge gave their consent, but the King of Hanover, the former Duke of Cumberland, refused, urged the Tories to object and persuaded the Duke of Cambridge to withdraw the consent he had given.

The King of Hanover was preparing to be disagreeable; he had refused to allow the Queen to be supplied with the 'creams and blacks' (cream and black horses from the Hanoverian stables which since the accession of the Hanoverian dynasty to the throne of England had drawn the English royal coach on state occasions), he refused to allow his apartments in St James's Palace to be occupied by his sister-in-law, the Duchess of Kent, and he was getting ready to lay claim to the Hanoverian Crown Jewels, bought with English money while England and Hanover were united.

Owing to the 'slovenliness' of Whig drafting, no provision had been made for the Prince supposing the Queen died before him without leaving a child, in which case the King of Hanover would succeed to the throne, a recurrent nightmare to the British nation. Nor had it been appreciated that if the Queen's wish was fulfilled and the Prince given the highest possible rank, next to the Queen herself, for the whole of his lifetime, he would take precedence over every eldest son and heir apparent of a sovereign, including—if the Queen should die without leaving children—the son of the King of Hanover, who would then succeed to the English throne, and if the Queen's death should occur after a son was born to her, over the heir apparent to the throne of England itself.

The Queen had taken the defeat on the annuity 'with great composure' but laid all the greater weight on the question of precedence. At dinner on 27th January Lord Melbourne said 'You've heard that we have had terrible work about this Bill. . . . We've been obliged to put it off to consider it till Friday.' The Duke of Wellington took exception to it. 'I grew quite frantic,' wrote the Queen,[27] 'declared I never would forgive it, never would look at the Duke again, etc. "Don't be angry", Lord M. said calmly. I was quite furious and raged away. . . . At near 11 Lord M. received a note . . . saying that we had been beat by 104; that it had been made quite a party question (vile, confounded, infernal Tories), that Peel had *spoken* and voted against the £50,000 (nasty wretch) and Graham too. As long as I live I'll never forgive these infernal scoundrels, with Peel at their head . . . for this act of personal spite!! . . . Talked of that fiend the Bishop of Exeter.'

The Bishop of Exeter, Dr Henry Phillpotts, had incurred the Queen's wrath, not only by supporting the reduction of the Prince's allowance, but by his reactionary opinions. Chartism was a burning issue, the country was restless with industrial and agricultural discontent and the policy of Melbourne's government was to avoid adding fuel to the flames. But on 24th January 1840 when the House of Lords spent the day debating socialism, the Bishop of Exeter presented a petition, signed by 4,000 persons in Birmingham, stating the government had done nothing against the socialists in spite of the danger they represented to the morals of the people as a whole. A statute did exist (57 George III Cap. 19) which declared that societies sending 'missionaries' should be deemed guilty of unlawful combination, but the Bishop pointed out how many other societies there were, instituted for the best and most pious purposes, which were in the same case. 'How was it possible then to carry that Act into effect? Indeed he believed it never had been carried into effect. If it had any effect at all, he thought it operated solely by means of terror. . . .' But, the Bishop went on, 'the object of the Socialists . . . was to alter the whole framework of society, and the whole framework of property'. On account of this and similar statements the Bishop was regarded as a fanatic.

The Queen's anger remained at boiling point. She declared she would not invite the Duke of Wellington to the Chapel [the Chapel Royal, St James's] for her marriage and 'Lord M. wrote twice begging I would. I said to Lord M. I really couldn't ask the Duke: "Why, I think," said Lord M., "his age, station and position require he should." I said I really couldn't. . . . I fear I was very eager and over violent.'

On Sunday, Lord Clarendon, who had been to see the Duke of Wellington, reported that the Duke considered Prince Albert should have the same precedence as Prince George of Denmark when he married Queen (then Princess) Anne and Prince (now King) Leopold when he married Princess Charlotte but not more; Lord Melbourne advised the Queen to give up voluntarily what it would certainly be very disagreeable to be forced to give up. Once more the Queen 'raged'. 'I was perfectly frantic,—this wicked old foolish Duke, these confounded Tories, oh! may they be well punished for this outrageous insult! I cried with rage. . . . Poor dear Albert, how cruelly are they ill-using that dearest Angel! Monsters! You Tories shall be punished. Revenge! Revenge!'

The Queen was persuaded to invite the Duke to the wedding but refused to ask him to dinner. ' "I don't think he means any disrespect," Lord Melbourne said amiably and kindly, "It's his conscience".'

Greville, an authority on procedure now, however, wrote a pamphlet giving it as his opinion that the Queen, by exercise of the royal prerogative, was entitled through letters patent to confer whatever rank and precedence she chose on the Prince, next to herself if she wished, except in Parliament and at the Privy Council. The Duke of Wellington, the Lord Chancellor and the Attorney General concurred. Letters Patent to this effect were issued by the Queen on 5th March 1840.[28]

A more difficult and intimate question was the formation of the Prince's household. On 29th November 1839 the Queen wrote to Prince Albert that she had had 'a good talk' with Lord Melbourne about the Prince's official attendants and Lord Melbourne told her that young Mr George Anson, his private secretary, 'greatly wishes' to be with the Prince. The Queen was 'very much in favour of it, because he is an excellent young man, very modest, very honest, very steady, very well informed and will be of much use to you. . . .'

Mr Anson's association with Lord Melbourne made it clear that he was a Whig; furthermore his uncle, Sir George Anson, who was proposed as Groom of the Prince's Bedchamber, was a well-known member of the Whig party. But it was the Prince's particular wish that the selection of his household should be made 'without regard to politics'. It was the Prince's conviction, one which remained the guiding principle of his political philosophy and of his life, that the Crown should be above party, and that personal appointments round the Crown should not be 'mere party awards. It is very necessary that they should be chosen from both sides— the same number of Whigs as of Tories. . . .'[29]

*

This principle, that the Crown is dissociated from party and above party, is Prince Albert's contribution to British politics. Queen Victoria's predecessors had identified themselves with one or other of the political parties: the Queen's uncle William IV had been a rabid Tory, the Queen herself was an equally determined Whig. Prince Albert's conviction, ultimately shared by the Queen, that the Crown should be non-party, is the fact to which the British Royal Family largely owes the present stability of its position in Europe and its place in the affections and loyalty of its subjects of differing political opinions.

It was therefore a blow to the Prince to be informed by the Queen, in a tone very different from her usual terms of adoring affection, 'As to your wish about your gentlemen, my dear Albert, I must tell you quite honestly that it will not do. You may entirely rely upon me that the people who will be round you will be absolutely pleasant people of high standing and good character ... you may rely upon my care that you shall have proper people and not idle and not too young and Lord Melbourne has already mentioned several to me who would be very suitable. ...'

In the midst of affection and longing the iron hand appeared within the velvet glove, as had already been the experience of Lord Melbourne. As Lady Lyttelton, when governess to the royal children, remarked, 'a vein of iron runs through her most extraordinary character' and Prince Albert had no choice but to submit. 'I am very sorry' he wrote 'that you have not been able to grant my first request, the one about the gentlemen of my household, for I know it was not an unfair one. ... As to your proposition concerning Mr Anson, I confess to have my doubts. ... I give you to consider, dearest love, if my taking the Secretary of the Prime Minister ... would not from the beginning make me a partisan in the eyes of many? As my Privy Purse cannot have so much to do, I hope that Schenck, whom as you know I have already appointed, will be quite adequate to the business. ... Think of my position, dear Victoria; I am leaving my home with all its old associations, all my bosom friends, and going to a country in which everything is new and strange to me—men, language, customs, modes of life, position. Except yourself I have no one to confide in. And is it not even to be conceded to me that the two or three persons who are to have the charge of my private affairs should be persons who already command my confidence?'

It was not conceded. Members of the Prince's household were to be appointed by the Queen. 'I am distressed to be obliged to tell you what I fear you do not like, but it is necessary. ...' Queen Victoria told the Prince on 23rd December 1839. The Prince had no choice but to give way. 'Albert ... I am glad to say, consents to my choosing his People. ...' the Queen wrote to King Leopold.[30] The only German permitted to the Prince was his secretary, Herr Doctor Schenck, who did not dine at the Equerries' table and occupied an inferior social position.

It is a tribute to Prince Albert's character that he became devoted to

Anson, and Anson to him. The Queen records that Prince Albert said to her later 'He was my only intimate friend. We went through everything together since I came here. He was almost like a brother to me', and the Prince's initial opposition became a standing joke between Mr Anson and himself.

On 14th January 1840, Lord Torrington and General Charles Grey (later author of *The Early Years of the Prince Consort*) left Buckingham Palace with three of the Queen's carriages to fetch Prince Albert from Gotha, taking with them the Garter, with which the Prince was invested in the throne room at Gotha on 23rd January 1840. The Prince's father, the Duke of Saxe-Coburg and Gotha, who was already a Knight of the Garter, was issued by the Queen with Letters Patent authorising him to invest the Prince with the insignia of the Order; Prince Charles of Leiningen, the Queen's half-brother, also a Knight, was to attach the Garter itself. The entire Court assembled, the ladies in boxes wearing their jewels, the gentlemen wearing full uniform. At the moment of the Prince's investiture a salute of 101 cannon was fired. A banquet for 180 persons followed, at which the Queen's health was drunk standing, trumpets sounded a fanfare, the band of the Coldstream Guards, brought over from England, played 'God Save the Queen' and the cannon fired a Royal Salute.

In Coburg itself the joy of the people when the marriage was declared had been so great 'that they went on firing in the streets with guns and pistols during the whole night, so that one might have imagined that a battle was taking place'.

On 27th January 1840 the Prince's visit to Gotha reached its last day. After a full-dress dinner every member of the Court passed before him to say farewell, many in tears, the Dowager Duchess being repeatedly overwhelmed by bursts of weeping.

Next day, when the journey to England began, 'the streets of Gotha were densely crowded; every window crammed with heads, every housetop covered with people waving handkerchiefs. . . .' At the Dowager Duchess's residence, the Prince, accompanied by his father, stopped his carriage and got out to bid her a last farewell. As the carriages drove off she came to the window, threw up her arms calling 'Albert, Albert' and was carried away in a fainting state by her attendants.[31]

Two vessels, the *Ariel Packet* carrying Mr Hamilton, one of the most experienced pilots in the service, and the *Firebrand*, were sent to Calais by the Admiralty to bring the Prince and his suite to Dover, both vessels being under the temporary command of Lord Clarence Paget for the passage.[32] Orders were given for 'suitable' refreshments to be prepared for both vessels, 'sufficient should his Serene Highness prefer to travel in *Firebrand*'.

The refreshments were never consumed. The 'passage to England was terrible'. The wind freshened to half a gale, it was impossible to board *Firebrand*, and the whole party embarked in the small packet *Ariel*. The passage took five and a half hours, the seas becoming heavier as the English coast approached, and the deck of the little steamer was a nightmare of misery and seasickness. The Duke of Saxe Coburg Gotha went below where the two Princes, one on either side of the cabin staircase, lay helpless with seasickness. When Dover was finally reached the piers were crowded with cheering people come to welcome the future husband of their Queen. By no common exercise of resolution Prince Albert managed to rouse himself and appear on deck to bow and smile to the enthusiastic crowds as the vessel drew in. His face, he remarked, was the colour of a wax candle.

The Prince was enthusiastically received, crowds gathering at every village the whole way to London. The 11th Light Dragoons escorted him, commanded by the seventh Earl of Cardigan, later leader of the Charge of the Light Brigade; in celebration of this event the name of the regiment was changed to the 11th Prince Albert's Own Hussars. Especially large crowds gathered at Canterbury where the Prince and his brother spent a night and attended afternoon service at the cathedral. In the evening the city was illuminated, the Prince was called for by name, appeared on the balcony of the hotel and was vehemently cheered. Lord Melbourne commented that the Prince's reception was such that he must take care not to become intoxicated by it. At half past four in the afternoon of Saturday, 8th February, the Prince's carriage and escort drove up to the door of Buckingham Palace. The Duchess of Kent, the whole household and the Queen were waiting, the Queen standing at the door itself. She took Albert by the hand and led him up to her sitting-room. She had been so agitated as to feel unwell: 'Most natural,' said Lord Melbourne, 'how could it be otherwise?' but when she and the Prince met, 'seeing his *dear dear* face again put me at rest about everything'.[33] Wedding gifts were exchanged. Prince Albert gave the Queen a superb brooch of an immense sapphire set round with diamonds; she gave him a diamond Garter and the Star and Badge of the Garter in diamonds. At 5 p.m. the Lord Chancellor administered the oaths of naturalisation, and the day ended with 'a great dinner', Prince Albert still feeling giddy and ill from seasickness.

The marriage was to take place on Monday 10th February. On the Sunday, the Prince came to the Queen's sitting-room in the afternoon 'and we talked of Anson's appointment . . . about which we had some little misunderstandings and he was so dear and *ehrlich* and open about it; he will appoint him. I embraced him again and again.' The Queen then watched his carriage drive away through an immense throng: the upper and prosperous middle classes might have their doubts about the Prince, but the crowds were delighted by the Queen's romance and the young Prince's good looks.

The Queen and the Prince met again before dinner, read over the marriage service together, and tried managing the ring. The Queen commented to Lord Melbourne that Albert was tired and agitated, which Lord Melbourne said he did not wonder at. She added that Albert had feared she loved him less before they had the explanation over Anson, but that all was right now.

That Sunday night, the Queen wrote in her Journal 'The last time I slept alone'.[34] She slept well, she was not nervous; the only thing she dreaded about marriage was the possibility of having a large family of children.

The ceremony was to take place at the Chapel Royal, St James's, at 1 p.m. Royal weddings had hitherto taken place late at night, so on 10th February, in spite of the weather—'a dreadful day,' wrote Greville, 'torrents of rain, and violent gusts of wind. Nevertheless a countless multitude thronged the park and was scattered over the town.' Later the day cleared and the sun broke through to bring the brilliant sunshine so regularly attendant on the Queen's activities that it was known as 'Queen's weather'. After breakfast the Queen disregarded tradition by seeing the Prince 'for the *last* time *alone* as my bridegroom'. At half past twelve the Queen left Buckingham Palace accompanied by the Duchess of Kent and her mistress of the robes, the Duchess of Sutherland. She wore a white satin gown, with a very deep flounce of Honiton lace, made in imitation of the antique, a diamond necklace and earrings and Prince Albert's magnificent sapphire brooch. Her twelve young train-bearers wore white with white roses. There was a flourish of trumpets, as the Queen entered the Chapel. The Prince wore the uniform of a Field Marshal, the rank awarded him in the British Army, with the Order of the Garter. The Queen was given away by her uncle, the Duke of Sussex. Both she and the Prince made the responses in the marriage service clearly and firmly. Miss Agnes Strickland, in her account of the marriage given in her suppressed biography, *Victoria from Birth to Bridal*, states that on entering the Chapel Royal the Queen 'moulded her blanched and trembling lips into a faint smile, was agitated and with difficulty restrained her feelings'. The Queen, reading this, commented 'Not true'. Miss Strickland alleged that the Queen on her return from the Chapel Royal after the marriage looked 'pale and thoughtful', 'a wife as well as a sovereign' and 'evidently felt acutely and strongly the alteration her position had undergone'. The Queen commented 'Not so. *Only* felt *so* happy.' Miss Strickland stated the Queen's smile after the marriage had 'a touch of melancholy'. The Queen wrote 'Not melancholy—joy!'[35]

Gossip had been busy with the Whig opinions of the persons invited by the Queen. 'She had been as wilful, obstinate and wrong-headed as usual about her invitations' wrote Greville 'and some of her foolish and mischievous Courtiers were boasting that out of above 300 people in the Chapel there would only be five Tories. Of these 5, two were the Joint Great Chamberlains, Willoughby and Cholmondeley, whom they could hardly omit, and one Ashley, the husband of Melbourne's niece; the other two were Ld. Liverpool, her own old friend, and the Duke [of Wellington] but there was a hesitation about inviting them.'[36] Among the sight-seeing crowds was Florence Nightingale who was in London for 'a little change' staying with her Aunt Mai. In common with the prosperous majority of the nation the Nightingales despised Prince Albert for being penniless, and Miss Nightingale wrote home that she had seen the Prince 'in the clothes which no doubt he borrowed to be married in'. She wrote a lively account of the ceremony.[37] 'There were but 3 Tories there. Ld Melbourne pressed the Queen to ask more, told her how obnoxious it was. Queen said "It is MY marriage and I will only have those who can sympathise with me." She asked D. of Wellington as a public character; Ld Liverpool and the Jenkinsons as her private friends and Ld Ashley because he married a Cowper—but not even the Duchess of Northumberland. . . . Mr Harcourt told Lord Colchester that there was a great levee to receive the Prince and they were all standing with the Queen ready to receive him. When his carriage was announced she walked out of the room. Nobody could conceive what she was going to do and before anyone could stop her, she had run downstairs and was in his arms.'

The wedding breakfast was held at Buckingham Palace, the Queen being led in by her husband and her train carried by four pages. She sat between Prince Albert and the Duke of Sussex. The Queen then went upstairs, took off her wedding dress and put on a white silk gown trimmed with swansdown and a white bonnet trimmed with orange flowers. Lord Melbourne came in and told her ' "Nothing could have gone off better" . . . I pressed his hand once more, and he said "God bless you Ma'am", most kindly, and with such a kind look. Dearest Albert came up and fetched me downstairs, where we took leave of Mamma and drove off at near 4, Albert and I alone which was *so delightful*.'

The fashion in which the newly married couple departed was not approved by Greville who was earning himself his subsequent nickname of 'Grumpy'. 'They went off in a very poor and shabby style. Instead of the new chariot in which most married people are accustomed to dash along, they were in one of the old travelling coaches, the postillions in undressed liveries, and with a small escort, three other coaches with post horses following.'[38]

The Queen wrote in her Journal that evening 'There was an immense crowd of people outside the Palace, and which I must say never ceased until we reached Windsor Castle. Our reception was most enthusiastic and hearty and gratifying in every way; the people quite deafening us; and horsemen and gigs etc. driving along with us. We came through Eton where all the Boys received us most kindly—and cheered and shouted. Really I was quite touched . . . We only arrived at 7.'[39]

When the Queen had looked over the rooms she and the Prince were to occupy and changed her dress, she joined the Prince in his room; he was playing the piano and had changed into his Windsor coat. He took the Queen in his arms and kissed and caressed her, and 'was so dear and kind. We had our dinner in our sitting room, but I had such a sick headache that I could eat nothing, and was obliged to lie down . . . for the remainder of the evening on the sofa; but ill or not, I *never, never* spent such an evening!! My *dearest dearest dear* Albert sat on a footstool by my side, and his excessive love and affection gave me feelings of heavenly love and happiness I never could have *hoped* to have felt before! He clasped me in his arms, and we kissed each other again and again! His beauty, his sweetness and gentleness—really how can I ever be thankful enough to have such a *Husband*! . . . to be called by names of tenderness, I have never yet heard used to me before—was bliss beyond belief! Oh! this was the happiest day of my life!—May God help me to do my duty as I ought and be worthy of such blessings!'

Next day to have the Prince's 'beautiful angelic face' to greet her in the morning was more joy than the Queen could express. They got up at half past eight, much earlier than the Queen's usual hour, and Greville, still grumpy, told Lady Palmerston the wedding night had been too short, this was 'not the way to provide us with a Prince of Wales'. Albert breakfasted in a black velvet jacket without any neckcloth so that his throat could be seen 'and looked more beautiful' wrote the Queen 'than it is possible for me to say'. They then walked on the Terrace and New Walk, alone arm in arm. It was now the turn of the Prince to feel sick, as he had not yet recovered from the effects of his seasickness followed by the festivities and banquets attendant on the marriage in addition to the strain of the ceremony itself. He lay down and dozed in the Queen's sitting-room while she wrote letters, getting up at one point to read her a funny story but feeling so poorly that he was forced to lie down again, resting his head on her shoulder. That evening, the second of the honeymoon, was not spent alone with the Queen. There were ten people at dinner, a 'very delightful, merry, nice little party' wrote the Queen. Prince Albert recovered sufficiently to be able to sing, though he still felt weak in his knees.

The following evening, Wednesday, the Queen collected an 'immense' party at Windsor and sent up to London in a hurry for one of her favourite

Pagets, Lord Clarence Paget, who had commanded the vessels which brought the Prince to England, to come down and organise a dance, 'a proceeding quite unparalleled'. Fashionable opinion was outraged. Lady Palmerston told Greville she was 'much vexed' that the Queen had nobody about her who could venture to tell her that this was not becoming and would appear indelicate. 'But She has nobody who dares tell her, or she will not endure to hear such truths.'[40]

The Queen was aware that the Prince would have preferred a period of retirement—the English custom after marriage.[41] He had written to her from Gotha that he wished they could remain at Windsor alone for a time after the wedding. 'It is usual in England, is it not, for newly married people to stay up to four to six weeks away from the town and society, and they seem to make a great point of this? It might perhaps be a good and delicate action not to depart from this custom altogether and to retire from the public eye for at least a fortnight—or a week.'

The Queen was annoyed. 'My dear Albert,' she wrote, 'you have not at all understood the matter. *You forget, my dearest Love, that I am the Sovereign, and that business can stop and wait for nothing. Parliament is sitting and something occurs almost every day for which I am required and it is quite impossible for me to be absent from London; therefore two or three days is already a long time to be absent. . . . I must come out after the second day . . . I cannot keep alone. This is also my own wish in every way.'*

In the same letter the Queen pronounced with equal firmness on the question of the arms to be borne by the Prince. He had no right to quarter the English Royal Arms with his own 'but the Sovereign has the power to allow it by Royal Command, and this was done for Uncle Leopold by the Prince Regent and I will do it again for you, but it can only be done by Royal Command'.

The Queen was bursting with happiness and spirits. Her joy and pride in Prince Albert never faltered, '. . . *his* love and gentleness is beyond everything, and to kiss that dear soft cheek, to press my lips to his, is heavenly bliss. . . . Oh! was ever woman so blessed as I am!' But she also longed for 'merriment'—for fun, jokes, laughter and dancing; quadrille music, she had observed, 'almost drove her mad'. After the dance, only two days following her marriage, she stayed up until ten minutes after midnight and went upstairs to find Prince Albert asleep on the sofa in their bedroom, 'looking quite beautiful'. She roused him with a kiss and they went amicably to bed. Next day when she dressed, the Prince put on her stockings for her, and she went in to see him shave, a great pleasure to her. Another dance took place in the Castle that evening at which the Queen danced a galoppe with Prince Albert, 'which gave me great delight'. On Friday the Queen and the Prince left Windsor for London, after three '*very very* happy' days which constituted their honeymoon. Lord Melbourne said it had been a 'whirl' and told the Queen she seemed very well. The Queen replied 'Very, and in very high spirits'. It was impossible to be otherwise, she said, living with the two young Princes, Prince Albert and Prince Ernest. Lord Melbourne replied 'That's a capital thing' and the Queen added Albert's kindness and affection towards her were 'beyond everything' and she could not say how much she felt it. She had now all but finished the twenty-eighth volume of her Journal which, she wrote on 16th February 1840, 'contains the most interesting and happiest time of my life'.[42]

*

Buckingham Palace,[43] which had superseded St James's Palace as the Sovereign's private London residence, was not satisfactory. It had originally been built by John Sheffield, Duke of Buckingham, in 1705 and bought by George III in 1762 as a dower house for Queen Charlotte. King George and Queen Charlotte moved in immediately, making few alterations and continuing to use St James's Palace for ceremonial occasions. When Queen Charlotte died in 1818 the Prince Regent contemplated rebuilding Buckingham House as a palace for himself, but sufficient money to execute his plans was not forthcoming until his accession to the throne, when he determined to carry out the conversion with John Nash as his architect. Both King George IV and Nash, however, were so much occupied with the building of the Brighton Pavilion, while the King was also absorbed in the alterations planned for Windsor Castle, that nothing was done to Buckingham House until 1825. Funds ran out in 1828 and public dissatisfaction with Nash's design and with the enormous sums already expended resulted in the appointment of a Select Committee to investigate. As a result of the Committee's report Parliament, in 1829, fixed a limit to expenditure on the completion of the Palace, which the King however ignored. Orders continued to be given until George IV's illness in 1829 brought work to a standstill; on his death in 1830 Nash was dismissed. During the first months of King William IV's reign Edward Blore was called in to make the Palace habitable. But King William IV did not care for it and offered to donate it for the use of the Houses of Parliament, which had just been burned down. The offer was declined and the King, without enthusiasm, prepared to live in it himself. Work did not proceed smoothly and Buckingham Palace was not completed until May 1837, only a month before the King died. Perhaps because of its architectural vicissitudes, Buckingham Palace was not a comfortable house. The chimneys without exception smoked 'so abominably' that when the young Queen spent the severe winter of 1837–8 there, the first after her accession, 'They are obliged to let the fires go down, even in this bitter weather and shiver in their magnificence.'

Gaining entrance to Buckingham Palace was easy. 'The boy Cotton', finally apprehended in December 1838, had spent a year there, inhabiting the domestic offices and servants' quarters. He was 12 years old, covered in soot, having concealed himself in chimneys, and blackened the beds he slept in. He had never attempted to penetrate to the state apartments or the Queen's suite, but had broken open a sealed letter addressed to the Queen, probably in the hope of finding money in it. He had picked up and hidden a number of articles of small value, ranging from two glass inkstands to a sword, a pair of trousers, which he put on, and 'a Book'. After trying to get out by the equerries' gate he was apprehended on the Palace lawn.[44]

Complaints were made, on the Queen's behalf, of '*smells* and bad ventilation' in the Palace, in addition to the risk to her safety represented by the episode of 'the boy Cotton'. Sir Benjamin Stephenson, one of three Commissioners of Woods and Forests etc., inspected Buckingham Palace a week after the Queen had left, Lord Duncannon, the First Commissioner, being ill, and was horrified.[45] 'None of the rooms had been cleaned or dusted, or any windows opened since the Queen's departure—on the Library Floor the smell was most offensive, and as it appeared to proceed from the basement storey Sir Benjamin proceeded there and ascertained that it proceeded from the kitchen offices, where he found the remains of garden stuff and everything else the most filthy and offensive, and evidently had not been touched since the Queen's departure—on speaking to the Housekeeper . . . she said she had nothing to do with it. When the Queen is resident the same objections may be made, the business is not properly done; if it was your house or mine, we should insist on all the work being done by ten o'clock at latest . . . in place of which, when you go to the Palace, you will find the lamplighters and persons of all occupations, finishing their work 2 or 3 hours later.'

Sir James Clark was alarmed at the danger to the Queen. After her serious illness at Ramsgate in 1835 he had insisted she should be moved to an airier, fresher part of Kensington Palace. There was no need for extravagance at Buckingham Palace but measures must be taken, for the sake of the Queen's health. Lord Conyngham, the Lord Chamberlain from 1835 to 1839, whose innumerable functions included the ventilation and cleaning of the Palace, sent Lord Melbourne a report in September 1838 which is revealing.[46] Windows in every room were opened daily from 8 a.m. until 10 a.m. or later and closed between 4 and 6 p.m. This had been done every day while the Queen was at Windsor but when it was pouring with rain this practice endangered the valuable furniture. Cleaning began the day after the Queen left; all the chimneys were swept, the bright fronts of the grates removed, the ornamented ceilings in several rooms had been brushed and the Queen's rooms cleared entirely to admit the workmen who were to carry out the alterations. Meanwhile the

208

women had been well employed in 'waterwashing' elsewhere. 'The whole palace however is in that apparent state of confusion consequent on such proceedings and it is unlucky that any opinion should have been formed on the subject at the present moment.' The noisome state of the kitchens and the accumulation of decaying food were not mentioned. 'Conyngham's first appointment as Lord Chamberlain was to place one of his mistresses as housekeeper in Buckingham Palace . . . a day or two after, this woman in the actual Palace of the Queen was suddenly checked whilst rushing into the arms of her patron, the Lord Chamberlain and quondam master of her Person.'[47]

The idea of lighting the Palace with gas gave rise to difficulties. Mr Peter Hogg, Clerk of the Works, reported that in his opinion though the upper part of the Palace might be lighted with gas 'done with care', he did not think it would be safe in the attics over the state apartment; several parts of the building were not fireproof and there were 'large enclosed spaces between the ceilings and the floors where any escape of gas can collect'. It was the *private* opinion' of the Hon. Charles Augustus Murray, Master of the Household, that gas was less dangerous in the garrets and upper passages of the Palace than in the damp confined vaults of the basement where it was already used. Eventually, however, it was decided that in deference to the Queen's safety, gas was not to be installed in the attics (though by some mistake it was in fact so installed), but that it should continue to be used in the basement and on Mr Murray's 'remote' staircase to his own apartments.[48]

At the beginning of 1840 Lord Duncannon was uneasy at the amount of work being done at the Palace and the amount of money expended. It was to be completed by the time the Queen came back from Windsor to meet Prince Albert for their wedding and it was with 'consternation' that Lord Duncannon 'heard a report that the Queen was coming on the 7th not the 9th of January. The Palace will not be ready on the 7th. Please let me know something' he besought Lord Melbourne.

However, it was 10th January before the Queen arrived and she was delighted: 'It is all so changed, fresh painted and gilded; my rooms fresh painted and the doors altered, and the ceiling gilt; and beautiful chintz curtains and furniture; it looks like a new house and so pretty.'[49]

Concealed by the freshness of new chintzes, paint and gilt, any possible accumulations of gas in the attics, insanitary conditions in the kitchens and bad smells in her own apartments passed unobserved by the Queen, and if the Prince noticed anything undesirable in the Palace when he arrived, for the moment he passed it by. He was in any case not in an observant condition after the rigours of his crossing.

*

The Prince was aware, as he had stated several times, that his life, in spite of the splendour of his destiny, would be strewn with thorns, but he was not prepared for the situation which confronted him when he began life at Buckingham Palace. Trouble might have been expected with Lord Melbourne, but there was no trouble in that quarter; the trouble was with the Queen herself, and with Lehzen. The Queen adored the Prince, she worshipped the ground he trod on but she was, as she had always been, jealous of her position and rights as Sovereign. A great deal had been written before her marriage to Prince Albert of the assistance he would be to her in her heavy duties, but she did not wish for his assistance. For the first few months of their marriage she would allow him no part whatsoever in state business. He was not allowed to see the contents of the boxes which brought documents from the various departments of state to the Queen, he was never invited to be present when the Queen saw her Ministers. This conduct Lord Melbourne considered was wrong; the Queen should gradually have imparted the whole business of the State to the Prince. The Queen writes in a memorandum 'Though Lord Melbourne expressed much anxiety that the Queen should tell him [the Prince] and show him everything connected with public affairs . . . he did not at this time take much part in the transaction of business.'[50]

The Queen was not in the position of an ordinary woman. 'It seems impossible' wrote Lord Palmerston to Lord Melbourne of the Queen and the Prince 'that the husband can have over his wife, those common and ordinary rights of authority. . . .'[51] She was at once above and beyond the Prince and after being married for three months the Prince wrote[52] to his great friend Prince William of Löwenstein in May 1840 'In my home life I am very happy and contented; but the difficulty of filling my place with proper dignity is that I am only the husband, and not the master in the house.'

The internal arrangements of the Royal Household were not under the control of the Prince. Since the Queen's accession internal arrangements had been the responsibility of Baroness Lehzen, whose long devotion to the Queen 'probably blinded her to the obvious truth that her former influence must, in the natural course of things, give way to that of a husband'.[53] For instance the Baroness had controlled the Queen's private expenditure. All 'minor' expenses, that is to say those which were not state expenses, were laid every three months before the Queen by the Baroness, and Sir Henry Wheatley, the Keeper of the Privy Purse, did not pay any bill until it had been signed by the Baroness. This had given Baroness Lehzen considerable financial power in addition to possessing the ear of the Queen at all times, though it is true that the communication made between her room and the Queen's in 1837 had now been blocked up.

At the end of May 1840 Lord Melbourne had a conversation with the Queen, recorded by Anson in a memorandum.[54] She told Lord Melbourne that the Prince complained of want of confidence on trivial matters and on all matters connected with the politics of the country, but said this proceeded entirely from her own indolence. She knew it was wrong but when she was with the Prince she preferred talking on other subjects. Lord Melbourne thought she was afraid of quarrels arising from differences of opinion. 'The Queen has not started on a right principle—she should by degrees impart everything to him, but there is a danger in his wishing it all at once. A case may be laid before him, he may give some crude unformed opinion, the opinion may be taken, the result disastrous, and a forcible argument is then raised against his advice being asked for the future.'

It was Lord Melbourne's opinion that the Queen was influenced more than she was aware of by the Baroness. '. . . I do not see the Baroness often now' Lord Melbourne said. 'I have spoken most seriously to her. I have told her she undertook great responsibility in standing between the mother and daughter, however much circumstances may have justified her—but, if she ventures, or puts herself in a position to appear so, to stand between husband and wife—she will draw down ruin on herself, entail misery on her she professes to be devoted to, and be execrated by the whole country.'

A crisis was approaching when nature intervened and the Queen found she was pregnant. Though no announcement was made, Lord Holland wrote to Lord Granville that 'the knowing ladies are all confident she is with child'. Her fear of having children, the one thing about marriage she had said she dreaded, had, for the moment at least, vanished and Lord Holland added 'none can see her without being satisfied that she is in spirits as well'. The new pictures and appointments of Buckingham Palace 'are really dazzling, if not magnificent'. The Queen's spirits continued high; six weeks later she gave a ball and danced more than Lord Holland if he had been 'a nurse or man midwife' believed he would have approved.

It was the situation above all in which husband and wife draw more closely together, especially when the child is the first and when, as in the case of the Queen, the husband has mental gifts which enable him to become her support and natural deputy.

Before the end of February Lord Holland was reporting to Lord Granville in Paris that 'the youth, demeanour and prepossessing appearance of the Court, both Albert and Victoria, are very rapidly effacing unfavourable impressions. His good looks . . . his modest answers to the Addresses please exceedingly.' A week or so later Lord Holland wrote 'It is now all the fashion to praise Prince Albert.'[55]

The Prince's first step into public life was to accept the office of President of the Anti-Slavery Society.

Throughout the British Empire slavery had already been abolished and the Prince decided to accept because the Society not only had such a good and useful object but was entirely unconnected with politics. Mr Buxton, the prominent Quaker abolitionist, calculated that the Emancipation Act would save 50,000 lives. The Queen in a memorandum said the Prince was very nervous, learnt his whole speech off by heart and repeated it to her that morning.[56] All went off well and the Prince's first public speech was received with 'great applause' on 1st June 1840.

A few days later the Queen's new popularity was increased by an attempt to assassinate her as she drove up Constitution Hill with the Prince in a small open phaeton at about 6 o'clock in the evening. 'We had hardly proceeded a hundred yards from the Palace' wrote the Prince 'when I noticed, on the footpath on my side, a little mean-looking man holding something towards us; and before I could distinguish what it was, a shot was fired, which almost stunned us both, it was so loud and fired barely six paces from us. Victoria had just turned to the left to look at a horse, and could not therefore understand why her ears were ringing, as from its being so very near she could hardly distinguish that it proceeded from a shot having been fired. The horses started and the carriage stopped. I seized Victoria's hands and asked if the fright had not shaken her, but she laughed at the thing. I then looked again at the man, who was still standing in the same place, his arms crossed, and a pistol in each hand. His attitude was so affected and theatrical it quite amused me. Suddenly he again pointed his pistol and fired a second time. This time Victoria also saw the shot, and stooped quickly, drawn down by me . . . the many people who stood round us and the man, and were at first petrified with fright on seeing what had happened, now rushed upon him. I called to the postilion to go on and we arrived safely at Aunt Kent's. From thence we took a short drive through the Park, partly to give Victoria a little air, and partly also to show the public we had not . . . lost all confidence in them. . . . My chief anxiety was lest the fright should prove injurious to Victoria in her present state, but she is quite well. . . .'

By the time the Queen returned from her drive, the news of the attempt on her life had spread very widely; it was already a matter of common knowledge that she was some four months pregnant. 'She was received with the utmost enthusiasm by the immense crowd that was congregated in carriages, on horseback and on foot. All the Equestrians formed themselves into an Escort and attended her back to the Palace, cheering vehemently, while she acknowledged with great appearance of feeling these loyal manifestations. She behaved on this occasion with perfect courage and self-possession and exceeding propriety.'

Next day Mr Anson saw the prisoner who proved to be one Edward Oxford, a waiter in a low inn, son of a mulatto jeweller of Birmingham and about 17 or 18 years old; he exhibited no sign of a guilty conscience but a 'stern sullenness'. There was some doubt at the trial if the pistols had ever been loaded with ball and a suggestion of mystery as the pistols were silver mounted and bore the monogram E.R., supposed to stand for 'Ernestus Rex', the unpopular King of Hanover, who had been Duke of Cumberland. What became known as 'the Hanover letter' was found at Oxford's lodgings but the contents were never made public. Stockmar told Mr Anson, however, that he 'did not think the King of Hanover would be likely to be implicated in the affair, for tho' a wicked man and possessed of a conscience callous to the perpetration of most crimes . . . he had a peculiar feeling about those which were contrary to his notion of a gentlemanlike crime—conniving at the murder of his own family, would come under the class which he would not be guilty of'. Dr Connolly of Hanwell Lunatic Asylum gave evidence that he considered the prisoner of unsound mind and Oxford was found guilty, but insane.

The immediate result of Oxford's attempt was a period of overwhelming popularity for the Queen. The courage of her behaviour during the attempt, her coolness and composure went far to obliterate the effect of the Bedchamber crisis and Lady Flora Hastings. At Ascot, where her reception had recently been tepid and occasionally hostile, 'dense multitudes demonstrated their attachment to her person and their joy at her recent escape'.

'Wherever the Queen and Prince showed themselves in public, for many days after the occurrence, they were enthusiastically cheered'; and when they went to the opera for the first time after it, 'the moment they entered the box' writes the Queen in her Journal 'the whole House rose and cheered, waved hats and handkerchiefs, and went on so for some time. . . . "God Save the Queen" was sung . . . and Albert was called for separately and much cheered.'[57]

Greville notes that from this time 'partly from a judicious influence [the Prince]', the Queen 'began to make her Court much less exclusive'.[58] One indication of this was that she at last consented to recognise Lady Cecilia Buggin, 'Cis', whom the Duke of Sussex had married as long ago as 1830 or 1831. The most likeable of the Royal Dukes, 'that good natured man the Duke of Sussex' had as a youth been forced by asthma to winter out of England. In Rome during the winter of 1792, when he was 19, Prince Augustus—not yet Duke of Sussex—had met, fallen in love with and married Lady Augusta Murray, daughter of the Earl of Dunmore, the lady being estimated as six to eleven years his senior. Since George III had not given his consent the marriage was null and void under the Royal Marriages Act. However, two children, a son and a daughter, were born, who took the name of d'Este, from an ancestor common both to Lady Augusta and Prince Augustus. In 1801 the marriage came to an end, the Prince retaining the custody of the children. The same year he was created Duke of Sussex and Earl of Inverness in the English peerage and received a Parliamentary grant, raised to £18,000 a year in 1806, out of which he allowed Lady Augusta £4,000 annually.

The Duke then became devoted to Lady Cecilia Buggin, widow of Sir George Buggin, Kt, Alderman of the City of London, born Lady Cecilia Gore, daughter of the second Earl of Arran. The pair lived together in a small house overlooking the north side of Hyde Park, until 1830 when Lady Augusta died, and in 1830 or 1831 the Duke married Lady Cecilia. Since the Sovereign had not given his consent this marriage was also void, but after the accession of Queen Victoria the Duke devoted his energies to trying to secure some official recognition for his wife. The Queen refused. Public opinion on the whole took the Duke's side. Lord Holland wrote to Lord Granville of 'the natural and surely not unreasonable desire of the D. of Sussex to get his marriage recognised at Court. I am afraid that much as that atmosphere has been improved, the noisome weed of foolish German pride is not so entirely eradicated as one could wish ... the notion of creating Lady Cecilia Duchess or Countess of Inverness even at the risk of appearing to introduce left hand or morganatic marriages' had been suggested.[59] In Lord Holland's opinion it was absurd for a young Queen of 20 to withhold her consent to the recognition of the marriage of an uncle of 70 (the Duke was in fact 67).

Lord Holland believed that if the position were explained to her, 'she would, as she almost always does, consent even to what she dislikes with a good grace.'

The Duke had been a friend to the Queen and had given her away at her marriage. He wrote to Lord Melbourne asking that Lady Cecilia should be made a duchess, that some Parliamentary provision should be made for her in the event of his death and that she should be given apartments.

Lord Melbourne, forwarding the letter to the Queen, remarked that whether Lady Cecilia could be made a duchess was for the Queen's consideration. 'It would be very ridiculous. But to undertake to ask a provision for her from Parliament is quite impossible. . . . I suppose your Majesty will have no objection to promise her apartments.' The Duke of Sussex already had apartments in Kensington Palace adjoining those occupied before the Queen's accession by the Duchess of Kent, who had annexed two of the Duke's best rooms while he was living with Lady Cecilia in the small house overlooking Hyde Park.

On 22nd March 1840 the Queen replied that she had read the letters to Prince Albert and Baron Stockmar, who both thought that conferring the title of Duchess on Lady Cecilia was 'the only way of settling this affair. . . . The Queen therefore gives Lord Melbourne full authority to do this. But I think it is absolutely necessary (as Stockmar also thinks) that you should get in writing a promise from the Duke to consider this as *final*.'

Lady Cecilia was created Duchess of Inverness. '. . . She and the Duke are, or affect to be, enchanted, though nobody can tell why' wrote Greville. 'She is Duchess of Inverness, though there would have been more meaning in her being Countess of Inverness, since Earl of Inverness is his second title. However, there she was last night at the ball at Lansdowne House, tucked under the Duke's arm, all smiles and shaking hands vehemently in all directions in acknowledgment of congratulations. . . . It is called a recognition of the marriage, which is just what it is not. It is a recognition of the cohabitation, and if it is considered an approval of it, it is a very indecent proceeding.'[60] However, Lady Lansdowne had written to the Queen to ask whether the Duchess of Inverness should be asked to sup at her table and the Queen replied she would not object provided care was taken that the Duchess of Inverness did not go out or take place before any other duchess.

Meanwhile within Buckingham Palace the underground war between the Prince and Lehzen continued. On 21st June Mr Anson had an interview with Lehzen about a certain Captain Childers who was making himself a nuisance by 'mad professions of love for the Queen'. Lehzen said she had done everything necessary by informing Lord Uxbridge, the Lord Chamberlain. Anson told her she ought to have informed the Prince, to which Lehzen replied that the 'Prince's conduct to her had rendered it impossible for her to consult with him. He had slighted her in the most marked manner and she was too proud not to resent it. . . . He had once told her to leave the Palace, but she replied he had not the power to turn her out of the Queen's house. . . . She tried again to impress upon me that the Queen would brook no interference with the exercise of her powers of which she was *most jealous*.' The Baroness spoke 'with great agitation and earnestness. I think she must mean well but is wanting in judgment and discretion.'[61]

The Prince's chief anxiety during Oxford's attempt on the Queen's life had been 'lest the fright should have proved injurious to the Queen in her present condition', and the passing of a Regency Bill was necessary to meet the possibility of the Queen dying, leaving a minor as heir to the throne.

Stockmar was anxious to act in the matter 'upon a full understanding with the Opposition', the Tories. Though the Prince was the natural guardian of the child, difficulties would be raised on account of his youth and his want of acquaintance with the country and its institutions; the

King of Hanover and the Dukes of Cambridge and Sussex would not wish to be passed over, but the Prince should be Regent, the only question being whether he should be sole Regent, as the Duchess of Kent was to have been, or Regent with a Council. Melbourne's recent advice to the Queen on her behaviour to the Tories, 'You should now hold out the olive branch a little', bore fruit. Sir Robert Peel was friendly and could not see the practical utility of a Council; the Duke of Wellington, on being consulted, replied 'that it could and ought to be nobody but the Prince'.

Only the Duke of Sussex wrote to say 'that he must oppose the Bill in the House of Lords, and that he must not allow the rights of the Family to be passed over'. His was the single dissentient voice. Otherwise the Regency Bill passed both Houses without opposition nor was there opposition in any one of the newspapers.

Lord Melbourne told the Queen 'Three months ago they would not have done it for him. It is entirely his own character.'

King Leopold told Mr Anson the passing of the Bill had helped the Prince immensely, the country thereby demonstrating the great confidence they placed in the uprightness of his character. 'The Baroness was the great future danger to be apprehended. She had completely deceived Her Majesty' in the past and was 'only stayed from interrupting the present domestic harmony by the fear of breaking her own neck in the attempt.'[62]

In Mr Anson's opinion 'the Queen is unquestionably a happier person since her marriage . . . she is far steadier in her friendships, not taking up a person and putting them down again, altogether more formed, softened and improved'.

On the night of 21st November 1840, just before the early hours of the morning, the Queen woke up feeling 'very uncomfortable', though the baby was not expected for another fortnight. She roused the Prince 'with difficulty', and he fetched Sir James Clark, who sent for the obstetrician, Dr Locock. The Queen tried to go to sleep again but by 4 a.m. was feeling 'very bad' and when Dr Locock came he said the baby was on the way but everything was all right. Inevitably, the death of Princess Charlotte was uppermost in everyone's mind. About 2 p.m. on 22nd November 'a perfect little child was born, but alas a girl and not a boy, as we both had so hoped and wished for. We were, I am afraid, sadly disappointed. . . .'

The Queen had expressed her objection to the number of persons being present who usually attend as witnesses to a royal birth and within her room were only Dr Locock, no other doctor (though Clark and another doctor came in after the birth), Mrs Lilly the monthly nurse, and the Prince. In the next room were the Cabinet Ministers, the Archbishop of Canterbury, the Bishop of London and Lord Erroll, Lord Steward of the Household, 'with the door open so that Lord Erroll said he could see the Queen plainly the whole time and hear what she said. . . .' When the child was born

Locock said 'Oh Madam it is a Princess'. She said 'Never mind, the next will be a Prince'. The baby was then brought stark naked into the room where the Councillors were, and laid upon a table (already prepared) for their inspection. The Queen's delivery was so little expected that the wet nurse was still at home in the Isle of Wight, and Whiting, a page (formerly favourite valet de chambre of George IV), 'went off for her, brought her over in an open boat from Cowes to Southampton, and had her at the Palace by two in the morning'.

The Queen passed an excellent night, enjoyed her breakfast next morning and the little Princess throve. 'Indeed from the first moment there was not the slightest excuse for anxiety' wrote Lord Clarendon to Lord Granville in Paris. 'Both the Queen and the Prince were much disappointed at not having a son. I believe because they thought it would be a disappointment to the country, but what the country cares about is to have a life more, whether male or female, interposed between the succession and the King of Hanover.'

During the time the Queen was laid up she records in a memorandum that '. . . the Prince's care and devotion were quite beyond expression. He refused to go to the play, or anywhere else, generally dining alone with the Duchess of Kent. . . . He was content to sit by her [the Queen] in a darkened room, to read to her, or write for her. No one but himself ever lifted her from her bed to her sofa, and he always helped to wheel her on her bed or sofa into the next room. For this purpose he would come when sent for instantly from any part of the house.' In short, the Queen adds, 'his care of her was like that of a mother, nor could there be a kinder, wiser, or more judicious nurse'.[63]

On 2nd December 1840, Mrs Lilly, the Queen's monthly nurse, heard a stealthy noise in the Queen's sitting-room shortly after one in the morning and summoned a page, who found a boy rolled up under the sofa, on which the Queen only three hours previously had been sitting. The sofa was one of 'the most costly and magnificent material and workmanship and ordered expressly for the accommodation of the Royal and illustrious visitors who call to pay their respects to Her Majesty.' The intruder was at once recognised as 'the boy Jones' who on a former occasion had, like the earlier 'boy Cotton', contrived to enter the Palace.[64] He alleged he could obtain an entrance into the Palace whenever he pleased, by getting over the wall on Constitution Hill and creeping through one of the windows. When asked why he entered the apartment of Her Majesty he replied 'I wanted to know how they lived at the Palace. I was desirous of knowing the habits of the people, and I thought a description would look very well in a book.' He had no weapon or stolen property about him. He declared 'that he had sat upon the throne, that he saw the Queen and heard the Princess Royal squall'. He had slept under one of the servants' beds and helped himself to 'eatables' at night, 'leaving his finger prints on the stock for the soup'. Enquiry by Home Office officials revealed him to be Edmund Jones, aged 17 but stunted in growth and looking younger, son of a poor but industrious tailor who earned a scanty living working in a shed in Derby Street, Cannon Row, Westminster. On his first appearance he had been declared insane and discharged, this time he was committed to the House of Correction in Tothill Street as a rogue and vagabond for three months and put on the treadmill. He affected an air of great consequence and repeatedly requested the police 'to behave towards him as they ought, to a gentleman who was anxious to make a noise in the world'.

His third visit to the Palace, on 15th March 1841, was followed by another three months on the treadmill in the House of Correction, after which he was sent to sea in the hope that his character might improve under naval discipline.*

*

The Queen's recovery was so rapid that the Court was able to return to Windsor for Christmas. According to what had become family custom, gifts were distributed from tables with Christmas trees on them, a separate table being arranged for the gifts intended for each person.

December 1840 saw a considerable advance in the Prince's position. Mr Anson returned on 20th December from ten days' absence to find that the Queen, after consultation with Lord Melbourne, had given the Prince the keys of the boxes containing Cabinet and confidential documents which he had previously been refused. 'This' wrote Mr Anson 'has been brought about by the fact of the Prince having received and made notes of all the Cabinet business during the Queen's confinement, this circumstance having evinced to the Queen his capacity for business and power to assist in searching and explanation.' He was now, with the full agreement of those who were responsible for the actions of the Queen, 'in fact, tho' not in name, Her Majesty's Private Secretary'.[65] It was a piece of good fortune for the Queen that the Prince not only possessed an excellent mind, patience and the capacity for taking pains, but that his philosophy was 'to sink his own individual existence in that of his wife—to aim at no power by himself, or for himself . . . but making his position entirely a part of the Queen's continually and anxiously to watch every part of the public business, in order to be able to advise and assist her at any moment in any of the multifarious and difficult questions brought before her. . . .'

* He joined H.M.S. *Warspite* on 22nd May 1842; five months later he 'left', but was recaptured. In December 1845 he was discharged from the *Warspite*, his conduct 'fair', and subsequently served in H.M.S. *Inconstant* and H.M.S. *Harlequin*, with conduct noted as 'good'. On 21st October 1847, no longer a boy, he applied for a discharge, was left to await a passage to England from Malta, and disappears from recorded history.

Mr Anson was angry to discover that Baroness Lehzen had 'meddled and made mischief wherever she has had the opportunity since I left. ... I can however forgive anything sooner than her taking advantage of the Queen's illness to complain of the P's conduct, at a moment when, from natural excitability it could not fail to work strongly on the Queen's mind and to increase her illness. Baron Stockmar's being here is lucky, as her critiques are [then] more subdued, but in her [the Baroness] we must be always subject to troubled waters. . . .'

About two months later Mr Anson had a long conversation with Lord Melbourne on the subject of Lehzen. There was a prospect of disagreement between the Prince and the Queen, on account of the Prince's determination to prevent the three great officers of the Household, the Lord Steward, the Lord Chamberlain and the Master of the Horse, having access to the Queen through Lehzen. Lord Melbourne said 'I think the Prince would be quite unjustified to make a stand upon such ground. I can understand that it must be irksome and annoying to him to feel this constant interference, but he cannot argue . . . and if he put it in a manner implying as the alternative that either the Baroness must go, or he would not stay in the House, looking to the Queen's determination and obstinacy of character, her reply would be "in this alternative you have contemplated the possibility of living without me, I will shew you that I can contemplate the possibility of living without you". '

'The Prince thinks' continued Anson 'that the Queen has more fear than love for the B[aroness] and that she would *really* be happier without her though she would not acknowledge it. If he goes out for several hours, the Queen then sees much of L[ehzen], is consequently tired and annoyed, and the P[rince] is set down as the cause. . . .'

Lord Melbourne said the Queen was as much in love with the Prince as ever; in his opinion 'no influence from without will shake it'. 'I said' wrote Anson 'I thought there could be no confidence for that, when she [Baroness Lehzen] was always in the Queen's path, pointing and exaggerating every little fault of the Prince, constantly misrepresenting him, constantly trying to undermine him in the Queen's affections and making herself appear a martyr, ready to suffer and put up with every sort of indignity for the Queen's sake. The effect of this state of things cannot be viewed but with alarm.'[66]

Nevertheless the Queen was happy in what she described as 'the solid pleasures of a peaceful quiet yet merry life . . . with my inestimable husband and friend'.

On 2nd January 1841 the Court left Windsor for Buckingham Palace, to the Queen's regret. The weather was freezing and early in February the Prince, an expert, went skating on the pond in the Buckingham Palace grounds accompanied by the Queen, who wore shoes with list soles to prevent her from slipping on the frozen ground. As she was admiring his performance the ice cracked and the Prince fell in, the water for a moment closing over his head. The Queen was the only person with presence of mind to assist him. Her lady-in-waiting was occupied in screaming for help, but the Queen stretched out her arms which the Prince caught and got back to the bank.[67]

On 10th February, the first anniversary of the marriage of the Queen and the Prince, the Princess Royal was christened Victoria Adelaide Mary Louisa in the Chapel Royal, St James's.[68] The little Princess was an attractive child, gay, intelligent and 'noticing'. She behaved herself 'with great propriety . . . was awake, but did not cry at all, and seemed to crow with immense satisfaction at the lights and brilliant uniforms. . . .' Lord Melbourne remarked to the Queen next day 'How she looked about her, quite conscious that the stir was all about herself.'

In spite of her rapid and satisfactory recovery the Queen had suffered a shock from the birth of the Princess Royal. She had always dreaded having children and she found her dread was justified. 'I think, dearest Uncle,' she wrote to King Leopold on 5th January 1841, 'you cannot *really* wish me to be the "Mamma d'une *nombreuse* famille" . . . men never think, at least seldom think, what a hard task it is for us women to go through this *very often*. . . .' In the spring of 1841 she was horrified to find that, almost at the first possible moment, she was pregnant again. Writing later to the Princess Royal, when Crown Princess of Prussia in April 1858, Queen Victoria declared 'what made me so miserable was—to have the first two years of my married life utterly spoilt by this occupation' (her successive pregnancies). 'I cld enjoy nothing, not travel about or go about with dear Papa. If I had waited a year—as I hope you will, it wld have been very different. . . .'[69]

It was a complication that the Queen did not feel as well as she had during her first pregnancy and was subject to depression.

Politically through the first six months of 1841, the Melbourne government was once more tottering. The atmosphere, however, was very different from the emotionalism of two years before. The Prince's influence had softened the Queen's feeling towards the Tories; while she remained a Whig, she was no longer an aggressive Whig and had become reconciled to the Duke of Wellington. At the christening of the Princess Royal, since the Duke of Saxe-Coburg and Gotha was not able to come to England to stand as godfather, the Queen and the Prince asked the Duke of Wellington to represent him, and the Queen wrote in her Journal 'The Duke is the best friend we have.'

Even more important, owing to the Prince's influence, the Queen was taking a greater interest in foreign than in home affairs. This did not mean that the Queen and the Prince were absorbed in the development of the vast areas which at the beginning of the Queen's reign had been blanks on the map of the world. The business of the Foreign Office in 1841 was for the most part a European business; foreign policy signified policy towards persons known, liked, or disliked, by the Queen, and usually related to her. She proposed that the Prince should enjoy free access to all foreign despatches and Lord Melbourne agreed. But the Prince did not stop at perusal. He soon claimed on behalf of the Queen a right to consultation before any action was taken by the government outside the United Kingdom. 'Under his guidance the Queen came to regard the supervision of foreign affairs as peculiarly within the Sovereign's province.'[70]

The Whig government failed to gain strength and by 4th May 1841 George Anson was writing a memorandum on its approaching fall headed 'The Government in Jeopardy'.[71] Lord Melbourne, with whom he had just had an hour's conversation, feared that 'Peel's doggedness and pertinacity might make him insist as a point of honour on having all discretion . . . in regard to the removal of Ladies.' Mr Anson repeated the Prince's suggestion that some negotiation should be entered into with Sir Robert, and both yield to some extent, but Lord Melbourne insisted the Prince must have no personal communication with Sir Robert, though he thought that Mr Anson might. Next day Lord Melbourne reported that he had seen the Queen who was perfectly calm and reasonable, prepared for the resignation of the government and to give way on the question of her ladies, but she did not mean to give up Lord Melbourne's society. Lord Melbourne said his opinion on any subject should be obtained through the Prince but the Queen said she must be able to communicate direct with him. The Queen leant towards sending for the Duke of Wellington, but Lord Melbourne told her she must make up her mind to sending for Sir Robert Peel.

Proceedings in the House of Commons showed how low the government had sunk in the estimation of the country. On 18th May the government was defeated by 36 votes; on 25th May voting was even and the government saved by the casting vote of the Speaker; on 4th June, following a speech by Sir Robert Peel, a vote of 'no confidence' in the government was defeated by only one vote.

Lord Melbourne, however, would not resign. In spite of the fact that Lord Normanby declared that the Whigs 'must go, it was clear the country had turned against them', Lord Melbourne continued in office, intending to hold a general election on the issue of a fixed duty of 8s. a quarter which the government intended to impose on imported corn, and which he believed would influence the agricultural and landed interests.

Parliament was dissolved by the Queen in person on 29th June. In the general election which followed, the Tories were returned by an overwhelming majority. Lord Morpeth, a Whig peer, wrote to Lord John Russell on 9th July 1841 'we are smashed'.

On 9th May Mr Anson had had a secret interview with Sir Robert Peel and told him the Prince was most anxious to overcome the difficulties upon Sir Robert coming into office. If Sir Robert would not insist upon reviving the question of the removal of the Ladies of the Bedchamber, the Queen would undertake to procure the resignation of any Ladies obnoxious to him but hoped that these might be confined to the Mistress of the Robes, the Marchioness of Normanby, and the Duchess of Bedford, both the latter being noted Whigs, the Duchess of Bedford a friend of the Queen's for many years. Sir Robert said 'I would waive every pretension to office, I declare to God, sooner than that my acceptance of it should be attended by any personal humiliation to the Queen.' Further secret interviews between Sir Robert Peel and Mr Anson took place on 10th, 11th and 12th May, at which the Bedchamber question was satisfactorily settled. On 10th May Sir Robert said 'It is essential to my position with the Queen that Her Majesty should understand that I have the feelings of a gentleman and, where my duty does not interfere, I cannot act against her wishes. Her Majesty doubtless must know how pressed I am as the Head of a powerful Party, but the impression I wish to create in Her Majesty's mind is that I am to defend her against their Encroachments.'[72]

The Queen agreed that while the Prime Minister, after consultation with her, should notify her Ladies of the Bedchamber of her intention to appoint them, she herself would announce their actual appointment. She gave up the right to appoint the three great officers of the household, the Lord Steward, the Lord Chamberlain and the Master of the Horse, also the Lords in Waiting, Grooms in Waiting and Equerries who were in Parliament, though 'the Queen considers it her right (and is aware that her Predecessors were peculiarly tenacious of this right) to appoint her own Household.' Mr Anson remarked that Sir Robert Peel showed every sign of goodwill.

Though this difficult question had been amicably settled, the Queen was still not tranquil in her mind. On being told by Lord Melbourne of the excellent reception the Prince had received at the Festival of the Sons of the Clergy, both on the way to St Paul's Cathedral and at the subsequent dinner, the Queen said 'Yes, so everyone tells me, but I don't like it—first of all because I don't like his being absent from me, and then because I dislike his taking my part in politics or in the general affairs of the country.'

As she approached the fourth month of her second pregnancy the Queen had second thoughts about the amicable settlement she had reached with Sir Robert Peel. When the Duchess of Bedford resigned the Queen declared that Lord Melbourne had compromised her and that she had never meant to give up so many ladies. If she submitted she would be vanquished and lowered before the world. The Prince then said he feared the ladies' gossip was getting about her again, on which the Queen burst into tears which could not be stopped for some time, and declared she did not know if she would consent to show him a private letter left for her with Lehzen by one of the Bedford family. The Prince told her she might show it or not as she pleased, but another quarrel with Sir Robert Peel would do her harm. Mr Anson reported 'The Queen was the whole day much depressed and said it weighed heavily on her mind and felt she had been hurried and compromised by the Prince and Lord Melbourne.'[73]

In September 1841 the Queen and the Prince went to Claremont for a few days' quiet 'as this place is so very private' and it was there that the Council at which the new Ministers were appointed was held. 'The Queen' wrote Greville[74] '. . . conducted herself in a manner which excited my greatest admiration and was really touching to see . . . She looked very much flushed, and her heart was evidently brim full, but she was composed and throughout the whole of the proceedings . . . she preserved complete self-possession, composure and dignity. . . . Peel told me she had behaved perfectly to him and that He had said to her that He considered it his first and greatest duty to consult her happiness and comfort; that no person should be proposed to her who could be disagreeable to her. . . . I asked him if She had taken this well, and met it in a corresponding spirit and he said "Perfectly". In short he was more than satisfied; he was charmed with her.'

Mr Gladstone, who held the first office of his political career as Vice-President of the Board of Trade, told Mr Anson '. . . There was not one of the new government who did not place the fullest confidence in Her Majesty's intended fairness towards them. . . . They admired the extreme dignity of the Queen at the Council, it was evidently painful to her but her conduct was beautiful.'[75]

The Queen was now in the seventh month of her pregnancy and sympathy for her was strong. Mr Baring, Chancellor of the Exchequer, and Sir George Grey were moved to tears, Lord Erroll, the Lord Steward, had to 'make a rush out of the room'.

The Queen had seen Lord Melbourne in a final audience at Windsor on 30th August. Mr Anson, who was present, was much affected by the way in which Melbourne said 'I shall see you again before I take my leave.' That evening, standing 'in the starlight' on the terrace at Windsor, Lord Melbourne told the Queen 'For four years I have seen you daily and liked it better every day.'

The final farewell was at Claremont on 3rd September 1841. The Queen was observed to be much affected but recovered herself. The following evening Lord Melbourne wrote the Queen a letter advising her to entrust herself to the Prince. 'Lord Melbourne cannot satisfy himself without again stating to your Majesty in writing what he had the honour of saying to your Majesty respecting H.R.H. the Prince. Lord Melbourne has formed the highest opinion of H.R.H.'s judgment, temper and discretion, and he cannot but feel a great consolation and security in the reflection that he leaves Your Majesty in a situation in which Your Majesty has the inestimable advantage of such advice and assistance. Lord Melbourne feels certain that Your Majesty cannot do better than have recourse to it, whenever it is needed, and rely upon it with confidence.'

The Queen was profoundly affected by the parting from Lord Melbourne, the removal of what Mr Anson termed his 'domestication' left her desolate: '. . . after seeing him for four years, with very few exceptions—*daily*—you may imagine that I *must* feel the change' the Queen wrote to her uncle, King Leopold, on 8th September 1841.[76] Nevertheless of the two it was Lord Melbourne who now depended on the Queen. He was alone, she had the husband she adored and an increasing family.

The little Princess Royal, called by her parents 'Pussy', flourished. Lady Robert Gardiner, one of the Queen's Women of the Bedchamber, describes her as 'smiling and springing in the nurse's arms', and Lady Portman reported from Windsor that the little Princess was 'in perfect health'.

This happy state of affairs unfortunately did not continue.[77] From the end of July there were anxieties; the little Princess was unable to digest her food, lost weight, and cut her teeth with difficulty.

The Queen's pregnancy was not easy, she felt 'wretched', depressed, and dreaded the ordeal which lay before her. Difficulties with the Princess Royal's health increased her distress. 'Till the end of August she was such a magnificent, strong fat child, that it is a great grief to see her so thin, pale and changed' the Queen wrote.

On 11th October it was feared that the birth was about to take place prematurely. 'We have been in great alarm since I wrote,' Mr Anson told Lord Melbourne. 'I hope however that all danger has subsided, and that the Q. will go on well to her proper time. . . .' A further alarm occurred on 26th October, when the Queen saw Dr Locock, who thought the moment of the confinement was fast approaching. 'Albert was so dear and kind, and anxious that this trying time of waiting should be over' but she 'was feeling low and depressed'.[78] On 28th October the Queen wrote 'I unfortunately was feeling very wretched and left the drawing-room early.' Next day she walked a little in the garden but was so done up she could not go far. Poor dear Pussy's ailing state 'though not dangerous fusses and worries me much'. The Queen wrote that from 3rd

November the little Princess was given '*only* asses' milk' and for the moment improved.

On 8th November the Queen felt wretched and uncomfortable but 'did not know what to think as I had had so many false alarms'. However, on the 9th November 1841, early in the morning, she summoned Mrs Lilly, who at once sent for Dr Locock and despatched a messenger to the Duchess of Kent. The Queen's forebodings were unhappily fulfilled, the confinement was not easy and she wrote[77] 'my sufferings were really very severe, and I don't know what I should have done, but for the great comfort and support my beloved Albert was to me'. At last, at 12 minutes to 11, the baby arrived safely, 'a fine large boy'.

Pussy was 'not at all pleased'.

Chapter Seven

The heir to the throne was a handsome baby 'with large, dark blue eyes, a good high forehead, a pretty but rather large nose, a nice little mouth and chin'. From the moment of his birth he 'flourished', digesting his food, gaining weight, crowing and smiling early. Reports to the Queen describe him as being 'in his usual high health', 'looking, if possible, better than ever'. His arrival was greeted with ecstasy. 'What a joy! . . . Oh God what a happiness, what a blessing' wrote the Duchess of Kent. The English people were delighted, no male heir to the throne had been born for almost eighty years. A crowd gathered in front of Buckingham Palace, a salute was fired, the Queen and the infant Prince were repeatedly cheered and 'God Save the Queen' was sung. The nightmare of the King of Hanover ascending the English throne had now all but passed away. When the Queen took the Prince of Wales to see the Duke of Wellington at Walmer Castle in the following year the crowds were immense: 'continual cheers, wreaths, bonfires, triumphal arches, peals of church bells and cannons . . . "Where's the Prince? Show him! Turn him this way! Bless his little face! What a pretty Boy! How like his father" was screamed incessantly.'[1]

But the Queen and Prince Albert did not have the joyous carefree pleasure in their son and heir usually enjoyed by young parents.

Anxiety darkened their view of the Prince of Wales from the moment of his birth; he was the future King of England, and his infantile actions, his first words, his smiles and his crows were judged as the conduct of England's future sovereign. Prince Albert Edward was created Prince of Wales by Letters Patent from the Queen on 4th December 1841; the title is not automatically hereditary. His parents' minds were haunted by the Royal Dukes, the Queen's uncles, whose extravagance, dissipation and disreputability had brought the country to the verge of revolution. The object, almost the sole object, of the Prince of Wales's education was to prevent any resemblance to the Royal Dukes. He was, the Queen prayed, in every respect to resemble his adored father. No reference was made to Prince Albert's own relatives though his father and brother Ernest were as dissolute and unprincipled as the Royal Dukes of England.[2]

The royal nursery did not run smoothly. In the beginning of 1841 Mrs Southey, a lady recommended by the Archbishop of Canterbury, was engaged to superintend the nursery establishment under the Queen and the Prince. Rules were strict. The children were to be shown to no one; four nursery staff were under Mrs Southey's authority and the children were never to be left alone. All plans for the children, including doctors' instructions, were to be submitted to the Queen and the Prince.

Within a few weeks of the Prince of Wales's birth, the Queen was dissatisfied with Mrs Southey, whose mind was not on her duties; she complained she was homesick and wanted to be continually out visiting friends. On 26th December 1841, Mrs Southey said she did not feel 'equal' to managing the royal nursery and would resign as soon as someone else could be found.

Three months later, on 24th March 1842, the Queen wrote to Lord Melbourne that owing to the duties their position involved, she and the Prince found the children were being left to 'low people' and surrounded by an atmosphere of constant quarrelling which Mrs Southey could not control.[3] Lord Melbourne agreed with the Queen a lady of high rank would have more authority and be less likely to have her head turned by the elevation of her position than someone from the middle class.

The appointment was offered to Sarah Lady Lyttelton, who accepted on 18th April 1842.[4] Lady Lyttelton had both rank and ability. Born Lady Sarah Spencer, she was the daughter of the beautiful Lady Lavinia who had been a Bingham and was a near relative of the third Earl of Lucan whose feud with the seventh Earl of Cardigan was later largely responsible for the Charge of the Light Brigade at Balaclava. Lady Sarah married William Henry Lyttelton in March 1813; he succeeded as third Baron Lyttelton in 1828 and died in 1837, leaving her with five children. She became Lady of the Bedchamber to Queen Victoria in 1838.

The Queen liked Lady Lyttelton and appreciated her many admirable qualities, but she disapproved of her High Church views and would never permit discussion on ecclesiastical subjects. Lady Lyttelton's first reception by the Princess Royal was discouraging; at the sight of her the little Princess burst into screams of 'unconquerable horror . . . nothing would pacify her but my leaving the room'.

Being possessed of both tolerance and patience, Lady Lyttelton gradually won the Princess Royal's confidence and was soon reporting her as no longer screaming but 'very grave and distant towards me, and her smiles, very sweet, are rare'. Lady Lyttelton did not believe in punishments: 'One is never *sure* they are fully understood by the child as belonging to the naughtiness', and she had considerable humour, noting that the Princess uttered the cry 'Wipe my eyes' all the time she was roaring. 'Princessy', as Lady Lyttelton called her, was 'over sensitive and affectionate and rather irritable in temper at present', subject to sudden fits of sickness and shivering and having difficulty in cutting her teeth. Whereas the Prince of Wales had a 'noble countenance and calm manner . . . and looks through his large clear blue eyes full at one'.[5]

Both the Queen and the Prince were inclined to be nervous about the children's health, and the Princess Royal's gave some grounds for anxiety. While the Prince of Wales enjoyed perfect health and 'crowing spirits', the Princess Royal had digestive troubles, was often sick and lost weight easily. The Queen remained loyal to Sir James Clark: he was 'very tiresome in the nursery but had the merit of not talking about the Queen herself which she lays great stress on'. She sent him to see the little Princess, whom he dosed with calomel.

Lady Lyttelton thought the Queen, like many young mothers, was too anxious; the Princess was 'over-watched and over-doctored; always treated with what is most expensive, cheaper and commoner food and ways being often wholesomer. She now lives on asses' milk, and arrowroot and chicken broth, and they measure it out so carefully for fear of loading her stomach, that I fancy she always *leaves off hungry*'.[6] Asses' milk, it was noted, is richer even than Jersey milk.

The Queen herself was not well after the birth of the Prince of Wales, and did not recover as quickly as she had after that of the Princess Royal. Her nerves were shaken by her two rapid pregnancies, she felt 'depressed' and low. When Eos, the Prince's favourite greyhound, was accidentally shot, both the Prince and the Queen were consumed with anxiety, the Queen even more upset than the Prince, as almost invariably happened in any matter which concerned him. Eos was attended by Mr Brown, the apothecary who attended the royal children when at Windsor, and the Queen agitated herself so much that she was unable to attend luncheon.[7] Eos made a satisfactory recovery.

*

The domestic tranquillity for which the Prince longed was far from existing either in Windsor Castle or Buckingham Palace. The Queen was irritable, 'wretched', unwell, and her feelings were inflamed by Lehzen who, wrote Anson, 'lets no opportunity of creating mischief and difficulty escape her,' hoping to keep her power through influence over 'the nursery darlings'. After the birth of the Prince of Wales, Lehzen proposed that the revenues of the Duchy of Cornwall, instead of being placed under the control of Mr Anson, who was to be appointed Privy Purse of the Duchy, should be handed over to herself for nursery expenses. Mr Anson, she declared, was too parsimonious.

Lehzen's position was painful. She had been everything to the Queen; during the years at Kensington she had endured miseries for the Queen's sake. In later years the Duchess of Kent's behaviour to her daughter was softened and explained away, but during the time at Kensington, when Conroy was ascendant, the fate of the young Princess Victoria would have been miserable indeed without Lehzen to protect her, and that period, covering many years, was never forgotten by the Queen.[8]

The Queen's success when she first ascended the throne and the Queen's affection had been Lehzen's reward. Now she was no longer wanted. The Prince was everything to the Queen and the Prince's confidant and friend was Anson. Lehzen was nothing, she had no official position, she had no official title, she no longer had any place in the Queen's life. Lehzen was a passionate, jealous woman and warfare between her and the Prince and Anson raged.

The Prince considered Lehzen to be 'a crazy, stupid intriguer, obsessed with the lust of power, who regards herself as a demi-God, and anyone who refuses to recognise her as such is a criminal. . . .' 'Victoria,' wrote the Prince, 'who on other questions is just and clear-sighted, does not see this because she has never been away from her, and, like every good pupil is accustomed to regard her governess as an oracle. Besides this, the unfortunate experience they went through together at Kensington has bound them still closer, and Lehzen, in her madness, has made Victoria believe that whatever good qualities she possesses are due to her.

'I, on the other hand, regard Victoria as naturally a fine character, but warped in many respects by wrong upbringing. Up to now I have suffered in patience, and will go on doing so for love of Victoria, if she wishes; I am not even irritated with her; on the contrary I pity her . . . but there can be no improvement until Victoria sees Lehzen, as she is. . . . I declare to you [Stockmar], as my and Victoria's true friend, that I will sacrifice my own comfort, my life's happiness to Victoria in silence, even if she continues in her error. But the welfare of my children and Victoria's existence as sovereign are too sacred for me not to die fighting rather than yield them as prey to Lehzen.'[9]

The same day the Queen wrote in misery to Stockmar.[10] The Prince's letter was the result of a quarrel between the Queen and the Prince over Lehzen. The Queen would rather not see Lehzen herself, but asked Stockmar to see her and explain 'there had been a little misunderstanding which has affected me a good deal . . . and my tears flow always afresh. I feel so forlorn and I have got *such* a sick headache!—I feel as if I had had a dreadful dream. I do hope you may be able to pacify Albert. He seems so very angry still. I am *not*.' Next day she begged Stockmar to impress on Albert the importance of speaking up 'when he sees anything amiss and then to believe me and not to credit stories which help to make trifles serious affairs. . . . Now will you promise me this? I forgive the thoughtless words of yesterday; they were said in grief and in anger and vexation.'

The Prince, however, was not easily pacified. He was furious and wounded and on 18th January he wrote to Stockmar[11] '... All the disagreeableness I suffer comes from one and the same person, and that is precisely the person whom Victoria chooses for her friend and confidante. I cannot mention anything that would not pain Victoria.

'I loathe complaining and am too proud to play the informer about trifles. ...

'Victoria is too hasty and passionate for me to be able often to speak of my difficulties. She will not hear me out but flies into a rage and overwhelms me with reproaches of suspiciousness, want of trust, ambition, envy, etc. etc. There are, therefore, two ways open to me: (1) to keep silence and go away (in which case I am like a school boy who has had a dressing down from his mother and goes off snubbed), (2) I can be still more violent (and then we have scenes like that of the 16th, which I hate, because I am so sorry for Victoria in her misery, besides which it undermines the peace of the home).

'On the 16th in the nursery, I only said to Victoria when Mrs Roberts threw out her hint [Mrs Roberts was one of the royal nursery staff and the Prince did not approve of the regime being followed for the Princess Royal] "that is really malicious". This was enough to make Victoria accuse me of wanting to send the mother out of the nursery, I could murder the child if I wanted to etc. etc. I went quietly downstairs and only said "I must have patience. ..."'

Enclosed, however, in this letter to Stockmar was a note to Victoria which revealed the violence and depth of anger seething within the Prince. 'Dr Clark has mismanaged the child and poisoned her with calomel and you have starved her. I shall have nothing more to do with it; take the child away and do as you like and if she dies you will have it on your conscience.'

Next day, 19 January 1842, the Queen wrote to Stockmar[12] 'If A's note is full of hard words and other things that *might* make me angry and unhappy (as I know, he *is* unjust) don't show it me but tell me what he wants, for I *don't wish* to be angry with him and really *my* feelings of justice would be too violent to keep in, did I read what was too severe. If you think it is *not* calculated to do this, let me see it.'

Stockmar then wrote the Queen an anxious confidential letter.[13] He had not communicated with her earlier in order to be quite sure that 'perfect coolness and evenness of temper had returned to everyone. ... He must express that he would have to consider a repetition of a similar collision as a certain cause for the greatest misery both to the Prince and your family. Language has not sufficient power to declare with what despondence he looks to the future if he allows for a moment that such violent emotions could be produced again from the same causes. There is another consideration which, though unimportant in itself from being merely personal . . . he ought to bring under the Queen's notice in time. A repetition of such distressing scenes would make his present position entirely untenable. . . . Never being able to be violent himself, he must foresee what his fate must be if opposed to mental vehemency. . . . He will most likely persuade no one and in the end certainly displease both your Majesty and the Prince.'

The Queen then wrote to Stockmar begging that Prince Albert should be persuaded to be open and speak up: 'Albert must tell me what he dislikes and I will set about to remedy it, but he must also *promise* to listen to and believe me; when (on the contrary) I am in a passion which I trust I am not very often in now, he must not believe the stupid things I say like being miserable I ever married and so forth which come when I am unwell. . . . I have often heard Albert own that everybody recognised Lehzen's former services to me and my only wish is that she should have a quiet home in my house and see me sometimes. A. cannot object to my having her to talk to some times . . . and I assure you *upon my honour* that I see her very seldom now and only for a few minutes, often to ask questions about papers and *toilette* for which she is of the greatest use to me. A. often and often thinks I see her, when I don't. . . . I tell you this as it is true, as you know me to be. . . . Dearest Angel Albert, God only knows how I love him. His position is difficult, heaven knows and we must do everything to make it easier.'

As a result of this letter Stockmar decided angry passions had subsided and sent the Prince's letter of 18th January to the Queen, who felt aggrieved. Lehzen might have been her confidante before her marriage but not since, she told Stockmar on 20th January. 'I *never* speak to her or anybody (but you) about it now if anything new has been settled about the Nursery, I *never* go to *her* to complain which I fear A. suspects I do; no, never. . . . The second thing is my being so passionate when spoken to; this I fear is irremediable as yet, but I hope in time it will be got over. There is often an irritability in me which (like Sunday last which began the *whole* misery) makes me say cross and odious things which I don't myself believe and which I fear hurt A., but which he should not believe . . . but I trust I shall be able to conquer it. Our position is tho' very different to any other married couples. A. is in my house and not I in his.—But I am ready to submit to his wishes as I love him so dearly.'[14]

Having engaged in battle with the Prince, Lehzen was, as might have been expected, defeated. Prince Albert was determined to be master in his own house. Greville commented 'Melbourne told me long ago that the Prince would acquire unbounded influence.' He was now 'all-powerful'. Lehzen was told she must go. 'It was not without great difficulty' Stockmar told Lord Granville 'that the Prince succeeded in getting rid of her.

She was foolish enough to contest his influence, and not to conform herself to the change in her position. . . . If she had done so, and conciliated the P., she might have remained in the Palace to the end of her life.' On 23rd September 1842 the Duchess of Kent noted in her diary that Lehzen had left for Germany that day. The Duchess 'would like to have taken leave of her, but she did not choose to ask for it and I would not make any advances to her.' Before Lehzen left, the Queen presented her with a carriage and she was granted a pension of £800 annually, at that period a good income. She went to Buckeburg, a small town in north-western Germany, to live with a sister, but unhappily in December the sister died and Lehzen's subsequent life was spent alone.

When Mr Theodore Martin was writing the *Life of the Prince Consort* the Queen with her usual generosity and fairness wished his treatment of the Baroness Lehzen to be modified. 'The Queen owed her so much— that only to speak of her *mistakes* would not be right. She thinks Mr Martin might alter those passages.' The Queen wrote again to Mr Martin in an undated letter: 'Observations relative to Bss. Lehzen. It was *not* "Personal ambition" *at all* but the idea that *no one* but herself was able to take care of the Queen and also she did not perceive till later, when before leaving the Queen told her herself, that *people* flattered her and made use of *her* for their own purposes. Her devotion to the Queen was so great, her unselfishness and disinterestedness so great, and the Queen owed her so much that she did *not* wish her faults to be brought forward (as they are *quite forgotten now*) and some tribute to her merits and faithfulness ought to be rendered.' In a second letter the Queen suggested to Mr Martin that it might even be better if reference to any particular difficulties the Prince experienced with Baroness Lehzen were omitted and merely a general allusion made to his many *difficulties* in the *household*, which he overcame. Mr Martin amended his text as the Queen wished, and an affectionate acknowledgment of Lehzen's services was all that was made.[15]

*

The departure of Lehzen was succeeded by a period of peace. The year 1842 proved to be one of 'respite'; the Queen did not have another child, she recovered her health and nerves and her relations with the Prince resumed their former happiness. When, late in 1842, she found that she was again pregnant, she remained calm though she wrote to King Leopold in February 1843 that while his kindness about the expected arrival touched her much she still did not wish for a child every year. 'My poor nerves, tho' thank God! nearly *quite* well *now* were so battered last time that I suffered *a whole year* from it. . . . Still those nerves were incidentals and I am otherwise so strong and well, that if only my happiness continues I can bear everything else with pleasure.'

On 25th April a princess was born. The birth was without complications and the Queen was shortly able to resume her usual habits. 'Thank God I am stronger and better this time than either time before, my nerves are *so well* which I am most thankful for. . . . My adored Angel has, as usual, been *all* kindness and goodness, and dear Pussy a very delightful companion. She is very tender with her little sister, who is a pretty and large baby and we think will be the beauty of the family.'[16] The little Princess was christened by what the Queen described as 'the old English name' of Alice; the King of Hanover was paid the compliment of being invited to be sponsor, a gesture of conciliation in spite of his previous rudeness. He arrived, wrote the Queen, 'Just too late to be in time' and was even ruder than before.

The marriage of Princess Augusta of Cambridge, sister of Prince George of Cambridge, on 28th June 1843 was turned into a farcical scramble by the King of Hanover's determination to take precedence of Prince Albert. As soon as the service was over, the King, who had become much bent with rheumatism adding to the unattractiveness of his appearance, 'hobbled round to where the Queen stood and told her she must now walk out with him'; it was his right as a sovereign. She refused, the King persisted and the Prince gave 'a slight push' to move him forward upon which he nearly fell down, but was caught and led out of the Chapel by force by the Lord Chamberlain, 'fuming with ire'; the Queen walked with the Prince. In the lower dining-room, where the signatures in the register were attested, the King of Hanover was more determined than ever to push forward and sign next to the Queen. The register was on the table and placing his elbow on it he demanded that the Queen should come and sign, intending to sign himself immediately after her. But the Queen was too quick for him and, hurrying to the other side of the table, commanded that the register should be handed across to her, thus enabling her signature and that of the Prince beneath it to be attached before 'the foaming King' had time to sign. 'He then protested that as he could not sign where he chose then he would not sign at all, and asked the Bishop of London whether it was necessary, and the Bishop replied (which only chagrined him the more) that it was quite unimportant.' Once the Duke and Duchess of Cambridge had written down their names, the King took up the pen and said with marked emphasis 'Well now, after "the Parents" I have no objection to sign'.

'On going up to the Drawing-rooms he was again bent upon taking the lead of the Prince and came up to the Queen, who was with the Prince and the Queen of the Belgians, and said he would now lead the Queen upstairs. The Queen on finding resistance useless, said that in her house she always gave the Queen of the Belgians precedence and that she would walk with the King but that the Prince must walk first with the

Queen of the Belgians and in this order they proceeded to the manifest annoyance of the King, who was foiled in every attempt to displace the Prince.'[17]

One difficulty remained, regarded by the Queen's advisers as certain to prove disastrous—the Queen's determination not to give up Lord Melbourne. In spite of the change of government in 1841 and the replacement of Lord Melbourne as Prime Minister by Sir Robert Peel, the Queen persisted in writing frequent letters to Lord Melbourne. Mr Anson, to whom Peel had taken a great liking, was warned by Baron Stockmar that nothing but the most serious harm could come out of the correspondence; no government could be expected to endure such an 'undermining influence', especially Peel, who had done his best to be generous to the Queen but whose stiffness and tendency to suspicion were well known.

The situation had changed since the Bedchamber crisis of 1839, when the Queen had despaired at the prospect of losing Lord Melbourne. She had then been the more agitated of the two, the more distraught, the more clinging. Now the positions were reversed. Greville had noted that Lord Melbourne's devotion to the young Queen was based on his being a man 'with a capacity for loving and nothing to love'; now he dreaded losing the Queen, while she was madly in love with her husband, had children, domestic problems and, at her elbow, Stockmar, of whose advice the Prince approved. She still loved Lord Melbourne with fondness, still hated the Tories, still disliked Sir Robert Peel, but the responsibility for prolonging 'the dangerous correspondence' lay with Lord Melbourne. Stockmar complained that Lord Melbourne had promised the correspondence would die a natural death after the Queen's confinement in 1841 and the birth of the Prince of Wales 'but instead of permitting it to do so, he before he left London, recommenced it and proffered of his own accord to write from time to time, thereby starting it again in full vigour.'

Peel in an interview had said to Stockmar that 'every private wish the Queen had should be by him respected and attended to to the utmost of his power, and all he asked in return was perfect honesty in public affairs towards him. If he ever had reason to suppose that H.M. took advice from any other quarter, that very instant, be the consequence what it might, he would throw up the office he held, and in so doing should feel that he was acting in strict accordance with the duty which he owed to the Country—before the Baron left him he [Peel] again emphatically repeated these sentiments.'[18] To make matters worse, Lord Melbourne had imprudently imparted the fact that he was corresponding with the Queen to Mrs Norton, the lovely daughter of the playwright Sheridan, known for her indiscretion, who boasted that Lord Melbourne retained his influence with the Queen and was in correspondence with her.

Apprehensions were in fact groundless. Lord Melbourne's letters to the Queen, preserved in a separate packet for this period, contain no political advice.[19] Compromising letters can, of course, be destroyed, but the correspondence follows on logically. In a letter endorsed No. 1 which might have been read by Sir Robert Peel with satisfaction, Lord Melbourne wrote to the Queen '. . . in the concerns of a great nation like this, these changes [i.e. the recent change of government] became difficulties and entanglements but upon the whole the present state is good and the prospect is good for the future. There is no reason to fear that Sir Robert Peel will be devious or liable to take a very different course from that which has been taken by Your Majesty's old servants, and some difficulties will certainly be [eased] and other obstacles smoothed by the change which has lately taken place. . . .' Succeeding letters deal with such subjects as Lord Melbourne's approval of the appointment of Mrs Anson as Woman of the Bedchamber—the Ansons were not wealthy and her salary would be of use to them—and the importance of the Queen confining her invitations to Windsor to Sir Robert Peel and the Lord Chancellor.

Anxiety nevertheless continued. Prince Albert and Stockmar were both in a frenzy of agitation, and in October 1841 Prince Albert asked Mr Anson to go and read to Lord Melbourne an opinion given by Stockmar, on a visit which Lord Melbourne was proposing to pay the Queen at Windsor.[20] Stockmar's opinion had been asked by the Prince because it was 'a case upon which he [the Prince] could exercise no control'. Stockmar wrote it would be better that 'Lord Melbourne's first appearance should be in London, where he would meet the Queen only on the terms of general Society'. It was unfortunate that Lord Melbourne had made a violent attack on the financial policy of Sir Robert Peel and his government, during the previous week in the House of Lords,[21] which 'had added another impediment to his coming at this moment, as it had identified him with and established him as the Head of the opposition party', which the Prince had hoped he would have been able to avoid. Lord Melbourne was then sitting on the sofa listening to Mr Anson; when he heard this, Anson reported, 'he rushed up and across the room in a violent frenzy'. 'God eternally D—— it, etc. etc. Flesh and blood could not hear that. I only spoke upon the *defensive*. . . . I cannot be expected to give up my position in the Country, neither do I think that it is to the Queen's interest that I should. . . .' Anson then went over the previous arguments, that no government could be expected to tolerate such a powerful underground influence, and the importance of calming the Queen's mind in her present condition, the eighth month of her pregnancy. But though the visit to Windsor did not take place the secret correspondence—at the request of the Queen herself—continued. On 26th December 1841 Anson reported the Queen was 'low' and Melbourne was ignoring the remonstrance on his correspondence with her, made to him by the Prince.[22]

The truth was that, as early as 1840, Lord Melbourne's health had begun to fail. He put on an enormous amount of weight assisted, in Lady Lyttelton's opinion, by the 'consommés, truffles, pears, ices and anchovies which he does his best to revolutionize his stomach with every day'. When Lady Lyttelton found herself in a carriage with him and he sat on her cloak, he was so unwieldy she did not like to ask him to move, and she observed he was looking 'as old as the hills'. Nevertheless he continued to eat hugely. The Queen noted that he began the day with a cold grouse, followed by three mutton chops. He made himself ill by eating too much lobster salad for supper at Lady Holland's house, and was in the habit of eating a large rich dinner after midnight when he returned home from the House of Lords. On 7th August 1839 he mentioned eating a pike, chicken, peas and raspberry tart and drinking a bottle of Madeira at 4 a.m. His house, No. 51 South Street, Mayfair, though filled with servants —there were sixteen of them, 'they all drink and he believes cheat'—was dirty and neglected. Lord Melbourne commented that all the accommodation he himself required was a bedroom on the ground floor, with two libraries opening off it.

He did not always seem to know what he was doing. A reporter from the *Morning Post* saw him walking alone on the terrace at Windsor, 'talking wildly and loudly to himself'; the Queen observed him at a dinner party 'talking so to himself and making fierce faces'. He was in a state of extreme sensitivity; his eyes, always apt to fill with tears, were now constantly brimming over. His wit and urbanity, his flashes of brilliance remained, so that since he had always been mildly eccentric, even his close relatives did not realize he was breaking up.

At the end of October 1842 Lady Lyttelton reported that 'Poor Lord Melbourne has had rather an alarming attack of giddiness in the head. He is said to be better now.'[23] Lord Melbourne's seizure was serious. He had had a stroke and his career was at an end. The stroke had effects from which he never recovered; after it his hair became white, he dragged one leg, he was melancholy, and his noted vitality and brilliance appeared only occasionally.

Fortunately, in 1842 his brother, Lord Beauvale, with his charming young wife, Lady Adine, returned to England after ten years spent as British Ambassador at Vienna. The affection between the members of the Lamb family was proverbial, and with the assistance of Lady Palmerston, Lord Melbourne's sister, the Beauvales took charge of Lord Melbourne. Much of his time was spent in the quiet of the country at Brocket, his house in Hertfordshire, or at Broadlands, Lord Palmerston's seat in Hampshire. He clung to the hope that he might hold office again and when Peel's government resigned in 1846 on the issue of the repeal of the Corn Laws Lord Melbourne was mortified not to be offered a seat in the Cabinet. Lord John Russell, the new Prime Minister, explained, kindly enough, on 3rd July, 'I submitted to the Queen yesterday the list of a new Ministry. I have not proposed to you to form a part of it, because I do not think your health is equal to the fatigues which any office must entail. . . .' Melbourne himself recognised that Lord John was correct and replied the same day 'You have judged very right and kindly in making me no offer. I am subject to such frequent accesses of illness as render me incapable of any exertion.'[24]

It was inevitable that Lord Melbourne's old age should be melancholy. The years of power, the courting, the flattery, were over, the crowds waiting outside his door, hanging on his every word, had gone elsewhere. He was fortunate in the faithful affection of his brothers and sisters and the consideration and love with which they surrounded him. But then there was the Queen, he longed for the Queen, and she wrote less and less frequently. He could not bring himself to accept that from the appearance of Prince Albert, in 1840, he had ceased to be important to her. He longed for their old association. 'Lord M. cannot say otherwise than that he continually misses and regrets the time when he had daily communication with Your Majesty'[25] he wrote.

His financial affairs were a source of anxiety to him and his state of health caused him to think his circumstances worse than they were.[26] He wrote to the Queen on 30th December 1847, telling her he was low and depressed in spirits owing to his 'straitened . . . pecuniary circumstances, & these embarrassments are growing now every day more & more urgent, so that he dreads before long that he shall be obliged to add another to the lists of failures & banqueroutes of which there have lately been very many. This is the true reason why Ld. Melbourne has always avoided the honour of the Garter when pressed upon him by . . . Your Majesty.' Lord Melbourne knew that 'the expense of accepting the blue riband amounts to £1,000 & there has been . . . no period at which it would not have been seriously inconvenient for Ld. Melbourne to lay down such a sum.'

He had been a very rich man when he succeeded to the title, but he had been 'generous, lavish and careless'. Estate accounts bored him and had not been examined for years on end.

Early in 1848 he applied to the Queen, who sent him a sum of money which he accepted, soliciting a pension. He asked the Queen to speak to Lord John Russell about it. '£2,000 . . . would greatly improve his circumstances but £3,000 will render him affluent.' Lord John Russell told the Queen that in order to obtain a pension for services in the higher offices of state it was necessary not only to serve for a fixed period of time but also to produce evidence that the person in whose favour the pension was to be granted 'has not a private fortune adequate to his station in life. . . . Now it appears to Lord John Russell that although the services of Lord Melbourne . . . would fully qualify him for a pension, it is impossible to affirm or to admit that he has not a private fortune adequate to his station in life.' The rent roll of his estate although diminished was still well over £17,000 annually.

The Queen then lent Lord Melbourne a considerable sum to cover his immediate requirements. The explanation of Lord Melbourne's anxiety was that his bankers had called on him to repay a sum of about £10,000 which they had advanced to him and which, in the existing circumstances of financial crisis, they wished to turn to a more lucrative account. 'Lord Melbourne allowed his mind to become very unnecessarily harassed by this pressure, and his estate being strictly entailed, he said he was at a loss how or where to procure this accommodation'.

On 8th February 1848 Mr Anson told Prince Albert that he had had a good deal of conversation with Lord Beauvale about Lord Melbourne's affairs. The loan from the Queen would be a great accommodation to Lord M., but as regarded the pension, Lord Beauvale was both *wholly* ignorant and a good deal distressed. 'He [Lord Beauvale] of course took entirely the same view that we do upon it, that . . . it would be most injurious to Lord M's reputation . . . besides, it is quite unnecessary as a little Energy & management will perfectly relieve the pressure. . . . Ld Melbourne's estates yield £18,000 a year . . . there is not a debt upon the property & the only charges upon it are settlements for life upon Ld Beauvale & Mr Lamb. . . . Ld Beauvale says that Ld M. is quite unfit to attend to his own affairs . . . but he will not allow any of his family to interfere with or speak to him about them, & broods over imaginary (to a great extent) difficulties. I think Lord Melbourne altered for the worse a good deal . . . & no wonder, for nothing can exceed his imprudence in Living, & after an unwholesome Dinner & much more wine than he ought to drink he generally goes to bed *before* 9 o'c—His Doctor & Head Nurse (Miss Cuyler) are not the least Check upon him. . . .'

Lord Melbourne had no further stroke but his health continued to decline and on 24th November 1848, less than a year later, he died at the age of 69. The Queen mourned him, in her own words 'truly and sincerely', recalling that for the first two and a half years of her reign he had been almost her only friend, except Stockmar and Lehzen, and that she used to see him daily. But her grief was gentle, melancholy and restrained.[27] The Prince was everything to her, Melbourne nothing. As Greville had predicted the Prince was all powerful. 'He is as much King as She can make him' Greville wrote.[28] 'She has just had a chair of State set up for him in the H. of Lords, the same as her own, another throne in fact.'

Every few months now brought the Prince an access in authority. When the Queen was laid up after the birth of Princess Alice in 1843 the Prince held levées in her place. 'Presentations to him were to be considered as equivalent to Presentations to the Queen herself . . . this step . . . provoked the animadversions of a certain Court party as an unwarrantable assumption of Royal functions; and . . . they . . . had the bad taste to follow up their complaints by conspicuously absenting themselves from the Levées.'[29] Among those who absented themselves were the Duke of Cambridge and the King of Hanover. The Queen was furious with them. When the Queen announced decisions to her Ministers not only was the Prince always present, but the Queen used the plural 'we' instead of the first person singular, 'I'. 'All this, however,' remarked Greville, 'does not make him more popular. . . . He is become so identified with her that they are one person, and as He likes and she dislikes business, it is obvious that while she has the title, he is really discharging the functions of the Sovereign. He is King to all intents and purposes.'[30]

After the birth of Princess Alice, the Queen's relief that the ordeal was over and the happiness of her relations with the Prince, no longer complicated by Lehzen, put her in a frame of mind to wish for a little 'merriment'. She longed to travel. The nation had just presented her with a yacht, the *Victoria and Albert*—launched the same day Princess Alice was born—and her beloved aunt, Queen Louise of the Belgians, had long been urging her to cross the Channel and pay a short visit to Queen Louise's parents, Louis Philippe, King of the French, and his wife Queen Amélie. The Queen decided the expedition should be made. The Prince, accompanied by Anson, went down the Thames to the West India Dock on 18th June 1843, the anniversary of the battle of Waterloo, to inspect the yacht's fittings, using the state barge, last employed to convey Nelson's body to burial.[31] The plan was to cross the Channel to Tréport in Normandy, where the French Royal Family owned a property, and to stay for a day or two informally at the Château of Eu which stood in the park. The visit was represented as one of family affection, but it was significant that Lord Aberdeen, Peel's Foreign Secretary, accompanied the Queen and the Prince, and that Guizot, the French Foreign Minister, came with King Louis Philippe. The Queen and the Prince were venturing into the tangled world of European politics.

Relations between France and Great Britain, once hereditary enemies, had been changed since 1830 by the situation in the Middle East. Turkey had become of vital importance, and the policy of France and Great Britain towards Turkey was, broadly speaking, the same; the Ottoman Empire, not yet 'the sick man of Europe', was to be maintained in order to preserve the European balance of power.

Towards the end of 1831 the situation in the Near East had become urgent through the rise of Mehemet Ali. This able Albanian, originally a tobacco merchant from the Aegean, had served in Napoleon's expedition to Egypt, risen to be Pasha (Governor), and now was determined to extend his power by gaining control of Palestine, Syria and Arabia. Picking a quarrel with the Pasha of Lebanon, he invested Acre, upon which the Sultan Mahmoud II declared Mehemet Ali a rebel but, far from crushing him, was defeated by Mehemet Ali in a series of disasters. By December 1832 it appeared as if the forces of Mehemet Ali might overrun Asia Minor and even capture Constantinople.

All powers with interests in the future of Turkey were concerned, and Metternich sought to promote collective action by which Mehemet Ali might be suppressed, but the French government was on cordial terms with Mehemet Ali and favoured mediation between the Sultan and his vassal, while in Britain Palmerston had not yet made up his mind what policy he meant to take. He wished London, not Vienna, to be the centre for diplomatic conversations between the powers, an idea unacceptable to Metternich who longed to restore Vienna to its former position as diplomatic capital of Europe. British attention had also been deflected by interest in the negotiations which in 1831 placed Prince Leopold of Saxe-Coburg on the Belgian throne and, faced with a lukewarm reception from both the French and English governments, the Sultan unwillingly turned to Russia.

In February 1833 a Russian naval force entered the Bosphorus, a Russian army encamped on the Asiatic shore and 5,000 troops were landed near Constantinople. The French attempted to make peace between the belligerents but failed, owing to their inclination towards Mehemet Ali whom they associated with Napoleonic glories. Great Britain, assisted by Austria, was more successful. The Sultan was induced to offer Syria and Adana to Mehemet Ali, terms so advantageous that Mehemet Ali hastened to accept and the Russian force withdrew. It may be noted that earlier Mehemet Ali had presented King George IV with the celebrated giraffe, the first specimen to be seen in England, which was visited by Queen Victoria when Princess, and whose portraits by Jacques-Laurent Agasse and Richard Barrett Davis hang in the Royal Collection.

Good relations between Great Britain and France were essential in 1843 having regard to the state of the Turkish Empire, the certainty of further trouble from Mehemet Ali and the menace of an extension of Russian power in Europe, but the French were suspected and Louis Philippe was considered a man in whom no trust could be reposed. The Citizen King, as he liked to be called, was of royal blood, the eldest son of that Duke of Orleans who had adopted the principles of the French Revolution with such fervour as to earn himself the name of Philippe

Égalité. Although descended in direct line from the younger brother of Louis XIV, Philippe Égalité voted for the execution of Louis XVI in 1793, only to be guillotined himself during the Terror later in the same year.

His son Louis Philippe was too young to vote for the execution of Louis XVI, but fought in the revolutionary army at the two actions of Valmy and Jemappes, was later discovered to be involved in a plot against the Republic and forced to fly from France, returning, after visiting the United States, only after the abdication of Napoleon in 1814. He emerged a unique figure, a Prince of the House of Orleans, not involved in the execution of Louis XVI, who had fought under the flag of the Revolution. France had become exhausted as the terror was succeeded by the torrents of blood poured out in the Napoleonic campaigns. In contrast the Revolution of July 1830, which, all but fifteen years later, placed Louis Philippe on the throne of France, was bloodless. He was proclaimed in the Chamber, 'King of the French by the grace of God and the will of the people', and made no claim to rule by divine right. The Palais Royal, where he began his reign, was, like the White House, Washington, open to all citizens who wished to call and shake him by the hand.

He cherished, nevertheless, secret ambitions. He wished to reinstate French power in southern Europe, and his wife was Maria Amélie, eldest daughter of the Bourbon King of Naples and the Two Sicilies, a Catholic monarch, noted for his bigotry, reactionary views and savage suppression of opposition. Their eldest daughter, Princess Louise of Orleans, married Queen Victoria's uncle Leopold, King of the Belgians, as his second wife. The Princess was a devout Catholic; King Leopold belonged to the Lutheran branch of the Protestant Church and each adhered to their separate religion. The children were brought up as Catholics.

It was Louis Philippe's ambition to unite the thrones of France and Spain. Such a union had been expressly forbidden by the Treaty of Utrecht, signed after the War of the Spanish Succession in 1713, and confirmed by the Quadruple Alliance of 1834 signed by Great Britain, Portugal, France and Spain.

The visit to Eu by the Queen of Great Britain and her husband the Prince was bound to have significance beyond an informal visit of family affection. Tension was heightened by the urgency of the marriage of the young Queen Isabella of Spain. Whom was she to marry and what would the consequences be?

In 1829 King Ferdinand of Spain, who had no children, became a widower for the third time and married Maria Christina, a Neapolitan princess. On 19th May 1830 Queen Christina gave birth to a daughter Isabella, who was recognised by the Spanish Cortes as the heir to the throne. Isabella was followed by another princess, the Infanta Louisa. In 1832 King Ferdinand died, leaving his infant daughter Isabella Queen of Spain with her mother Queen Christina as Regent. In 1843 she was 13, mature for her age, and a marriage for her in the near future was considered wise. Rumour, supported by responsible Ministers of European governments, credited Louis Philippe with an ingenious plan. The young Queen Isabella was to marry her cousin, the Duke of Cadiz, while her sister and next heiress, the Infanta Louisa, married one of Louis Philippe's sons, the Duke of Montpensier. It was believed that the Duke of Cadiz was incapable of having children. If his marriage with Queen Isabella proved barren, the crown of Spain would pass to the Infanta Louisa and her husband.

In these circumstances the Queen's project of a visit to Eu appeared politically significant. Her Ministers were dubious. Might the British government be suspected of embarking on political intrigue? The Queen, however, was determined—a visit to France, a journey in her new yacht over the Channel, which she had never crossed, were irresistible. As usual when the Queen was determined, she had her way. There were formalities to be dealt with. This would be the first time an English sovereign had visited a French sovereign since Henry VIII and Francis I met in 1520 at the Field of the Cloth of God. Hitherto the Sovereign on leaving the realm had always left behind Lord Justices, Deputies and an Act of Regency to represent the royal authority. Queen Victoria refused to be involved in any of these. Though opposed by the Duke of Wellington, the precedent was established and on the Queen's numerous subsequent visits abroad the royal authority was not, except in special circumstances, delegated.[32]

In England, the visit continued to be regarded with suspicion; a plot by Louis Philippe was suspected and Lord Melbourne, who in 1843 still retained much of his health, wrote to the Queen 'Your Majesty is quite right in supposing that Lord Melbourne would at once attribute Your Majesty's visit to the Château d'Eu to its right cause—your Majesty's friendship and affection for the French Royal Family and not to any political object. The principal motive now is to take care that it does not get mixed either in reality or in appearance with politics. . . . Do not let them make any treaty or agreement there. It can be done elsewhere just as well, and without any of the suspicion which is sure to attach to any transaction which takes place there.'[33] King Leopold of the Belgians, on the other hand, exhorted the Queen not to be suspicious.[34] He was sure the 'personal contact with the family at Eu . . . would remove some impressions on the subject of the King, which are really untrue. Particularly the attempt of representing him like the most astute of men, calculating constantly everything to deceive people. His vivacity alone would render such a system extremely difficult, and if he appears occasionally to speak too much and to seem to hold a different language to different people, it is a good deal owing to his vivacity and his anxiety to carry convictions to people's minds. . . .'

Queen Louise cautioned her mother not to allow her father King Louis Philippe to talk politics to Queen Victoria. He might be tempted to discuss the situation in Spain, and Queen Victoria never talked politics. She was naturally suspicious and always afraid of committing herself or making some verbal assent, '. . . if I may say so it is the paternal character, the father of a family, that Victoria would like to see. My excellent Father then should be natural, patriarchal, without ceremony, as he is always, but, unless she begins the subject, which she certainly will not . . . he should not enter into politics and avoid everything which could suggest he was trying to use her visit to influence her.'[35]

On 2nd September 1843 the *Victoria and Albert* dropped anchor at Tréport. The Prince de Joinville, one of King Louis Philippe's sons, had joined the *Victoria and Albert* at Cherbourg; when he reported the approach of the French royal barge containing King Louis Philippe the Queen felt agitated. However, the King could hardly be persuaded to wait, wrote the Queen, until the barge was near enough before he hastened out, came up and embraced the Queen warmly, saying over and over again how delighted he was to see her. The French barge was very fine, with a large number of oarsmen, dressed in white, with red sashes and red ribbons round their hats. The Queen and the Prince went on board 'and presently the novel spectacle was seen of the Royal Standards of England and France floating side by side over the Sovereigns of the two countries as they were rowed to shore'.[36] The Queen and the Prince were given a magnificent reception, the whole Court assembled on the shore, with numbers of troops and large crowds of cheering citizens shouting 'Vive la Reine d'Angleterre'.

The weather was magnificent 'even at Eu where the sea is usually agitated and troublesome'[37] and the Queen felt gay and happy. The visit was arranged as a private family meeting, the party drove to the forest where there was a déjeuner out of doors, the Queen went over the Château with the Queen of the French, 'for whom I feel a filial affection', Albert swam in the sea, another déjeuner took place in a tent in the garden. King Louis Philippe had taken a great deal of trouble to please what he conceived to be the English taste by sending to England for quantities of bottled beer and cheese. 'No exchange of views on political subjects took place' according to an official account 'beyond the voluntary declaration of the King in a conversation with the Queen, the Prince and Lord Aberdeen . . . that no designs were entertained which could have the effect of placing any of his sons on the throne of Spain.'[38]

The Prince wrote to Stockmar that '. . . the old King [Louis Philippe] was in the third heaven of rapture, and the whole family received us with a heartiness, I might say affection, which was quite touching'.[39] The promise volunteered by the King of the French on the Spanish marriages was accepted as trustworthy and sincere.

On Monday, 7th September, the Queen and the Prince returned to England. The French Royal Family went with them on the barge where farewells were regretfully said; the French Royal Family then transferred to a small steamer and the Queen and the Prince were rowed to the yacht in the barge, and stood on the paddle box of the yacht while the steamer passed, King Louis waving his hand and calling out 'Adieu, Adieu'. The Prince de Joinville accompanied the Queen and the Prince to Brighton and spent two nights at the Pavilion. 'He was very much struck with the strangeness of the building' wrote the Queen. Prince Albert told Stockmar that he had 'rarely been so pleased with any young man' as with the Prince de Joinville. He was 'straightforward, honourable, gifted and amiable'.

The Queen's nerves were tranquil, in spite of the fact that the birth of Princess Alice was succeeded by another pregnancy in the following year. She delighted in the *Victoria and Albert*, and after returning to Windsor to see her three children crossed the Channel again on 12th September to visit Leopold, King of the Belgians, and Queen Louise, and become acquainted with the cities of Bruges, Ghent, Brussels and Antwerp.

In two letters dated 21st and 26th September[40] the Queen describes the visit as 'painfully short! It was such a joy for me to be under the roof of one who has ever been a father to me!' They returned to 'find Pussy amazingly advanced in intellect, but alas also in naughtiness'.

Prince Albert steadily gained ground. Chartism was once more arousing anxiety but the Prince insisted on visiting Birmingham, its stronghold, and received a warm welcome. 'The 280,000 people [of Birmingham] seemed to have turned out on the occasion,' wrote Mr Anson,[41] 'the streets were literally jammed but nothing could exceed the good humour, good feeling and apparent excess of loyalty which pervaded the whole multitude. There was not a single instance to the contrary amidst those dense masses.'

In another aspect of English life, the Prince carried off honours by showing at a meet at Belvoir, the Duke of Rutland's seat, that he excelled in the hunting field. 'We had a capital run, and the Prince rode admirably to the amazement of most' wrote Mr Anson, himself an ardent follower of hounds. 'One can scarcely credit the absurdity of people here' the Queen told King Leopold 'but Albert's riding so boldly and hard has made such a sensation that it has been written all over the country, and they make much more of it than if he had done some great act!'[42]

*

On 29th January 1844 Prince Albert's father, the Duke of Saxe-Coburg and Gotha, died after a few days' illness. He had been extravagant, dissolute and heartless. His bad treatment of Prince Albert's mother had been notorious, he had caused embarrassment by trying to borrow money from Queen Victoria, and endeavouring to make use of her great position to aggrandise his own. Nevertheless the Queen and the Prince, especially the Queen, plunged into ecstasies of mourning: '*You* must now be the father of us two poor bereaved heart broken children' the Queen wrote to King Leopold[43] on 6th February 1844. 'To describe to you *all* that we *have* suffered, all that we do suffer, would be difficult. God has heavily afflicted us. We feel crushed, overwhelmed, bowed down by the loss of one who was so deservedly loved, I may say adored, by his children and family. I loved him and looked on him as my own father. . . .' The Queen was, as always, thinking first of the Prince and the extravagance of her grief was inspired by her concern for him. 'My darling stands so alone' she told Stockmar[44] 'and his grief is so great and touching. . . . He says (forgive my bad writing, but my tears blind me), *I* am now *all* to him. Oh! if I can be, I shall be only too happy. . . .'

Lady Lyttelton wrote that she had been a good deal with the Queen who is 'very affecting in her grief . . . [which is], in truth, all on the Prince's account, and every time she looks at him her eyes fill afresh'.[45]

Prince Albert mourned his vanished youth, the scenes at Rosenau and Coburg he had so dearly loved, the pleasures of boyhood he had enjoyed. He wrote to Stockmar that while his father would no doubt have been doomed to a dreary old age, as far as Prince Albert himself was concerned a great piece had been taken out of his life. His early life in Germany was finally over and a new era had begun. 'I will, therefore, at once close accounts there, and set about putting the machine into a state in which it may go working on for the future. . . . These considerations have decided me to go over. Ten to twelve days are enough to despatch the whole business.'[46] The affairs of the Duchy of Saxe-Coburg and Gotha were in some confusion, especially its finances, and the new Duke, Prince Albert's brother Ernest, already known to be dissipated, was showing disquieting signs of resembling his father.

Prince Albert was in Germany from 28th March to 11th April 1844. Short though the separation was, the Queen suffered; during the four years of her marriage she had hardly been separated from the Prince for a day. The King and Queen of the Belgians came over to be with her, the two persons she often said whom 'next to her husband she loved best in the world'.[47] 'I shall be thankful when the trial is over' wrote Lady Lyttelton. 'We all feel sadly wicked and unnatural in his absence, and I am actually counting the days de mon coté, as Her Majesty is.'

At the end of May 1844 the Prince de Joinville alarmed the governments of England and France by publishing without warning a pamphlet, under his own name, entitled *On the State of the Naval strength of France in comparison with that of England.*[48] The pamphlet created a sensation; it went through at least three editions in French and four in English and roused the old hatreds and antagonisms which the Queen and the Prince had visited Eu to soften. On page 7 he wrote 'My well-grounded and decided idea is, that it is possible for us to sustain war against any power, even that of England. . . . Who can doubt, but that with a well-organized steam navy we should possess the means of inflicting losses and unknown sufferings on an enemy's coast, which has never hitherto felt all the miseries that war can inflict? With her sufferings would arise the evil, till then unknown to her, of confidence destroyed; the riches accumulated on her coasts and in her harbours would cease to be in security; while by means of well-appointed privateers, the plan of which I shall develop by and by, we could act efficiently against her commerce, spread over the whole surface of the ocean.

'The struggle then would no longer be unequal. . . .' He quoted observations made by *The Times* in its condescending manner. '. . . France can equip a powerful fleet; but if she were plunged in a war of aggression, and opposed to England, we are confident that neither the money lavished on the navy, nor the indisputable courage of her naval officers, would rescue her vessels from the cruel alternative of inaction in her ports, or of destruction out of them. She is the second maritime Power, but in order to remain so she must be at peace with the first.'

The Queen wrote to the King of the Belgians 'I must write you a line to say *how vexed* we are at this *most unfortunate* and *most imprudent brochure* of Joinville's; it has made a *very bad* effect here, and will rouse all the envy and hatred between the *two Navies* again, which it was our great effort to subdue. . . . I can't tell you how angry people are. . . . If he comes here, *what* shall we do? Receive with open arms one who has talked of ravaging our coasts and burning our towns? . . . We shall forgive and forget, and feel it was *not* intended to be published—but the public *here* will *not* so easily . . . what *could* possess Joinville to write it, and still more to have it printed?'[49] On 29th May the Queen wrote to Lord Aberdeen recommending him to read the pamphlet, 'as one cannot judge fairly by the extracts in the newspapers. Though it does not lessen the extreme imprudence of the Prince's publishing, it certainly is *not* intentionally written to offend England, and on the contrary frankly proves *us* to be immensely superior to the French Navy. . . .'[50] Eventually it was decided that the Prince de Joinville's indiscretion had better be overlooked and his relationship with the Queen and the Prince remained unchanged.

On 1st June the Emperor of Russia, Nicholas I, arrived in London for an unexpected visit.[51] Though taken by surprise and advanced in her fourth pregnancy the Queen exerted herself to fête him. He went with the Court to Windsor, was given two dinners in the Waterloo Chamber, accompanied the Queen to a large and brilliant review in Windsor Great Park and expressed himself as 'quite enchanted' by Windsor Castle. He accompanied the Queen to Ascot races and made himself popular by establishing a race with an annual prize of £500. In London he stayed at Buckingham Palace, a grand concert was given in his honour, and he went with the Queen to the opera where they were most brilliantly received. The Prince also took him to a breakfast at the Duke of Devonshire's celebrated villa at Chiswick, though in the Queen's state of health it was thought wiser for her to stay at home. The Emperor's elder brother, the Emperor Alexander, had been the Queen's godfather and the present political situation made the strengthening of the personal tie desirable. The visit was a success.

The Emperor's object was to discover what prospect, if any, existed of detaching England from her alliance with France. He was convinced that Turkey was in a moribund state and must soon fall to pieces. 'I do not covet one inch of Turkish soil for myself, but neither will I allow anybody else to have one' he told Sir Robert Peel. This remark was aimed at France whose support of Mehemet Ali indicated an intention of securing a footing on Turkish territory. Both Sir Robert Peel and the Prince made it clear that England's only intention in the East was to make sure that no government in Egypt was powerful enough to prevent the passage of English trade and English mails across Egypt. As far as France was concerned Sir Robert Peel stated that it was one of the main objects of his policy to make certain that the French throne on the death of Louis Philippe descended to the next legitimate heir of the Orleans dynasty. Great Britain intended to maintain the status quo in Turkey.

Public opinion in France was incensed by the Emperor of Russia's visit to London, and unfavourable comments in the French Press were already irritating the British nation when fresh trouble arose. The French were not easy allies. The distant island of Tahiti was to all intents and purposes seized by the French from its ruler Queen Pomare, an old ally of the British, in 1842. A rupture between Great Britain and France had been averted only by a narrow margin, when the French authorities, who had made themselves detested in the island, committed an unprovoked outrage on a Protestant missionary, Mr Pritchard, who was also British Consul in Tahiti. He was seized, imprisoned and finally expelled from Tahiti without being allowed to see his family. Anger in England exploded in fury, Sir Robert Peel himself lost his temper and war with France seemed probable. 'M. Guizot has been himself alone to blame for what has occurred' wrote Sir Robert to Lord Aberdeen. 'If he chooses to send out expeditions to occupy every place where they can find the pretence for occupation . . . and if M. Guizot has not the power or courage to disavow them, *he* is responsible for whatever may occur in consequence of such proceedings. It is absurd to throw the responsibility on Mr Pritchard. If the French Consul got up a plot with the French naval officer to swindle Queen Pomare out of her sovereignty, can M. Guizot be surprised that English residents in Tahiti feel indignant . . . that the language they hold adds to the excitement among the natives; and makes an unjust usurpation uncomfortable for usurpers? . . . there is anything but advantage to us in his [Guizot's] continuance in power.'[52] Calmer counsels, however, prevailed and after months of negotiation an explanation was made by the French government and an indemnity paid to Mr Pritchard.[53]

In the midst of the negotiations the Queen's fourth child and second son, Prince Alfred, was born on 6th August 1844. The Queen had hoped for a son and the arrival of a prince was greeted with delight. She now had two sons and two daughters and her satisfaction was great. Her nerves had supported the strain of the confinement without ill effects. 'The *only* thing almost to mar our happiness' she wrote to King Leopold in her first letter after her confinement 'is the heavy and threatening cloud that hangs over our relations with France which *distresses* and *alarms* us sadly. The whole nation here are *very angry*. . . .'[54] On 15th September she wrote again to her uncle 'The good ending of our difficulties with France is an immense blessing, but it is really and truly necessary that you and those at Paris should know that the danger was *imminent*'.

The settlement of the Pritchard affair left the way clear for King Louis Philippe to visit England. On 8th October 1844 Prince Albert got up at 6 a.m. to go to Portsmouth to meet the King, accompanied by the Duke of Wellington.[55] The Queen waited in the state apartments at Windsor with her ladies and the Duchess of Kent and as the carriage with the King drove up, went and stood under the portico. The King, who embraced her warmly, seemed 'quite touched' at seeing the Queen again. 'What emotions must he feel' wrote the Queen. 'He is the first King of France who ever came to pay a visit to the Sovereign of this country.' He admired Windsor and said of the grand staircase leading to his apartments 'Dieu comme c'est beau'. He thanked the Queen for the kindness of the British government over Prince de Joinville's pamphlet—'very dangerous for a Prince to publish'. The Duc de Montpensier told the Queen next day, 9th October, that 'all but fifty copies had been locked up, but the King said this was enough to do the damage'. 'M. Guizot left England four years ago when there were no children, now he returns and finds four!' wrote the Queen. The King went over the Castle, was 'enchanted' by the Library, and with the whole Castle, pronouncing St George's Chapel 'the most beautiful he had ever seen'. Dinner was in St George's

Hall. 'The King was enchanted with the whole thing, which is very splendid and said "C'est superbe".'

On 10th October King Louis Philippe visited Twickenham where he had lived in exile with his uncles. He was rapturously welcomed and said he never had a reception to compare with it. 'We are so pleased at this' wrote the Queen 'as he truly deserves it.'

Immediately after lunch on 11th October the Queen dressed in her robes of the Garter and King Louis Philippe was invested. Prince Albert placed the Garter round the King's leg, the Queen pulled it through while the admonition was being read, the Duke of Cambridge assisted the Queen in placing the ribbon over King Louis Philippe's shoulder. 'He was in transports of delight.' Afterwards the Queen expressed regret to King Louis Philippe that the Bourbons had not profited by their lesson in the French Revolution. (In a well-known saying the Bourbons are described as having learned nothing and forgotten nothing.) King Louis Philippe said he had disliked Louis XVIII who was very inimical to him, but had liked Charles X, though he was never allowed to see or be with him. If he had, things might have been very different.

The Queen notes that no parties or dinners were given in the Waterloo Gallery during the King's stay, 'a delicate attention much appreciated'. In spite of Prince de Joinville's injudicious pamphlet the royal party went on board the French battleship *Gomer*, off the Isle of Wight, on 15th October and were given a French salute, a full broadside, three times. The Queen considered that the officers of the two navies having lived together and the excellent reception given King Louis Philippe must do good; the visit, she told Lord Aberdeen, had gone off admirably. The King's satisfaction, his expressions of affection and hopes of peace were he said 'quite from the heart' of Guizot, with whom Sir Robert Peel had every reason to be satisfied.

King Louis Philippe had blessed the Queen's children, telling her that her father, the Duke of Kent, 'had been his very great friend'.

It seemed, from this visit beyond all others, that a new era of peace in western Europe was about to commence. On 28th October the opening of the new Royal Exchange by the Queen in person brought an extraordinary demonstration of loyalty and affection. The crowds were calculated to be even greater than at the coronation, Albert was enthusiastically received and the articles in the papers were 'most kind and gratifying; they say' wrote the Queen[56] '*no* Sovereign *was more* loved than I am (I am bold enough to say) and *that*, from our *happy domestic home*—which gives such a good example'.

*

The Queen's relations with Sir Robert Peel had been transformed. The violent antagonism which she had felt towards him and had expressed in language of unmeasured fury, the anxiety caused by the fear of an open rupture between them, her alarming indiscretions, for instance the correspondence with Lord Melbourne after Sir Robert became Prime Minister, had ceased. The truth was that Sir Robert Peel's character, his paternalism, protectiveness and probity were calculated to appeal to the Queen. Prince Albert placed the highest confidence in him and always had done so.

Six months after assuming office Sir Robert Peel wrote 'My relations with Her Majesty are most satisfactory. The Queen has acted towards me not merely (as everyone who knew Her Majesty's character must have anticipated) with perfect fidelity and honour, but with great kindness and consideration. There is every facility for the despatch of public business, a scrupulous and most punctual discharge of every public duty and an exact understanding of the relation of a constitutional Sovereign to her advisers.'[57]

1845 was another year of 'respite'. Princess Helena was not born until May 1846, and in August 1845 the Queen left England for a tour in Germany, visiting Coburg, the Rosenau and other scenes of Prince Albert's youth. A difficulty over the precedence accorded to Prince Albert by the Prussian Court and the refusal of Prussian Court officials to give him the seat next to herself, awarding the place of honour to the uncle of the Emperor of Austria, caused her such annoyance that for some years she was unwilling to accept offers of hospitality from the Prussian Court.

The German visit was not altogether a success.[58] The Queen was put into a bad temper by the behaviour of the Court and public opinion in England was outraged by her presence at the slaughter of several hundred deer which according to continental custom had been herded into an enclosure to be shot. 'We hear of nothing' wrote Greville 'but the dissatisfaction which the Q. gave in Germany, of her want of civility and graciousness, and a great many stories are told which are probably exaggerated or untrue. It is clear however that the general impression was not favourable. Nothing can exceed the universal indignation felt here by people of every description at the brutal and stupid massacre of the deer which Albert perpetrated and at which she assisted. It has been severely commented on in several of the papers, and met by a very clumsy (and false) attempt to persuade people that She was shocked and annoyed. No such thing appeared and nothing compelled her to see it. But the truth is, her sensibilities are not acute, and though she is not at all ill-natured, perhaps the reverse, she is hard-hearted, selfish and self-willed.'

On 8th September 1845, accompanied by Lord Aberdeen, the Queen and Prince Albert again visited Eu. King Louis Philippe was once more accompanied by Guizot. The Spanish marriages were discussed in detail.

The Queen and Prince Albert wished Queen Isabella to marry one of the Catholic Coburgs, Leopold, the younger brother of Ferdinand who had married the Queen of Portugal. Unfortunately the results of that match were not encouraging. Ferdinand's dictatorial methods had provoked revolution, and in the present discussions at Eu the candidates were reduced to two, the Duke of Cadiz and his younger brother Don Enrico. But, as we have seen, not only the marriage of the Queen of Spain had to be considered but that of her younger sister, the Infanta Louisa, who possessed riches, and whom King Louis Philippe intended to marry his son, the Duc de Montpensier. To this the British government could not at once agree because if, as seemed probable, the marriage of Queen Isabella proved childless, the children of the Duc de Montpensier and the Infanta Louisa would inherit the Spanish throne, contrary to the Treaty of Utrecht which not merely forbade the union of France and Spain, but debarred the heirs of the House of Orleans from ever succeeding to the Spanish throne. Hence the British and French Ministers at Eu came to an agreement and declared in the most explicit terms that *until Queen Isabella was married and had children* they should consider the Infanta in precisely the same light as her sister and any marriage with a French Prince would be entirely out of the question.

Guizot himself in the summer of 1845 repeated to Mr Henry Bulwer, the British Ambassador at Madrid, that both King Louis Philippe and Queen Christina were anxious to settle the marriage of the Duc de Montpensier and the Infanta Louisa for private personal reasons, into which the Infanta's fortune entered, but that it would not take place for some time, nor until Queen Isabella had children.[59] Lord Aberdeen also wrote to Sir Robert Peel from the Château d'Eu, 8th September 1845, 'I distinctly understood, that it was not only a marriage and a child, but *children, that were necessary to secure the succession.*'

A close watch was kept on Queen Isabella, so close that on 3rd April 1846 the French Ambassador in Madrid sent a message to the Ministry in Paris '—la reine est nubile depuis deux heures'. Pressure on Queen Christina to decide her daughters' marriages increased.

Meanwhile a government crisis developed in Britain. For some years Sir Robert Peel had been moving towards the conclusion that the high cost of bread was an unwarrantable burden on the working mass of the population. The cost of bread depended on the price of corn and wheat which was, in effect, kept up artificially and upon which largely depended the prosperity of farmers and landed gentry. The 'hurricane' of the Irish famine, due to the failure of the potato crop in Ireland, with the pressing need for a cheap food was the deciding factor.

Sir Robert Peel, after a personal crisis, aware what the consequences to his party and himself must be, considered his duty was to propose the total abolition of the Corn Laws. Prince Albert gave offence to the House of Commons by coming down on 27th January 1846 to hear the debate. Lord George Bentinck declared the object was 'by reflection from the Queen, to give the semblance of a personal sanction of Her Majesty to a measure, which, be it for good or for evil, a great majority, at least of the landed aristocracy of England, of Scotland and of Ireland, imagine fraught with deep injury, if not ruin, to them. . . .'[60] Prince Albert never went to the House of Commons again.

Following his introduction of the Bill for repeal a storm of rage broke on Sir Robert Peel's head, he was boo-ed, hissed, shouted down, 'hunted like a fox'. The Queen's unhappiness at the prospect of parting from him was almost as great as she had felt when parting from Lord Melbourne nearly five years ago and the arrival of her third daughter, Princess Helena, on 25th May 1846, hardly distracted her attention. On 26th June the Bill for the Repeal of the Corn Laws passed its third reading in the House of Lords but by an ingenious political stratagem Peel was defeated on an unrelated Irish issue by seventy-three votes in the House of Commons. He had lost the confidence of the House.

With regret the Queen had no choice but to invite the leader of the Opposition, Lord John Russell, to replace him, and with Lord John Russell as Prime Minister came Lord Palmerston in place of Lord Aberdeen as Foreign Secretary. The Queen mourned Sir Robert Peel and Lord Aberdeen. 'We felt so safe with them' she wrote[61] to the King of the Belgians.

The question of the Spanish marriages now emerged again with added complications. Prince Leopold of Coburg, who had earlier been rejected, was proposed again in May 1846 by Queen Christina, the Queen's mother. Contrary to diplomatic propriety she wrote direct to Prince Albert's elder brother Ernest, now Duke of Saxe-Coburg and Gotha, and not to one of his Ministers, asking him to enlist the personal assistance of Queen Victoria in marrying Queen Isabella to Prince Leopold of Coburg.

The scheme was known to be regarded by the French with hostility and though Ernest Duke of Saxe-Coburg and Gotha and King Leopold visited England and discussed the matter thoroughly with Queen Victoria and Prince Albert, it was agreed that since both the English and French Ministers had refused to consider Prince Leopold of Coburg as a candidate he must be rejected.[62]

Nevertheless on 18th July 1846 Lord Palmerston wrote his celebrated despatch which did put forward the name of Prince Leopold of Coburg as a possible candidate for the Queen of Spain's hand. The despatch was addressed to Mr Bulwer in Madrid, but Lord Palmerston inexplicably showed it to Count de Jarnac, the French Ambassador in London.[63] The French King and his Ministers were incensed, matters were brought to a crisis and at home the English government was accused of letting Louis Philippe unite with the Spanish government, instead of supporting the Spanish government against the French. Mr Bulwer was asked 'Are your Ministers mad?' but Lord Palmerston did at this time place reliance on the promises of the French. The French government, however, considered that by the despatch they were 'freed a thousand times' from the promises made at Eu, while a further paragraph provoked anger in Spain by adjuring them to lose no time in returning to the ways of the Constitution and obedience to the law, that is to relinquish their pro-French policy.

Events now moved quickly. Without further discussion French and Spanish Ministers at Madrid arranged that Queen Isabella should marry the Spanish Duke of Cadiz, and that on the same day her sister, the Infanta, should marry the Duc de Montpensier, son of King Louis Philippe.

On 8th September 1846 Queen Marie Amélie, Queen of the French, announced the marriage of her son with the Infanta Louisa in a bland letter to Queen Victoria: 'Madame, Trusting to the much prized friendship of which Your Majesty has given us so many proofs and to the kind interest you have always shown in all our children, I hasten to announce the settlement of the marriage of our son Montpensier with the Infanta Louisa Fernanda to you. This family event overwhelms us with joy, because we believe it will ensure the happiness of our cherished son and that we shall find in the Infanta another daughter, as good and lovable as our daughters who will be her elder sisters. I beg in advance that you will bestow your friendship on our new child, confident that she will share the feelings of devotion and affection we all have for you. . . .'[64]

The double Spanish marriages provoked an outburst of anger in Britain. Charges of breach of faith abounded on both sides; in her letter Queen Victoria plainly told the Queen of the French that the King had broken his word. Writing with indignation on 10th September Queen Victoria replied[65] 'Madame—I have just received Your Majesty's letter of the 8th . . . you will perhaps remember what took place at Eu between the King and myself, and you are aware, Madame, of the importance I have always attached to our Entente Cordiale and the enthusiasm with which I have worked for it. You have no doubt learned that we ourselves declined to arrange the marriage between the Queen of Spain and our cousin Leopold (which both Queens [i.e. Queen Isabella and her mother Queen Christina] greatly desired) with the sole object of making it possible for us to take a step which might be more agreeable to your King. . . . You can easily understand, that the sudden announcement of this *double marriage* can only cause us surprise and very keen regret. I ask your forgiveness for talking politics at this moment, but I like to be able to say to myself that towards you I have always been *sincere*. . . .'

To King Leopold the Queen wrote[66] 'The settlement of the Queen of Spain's marriage *coupled with Montpensier's* is *infamous* . . . & we *must* remonstrate. Guizot has had the barefacedness to say to Lord Normanby that tho' *originally* they said that Montpensier shld *only* marry the Infanta *when* the Queen *was married & had children*, that Leopold's [the Coburg Prince] *being* named one of the candidates has changed all and that they must settle it now!!! . . . The King shld know that *we* are extremely indignant. . . .' '*How* the King *can* wantonly throw away the friendship of one who had stood by him with such sincere affection, for a *doubtful* object of personal and family aggrandizement, is to me and to the whole country, inexplicable. Have *confidence* in *him* I fear I never can again. . . .'

The Duke of Beaufort wrote to Thomas Raikes, author of *Raikes' Diary* '. . . he has forfeited his word of honour as a gentleman *to her personally*, while pretending the most sincere friendship. She will not allow his picture to be put up in the castle.'[67] Public opinion declared that the French knew the Duke of Cadiz was unfit for matrimony and that the marriage of the Infanta was a typical French plot to secure the Spanish crown for France. Queen Victoria considered Palmerston 'mismanaged it'.

Lord Palmerston summed the matter up in a letter to Queen Victoria on 12th September 1846:[68] '. . . with regard to the marriage of the Queen of Spain . . . the British government . . . deeply regret that a young Queen should have been compelled . . . to accept for husband a person whom she can neither like nor respect, and with whom her future life will certainly be unhappy at home. . . . But these are matters which concern the Queen and people of Spain more than the Government and people of England. But the projected marriage of the Duke of Montpensier is a very different matter, and must have a political bearing that must exercise a most unfortunate effect upon the relations between England and France.'

The Queen was angry at the contemptuous treatment of the Coburg candidate, Prince Leopold of Coburg, and, as invariably happened, her anger was more bitter because it was on account of Prince Albert than if it had been on her own account.

On 10th October 1846 the marriages were celebrated in Madrid and proved a failure for France but not for Spain. Queen Isabella was not happy, but she had five children of whom the Duke of Cadiz was presumably the father.

France lost her best friend in Great Britain, the first Entente Cordiale was ended, Austria broke the Treaty of Vienna and Russia annexed the Republic of Cracow in November 1846. The effect of the Spanish marriages on British prestige was small, but it is not an exaggeration to say that in the coming years of revolution the Spanish marriages cost King Louis Philippe his throne.

*

Side by side with the complications of the Spanish marriages another series of difficulties arose with the Duchess of Kent and Conroy. Conroy had gone abroad, induced by the Duke of Wellington, in 1839 and was now living in Rome with a semi-invalid son—a tendency to tuberculosis existed in the Conroy family. But the Duchess of Kent had not severed all connections with the Conroys. In January 1843 Prince Albert remonstrated with her for 'keeping up' with them.[69] She dreaded loneliness. Apart from Sir John Conroy, the Conroy Papers contain many packets of notes from the Duchess to Jane Conroy, who was 'delicate' and died young, showing that the Duchess visited Jane several times a week. When Victoire Conroy married, the Duchess wished to settle £200 a year on her, a scheme which Prince Albert 'nipped in the bud'.[70]

Though the Duchess had unwillingly accepted that she could not continue to live in Buckingham Palace with the Queen and Prince Albert after their marriage, finding a residence which satisfied her was difficult. An offer to give Kensington Palace to the King of Hanover in exchange for his apartments in St James's Palace, which he never used, was 'insolently refused' and Lord Melbourne told the Queen she would have to pay the rent of a furnished house for her mother.[71] The Queen was irritated. It was wrong for the Duchess to be always applying to her daughter for money and she would only consent to commit herself for four years at a rental of about £1,500. The Queen had suggested at the time of her engagement that the Duchess should be given a gentleman to be comptroller of her household and manage her financial affairs, and the Queen's advisers selected Colonel George Couper, who had been man of business to Lord Durham in Canada, an exceptionally difficult post, and given unqualified satisfaction. His manners were gentle and mild yet he possessed energy and persistence; but the Duchess did not cease to long for Conroys round her. She was not attracted by Colonel Couper, she wanted someone more dashing, with more 'presence' and 'more brilliant qualities'. Lord Dunfermline, ex-Speaker, her principal friend and adviser, told her an application for one of the Conroy family would be refused.

While the negotiations were proceeding consternation was aroused by rumours that Conroy intended to leave Rome and come to London. Lord Dunfermline's patience became exhausted and in a series of irritated letters[72] he told the Duchess she must make up her mind either to accept or refuse Colonel Couper. She then suggested that Colonel Couper should come on a year's trial. This was impossible. If the Duchess was determined to refuse Colonel Couper the matter must be placed in the hands of the Duke of Wellington.

The Duchess gave way and Colonel Couper was appointed. He was to have the title of First Equerry and be in charge of the Duchess of Kent's household and finances. Lord Duncannon, the First Commissioner of Woods and Forests, told the Duchess she could not have made a better choice. The Queen commented in her Journal that Colonel Couper seemed a little alarmed at what he had undertaken and found the Duchess's affairs in a state of great confusion.[73]

The Duchess's advisers suspected the integrity of Sir John Conroy's dealings with her affairs and Lord Dunfermline wrote the Duchess a letter warning her to be cautious in having communications of any kind with Sir John Conroy.[74] 'I dare not suppose that the affairs of your Royal Highness are in a more orderly state than when I had the honour of seeing your Royal Highness. If things go wrong now . . . it is vain to disguise that the consequences could be very injurious to Your Royal Highness.'

The Duchess was eventually persuaded to accept Ingestre House in Belgrave Square, taken for her by the Queen for an annual rental of £2,000 a year, and moved there on a '*sad* and momentous day', 15th April 1840. Colonel Couper was waiting to welcome her and take up his duties. The Duchess at once complained saying Ingestre House was too small, but five months later, in September, Princess Augusta, daughter of George III, died and the Queen gave the Duchess of Kent both the houses which her aunt had occupied: Clarence House, St James's, where William IV and Queen Adelaide had lived, together with Frogmore House at Windsor.[75] On 21st April 1841 the Duchess, accompanied by Colonel Couper, moved into Clarence House.

The facts of Conroy's administration of the Duchess of Kent's financial affairs now began to emerge.

When Colonel Couper was appointed on 1st January 1840 he was told by Lord Dunfermline that he was to have nothing whatever to do with any accounts prior to this date. 'This arrangement' wrote Colonel Couper 'was rigidly and jealously adhered to, both by Her Royal Highness and by Rea, the Clerk of the Works.'[76] Within a fortnight of his appointment Colonel Couper was beginning to doubt the integrity of Rea, who had worked with Conroy.

In 1845 Rea was removed from the Duchess of Kent's service, locked up all the accounts prior to Colonel Couper's appointment in two commodes in the library at Clarence House and gave the keys to the Duchess. 'Of this arrangement Colonel Couper was not cognizant.' Meanwhile Sir John Conroy had returned to England and was living at his house, Arborfield Hall, near Reading, pressing his claim to the Irish peerage which, he alleged, Lord Melbourne had promised him in 1837.[77] The Queen would have it in her power to create a new Irish peerage in 1845.

Conroy was not successful. Lord Melbourne had given his promise conditionally on being in office, and his government was not in office. Sir Robert Peel, who was in office, refused, and Conroy was forced, at least for the moment, to relinquish his claim. Two years later he renewed his demand for an Irish peerage, but only to be rebuffed by Lord John Russell.

Colonel Couper was a man of ability and integrity; very few such men had entered the Duchess's life. With time their relationship improved and an attachment grew up between them. When a knighthood was conferred on him she wished with characteristic generosity to pay the fees, an offer which was, also characteristically, refused.[78] Colonel Couper wrote he had already sold out sufficient stock. Several years passed but the Duchess still did not give the keys of the commodes to Sir George Couper. She was uneasy and nervous; gossip about Conroy was general, and she was afraid of the disclosures which might result. Throughout 1849 she discussed the contents of the commodes repeatedly with Sir George, telling him she intended to give him the keys, but it was not until February 1850 that he received them with the request that he would put the private accounts in a box and send them to her. 'With the other papers' she added 'you may do what you like.'[79]

When the commodes at Clarence House were unlocked a deplorable state of affairs came to light. In a long memorandum,[80] Sir George Couper informed the Duchess that from 1829 onwards no books whatever were to be found; Conroy had conspired with Rea to defraud her. Some lists of what Rea termed 'incidentals' had been kept, but not with regularity, some bills paid, but again irregularly. 'From 1829–1840, it is not possible to shew the expenditure of any quarter of any year. Neither is it possible to ascertain how the money drawn from the bankers has been expended.'

The memorandum in full was sent to the Duchess by Sir George Couper on 16th February 1850, with a personal note expressing his concern at the contents which he was sure 'would greatly shock Her Royal Highness'. The Duchess was horrified. She could no longer shut her eyes to Sir John Conroy's dishonesty towards her, dishonesty extending over many years. 'Be so good as to keep this paper' she wrote in a note sent by hand. 'I wish to speak to you about it. I have no *head* and no time to think and write about anything distressing. You will understand that the past is very painful to my heart and feelings. If others have been *wrong*, I have also been wrong. I blame myself severely.'

In a note sent by return Sir George Couper wrote 'I hope Your Royal

Highness will pardon the liberty I venture to take in humbly expressing my opinion, that, with the kindness and generosity which belongs to Your character, Your Royal Highness deals far too severely with yourself, far too leniently with others. When free from suspicion Your Royal Highness's nature appears to be confiding to a degree that no good heart could withstand or betray. In your Royal Highness's former great position, it was most natural to pursue the course with respect to accounts which Your Royal Highness has done. Surely Your Royal Highness cannot be blamed for that? But I will not venture to trust myself to express the opinion I entertain of those who seem to have abused so grossly such confidence, so unreservedly, so kindly and so graciously, reposed in them.'

On 18th February Sir George Couper had to explain to the Duchess that more serious frauds had taken place. No good purpose could now be served by going into details of the old accounts but large capital sums were missing. Sir George had been assured both by Stockmar and King Leopold himself that King Leopold, while still Prince, had made a gift of £16,000 to the Duchess of Kent, with which her accounts had never been credited. This sum should have been paid into Coutts Bank and used to meet the expenses of her 'Journies' with the Princess Victoria. Investigation was impossible because all the Duchess of Kent's private bills from 1830 to 1840 were missing. In the opinion of Lord Melbourne, Baron Stockmar and King Leopold, Rea had been the instrument of carrying Conroy's schemes into effect. It was known that Conroy had paid £35,000 for his estate in Wales—and that he had no means to pay such a sum; the general belief was that he had paid out of the Duchess of Kent's money. Colonel Wylde, for instance, who had been on intimate terms with Conroy, 'cut' him stating that he should continue to do so until Conroy could explain the means by which he had purchased the estate.

In the Conroy Papers[81] a different explanation is given. It is asserted that Princess Sophia, daughter of George III, whose finances Sir John Conroy controlled and who was described by Mr Anson as his 'chère amie', 'had made him her heir' *de facto* 'for she gave him nearly all her large income'. It was the money given to Conroy by Princess Sophia which enabled him to buy the Llanlogmaes estate in Montgomeryshire for £18,000. Sir John Conroy then added to the estate by other purchases, the extent of which is not specified. He also bought the lease of a mine from Sir William Wynn, but got next to nothing from it in spite of a 'vast outlay'.

Sir John Conroy's house, Arborfield Hall, near Reading, was bought for him by Princess Sophia. She gave £20,000 towards the price and engaged to contribute annually until the purchase was completed. On her death on 27th May 1848 her family was astonished to find she had left almost nothing. Mr Parkinson of 66 Lincoln's Inn Fields, a solicitor of high reputation, was asked by the Duke of Cambridge and the Duchess of Gloucester to look into her affairs, but could find no property 'except the furniture in the House, a balance at her Bankers, Messrs. Drummonds of £1,607.19.7 and some shares in the Reversionary Society and the Great Western Railway, both of which are of little value. This is a matter of great surprise . . . inasmuch as her income was so large and her expenses so trifling.'[82]

Sir George Couper's report was detailed and damning.[83] 'From the time of Queen Charlotte's death to the death of Princess Augusta, Princess Sophia had an income of £15,000 a year and from the death of Princess Augusta to her own death Princess Sophia had an annual income of more than £17,000. Her Royal Highness had a house from the public. She saw no company, had a very small establishment. . . . £3,000 a year must have been the very utmost of her expenditure, for Captain Garth had been provided for. [Captain Garth was Princess Sophia's illegitimate son.] This would give a saving on the Princess's income of nearly four hundred thousand pounds. Where that money is gone no one can say. Sir John managed the Princess's affairs and declined to give any account of her money. The world therefore believes that it was given, *from time to time*, by the Princess to him. She drew all the cheques on the Bankers and nothing of the disposal of the money so drawn after she had received it is known.'

The revelations of the frauds practised on Princess Sophia did not take place until 1854, which was to prove the last year of Conroy's life. He died of a heart attack at 2 a.m. on 2nd March 1854, his death being announced to the Duchess of Kent later that morning. The Duchess behaved with dignity, though the trembling of her handwriting shows shock. 'I was painfully affected when I heard of the death of Sir John' she told Sir George Couper. 'The recollection of the past disturbed my mind very much.' She wished to know if she should write to Mr Edward Conroy, now the head of the family, and advise him to announce his father's death to the Queen. Lady Conroy had always been delicate and the Duchess feared Jane Conroy, her favourite, would not long survive her father.[84] The Queen wrote generously to her mother[85] on the same day, 'I quite understand your feelings on the occasion of Sir John Conroy's death. . . . I will not speak of the *past* and of the many sufferings he entailed on us by creating divisions between you and me which could never have existed otherwise, they are buried with him. For his poor wife and children I am truly sorry. *They are now free* from the *ban* which kept them from ever appearing before me! . . .'

Thanking the Queen for her letter the Duchess of Kent wrote 'Yes, Sir

John Conroy's death was a most painful shock. I shall not try and excuse the many errors that unfortunate man committed, but it would be very unjust if I allowed all the blame to be thrown on him. I am in justice bound to accuse myself. . . . I *erred* in *believing blindly*, in *acting without reflexion* . . . I allowed myself *unintentionally* to be led to hurt you, my dearest child, for whom I would have given at every moment my life! Reflexion came always too late, but not the *deserved punishment*! my sufferings *were great, very great.* God be praised that those terrible times are gone by and that only death can separate me from you My beloved Victoria.'[86]

Sir John Conroy's estate proved insolvent and the Conroy family ended by depending largely on the Queen for the means to exist. Edward Conroy turned out badly, possessing his father's disregard of truth and overbearing character, without his charm. However, his grandson, John Conroy, possessed scientific talents of a high order and after a distinguished academic career became fellow and science tutor of Balliol College, Oxford, as well as fellow of the Royal Society, and was responsible for depositing the Conroy Papers in the Library of Balliol College.

Chapter Eight

The Queen lived in considerable discomfort. She possessed the British characteristic of indifference to cold; when she first went to Buckingham Palace after her accession the fires could not be lighted because all the chimneys smoked; the Court 'shivered in icy magnificence', but the Queen was not affected. Later the chilliness of Balmoral was dreaded by her Court. Buckingham Palace also contained more dangerous defects, drains which did not function, unsatisfactory ventilation, accumulations of vile-smelling rubbish unseen below stairs, and a degree of confusion and lack of discipline in staff organisation which had made it possible for 'the boy Cotton' to live unobserved for twelve months in the kitchen quarters. Armies of servants did not produce service. The Queen's guests lost their way and could find no one capable of directing them, fires were unlighted, luggage left behind, orders unexecuted.

Shortly after the Queen's marriage, Baron Stockmar and the Prince investigated the organisation of the household. New paint and gilding, fresh chintzes, had not concealed the defects of the Palace from the Prince, but he was then only at the beginning of his career in England. Stockmar drew up a long memorandum setting out what was wrong and what should be done.[1] This was in 1841, but it proved impossible to put the memorandum into effect while Baroness Lehzen was still with the Queen.

In 1842 Lehzen departed and the Prince asked Stockmar to come over from Coburg to help him.[2]

When the Queen succeeded, the Royal Household in England was divided into three departments under the Lord Steward, the Lord Chamberlain and the Master of the Horse. But these three officials were at the same time great officers of state who changed with every change of government. They were always noblemen of high rank; the only quali-fication required for their respective offices was political. Since 1830 there had been five different Lord Chamberlains and six different Lord Stewards. None of the great officers lived in the Palace, daily inspection of their departments was impossible; the limits of those departments had never been properly defined and frequent delegation of authority to servants in the Royal Household inferior in rank produced undesirable and 'ridiculous' results.

The Palace building itself ought to have been in the charge of one department. Not only was it under the charge of three departments, but it had never been decided which parts of the Palace were under the charge of the Lord Chamberlain and which under the Lord Steward. 'In the time of George III the Lord Steward had the custody and charge of the whole palace, excepting the Royal apartments, drawing rooms etc., etc. In George IV's and William IV's reign, it was held that the whole of the ground-floor, including halls, dining rooms, etc., were in his charge. In the present [i.e. Queen Victoria's] reign, the Lord Steward has surrendered to the Lord Chamberlain the grand hall and other rooms on the ground floor; but whether the kitchens, sculleries, pantries, remain under his charge . . . is a question which no one could perhaps at this moment reply to.'[3] The exterior of the Palace was the responsibility of the Office of Woods and Forests, a department noted for its dilatoriness; as a consequence the inside cleaning of the windows was done by the Lord Chamberlain's department, the outside by the Office of Woods and Forests. Thus the amount of light admitted into the Palace depended on co-operation and good understanding between the Lord Chamberlain's office and the Office of Woods and Forests. If there should be a disagreement the Queen must look at the world through obscured and dirty windows.

The household staff of the Palace, for the sake of order, industry and discipline, should have been placed under one controlling authority, but, instead, responsibility was divided between three. Housekeepers, pages and housemaids were under the authority of the Lord Chamberlain, but footmen, livery porters and under-butlers under the Master of the Horse, by whom they were not only paid but clothed. The remainder of the Palace servants, the clerk of the kitchen, cooks, porters etc. were controlled by the Lord Steward. Strange results were produced by this system. When the Queen asked for the fire in the dining-room to be lighted and enquired why this had not been done already, she was 'gravely' answered by an official representing the Lord Steward's department 'You see, properly speaking, it is not our fault; for the Lord Steward lays the fire only, and the Lord Chamberlain lights it.' The Lord Chamberlain provided the lamps: the Lord Steward cleaned, trimmed and lighted them. If a pane of glass or the door of a scullery cupboard required mending, six separate officials each had to sign an authorisation 'and consequently many a window and cupboard have remained broken for months'. 'There is, indeed, in the palace a resident officer, called a Master of the Household, who belongs to the Lord Steward's department. But in the Lord Chamberlain's department . . .

the authority of the Master of the Household is entirely unrecognised, and even in the Lord Steward's department it is quite undefined. It depends altogether upon the chief officers, whom political changes place over the Master of the Household, to what extent they will delegate their power to him. . . . The Master of the Household's office . . . may therefore be pronounced to be, to all practical intents and purposes, a nullity.' As a result 'more than two-thirds of all the male and female servants are left without a master in the house. . . . They may commit any excess or irregularity: there is nobody to observe, to correct, or to reprimand them . . . if smoking, drinking, and other irregularities occur in the dormitories, where footmen etc. sleep ten and twelve in each room, no one can help it.

'There is no one who attends to the comfort of the Queen's guests, on their arrival at the royal residence. When they arrive, at present, there is no one prepared to show them to or from their apartments; there is no gentleman in the palace who even knows where they are lodged, and there is not even a servant who can perform this duty, which is attached to the Lord Chamberlain's department. It frequently happens at Windsor, that some of the visitors are at a loss to find the drawing room, and at night, if they happen to forget the right entrance from the corridors, they wander for an hour helpless and unassisted. There is nobody to apply to in such a case, for it is not in the department of the Master of the Household, and the only remedy is, to send a servant, if one can be found, to the porter's lodge, to ascertain the apartment in question.' It was this state of affairs, notes Baron Stockmar, which enabled 'the boy Jones' to gain access to the Queen's private sitting-room shortly after the birth of the Princess Royal. '. . . The public attached blame, and I think with much reason' continued Stockmar 'to the person or persons on whom depend the regulations for the protection of the Queen's person. But . . . there was no person in the palace on whom such responsibility could rightly be fixed; for it certainly did not fall on the Lord Chamberlain, who was in Staffordshire, and in whose department the porters are not; nor on the Lord Steward, who was in town, and who has nothing to do with the disposition of the pages and other parties nearest to the royal person; nor, finally, on the Master of the Household, whom we have above shown to be only a subordinate officer in the Lord Steward's department.

'On whom does it then fall? Entirely on the absence of system, which leaves the royal palace without any responsible authority.'[4]

The process which converted the confusion of the Palace into a smooth-running machine, officiating with economy, precision and regularity was conducted by Prince Albert with the aid of Stockmar. Encouragement was not universal. Sir Robert Peel doubted the wisdom of reform and in November 1841 wrote he did not wish to make any change which should impair, or even seem to impair the authority of the three great officers of state and render their offices 'less an object of ambition than they at present are to very distinguished Members of the House of Peers'.[5] The Prince agreed and added 'Ancient institutions and prescriptive usages in the Court ought never to be touched by the Queen but with the maturest reflection and caution . . . [but] much as I am inclined to treat the Household machine with a sort of reverence from its antiquity, I still remain convinced that it is clumsy in its original construction, and works so ill, that as long as its wheels are not mended there can neither be order nor regularity, comfort, security, nor outward dignity in the Queen's Palace.'

Progress was slow. The proposed changes were equally distasteful to both political parties and a body of subordinate employees in the household united to oppose reform for fear of losing their posts and of the cessation of the previous lavish expenditure. Finally the Prince himself drew up a scheme which laid down that the three great officers of the Court were to be maintained with their respective departments in *connection* with the political system of the country but must be induced, each in his own sphere, to delegate as much of his authority as was necessary to the maintenance of the order, discipline and security of the palace, to two officials one of whom should always reside at Buckingham Palace and one at Windsor, possess absolute authority and be called Inspectors, responsible to the Master of the Household.

'Lord Chamberlain's Office, 18th June 1846. Minute of Regulations as regards the Master of the Household in connection with the Lord Chamberlain's Department within the Palaces . . . at Windsor and Buckingham Palace.

'The Master of the Household is considered as the resident representative of the Lord Chamberlain in the Palaces.

'He receives his instructions from the Lord Chamberlain, or if it should so happen, from the Queen or from H.R.H. Prince Albert.

'The Master of the Household will be in constant communication on all matters respecting the conduct of the Department within the Palace, with the Lord Chamberlain.

'In each Palace there is an Officer called an Inspector who will execute all orders given by the Lord Chamberlain or Master of the Household for the Service of the Palace in the Department of the Lord Chamberlain, and will have the general superintendence of the tradespeople, workmen, etc. in the Palace, employed and paid by the Lord Chamberlain.

'He will keep the Accounts of the expenditure on the 3rd or Bill Class of the Civil List relating to the Palace and will make up and transmit them monthly to the Office of the Lord Chamberlain. . . .'[6]

'Waste, the canker of all, but especially of all great, establishments, should be made as difficult as possible, at the same time that nothing was spared which was essential for the befitting splendour of a great Monarchy.'[7]

The reform of the Royal Household was successfully carried out according to these principles by the Prince.

*

In January 1847 the Queen and the Prince had been married a few days less than seven years. The Queen already had five children. Both the Queen and the Prince devoted hours of anxious consideration to the education and character training of their children, to the education and character training of the Prince of Wales above all, but also to the education of the Princesses and Prince Alfred. A Memorandum written by the Queen and the Prince in January 1847 laid down the system to be pursued with their present and any subsequent children. The Queen wrote later that all plans originated with the Prince.[8]

The children in the royal nursery were to be divided into classes.

The first was to be a nursery class—to the age of 5 or 6 years. At the moment the Princess Royal was 6 years old, the Prince of Wales 5. Next came Princess Alice 3, Prince Alfred 2. The fifth child, born in May 1846, was Princess Helena. Lady Lyttelton would be in charge and the children would receive instruction in English, French, German and the elements of religious instruction. At the age of about 6 years the child would move into Class II. A new governess was to be engaged and the subsequently well-known Miss Hildyard had been selected. Her salary was to be £200 a year and she was to have a bedroom and a schoolroom. She and two further governesses who had been engaged, German and Swiss, would all be under Lady Lyttelton.

The children were to continue to sleep in the nursery, where there was now a satisfactory nurse, Mrs Thurston, with nursery maids to assist her. Miss Hildyard was to treat the Princess Royal and the Prince of Wales with perfect equality.

Religious instruction was to be imparted to the Princess Royal by the Queen herself, to the Prince of Wales by Lady Lyttelton and Miss Hildyard. The Queen never wished for a particularly close relationship with her eldest son, it apparently never occurring either to her, or to the Prince, that this was a regrettable Hanoverian characteristic. When the Queen was unable to give religious lessons to the Princess Royal, as for instance during her coming confinement, Lady Lyttelton and Miss Hildyard would do so and Miss Hildyard would always be present when the children said their prayers. Sunday was to be a happy day with no lessons and more play. The Queen laid emphasis on the need for the children to be able to converse in foreign languages as well as learning grammar. All details and problems of every kind, punishments, outings, education, were to be discussed with the Queen herself.

The Prince of Wales and the Princess Royal were to begin in Class II, towards the end of February. Out of their working hours one hour a day each was to be devoted to German and French. The Queen intended to continue the religious instruction of the Princess Royal herself, while Lady Lyttelton continued with the Prince of Wales. The Queen had a discussion with Princess Feodora about the children kneeling by their beds to say their prayers. Princess Feodora's children 'say their prayers in their beds but not kneeling; how absurd to find *that* necessary; as if it could have anything to do with making our prayers acceptable to the Almighty. . . .'[9] Queen Victoria's children continued to kneel. When Princess Alice was sufficiently advanced the Queen meant to give her her first lessons herself and to make the Princess Royal entirely over to Miss Hildyard. A scheme for the day would show what was to be done and each hour of it would be regulated by the seasons. Arithmetic, geography and English grammar would be regularly taught. The Prince of Wales was to remain in this class until his sixth or seventh year when he would enter into a third class, having a tutor and a valet to attend on him. The Princess Royal was to have a maid to herself, and she would remain with Miss Hildyard until her ninth or tenth year, when she would receive a 'Lady Governess' and begin to be trained to go into society later, this Governess to remain with her until she married. 'The acquirement of good manners' would then be 'one of the main objects' of her education, but she also would have masters for the various sciences and arts and 'her religious instruction will be made over to a clergyman'.

'It is intended that these classes and persons are to do for *all* the children now extant and possibly to come, and that the children are to pass successively through these classes and through the hands of these persons. Victoria R. Albert.'

The Prince of Wales would have to work very hard to acquit himself as he ought. When he was 2, Lady Lyttelton reported to the Queen that the Prince of Wales was 'just as forward as the majority of children of his age, and no more. . . .' By the time he was 4 he was 'uncommonly averse to learning and requires much patience from wilful inattention and constant interruptions, getting under the table, upsetting the books and sundry other anti-studious practices'.[10] He had also developed 'impetuous spirits', a liking for 'violent exercise and enjoyment of life' and began to stammer. It was decided that the solution of the problem was to apply extra pressure and a scheme was drawn up in which, Stockmar observed, the tutors 'seem to recommend that the Prince's whole time, except what is passed in sleep should be occupied, [in] lesson or pursuit. It is unnecessary to remark that such a system, if fully carried into effect and especially in the earlier years of the Prince's life would, if he were a sprightly boy, speedily lead to a cerebral disease, and if he was constitutionally slow, induce inevitable disgust. . . .'[11]

The Queen considered the Prince of Wales, whom she called 'the Boy', at 6 years old at latest 'ought to be given entirely over to the Tutors and taken *entirely away* from the women'.[12]

Phrenology was the fashion and in the anxious watch kept on the Prince of Wales's progress numerous and lengthy reports were regularly submitted by a phrenological expert. One such report states '. . . in the Prince of Wales the organs of ostentativeness, destructiveness, self esteem etc. are all large, intellectual organs only moderately developed. The result will be strong self will, at times obstinacy. . . .

'In the Prince self esteem is so large that he will be unusually sensitive to everything that affects himself, whether in his feelings or his rights, and the way to moderate this sensibility is not to attempt to lower him in his own esteem by disrespectful treatment, even when he is in the wrong, not to *force* self denial on him or any degree of harsh authority, but kindly yet softly to show that he is acting improperly and to appeal to his sense of honour, his dignity, justice, kindness and benevolence . . . it may take hours.'[13] This advice was not followed.

From infancy the Prince of Wales was conscious that he was a disappointment to his parents, that it was a blow to them that the Princess Royal should be noticeably his superior in intelligence, and it is a tribute to his character that he grew up devoted to his sister. The Princess Royal had rare abilities and was studious as well. At the age of 6 the Prince of Wales had only advanced as far as Princess Alice, who was more than eighteen months younger, and the Queen must remember that Princess Alice was 'neither studious nor so clever as the Princess Royal'.[14]

Lady Lyttelton found the Princess Royal, whom she called 'Princessy', '. . . all gracefulness and prettiness, very fat and active, running about and talking a great deal' but '*over* sensitive' and inclined to be temperamental.[15] The Princess Royal told untruths of a childish kind, for example assuring her French governess Mlle Charrier that Lady Lyttelton had given her permission to call her Charrier and drop the Mademoiselle. Lady Lyttelton feared she might be forced to 'try a very severe course'.[16] On 23rd August 1845 the Princess Royal declared that Lady Lyttelton had desired her to 'walk out after supper in her *pink bonnet*' when Lady Lyttelton had never even mentioned the subject. 'She was imprisoned with tied hands and very seriously admonished and I trust was aware of her fault in the right way.'[17] She was inclined to be rebellious, given to fits of rage, with shrieking, roaring and threats of naughtiness, but 'forcible arguments' were used with success. The Princess Royal's language was droll. While she was playing at being a kitten, Mademoiselle Charrier asked 'Comment vous portez vous, petit chat?' The Princess said 'Bien, gros chat! Et vous?'[18]

The Princess Royal was the favourite of Princess Feodora.[19] 'It is the vivacity and animation in her countenance and manners which make her so irresistible in my eyes. She is a treasure. . . .' 'I love that darling child more than I dare say! She has quite blinded me for my poor Feo [her daughter], because I must always compare, which is very foolish and greatly to the disadvantage of Feo.'

Punishments were severe. Princess Alice at the ate of 4 was given a whipping for not speaking the truth, and 'roaring'. She was given to attacks of ungovernable rage, flinging herself down and beating her head on the floor, as well as disregard for the truth. 'I thought the case very grave' writes Lady Lyttelton[20] 'and that I should obey his Highness's instructions best by administering a real punishment by whipping.'

Prince Alfred was pronounced at the age of 18 months to show signs of having 'a very good manly temper; much more like that of most children than that of the Princess Royal or Prince of Wales'. On 7th March 1849, when Prince Alfred was approaching 5, she wrote: 'The Prince has very uncommon abilities; and a mind which will make the task of instructing him most smooth and delightful. . . .'[21] Miss Hildyard was 'a great success . . . it is really a blessing to have met with such a person. . . . I earnestly wish for her continued success in managing the Prince of Wales's wayward temper. . . .'[22]

Prince Albert enjoyed playing with his children and their toys. He is described in the nursery at Claremont, building a house with the Princess Royal's wooden bricks, so tall that he had to stand on a chair to finish it and reach above his head. 'Such a fall as it made! He enjoyed it much the most.'

'It was pretty to see him [Prince Albert] yesterday, after Mrs Sly [one of the nurses] had vainly endeavoured to get on the Prince of Wales's glove (you know what a difficulty) and thrown it aside at last as too small, just coax the child on to his own knee, and put it on, without a moment's delay, by his great dexterity and gentle manner; the Princey, quite evidently glad to be so helped, looking up very softly at his father's beautiful face. It was a picture of a nursery scene. I could not help saying "It is not every Papa who would have the patience and kindness" and got such a look of flashing gratitude from the Queen!'[23]

Amongst his talents Prince Albert could dance like a ballet dancer. The Queen had been criticised for her disagreeable expression at Coburg,[24] and admitted she was tired and fatigued and might have looked cross, 'saying like a good child "What *am* I to do another time?"' The Prince advised her '. . . to behave like an opera dancer after a pirouette, and always to show all her teeth in a fixed smile. . . . He accompanied the advice with an immense pirouette and prodigious grin of his own, such as few people could perform just after dinner without being sick, ending on one foot and t'other in the air.'[25]

*

In spite of the immense size of Windsor Castle and the alterations to Buckingham Palace carried out at the time of the Queen's marriage, the Royal Family lacked suitable accommodation. Windsor had no private garden; Buckingham Palace had a private garden but not enough rooms: the children had to sleep in the attics and finding rooms suitable for the Queen's distinguished visitors and their suites was almost impossible. On 10th February 1845, when the Queen had four children, she wrote to Sir Robert Peel[26] 'Sir Robert is acquainted with the state of the Palace and the total want of accommodation for our little family, which is fast growing up. Any building must necessarily take some years before it can be safely inhabited. [Modern building methods have obviated the necessity for drying out.] . . . If it [building] were to be begun this autumn, it could hardly be occupied before the spring of 1848, when the Prince of Wales would be nearly seven, and the Princess Royal nearly eight years old and they cannot possibly be kept in the nursery any longer. A provision for this purpose ought therefore to be made this year. Independent of this, most parts of the Palace are in a sad state and will ere long require further outlay to render them *decent* for the occupation of the Royal Family or any visitors the Queen may have to receive. A room capable of containing a larger number of those persons whom the Queen has to invite in the course of the season to balls, concerts, etc. than any of the present apartments can at once hold, is much wanted. Equally so, improved offices, servants' rooms, the want of which puts the departments of the household to great expense yearly. It will be for Sir Robert to consider whether it would not be best to remedy all these deficiencies at once, and to make use of this opportunity to remedy the exterior of the Palace such as no longer to be a *disgrace* to the country, which it certainly now is. The Queen thinks the country would be better pleased to have the question of the Sovereign's residence in London finally disposed of, than to have it so repeatedly brought before it.'

Sir Robert Peel replied that finance was difficult. He was being forced to propose the continuance of income tax in his Finance Bill. It would be a pity if improvements to Buckingham Palace were to become connected with income tax in the public mind. The Queen persisted; of course she never intended Sir Robert Peel to bring Buckingham Palace before Parliament with his financial statement next Friday but '*something* must absolutely be done during this Session'. Nothing was done and in May the Prince pressed urgently for a vote for Buckingham Palace from Parliament this session. 'May is not really so late . . . the Palace is admitted by every-body to be a disgrace to the Sovereign and the nation.' The Queen was about to give up the Pavilion at Brighton 'and all that is asked for is the surplus expense (perhaps 30 or 40 thousand pounds in addition to be spread over 3 years), I cannot believe that to such a statement reasonable objections could be made'. Peel told the Prince on 20th May that the Pavilion could be pulled down and the site and building materials sold. If the proceeds of the sale were sufficient, that money might be used, but it was not possible to ask for a vote of public money this session.[27]

On 23rd May 1846, however, Sir Robert Peel informed the Com-missioners of Woods and Forests, custodians of the fabric of the Palace, that a Commission had been set up and the names of Commissioners approved by the Queen 'for the purpose of considering the plans and estimates which may be submitted for effecting the enlargements or improvement of the Palace'. Mr Edward Blore, an architect with an extensive practice, had been called in and would submit a report.

The Prince's anxiety over Buckingham Palace led him to maintain pressure on Sir Robert Peel through the Repeal of the Corn Laws crisis and the disaster of the Irish potato failure. While Sir Robert Peel's fate hung in the balance, the Prince dwelt on the Palace. 'The fear about the fate of the Government . . . naturally led us to consider the effect all this will have upon the execution of the Building Scheme of this Palace. You know that this execution is *absolutely* necessary . . . you admit the justice and urgency of the demand and that there will be no difficulty in carrying the measure through the House of Commons. What do you intend to do now? You have got part of the Estimates noted and you might still introduce this one at least,' the Prince wrote to Sir Robert Peel on 9th June 1846.[28] Peel replied next day that 'if the Government remains in power he will be prepared to propose a vote at as early a date as he can' after the Report of the Commissioners.

The government did not stay in power and on 30th June Sir Robert Peel, at his first official interview with his successor Lord John Russell, explained all that had passed with regard to Buckingham Palace.[29] 'A new government might probably be startled at having to propose a vote for that addition at the very outset of their career. He [Sir Robert Peel] would bear the whole responsibility for such a vote and Lord John might say in the House of Commons that he found the whole matter arranged by his predecessor.'

Prince Albert told Sir Robert Peel on 1st July 1846 that 'Lord John Russell, who left us this moment, has accepted the task of forming an administration. . . . He professes himself ready to undertake the scheme of Buckingham Palace, being able to say, that it had been all settled when he came into office.' Blore's report was submitted on 4th August.[30] The problem was all but insoluble. Buckingham Palace was too small and space to enlarge did not exist. The nurseries consisted of 'a few rooms in the attics of the North Wing . . . these rooms are very small and very low . . . in order to extend the accommodation within this very limited space to meet the growing wants of an increasing family . . . every possible expedient has been resorted to; rooms not exceeding 15 feet high, and of small area, have been divided in their length and width to convert them into smaller rooms; and as the Royal children could only occupy attics intended for servants, it has been found necessary to cut the height of the ground floor storey into two, by the assistance of a false ceiling, which has consigned the servants to darker and more uncomfortable rooms than has been agreeable to Her Majesty's wishes.' The royal children were growing up, further accommodation would be required for tutors and additional attendants and there was not 'the slightest means of extension or improvement within the existing building'. For the reception of distinguished foreign visitors only a single suite of rooms could be spared and if more than one guest was entertained, this could 'only be accomplished by devoting unsuitable rooms to the purpose'. In the House of Commons the Earl of Lincoln commented that 'so great was the necessity for additional room in the palace that before the birth of the last princess [Princess Helena, on 25th May 1846] . . . it was almost impossible that the royal family could be accommodated, not merely with convenience or comfort but absolutely with decency.'[31]

The Palace, as designed by Nash, had a large open courtyard with two wings. Blore's principal suggestion involved substantial additions, joining the two wings and thus providing space for more rooms by turning what had been an open into an enclosed courtyard.

The alterations recommended by Mr Blore would, the Chancellor of the Exchequer estimated, cost about £150,000, part of which would be covered by the proposed sale of the Pavilion, but before any building began plans and estimates would be submitted. Mr Joseph Hume, the Radical M.P., suggested that if only £150,000 was to be spent 'the palace would never be worthy of the sovereign'; why not demolish Kensington Palace and build a new and suitable one in Kensington Gardens, turning Buckingham Palace into a museum for the public? Mr William Williams, M.P. for Coventry, asserted that since the death of George III no less than £2 million had been spent on erecting palaces; if the English were so wealthy it might be noted that '$2\frac{1}{2}$ millions of Irish fellow subjects were in a state of starvation such as was unknown in any other part of the world'. No less than eight royal palaces were supported by the nation, including one for King Leopold of the Belgians and two in Scotland.

Lord John Russell rose to point out that only two out of the eight palaces were occupied by Her Majesty. The whole expense of Osborne

House had been borne from Her Majesty's private funds. The re-building of Kensington Palace was too costly to consider.

At the beginning of the first Parliamentary session of 1847, £150,000 was voted for the execution of plans submitted by Blore which comprised building the east side of the courtyard, re-planning the south wing, removing the Marble Arch and erecting new kitchens and a ballroom.[32] The builder was to be the great entrepreneur Thomas Cubitt, who was responsible for the development of Pimlico and other districts in expanding London.

From the first doubts were felt. 'Let Mr Blore take a few lessons in the grandiose and scenic from Greenwich Hospital, but alas he never did' remarked *The Builder* on 18th August 1847.

The necessity to provide as many rooms as possible of secondary importance handicapped Blore in his fenestration (the design of the windows), but after allowance has been made the façade 'cannot be described as anything but a dull and mediocre version of French Baroque lacking the refinement of Nash. . . .' *The Builder* described the work of Blore and Cubitt as 'little more than an ordinary piece of street architecture, built in stone instead of stucco'.[33]

Before work began, Nash's open colonnades which ran along the sides of the courtyard were filled in 'to provide sheltered access to the main part of the Palace whilst building operations were in progress . . . whilst the gain in comfort is undoubted, the lateral faces of the courtyard were thus deprived of their one decorative feature'.

The Marble Arch, planned by Nash to be the grand entry to the Palace, had, owing to Blore's alterations, to be moved and was eventually placed in its present position at a cost of £11,000. The arch, though faced with marble, was never enriched by the statuary, sculpture and bronzes Nash had intended.[34]

At this point a fortunate change of policy brought about a change of architect. James Pennethorne, sole architect and surveyor to the Commissioner of Woods and Forests, and nephew to John Nash, in whose office he had been trained, was chosen to design a new block at the south-west corner of the Palace, containing kitchens and domestic offices with a ballroom over. James Pennethorne was 'the best architect who had as yet been associated with the Palace';[35] his work began in the early 1850s and the new block was inaugurated by a state ball on 8th May 1856. No further alterations of importance to Buckingham Palace were carried out in the Queen's lifetime. There were, however, minor defects; Blore's stonework, for instance, did not wear well and the want of space round the Palace due to building up having been permitted on the Pimlico side was, and remains, a drawback. Buckingham Palace was to pass through further vicissitudes and has never been entirely satisfactory or beloved.

20   THE QUEEN WITH PRINCE ARTHUR
(later Duke of Connaught)
from the painting by Winterhalter

21 PRINCESS FEODORA, 1843
from the miniature by William Charles Ross

22 THE DUCHESS OF KENT, 1844
from the drawing by Sir George Hayter

23   LORD JOHN RUSSELL
detail from the painting by F. Grant

24   'A CASE OF REAL DISTRESS'

'*Good People, pray take compassion upon us. It is now nearly seven years since we have either of us known the blessing of a Comfortable Residence. If you do not believe us, good people, come and see where we live, at Buckingham Palace, and you will be satisfied that there is no deception in our story. Such is our Distress, that we should be truly grateful for the blessing of a comfortable two-pair back, with commonly decent Sleeping Rooms for our Children and Domestics. With our slender means, and an Increasing Family, we declare to you that we do not know what to do. The sum of One Hundred and Fifty Thousand Pounds will be all that will be required to make the needful alterations in our dwelling. Do, good people, bestow your Charity to this little amount, and may you never live to feel the want of so small a trifle.*'

from Punch, *1846*

25   THE PRINCE OF WALES, 1859
from the painting by Winterhalter

26   QUEEN VICTORIA AND PRINCE ALBERT
from a photograph, about 1860, by Mayall

27 THE PRINCE'S DRAFT MEMORANDUM
ON THE TRENT QUESTION
1 December 1861
*with a note above it in the Queen's handwriting: 'This Draft was the
last the beloved Prince ever wrote; he was very unwell at this time
and when he brought it to the Queen, he said "I could
hardly hold my pen". V.R.'*

28   THE PRINCE CONSORT
DURING HIS LAST ILLNESS
HOLDING THE TRENT MEMORANDUM
from the water-colour,
after a photograph, by Smith

The Queen had never liked Brighton Pavilion. When in 1787 George IV, then Prince of Wales, first took a lease of the ground in Brighton on which to erect his 'Marine Pavilion', there were scarcely any houses on the Steine so that the house commanded a full view of the sea.[36] Since then a fashion for the sea had set in, the tonic effect of sea air, especially for children, was recognised, sea bathing began to be popular, and the small impoverished fishing village of Brighthelmstone had been transformed into modish Brighton. The town was built up, and land that had been downland in the time of George IV was covered with streets, not only stately villas but small houses. The people of Brighton were loyal but inquisitive. Walking to the Chain Pier during their winter visit in 1845, 'the crowd behaved worse than I have ever seen them do' wrote the Queen in her Journal[37] 'and we were mobbed by all the shopboys in the town, who ran and looked under my bonnet, treating us just as they do the Band, when it goes to the Parade! We walked home as fast as we could.'

The romantic oriental decorations of the Brighton Pavilion attracted neither Queen Victoria nor Prince Albert, though the decorations were a development of the 'Chinoiserie' of the eighteenth century which Chippendale admired and a taste in which he executed some of his finest pieces. The fate of the Pavilion hung in the balance.

In 1846 its stripping began and during 1847 and 1848 143 vanloads of furniture, decorations, porcelain, clocks and carpets were removed to Buckingham Palace, Windsor Castle and Kensington Palace. In 1847 a sale of furniture, decorations and objets d'art was held; on 6th June 1848 the remaining items were sold out of doors on the lawns, the plants and garden implements disposed of, and on 7th June the doors locked and the keys sent to the Lord Chamberlain. The acquisition of the Pavilion by the government for demolition now met with opposition. The Brighton Town Councillors wished to buy it; curiosity concerning the buildings was intense and in the summer of 1849, when the Pavilion was open for inspection, 27,563 people passed through the empty stripped rooms in a single week. A loan of £60,000 was arranged with the Bank of England and on 19th June 1850 the Royal Pavilion Estate became the property of the town of Brighton. It was said that Mr Cubitt had offered £100,000 to purchase the site for development. The work of rehabilitation began almost immediately, £4,500 being spent on restoring ten rooms in September 1850. It was hindered by the behaviour of the Board of Woods and Forests, owners of the fixtures, who to remove copper bell wires (subsequently sold for threepence a pound) tore away skirting boards and attacked floors with pickaxes, took down mirrors, destroying brickwork with crowbars and ripping quantities of hand-painted Chinese papers from the walls, and, in order to wrench pedestals free, smashed sculptures and defaced friezes. Nevertheless the work of 'restoration' proceeded, with private donors returning pieces purchased at the 1847 sale. Queen Victoria with 'regal generosity' contributed several vanloads of new and priceless chandeliers and wall paintings never yet used at Brighton, and her generosity has been followed by the Royal Family, notably later by Queen Mary and King George V. The complete *batterie de cuisine* of the great Duke of Wellington from Apsley House, of the right period, size and splendour, was donated by his descendant, the seventh Duke; carpets have been replaced with financial help from the Regency Society and the tens of thousands who visit the Brighton Pavilion every year now see it very much as it was intended to be.[38] Its total eclipse lasted only three months.

In 1843 the Queen and the Prince had their attention drawn by Sir Robert Peel to the possibilities of purchasing a private retreat in the Isle of Wight. The Queen wished to pay the purchase price out of her own money. The property was to belong to the Prince and to her, there was to be no asking for finance or permission to do what they wished from the Treasury. Above all the Queen longed for 'a place of one's own, quiet and retired', preferably a marine residence, where she could enjoy a normal family life, with her growing family and her beloved husband. The Queen had happy memories of holidays spent in the Isle of Wight at Norris Castle and sailing in the Solent in the 'little schooner' given her by her mother. Sir Robert Peel had heard that Lady Isabella Blatchford wished to sell Osborne House with an estate of about 1,000 acres, and on 1st November 1843 Prince Albert wrote a detailed letter[39] to Sir Robert, enquiring about the sea view, the water supply, the possible existence of a public footpath or right of way through the Park or grounds which would be fatal to privacy, the position of the farms and woods, and asking for a coloured Ordnance map 'to show what does belong to the property'.

Lady Isabella Blatchford proved difficult. After a price of £28,000 had been agreed she demanded £30,000. The Queen and Prince Albert then offered £26,000 without furniture or crops, which was apparently accepted.[40]

A few weeks later Mr Anson reported to Prince Albert that Lady Isabella was behaving 'very ill'. She insisted she was entitled to the fixtures and would rather give up the whole contract than give way. She considered she had been ill used by the Queen because her furniture had not been taken at a valuation. She had, however, signed a contract which could be enforced in the Court of Chancery, though this would be most undesirable.[41] On 17th April Sir Robert Peel advised the Prince to be firm. In his opinion Lady Isabella was being incited by the auctioneer and Anson thought the agent did not want to face Lady Isabella's fury.

In spite of these difficulties the Queen and the Prince had taken possession by 3rd April 1845, when she wrote to Lord Melbourne[42] 'The Queen . . . thinks it is impossible to imagine a prettier spot—valleys and woods which would be beautiful anywhere; but all this near the sea (the woods grow into the sea) is quite perfection; we have a charming beach quite to ourselves. The sea was so blue and calm that the Prince said it was like Naples. And then we can walk about anywhere by ourselves without fear of being followed and mobbed, which Lord Melbourne will easily understand is delightful.'

On 22nd June the Queen wrote to Sir Robert Peel[43] 'We are more and more delighted with this lovely spot, the air is so pure and fresh, and in spite of the hottest sun which oppresses one so dreadfully in London and even at Windsor . . . really the combination of sea, trees, woods, flowers of all kinds, the purest air . . . make it—to us—a perfect little Paradise.'

The Queen's original purchase at Osborne had been Osborne House with an estate of about 1,000 acres, but the original house proved to be too small, and the Queen laid the foundation stone of the new building on 23rd June 1845, during the first summer spent at Osborne.[44]

Greville went over to Osborne for a Council on 14th September 1845, found the trip—special train to Gosport in $2\frac{1}{4}$ hours and Black Eagle steamer to East Cowes—'very agreeable' but Osborne itself 'a miserable place and such a vile house that the Lords of the Council had no place to remain in but the entrance Hall, before the Council. Fortunately the weather was fine, so we walked about, looking at the new house the Q. is building; it is very ugly, and the whole concern wretched enough. They will spend first and last a great deal of money there, but it is her own money and not the nation's.'[45] In 1847 Mr Anson told Greville that the Queen would be able to provide for the whole expense of Osborne out of her income without difficulty 'and that by the time it is furnished it will have cost £200,000'.

The new Osborne House was designed by Prince Albert himself, with the assistance of Thomas Cubitt, who prepared the drawings and executed the work using new techniques, for instance cast-iron girders in place of wooden beams. Prince Albert designed the mansion in the style of an Italian villa 'rather coarsely detailed in Cubitt's London stucco, but made effectively picturesque by asymmetrical grouping'.[46] There are two 'campaniles', the flag tower and the clock tower, and a first-floor loggia: gardens descend to the sea in terraces, with fountains and statues in the Renaissance manner. The furniture and decorations of Osborne reflect the personal taste of the Queen and the Prince; a large number of pieces were designed by Prince Albert himself, one of the best-known being a painted billiard table. In the drawing-room is a collection of marble replicas of the limbs of the royal children as infants and a marble carving of one of Queen Victoria's hands, executed in 1842. Outside the Queen's sitting-room is the balcony, on which the Queen and the Prince stood on summer evenings to hear the song of the nightingales. Of all the songs of birds Prince Albert loved these the most, 'listening for them in the happy peaceful walks he used to take with the Queen in the woods, and whistling to them in their own peculiar long note, which they invariably answer!' or standing out at night on the balcony to hear their song.[47]

On 15th September 1846 the Royal Family spent their first night in the new Osborne House. 'Nobody' wrote Lady Lyttelton 'caught cold or smelt paint. . . . Everything in the house is quite new, and the dining room looked *very* handsome. The windows lighted by the brilliant lamps in the room must have been seen far out at sea. After dinner we all rose to drink the Queen's and Prince's health as a *housewarming*, and after it the Prince said, very naturally and simply but sincerely, "We have a hymn" (he called it a psalm) "in Germany for such occasions. It begins"— and then he quoted two lines in German which I could not quote right, meaning a prayer to "bless our going out and coming in". It was dry and quaint being Luther's; but we all perceived that he was feeling it. [The quotation was

'Gott behüte dieses Haus
Und die da gehen ein und aus.']

And truly entering a new house, a new palace, is a solemn thing to do.'[48]

In the grounds of Osborne the royal children were given an elaborate playground. The Swiss cottage, standing about half a mile from the mansion, was brought in sections from Switzerland and presented to them, for the boys to learn carpentry and cultivation of the soil and the girls cookery and housekeeping. The Queen and Prince Albert were invited here by their children to tea. All the furniture is on a small scale, including two dwarf charcoal ranges with saucepans to match and a miniature grocer's shop.

*

Osborne was mild in climate, luxuriant and flower-wreathed; the next venture of the Queen and Prince was bracing, mountainous and majestic. The Queen had continued loyal to Sir James Clark who was still her personal physician. Clark was very well acquainted with the Highlands and believed in the tonic properties of pure mountain air, especially for the Prince and the Queen. In September 1842 the Queen and Prince stayed with Lord Breadalbane at Taymouth Castle and from the first the Prince was enchanted. 'Scotland has made a most favourable impression upon us both' he wrote.[49] 'The country is full of beauty, of a severe and grand character; perfect for sport of all kinds, and the air remarkably pure and light in comparison with what we have here. The people are more natural, and are marked by that honesty and sympathy, which always distinguish the inhabitants of mountainous countries, who live far away from towns. There is, moreover, no country where historical traditions are preserved with such fidelity, or to the same extent. Every spot is connected with some interesting historical fact, and with most of these Sir Walter Scott's accurate descriptions have made us familiar. . . .'

Two years later, in 1844, when a proposed visit of the Queen to Ireland was cancelled owing to the disturbed state of the country, Lord and Lady Glenlyon turned out of Blair Atholl Castle to accommodate them, and in 1847 a cruise up the West Coast in the Queen's yacht terminated in a stay at the fishing and shooting lodge of Ardverikie. This expedition was not a success.[50] The sea had a heavy swell which made the Queen sick, mists obscured the magnificent views and at Ardverikie rain poured.

The idea of settling in the west of Scotland was given up.

Meanwhile Sir James Clark had been investigating and reached the conclusion that Deeside, in the east, near Aberdeen and with its fine scenery was one of the driest districts in Scotland, and Balmoral above all. This was due to the sandy gravelly nature of the soil and the fact that the rain clouds from the sea broke and discharged themselves upon the mountains between Braemar and the ocean before they reached Deeside.[51]

In 1847 Sir Robert Gordon, tenant of Balmoral, unexpectedly died and the Queen and the Prince bought a lease of the house. On Friday, 8th September 1848, the Queen wrote 'We arrived at Balmoral at a quarter to three.' Day after day of glorious weather followed, 'exceeding my expectations, great as they were' wrote Sir James Clark.[52]

Balmoral was 'a complete mountain solitude, where one rarely sees a human face, where the snow already covers the mountain tops and the wild deer come creeping round the house' wrote the Prince.[53] The Prince's idea of sport was not thought well of in England, where the 'battue', the great pile of slaughtered game popular on the Continent, was not practised. The slaughter of three hundred roe deer in a single drive was condemned by Greville as 'a massacre' and he was shocked that the Queen watched. The Prince was not a first-class shot and had an unattractive approach to the subject. Of the deer at Balmoral he wrote 'I, naughty man, have also been crawling after the harmless stags, and today I shot two roe deer, at least I hope so, for they are not yet found.' The little castle of Balmoral was built of whitewashed granite with numerous small turrets, situated on rising ground close to the Dee. The 'glorious and clear but icy cold' air benefited both the Queen and the Prince. Like Osborne, Balmoral Castle was too small. As the Queen's family continued to increase, additions were built but they were inadequate. The Queen and the Prince, however, held Balmoral only on a lease which had four years to run. At this point news reached the Queen that a very handsome fortune had been unexpectedly bequeathed her by a Mr John Camden Nield. He knew, she remarked, that she would not squander it. Out of this bequest, after protracted negotiations, the castle and estate of Balmoral, 17,400 acres, was bought from the Trustees of the Earl of Fife in 1852 and the Queen laid the foundation stone of a new castle on 28th September 1853. The house was designed by the Prince. 'My dearest Albert's own creation, own work, own building, own laying out, as at Osborne' wrote the Queen.

At Osborne the Prince had had the help of Thomas Cubitt; at Balmoral he was assisted by Mr William Smith, the foremost builder in Aberdeen.

The Prince developed a particular affection for Balmoral; the mountain air suited him, he enjoyed the shooting and admired the character of the people. He told Stockmar that he and the Queen intended to start 'the day Parliament rises on a visit for 14 days to Balmoral, my new property in Aberdeenshire, to which we are strongly urged by Clark. . . .'[54]

*

The most important palace in the kingdom is Windsor Castle, but little of importance was done at Windsor during the reign of Queen Victoria and what was done was not, on the whole, admirable. Enormous sums of money had been spent by George IV and his favourite architect, Sir Jeffry Wyatville in making the Castle into a Victorian Gothic dream, with, it is now acknowledged, success. Earlier George III had spent large sums in transforming the Castle into a comfortable residence. In 1839 a grant of £70,000 was made by Parliament towards the erection of new stables to the designs of Wyatville, who died in 1840.[55] In 1843 a new chapel was designed by Edward Blore, using space partially occupied by a gatehouse, and later in Queen Victoria's reign the Grand Staircase designed by Wyatville, and executed at a cost of £30,000, was demolished and replaced by one designed by Anthony Salvin with no direct access from the courtyard. Salvin had established himself as the leading authority on castles and was frequently employed by Queen Victoria, chiefly on works of destruction. The 'lodging for five poor Knights' erected about 1657 at the end of the lower ward of the Castle was pulled down and replaced by the existing guard house, 'a destruction much to be deplored'; the Curfew Tower underwent restoration and partial re-building, assuming its present extinguisher top, all the ancient features of the north front of the Canons' houses were destroyed, and the 'Hundred steps' re-made. Between 1840 and 1850 works of destruction and re-building costing nearly £10,000 were executed by Blore, including the demolition of the ancient walls of the Military Knights' lodgings and their replacement by heavy stone enclosures. At the same time windows were pierced in the hitherto unbroken front of the outer wall and the beauty of the west side

278

of the Castle was lost. The old Chapter House of the canons, to the west of the Erary porch, and the ancient hall known as Dentons Commons perished.

In 1859 a more worthy work was undertaken, the clearing of the Castle 'ditch' under the superintendence of James Pennethorne, now sole architect to the department of Woods and Forests. Buildings, picturesque in themselves, had filled the 'ditch' especially towards Thames Street. Lord Melbourne complained that when he opened his bedroom window he looked directly into a butcher's shop. Houses and shops were now cleared away and the beauty of the great thirteenth-century wall and towers revealed.

But the splendour of Windsor concealed dangers. In 1848 the Lord Chamberlain reported to the Department of Woods and Forests that the works most urgently required for the safety of Windsor Castle were the completion of the drainage, begun in 1846. The main drains had then been constructed 'but nothing was then or has since been done to improve the drains in connection with the various water closets, sinks etc. within the Castle. The noxious effluvia which escapes from the old drains and numerous cesspools still remaining, is frequently so exceedingly offensive as to render many parts of the castle almost uninhabitable, and scarcely any portion can be said to be entirely free from the effects of imperfect drainage. It is therefore highly desirable that the completion of the work should be recommenced. . . .'[56] Beneath the splendour, Windsor Castle was more dangerous than a jungle.

Chapter Nine

The year 1848 has often been called the 'annus mirabilis' of nineteenth-century history; it was a year of upheaval and revolt, of shock for the rulers of Europe, of trembling thrones and upsurging masses. A new era was born and though not all that was achieved proved lasting, the political structure of Europe was never the same again.

The upheavals of 1848 are difficult to follow because each was a separate phenomenon. There was no concerted plan, no common revolutionary philosophy. Two threads run throughout, the thread of nationalism and the thread of economic change. Sometimes, as in Ireland, the two unite, but not invariably. It is an indication of the state of Europe that so many countries should have come, as it were, to the boil at the same moment. Metternich, the veteran reactionary statesman, as early as August 1847 addressed appeals to the powers urging them to remain united in face of the coming revolution. In fact the post-Waterloo system in Europe, based on the treaties of 1815, was beginning to break up.

Before the year opened revolt was in the air, and 1847 was dark with forebodings of disaster. Almost every country in Europe, including Britain, was seething with discontent; the only exceptions were Belgium, industrialised, prosperous and constitutionally ruled by King Leopold, and Russia held down by the autocrat Tsar Nicholas I.

In Portugal Queen Victoria's contemporary, Queen Maria, and her Coburg husband Ferdinand struggled with the Pretender to the throne, Dom Miguel, while conflict raged between reactionaries and progressives. In Spain civil war between Carlists and Christinists continued, complicated by difficulties arising from the 'Spanish Marriage' of Queen Isabella with her degenerate cousin Don Francisco, with whom she had quarrelled beyond hope of reconciliation. Within the Hapsburg Empire Czechs, Poles, Magyars, Roumanians, Hungarians and Lombards clamoured for self-rule. Italy, encouraged by the election of the liberal Pope Pius IX, 'Pio Nono', was openly preparing for another effort to expel the Austrian invaders, the hated 'white coats', and achieve a free united Italy. France was bored and disgusted with the dullness and corruption of the Orleanist regime of Louis Philippe and his reactionary minister Guizot. 'The political horizon grows darker and darker, Italy, Greece, Spain, Portugal are in a state of ferment' wrote Prince Albert to Stockmar on 11th September 1847.[1]

In Greece the German Prince Otho, created King of Greece in 1830 by Britain, France and Russia, after King Leopold had declined the throne in favour of that of Belgium, was flouting the liberal constitution he had been forced to accept. His regime was corrupt and despotic, he himself was detested and despised, and, though he was supported by the reactionary powers, Great Britain treated him with hostility. Palmerston said he was an idiot and the 'enfant gâté de l'absolutisme'.[2] Greece was primitive, with poor communications and a high rate of illiteracy; nevertheless in 1847 a number of provincial risings had already occurred.

The position of Britain was difficult. The Queen wrote to King Leopold in the early autumn of 1847 'The state of politics in Europe is very critical and one feels *very* anxious for the future.'[3] During 1847 in Great Britain itself several factors combined to produce a major financial panic. Chartism, the working-class movement in Britain which aroused universal alarm, had by then recovered from its defeat in 1839. Most Chartist agitators had been released from jail, a method had been found to evade the Act of 1799 which made any association of political societies illegal and a union of local groups had been successfully carried through. The six points of the People's Charter—manhood suffrage, the ballot, payment of Members of Parliament, abolition of the property qualification for members, equal constituencies and annual Parliaments—remained the Chartist policy and the movement appeared as vigorous as ever.[4] It is worth noting that all six points are in force today with the exception of annual Parliaments, which would hardly be welcome. Meanwhile in Ireland the potato famine had been becoming desperate. The first partial failure of the potato in 1845 had been followed by total failure in 1846, in which year cereal crops not only in Ireland but all over Europe wholly or partially failed. By bad luck the winter of 1846–7 was the most severe recorded and by 1847 the sufferings of the Irish people had become too terrible to contemplate.

At this point financial panic in London occurred. During the shortage of 1846 wheat prices rocketed, reaching 115s. in Mark Lane during May. Widespread speculation was not confined to wheat; wilder gambling was taking place in railway shares. The harvest of 1847 was magnificent and wheat had tumbled to 49s.6d. by mid-September; in addition the operations of railway speculators were curtailed by Sir Robert Peel's Bank Charter Act of 1844, which restricted the issue of Bank of England notes to a sum backed by the gold held by the Bank in their issue department. Because gold had been sent abroad in the course of the speculation boom the Bank was short of gold, therefore unable to lend freely, and panic in the money market followed.[5] By the end of September, among first-class firms, losses of nine to ten million pounds were sustained. During the course of the panic 117 firms failed, eleven banks broke and the state of the City was described by Lord John Russell as 'disastrous'. Hope of financial help for Ireland vanished. 'You must not expect any money' Sir Charles Wood, Chancellor of the Exchequer, told Lord Clarendon, the Lord Lieutenant of Ireland, '. . . there will be no money. You cannot have what I have not got.'[6]

The magnificent wheat harvest of 1847 was useless to the starving Irish. They had been allowed to become so dependent on potatoes that if grain had been given to them they had no means of milling or using it. Their sufferings not merely continued but increased and plans began for rebellion. The links between Chartism and Ireland were close. Feargus O'Connor, leader of the Chartists, was the Irish Nationalist leader; another leading Chartist, Bronterre O'Brien, was also a leading Nationalist Irishman. The apprehension felt throughout Britain sprang from two fears now united, the known misery of the workers and the menace of Ireland.

The first serious revolution of the year of revolutions, however, took place in Paris on 24th February 1848, and was totally unexpected. The existence of a movement against the regime and the general unpopularity of the Orleans family was common knowledge; as Lamartine remarked 'La France s'ennuie'. But 'up to the very moment at which the explosion took place . . . no human being dreamt of a revolution and of the dethronement of the King . . . no one imagined that the King, defended by an Army of 100,000 men and the fortifications of Paris (which it was always said he had cunningly devised to give himself full power over the capital) was exposed to any personal risk and danger . . . the principal leaders of Opposition were understood to have no designs against the Monarch.'[7] The campaign against the regime was conducted through a series of democratic banquets, the first having been given on 9th July 1847. The final banquet, arranged for 22nd February 1848, was forbidden by the government and a procession accompanying it banned. The organisers nevertheless determined both should proceed. Throughout the 22nd February the city was disturbed but the 'extraordinary and incredible things' which followed came 'like an unbelievable clap of thunder'.[8]

The bourgeois National Guard, backbone of the regime, sent a deputation to the Tuileries declaring they could answer for nothing if the King did not change his government. The King yielded and Guizot was dismissed. All seemed quiet but on the evening of 23rd February a long procession of demonstrators formed along the boulevards and outside the Ministry of Foreign Affairs 'a single shot, by whom fired will, perhaps, never be ascertained . . . broke the leg of the horse on which the major commanding the detachment of the 14th regiment of the line was mounted. He immediately, without the slightest notice, gave an order to fire a volley into the crowd. . . . It is stated that no less than fifty-two people, many of them women and children were killed or wounded. . . . The crowd immediately dispersed into the different quarters of Paris from which they had been collected, shouting "Vengeance!" and "Treachery!" '[9] The suburbs of Saint Honoré, Saint Martin and Saint Antoine, names of terror in the first revolution, rose; gunsmiths' shops were raided and by the morning of 24th February 1848 Paris was in armed revolt. Barricades were thrown up in central districts, and a mob, in which the National Guard mixed with the people, marched upon the Tuileries, threatening the life of the King. Emile Girardin, founder of the newspaper *La Presse*, and an officer in the National Guard, 'hastily drew up an act of abdication and placed it before his Majesty, as the only means of safety'.[10] Among his faults Louis Philippe did not include want of courage. At first he refused to sign, saying he would rather die, but was persuaded by the Duc de Montpensier. Having signed the abdication, the French Royal Family 'retired' through the garden, 'the King saying to everyone he passed "J'abdique, J'abdique".'[11] Retirement was only just in time; an hour later the mob broke into the Tuileries and ransacked the Palace, the French Royal Family escaping in almost nothing but the clothes they stood up in. Queen Victoria wrote to King Leopold 'Certainly at the *very last* if they had not gone they would all have been massacred . . . but there is an impression they fled too quickly.'[12] Montpensier ought at least to have gone to Vincennes and the King to have put himself at the head of the Army.

Paris was in confusion. Threatening mobs patrolled the streets, looking for the King, a provisional republican government was set up in the Chamber, and the widowed Duchesse de Chartres, leading the heir, the young Comte de Paris, was rejected with insults. The Palais Royal was plundered as well as the Tuileries; members of the French Royal Family lost touch with each other, and the Duchesse de Nemours barely escaped after being dragged from her carriage.[13]

The King was in immediate danger and the British Consul at Le Havre, Mr G. W. Featherstonehaugh, determined on a daring scheme.[14] He would bring the King and Queen of the French into Le Havre itself and send them by the packet to England. The weather was stormy, the sea 'in a furious state', and the original plan of transporting the King and Queen in a fishing boat had to be abandoned. The King was brought from Paris and concealed in a small house at Trouville. News that some person of importance was hidden there, probably Guizot, leaked out; a mob assembled outside the house and the King had to be 'rushed out of the back door' by Mr Featherstonehaugh, and to walk two leagues on foot to Honfleur where the Queen was waiting in a cottage.

Meanwhile Captain Paul, commander in H.M.'s Navy, was instructed to have steam up in the *Express* packet by 7.30 p.m. when it would be dark, and to moor her by a single rope only. The King was to walk to the ferry which ran from Honfleur across to Le Havre, a distance of three-quarters of a mile, armed with a British passport in the name of Mr William Smith and accompanied by the Vice Consul, Mr Jones. If his passport was questioned he was to say he was Mr Featherstonehaugh's uncle. The Queen was to follow separately, and the rest of the suite to board the ferry one after the other but no one in the party was to speak or appear to know his or her companions. Mr Featherstonehaugh feared trouble with the police, who had been unusually active. When the ferry arrived in Le Havre a white handkerchief was to be shown twice as a signal that all was well. Mr Fatherstonehaugh had confidentially communicated to the greatest gossips in the town that he had seen a written statement that the King had been landed in England from a Tréport fishing boat, and had also arranged that if any difficulty arose over 'Mr Smith's' embarkation, two persons should pretend to quarrel and exchange blows which would divert the attention both of the police and the crowd. 'At length' wrote Mr Featherstonehaugh 'the anxiously expected moment arrived. The ferry boat came to the quay. It was almost dark but I saw the white handkerchief. There was a great number of passengers . . . when half of them were out the trembling Queen came up the ladder. At last came the King disguised, his whiskers shaved off, a sort of casquette on his head . . . and immense goggles over his eyes. . . . I advanced, took his hand and said "Ah, my dear Uncle, I am delighted to see you" upon which he answered "My dear George, I am glad you are here". The English about me now opened the crowd for their Consul, and I moved off to a quiet part of the quay. But my dear uncle talked so loud and so much that I had the greatest difficulty to make him keep silence. At length we reached the steamer . . . the crowd was again opened for me: I conducted the King to a stateroom below . . . and having personally ascertained that the Queen was in her cabin and being very much touched with her tears and her grateful acknowledgments, I respectfully took my leave, gave the Captain the word to cut loose, and scrambled ashore. In twenty minutes the steamer was outside, steaming away for England. . . .' In a P.S. Mr Featherstonehaugh added 'Information has just reached me that one hour after the King and Queen left their hiding place last night, and just as I was embarking them, an officer and three gens d'armes came to the place to arrest him. It appears that the man who gave him refuge had confessed who he was as soon as the King had left Trouville and had betrayed the King's hiding place at Honfleur. What an escape . . .!'

On 4th March 1848 the Queen wrote in her Journal that the King and Queen of the French had arrived safely at Claremont, after landing from the packet at Newhaven. The King wrote immediately on landing asking the Queen to give him refuge, to which Lord John Russell agreed she should assent.[15] On 4th March Prince Albert went down to Claremont to see the French Royal Family and on 5th March Lord Palmerston, Foreign Secretary, consented to the King and Queen visiting Buckingham Palace. '. . . They came here with Montpensier' wrote the Queen to the King of the Belgians on 7th March.[16] 'They both look very *abbatu* and the poor Queen cried much in thinking what she had gone through and what dangers the King had incurred. In short, humbled poor people they looked . . . they are still very much in want of any means & live on a very reduced scale.' A week later the Queen wrote '. . . the poverty of the poor exiles is most lamentable. I cannot say *how* dear and excellent, dearest Victoire [wife of the Duc de Nemours, son of the King of the French] shows herself. . . . They really have hardly the means of living; it is a gt happiness for me to be able to help her in little trifles.'

Though no one would dream of disturbing the 'poor old King', wrote the Queen to King Leopold on 16th March, he 'was to be left in peace and quiet to end his days here . . . and will easily be assisted to hire or buy a little place . . . Claremont is another thing.' The Queen did not doubt that in a few week the French Royal Family would be able to leave Claremont. It was not wise for the King of the French to be occupying one of the English royal palaces, the more he stayed aloof from politics the better. '. . . Those unlucky Spanish marriages. Oh!! *they have* brought on much of all this.' 'One does not like to attack those who are fallen but the poor King L.P. has brought much of this on, by that ill-fated return to a *Bourbon Policy*. I always think he *ought not* to have abdicated.'[17] The Queen told Lord John Russell she was angry at the poverty of the French Royal Family, they had been 'shamefully treated'. Lord John replied he would speak to the British Ambassador in Paris, Lord Normanby, about the Orleans property, but the Orleans Princes were known to retain their pretensions to the French throne and the Republic could hardly be expected to furnish funds for its own overthrow.[18]

On 26th October 1848 Lord Normanby wrote in his Journal[19] that he was 'happy to say that the decree restoring to the Orleans family the possession of their personalities and the enjoyment of their incomes was yesterday passed by the National Assembly almost without discussion and with hardly a dissentient voice', and at the end of November Lord John Russell told the Queen that when everything had been arranged he thought that King Louis Philippe would have more than a million pounds sterling.

The misfortunes of the French Royal Family were not quite over. In November the inhabitants of Claremont, who had all been suffering mysterious attacks of illness, became 'sharply' ill. The Queen's state caused anxiety and the Ducs de Nemours and de Joinville, who had been ill for the longest time and most seriously, both had a relapse. Analysis of the water at Claremont showed it contained dissolved lead from a newly installed cistern, the King's doctor recommended an immediate change of air, and the family decided to go for several days to the Star and Garter at Richmond.

Elsewhere the year of revolutions was already on its way. On 3rd January 1848, a clash between the Austrian garrison and the Lombard inhabitants revealed Milan to be on the verge of explosion. On 12th January Sicily revolted at Palermo against the Neapolitan Bourbons and on 27th January Naples rose; the Bourbon King Ferdinand was forced to yield and granted a constitution on 10th February. Events in Paris were followed by outbreaks in Piedmont and in Rome, where Pope Pius IX appointed a ministry with a lay majority. In Central Europe, with the meeting of the lower Austrian Diet on 13th March, the crisis came to a head. Demonstrators clashed with troops, the suburbs of Vienna rose, the Court panicked and Metternich fled in disguise. His flight was decisive. Austrian domination collapsed, and in a movement of liberation irresistible as the mass movements of the first French Revolution, and notwithstanding their lack of arms, the people of Lombardy, followed by Venetia, set themselves free.

Nearer home the impetus given to rebellion, particularly Irish rebellion, was electric. The news that France was free, that the government which had starved the people and refused all reform was overthrown and a republic proclaimed with the poet Lamartine as Minister for Foreign Affairs, seemed to be the dawn of a golden age. 'Ireland's opportunity— thank God, and France—has come at last!' wrote Charles Gavan Duffy.[20] 'Its challenge rings in our ears like a call to battle, and warms our blood like wine. . . . We must answer if we would not be slaves forever. . . . We must unite, we must act, we must leap all barriers . . . if needs be, we must die, rather than let this providential hour pass over us unliberated.'

Equally strong was the impetus given to Chartism. Times were bad, unemployment increasing as conditions in Europe diminished trade. London contained thousands of hungry, miserable, workless men, tens of thousands of starving barefoot children. Julian Harney, the Chartists' leader, was addressing a meeting at a tavern in Drury Lane when the news of the unexpected revolution in Paris, the abdication of Louis Philippe and the proclamation of the republic was brought in. The effect was startling, wrote an eye witness: 'the audience including a dozen nationalities sprang to their feet, embraced, shouted in the wildest enthusiasm ... then the doors were opened and the whole assemblage ... with linked arms and colours flying marched to the meeting place of the Westminster Chartists in Dean Street, Soho.'[21] That night a large crowd paraded the main thoroughfares, shouting and singing, and Chartist meetings continued for many weeks. All the Chartist leaders had now been released from jail, and a campaign was decided on but violence was not to be used; a monster meeting was to be held on Kennington Common from which a procession would convey a petition to the House of Commons signed by more than a million and a half persons demanding the six points of the charter. The date was fixed for 10th April 1848. Alarm was universal. The continental risings, the bands of miserable workless men parading the London streets, the recent revelations of the horrors of poverty behind the luxurious splendour of London[22] inspired terror. Was a revolution on the model of the first revolution in France about to occur?

'The organisation of these people is incredible' wrote Prince Albert.[23] 'They have secret signals and correspond from town to town by means of carrier pigeons.'

As 10th April came nearer general apprehension increased and formidable measures of defence were taken under the command of the Duke of Wellington. Yeomanry regiments were called up, artillery made ready, 150,000 special constables enrolled. 'Every gentleman in London was sworn'[24] wrote Greville, among them Prince Louis Napoleon Bonaparte, who within three years would be President of the French Republic and later Emperor of the French.

No troops were to appear in the streets, only police, but it was generally known that four batteries of artillery commanded the Thames bridges and that a total of 9,000 troops had been brought into London and concealed at strategic points. Ships were commandeered and armed on the Thames and behind the barricaded windows of government offices stood more armed men.

On 9th April the veteran Chartist Bronterre O'Brien told a meeting that the government was too strong for the workers and walked off the platform to a chorus of groans.[25]

Princess Louise, christened after Prince Albert's mother, whom the family recognised as having been badly treated by his father, had been born on 18th March. Three weeks later, on the morning of 8th April, the platform at Waterloo station was cleared of spectators, several hundred special constables moved into their place, and an express with steam up was waiting to convey to safety a party consisting only of the Queen, the Prince, the royal children and their suites. Punctually at 10.30 a.m., the Queen appeared. There was no disturbance of any kind; she boarded the train, which immediately steamed off for Gosport, and lay on her couch during the journey. After crossing the Solent, she reached Osborne, 'our dear Osborne', at 2.15 p.m.[26]

On the night of 9th April Colonel Phipps, Equerry to Prince Albert, went out into the streets to see if he could hear any comments on the Queen's departure but heard none. 'Her reputation for personal courage stands so high, I never heard one person express a belief that her departure was due to personal alarm.'[27] Colonel Phipps did not wish the Prince to return to London but pressed him to remain at Osborne and support the Queen through the coming crisis.

That day the government had seized the telegraph system to prevent false reports being spread throughout the country.[28]

The 10th April 1848 dawned in an atmosphere of apprehension in London. It was not unreasonable for British citizens to fear—or hope—that the meeting on Kennington Common marked the opening of the English revolution. The true situation was different. On 6th April a proclamation had been issued forbidding the procession to the House of Commons as an attempt to intimidate the House. Meanwhile the determined preparations, the troops pouring into London, though kept out of sight, the presence of batteries of artillery, the legendary abilities and legendary inflexibility of the Duke, were breaking down Feargus O'Connor, the Irish patriot leader of the Chartists, who was suffering from a disease later to prove fatal. He became ill, unable to sleep, and adopted a tone of conciliation.[29] From his seat in the Commons he assured the House he would not allow the meeting to assemble if he thought a single breach of the peace likely to occur and he had no intention of attempting to intimidate the House.

At a few minutes before 10 a.m., the procession to Kennington left the Chartist headquarters in the John Street Institute, Westminster, headed by a waggon drawn by six horses carrying the National Petition and decorated in the Chartist and Irish colours, followed by a second waggon in which sat O'Connor and the other leaders. Irish inhabitants of London were prominent in the crowd and trouble was expected. Shops were shut, special constables lined the streets, as throughout the morning processions converged on Kennington Common. The estimated numbers differed: O'Connor estimated four to five hundred thousand, *The Times* estimated twenty thousand, Lord John Russell told the Queen he calculated twelve to fifteen thousand. One of the processions was of Irish confederates with a banner 'Ireland for the Irish'. No violence was shown and no disturbance except that as the waggon in which O'Connor was seated crossed the Common it was stopped by a messenger known to come from Mr Mayne, the Metropolititan Commissioner of Police, asking O'Connor to come and have a word with him. Seeing O'Connor accompanied by a police inspector someone shouted he had been arrested and the crowd made an ugly rush forward. O'Connor, however, went readily and the excitement subsided. In a neighbouring public house, O'Connor met Mr Mayne looking, Lord John Russell reported to the Queen, 'pale and frightened'. Mr Mayne told him the meeting might continue, but no procession would be allowed to cross the bridges over the Thames. O'Connor 'expressed the utmost thanks and begged to be allowed to shake Mr Mayne by the hand. He then addressed the crowd advising them to disperse and . . . went off in a cab to the Home Office, where he repeated to Sir George Grey his thanks, his fears and his assurances that the crowd should disperse quietly. Sir George Grey said that he had done very rightly but the force at the bridges should not be diminished. Mr F. O'Connor: "Not a man should be taken away. The Government have been quite right. I told the Convention that if they had been the government they never would have permitted such a meeting." '[30] O'Connor then returned to Kennington Common and besought the crowd to depart. The meeting broke into groups and was addressed by various Chartist leaders. By 1.45 p.m. all was over.

At 2 p.m. the government sent a telegraphic message to the Queen from Admiral Ogle on board the *Victory* in Portsmouth Harbour, 'For the Queen. The meeting at Kennington Common has dispersed quietly—the procession has been given up—the petition will be brought to the House of Commons without any display. No disturbance of any kind has taken place and not a soldier has been seen.'[31] Three cabs drew up on the Common, the bales of the National Petition were put inside them and O'Connor drove with them to the House of Commons. During the afternoon heavy rain began to fall and the remaining participants in the giant meeting, wet through, were allowed to trickle across the bridges. Chartism was dead. 'Thank God!' wrote the Queen[32] 'the Chartist meeting & Procession has turned out a complete failure; the loyalty of the people at large has been very striking & their indignation at their peace being interfered with by such wanton & worthless men—immense.'

Owing to the local structure of Chartism, necessitated by the provisions of the anti-combination statute, small independent meetings continued. 'We have Chartist riots every night which lead to numbers of broken heads,' Prince Albert told Stockmar on 5th June 1848. 'In a single night the police broke the heads of three to four hundred people with their truncheons.'[33] Similar meetings were held outside London, but nevertheless Chartism was ended.

The rising of 1848 in Ireland was also a failure.[34] A meeting held in the Prince's Theatre, Dublin, to form an alliance with the Chartists was attended by less than 300 persons. The leaders of the Young Ireland rebellion had failed to realise the effect of four years of famine; 'men

289

must eat to be able to fight' wrote Palmerston. Hunger had deadened the Irish nation, desperation had changed into the apathy of starvation, anger into despair. Tipperary, for instance, once 'a county of tigers', was inhabited by hordes of filthy scarecrows, with no thought beyond a daily ration of yellow meal. When the country was called out in July the Irish people failed to rise and the rebellion of 1848 was an ignominious failure.

England was safe. Chartism had failed, Irish armed rebellion had failed and the Queen had reason for satisfaction. 'If only dear Germany would settle down' she wrote to King Leopold.

Germany was in a situation different from that of any other country in Europe.[35] It comprised a federation of thirty-nine states, created by the Congress of Vienna under the peace treaties following Waterloo in 1815, embracing small Lutheran states in the north and Catholic provinces in the south.

Much the most active state in the federation was Prussia which was endeavouring to oust Austria from the formal primacy of Germany. Prussia had also established a 'Zollverein', or Customs Union, controlled by her and was virtually in command of German trade. Prussia was the leading Protestant state and in spite of her past—in the previous century she had been the terror of Europe, with a savage military system under Frederick II (Frederick the Great)—she was now the liberal hope of Europe. The Prussian government consisted of a king and an assembly, but the King, Frederick William IV, was far from the English idea of a constitutional sovereign; his power was absolute and the assembly was summoned at his will. He had already dissolved one assembly in 1847 because its proposals conflicted with his notion of the divine right of kings. Nevertheless he professed liberal opinions and was regarded by the liberal and reforming party with the same hope as the Italians regarded 'Pio Nono', but only to turn out an equal disappointment. King Frederick William IV has been described as a 'vain, versatile and romantic ruler, learned but without political grasp or stability'. In 1857 he became insane but lived until 1861, while his brother William the Prince of Prussia ruled as Regent. (It is important to bear in mind that it was the Prince of Prussia, not Frederick William IV, who was the friend of Queen Victoria and Prince Albert, and whose son married the Princess Royal.) In the spring of 1848 the majority of Germans, not only in Berlin but throughout Germany, were liberals and wished for some degree of reform. Germany was rapidly changing under the influence of industrialisation. In 1840, for instance, Germany possessed only 282 miles of railway line, increased to 5,134 in 1850. The old Germany of peasants and princes was disappearing, industries were being founded, machinery introduced and during the twenty-five years preceding 1848 a new middle class came into being, business and professional men, manufacturers, office workers and, with industrialisation, an increasing proletariat.

The rising of the population of Vienna followed by Metternich's fall and flight on 13th March coincided with a period of hardship and unemployment in the great working-class city of Berlin and the effect of Metternich's fall was immediate. Public meetings and street demonstrations became frequent and violent, disorder universal. The army was mobilised and behaved with brutality. On 15th March Uhlans drove a crowd with violence from Palace Square, inflicting casualties; the rioting became more serious, and King Frederick William IV gave way, on 17th March promising among other reforms an elected Parliament, national citizenship and a free press. The crowd cheered but demanded the withdrawal of the military forces, upon which the troops opened fire on the unarmed mob. Bystanders were mown down wholesale and the situation changed in a flash. Transported by fury, middle-class people who had taken no active part ran to help in erecting barricades and a bloody battle between the population and the army began. The people seized Berlin, as a few days earlier the people had seized Vienna, in a rising comparable with the mass risings of the first French Revolution. The King was forced to bare his head before the bodies of the victims of the massacre. He rode through Berlin escorted by the newly-formed civic guard, not by regular troops, and the 183 bodies of the slain were buried with full rites.

Throughout Europe the conduct of the German troops in Berlin was deplored and condemned, and a delicate situation resulted from the friendship between the Queen and Prince Albert and the Prince of Prussia. It had been suggested that the Prince of Prussia should visit the Queen and Prince in London and be one of Princess Louise's godfathers, but Prince Albert wrote to Stockmar on 30th March 1848 'We cannot let the Prince of Prussia come now. He has made enemies, because he is dreaded; but he is noble and honourable, and wholly devoted to the new movement for Germany. He looks at the business with the frank integrity of the soldier.'[36] Lord John Russell, now Prime Minister, advised the Queen that 'he thinks it better the Prince of Prussia should not be the godfather of the young Princess'.

Meanwhile the liberals of Germany, encouraged by the overthrow of Louis Philippe and the fall of Metternich, summoned an assembly to meet at Frankfort to prepare a plan for the election of a national Parliament. The Frankfort Assembly first met on 31st March 1848. It comprised the best minds and noblest characters in the country, it was of unimpeachable integrity, hard-working and patriotic. But it was also far too large. With 800 members, an assembly of intelligentsia, it failed to represent the princes and the nobles, the growing class of industrial magnates, or, for that matter, the workers. It was also without administrative experience; its progress was slow, it became entangled in procedure, and was evidently unlikely to achieve its aim.

At this juncture in 1848 a problem first made itself felt which was destined to be of immense importance to Britain, the British Royal Family and British foreign policy, through the marriage of the Prince of Wales, later King Edward VII, with the beautiful Danish Princess Alexandra—the Schleswig Holstein question. Events in 1848 were, however, only the overture.

The problem of the Schleswig Holstein Duchies was notoriously complicated. Lord Palmerston said he had known only three men who understood it: one was dead, one had gone mad on account of it and he himself, the third, had forgotten what it was all about. Reduced to its elements, the problem was one of nationality, entangled by feudal and dynastic custom. Since 1448 Denmark had been ruled by the house of Oldenburg, but the same house had possessed the Duchies of Schleswig and Holstein before their election to the Danish crown and, in the event of the failure of the male Oldenburg line, Denmark and the Duchies were likely to be separated, following different rules of inheritance. From the early nineteenth century a strong policy of Danish centralisation had antagonised the Duchies and this sentiment was fanned by the rising tide of German nationalism. Schleswig's sympathies were with the German landed nobility though the majority of the population was, by a small margin, Danish. German, however, was usually spoken in the schools. There was also an ideological difficulty since the German aristocrats of Schleswig were anathema to the democrats of Denmark.[37]

In July 1846 Christian VIII of Denmark, King-Duke of Schleswig and Holstein, who seven years earlier had succeeded to the throne of Denmark in middle age, announced to the world in an 'Open Letter' that, with the concurrence of the Danish Parliament and the Danish people, it had been agreed that the union between the Kingdom of Denmark, the Duchy of Schleswig and part of the Duchy of Holstein was permanent and indisputable. Angry protests were made by the Schleswig population and nobility, headed by the Duke of Augustenburg and the Grand Duke of Oldenburg, but 1847 passed without hostilities. In January 1848 Christian VIII died and was succeeded as King of Denmark by Frederick VII.

On 18th March at Kiel the Duchies rose against Denmark, proclaimed their independence and set up a provisional government under a brother of the Duke of Augustenburg. Fighting began. The Prussian army supported by German volunteers hastened to the assistance of the Duchies and by the end of April 1848 the Danish army had been thrown back across the river Eider, Denmark's frontier.

Prince Albert correctly interpreted British opinion when he wrote

'. . . Germany's only object in separating Holstein with Schleswig from Denmark is to incorporate them with herself. . . . Denmark will then become a State too small to maintain a separate independence. . . .'[38]

Germany had not yet emerged as Britain's chief enemy and rival. Britain was apprehensive of an attack from France, or from Russia, or, worse still, from both combined and it was vital that Denmark in the event of an attack should be strong enough to hold the straits leading to the Baltic Sea. Of this the Danes were aware and fought with such obstinacy and desperation for survival that the Germans and Prussians were taken aback and in August 1848 a truce was proposed at Malmö. But the Truce of Malmö did not settle the Schleswig Holstein question. Occasional hostilities, interrupted by minor truces and frequent arguments, dragged on year after year, until, fourteen years later, serious fighting broke out again. By then the beautiful Princess Alexandra of Denmark, an impassioned Danish patriot, had become Princess of Wales, and Britain was inevitably involved.

In the autumn of 1848 the tide of revolution turned. In the spring it had seemed that a new Europe based on principles of democracy and national freedom was about to be born. Less than six months later the tide was ebbing. Europe was liberal but there was a dread of disorder, violence and bloodshed. When in France the idealism of the February revolution failed to overcome the problems of unemployment and food shortage and fighting broke out again in the streets of Paris, this time with many casualties, the effect was felt throughout Europe. As early as 29th April Pope Pius IX dealt a mortal blow to the Italian national movement by becoming reconciled with Italy's oppressor Austria. His argument was that he was head of the Catholic Church, a spiritual not a temporal sovereign, and he issued a plea for peace. From July onwards liberal movements were crushed. The workers of Vienna protesting against reduced wages were defeated by the National Guard, and in August the Imperial Court, without Metternich, returned to Vienna. In Germany on 2nd November 1848 the King of Prussia embarked on a policy of reaction, dismissing his ministers, his assembly and the Civic Guard, while the Frankfort Parliament, in 'utter weariness of heart' at project after project having become confused and lost in wordy debates, came to the view that 'the best chance of uniting the thirty-two millions of Germans into one great nation lay in placing the Imperial Crown in the hands of the King of Prussia as the head of a consolidated State. His Majesty rejected the proffered crown, because it was offered to him by the nation, and not by the Princes, whom alone his principles permitted him to regard as the depositaries of power.'[39] The King of Prussia had 'long walked in the leading-strings of Metternich, and was so deeply imbued with the spirit of Absolutism'.[40]

By the spring of 1849 the wave of liberalism which resulted in the revolutions of 1848 had receded. The tangible result was small, the intangible result important. The tangible result was that Metternich had gone, and without his genius and his cunning Austria never regained the reactionary domination of Europe; the intangible result was the revelation of an unsuspected strength of liberal opinion in every country in Europe. All absolute rulers were given food for reflection.

Of the great powers, Britain alone remained undisturbed in spite of the strongest social reasons for revolution; the appalling poverty of the mass of the population in both rural and urban areas and the appalling conditions of the industrial workers contrasted with the splendour and wealth of the upper classes and the comfort enjoyed by the middle ranks of society.[41] Visitors from the continent were astonished by the contrast.

The Queen was proud of the loyalty of her subjects. On 30th December 1848 she wrote to King Leopold[42] '. . . I write to you *once* more in this *old* & *most dreadful* year . . . but I must not include myself or my country in the misfortunes of this past year:—on the contrary I have nothing but thanks & most grateful thanks to offer up for *all* that has happened *here*. . . .'

*

One of the most important events of the succeeding year 1849 was to pass virtually unnoticed. Two quiet youngish Germans came to settle in London, the name of one was Karl Marx, of the other Friedrich Engels. They had been living in Brussels where at the end of 1847 they wrote the Communist Manifesto. In May 1848 they moved to Cologne and founded a daily paper which preached revolution, the *Neue Rheinische Zeitung*. In November 1848 when the King of Prussia dissolved the National Assembly, the editors of the *Neue Rheinische Zeitung* advocated non-payment of taxes and the organisation of armed resistance. A state of siege was declared in Cologne, the newspaper suspended and Marx tried for high treason but unanimously acquitted. Expelled from Prussian territory in 1849, Marx and Engels went to Paris but were ordered to leave at once, and in the same month, May 1849, settled in London, where their activities attracted little, if any, attention.

*

Early in 1849, partly in a spirit of thankfulness, partly in ignorance—and as far as the Queen's advisers, Lord Clarendon, the Lord Lieutenant, and Lord John Russell, the Prime Minister, were concerned, from faith in the magical effect of the royal presence—it was decided that the visit of the Queen and the Prince to Ireland, originally planned for 1848, should take place in 1849. It was a remarkable decision since the state of Ireland was more desperate in 1849 than it had ever been. The rising of 1848 had failed, not because anti-English feeling had subsided, but because the

Irish were too weak with hunger to fight. Another total failure of the potato crop had taken place in 1848 but no further help was or could be given because relief funds had been expended. It was against a background, especially in the west and south-west, of thousands 'literally *screaming* for food who can't be relieved', packed workhouses, wholesale evictions, estates which could find no purchaser, that the royal visit was planned. On 6th June 1849 Lord John Russell informed Lord Clarendon that the Queen intended to come over to Dublin during the summer. 'She will live at Vice-Regal Lodge for a week in some splendour and hold a levée and a drawing-room.' Later the visit was to include Cork. Lord Fitzwilliam refused to have anything to do with the visit. '. . . A great *lie* is going to be acted there [at Dublin Castle]' wrote Lord Fitzwilliam. '. . . I would not have her go *now* unless she went to Killarney workhouse . . . Galway, Connemara and Castlebar. *That* would have been my tour for her instead of Cork, Dublin . . . unless she draw the right conclusion by seeing the Cove of Cork without a ship in it.' On 18th July 1849 the Dublin *Evening Mail* sarcastically suggested that since it was desirable that Her Majesty should not have the decay of Ireland thrust on her notice, the Dublin streets through which she would pass should be occupied for the time being by decently dressed persons sent in for the purpose while the fine houses in Dame Street, Grafton Street and elsewhere now 'in a dirty and dilapidated condition, the windows broken, patched with brown paper, or here and there . . . stuffed with an old hat, the shops closed and the wooden shutters covered over with auction bills . . . and notices from the Insolvent Court' should be 'cleaned as well as the short time allows and fully furnished with window curtains, muslin blinds and flower pots.'

As a demonstration of the Queen's desire for economy and informality, Sir Charles Wood, Chancellor of the Exchequer, received an intimation that Her Majesty 'does not desire State beds'.

The Queen was to land at Cork and go by sea up the East Coast to Dublin.

At 9 p.m. on 1st August 1849 the royal yacht was reported to be passing Portland Bill; at 10 p.m. on the 2nd she steamed into Cove (Cobh) harbour, Cork. Next day the mayor of Cork hastened off to implore her to delay her landing as preparations were not completed. But the Queen's timetable made delay impossible and at 2 p.m., to loud cheers, the Queen, 'the virtuous and honoured embodiment of fashion' as the *Freeman's Journal* commented, boarded the *Fairy* tender, toured the harbour and stepped ashore on Columbine Quay, where a marine pavilion had been erected, while the roar of cannon, which had been placed too close, shook the pavilion. She was the first British sovereign ever to set foot in the county of Cork.

Addresses were presented, the Queen gave her sanction to the name of the town being changed to 'Queenstown', a new flag was hoisted and the Queen steamed up to Cork where the mayor was knighted on the *Fairy*, '*on deck* like in times of old'. The Cork shops were closed and the streets decorated; the Queen noted 'Cork is not at all like an English town and looks rather foreign. The crowd is a noisy, excitable, but very good humoured one, running and pushing about, and laughing, talking and shrieking. The beauty of the women is very remarkable . . . almost every third woman was pretty and some remarkably so.'

The passage up the coast to Dublin was rough and the Queen and her children were 'very seasick', but on Monday 6th August the weather had cleared. The Queen came ashore in brilliant sunshine at 10 a.m. Accounts of the warmth of her reception differed; the *Freeman's Journal* reported the stands only a quarter full, but the Queen wrote of immense multitudes 'shrieking instead of cheering', flowers strewn in her path, a scene 'wonderful, striking, never to be forgotten'. She noticed the poverty; 'You see more ragged and wretched people here than I ever saw anywhere else' she wrote but commented again on the good looks of Irish women. '*En revanche* the women are really very handsome—quite in the lowest class . . . such beautiful black eyes and hair and such fine colour and teeth.'

Dublin delighted her. She drove about without any escort admiring the city and was amused not irritated by the jaunting cars and riders following her and the people running and screaming, not cheering as in England. The city was illuminated and crowds gathered in the streets. A very large levée was held at the Castle, the Queen wearing evening dress of brilliant green Irish poplin with a magnificent diamond tiara. She continued her practice of driving informally round Dublin in an open carriage, visiting the buildings for which the city is famous. The absence of any escort was felt to be flattering.

The inhabitants responded with excitement to decorated streets, illuminations and band music. Dublin had lost her splendour after the Union, now she was sunk in the despair of the famine. The Queen, though not beautiful, was still young (she had been 30 in May) and her simplicity, her lack of stiffness and touchiness, her admiration of Dublin, all had their effect. The *Freeman's Journal*, previously hostile, changed its tone. 'The personal demeanour, the frank and confiding manner of the Queen have won for her golden opinions' declared a leading article on 8th August 1849. Irish people are fond of children and the Queen had brought four of hers with her. The climax of the visit was reached on 9th August in a review in the Phoenix Park, with infantry movements and two grand charges of about 6,000 men, stopping dead only twenty yards from the royal carriages. The same evening a drawing-room was held at the Castle.

The Queen again wore Irish poplin, pink, elaborately figured with gold shamrocks, and again a magnificent tiara. Crowds watched the guests arrive, and the Queen asked the Castle authorities to let the people come closer to have a better view. She estimated that between two and three thousand ladies passed before her and 1,700 were presented.

On her last day, 10th August, she had been invited to a déjeuner at Carton, the seat of the Duke of Leinster, Ireland's only Duke, in Co. Kildare and was to embark at Kingstown (Dun Laoghaire) at 6.15 p.m. In the farewell to the Queen, the visit reached its climax. Every pier, every roof, every wharf in Kingstown was black with people, every boat in the harbour crammed. The crowd was delighted to see the four children with her, especially the Prince of Wales in his sailor suit; he and his sister the Princess Royal had been doing their lessons every day throughout the visit. Peal after peal of cheers and shrieks and shouts greeted the Royal Family and the Queen, leaving the deck, mounted the paddle box with astonishing lightness. There she was joined by the Prince, who removed his hat while she took his arm and with her other hand waved to the crowds. Cheers and shrieks redoubled, and at a word from the Queen the paddles ceased to move. The *Victoria and Albert* slowly drifted past the immense crowds, as near as safety allowed, with the Queen remaining on the paddle box until the pier was fully half a mile behind. It was, said Lord Lansdowne who was present, a scene impossible to witness without being moved.

Though the visit had been a success, Ireland was past the point where the Irish could be made governable with a few kind words, and no result was achieved.[43]

*

Through these anxious years a personal sorrow was hanging over the Queen. Her beloved aunt by marriage, Queen Louise of the Belgians, who had been responsible for the few bright intervals in the Queen's youth, visited her at Ramsgate during her illness in 1835, taught her to arrange her hair, and sent her clothes from Paris, was becoming alarmingly ill. She had a cough, which grew steadily worse, but her husband King Leopold did not seem to realise her condition and the Queen wrote admonishing him: 'Louise must get rid of her cough, it is not right to allow it to go on. . . . She ought to change air; Clark always says you ought to let both her and children change air more often.'[44] King Leopold expected too much of Queen Louise. 'She was in such anxiety always if you had the slightest *annoyance* or *inconvenience* . . .' the Queen wrote on 25th October 1850.[45] King Leopold wished Queen Louise to come to England, and, though she felt the journey was too much for her, she obeyed. But her condition was already desperate. On 7th October King Leopold was still writing 'She is so contented, so cheerful, that the possibilities of danger appear to me impossible.' Nevertheless on 11th October she died and three weeks afterwards Queen Victoria wrote '. . . But oh dearest Uncle, you can't think *how* ill she was *then*. Clark had in fact little or *no* hope of her life being long preserved.'[46]

Queen Victoria's grief was overwhelming. She could never forget Queen Louise's kindness to her during the days of the 'Kensington System'; the Queen seldom forgot kindness, though she could forget injury, and a long entry in her Journal for 13th October 1850 speaks in the voice of true sorrow.

*

The Queen and the Prince now embarked on a struggle which absorbed their energies and irritated their tempers for many months to come—a struggle with the Queen's Foreign Secretary, Henry John Temple, third Viscount Palmerston. Born in 1794, Palmerston possessed good looks, charm and brains, together with a graceful elegance reminiscent of the manners of the eighteenth century. Though attractive to women—the number of his love affairs earned him the nickname of 'Cupid'—he did not marry, owing, his friends were aware, to his attachment to the Countess Cowper, born Lady Emily Lamb, sister of Lord Melbourne. On 21st June 1837 Lord Cowper died and Palmerston urged Lady Cowper to marry him. She was fifty-two, he was fifty-five, and she hesitated. She was a grandmother, the marriage would be ridiculed; her children, to whom she was devoted, might object. After two years of Lord Palmerston 'always wanting her to marry him', she gave way and the marriage took place on 16th December 1839. Palmerston's happiness was touching; the day of the marriage was wet, gloomy and cold but he saw blue skies and brilliant sunshine.[47] The union proved idyllically happy and twenty-six years of bliss followed until Palmerston's death on 18th October 1865, within two days of his 81st birthday.

There had not always been antagonism between the Queen and Lord Palmerston. When she was a young girl he had been a favourite. She enjoyed sitting next him at dinner, 'always so gay and amusing', and when she came to the throne he was one of the statesmen who trained her in the business of being a Queen, teaching her how to address foreign sovereigns, princes and statesmen in their correct styles, instructing her in diplomatic etiquette, supplying her with a copy of the Gotha Almanach, and having 'Atlases' drawn to make foreign despatches easier for her to understand.[48]

The Queen was tenacious, and even as a girl had insisted on her rights. On this account she had rebuked Melbourne himself, even when her affection and dependence on him was at its height.

When the Queen, after her marriage to the Prince, began to assert what Stockmar termed 'the right of supervision and control belonging to

298

the Crown in foreign politics',[49] disagreement with Palmerston followed. On 4th May 1841 the Queen complains she 'has not received a [Foreign Office] Box *for the last 5 days* . . . she has also perceived that they have sent to her drafts to approve when the originals have already been sent away which of course renders her doing so useless.'[50] On 31st May 1841 Palmerston circulated a minute: 'The Queen says she has had no Despatches sent her for some days and she wishes Despatches to be sent to her every day. . . . The Queen also remarks that Drafts have been sent off. This should never be done! The Despatch should not go till the Draft is returned from the Queen. Make this known in the several rooms in the office.'[51] It was a typical example of his method with the Queen and the Prince. He wrote blandly, courteously, respectfully, assented to all they wished, and then continued to behave as, from the beginning, he had intended to behave.

Palmerston was, above all, a professional diplomat. The amount of work he performed was prodigious. Twenty-eight thousand despatches passed through the Foreign Office in a year—1848.[52] 'It is indeed hardly possible to read the letters and despatches which he poured forth in a torrent during this crowded and critical period without coming to the conclusion that he thoroughly enjoyed the game of diplomacy, which he played with the skill and precision of an incomparable master. He seemed thoroughly to know the politics and parties of every Court and Cabinet in Europe; he appeared to be familiar with the leading statesmen of every land and to have an accurate estimate both of their character and their capacity. . . . He desired to advance the cause of constitutional government in the world because he felt that by no other means could the reasonable demands of reformers be so satisfactorily met, the agitations of revolutionaries stopped, and the peace of mankind assured.'[53]

Sometimes he made mistakes with serious consequences. On 16th March 1848, for instance, he sent to Sir Henry Bulwer, the British Ambassador in Madrid, in direct defiance of Lord John Russell, then Prime Minister, a letter instructing him to advise the Queen of Spain how she should conduct her government, which resulted in the Ambassador being dismissed from his post. As a colleague he was 'unquestionably irritating'. He kept important and pompous persons waiting, he left letters unanswered for months. He wrote with undiplomatic pungency employing expressions which 'roused the recipients to an ecstasy of fury'. Lord Ponsonby for instance told Lord John Russell that 'he had received from Lord Palmerston letters which are not to be submitted to by any man'.

He conveyed, to those who disliked him, an impression of levity. He disliked discussion; his step, to the end of his life, was 'gay and somewhat jaunty';[54] he had 'an undisturbed and half careless air' and 'no one went more into . . . fashionable society'.

His was not a character likely to commend itself to the Queen and the Prince, particularly not to the Prince, and Stockmar notes that 'antagonism between them had long existed'.[55]

The policy favoured by Palmerston was often opposed to that favoured by the Queen and the Prince. A gulf yawned perpetually between them. The Queen and the Prince considered that Palmerston's hostility to Louis Philippe and the Orleans family had been responsible for the Spanish marriages; they supported Schleswig in the Schleswig Holstein dispute and resented Palmerston's support of the Danes; they wished to see a Prussian predominance over Germany; they favoured Austria, while Palmerston, who had become devoted to Italy as a very young man and spoke Italian fluently, was devoted to the cause of United Italy. Palmerston's Italian policy so infuriated Austria that when Francis Joseph was made Emperor in December 1848 no representative was sent to announce his accession to Queen Victoria, a public slight which she felt deeply. Palmerston acted behind the back of the Cabinet in support of Italian revolt, diverting arms from Woolwich Arsenal without permission and sending them to the rebels in Sicily.

*

In the midst of these perplexities, as the situation with Lord Palmerston daily grew more tense, the Prince suffered a crushing blow. George Anson, who had been the Prince's Treasurer and Private Secretary during his first seven years in England and Keeper of the Privy Purse since 1847, died suddenly at the age of 37. For some years his health had not been good; in 1843 Sir Denis Le Marchant, Under Secretary for the Home Office, had written urgently advising him to take more care of himself.[56]

On 11th April 1848 the Queen wrote to King Leopold 'Poor Anson is very unwell with one of those attacks in his head.'[57] On 8th October 1849 he suddenly fell down dead when alone with his wife, who was expecting a baby with more than usual anxiety because her previous children had died. 'I cannot describe the painful surprise and grief it was to me' wrote the Queen in her Journal 'for he was such a valuable old and faithful friend. . . . To see my poor dear Albert's deep distress made me wretched, for he loved and valued Anson who was almost the only intimate friend he had in this country, and he mourns for him as for a brother. To think of poor unfortunate Mrs Anson who was wrapped up in him, & is now expecting her confinement—makes one's heart ache . . . he was sincerely attached to my beloved Albert . . . saw him constantly and was on terms of such great intimacy and confidence with him . . . he was most useful *discreet* and assiduous in those difficult and trying times for my poor Albert when 1st married and laboured incessantly to [make] my beloved husband's position what it ought to be. Anson and Albert worked together for the reformation of the Household & finances, & had the happiness of seeing everything succeed. The sorrow is universal and there is hardly a dry eye in the house from highest to lowest.'[58]

It was decided to appoint Colonel Grey to be Prince Albert's Private Secretary, Colonel Phipps to fill three offices, Privy Purse and Treasurer to the Prince and Cofferer to the Prince of Wales, and to appoint a new Equerry.[59] Mrs Anson's baby arrived safely on 8th December and proved to be a daughter.

*

Throughout 1849 Lord Palmerston's independence persisted; threats, remonstrances, appeals, had no effect. Rebuked he readily apologised, promised amendment and then proceeded precisely as before. The differences between the Queen and Palmerston had become 'almost invariably' irreconcilable[60] and as within the minds and hearts of the Queen and the Prince anger against Palmerston rose, they reached the decision that he must be dismissed and replaced.

Four major events brought matters to a climax. The first was the affair of Dom or, as he is always called, Don Pacifico. Don Pacifico was a Portuguese Jew, living in Athens where he was Portuguese Consul General, but the fact that he had been born in Gibraltar made him a British subject. During Easter 1847 his house was attacked and gutted in broad daylight by an anti-semitic mob headed by the sons of the Minister of War. He claimed the immense sum of £81,000 from the Greek government and when his claim was refused applied to the British government for help on the ground of his British citizenship. The Greek administration was already disliked by Palmerston. Prince Otho, the German Prince who had been sent by the powers to occupy the throne of Greece, was despotic and stupid, and other disputes had been dragging on for several years. After twenty months of fruitless negotiation on Don Pacifico's behalf Palmerston acted. In January 1850 the British Mediterranean fleet was ordered to enter the port of Piraeus, the principal harbour of Greece, and seize sufficient Greek shipping to pay the claim. The Greek so-called navy consisted of a handful of vessels in poor order; the Greek government gave way and a settlement was made. Palmerston's action caused acute irritation, both at home and abroad, and with reason. The size of Don Pacifico's claim was preposterous, the use of the Mediterranean fleet to collect it for him indefensible; the French withdrew their Ambassador, the Russians threatened to do the same.

The Queen, with the full support of the Prince, decided the time had come for Palmerston to be dismissed from the Foreign Office. '. . . One conviction grows stronger and stronger with the Queen and myself (if it is possible), viz that Lord Palmerston is bringing the whole of the hatred which is borne to him—I don't mean here to investigate whether justly or unjustly—by all the Governments of Europe upon England, and that the country runs serious danger of having to pay for the consequences . . . the Queen may feel that her duty demands her not to be content with mere warning without any effect, and that for the sake of one man the welfare of the country must not be exposed.'[61]

A rebuke of the sternest nature was also transmitted to Lord Palmerston.[62] 'With reference to the conversation about Lord Palmerston which the Queen had with Lord John Russell the other day . . . she thinks it right, in order to *prevent any mistake* for the *future*, shortly to explain *what it is she expects from her Foreign Secretary*. She requires: (1) That he will distinctly state what he proposes in a given case, in order that the Queen may know as distinctly to *what* she has given her Royal sanction; (2) Having *once given* her sanction to a measure, that it be not arbitrarily altered or modified by the Minister; such an act she must consider as failing in sincerity towards the Crown, and justly to be visited by the exercise of her Constitutional right of dismissing that Minister. She expects to . . . receive the Foreign Despatches in good time, and to have the drafts for her approval sent to her in sufficient time to make herself acquainted with their contents before they must be sent off. The Queen thinks it best that Lord John Russell should show this letter to Lord Palmerston.'

Lord Palmerston was extremely angry when Lord John Russell later read this memorandum aloud in the House of Commons and was unwilling to serve under him ever again.[63]

Lord Stanley had put down a motion in the House of Lords challenging the government's action in the Don Pacifico affair. But Lord John Russell, the Prime Minister, delayed until the end of the session, and Palmerston was saved. On 24th June 1850, during a four days' debate on the Greek question, Palmerston made a speech lasting nearly five hours.[64] Brushing aside the preposterous size of Don Pacifico's claim, reflections on Don Pacifico's character or the propriety of the use made of the British fleet, he finished with the famous declaration 'I fearlessly challenge the verdict . . . whether the principles on which the foreign policy of Her Majesty's government has been conducted and the sense of duty which has led us to think ourselves bound to afford protection to our fellow subjects abroad are proper and fitting guides for those who are charged with the government of England; and whether, as the Roman in days of old, held himself free from indignity when he could say "Civis Romanus sum" (I am a Roman citizen), so also a British subject, in whatever land he may be, shall feel confident that the watchful eye and the strong arm of England will protect him against injustice and wrong.'

Palmerston sat down to 'loud and prolonged cheers'. He had scored a great triumph, turned the tables on his adversaries and vindicated his actions as Foreign Secretary. His political opponent Sir Robert Peel declared 'It has made us all proud of him.'[65] At one stroke he had become a national idol and henceforward those who opposed 'Pam' had to reckon with a popularity such as few statesmen have enjoyed before or since.

The day after Palmerston's triumph the Queen and the Prince received another blow. As Peel was riding up Constitution Hill on his brown cob, the horse slipped and fell on him. Three days later Peel died in great pain. Palmerston wrote[66] '. . . He was a very bad and awkward rider, and his horse might have been sat by any better equestrian; but he seems, somehow or other, to have been entangled in the bridle, and to have forced the horse to step or kneel upon him . . . that which killed him was a broken rib, forced with great violence inwards into the lungs.'

The loss to the Queen and the Prince was incalculable. The Queen's former dislike had disappeared, she had become deeply attached to him and relied on him politically far more than she ever had on Lord Melbourne. The Prince 'felt and feels Sir Robert's loss *dreadfully*. He feels he has lost a second father' wrote the Queen to the King of the Belgians, while the Prince himself wrote 'We have lost our truest friend and trustiest counsellor, the throne its most valiant defender, the country its most open minded and greatest statesman.'[67] Public concern was intense, the Queen records that the entrance to Sir Robert Peel's house was besieged by crowds to whom a bulletin of his progress was from time to time read aloud by a policeman.

Faced with Lord Palmerston's triumph, it was difficult for the Queen and the Prince to proceed with a scheme for his removal, and, as the Queen herself observed, there was 'no chance of Lord Palmerston reforming himself in his sixty-seventh year'.[68]

Relations between them had thus to proceed on their uneasy way until the second of the four Palmerston storms blew up. This centred round the Austrian General Haynau, nicknamed 'General Hyaena', possessed of an evil reputation in Hungary and Italy for his cruelty and the atrocities he had committed, especially the flogging of women. Palmerston considered that a visit he paid to London 'without rhyme or reason, so soon after his Italian and Hungarian exploits, was a wanton insult to the people of this country, whose opinion of him had been loudly proclaimed at public meetings and in all the newspapers . . . Metternich and Neumann strongly advised him, as he passed through Brussels, not to come to England at present; and Koller [the Austrian Ambassador] tried to persuade him to cut off his long yellow moustaches. But he would not shave, and he professed to think that his presence in England could turn public opinion in his favour.'[69] On 5th September General Haynau chose to pay a visit to Barclay and Perkins' London brewery.[70] As soon as he arrived he was recognised and attacked by a number of draymen with brooms; shouting 'Down with the Austrian butcher', they gave him a beating and covered him with dirt. General Haynau fled with the draymen at his heels and took refuge in a public house till a force of police came to his rescue and took him away in a van to a place of safety.

The Queen felt that Palmerston, in his letter to Baron Koller, had made it clear that 'he is not sorry for what has happened'.[71] In a letter to the Queen Lord Palmerston assured her that 'feelings of just and honourable indignation have not been confined to England, for he had good reason to know that General Haynau's ferocious and unmanly treatment of the unfortunate inhabitants of Brescia and of other towns and places in Italy, his savage proclamations to the people of Pesth, and his barbarous acts in Hungary excited almost as much disgust in Austria as in England, and that the name of "General Hyaena" was given to him in Vienna long before it was applied to him in London'.[72]

The Queen was once more infuriated to find that the despatch had already been '*sent*'; she had merely a useless copy. She insisted on the despatch being recalled and Palmerston undergoing the indignity of his original being repudiated. 'The Queen is very glad' she wrote[73] to Lord John Russell on 19th October 1850 'of the result of the conflict with Lord Palmerston. . . . The correspondence, which the Queen now returns, shows clearly that . . . Lord John has the power of exercising that control over Lord Palmerston, the careful exercise of which he owes to the Queen, his colleagues, and the country, if he will take the necessary pains to remain firm.'

Lord John Russell had alarmed the Queen and the Prince by suggesting that Palmerston might be removed from foreign affairs by being made Leader of the House of Commons, a position in which since the death of Peel and his parliamentary triumph he could exercise possibly even more power.[74] The Radicals were rallying round him and he was cheered on entering the House of Commons.

The Prince and the Queen made one of their chief objections against Palmerston a charge of immorality,[75] the Prince alleging that 'while a guest under her [the Queen's] roof at Windsor Castle he had committed a brutal attack upon one of her ladies in waiting, had at night by stealth, introduced himself into her apartment, barricaded afterwards the door and would have consummated his fiendish scheme by violence had not the miraculous efforts of his victim and assistance attracted by her screams saved her.'

How could the Queen consent to take such a man as her adviser and counsellor of state? The Prince did not mention that the incident had taken place in the earliest part of the Queen's reign and before Lord Palmerston's marriage. There had been a change in accommodation at Windsor and the room entered by Lord Palmerston was normally occupied by a lady not averse from his attentions, whom he was accustomed to visit there.

In the following autumn the third of the quarrels which led to Palmerston's dismissal blew up over the question whether he was or was not to receive the patriot Hungarian leader Kossuth. In 1849 Lord Palmerston had saved the life of Kossuth in addition to the lives of a number of other Hungarian refugees by preventing them from being extradited from Turkey and handed over to the Austrians. On 23rd October 1851 Kossuth landed in England and began a series of speeches denouncing the Emperors of Austria and Russia. The Queen and the Prince, who were anxious to preserve friendship with the two Emperors, stated in the strongest terms that any reception of Kossuth by Lord Palmerston would be highly improper. Palmerston had already made an appointment to receive Kossuth at his private house, but when the question was referred to the Cabinet a majority disapproved. Palmerston was extremely angry and wrote to Lord John Russell on 30th October 'There are limits to all things. I do not choose to be dictated to as to who I may or may not receive in my own house. . . . I shall use my own discretion. You will, of course, use yours as to the composition of your Government. I have not detained your messenger five minutes.'[76] Nevertheless he did submit and the appointment was cancelled. In a few weeks the Kossuth question had flared up again. Palmerston did not see Kossuth, but he described himself as 'extremely flattered and highly gratified' when he received an address from a deputation of Radicals from Finsbury and Islington in which the Emperors of Russia and Austria were described as 'odious and detestable assassins' and 'merciless tyrants and despots'. The Queen and the Prince were transported with fury and only the embarrassing popularity of 'Pam', and of Kossuth, who was regarded by the populace as a martyr, saved Lord Palmerston from instant dismissal. The Queen once again told Lord John Russell she would like Lord Palmerston to go but Lord John wavered—Palmerston's dismissal must break up the Cabinet.[77]

While these domestic and political crises absorbed the attention of the Court and the country, events of world-shaking importance were happening in British territory thousands of miles away. In 1849 gold had been discovered in California, and the Californian gold rush took place; early in 1851 gold was struck in New South Wales, Australia, with a similar sequel. The existence of gold in New South Wales had been known to the authorities for years, but the discovery of gold in a community containing 45,000 convicts provoked dread: the first convict, in a road gang, who turned up a nugget as early as 1823, was immediately flogged on the ground that he must have stolen the gold and melted it down. Subsequent discoveries were kept secret; not until February 1851 did the

Chief Secretary in Sydney decide to issue licences to dig. By May there were 400 prospectors on the Bathurst field.

The population of New South Wales was too limited to produce a real gold rush but with the discovery of new and richer fields farther south at Ballarat and, in December 1851, the riches of Bendigo, emigrants began to pour into Australia, a hundred persons arriving at Ballarat every day. Many were totally unfit for the toil of gold digging, exhausted by the hardships of the voyage, and varying in class from the sons of the English aristocracy to ex-convicts, from clergymen and schoolmasters to Scotch, Welsh and English miners. Within a few years the gold rush was to transform Australia from a community of convicts and farmers to a colony of importance. In June 1851 a reward of £200 was offered by a Gold Discovery Committee, for the discovery of gold within 200 miles of Melbourne, but perhaps fortunately for Melbourne, gold was not found.

*

At home in England political strife continued and Palmerston became involved in a further serious matter. On 2nd December 1851 Louis Napoleon's *coup d'état* took place. The news was received with horror in Britain. 'By that contrivance of consummate force and fraud, breaking an oath, violating a constitution, imprisoning many leading soldiers and politicians and shooting some twelve hundred innocent citizens in the streets of Paris, Louis Bonaparte made himself master of France.'[78] The chamber was dissolved and Louis Bonaparte's power became absolute.

King Leopold of the Belgians, celebrated for his political experience, told the Queen[79] he was 'inclined to think that Louis Bonaparte will succeed. The country is tired and wish quiet, and if they get it by this *coup d'état* they will have no objection, and let *le Gouvernement Parlementaire et Constitutionnel* go to sleep for a while. I suspect that the great Continental powers will see a military Government at Paris with pleasure; they go rather far in their hatred of everything Parliamentary.'

On 3rd December news of the *coup d'état* was announced to Lord Palmerston by the French Ambassador, Count Walewski. Lord Palmerston expressed his 'entire approbation of the act of the President and [his] conviction that he could not have acted otherwise'.[80]

The issue of Palmerston and the *coup d'état* is obscure. Hitherto his indiscretions, however infuriating, had always been popular in the country. They had been democratic and Palmerston himself was idolised by the nation as a democrat. Now he had been caught on the wrong foot. The *coup d'état* was an act of tyranny and he could safely be dismissed. Greville with penetrating judgment considered the dismissal of Palmerston over the *coup d'état* was a 'pretext' as the real cause was undoubtedly the reception of the Radical deputation from Finsbury and Islington and his conduct in the Kossuth affair. Lord John Russell 'did not dare to quarrel with him on grounds which would have enabled him to cast himself on the Radicals, to appeal to all the Kossuthian sympathies of the country',[81] but now he had a sufficient cause of quarrel in which Palmerston took the anti-democratic side and he seized upon it. On 13th December 1851 Lord Palmerston was officially requested to explain his action in expressing the approval of the British government of the *coup d'état* to the French Ambassador without any previous consultation with the Cabinet. The fact that 'the entire approval, of the British government had been conveyed by Lord Palmerston to the French Ambassador was declared by the Queen to be something 'the Queen cannot believe', especially as it would have been in direct contradiction to the policy of strict neutrality which had been laid down.[82] Palmerston replied by a long letter which was a reasoned exposition of his opinion of Louis Napoleon's action. Such antagonism had grown up between the Prince-President and the Assembly that they could not long continue to exist together and what had occurred was for the good of France. On these grounds he had formed the opinion he expressed to Walewski. The terms of that opinion and the accuracy of Walewski's report he did not deny.[83] Lord John replied that the question at issue was not the grounds for the opinion Lord Palmerston had formed but whether he ought to have given any opinion without previously consulting the Cabinet and getting the sanction of the Sovereign. These conditions Lord Palmerston refused to accept and on 19th December Lord John Russell wrote he had no other course left 'than to submit the correspondence to the Queen, and ask Her Majesty to appoint a successor to you in the Foreign Office'.[84]

The same day Lord John Russell advised the Queen[85] that Lord Palmerston should now be informed that his reply was not satisfactory and that she should inform Lord Palmerston she was now 'ready to accept the Seals of Office, and to place them in other hands'.

On 23rd December Greville wrote[86] 'Palmerston is out!—actually, really, and irretrievably out. I nearly dropt off my chair. . . .'

Chapter Ten

On 28th December 1851 Lord Palmerston was replaced as Foreign Secretary by Lord Granville, son of the Lord Granville, 'Granville beautiful Granville', whose correspondence with Lord Holland illuminates Queen Victoria's accession and the first years of her reign.[1] The younger Lord Granville was persona grata with the Queen, and had already worked throughout the past year with the Prince, who, in addition to his struggle with Palmerston, was toiling at the organisation of the project which emerged as the Great Exhibition of 1851. Lord Granville, who succeeded his father in 1846, had been Under-Secretary for Foreign Affairs in 1840–41, Paymaster General in 1847 and the first President of the newly constituted Board of Trade in 1848. He therefore had experience of business both at home and abroad, was a good linguist and in 1850 was appointed President of the Royal Commission in charge of preparations for the exhibition, working under the Prince.

Prospects at the outset were not encouraging. The Prince had been meditating on the scheme for some time. He first discussed it semi-officially with Sir Robert Peel and Mr Labouchere in July 1849, followed by a meeting in Buckingham Palace at the end of the month with Mr Thomas Cubitt, the well-known builder of Belgravia, and three of the most active members of the Society of Arts, Mr (later Sir) Henry Cole, Mr Francis Fuller and Mr John Scott Russell. Henry Cole, who joined the Society of Arts in 1846, almost immediately became the dynamo of the new undertaking. 'He started his career in the Public Record Office [Cole was nominally on the staff of the Public Record Office until 1852], and from there was seconded to promote one project after another. He helped Rowland Hill to launch the penny post; he focussed the attention of manufacturers on industrial design ... worked successfully for the introduction of standard gauge railway track; was responsible for the Royal College of Music, for the Albert Hall, a School of Cookery and ... was chiefly responsible for the extraordinary success of ... the South Kensington Museum, when he was in overall charge of its affairs from 1853 to 1873.'[2]

After the Royal Society of Arts received its Royal Charter in 1847,

Henry Cole and the Prince worked together in mounting a series of exhibitions; the first attracted 20,000 visitors, the second, in 1848, 70,000, the third, in 1849, over 100,000. Cole asked the Prince whether the exhibition now planned should be international or national. The Prince thought for a minute and then said 'It must embrace foreign productions. . . .' and added emphatically 'International certainly'.[3] It was to be the first international exhibition ever held.

A space within Somerset House was offered to house the Exhibition by the government, but was too small. The Prince inclined towards Leicester Square, but Cole persuaded him a much larger and more ambitious site was required and pressed the Prince to decide on Hyde Park. This would solve all considerations of space and prestige, and the Prince agreed.

An explosion of fury, which came as a surprise to the Prince, followed the announcement of the site. On 25th June 1850 *The Times* delivered a broadside: 'The whole of the Park, and, we venture to predict the whole of Kensington Gardens, will be turned into the bivouac of all the vagabonds of London so long as the Exhibition shall continue. . . . The annoyance inflicted on the neighbourhood will be indescribable. . . .' A building committee had been appointed and on 27th June *The Times* attacked their plans: 'In fact a building is to be erected in Hyde Park to the full as substantial as Buckingham Palace. . . . Not only is a vast pile of masonry to be heaped up in the Park but one feature of the plan is that there shall be a dome of 200 feet in diameter, considerably larger than the dome of St Paul's. . . . By a stroke of the pen our pleasant Park, nearly the only place where Londoners can get a breath of fresh air, is to be turned into something between Wolverhampton and Greenwich Fair. The project looks so like insanity that even with the evidence we have before us we can scarcely bring ourselves to believe that the advisers of the Prince have cared to connect his name with such an outrage to the feelings and wishes of the inhabitants of the metropolis.' The Prince wrote in despair to Stockmar 'If we are driven out of the Park the work is done for.'[4]

Meanwhile in the House of Commons both the Exhibition and its site in Hyde Park were being furiously attacked by Colonel Charles de L. Waldo Sibthorp, an arch Tory in his 68th year. 'As for the object for which Hyde Park is to be desecrated' he fulminated 'it is the greatest trash, the greatest fraud and the greatest imposition ever attempted to be palmed upon the people of this country. The object of its promoters is to introduce among us foreign stuff of every description. . . . All the bad characters at present scattered over the country will be attracted to Hyde Park. This being the case I would advise persons residing near the Park to keep a sharp look out over their silver forks and spoons and servant maids.'[5] A strong point was made over an alleged proposal to cut down a clump of young elm trees on the site of the Exhibition, which he described as the beginning of a total sacrifice of natural beauty. It is worth noting that Colonel Sibthorp had put up equally violent opposition to the Public Libraries Act of 1850, on the ground that he himself did not like reading at all.

The Prince became increasingly depressed. He was in a perpetual state of irritation with Lord Palmerston, and overworked through the endless unexpected difficulties presented by the Exhibition. On 1st May the Queen had a third son, their seventh child. This was a happy event, for both he and the Queen had wished for a third boy and by a fortunate chance the Prince was born on the Duke of Wellington's 81st birthday. He was to be christened Arthur after the Duke, with the Duke standing as his godfather. When the Queen had barely recovered from her confinement, two further attempts on her life took place. On 19th May 1850 an Irishman, William Hamilton of Adare, fired directly at her as she drove up Constitution Hill. The pistol was loaded with blank but the Queen did not know this and the shock was great. On 27th May 1850 Robert Pate, 'a dandy who had made himself conspicuous in the Park', a man of good family who had held a commission in the Army for five years, started forward from the crowd as the Queen left Cambridge House, where the Duke of Cambridge was seriously ill, and struck a violent blow at the Queen's face with his cane. The force was fortunately broken by the brim of her bonnet, but she was severely bruised on her forehead and though she did not become hysterical her nerves were badly shaken. Robert Pate refused to speak or disclose his motives and was manifestly deranged. 'All this does not help' the Prince told Stockmar.

On 2nd July 1850 the Prince urgently asked Stockmar to come to England. 'We are on the point of having to abandon the Exhibition altogether . . . if you can come pray do so, for we have need of you.'[6]

The Queen's grief at the death of Peel was, as always, intensified by the Prince's suffering. She was anxious about his health and the effect on him of disappointment over the Exhibition, after his gruelling work. She wrote several times beseeching Stockmar to come to England.[7] 'You do not answer my anxious letters. Pray, do listen to our entreaties to come. It will do you good to be with my beloved Prince. He longs for you. . . . Clark admits that it is the mind . . . he has likewise been so shamefully plagued about the Exhibition . . . if a little knot of selfish people had succeeded in driving him out of the only place where the architects said it could be. He felt their conduct much and thought much about it. . . .'

However, when the debate on the site finally took place, Parliament had a change of heart. Sir Theodore Martin, the Prince's biographer, attributes the new feeling of the House to the effect of the death of Peel whose loss was felt daily and whose wisdom and integrity were almost hourly more regretted. It was known that Sir Robert had been in favour of the site in Hyde Park and in the House of Commons on 4th July the motion in opposition was defeated by a large majority, while in the House of Lords the motion was withdrawn.[8] A few days later the Prince wrote in his diary 'The feeling respecting Hyde Park is quite changed.'[9]

Difficulties, however, were not yet over. Want of money was the next obstacle. The average estimate of the cost of the building was £100,000 and subscriptions were 'very backward'.[10] A guarantee fund was established, several of the Commissioners gave substantial sums and £200,000 was collected in case of a possible deficit. All now seemed plain sailing; apparently it remained only to put the Exhibition building up when controversy over the plan broke out again. It was too solid, people complained; it could never be demolished, it would remain permanently. 'Can anyone be weak enough to suppose that a building erected on such a scale will ever be removed?'[11] All the previous arguments were brought out, the Park would be ruined, the people deprived of enjoyment and the Prince's name connected with an outrage.

The solution was unexpected. In 1834 both the House of Commons and the House of Lords had been burnt to the ground in a conflagration started by reckless burning of old wooden Exchequer tally rods, used in past centuries for keeping accounts. The Houses of Parliament were rebuilt and on 7th June 1850, when the House of Commons was substantially completed, a trial session had been held, at which a certain Joseph Paxton was present with a friend, Mr Ellis M.P.[12] Joseph Paxton was one of the most remarkable men of the century. Starting life as a gardener's boy, he had become the protégé of the Duke of Devonshire, and though without architectural qualifications had become celebrated as the designer of the great conservatory at Chatsworth, the Duke's seat in Derbyshire. Disputes over a building to house the Exhibition had now reached a point at which 13,937 applications for space to exhibit had been received, finance for a building had been raised, subscriptions were coming in, but no plan for a building had been agreed and the opening date for the Exhibition was only ten months ahead, May 1851. Once more the undertaking hung in the balance.

Scribbling on a blotting pad, Paxton produced a rough sketch for a 'palace of glass', a giant greenhouse, on an undreamt-of scale, a revolutionary design which could be swiftly erected, and was novel, light, glittering. The Committee, faced with the necessity of committing themselves, hesitated, raised objections, became nervous. Paxton went over their heads. Working night and day with a small staff he completed plans and appealed direct to the public by publishing his design in the *Illustrated London News* for 6th July 1850. The aesthetic conception of the Crystal Palace is thought to have been inspired by Paxton's study of the structure of the water-lily *Victoria Regia*.[13] In 1837 an English traveller in British Guiana had been startled by the sight of a giant water-lily, the seeds of which had been brought back to England where they germinated; but the plants had not flowered. In 1849 Paxton secured a plant for Chatsworth, placing it in a specially heated tank stirred by water-wheels of his own design. In three months' time it flowered: eleven leaves 5 feet in diameter lay about the gigantic bud. *Victoria Regia* attained a stupendous growth. One day Paxton set his small daughter to stand on one of the lily's great leaves; it easily bore her weight. Impressed by the plant's slender strength, he studied its structure; strong ribs radiated outwards, being held tautly by delicate cross-ribs. It was a marvel of natural economy. Faced with the necessity of re-housing the growing lily, he built the lily-house, itself another marvel of economy and delicate strength capable of withstanding both wind and hail.

Paxton's design for the Exhibition building created a sensation. The public was enchanted and public opinion compelled the Committee, still somewhat unwilling, to adopt the plan for what *Punch*, by a stroke of genius, christened in November 1850 'The Crystal Palace'. No trees were to be cut down in Hyde Park; three tall elms which grew across the site from north to south were roofed in by an immense transept and added to the fairy-like charm of the interior.

Prophecies of disaster abounded. Paxton had no official qualifications as architect, engineer or scientist; it was declared that the building would collapse, the footsteps of the walking multitudes would set up vibrations which must shake it down. Colonel Sibthorp declared that the dearest wish of his heart was that 'the confounded building called the Crystal Palace would be dashed to pieces'. Hail was certain to crack it, thunder to shatter it, rain to swamp it. But, as the vast glittering building rose above the tree tops, public opinion prevailed. Nothing like this had ever been seen before. The people had been fascinated by the conception of the Crystal Palace from the first; now as it approached completion there was mounting excitement, and it was generally felt that something very extraordinary was about to take place. The first ribs of the great transept were hauled up on 4th December 1850. In 1851 armies of workmen began their labours, 2,112 in January and an average of 2,000 until the end of March.

The Queen and the Prince paid frequent visits, several times a week. Though flattering, these were not altogether welcome to the contractors. Mr Cole wrote in his diary that Mr Fox of Messrs Fox & Henderson, the contractors, reckoned each royal visit excited the workmen so much that it cost £20 in loss of time.[14]

Considerable sums were paid for auxiliary services. Thomas Masters, confectioners, paid £5,500 for the right to sell refreshments. No alcoholic beverages were allowed; the choice, besides tea and coffee at 6*d.* a cup, included raspberry vinegar, lemonade, soda water, spruce beer, ginger beer and orangeade at 6*d.* a bottle. Jellies and blancmanges were 6*d.* a glass, ices of various flavour 6*d.* but fresh strawberry and fresh pineapple 1*s.* Eatables were restricted to sandwiches, savoury pies and patties and bread, butter and cheese. Some disappointment was felt at the absence of beer, for which a strawberry ice and a wafer were not felt to be an adequate substitute. The cost of extra police to be on duty outside the building was £5,043 19*s.* 6*d.* Within the Crystal Palace itself, the Commissioner of the Metropolitan Police and the Head of the Metropolitan Fire Brigade took responsibility. The crowds who attended were peaceable and orderly: 'Not a flower was picked, not a picture smashed.'[15]

About 14,000 exhibits, from all over the world, were divided into four sections, raw materials, machinery and mechanical inventions, manufactures, and sculpture and plastic art. Exhibitors had to deliver their exhibits at their own expense but were charged no rent. More than half the total area of the building was allotted to foreign exhibitors, 213,000 square feet. This had subsequently to be increased, especially in the case of France. The British Colonies were allowed 51,000 square feet. When applications from the United Kingdom were received they exceeded 417,000 square feet (210,000 square feet more than was available) and wall space of 200,000 square feet was requisitioned. The number of exhibitors who applied was 8,200. An important point was that the Exhibition was kept contemporary. In the fine arts section, for instance, only the work of artists still living or less than three years dead might be shown. The emphasis was to be on modernity, invention, discovery, and to this policy the Great Exhibition owed its remarkable success. The 1st of May 1851 was fixed as the day of opening and as exhibits began to arrive from all parts of the world public excitement mounted.[16] Unloading was done by men of the sappers and miners and the exhibits were fitted, not without difficulty, into their intended places.

Crowds of people thronged Hyde Park and its approaches daily. Plans were made to form clubs for travellers from the country to take advantage of the low excursion rates while foreign visitors were expected in thousands. Endless problems arose over stalls, display stands, delayed and erroneous deliveries. 'Just at present' wrote the Prince[17] 'I am more dead than alive from overwork. The opponents of the Exhibition work with might and main to throw all the old women into panic, and to drive myself crazy.'

Even the birds of the air conspired to add to the Prince's difficulties. It was alleged that the three large elms in the transept harboured so many sparrows that all the rich goods displayed would be spoiled by them. The Queen suggested that Lord John Russell should be sent for. Lord John advised that soldiers from the regiment of Guards should be sent into the building to shoot the sparrows. The Prince pointed out that in that case the glass would be destroyed. Lord Palmerston was called into consultation and proposed bird lime on the branches of the trees. The Prince replied that the birds no longer roosted on the trees but sat on the iron girders of the building. The infallible remedy was then employed: 'Send for the Duke of Wellington.' After remarking he was not a bird catcher, the Victor of Waterloo presented himself at Buckingham Palace. After a consultation had been held, the Duke went to the Queen and oracularly uttered the words 'Sparrow Hawks'. At the sight of the Duke of Wellington and the words 'Sparrow Hawks', Lord Playfair reports,[18] the sparrows flew out of the Crystal Palace in a body and were never seen again.

The final straw was a criticism of the Queen because, with the memory of Robert Pate's assault on her in mind, the authorities were endeavouring to arrange for her to open the Exhibition in private. The last accusation that could be levelled against the Queen was want of personal courage, but *The Times* did so: 'Surely Queen Victoria is not Tiberius or Louis XI that she should be smuggled out of a great glass carriage into a great glass building under cover of the truncheons of the police and the broad swords of the Life Guards? Where most Englishmen are gathered together there the Queen of England is most secure.'[19] The Queen never had any intention of not opening the Exhibition in person.

Though the mounting excitement indicated eventual success, the Commissioners displayed financial courage approaching recklessness.[20] True a guarantee fund existed of £230,000, largely subscribed by themselves, but on 22nd April 1851, when the Exhibition was due to open on 1st May, the Commissioners were working on an overdraft at the Bank of England, subscriptions were slower coming in than expected and the Treasury had washed its hands of all liability.

'Everyone is occupied with the great day & afternoon' wrote the Queen in her Journal on 30th April 1851[21] '& my poor Albert is terribly fagged. *All* day some question or other, or some difficulty, all of which my beloved one takes with the greatest quiet & good temper.' After breakfast the Queen and the Prince with the elder children and the Prince and Princess of Prussia, also accompanied by their children, visited the Exhibition. 'The noise and bustle, even greater than yesterday, as so many preparations are being made for the seating of the spectators, & there is certainly still much to be done.'

A substantial contribution to the success of the organisation was made by the tact and good humour of Lord Granville. 'On the day of opening when at the last moment the arrangements were found to be a little backward, he was seen, broom in hand, vigorously sweeping up the refuse scattered about the dais, half an hour before the time fixed for the arrival of the Royal personages . . . who were to perform the ceremony.'[22]

At length on 1st May 1851 the opening day of the Exhibition came.

'This day is one of the greatest & most glorious days of our lives, with which, to my pride & joy the name of my dearly beloved Albert is forever associated! It is a day which makes my heart swell with thankfulness' wrote the Queen in her Journal for 1st May 1851.[23] 'The Park presented a wonderful spectacle, crowds streaming through it,—carriages & troops passing, quite like the Coronation Day, & for *me*, the same anxiety. The day was bright, & all bustle & excitement. At $\frac{1}{2}$ p. 11, the whole procession in 9 state carriages, was set in motion. Vicky & Bertie were in our carriage. Vicky was dressed in lace over white satin, with a small wreath of pink wild roses, in her hair, & looked very nice. Bertie was in full Highland dress. The Green Park & Hyde Park were one mass of densely crowded human beings, in the highest good humour & most enthusiastic. I never saw Hyde Park look as it did, being filled with crowds as far as the eye could reach. A little rain fell, just as we started; but before we neared the Crystal Palace, the sun shone & gleamed upon the gigantic edifice, upon which the flags of every nation were flying. We drove up Rotten Row & got out of our carriages at the entrance on that side. The glimpse through the iron gates of the Transept, the moving palms & flowers, the myriads of people filling the galleries & seats around, together with the flourish of trumpets, as we entered the building, gave a sensation I shall never forget, & I felt much moved. We went for a moment into a little room where we left our cloaks & found Mama & Mary. Outside all the Princes were standing. In a few seconds we proceeded, Albert leading me having Vicky at his hand, & Bertie holding mine. The sight as we came to the centre where the steps & chair (on which I did not sit) was placed, facing the beautiful crystal fountain was magic & impressive. The tremendous cheering, the joy expressed in every face, the vastness of the building, with all its decorations & exhibits, the sound of the organ (with 200 instruments & 600 voices, which seemed nothing), & my beloved Husband the creator of this great "Peace Festival", uniting the industry & art of *all* nations of the earth, *all* this, was indeed moving, & a day to live forever. God bless my dearest Albert, & my dear Country which has shown itself so great today. . . . After the National Anthem had been sung, Albert left my side, & at the head of the Commissioners—a curious assemblage of political & distinguished men—read the Report to me, which is a long one, & I read a short answer. After this the Archbishop of Canterbury offered up a short & appropriate Prayer, followed by the singing of Handel's Hallelujah Chorus.'

During the singing of the Hallelujah Chorus there occurred what became known as the incident of the Chinese Mandarin. According to Lord Playfair[24] 'a Chinaman, dressed in magnificent robes, suddenly emerged from the crowd and prostrated himself before the throne. Who he was nobody knew. He might possibly be the Emperor of China himself who had come secretly to the ceremony, but it was certain he was not in the programme of the procession and we who were in charge of the ceremony did not know where to place his Celestial Highness. The Lord Chamberlain was equally perplexed and asked the Queen and the Prince Consort for instructions. We were then told there must be no mistake as to his rank, and that it would be best to place him between the Archbishop of Canterbury and the Duke of Wellington. In this dignified position he marched through the building to the delight and amazement of all beholders. Next day we ascertained that this Chinaman was a keeper of a Chinese junk that had been sent over to lie in the river Thames and which anyone could visit on payment of a shilling!'

'This concluded the Procession of great length' wrote the Queen 'which was beautifully arranged, the prescribed order being exactly adhered to. The Nave was full of people, which had not been intended & deafening cheers & waving of handkerchiefs, continued the whole time of our long walk from one end of the building, to the other. Every face was bright, & smiling, & many even had tears in their eyes. Many Frenchmen called out "Vive la Reine". One could of course see nothing, but what was high up in the Nave, & nothing in the Courts. The organs were but little heard, but the Military Band, at one end, had a very fine effect, playing the March from *Athalie*, as we passed along. The old Duke of Wellington & Ld. Anglesey walked arm in arm, which was a touching sight. I saw many acquaintances, amongst those present. We returned to our place & Albert told Ld. Breadalbane to declare the Exhibition to be opened, which he did in a loud voice saying "Her Majesty commands me to declare the Exhibition opened", when there was a flourish of trumpets, followed by immense cheering. Everyone was astounded & delighted. The return was equally satisfactory,—the crowd most enthusiastic & perfect order kept. We reached the Palace at 20 m. past 1 & went out on the balcony, being loudly cheered. The Pce. & Pss. [of Prussia] were quite delighted & impressed. That *we* felt happy & thankful,—I need not say,— proud of all that had passed & of my beloved one's success. Dearest Albert's name is for ever immortalised & the absurd reports of dangers of every kind & sort, set about by a set of people,—the "soi-disant" fashionables & the most violent protectionists—are silenced. It is therefore doubly satisfactory that all should have gone off so well, & without the slightest accident or mishap. Phipps & Col Seymour spoke to me with such pride & joy, at my beloved one's success & vindication after so much opposition & such difficulties, which no one, but *he* with his good temper, patience, firmness & energy could have achieved. Without these qualities his high position alone, could not have carried him through.'

The original Crystal Palace which the royal party saw before them on that May morning was a gigantic glass house 1,851 feet in length from east to west and 408 feet from north to south, four times the area of St Peter's in Rome. The ground floor was 24 feet high, surmounted by a first storey of 20 feet in height which ran the whole length but was 264 feet in width. This in turn was crowned with a second storey 20 feet in height rising in three tiers like an immense Babylonian ziggurat. The feature of the building best remembered was a 'transept' 120 feet wide which ran across the building, roofed by a semi-circular vault which raised the height to over 100 feet. The framework of the building was light blue picked out with orange and scarlet, and the successive storeys were adorned with flags of all nations.

The morning had been dull, with even a little rain, but as the royal party entered the sun broke through, the 'Queen's weather', proverbially lucky, set in and the whole building glittered in sunlight. Before the Marquess of Breadalbane declared the Exhibition open on the Queen's behalf, she had assumed her royal robes and ascended the throne erected at the northern end of the great transept, while Prince Albert joined the Commissioners, subsequently reporting to her the gradual achievement of the Exhibition and handing her the catalogue, while the Queen's attendants, about fifty in all, grouped themselves under the elm tree in the transept. Before the Queen's procession withdrew, the Hallelujah Chorus was sung by the united choirs of the Chapel Royal, St Paul's Cathedral, Westminster Abbey and St George's Chapel, Windsor Castle, but far from being overpowering so vast was the building that the effect seemed distant and almost faint.[25]

The enormous size of the building struck contemporary commentators more than any other feature. Nothing like this vast glittering structure, dazzling, glowing with colour, had ever been seen before. National pride gloried in success. Britain had been industrialised before other countries, now she led the world in machinery and mechanical invention. She retained from the previous century some of her supremacy in the arts— Minton china, for instance, Crown Derby, silver, painting. She ruled an Empire with sincere faith that she ruled for its good. More than six million persons visited the Great Exhibition between 1st May and the closing date, 15th October 1851. 'The whole period of the Great Exhibition will be remembered with wonder and admiration by all . . . enormous excursion trains daily poured their thousands. . . . Throughout the season there was more of unrestrained and genuine friendship . . . than has ever been known. It was like a gigantic picnic . . . large numbers of work people received holidays for the purpose . . . 800 agricultural labourers in their peasant's attire from Surrey and Sussex [were] conducted by their clergy at a cost of two and twopence each person, numerous firms from the North sent their people . . . an agricultural implement maker in Suffolk sent his people in two hired vessels provided with sleeping berths, cooking apparatus and every comfort . . . which were drawn up to a wharf in Westminster.'[26] For the Prince it was an apotheosis, he was vindicated, applauded, admired. The Queen was in ecstasies, visiting the Exhibition several times a week. She noted in her Journal on 17th June 1851 there had been 67,800 attendances on that day and on the previous day 65,000.[27] 'It is wonderful!'

For a large mass of the people the Exhibition was a revelation. Many had never seen a railway train before, machinery of any kind was a novelty and here Indian silks, black lace mantillas from Spain and intricate weaving machinery from France vied for attention with naval architecture and japanned trays. The Koh-i-noor diamond was on view. Groups of statuary, as well as single figures, all but nude in the classical style, attracted gaping wonder. 'It was such a time' wrote the Queen in her Journal on 18th July 1851 'of pleasure, of pride, of satisfaction & of deep thankfulness, it is the triumph of peace & goodwill towards all,—of art, of commerce,—of my beloved Husband—& of triumph for my country. To see this wonderful Exhibition which has pleased *everyone* looked upon as dearest Albert's work, this has, & does make me happy. . . .'[28]

On 15th October 1851 the Exhibition formally closed and it was estimated that £150,000 to £200,000 would be left as surplus. In a memorandum[29] the Prince drew attention to the fact that some plan for using it must be made. One scheme suggested that the Crystal Palace should be purchased and maintained in Hyde Park as a winter garden for the use of the public. The Prince pointed out that the object of the Exhibition had been the promotion of every branch of human industry, and the promotion of kindly feelings by the nations to each other 'by the practical advantages which may be derived by each from the labours and achievements of the others'. A 'lounging place' for the public in Hyde Park did not fulfil the objects even though the suggestion was made that the Crystal Palace should also be a museum of antiquities. 'Our connexion with the building has been . . . merely as a covering to our collection and ceases with the dispersion of the latter and therefore even if we were not bound by legal contracts to remove the building on a specified day, we the Commissioners have not the power to divert any part of the surplus towards providing the English public with a place of recreation.' 'If *I* am asked what *I* would do with the surplus, I would propose the following scheme; I am assured that between 25–30 acres of ground, nearly opposite the Crystal Palace on the other side of the Kensington Road, called Kensington Gore . . . are to be purchased at this moment for about £50,000. I would buy that ground & place on it four Institutions, corresponding to the 4 great sections of the Exhibition, Raw materials, Machinery, Manufactures and Plaster [Plastic?] Art. I would devote these Institutions to the furtherance of the industrial pursuits of all nations in these 4 divisions.' The Prince considered 'progress is to be obtained in human knowledge, (1) by personal study from books, (2) oral communication of knowledge to those who wish to acquire it, (3) ocular observation, comparison and demonstration, (4) exchange of ideas by *personal discussion*. The Prince proposes to provide each institution with opportunities for each of these also, (1) a library and rooms for study, (2) lecture rooms, (3) an acre of glass for exhibitions, (4) rooms for conversations and discussions [in fact a university].'

On 30th September Mr Cole suggested moving the Crystal Palace to Battersea Park, now in course of being planned, and putting it to a slightly less academic use than the Prince suggested.[30] 'A sheltered promenade and rendezvous for large meetings, may be rendered attractive and instructive with plants, flowers and sculpture.' The building was to be named 'Great Exhibition of the Works of Industry of all Nations 1851. President His Royal Highness Prince Albert K.G. etc. etc.' and Mr Cole calculated 6 per cent could be paid on a capital of £500,000.

However, on 10th June 1852, Mr Disraeli, now Chancellor of the Exchequer, informed the Prince that he had obtained the consent of the Governor of the Bank of England to an advance of £150,000 (subsequently modified to £110,000 as the larger sum would have caused delay), for the purchase of land adjoining Hyde Park, a further £120,000 being provided from the surplus funds from the Exhibition. Mr Cubitt on 7th August 1852 anticipated that the purchase of the land would be arranged in about a month and on 6th December 1852 Mr Disraeli reported that the vote for the purchase of the land, as suggested by the Prince, at Kensington Gore, had been carried unanimously by Parliament that evening.[31]

The Prince's educational scheme, supported by Mr Gladstone, was carried through with modifications, and a group of colleges and museums now occupies the land in South Kensington bought with the money made by the Great Exhibition, including the Imperial College, the City and Guilds College of Engineering and the Royal College of Music. The Natural History Museum contains the collections originally in the British Museum at Bloomsbury and has more recently added the exhibits from the Geological Museum in Jermyn Street; the Science Museum dates in its present form from 1912 and in addition to being available to scientists, enjoys popularity with youthful visitors. It contains Stephenson's 'Rocket' and the first jet engine designed by Sir Frank Whittle.

The Crystal Palace building itself was bought by the London Brighton and South Coast Railway for £70,000, and the transaction completed in May 1852.[32] The building was taken to Sydenham and re-erected there, with the alteration of a barrel roof and the addition of ornamental courts.

To handle the traffic, a down line was laid from London Bridge, with a branch to the Palace grounds, and in 1864 a further connection was opened by the London Chatham and Dover Company to handle traffic from the metropolis with access to King's Cross.

On its new site the Crystal Palace was a success and remained at Sydenham, one of the sights of London until it was destroyed by fire in 1936.

The Victoria and Albert Museum was originally opened in 1857 under the title of the South Kensington Museum and was founded on the collections from Somerset House with the addition of objects from the Great Exhibition bought with £5,000 voted by Parliament 'to be selected without reference to styles but entirely for the excellence of their workmanship'. In 1899 the foundation stone of the present museum was laid by Queen Victoria—her last appearance at a public ceremony—and ten years later, on 26th June 1909, the 'Victoria and Albert' was opened by King Edward VII, and has progressed from strength to strength.[33]

The Great Exhibition, entailing a mountain of detail work, had imposed a strain on the Prince's health. Conscientious to a fault, he fretted over trifles, his digestion was weak and he was subject to 'attacks' in his stomach. On 10th October 1851, just before the Exhibition closed, the Queen mentions in her Journal that the Prince was 'unwell' from 1 a.m. throughout the night.[34] He was living in a state of over-fatigue, concealed by what Sir Robert Peel had described as his 'extraordinary powers of self control', but wearing himself out. Sir Robert told Lord Kingsdown he had never seen the Prince's temper disturbed, though 'very often tried' and he was always ready to listen to 'any suggestions, though against his own opinions'.[35] But he was not robust, and during 1850 and 1851 he was hard pressed, by the struggle with Palmerston, the labour entailed by the Great Exhibition and, besides these, by a national 'religious ferment' involving an explosive issue—the relations of the Church of England and the Church of Rome.

The years of the 1848 period were a time of intense religious feeling in England. They were the years of the Oxford Movement, headed by such men as Newman, Keble, Pusey and W. G. Ward, the 'Tractarians', who set out to achieve the sorely needed reform and revitalising of the Church of England. In 1845 Newman's conscience impelled him to leave the Church of England and join the Church of Rome: a considerable number of conversions from the Church of England to the Church of Rome followed, especially in the upper classes of society. Members of the Oxford Movement, for instance Dr Pusey, used practices such as confession not usually associated with Protestantism, and the Oxford Movement and the clergy connected with it came under suspicion of Romanism.

Religious feeling at the time was of an intensity unknown in the Church of England for more than a century, and manifested itself in an interest in doctrinal and ecclesiastical matters. Two proposed appointments aroused especially violent opposition: that of Dr Hampden, late Professor of Divinity at Oxford and a pioneer in Biblical criticism, to the Bishopric of Hereford, and that of the Rev Mr Gorham to the living of Brampford Speke, in Devon.

Dr Hampden was alleged to hold the church authority to be fallible and inferior to the infallibility of the Bible; Mr Gorham, an elderly and scholarly botanist, who wished to end his days in rural peace, was refused induction into the living of Brampford Speke on the ground that he held Calvinistic views on baptismal regeneration.

Feeling on both controversies ran high. On the case of Dr Hampden, more than thirty books were written; on the case of Mr Gorham, more than fifty, and torrents of ink were poured out in the columns of the daily newspapers. Dr Hampden, after being opposed by the Dean of Hereford, was confirmed in his bishopric by the Chapter of Hereford and instituted on 28th March 1848.

The case of Mr Gorham and the living of Brampford Speke, worth £216 annually, created even greater controversy. The action was fought out first in the Court of Arches, the Ecclesiastical Court, and then, after Dr Phillpotts, the unpopular Bishop of Exeter, had refused to induct Mr Gorham, by an appeal to the Privy Council. On 8th March 1850 judgment was given at the Privy Council Office. Greville, as Clerk to the Privy Council, was present. 'The crowd was enormous, the crush and squeeze awful' he wrote. He saw Cardinal Wiseman, 'a smooth, oily, agreeable Priest', and Baron de Bunsen, the evangelical Prussian Ambassador, 'sitting cheek by jowl, probably the antipodes of theological opinions'.[36] Judgment was given in Mr Gorham's favour and he was inducted into the living in August 1851 after an action which had lasted for more than two and a half years. A subscription was raised to pay his costs and enough came in to enable him to buy a silver tea set as well.

These events, the success of the Oxford Movement and the number of converts from the Protestant to the Roman Catholic Church, were supported by the arrival of hordes of immigrants pouring over, by tens of thousands, from famine-stricken Ireland, almost without exception observing Catholics. At this period it was possible to cross from Ireland to England for 2s. 6d. or less and the religious plight of the Irish in Liverpool, Glasgow and the ports of South Wales was urgent. Influenced by these considerations, Pope Leo IX, on 24th September 1850, issued a Bull, without notifying the Queen or the British government, which divided England into a hierarchy of Bishops in place of the Vicars Apostolic who had exercised spiritual authority over Roman Catholics since the Reformation, appointed at the head of the new Bishops a Roman Archbishop of Westminster and used language which could not fail to provoke Protestant feeling in the country. He asserted amongst other pronouncements 'that every day the obstacles were falling off which stood in the way of the extension of the Catholic religion'. The Protestants exploded with fury and the Queen was extremely angry at what she termed 'an extraordinary proceeding of the Pope, who has issued a Bull, savouring of the times of Henry VIII's reign, or even earlier—restoring the Roman Catholic "Hierarchy", dividing this country publicly and openly into an Archbishopric and Bishoprics, saying that England was again restored to the number of Catholic Powers, & that her religious disgrace had been wiped out. He has appointed Dr Wiseman, whom he had elevated to the dignity of a Cardinal, to be metropolitan Archbishop of Westminster.'[37]

Cardinal Wiseman's first pastoral letter poured oil on the flames. 'The Cardinal has desired the Pope to be prayed for before me' wrote the Queen 'and the Bishop of Birmingham, Dr Ullathorne, has been publicly and pompously enthroned, Dr Newman, the head of the Oratorians, preaching the sermon! All this is inconceivable, & it is in the highest degree wrong of the Pope to act in such a manner, which is a *direct* infringement of my prerogative, without *one* word as to his instructions having been communicated to this Govt.'

The Queen was not intolerant; she had dearly loved Queen Louise, who was a devout Catholic. Her personal leanings were evangelical but she had not the anti-Catholic prejudices of the Prince. Her antipathy was directed towards the High Church 'Puseyite' party whom she described as 'snakes in the grass' and '. . . in fact the hidden Jesuits of this country. . . . I repeat the "priests" of the present day are *not* the clergymen of former times and it is from this *priestly domination* that I recoil with horror & against them that I protest in the name of Protestantism.'[38] The present crisis, she wrote, 'is, I fear, the result of such a number of our clergy having at the present time such a leaning towards the Romish Church, and shows how it is straining for power. It will, I fear, raise intolerant cries against innocent Roman Catholics, which I should deeply deplore and regret. I see that the clergy are addressing the Bishop of London, who has written a very proper reply, but I hope it may open the eyes of many who have gone too far towards the Church of Rome.'

Lord John Russell held strong Protestant views and agreed with his friend the Bishop of Durham in describing 'the late aggression of the Pope' as 'insolent and insidious'. He was also at one with the Queen in finding a danger more alarming than papal aggression in 'clergymen of our own church, who have subscribed the Thirty Nine articles and acknowledged in explicit terms the Queen's supremacy [and] have been most forward in leading their flocks step by step to the very verge of the precipice. . . . The honour paid to saints, the claim of infallibility for the Church, the superstitious use of the sign of the cross, the muttering of the liturgy so as to disguise the language in which it is written, the recommendation of auricular confession and the administration of penance and absolution—all these things are now pointed out by clergymen of the Church of England as worthy of adoption. . . . What then is the danger to be apprehended from a foreign prince of no great power compared with the danger within the gates from the unworthy sons of the Church of England herself?

'I have little hope that the propounders and framers of these innovations will desist from their insidious course. . . . But I will not bate a jot of heart or hope so long as the glorious principles and the immortal martyrs of the Reformation shall be held in reverence by the great mass of a nation which looks with contempt on the mummeries of superstition. . . .' Lord John concluded by stating that the Bishop of Durham had his full permission to publish the letter.[39]

The letter was received with a chorus of approbation, but even in the midst of overwhelming enthusiasm, whispers of dissatisfaction were heard. 'High Churchmen not unnaturally resented being called "the unworthy sons of the Church of England". Moderate Roman Catholics deplored the application of such a phrase as "the mummeries of superstition" to a service which they regarded as sacred.'

The 'No Popery hubbub', as Greville called it, ran its course furiously over the length and breadth of the kingdom and no possibility of a European war, no urgency of the political situation could compare with the interest it evoked. 'I view the whole of this from beginning to end and the conduct of all parties with unmixed dissatisfaction and regret' wrote Greville.[40] 'The Pope has been ill-advised and very impolitic, the whole proceeding on the part of the Papal Government has been mischievous and impertinent and deserves the severest censure. On the other hand the Protestant demonstration is to the last degree exaggerated and absurd. The danger is ludicrously magnified, the intention misunderstood, and the offence unduly magnified. 'A "No Popery" cry has been raised and the depths of theological hatred stirred up for most inadequate cause. . . . Clarendon writes me word that the effect it has produced in Ireland is not to be told. . . . Two days ago Bowyer came to me from Cardinal Wiseman . . . to ask my opinion whether anything could be done, and what. I said if he had sent to me some time ago and told me what was contemplated I might have done him some service by telling him what the consequences would be; but that now it was too late to do anything, John Bull had got the bit in his mouth, and the devil could not stop him.' To her aunt, the Duchess of Gloucester, who had sent a letter

323

congratulating her on the moderation of her reply, the Queen wrote[41] 'I would never have consented to say anything which breathed a spirit of intolerance. Sincerely Protestant as I always have been and always shall be, and indignant as I am at those who call themselves Protestants, while they are in fact quite the contrary. . . . I cannot bear to hear the violent abuse of the Catholic religion, which is so painful and so cruel towards the many good and innocent Roman Catholics. However we must hope and trust this excitement will soon cease. . . .'

When the Queen opened Parliament on 4th February 1851, though she never remembered such vast crowds or such enthusiasm, she was annoyed to hear shouts of 'No Popery' mingled with the cheers.[42] On their part the Protestants had to contend with the effect of Lord John Russell's letter which, instead of smoothing things over, 'filled with stupid and fanatical enthusiasm all the Protestant Bigots and stimulated their rage; and on the other [hand] it has irritated to madness all the zealous Catholics, and grieved, shocked and offended even the most moderate and reasonable'.[43]

In the first flush of excitement following Lord John's letter, the House had enthusiastically endorsed words which Lord John put into the Queen's mouth in her speech announcing a measure to resist 'the Pope's aggression' introduced as the Ecclesiastical Titles Bill on 7th February 1851.[44] The establishment of Roman Catholic sees was prohibited and the forfeiture to the Crown of money willed to persons holding prohibited titles was re-affirmed and stimulated.

The Prince was anti-Catholic but he wished for moderation. He foresaw the alarming results further controversy was bound to produce and pressed the government to postpone its Ecclesiastical Titles Bill, first making an effort to persuade the Pope to revoke his late Bull, but the hostility of the Protestants had been raised to extraordinary heights and nothing but the revocation of the Bull would allay it. The Prince understood that Bulls which had no reference to doctrine had more than once been withdrawn in other countries. It would be very difficult, in the present state of public feeling, to protect Roman Catholics from further restrictions, if the Bull was persevered in. The Prince was insistent that the Pope should be impressed that the British government was well-meaning and kindly disposed towards Catholics 'but no negotiations could be entered into; if by some indiscretion it should transpire that the British government was "tampering" with Rome, public indignation would be intense. . . .'[45]

Since the Catholic powers were hostile to Britain, and France was, in the Prince's opinion, 'not to be trusted in any way', the Prince suggested that a letter from King Leopold of the Belgians to the Pope might be 'a desirable auxiliary'. King Leopold, it will be recollected, though married to a devout Roman Catholic, had remained a Lutheran. Lord John disappointed the Prince by refusing to delay the Ecclesiastical Titles Bill, which passed by a majority of 217 on 4th July 1851,[46] but proved a source of continual internal difficulty. The followers of Sir Robert Peel, including Mr Gladstone, Lord Aberdeen and Sir James Graham, agreed in their dislike of penal measures of any kind aimed at the Catholic Church which they considered would make Ireland ungovernable, and they therefore would not unite with the Russellite Whigs. The Duke of Wellington was consulted and gave as his opinion that the Papal Aggression Bill . . . might be modified, but that a Bill must be persevered in and the government of Lord John Russell should continue. Substantial modifications were made, clauses dealing with the introduction of Papal bulls and the confiscation of money willed to persons holding prohibited titles were dropped. The Bill received the Royal Assent on 29th July 1851 but it was never enforced and, to the Queen's satisfaction, was repealed in 1871.[47]

On 14th September 1852 the Duke of Wellington died. The Queen, who was at Balmoral with the Prince, was startled to receive the news by telegram on 16th September, quoting a newspaper report, and refused to believe it. 'Would to God that *we* had been right' she wrote in her Journal.[48] That afternoon she and the Prince were making an expedition when she missed her watch which the Duke had given her and sent a ghillie back to see if she had left it behind. He returned with the watch and letters including one from Lord Derby. 'Alas!' wrote the Queen, 'it contained the confirmation of the fatal news, that Britain's pride, her glory, her hero, one of the greatest men she ever produced, was *no more*! What a great & irreparable loss! Ld. Derby enclosed a few lines from Ld. Charles Wellesley saying that his dear Father had died . . . after a few hours illness & no suffering, God's will be done! The day must have come, & the Duke was 83. . . . One cannot think of this country *without* "*the Duke*", our immortal hero! In him centered almost every earthly honour a subject could possess, his position was the highest a subject ever had, above all Party—looked up to by all,—revered by the whole nation, the trusted friend of the Sovereign! And how simply he carried these honours! By what singleness of purpose, what straightforwardness, what courage, were all the motives of his actions guided. The Crown *never* possessed, & I fear never will again, such a loyal, faithful subject, & such a *staunch* supporter. To us . . . his loss will be quite irreparable. . . . There will be few dry eyes in the country,—We hastened home on foot . . . A gloom cast over everything! Albert dreadfully sad at the news.'

The death of the Duke evoked unexampled national grief. Even 'Grumpy' Greville was devoted to him and wrote 'In spite of some foibles and faults, he was, beyond all doubt, a very great man—the only great man

325

of the present time—the Crown never possessed a more faithful, devoted and disinterested subject. Without personal attachment to any of the Monarchs whom he served, and fully understanding and appreciating their individual merits and demerits, he alike reverenced their great office in the persons of each of them, and would at any time have sacrificed his ease, his fortune or his life to serve the Sovereign and the State. . . . His position was eminently singular and exceptional, something between the Royal Family and other subjects. He was treated with greater respect than any individual not of Royal birth, and the whole Royal Family admitted him to a peculiar and exclusive familiarity and intimacy in their intercourse with him, which, while he took it in the easiest manner, and as if naturally due to him, he never abused or presumed upon. . . . Upon every occasion of difficulty, public or private, he was always appealed to. . . . He held popularity in great contempt, and never seemed touched or pleased at the manifestations of popular admiration and attachment of which he was the object. Whenever he appeared in public, he was always surrounded by crowds of people, and when he walked abroad everybody who met him saluted him; but he never seemed to notice the curiosity or the civilities which his presence elicited.'[49]

To British troops he was a legend and more than three-quarters of a century after his death men in the ranks were still using the phrase, 'It wouldn't have done for the Duke.'

The body of the Duke was brought from Walmer Castle, to lie in state in the Hall of Chelsea Hospital from 11th to 17th November 1852. So great was the crowd, that on 13th November, the first day the public were admitted, two women and a man were crushed to death.

The day of the Duke's funeral, 18th November 1852, was cold, windy and wet and the tens of thousands who had waited all night in the rain were drenched. 'It was impossible to convey any idea of the emotion felt by the nation, nothing like it had ever been manifested before' wrote *The Times*.[50] The lying-in-state of the Duke's body ended at 5 p.m. on 17th November and during that day 65,073 persons filed past. Stands to view the procession were finished during the night by the light of flares.

At 7.45 a.m. on the 18th, 17 minute guns were fired in the Park to signal the start of the procession, watched by the Queen from the balcony of Buckingham Palace, and the great bell of St Paul's Cathedral began to toll. The cortège was led by six battalions of infantry, including the Rifle Brigade and regiments of the Brigade of Guards, marching in slow step to bands with muffled drums, playing funeral marches, most frequently the Dead March in *Saul*. The long roll of muffled drums with which that march opens moved the Queen unbearably, her eyes overflowed with tears; few eyes, she observed, were not wet. Five squadrons of cavalry followed and further foot guards brought up the rear, their band, too, playing the Dead March in *Saul* and their arms reversed. Fortunately the weather had now cleared. At Charing Cross the procession was joined by 83 Chelsea pensioners and representatives of the East India Company's Army accompanied by thirteen trumpets and a kettle drum. The Queen noted in her Journal the melancholy effect produced by the succession of bands. The Guidon (standard) and the Banner of Wellesley, carried by mounted army officers, were succeeded by a large number of deputations from public bodies in carriages, by Prince Albert in a coach drawn by six horses, followed by foreign military officers of high rank. The Queen was much incensed that Austria refused to send any representative on the grounds of the treatment of General Haynau. She observed the true reason was Austrian fear of displeasing France.

Meanwhile the vast funeral car, largely designed by the Prince, had met with trouble. This gigantic vehicle, 27 feet long, 10 feet broad, 17 feet high, weighed between ten and eleven tons, and was made to a considerable extent of bronze. Lions projected from the bosses of the wheels, figures of victory formed the flanges, 'playfully interposed' with dolphins; on each side of the car was a list of the Duke's many victories decorated with swords sheathed and wreathed in laurel; a 'magnificent' bronze casting of the Duke's arms stood in front of the car. The coffin itself, covered with a silver pall, stood on a bier richly gilt. Twelve horses, chosen for their size and strength, were needed to get the huge car in motion. Owing to their voluminous sable trappings they were thought to look like black elephants. Nevertheless, owing to the night's rain, opposite the Duke of York's column the car became embedded in mud. The delay while a force of police extricated it was the only mishap though the car was thought to look dangerously top-heavy. As it passed all men removed their hats. Garter King of Arms followed the car. Behind him came the Duke's horse, led by a groom, and next the Queen's carriage, empty according to custom, succeeded by the carriages of the Duchesses of Kent, Gloucester and Cambridge and followed by a representative of every regiment in the British Army.

At Temple Bar, which marks the limits of the jurisdiction of the Lord Mayor of London and within which his authority equals if not transcends that of the Queen, the procession was joined by the Lord Mayor, bearing the City Sword, the City Recorder and their suites. At the door of St Paul's Cathedral the bands became silent, all civilians uncovered and only the tolling of the bell was heard.

The Duke's coffin was received by the Bishop of London and the Dean and Prebendaries of St Paul's, with other ecclesiasticals. Inside the cathedral 18,000 persons waited. The Duke's insignia followed, his spurs borne on a cushion by York Herald, his helmet and crest by Richmond Herald, his sword and target by Leicester Herald, his surcoat by Chester

Herald, his coronet by Clarenceux King of Arms, his Duke's baton by the Marquess of Anglesey, supported by the Duke of Richmond. The baton was placed on the coffin. At the close of the burial service the Duke's titles and styles were recited by Garter King of Arms; when the long list had finished the Duke's Comptroller broke his staff of office into pieces and Garter King of Arms placed the pieces in the grave. At that moment the Tower guns fired to signal the ceremony was completed, the Great Bell of St Paul's stopped tolling and civilians replaced their hats. The great Duke had gone.

*

The last three years had been years of strain for the Queen. She had been deeply concerned at the damaging effect which his overwork on the Great Exhibition had had on the Prince's health. It was alarming to contrast the beautiful, elegant youth he had been in 1840 with the paunchy, balding, prematurely middle-aged man of 1851, though the Queen, blinded by love, did not notice the disappearance of his good looks. The death of the Duke of Wellington shook her nerves. One by one, the props of her younger life were disappearing. Lord Melbourne, Sir Robert Peel, Lord Liverpool, now the Duke.

On 7th April 1853 the Queen's fourth son and eighth child, Prince Leopold, was born. For the first time the Queen had chloroform, 'that blessed chloroform', administered by the well-known anaesthetist Dr John Snow. '. . . The effect' wrote the Queen in her Journal for 22nd April 1853 'was soothing, quieting and delightful beyond measure.'[51] Dr Snow was a remarkable man; his attention had been arrested by ether when it was first adopted in America in 1846, and he became so skilful in the technique of its administration that nearly all the practice in London came into his hands. He then turned his attention to the technique of administering other anaesthetising drugs, especially chloroform. He has a claim to fame in the fact that he was responsible for the discovery that cholera is transmitted by a contaminated water supply.

In spite of the ameliorating effect of chloroform, the Queen's nerves were upset. She dreaded child-bearing and resented it, she was capable of feeling something approaching rage against the Prince because he was a man and exempt from this duty. At the same time she adored him. Of his love for her there is no doubt; she was precious to him, she gave him the affection he needed, and needed none the less because he found his need difficult to express. It was her nature to be the one who gave the kiss, his nature to turn the cheek and receive it, but the kiss was not less important to him because their natures differed.

After the birth of Prince Leopold, the Queen told King Leopold, his great-uncle after whom the new baby was named, that she had never been so well and that the child was 'a jolly fat little fellow, but *no* beauty'.

For the first few weeks of his life little Prince Leopold seemed to flourish, but he was in fact extremely fragile, a victim of the incurable disease of haemophilia, and a constant anxiety to his parents. He lived, however, until he was 31, long enough to grow up and marry.

Within days of his birth, however, the Queen's mood changed; she underwent a nervous hysterical crisis and made a series of scenes. Early on 2nd May 1853[52] the Prince wrote her a soothing letter: 'Dear Child. I have read your letter over several times. . . . Now it will be right to consider calmly the facts of the case. The *whole* offence which led to a continuance of hysterics for more than an hour, and the traces of which have remained for more than 24 hours more, was: that I complained of your turning several times from inattention the wrong leaves in a Book which was to be marked by us as a Register & test the completeness of a collection of Prints. This miserable trifle produced the distressing scene. In which, in case I am accused of making things worse by my false method of treatment, I admit that my treatment has on this occasion as on former ones signally failed, but I know of no other. I either try to demonstrate the groundlessness and injustice of the accusations which are brought against me, then I increase your distress . . . you undervalue your own capacity & are unnecessarily diffident on that account. I never intend or wish to offend you. . . . If you are violent I have no other choice but to leave you . . . I leave the room and retire to my own room in order to give you time to recover yourself, then you follow me to renew the dispute and to have it *all out*. . . . Now don't believe that I do not sincerely and deeply pity you for the sufferings you undergo, or that I deny you do suffer really very much, I merely deny that I am the *cause* of them, though I have unfortunately often been the *occasion*. . . . I am often astonished at the effect which a hasty word of mine has produced. . . . In fact in your candid way you generally explain later what was the real cause of your complaint. . . . It appears now that the apprehension, that you might be made answerable for the suffering, perhaps the loss of health, of the Baby (occasioned by the milk of the Wet nurse not agreeing on account of your having frequently expressed a wish to have a Nurse from the Highlands of Scotland) was the real *cause* of your distress which broke out on the occasion of the Registration of the prints. . . . Your letter now contains a hint about something concerning Stockmar which you have treasured up!'

The scenes continued at intervals over several years, embittering the life of the Queen and the Prince. On 9th February 1855[53] the Prince, imploring her to be reasonable, asked her 'What are you really afraid of in me? What can I do to you, save, at the most, not listen to you long enough when I have business elsewhere. . . . So be comforted and keep cheerful, and show a *little* confidence in me.'

Later in the year and in 1856 the Queen's nerves improved and she had several periods of tranquillity, 'four weeks of unbroken success in the hard struggle for self-control'.[54] The Prince congratulated her readily. He admitted she was right in accusing him of not saying much, but 'that does not mean that I have realised any the less how unselfishly you have behaved. . . . It is indeed a pity that you find no consolation in the company of your children. The root of the trouble lies in the mistaken notion that, the function of a mother is to be always correcting, scolding, ordering them about and organising their activities. It is not possible to be on happy friendly terms with people you have just been scolding.'[55]

A few weeks later tranquillity had passed and the situation was as bad as ever. On 5th November 1856[56] the Prince wrote 'Dear Child. I have read your letter and am answering it because you ask me to do so, but I really don't know what I am to say ? . . . I don't yet know why my question while we were slowly and quietly reading the Princess's letter [the Princess of Prussia], "What makes you so bitter ?", produced such an outburst. It is my duty to keep calm, and I mean to do so, but unkindness or ingratitude towards others makes me angry like any other kind of immorality. Fritz is prepared to devote his whole life to your child [the Princess Royal was now betrothed to the son of the Prince of Prussia]—whom you are thankful to be rid of—and because of that you turn against him! Stockmar, who had shown us nothing but kindness for as long as we can remember, is suddenly asked, old and ill as he is, to drag himself over here. . . . This is not a question of bickering, but of attitudes of mind which will agree as little as oil and water and it is no wonder that our conversations on the subject cannot end harmoniously. I am trying to keep out of your way until your better feelings have returned and you have regained control of yourself.'

The Queen, the Prince told her, made a parade of her suffering before his eyes as much as to say 'See, this is all *your* work' which was not calculated to encourage him 'in any move towards reconciliation'. 'Neither will I play the part of Greatheart and *forgive*, that is not at all how I feel, but I am ready to ignore all that has happened and take a new departure, as the sailors say (although I shall probably be accused of being unfeeling) and try in future to avoid everything which might make your unhappy state of mind worse. *Cure* it I cannot, you alone can do that. . . .' 'Good! Let Vicky have her meals by herself. I, too, think it would have been better if you had allowed yourself the distraction of company. However, as it can no longer be so, we must make the best of it.'[57] 'I am only sorry that the week here, which was intended to make you stronger and better able to face what the coming weeks may bring, has been wasted.'[58] The Queen was in the final months of pregnancy before the birth of Princess Beatrice, her ninth and last child. Princess Beatrice was born on 14th

April 1857, and Dr Snow again administered chloroform. 'I, like everyone else in the house,' wrote the Prince, 'make the most ample allowance for your state. . . . We cannot, unhappily, bear your bodily sufferings for you—you must struggle with them alone—the moral ones are probably caused by them, but if you were rather less occupied with yourself and your feelings . . . and took more interest in the outside world, you would find that the greatest help of all. . . .'

The Queen did not find this letter satisfactory and the Prince wrote again in order to 'calm' her.[59] He had no intention whatsoever of questioning her maternal authority with the children. He had not realised the extent to which her nerves were shaken, he promised in future never even to express a difference of opinion until she was better.

'As regards your condition I cannot, unfortunately, help you. You must fight it out for yourself with God's help. Trust in his wisdom and goodness should lift you above the feelings of degradation, indignation etc. etc. which you describe. That relationship is sacred, in spite of the pains and trials which women have to suffer. My love and sympathy are limitless and inexhaustible.'

It would not be true to convey the impression that painful scenes with the Queen were continuous—the Prince's letters cover eight years. Nor is it true that her emotional outbursts were solely the result of her pregnancies. Two years after the birth of Princess Beatrice, on 12th October 1859,[60] the Prince writes at Balmoral that he wants 'to tell you how glad I am that you have felt so well and happy here. I have noticed with delight your efforts to be unselfish, kind and sociable, and your success is in no small degree responsible for your contentment. It cannot fail to be so. . . .'

Peace and tranquillity did not endure. The Prince's next letter, undated, is written in sadness: 'You have again lost your self-control quite unnecessarily. I did not say a word which could wound you, and I did not begin the conversation, but you have followed me about and continued it from room to room. There is no need for me to promise to *trust* you, for it was not a question of trust, but of your fidgety nature, which makes you insist on entering, with feverish eagerness, into details about orders and wishes which, in the case of a Queen, are commands, to whomever they may be given. This is your nature; it is not against Vicky, but is the same with everyone and has been the cause of much unpleasantness for you. It is the dearest wish of my heart to save you from these and worse consequences, but the only result of my efforts is that I am accused of want of feeling, hard heartedness, injustice, hatred, jealousy, distrust etc. etc. I do my duty towards you even though it means that life is embittered by "scenes", when it should be governed by love and harmony. I look upon this with patience as a test which has to be undergone, but you hurt me desperately and at the same time do not help yourself.' This letter is followed by one, also undated, testifying that things have gone much better during the last two years.[61]

The Queen and the Prince were not unhappy together. They were devoted to each other; the Prince's letters to the Queen are repeatedly written in the language of a lover, he longs for her physical presence, he is counting the hours until he will be in her embrace.

In January 1862 the Queen described her life with the Prince in detail.[62]

'I will now describe our life in the most minute and detailed manner I can.' At 7 a.m. the wardrobe maid came in and opened the shutters and generally also the window. Almost always the Prince got up then. He slept in long white drawers, which enclosed his feet as well as his legs, like the sleeping suits worn by small babies.

'He then went to his room—sitting room, where in the winter a fire was made & his green German lamp lit, he brought the original one from Germany, & we always have 2 on our 2 tables which everywhere stand side by side in my room (& shall ever do so) & wrote letters, read etc. & at a little after 8, sometimes a little sooner or later, he came in to tell me to get up, "Es ist zeit, stehe auf!" and constantly he brought me in his letters (English ones) to read thro': "Lese recht aufmerksam, & sage wenn irgend ein Fehler da ist" & so I did. . . . Also drafts of answers & letters to the Ministers (all of which are preserved as most precious & invaluable documents, in those invaluable books of political & family events which he compiled so beautifully). . . . He used to write quite a short diary in a little book, a "remembrancer", with the days printed on the leaves into which he entered his letters. . . . Formerly he used to be ready frequently before me . . . & he would either stop in my sitting room next door to read some of the endless numbers of despatches which I placed on his side (on H.R.H.'s) having either read them or looked into them before & turned the label.' A foolish despatch or draft upset his stomach. 'If he was *not* ready—Baby [Princess Beatrice] generally went into his dressing room (oh! that poor dear dressing room so full of *dear* & *sad* recollections) & stopped with him till he followed with her at his hand coming along the passage with his dear heavenly face. . . . Poor darling little Beatrice used to be so delighted to see him dress & when she arrived and he was dressed she made dearest Albert laugh so, by saying "What a pity"!'

Perhaps because she was the youngest and not nervous of her parents, Princess Beatrice enjoyed greater freedom than her brothers and sisters in her relations with them. A story is related of her lunching with the Queen when a rich iced pudding appeared.

'Baby must not have any of that, it is not good for Baby,' said the Queen.

'But Baby likes it, my dear,' rejoined the little Princess.

The Prince 'went out shooting three or four times a week, hunted once a week, wore a green coat with gold buttons, white breeches and high black boots and a cord in his hat. Walked very fast, worked eating his luncheon. Dr Jenner suggested he should eat less lunch, a little cold meat, a little sweet or fruit and a little more claret. This did good. . . .'

'When he went out shooting he always came in his shooting jacket or short coat, either black (latterly at Windsor on account of our deep mourning) or in one of Balmoral mixture, & thick or thin according to what the weather might be, checked or other trousers & always wore straps to them which made him look so nice and gentlemanlike. . . . He never went out or came home without coming thro' my room or into my dressing room—dear, dear Angel with a smile on his dearest beautiful face . . . & I treasured up everything I heard, kept every letter in a box to tell & show him, & was always so vexed & nervous if I had any foolish draft or despatch to show him, as I knew it would distress & irritate him and affect his poor dear stomach. . . .

'My Angel always wore the blue ribbon of the garter under his waistcoat which looked so nice. At breakfast & luncheon & also our family dinners he sat at the top of the table & kept us all enlivened by his interesting conversation, his charming anecdotes & funny stories of his childhood & people at Coburg—of our good people in Scotland & endless amusing stories which would make him laugh so heartily & which he repeated with the most wonderful mimicry. . . . One of the children, or a visitor like Feodore, Marie L[einingen], or others who sometimes came to us, sat between me and him & one of the younger children whom he constantly kept in order if they ate badly or untidily. . . . He could *not* bear bad manners & always dealt out his dear reprimands to the juveniles & a word from him was instantly obeyed. . . .' He always played Mendelssohn every evening on the piano before dinner, arrangements as well as solos; among other favourites were Beethoven's Egmont and Leonora No. 1. In winter the Prince played hockey on the ice and all the children skated. Birthdays were celebrated by a festive breakfast, new clothes and dancing in the evening. There was also dancing on New Year's Eve when 'Hands across the middle' and 'Pousette' were always danced by the Prince. The two dearest to her, wrote the Queen, the Prince and her mother, brought the fashion for Christmas trees from Coburg and 'it has been adopted ever since'.

Returning from Windsor to London, the Prince and the Queen went by Great Western Railway, taking the two eldest children and often the youngest with them as a treat. The Queen now went to London with regret, she shrank from the 'snobs' of the Court to the safety and security of her family. Albert was all in all to her, Albert with his beautiful face,

333

Albert looking enchanting in shooting clothes, Albert wearing the Garter with elegance, Albert playing Mendelssohn, Albert skating, riding, with the children, Albert, Albert, Albert.

There was one blot on her domestic happiness, the want of progress of the Prince of Wales. He was, there was no disguising the fact, backward. At 3 years old he was 'not articulate like his sister, but rather babyish in accent. He understands a little French and says a few words, but is altogether backward in language ... most exemplary in politeness and manner, bows and offers his hand beautifully, besides saluting à la militaire—all unbidden. He is very handsome, but still very small in every way.'[62] He was a difficult and troublesome child to teach. 'He ... requires much patience, from wilful inattention and incessant interruptions, getting under the table, upsetting the books, and sundry other *anti-studious* practices.'[63] The Prince was then only 4 years old. Two years later Lady Lyttelton wrote in the report which she sent to the Queen[64] that the continued want of progress of the Prince of Wales was the 'greatest distress' to his governess Mlle Hollande. 'No effort shall be spared to improve him'; now winter was coming hours of work could be lengthened. The Prince was doing lessons out of the same book as Princess Alice 'and Your Majesty knows Her Royal Highness is neither studious nor, certainly so clever as the Princess Royal'. Prince Albert considered that the Prince of Wales should learn his catechism at 8 years old, but he was too backward to begin.[65] Some realisation of the mistakes being made in attempting to force learning on the Prince did strike the Queen and on 8th September 1847, when the Prince was not quite 6, Lady Lyttelton promised the Queen 'he shall not be overworked as long as I have my senses at all about me'.[66]

Stockmar had reported adversely on the plan for the Prince of Wales' education when Prince Albert and the Queen first framed it and what he had predicted was now coming to pass. The Prince of Wales, called Bertie in his family, was being subjected to overwhelming pressure and exhibiting the classic responses, fits of rage, insolence, destructiveness, refusal to learn, disobedience. Every day was divided into hourly or half-hourly periods totalling five hours. Lessons were seldom if ever discontinued entirely; when the Prince of Wales and the Princess Royal went with their parents to Ireland in 1849 lessons went on. Naturally affectionate, the Prince of Wales was particularly devoted to his sister, the Princess Royal, in spite of the fact that she was intellectually his superior, and he was anxious to earn his parents' praise. But he could not endure chaff or play at any game or attempt anything new or difficult without losing his temper. His tutor Mr Henry Birch[67] thought it wisest to ignore the Prince of Wales' 'dislike of chaff' and treat him exactly as he had treated his pupils at Eton, where he had been a master; at the same time he thought the Prince too isolated in his lessons and tried the experiment of uniting his education with that of Prince Alfred, which was a success. There was a 'marked improvement in his temper, disposition and behaviour . . . he is far less selfish, far less excitable, and in every way more amiable and teachable'.[68] Dislike of being 'chaffed' remained a characteristic of the Prince throughout his life, united with a strong, sometimes an excessive, sense of his personal dignity.

Before teaching boys at Eton, Mr Birch had been at King's College, Cambridge, where he took four University prizes. He began his duties as the Prince's tutor in April 1849 and told Stockmar later that for the first year, up to the Prince of Wales' 9th birthday, the Prince was in such a state that he despaired of ever being able to influence him, or do him any good. The Prince was highly excitable, and subject to fits of rage which left him too physically exhausted to be able to work '. . . indeed I felt it to be my duty to offer H.M. and H.R.H. to resign my post at once if they knew of anyone who would be more likely to succeed in the management of so young a child. Happily all this is changed—the boy is influenced by me just as my Eton pupils used to be, and in a way that I dared not expect, and I feel that I am very sincerely attached to him which for some time I could not feel.'[69]

There were other difficulties. Mr Birch found the Queen and the Prince expected him to devote every moment of his time to the Prince of Wales. Surely, Mr Birch asked Stockmar, it would be a good thing for him (Mr Birch) to have a little time to himself? Surely it would be a good thing for tutor and pupil to be occasionally apart, so that the tutor might rub off some of the ennui and morbid feelings which must result from being morning, noon and night in the company of a child, while the pupil should see other boys of his own age?[70]

Another obstacle was that Mr Birch had always meant to take orders as a clergyman; the Rectory of Prestwich, near Manchester, was being kept open for him until 1851 by Lord Wilton, and he also had expectations. He would inherit a considerable sum of money. His circumstances were therefore easy. Both the Queen and the Prince were opposed to Mr Birch taking orders while in charge of the Prince of Wales. The Queen was nervous of 'Puseyism'. Mr Birch must promise not to be 'aggressive' in religiousness; there must be no refusal to attend the services of the established Church of Scotland while at Balmoral, or to take part in innocent amusements, shooting, theatricals at Windsor, dances. She was assured that Mr Birch was 'plain straightforward Church of England'.[71]

Eventually Mr Birch remained with the Prince of Wales for more than two years, until the beginning of 1852, and the Prince became attached to him. 'I seem' wrote Mr Birch to Stockmar[72] 'to have found the Key to his heart, and for the last two months . . . he has been giving me much cause for satisfaction. ... Taking into consideration the nature and disposition evinced by the Prince of Wales, will a change of tutor within a year be good or bad for him? ... If his parents are dissatisfied with my treatment of him, as sometimes I have feared that they may be, and if they think that a fresh tutor would do the work better, well and good. ... If, on the contrary, they or you feel I can be of any service to the Prince of Wales by remaining with him beyond January 1852 I wish you would so far act out the part of a private friend as to tell me so.'

Baron Stockmar, however, showed Mr Birch's letter to the Queen and the Prince and the latter was very much annoyed.[73] He wrote that he was looking for a suitable successor at the end of the appointed period.

Lady Canning, one of the Queen's ladies-in-waiting, wrote of the departure of Mr Birch 'It has been a trouble and sorrow to the Prince of Wales who has done no end of touching things since he heard he was to lose him, three weeks ago. He is such an affectionate dear little fellow; his notes and presents which Mr Birch used to find on his pillow were really too moving.'

The successor chosen to Mr Birch was Frederick Waymouth Gibbs, a man of strong character and opinions. He had been recommended to Prince Albert, who was Chancellor of Cambridge University, by Sir James Stephen, Professor of Modern History at Cambridge, and grand-father of Virginia Woolf. Because his mother was hopelessly insane and his father financially ruined, Mr Gibbs had been brought up with Sir James Stephen's sons. His intellectual abilities won him a fellowship at Trinity College, Cambridge, and he had then been called to the Bar but achieved little success. Precise in manner and with a 'prim' bearing, Mr Gibbs became the inseparable companion of the Prince of Wales from the Prince's 10th until his 17th birthday.[74]

The Prince of Wales' natural sensitiveness and politeness were demon-strated in his first contact with Mr Gibbs. Mr Birch left on 20th January 1852, and next day the Prince of Wales and Prince Alfred went for a walk with Mr Gibbs. The Prince of Wales apologised for their depression. 'You cannot wonder if we are somewhat dull today. We are sorry Mr Birch has gone. It is very natural, is it not?'

Acting on orders from Prince Albert, Mr Gibbs extended the Prince of Wales' lessons to cover six- or seven-hourly periods between 8 a.m. and 6 p.m. six days a week. The Queen noticed when the Prince of Wales 'hangs his head and looks at his feet, invariably in a day or two he has one of his fits of unmanageable temper'.[75] Dr Becker, Prince Albert's librarian, was courageous enough to warn him that the Prince of Wales was being overtaxed and that overtaxing was responsible for his outbursts of 'blind destructive rage'—'the gusts of elemental fury "in which he takes every-thing at hand and throws it with the greatest violence against the wall or window, without thinking the least of the consequences of what he is doing; or he stands in the corner stamping with his legs and screaming in the most dreadful manner"'.[76] This behaviour is common in young children when overtired and frustrated—Princess Alice suffered from similar fits of rage as a baby[77]—and is normally outgrown as the child becomes articulate. But the Prince of Wales remained given to rages all his life, in spite of his charm.

At this moment a transformation took place in Europe. The alignment of nations changed, alliances which had seemed unthinkable were made, and a situation of gravity impossible to exaggerate ended in the Crimean War. For the moment the attention of the Queen and the Prince was, at least partially, deflected from their eldest son.

Chapter Eleven

The outbreak of the Crimean War was preceded by changes in the relations of the European powers, so rapid, involving the break-up of so many old friendships, the abandonment of so many ancient enmities and so complicated by religious problems as to produce an impression that the causes of the Crimean campaign were intricate and difficult. On the contrary they are simple, easy to understand, and the outcome of war was inevitable.

The principal enemy of England in Europe throughout history has been France. France has been the bogey, whether monarchist or revolutionary, the nearest enemy and the most inveterate.

In 1844, ten years before the declaration of the Crimean War, a meeting was held in London at which Sir Robert Peel, then Prime Minister, Lord Aberdeen, his Foreign Secretary, the Duke of Wellington and the Tsar of Russia, Nicholas I, were present. At the end of the meeting a memorandum was drawn up, pro-Russian and anti-French, 'the spirit and scope of which was to support Russia in her legitimate protectorship of the Greek religion and the Holy Shrines, and to do so without consulting France'.[1] In the course of conversation the Tsar remarked to Sir Hamilton Seymour, British Ambassador to St Petersburg, that the European powers had a 'sick man' on their hands, the sick man being the Turkish Empire. No discussion followed.

Yet danger from Russia was evident. Russia was the largest Empire the world had ever seen. More than half the territory of Europe was already Russian; beyond Europe in Asia lay further vast Russian possessions, including Siberia; farther east across the Bering Straits, only 56 miles wide, tens of thousands of square miles in North America belonged to Russia. This huge giant was by no means benevolent. The Russian Empire was ruled with barbarism and cruelty; it contained a number of half-oriental races. Russia was the last country in Europe in which serfdom survived. With the exception of serving soldiers, barely five per cent of the population were free. The name 'Cossack' chilled the blood of Europe with terror. The Tsar was absolute autocrat, and absolute head of the Russian Church; the Russian religion, though Christian, was primitive,

338

difficult and obscure. The British people had no love for Russia, viewing the Russian government, always on the side of reaction and oppression, with suspicion, but Russia was remote, remote as a province in Africa. France was the bugbear, the hereditary enemy just across the Channel. It was not realised, certainly not by the mass of the British people, that Nicholas I, who had succeeded his more amiable brother Alexander I as Emperor of Russia in 1825, was an imperialist. Nicholas meant to expand. No power in Europe had ever yet succeeded in forcing Russia to relinquish a single acre she had seized, and the Tsar's concern for the well-being and religious liberty of the twelve million members of the Orthodox Church who were Turkish subjects in the Danubian principalities, viewed in the light of his imperialistic ambitions, was ominous.

In February 1852 the British government changed. Lord John Russell fell and Lord Derby became Prime Minister with Lord Malmesbury as Foreign Secretary. Lord Malmesbury was in many respects an excellent choice. Russia's ambitions were beginning to cause alarm; friendship with France was essential to balance the Russian menace and Lord Malmesbury was an intimate friend of Louis Napoleon Bonaparte. He had visited Louis Napoleon during his imprisonment in the Castle of Ham, which followed Louis Napoleon's dramatic and unsuccessful attempt to land at Boulogne and seize power in 1840 with a dejected-looking eagle tied to the mast of his vessel. Unfortunately when Lord Malmesbury became Foreign Secretary in 1852, relations between England and France had never been worse. Malmesbury found Persigny, the Minister for the interior, 'blustering about war and empire'[2] throughout May. In the early spring there had been a crisis when France appeared to be intending to invade Belgium which must have meant war with England; later in the year France appeared to be planning a descent on the coast of England itself. Meanwhile Louis Napoleon Bonaparte was absorbed to the exclusion of every other consideration in his determination to convert the Presidency, to which he had been elected in 1849 by the enormous majority of seven million votes, into a hereditary Bonapartist Empire with himself as Emperor. It was a moment when popularity was everything to him and he was in the hands of the Army, an army burning to avenge Waterloo.

Malmesbury was fortunate in having personal relationships with Lord Palmerston, as well as with Louis Napoleon Bonaparte. His grandfather, James Harris, the celebrated diplomat first Earl of Malmesbury, had been Lord Palmerston's guardian. Palmerston offered to call privately on the new Foreign Secretary and 'give him a sketch of the status quo in Europe'. The offer was gratefully accepted, and the sketch was 'masterly'. The burden of Palmerston's advice was 'keep well with France'.[3] In this he was supported by the Duke of Wellington who adjured Lord Malmesbury to 'look after France'.

On 2nd December 1852 Louis Napoleon Bonaparte took the decisive step. The second French Empire was proclaimed and he himself, from being Prince President, became the Emperor Napoleon III.

The rage of the Tsar was 'prodigious'. He refused to recognise the title Napoleon III, holding that the numeral III implied a Bonapartist dynasty. He declined to call Napoleon III brother. Queen Victoria, however, was not infuriated. She had written to King Leopold at the end of 1848 that she was glad there was 'no doubt' of Louis Napoleon Bonaparte's election as President, 'but that we should *have to wish* for *him* is really wonderful'. On 19th January 1849 she wrote that 'Louis Napoleon has really behaved very well . . . and his death would be the signal for terrible confusion, so much daring somehow disarms bad feeling.'[4]

After he had made himself Emperor, the Queen remained calm: 'Watchful we certainly shall and must be . . . and keep on the best terms with the President [now the Emperor Napoleon III]' she wrote on 20th January 1852 'who is extremely sensitive and sensible,—and for whom I must say I have never had any *personal* hostility; on the contrary I thought that during '49 and '50 we all owed him a good deal. . . .' She was in any case bound by her duty as a constitutional sovereign to take Lord Malmesbury's advice as her Foreign Minister and on 4th December addressed Louis Napoleon Bonaparte in a letter as 'Sir, my brother' ending 'Your Imperial Majesty's good sister'. The same day Lord Malmesbury wrote in his memoirs 'Official recognition of French Empire'.[5]

The Queen's letter was preceded by a secret protocol signed on 3rd December 1852 in London at the Foreign Office by Britain, Austria, Prussia and Russia, which recognised Louis Napoleon as Emperor. The Tsar, however, though he recovered himself sufficiently to sign the Protocol, refused to address Napoleon III by any other title than 'Mon cher Ami'.

*

In accounts of the origins of the Crimean War the question of the Holy Places bulks large, but the Crimean campaign was in no sense a religious war. The Holy Places were screens behind which international issues were pursued and were treated as being of vital importance by the Tsar because he considered them to have more popular appeal than the second choice of a casus belli, the alleged persecution of members of the Greek Orthodox Church in the Danubian principalities.

Briefly, Palestine, then a Turkish possession, contained a number of Christian shrines of which the chief were the Church of the Holy Sepulchre in Jerusalem, believed to cover the site of the tomb of Christ, a church in Nazareth believed to cover the home of the Virgin Mary, and the great church in Bethlehem with its natural trough in the rock believed to have been used as a manger and to be the birthplace of Christ.

These Holy Places had been placed in the care of the monks of the Latin Church. The Latin Church survived from the church established by the Frankish Crusaders when they founded the Kingdom of Jerusalem in 1099, and Catholic pilgrims from Italy and Western Europe traditionally looked to the Latin monks as their spiritual overseers. But the majority of pilgrims to the Holy Land—by a hundred to one—came from eastern Europe and Russia and were members of the great eastern Orthodox Church centred on Constantinople. Their welfare was catered for by Orthodox clergy in Jerusalem. Incessant bickering between Latin and Orthodox monks resulted and as early as the reign of Francis I, known in England for his meeting with Henry VIII at the Field of the Cloth of Gold in 1520, the Latin monks were placed under the protection of France, and the Orthodox monks under the protection of Russia. On the whole the description of the Holy Places disputes as a series of 'church-wardens' quarrels' is justified, but at the inflammatory point of the eighteen-fifties the Latin monks stood for France and the Orthodox monks for Russia.

'It must be remembered', wrote Anthony Trollope, 'that Eastern worshippers are . . . wild men of various nations and races—Maronites from Lebanon, Roumelians, Candiotes, Copts from Upper Egypt, Russians from the Crimea, Armenians and Abyssinians . . . clad in skins or hairy cloaks with huge hoods. Their heads are shaved, and their faces covered with short, grisly, fierce beards. They are silent mostly, looking out of their eyes ferociously.' On the whole neither Latin nor Orthodox pilgrims were of a high level of sophistication and the Holy Places were regularly the scene of unseemly riots; at times of Christian festivals hordes of pilgrims, greater than the churches could contain, trooped in, especially from the Orthodox Church; invariably violence broke out, blows were exchanged between the two groups of monks and heads broken.[6]

This was the period during which the new Emperor Napoleon III was searching everywhere for opportunities to assert the glory and power of France in order to gratify his subjects and maintain his position. On 22nd December 1852 the Latin monks under the protection of France marched in state into the church at Bethlehem, headed by their Patriarch, and, exercising an ancient right, placed a silver star engraved with the arms of France in the sanctuary while 'the key of the great door of the church, together with the keys of the sacred manger, was handed over to the Latins'.[7]

Once more the wrath of the Tsar was prodigious and on 9th January 1853 he had the first of four conversations with Sir Hamilton Seymour, British Ambassador at St Petersburg. As the Tsar was leaving a reception, Sir Hamilton with considerable audacity ventured to retain the hand the

Tsar extended to him in farewell, and begged him for some quietening news respecting Russia's intentions towards Turkey. The Tsar, reverting to his conversation with Lord Aberdeen in 1844, stated that they had now a very sick man on their hands, and that before his death the two powers Russia and Great Britain must take the necessary steps to secure the correct disposition of his property. Without waiting for any further proposals from Great Britain, the Tsar despatched Prince Menshikov to make Turkey his vassal, under the pretence that Menshikov's mission was solely concerned with the Holy Places and the protection of the Greek Orthodox Christians in the Danubian principalities.

Prince Menshikov made an alarming and warlike entry into Constantinople on 28th February 1853, refused to have any dealings with the Turkish Foreign Minister who had made concessions to the French, and gave the impression that an immediate attack on Constantinople by the Russians was about to follow.

In February 1853 Lord John Russell before resigning office as Foreign Secretary had sent back to Constantinople a celebrated authority on Near Eastern affairs, Stratford Canning, Viscount Stratford de Redcliffe. Internationally known for his attachment to Turkey and his distrust of Russia, Lord Stratford was so disliked by Nicholas that the Tsar had refused to accept him as British Ambassador to St Petersburg. Moreover the Cabinet was forced to allow him to follow his own judgment, since at the time communications with Turkey were so slow that any despatch from the Cabinet must take many days, if not several weeks, to reach him.

During this brief period several changes had taken place in the British government. Lord Malmesbury remained Foreign Secretary only until December 1852, when Lord Aberdeen became Prime Minister with Lord Palmerston as Home Secretary and Lord John Russell as Foreign Secretary. Lord John was not satisfied with the office and though when Parliament met on 10th February 1853 he held the seals, he resigned in less than a fortnight and led the House of Commons until the end of the session without taking charge of any department. He was succeeded by Lord Clarendon, who held office from February 1853 to 1858.

George William Frederick Villiers, fourth Earl of Clarendon, born in 1800, was much liked by the Queen. By character and training he was fitted to be a minister for foreign affairs.[8] He was accustomed to work for fourteen hours a day, was both an aristocrat and a liberal, master of the majority of European languages, learned in diplomatic affairs, witty, charming, loved by his subordinates and endued with the virtue of compassion. He had been the most successful Lord Lieutenant of Ireland during the famine.

Landing at Constantinople on 5th April 1853, Lord Stratford was aware that though the Russians had demanded satisfaction on the matter of the Holy Places, their true object was to establish sovereignty over all the twelve million Christians of the Orthodox Church in the Danubian provinces of Turkey, to which England could not agree. With the diplomatic skill for which he was famous he set to work to disentangle the Russian position and on 22nd April 1853, nearly a year before the declaration of the Crimean War, the Question of the Holy Places, together with special privileges, special doors, silver stars and silver keys, was settled and the long-drawn-out squabble of the 'rival churchwardens' was at an end.[9] Once more the Tsar was convulsed with rage, declaring he felt the smart of the Sultan's fingers on his cheek, but he could do nothing, and the Russian representative, also boiling with fury, was forced to pack his bags and return to St Petersburg.

Though notes between the powers were exchanged, not enough force was displayed to make the Tsar pause in his 'mad plunge towards war' and on 22nd June 1853 the invasion of the Danubian principalities, ostensibly to protect the religious rights of the inhabitants, began.

On 11th October 1853 Queen Victoria sent Lord Clarendon an admirable despatch, in which the hand of the Prince is evident. '. . . As matters have now been arranged, it appears to the Queen that we have now taken upon ourselves, in conjunction with France, all the risks of a European war, without having bound Turkey to any conditions with respect to provoking it. . . . England and France have bound themselves to defend the Turkish territory! This is entrusting them with a power which Parliament has been jealous to confide, even to the hand of the British Crown.'[10] The Prince in a conversation with Lord Aberdeen on 16th October 1853 pointed out that Turkey had every inducement to go to war with Russia. The Christian world had declared Turkey to be in the right, and England and France had made it clear they would take Turkey's side.

Even before the memorandum was written, the Turks had acted. An ultimatum had been sent to Prince Gorchakov, Commander of the Russian Army of occupation in the principalities, and received by him on 8th October 1853, requiring him to evacuate his troops within fifteen days on pain of hostile action. He instantly rejected it and Turkey and Russia passed into a state of war on 23rd October 1853. The Russian military organisation was, as it continued to be throughout the Crimean campaign, inefficient and the Turks, burning with hatred and longing for revenge, compelled the Russian forces to retreat. Blinded by one of the rages which originated in his physical condition, the Tsar took two fatal steps. He decided to attack Turkey proper and he ordered the Russian Black Sea Fleet to operate on the Turkish coasts. On 30th November 1853, without warning, a Russian fleet of war sailed out of Sevastopol

343

into the harbour of Sinope on the Black Sea and destroyed a Turkish fleet at anchor there. The massacre at Sinope was decisive. Britain exploded in rage. The British were accustomed to look on the ocean as their private property and the nation clamoured for war; Sinope was not only an atrocity but an insult to Britannia who ruled the waves.

The Queen at first hesitated to credit the news which reached her on 12th December; on the 15th she was still dubious whether the Russians had attacked the Turks in the harbour or gained a victory over them in a meeting at sea. She distrusted what she described as 'absurd and mischievous blusterings of newspapers and public and popular meetings'.[11]

One more effort was made with the consent of the French and British governments. Napoleon III addressed a letter to the Tsar, asking in temperate language that hostilities should be suspended, troops withdrawn, fleets recalled and fresh negotiations opened between St Petersburg and Constantinople. The Tsar's reply was an insult: 'Russia would prove herself in 1854 what she had been in 1812', when the retreat from Moscow ruined Napoleon I. With this remark the last hope of peace vanished. During the first week in February the Russian ambassadors were withdrawn from London and Paris and in reply the British and French ambassadors were called from St Petersburg. Both sides had now lost their tempers, the British public was in a frenzy of rage and peace would have been unwelcome. On 27th February a Franco-British ultimatum was presented to the Tsar, who did not deign to answer it. On 19th March 1854 a state of war with Russia was declared to exist and formally proclaimed in Paris on 27th March and in London on 28th March 1854. The Crimean campaign had officially begun.

*

Before the official declaration, when public opinion approached frenzy, the Prince became a victim of war fever. The wildest rumours were current against him. 'We might fancy we were living in a mad house' he wrote to Baron Stockmar on 24th January 1854.[12] Though the upper classes, who governed England, had been dubious about him, the Prince had previously been popular with the masses of the people. Now they, too, turned against him. Articles were printed in *The Times*, the *Daily News* and the *Morning Advertiser*, the favourite paper of the licensed victuallers; the matter became sufficiently serious to be dealt with at length in the House of Lords and the House of Commons. The people were excited to a degree 'which led thousands' stated Lord Derby 'to attend at the doors of the Tower to see His Royal Highness go in—and which led individuals to say he was sure to have been sent there if the Queen had not announced her intention to go with him. . . .'[13]

In this fantasy there was a grain of truth. The upper classes levelled charges against the Prince of interference with the administration of the Army and Navy, exercising undue influence over the Queen, arrogating authority which was not his right; allegations described in the House of Lords as 'miserable calumnies'. It had, for instance, been forgotten that it had been the 'great desire' of the Duke of Wellington that the Prince should succeed him as Commander in Chief of the Army and the Prince had refused. The real reason for his unpopularity was that he was a foreigner. His excellent work for the nation, his chancellorship of Cambridge, his presidency of the Anti-slavery Society, his many non-controversial activities, counted for nothing. 'First of all' wrote Stockmar 'he was a foreigner, a German: and this the insular Englishman, with his intolerant instincts, could hardly forget or forgive. . . . That he [the Prince] did not dress quite in the orthodox English fashion, that he did not sit on horseback in the orthodox English way, that he did not shake hands in the true orthodox English manner etc., etc.; all this, even those who were in closer contact with the Prince, who knew and esteemed him, could not easily get over. One heard them say: "He is an excellent, clever, able fellow, but look at the cut of his coat, or look at the way he shakes hands." '[14]

Anti-German feeling already existed in England. 'Why should we be ruled by Germans?' Lady Jersey had burst out angrily years ago at a party. Prince Albert was German to the core and took a pride in being German. He had vowed, in spite of being transplanted to England, 'Ein treuer fester Coburger zu sein.' The Queen was habituated to German conceptions, intonations, ideas. Lehzen, who brought her up, was German; the Duchess of Kent was German and in her household German was frequently—malicious gossip said almost exclusively—spoken. When the Prince went hunting in thigh-length boots of soft leather and an open-necked shirt, he appeared marvellously handsome in the Queen's eyes, but to English gentlemen, though admittedly handsome, he looked like a foreign tenor.[15] The Prince was reserved and stiff, had no free and easy manner. Mr Anson was told that the upper classes 'complain of his reserve and of his attaching undue importance to etiquette in everything relating to *himself* or rather of his exacting a degree of homage which they consider more than his right.' It was alleged that the Prince spoke more German than he ought, which the Queen indignantly denied.[16] 'First of all the Prince and Queen speak English . . . quite as much as we do German. . . . It is that continual and unbounded dislike (in England) of foreigners and *everything foreign* which breaks out continually, and is *very* painful to the Queen—whose husband, Mother and all her dearest relations and friends *are foreigners*.'

The Prince was stiff because he was nervous and shy and because his morals were strict. He never gambled or laid a bet. 'They call him slow because he does not gamble, does not use offensive language and does not keep an opera dancer' ran a letter in *The Times*.

'Nothing' wrote the Prince himself to Stockmar 'has been brought up against me which is not absolutely untrue,' and with shrewdness he commented: 'All the gossip and idle talk of the last fourteen years have been brought to light by what has occurred.' These were the fourteen years since his marriage to the Queen, when he had come as a boy of twenty to undertake a task of appalling difficulty.

The agitation against the Prince gradually died down. Little more of it was heard after the discussion in the Houses of Parliament and the declaration of war against Russia. The story of Prince Albert being committed to the Tower for high treason must take its place among the major rumours of history, a companion for the rumour of World War I, when a Russian army of immense size was declared to have passed through Britain on its way to the help of the Allies; it was easy to discern the troops were Russian because there was snow on their boots.

Both the Queen and the Prince took the attacks 'greatly to heart' and were made ill with headaches and indigestion. 'Since yesterday I have been quite miserable,' the Prince wrote to Stockmar, 'today I have had to keep to the house. . . .'

One other undertaking of importance was negotiated before the declaration of war. The new Emperor, Napoleon III, was anxious to stabilise his position and found a dynasty by a suitable marriage. Success beyond all expectations had attended him but, as he told Lord Malmesbury, he had no time to lose 'if he were to leave an heir grown up'.[17] Without good looks—he was described as having 'the appearance of an opium eater'—he nevertheless possessed charm for women and the number of his love affairs was notorious. Women became attached to him; for many years, including the time while he was President in Paris, a certain well-known Englishwoman, Miss Howard, had been his mistress. She lent him money, gave him support and encouragement, and he treated her with gratitude and respect. She was now retired with a handsome pension, and the Emperor wished for a royal bride. He first renewed his suit to Princess Mathilde Bonaparte, to whom he had been betrothed until her father broke off the match following the failure of Louis Napoleon's descent on Strasbourg to seize the French throne in 1836. Princess Mathilde refused. In June 1852 Princess Caroline Wasa, granddaughter of Stephanie Beauharnais, refused him and married the Prince Royal of Saxony.[18] In December 1852, the month in which Louis Napoleon made himself Napoleon III, he raised his eyes higher. On 13th December Count Walewski, the French Ambassador, called on Lord Malmesbury and told him the Emperor was anxious to make a marriage which would strengthen the ties of friendship between England and

France; would Lord Malmesbury ascertain from the Queen whether any objection would be raised by the Queen herself or by the family of Prince Albert to the Emperor contracting a marriage with Her Serene Highness Princess Adelaide of Hohenlohe, aged 17, daughter of the Queen's half-sister and greatly loved intimate friend, Princess Feodora of Hohenlohe-Langenburg? Lord Malmesbury gave an assurance that he would submit the Emperor's proposal to the Queen but foresaw difficulty because the Princess was a Protestant. Nevertheless Count Walewski urged Lord Malmesbury to submit the proposal; the Emperor was evidently sincere. The proposal annoyed the Queen and on 14th December she sent a reproof to Lord Malmesbury through Lord Derby, the Prime Minister.[19] He had put her in a situation to which she should never have been subjected, considering her close relationship with Princess Adelaide and the delicacy of Britain's political position with France. On the same day she wrote an irritated letter to Lord Malmesbury himself. She felt herself '... conscientiously precluded from forming an opinion of her own and from taking the slightest part in it either directly or indirectly. The only proper persons to refer to ... are the Parents of the Princess and the Princess herself.' Greville remarked that Princess Ada was staying with the Queen at the time and 'in her charge'. The Queen set her face against the match 'and made the girl refuse, who desired no better and if left to herself would have accepted the offer'.[20]

Princess Feodora thought the whole affair a 'very disagreeable business', which 'poor Ada ... would rather like'. As long as possible the Duchess of Kent must be kept in ignorance—'she will fuss dreadfully'. 'Oh! if we could say *no* at once. ... I shudder at the idea of giving a child into such hands, and *such a child* as poor Ada is, what will become of her!'[21] Princess Ada's health was not robust, she was late in developing physically, doctors had told her parents she should not marry for two or three years at least, and, brought up in the seclusion of Langenburg, she was incapable of even comprehending the complications of Second Empire politics. Above all she was a Protestant.

Princess Ada, however, of her own free will, refused the Emperor. She told her father in the 'clearest and most explicit terms' she did not feel she was 'endowed with enough strength of character, nor cleverness, nor ambition to accept a position as elevated as it is perilous',[22] a message which Prince Hohenlohe conveyed to the Emperor.

Queen Victoria now felt she could express her emotions—though her estimate of the Emperor was to alter radically during the next two years—and wrote to Princess Feodora on 6th January 1853.[23] 'Now that this terrible affair about our dear Ada has been decided by herself—I can and will write to you what I have felt and what mature reflection has made me feel *more* strongly even than I did at first. I feel that your dear child is

347

saved from *ruin* of every possible *sort*. You know what *he* is, what his moral character is—(without thinking him devoid of good qualities and even valuable ones) what his entourage is, how thoroughly immoral France and French society are—hardly looking at what is wrong as more than fashionable and natural—you know how very insecure *his* position is— you know his age, that his health is indifferent, and naturally his wish to marry Ada [is] merely a political one, for he has never seen her. . . . I ask you if you can imagine for a moment anything more awful than the fate of that sweet, innocent child . . . a prey to every ill natured remark and observation and to every wicked Counsellor, without a female friend in the world!' From a political point of view the Queen considered the marriage must have done Britain harm and the British Royal Family would have been accused of sacrificing their relations to sordid interest, but it would have been 'more than could be expected' that Ada should not have been dazzled, especially considering the young Princess's character.

The Emperor had since the previous autumn been paying marked attention to a Spanish lady of great beauty, ten years older than Princess Ada, Eugénie de Montijo. Wonderfully good-looking, she spent much of her time in Paris, chaperoned by her widowed mother, and was now 27, eighteen years younger than the Emperor, but not, according to the ideas of the period, any longer in the bloom of youth. She was not such a match as the Emperor had dreamed of, or the French nation desired. There was a suggestion of the dubious about her. When the Duke of Alba proposed to her sister, not to herself, she took poison and nearly died. Her betrothal to the Emperor was followed by the suicide of one of her admirers. Her demeanour left something to be desired; she had not been born or trained to the position she was to fill and alternated between a kindness and ease native to her and sudden accesses of haughtiness, when she recollected she was an Empress. Eugénie Montijo was sufficiently near an adventuress to make her a bad choice for an Emperor who was himself an adventurer.[24] Religiously she was a devout Catholic and had developed a cult of Queen Marie Antoinette, with whose career she contrived to identify what she believed would be her own. She felt sympathy for the Bourbons, who were universally detested for their bigotry and cruelty by the British. Nevertheless she won and retained the affection of Queen Victoria by her sweetness and gentleness. On 16th January 1853 the Emperor summoned family friends and Ministers and announced his forthcoming marriage to Mademoiselle de Montijo. 'Universal disappointment' reported Lord Cowley, the British Ambassador.[25] In a private letter Lord Cowley told Lord John Russell that, at a ball at the Tuileries, the Emperor said to Lady Cowley 'Well, I can confide to you that I took no determination till I received Prince Hohenlohe's answer.

Had that been favourable, my present marriage never would have taken place.' 'Now that it is all over I may say' wrote Lord Cowley 'that I have been aware of what has been going on in regard to the projected Alliance, but that the near relationship in which the Princess stood to the Queen prevented my even alluding to it. What however the Emperor says is true. He waited until he received Prince Hohenlohe's final answer. It reached Paris on the morning of the 18th, and on the evening of the same day he proposed to Mademoiselle de Montijo, and I believe that had Prince H's answer been favourable, the Montijo would have been sent to the right about.'

She was, as Lord Cowley wrote, 'very handsome, very coquette, very clever as her success shows'. To the Queen Lord John Russell wrote[26] 'Had the lady been unexceptionable in character and conduct and had she been French, it would perhaps have been the best decision the Emperor could take. As it is, the character of the Court will not be improved, and the best part of France will keep away from it.'

The Emperor married Eugénie de Montijo in the cathedral of Notre Dame on 29th January 1853. She wore the diamond coronet which Marie Louise, daughter of the Emperor of Austria, had worn to her wedding with Napoleon I; the same coach of glass and gold was used. The Minister of the Interior, Persigny, had reproduced every past splendour with care, an amnesty for those involved in the *coup d'état* (some three thousand persons) was proclaimed and large sums were distributed in charity, but there was a total absence of enthusiasm; indeed, the evening before, the bride had been hooted.[27]

Neverthless the Empress Eugénie accomplished a great deal for the Second Empire; it is impossible to imagine its gaslit splendours without her beauty, her charm, her chic. The Emperor became proud of his non-royal bride; he had, he declared, 'preferred a woman I love', and though Florence Nightingale described her as 'the Empress who was born to be a dressmaker', she displayed a courage, when misfortune came and glories faded, which won her universal respect.

*

The declaration of war in February 1854 was succeeded by a pause. The commanders of the British Army were nerving themselves to a decision of supreme importance; the fortress and port of Sevastopol was to be destroyed by action from the land. It was from Sevastopol that the Russian fleet had sailed out to destroy the Turkish fleet at Sinope, and it was to Sevastopol that the Russian fleet had returned afterwards in perfect safety. Sevastopol menaced Constantinople and threatened the control of the Dardanelles. Intelligence work barely existed at the period of the Crimean campaign and the British commander attached no more importance to the work being done at Sevastopol by Todleben, than to the work of any other Russian engineer. Todleben was, however, a genius, one of the two geniuses the Crimean campaign produced, the other being Miss Florence Nightingale, and he was rapidly converting Sevastopol into an impregnable fortress. The decision, however, was taken; Sevastopol was to be captured and destroyed and the British and French armies, together with a force of about seven thousand Turks, were to be re-embarked at Varna for the descent on the Crimea. The sorry oft-told tale of mismanagement, inefficiency and misfortune was about to begin. Varna was notoriously a hotbed of cholera and when the troops sailed for the Crimea cholera went with them. Not enough transport had been provided; Lord Hardinge had warned the Queen only 20,000 could be taken at a time. Thirty thousand men were crammed in but regimental medicine chests and hospital tents had to be left behind, finally even the men's packs had to be abandoned. Cholera was raging, with dysentery and colic as well; in the opinion of their medical officers the men were too weak to carry their packs and transport animals failed to materialise from the countryside. They did not exist. In any case there was no room to transport them. Hundreds of men were taken ill during the night of the landing, 14th September 1854, and when the army moved the line of march was marked by men who fell out to lie writhing in agony, many in their death throes.

Long before the terrible winter of 1854, the Crimean disaster was in being.

At home faith in the British army was complete. The British army had won Waterloo and the Peninsula, the mantle of the great Duke of Wellington was assumed to have fallen on his successors; the appearance of the Guards as they swung past the Queen on their way to embarkation, a line of drummer boys drumming at their head, was superb, they were in fact the finest troops in Europe.[28] No one suspected there were no adequate reinforcements behind them, no adequate supplies to support them.

While the British army was in course of descending on the Crimea, alighting like a flock of birds with no means of flying away, Prince Albert was visiting the Emperor Napoleon III at Boulogne. The Prince stayed four days completely alone with the Emperor and afterwards dictated a memorandum[29] to General Grey which illuminates the character of both men. The Emperor appeared to be completely open and the Prince trusted he himself was the same. Napoleon III appeared quiet, indolent and humorous, spoke French with a German accent and pronounced German better than English. 'A good deal remains of the gymnasium [school] at Augsburg where he was brought up.' His entourage was not 'distinguished' by birth, manners or education; they all seemed afraid of him. 'He does not care for music, smokes a great many cigarettes, which the Prince refused, was proud of his horsemanship in which the Prince could discover nothing remarkable.'

The Emperor's general education seemed to the Prince very deficient, even in such subjects of importance as political science, but he did not pretend. He showed the greatest candour in not feigning to know what he did not. He asked many questions about the Queen's administration and was astonished that all despatches went through the Queen's hands, whereas he himself only read extracts. He seemed in fact to have little time or inclination for reading, but allowed his Ministers to do business only through him. The Prince was left with the impression that the Emperor's difficulty was day-to-day government. 'Having deprived the people of every active participation in the Government and having reduced them to mere passive spectators' he was bound to provide a series of 'spectacles' to divert the public and whenever a pause occurred, the public immediately became impatient. 'Still he [the Emperor] seems to be the only man who has any hold on France, relying on the "nom de Napoléon" which is the last thing left to a Frenchman's faith.' He was decidedly benevolent, but he 'runs the risk of all absolute monarchs that he will be crushed under the weight of a mass of unimportant detail, while the real direction of affairs is filched from him by his irresponsible ministers.' The Emperor took the Prince to St Omer, to the camp where the French army was being fitted out for service in the Crimea, and three times the Emperor's carriage was stopped for him to receive packets of police reports.

Meanwhile from 'the army in the East', the term denoting the force marching to attack Sevastopol, little news trickled through. The army had vanished behind a haze of bad communications and disquieting rumours and it was with inexpressible relief that the Queen received the news of the victory of the Alma, won on 20th September 1854. In spite of cholera and inadequate supplies, the British army had stormed the heights above the river Alma, the men so short of water that they had paused to drink as they crossed the river at the risk of their lives. The position, telegraphed Lord Raglan, was formidable and defended by guns, the victory a tribute to British courage and British morale. National relief was intense and wildly optimistic rumours circulated, the Queen receiving a telegram from Lord Clarendon that a despatch from Constantinople reported the capture of Sevastopol with huge Russian casualties. A similar communication came from Lord Westmorland. 'This is indeed glorious news, if we could feel *quite sure* of its truth. God grant that it may be so' wrote the Queen. On 4th October, while the Queen and the Prince were at Balmoral, Sir James Graham brought another and longer telegraphic despatch, but the Queen noted there were still '*no official sources*'. On 6th October the fall of Sevastopol was contradicted and the British army base reported to be established at Balaclava.[30] The choice was either to march on and assault Sevastopol immediately after the victory of the Alma, or to establish a base and besiege. It has been held that the decision to establish a base at Balaclava was the major mistake of the campaign. This is dubious. Todleben was a genius and the geography of Sevastopol made assault difficult. Southern Sevastopol, containing the arsenal and fortress, was separated from the lesser defences on the north by an inlet over 1,000 yards wide. It was southern, not northern, Sevastopol which was the objective, and to reduce it might have been proved unexpectedly difficult. Both the French and the British armies were in poor shape, pursued by cholera to the very battlefield of the Alma, and the Alma had been a costly victory. A base was therefore established at Balaclava and the British army set off to march round Sevastopol to assault it from the south.

The initial disasters of the Crimean campaign, the cholera, the want of medical supplies and attention, were no longer a secret. For the first time in history a war correspondent, William Howard Russell, was accompanying the army and his despatches to *The Times* were being read at home with mounting indignation. Disaster succeeded disaster, the battle of Balaclava was won with difficulty, and the picturesque harbour of Balaclava itself became a sewage pond, in which arms and legs amputated after the battle floated and stank. During the battle of Balaclava the magnificent courage displayed in the Charge of the Light Brigade was useless, the Charge itself a military disaster. The Heavy Brigade had charged successfully but, through ineptitude, the fruits of their victory were thrown away. Balaclava was succeeded by Inkerman, when the British army came within an ace of being overwhelmed by unexpected multitudes of Russian troops; in a costly battle fought in swirling mist a victory was won but the revelation of Russian strength was alarming. On 14th November 1854 Balaclava was devastated by a storm which wrecked more than a dozen ships in Balaclava harbour laden with winter supplies, swept away the tents which alone sheltered the besieging army on the heights above Sevastopol and converted the greater part of the six-mile track, the sole link between the camp and the base, into an impassable morass. The troops besieging Sevastopol were now as effectively marooned as on a lighthouse and winter set in, the worst Crimean winter within living memory. Shiploads of cholera cases poured in continuously from Varna, but there was no means of sheltering them, much less of providing medical attention. Active troops and sick were alike starving; if food had existed there was no means of cooking it. It was a well-known fact that timber did not exist in the Crimea and every root of every bush had been grubbed out of the ground for fuel. Colonel McNeill and Colonel Tulloch in their report[31] stated that during the winter of 1854–55 mortality in the British army apart from battle casualties was 45–75 per cent.

George Duke of Cambridge, the Queen's cousin,* had endured as much as he could bear. Inkerman had horrified and disgusted him. He went sick to Malta and did not return.

The Queen was aghast. She did not accept the custom which exempted highly placed officers of the British army from the hardships of war. When the Duke wrote he 'was not fit for a winter campaign, he had asked Lord Raglan to come home on sick leave', the Queen entered in her Journal 'We were horrified, as I am sure this will have the very worst effect.' The same day the Duke received a 'significant letter from the Queen as to my return to the Crimea which put me out a good deal.' '. . . I hope you will be back in the Crimea by this time' the Queen had written. 'Forgive my telling you frankly that I hope you will not let your low spirits and desponding feelings be known to others; you cannot think how ill natured people are here, and I can assure you that the Clubs have not been slow in circulating the most shameful lies about you.'[32]

Want of courage was not a fault of which English officers were often accused. Lord Cardigan himself after leading the Charge of the Light Brigade went home observing it was no part of his duty to fight the enemy as a private soldier. The Duke of Cambridge was soft-hearted: after the battle of the Alma he burst into tears; after riding over the bloody field of Inkerman, a costly, hard-won victory, he collapsed. He felt resentment: 'Why doesn't he [Prince Albert] come himself and have a try? he wouldn't stay 24 hours I know, the fine gentleman.'[33] He reached England from Malta, after a short stay in Paris, on 30th January 1855, looking, wrote the Queen, 'ill & much broken'. He did not return to the Crimea.

The Queen's pain for the sufferings of the rank and file who were enduring the horrors of the war was real, nor did she confine her sympathies to officers. 'After luncheon' she wrote in her Journal[34] 'we went down into the Marble Hall in which were drawn up, to the number of 32, wounded men of the Grenadier Guards, who had returned from the Crimea. It was a touching sight, and one could not see a finer set of men, tall, noble-looking, whom it made one's heart bleed, to see so mutilated. However, the greater part of them looked well in the face. The Sergeant, Dawson, a fine, tall man, had, early in the day, at the Alma, lost his left arm, very high up. Two others had lost their arms, several were shot in the hand, others in the arms, shoulders, legs, hips, thighs,—one, in the instep,—another (an extraordinary case of recovery) had had a severe contusion of the chest, from a cannon ball,—one, had lost his leg,—

* This is the Prince George of Cambridge once spoken of as a possible husband for the Queen. His father Adolphus Frederick, the first Duke of Cambridge, died in July 1850.

353

another shot in the arm & neck,—one in the spine, which paralysed the arm; & the poor man said he suffered a good deal. A Private Challis had been given up & returned as dead, but he has quite recovered, though he has lost his arm. . . . They were all in their grey coats, the same, in which they had fought. . . . Almost ½ of the men had been wounded at the Alma, the others at Inkermann & a few in the trenches. . . . I had meant to make some kind of general speech, but I was so agitated, that it all stuck in my throat & I could only say to Col. Ward, that I hoped all would soon get their medals, which they well deserved. Afterwards they had a dinner in the Servants' Hall.'

A few days later she wrote in her Journal 'Immediately after luncheon, we went down into the Hall again, just as the other day, and saw 26 of the sick & wounded of the Coldstreams. I thought they looked worse than the others—more suffering & sickly, & less fine looking men. There were some sad cases;—one man who had lost his right arm at Inkermann, was also at the Alma, & looked deadly pale;—one or two others had lost their arms, others had been shot in the shoulders & legs,—several, in the hip joint, which impeded the action of the leg, rendering them unfit for further service. A private, Lanesbury, with a patch over his eye, & his face tied up, had had his head traversed by a bullet, penetrating through the eye, which was gone,—through the nose, & coming out at the neck! He looked dreadfully pale, but was recovering well. There were 2 other very touching & distressing cases, 2 poor boys, the one, (P. Randle) aged 19, lost his leg by the bursting of a shell, in the trenches, the leg having had to be amputated quite high up—the other, (P. Gilden) aged 20, looking particularly young, had had his arm so severely wounded, that it will wither & become useless. . . . I cannot say how touched & impressed I have been by the sight of these noble, brave, & so sadly wounded men & *how* anxious I feel to be of use to them, & to try & get some employment for those who are maimed for life. Those who are discharged will receive very small pensions but not sufficient to live upon. About 6 or 7, were sick with fever, & 2 quite crippled with rheumatism, got by falling into the river Alma.'

In January 1855 a great upsurge of popular indignation turned out Lord Aberdeen, for whom the Queen and the Prince had always felt affection, and she was forced to accept as Prime Minister the man she had dismissed from the Foreign Office three years earlier, Lord Palmerston. The nation was convinced that only his energy, his fearlessness, could save what was left of the British Army. The Queen did not give way without a struggle. On 29th January 1855 Lord Aberdeen was hopelessly defeated by 157 votes on Mr Roebuck's motion for an enquiry into the condition of the army outside Sevastopol (148 votes in his favour, 305 against him) and his retirement was inevitable. The Queen appealed to Lord Derby, who could not form a government without

354

support from other parties which he failed to secure. She appealed to Lord Lansdowne, who was equally unsuccessful. Lord John Russell was approached, in spite of the fact that he had acted against Lord Aberdeen, and the Queen even brought herself to express hope that Palmerston might join his government, but Lord John Russell also refused the attempt, not feeling himself to be strong enough.[35]

The Queen was compelled to send for Lord Palmerston. Lord John Russell stated, wrote the Queen in her Journal, that 'there was the most ample cause for enquiry, & that the whole country . . . cried out for Ld. Palmerston, as the only man fitted to carry on the war with success'.

The Queen had her first interview with Lord Palmerston on 3rd February 1855. It passed off smoothly. Lord Clarendon assured her that the course she dreaded was the only course open to her to follow; Palmerston would prove conciliatory if frankly treated and 'none other could take the helm'. The Queen yielded to necessity and, as was always the case, having yielded, did so with sincerity and a good grace, though she wrote in her Journal on 5th February 1855 that to change 'my dear kind, excellent friend Ld. Aberdeen . . . for Ld. Palmerston is somewhat of a *trial*'.[36] Lord Palmerston came to Windsor and kissed hands as Prime Minister that day. 'A month ago' he wrote to his brother Sir William Temple 'if any man had asked me to say what was one of the most improbable events, I should have said my being Prime Minister. . . . I think our Government will do very well. I am backed by the general opinion of the whole country, and I have no reason to complain of the least want of cordiality or confidence on the part of the Court.'[37] Less than eight weeks later the situation in Europe was radically changed by the unexpected death of the dreaded Tsar Nicholas. His gigantic physique, the austerity of his habits, seemed to promise him a ripe old age, but, as his rages indicated, he had been in a pathological condition during the negotiations preceding the declaration of war. The news of his death was received with outbursts of applause in England; in France, French stock rose five per cent on the Paris Bourse and, in the words of the Austrian Ambassador, 'All Europe breathed more freely'.[38]

The terrible winter of 1854–55 was now almost over, spring flowers carpeted the plains before Sevastopol, Miss Nightingale had brought some degree of elementary order into the treatment of the sick. The arrangements for supplying food to the troops had also, to some elementary degree, been reformed. In Miss Nightingale's words the men began to swear again, and a difficult situation developed between the French and English allies.

The Crimean campaign was, and continued to be, desperately unpopular in France. It was felt in France that England had led France into war—and such a war—in defence of English, not French interests. England was an unpopular ally, more unpopular than the enemy, Russia, and the British Ambassador, Lord Cowley, told Lord Clarendon in strict confidence that difficulty was anticipated in raising money for the war in France; it might be necessary to raise a joint loan with bonds payable in London or Paris.[39] France had sustained losses in men very nearly as terrible as the British, which were so heavy that the ranks could not be filled. At Inkerman alone half the British troops engaged had perished and Lieut. General Sir John Burgoyne, Inspector General of Fortifications, described as the second man in the British army, who had served throughout the Peninsular War, estimated that less than half of the original force landed now survived. Prince Albert had already suggested that a force of fifteen thousand foreigners should be raised, drilled in England and sent out to fight in the Crimea, but the objection of the Cabinet to the employment of mercenaries was insuperable. Lord Palmerston pointed out that the British army was '40,000 men short of the number voted by Parliament. . . . Let us get as many Germans and Swiss as we can . . . let us enlist Italians; and let us forthwith increase our bounty at home without raising the standard. Do not let departmental, or official, or professional prejudices and habits stand in our way . . . we *must* have troops.'[40]

In the midst of these deliberations Napoleon III exploded a bombshell.[41] For some time past he had not been satisfied either with the part he was playing in the war, or with the conduct of it. He was, as the Prince had noted during his visit to Boulogne, pursued by the necessity of perpetual successes, of providing show after show to demonstrate the glory and power of France under his rule, and he now proposed to go in person to the Crimea, assume supreme command and bring the siege of Sevastopol to a victorious conclusion. He believed he could achieve this before 1st May by a surprise attack. The Russians at the moment, according to the Emperor, had a force of only 30,000 at Sevastopol.

The announcement was received with consternation. The objections to the Emperor's scheme were overwhelming but from a French viewpoint it was irresistibly tempting. The blame attached to the British generals had not passed unnoticed in France; how glorious then for British troops (the victors of Waterloo) to be led to victory by a French Emperor bearing the name of Napoleon when their own generals had failed. The problems of popularity and prestige which haunted Napoleon III would be solved for ever. The British, whose losses in the past winter had been so high that there was no time to train fresh troops, would be reduced to auxiliaries and carriers, and the honours of a new victorious campaign would go to France.

Clarendon, who was friendly with the Emperor, hurried over to

Boulogne for a lightning visit on 3rd March, returning on the 5th to report hopefully to the Prince and the Queen.[42] The Emperor's 'most confidential officer', Colonel Fleury, told Lord Clarendon the Emperor was mistaken in believing the army would welcome his command. The French army was loyal to the Emperor, but did not wish to be commanded in the field by one whom they looked on as a civilian. Clarendon had taken the opportunity to indicate the practical difficulties of the scheme. These came to the Emperor as a surprise. The French were to provide the troops. He had promised Palmerston to bring up the French numbers to 62,000 men, and the British were to transport them, a somewhat ignominious role which would be unpopular. Clarendon pointed out there were at the moment 102 large British steamships fully occupied in the Black Sea, that a voyage from Marseilles to the coast near Sevastopol involving loading and unloading of stores, coaling, embarkation of troops, could not be accomplished in less than four weeks. The Admiralty had already engaged to transport 15,000 Sardinian troops to the Crimea and the utmost they could undertake would be the transport of another 10,000 French, and then not until six to eight weeks after the order had been actually given. Clarendon ventured the opinion that the Emperor should wait until all preparations had been made and then, when success seemed assured, appear in person to deliver 'le dernier coup de main'. The Emperor's attention was caught by the phrase and he repeated it: 'le dernier coup de main'. Lord Granville added his arguments to those of Lord Clarendon and a happy scheme was arrived at. Instead of going to the Crimea, why should not the Emperor and Empress of the French please the French people and add excitement and glory to the Emperor's reign by paying a state visit to Windsor first, and then receive the Queen and the Prince, also in state, in Paris during the summer? The Emperor allowed himself to be persuaded. 'He did not go to the Crimea, he went to England instead.'

On Monday, 16th April 1855, the Emperor Napoleon III and the Empress Eugénie landed at Dover, and were received by the Prince and escorted to London.[43] It was noted with approval that as the carriage drove through St James's Street the Emperor pointed out to the Empress the small house in King Street where he had lived during the most poverty-stricken years of his exile. The Queen herself received him at the grand entrance of Windsor Castle, while bands played the famous song written by the Emperor's mother and adopted by the French army almost as their national anthem, 'Partant pour la Syrie'. The Queen was moved: 'I cannot say what indescribable emotion filled me,' she wrote in her Journal,[44] 'how much all seemed like a wonderful dream. I advanced and embraced the Emperor, who received two salutes on either cheek from me having first kissed my hand. I next embraced the very gentle, graceful and evidently very nervous Empress.' At dinner, magnificent in St George's Hall, conversation turned to the war immediately and the Emperor said the French generals were always afraid of taking responsibility, which was why he wanted to go out. When the Queen urged the distance and the danger, the Emperor remarked there were dangers everywhere. Indeed attempts to assassinate him were so frequent that it appeared a regular stream of would-be murderers was passing to France after being supplied with a refuge in England. 'You know' the Emperor had told Lord Malmesbury 'I am neither fanciful, nor timid, but I give you my word of honour that three men have been successively arrested within fifty yards of me armed with daggers and pistols. . . . These men all came straight from England, and had not been twelve hours in France. Your police should have known it and given me notice.'[45]

In the evening there was a Ball in the Waterloo Gallery, tactfully re-christened the 'Picture Gallery' for the Emperor's visit, and next day the Emperor, when invested with the Order of the Garter, was visibly moved. The Queen's Journal records the Emperor's steady progress in her esteem. He was a master of the art of pleasing and his conquest of Queen Victoria was a major triumph. She was passionately Orleanist in her sympathies; her Uncle Leopold, King of the Belgians, having married the Orleanist Princess Louise to whom she was devotedly attached, she had come to love the whole Orleans family. While a visit from Napoleon III had been forced on her by political necessity, he achieved the feat of making it into a friendship. 'He has done his best to please her,' wrote Greville 'talked to her a great deal, amused her, and has completely succeeded.'[46] From being 'so very quiet, his voice low, & soft,' his manners become 'particularly good, easy quiet and dignified as if he had been born a King's son and brought up for the place'. Finally the Queen breaks into enthusiasm: 'That he *is* a very *extraordinary* man with great qualities there can be no doubt—I might almost say a mysterious man. He is evidently possessed of *indomitable courage, unflinching firmness of purpose, self reliance, perseverance and great secrecy*; to which should be added a great reliance on what he calls his *star* and a belief in omens and incidents as connected with his future destiny . . . at the same time he is endowed with a wonderful *self-control*, great *calmness*, even *gentleness* and with a power of *fascination*, the effect of which upon those who become more intimately acquainted with him is most sensibly felt.'[47]

*

Over in the Crimea, in spite of the amelioration brought by the end of winter, progress was not being made. The English losses recently had been greater than the French. As early as January 1855 the effective English force had dwindled to 11,000 men, while the French had increased to

78,000 and there was no immediate prospect of the mercenaries whom the British had reluctantly agreed to hire being on their way.[48]

The position of Sevastopol was not that of a besieged city in the normal sense. At the beginning of the 'siege', all non-combatants had been allowed to withdraw, but at no time had Sevastopol been cut off from the interior. Throughout the siege it received men, ammunition and supplies.[49] Napoleon III was determined on carrying Sevastopol by assault, preceded by a pitched battle. The French Commander-in-Chief resigned and was replaced by General Pélissier, a stern Norman who had no scruples in sacrificing the lives of his men. On 18th June 1855, the anniversary of Waterloo, an assault on Sevastopol was delivered by both English and French armies. The English force now represented only one-sixth of the effective combatants. After some preliminary success in capturing the outer line of the Russian fortifications, though at a cost of 6,000 French casualties and 600 English who could ill be spared, the assault failed. The prospect was bleak, summer was passing, another winter on the way; Sevastopol, though partially in ruins, remained unconquered. Worst of all cholera, Asiatic cholera, reappeared and decimated the new Sardinian recruits. Napoleon III displayed determination, the defeat was admitted; the power of his police crushed public outcry, and a new war loan was five times over-subscribed.[50]

Meanwhile magnificent preparations were put in hand for the return visit of the Queen and the Prince to Paris. The Emperor's necessity to maintain his throne by shows of glory was more urgent than before, and by good fortune on 16th August 1855, the eve of the visit of the Queen and Prince, the first victory over the Russians was achieved by the French fighting on their own at the Traktir bridge over the river Tchernaya. Sixty thousand Russians, an army intended to relieve Sevastopol, now concealed as at Inkerman by a mist, delivered an assault and were repulsed. The Tchernaya was an important battle. The hope of any successful relief of Sevastopol from without was at an end. The outlying fortifications had already been lost in Pélissier's costly success of the early spring. Sevastopol now lay open to constant bombardment.

In Paris a flush of success was already being felt in regard to the Queen's visit. Four centuries, during which the English and French had fought each other in almost every continent and country in the globe, had passed since the ten-year-old Henry VI had been crowned there. But during these blazing sunlit August days—the visit was blessed by the proverbial 'Queen's weather'—it seemed that perpetual warfare might at last end. Paris was 'en fête', decorated with banners, flags, arches of flowers, illuminations, full of people. There were endless cries of 'Vive la Reine d'Angleterre', 'Vive l'Empereur', 'Vive le Prince Albert'. The young Prince of Wales, now aged 13, and the Princess Royal, a year older, accompanied their parents; the other children were in quarantine for scarlet fever. The Queen writes of the 'blaze of light from lamps & torches—amidst the roar of cannon, bands, & drums, and cheers. . . . I felt quite bewildered,—all was like a fairytale, *so* beautiful and enchanting!'[51] Late at night on Friday, 24th August 1855, the Queen visited the tomb of Napoleon, and, leaning on the arm of another Napoleon, the granddaughter of George III surveyed the tomb of the arch-enemy of her family and her country to the light of flickering torches while bands played 'God Save the Queen'.

*

Napoleon III had conquered the Queen completely, and on her return she wrote of her 'delight at our triumphant, most interesting visit to Paris . . . the wonderful beauty and magnificence of *everything*. I never enjoyed myself more, or was more delighted or more interested, *& I can think* & talk of nothing else . . . we have come back with feelings of *real* affection for and interest in France. . . . For the Emperor personally I have conceived a real affection and friendship, & so I may truly say on behalf of the Prince. You know what *I felt* the moment I saw him. . . . Well we have now seen him for full *10 days* from 12 to 14 hours every day —often alone, and I cannot say *how* pleasant and easy it is to live with him, or how attached one becomes to him. I know *no* one who puts me more at my ease, or to whom I feel more inclined to talk unreservedly.' They had even, the Queen wrote, discussed the Orleans family. 'Wonderful it is that this man—whom certainly we were not over well disposed to, shd. by the force of circumstances be drawn into such close connection and become personally our friend and this entirely by his own personal qualities in spite of so much that could be & was, said against him! To the children (who behaved beautifully & had the most extraordinary success) his . . . judicious kindness was great & they are *excessively* fond of him. Without doing anything particular to *make* one like him, or *any* personal attraction in outward appearance, he *has* the power of attaching to him those who come near him and know him which is *quite* incredible. . . . The Prince, tho' less enthusiastic than I am, I can see well, shares this feeling, it is very reciprocal on the Emperor's part . . . the dear Empress, who was all kindness & goodness whom we are very fond of we saw comparatively little of—as for *really & certainly very good* reasons she must take great care of herself.'[52]

Lord Clarendon told Greville[53] the Queen was delighted with everything in Paris 'and especially with the Emperor himself, who, with perfect knowledge of women, had taken the surest way to ingratiate himself with her, by making love to her. This it seems he began when he was in England, and followed it up in Paris. As his attentions tickled her vanity without shocking or alarming her modesty, and the novelty of it (for she never had any love made to her before) made it very pleasant, his success was complete. After his visit the Queen talked it all over with Clarendon, and said, "It is very odd; but the Emperor knows everything I have done and where I have been ever since I was twelve years old; he even recollects how I was dressed, and a thousand little details it is extraordinary he should be acquainted with." "Le coquin, thought I" said Clarendon to me [Greville], "he has evidently been making love to her,"—and he [the Emperor] continued in the same tone at Paris much to her delight. She has never before been on such a social footing with anybody, and he has approached her with the familiarity of their equal positions, and with all the experience and knowledge of womankind he has acquired during his long life, passed in the world and in mixing with every sort of society.'

Both the children were delighted with their stay in Paris, and when the visit was coming to an end the Prince of Wales asked the Empress if she could not 'get leave for them to stay there a little longer', as he and his sister had enjoyed themselves so much and were very sorry to leave. 'The Empress said she was afraid this would not be possible, as the Queen and the Prince would not be able to do without them; to which the boy replied, "Not do without us! don't fancy that, for there are six more of us at home and they don't want us." ' In Paris, the Prince of Wales was put under Clarendon's charge by the Queen, to tell him what to do and how to behave. In Lord Clarendon's opinion the Queen's severe way of treating her children was 'very injudicious' and there would be trouble later with the Prince of Wales, who would be 'difficult to manage, as he has evidently a will of his own and is rather positive and opinionated', though his manners were good. The Princess Royal was 'charming, with excellent manners, and full of intelligence'.[54]

For the Emperor, the visit was equally successful. Above all things, almost more than success in the war itself, he wished to be received on an equality in the family of European sovereigns. England was still the most powerful nation and after the visit to Paris there was no doubt of the intimacy of his relations with the Queen.

*

A startling change took place in the Crimea due to the French victory in the battle of Tchernaya, which had left Sevastopol open to incessant cannon fire. On 17th August a bombardment of southern Sevastopol began and continued almost without a pause for all but three weeks.[55] Because the outer defences were no longer effective the continuous pounding of the city was more deadly than ever before. Southern Sevastopol, where the stores of ammunition and supplies were held, was swiftly becoming untenable, but the defenders resolved to hold it to the last whatever the cost. The decision was as useless as heroic, but there are moments in war, especially in defence, when the effect on morale not only for the present but the future, makes the sacrifice worth while. The Russians decided the defence must continue. For three weeks, the last two weeks in August and the first week in September, during the Queen's brilliant visit to Paris, Sevastopol was pitilessly bombarded at a cost to the defenders of 1,000 men a day, while during the night the exhausted garrison laboured frantically to repair or at least to conceal the damage done by day. But as the doomed garrison shrank, the fortress crumbled; on 7th September 1855, French troops attacked the Malakoff and in half an hour the key to Sevastopol was in their hands. All that day from before noon until after seven the Russians struggled to re-capture the fort, in a series of attacks, carried out with desperate courage, but without success; the Malakoff remained in the hands of the French.[56] A pontoon bridge had been constructed across the stretch of water separating the south from the north of Sevastopol and during the night of the 8th September in what has been described as 'one of the most brilliant feats of the entire war',[57] the Russian general succeeded in withdrawing the survivors of the garrison to the northern shore. Todleben than sank the last ships, destroyed the bridge itself and exploded the last of the great ammunition magazines setting the city behind on fire, a fitting conclusion to his historic defence of Sevastopol. For more than twenty-four hours the city blazed, and not until the morning of 10th September was it possible to endure the heat and enter the smoking ruins where Sevastopol had stood—destined, however, to rise again and in the war of 1939–1945 to be the scene of another historic defence.

The report of the fall of Sevastopol, which reached the Queen on 10th September 1855, stated shortly that the Malakoff was in the hands of the French, but the British assault on the Redan, the second key fortress to Sevastopol, had failed. Behind the bare statement lies one of the most painful pages of English history. The assault on the Redan failed because the British troops could not be brought to attack. The morale of the British army had collapsed, broken by the sufferings of the Crimean winter of 1854–55, by starvation, disease and exposure. The men who had stormed the heights of the Alma and fought like demons against odds at Inkerman, were dead, and their places taken by raw recruits. By an ill-judged decision the troops chosen to deliver the assault had been employed defending the British batteries against attacks in force from the Redan, and their losses had been heavy. The men had lost confidence in their generals and refused to stir. Painful scenes took place, young officers exposed themselves recklessly beckoning their men to follow them, some beat the men with their fists. Efforts were unavailing, the British would not leave the shelter of the parapet and were driven by the Russians back to their trenches in retreat. 'The greatest disgrace that had ever fallen on the British soldier' wrote Colonel Windham, who became known as 'Redan' Windham for the extreme courage he had displayed in leading the assault. It had failed, he told General Simpson, 'from want of pluck and method'.[58] Windham was the only man to emerge with enhanced reputation from that unhappy action.

At Balmoral the Queen, however anxious and concerned she might be as to what lay behind the terse report of British failure from the Crimea, must celebrate the fall of Sevastopol. A bonfire was lit, whisky liberally distributed, pipers played, rifles were fired into the air. The Queen sent a warm personal telegram of congratulations to the Emperor and remained at the celebrations until nearly midnight.[59]

The fall of Sevastopol, which did not solve the problem of the Crimean War, was succeeded by an event not merely of intense domestic interest to the Queen but one with fateful international consequences. The Princess Royal, called Vicky by her parents, became privately betrothed to Prince Frederick William, called Fritz in the family circle, only son of the King of Prussia's brother. His uncle the King had no children and Prince Fritz was heir to the throne. The affection between Prince Fritz and the Princess Royal dated from her childhood. They had first met when he came to England with his parents for the opening of the Great Exhibition in 1851. He was then a remarkably handsome young man of 22 and the Princess Royal a noticeably intelligent and attractive child of ten. A friendship sprang up between them. Prince Fritz stayed from 29th April until 27th May 1851, including several days at Osborne in an informal atmosphere, and they wrote affectionate letters to each other, the Princess Royal signing herself 'your loving and devoted Vicky', the Prince signing himself 'your loving Frederick William'.[60] That eventually they would marry was even then understood and approved by both sides, and when in 1855, the Princess Royal being then 14, Prince Fritz asked permission to begin to pay his addresses to her, bringing with him the blessing and consent of his parents, he received ready permission from the Queen and the Prince. The affection of the young couple for each other caused unexpectedly rapid progress.

On 29th September 1855 the Queen wrote[61] 'I must write down at once *what* has happened—what I *feel* & how grateful I am to God for *one* of the happiest days of my life! When we got off our ponies this afternoon Fritz gave me a *look* which implied that his little proposal to Vicky, wh. he had begged us to let him make—had succeeded. . . . He said in answer to my question whether anything had occurred, yes—that while riding *with her*—just at the very beginning, he began to speak of Germany, his hope that she would come there and stay there, they were interrupted in fact 3 times, upon one occasion by the picking up of some white heather,

363

which he said was good luck—which he wished her—and she him;—at last towards the end of the ride, he repeated again his observation about Prussia; she answered she would be happy to stay there for a year; he added he hoped always always—on wh. she became very red—he continued, he hoped he had said nothing which annoyed her—to which she replied "Oh! no,"—he added might he tell her Parents, wh. she then expressed a wish to do *herself*. He then shook hands with her—said this was one of the happiest days of his life. I tell this all in a hurry. We approved all this. . . . Vicky came into my room, where we both were . . . seemed *very* much agitated. . . . Her Papa asked her if she had nothing more to say "Oh! yes a great deal". We urged her to speak & she said: "Oh! it is that I am very fond of the Prince". We kissed & pressed the poor dear child in our arms & Albert then told her how the Prince . . . on the 20th had spoken to us—how we allowed him to pay her attention . . . [how he] wished to offer her his hand . . . & to see more & more of her. I asked did she wish the same? "Oh, yes, everyday" looking up joyously and happily in my face—she was kneeling. Had she always loved him? "Oh always!" . . . Albert came in to say that Fritz was there—& I took her in. She was nervous but did not hesitate or falter in giving her very decided answer. . . . He kissed her hand twice, I kissed him & when he kissed her hand again . . . she threw herself into his arms, & kissed him with a warmth which was responded to by Fritz again and again & I would not for the world have missed so touching and beautiful a sight. . . . It is his first love! Vicky's great youth makes it even more striking, but she behaved as a girl of 18 would, so naturally, so quietly and modestly & yet showing how very strong her feelings are. . . .

'Albert told her *in fact* she was too young to receive an actual proposal but that we felt for *both* their sakes her own feelings should be ascertained before he left but that no one but ourselves and Fritz's parents and sister shd. know. . . . My joy, my gratitude to God knows no bounds! To witness that dear child's innocent joy—to see the happiness of two such dear, pure, young Beings—is more happiness than I cd. ever have expected.'

Politically the betrothal of the Princess and Prince Fritz, 'the Prussian marriage', was enormously important. It was a maxim of European diplomacy that the peace of Europe would not be disturbed as long as the four powers, England, France, Austria and Prussia, were in agreement. But during the Crimean War a rift had appeared. Prussia and Austria, without being actively hostile, stood aloof. Frederick William IV, King of Prussia, was 'timidly obsequious' to his powerful brother-in-law, the Tsar of Russia, and 'too weak to be honest'.[62] The British Ambassador to Berlin, Lord Bloomfield, wrote angrily to Lord Clarendon 'It is impossible to make these people [the Prussians] understand the duties and responsibilities of a Great Power.'[63] Frederick William IV regarded the alliance between England and France as 'shameful', he had hopes of making great financial profits if Russia were blockaded and in spite of the fact that Austria stood for Catholicism and reaction, he had concluded an offensive and defensive alliance with the Austrian Emperor by April 1854. The policy of Prussia in the Crimean War was to be an 'ostentatious neutrality'.

Prussia and Britain were the two great Protestant states of Europe, and Prince Albert cherished very different hopes. His dream, as he had explained in 1848, was the unification of Germany. He longed to see a Protestant Prussia dominating a united Germany;[64] thus unknowingly he prepared the way for Bismarck.

Prince Albert wrote to Stockmar that the possibility of the marriage would have to remain a secret for about two years, by which time the Princess Royal would have been confirmed and have passed her 17th birthday. But the Prince was too much in love with the young Princess to keep silent.

To Lord Clarendon Prince Albert wrote that absolute secrecy was to be observed over the Princess Royal's marriage, but that to prevent the French people from suspecting a change of alliance, the Queen intended confidentially to inform the French Emperor.[65]

The news, however, leaked out and the general belief in Prussia's timidity and inclination towards Russia made the match unpopular. One of a series of articles in *The Times* described Prussia as 'a paltry German dynasty' which would not survive the downfall of Russia. Prince Fritz was actually spoken of as being likely to enter the Russian service in spite of the fact that both he and his father were well-known to be hostile to Russia. His uncle Frederick William IV's policy, although professedly liberal, united despotism with weakness and betrayed pro-Russian leanings. The result, however, was to make the proposed marriage suspect in both countries, and the difficulties of the task which awaited the Princess Royal, admittedly formidable, were increased.

*

The fall of Sevastopol, as has been said, brought no solution to the Crimean campaign. Lord Palmerston wrote[66] that after the capture of Sevastopol and the expulsion of the Russians from the Crimea, 'our danger will then begin, a danger of peace, and not a danger of war ... and we shall not yet have obtained those decisive successes which would enable us to insist on such terms as will effectually curb the ambitions of Russia for the future. I must try to fight the battle of negotiation as well as the battle of war.'

The position of the Allies had become reversed. The French longed for peace, the British burned for war. The British army which landed in the Crimea in September 1854 had virtually ceased to exist, hardly a man survived the disasters and the hardships of winter. The French troops were now more numerous, apparently fresher, the honour and glory of the recent fighting was theirs; they had assaulted and captured the Malakoff and in consequence Sevastopol, they had won victory at the Tchernaya, while the British were smarting from the shameful failure of the assault on the Redan. But in organisation, health and sanitation the French were behind the British, who had learned valuable lessons from the terrible winter of 1854–55. With the warm summer weather, Asiatic cholera had once again reappeared. In spite of the French military success, the last four months of 1855 showed an increase, compared with the previous year, of over 60 per cent in the French mortality, and a decrease of over 80 per cent in the British mortality compared with the disastrous winter of 1854. The French longed for the end of the war which had already vindicated their military honour. In Paris the news of the fall of Sevastopol had been greeted as bringing hope for the return of peace; the feelings of the British, owing to the failure at the Redan, were of humiliation and London was not illuminated. The Duke of Cambridge wrote to the Queen from Paris 'The feelings universally expressed here . . . are so different from those felt in England that it is extremely difficult to produce any impression. . . . France wishes for peace more than anything else on earth and this feeling . . . extends itself to all classes. The Emperor alone is reasonable and sensible in this respect but his position is a most painful one and he feels it very much.'[67]

Moreover the Emperor was aware that the position of France was not as triumphant as it seemed. The financial burdens of the war were heavy, so heavy that it would be difficult to continue such expenditure without injury to the finances of the country, and the large number of troops France was employing in the war was draining the vitality of the nation. As always, the Emperor's imperial position was not secure; in order to maintain his status he was compelled to progress from success to success. The prospect of facing another Crimean winter was alarming and he had in October signified his intention of withdrawing 100,000 men from the Crimea, since public opinion in France would not endure the expense of so large a force doing nothing and exposed to the hardships of a Crimean winter. Prince Albert wrote to Stockmar on 29th October 1855[68] that only some object of great national interest to France such as the Rhine frontier would stir the French to action. Meanwhile the inactivity of the armies in the Crimea and their failure to exploit the advantages of recent victories was attributed to the weak stand taken by Austria and Prussia and their alleged inclinations towards Russia. 'The position taken up by Austria and Prussia is alone to blame for all, and I tremble for the Nemesis' wrote the Prince to Stockmar.

Relations between Britain and France became heated. On 21st November 1855 Lord Palmerston wrote[69] he would rather continue the war with no other ally than Turkey than be dragged into a peace on unsatisfactory terms.

Conscious of his difficulties, for the critical state of French finances was known and had already produced a very mischievous effect in Vienna, Berlin and St Petersburg, the Emperor took the unusual step on 22nd November 1855 of addressing a long letter direct to Queen Victoria.[70] Divested of details, this letter made the startling suggestion that either the map of Europe ought to be re-adjusted, Poland freed, the Crimea given to Turkey and Finland to Sweden, or some agreement be arrived at with Austria, so that Austria might be driven to carry Prussia along with her and compel Russia to propose equitable conditions of peace.

In her reply, drafted by the Prince, to this letter the Queen emphasised that she, like the Emperor, desired an honourable peace: 'I am sincerely anxious to be at one with your Majesty'; but the peace must be supported by Parliament and acceptable to the nation. Her position as Queen of Great Britain was very different from that of the Emperor. With an overtone of regret she explained she was a constitutional while the Emperor was an absolute monarch. 'You are answerable to nobody, you can keep your own counsel, employ in your negotiations whatever person or form you choose, you can alter your course when you please. .... I, on the other hand, am bound by certain rules and usages; I have no uncontrolled power of decision; I must adopt the advice of a Council of responsible Ministers, and these Ministers have to meet and to agree on a course of action after having arrived at a *joint conviction* of its justice and utility. They have at the same time to take care that the steps which they wish to take are not only in accordance with the best interests of the country, but also such, that they can be explained to and defended in Parliament, and that their fitness may be brought home to the conviction of the nation.'[71]

Once more a period of fruitless negotiation intervened. Once more counter-proposals succeeded proposals. At St Petersburg, Prussia would have been preferred to Austria as a mediator.[72] Agencies working for Russian interests in Paris were identified and well known, and it was no secret that Austria's intention was to submit an ultimatum to Russia. Austria was aware that her conduct and that of Prussia had offended her allies and wished to establish their previous neutrality. The French government was approached through Baron Seebach, the Saxon Minister of the German Federation in Paris, but the Emperor refused to entertain any proposal except in concert with England. The terms were then stated in writing and described by the Queen as '... really too "naif". The Straits [Dardanelles] are to be closed and every flag excluded from the

Black Sea except the Russian and the Turkish, who will settle together what they think right.'[73] A clause in the Austrian proposals required a small cession of territory. Never before in history had Russia ceded territory she had appropriated, and the cession of this small portion of Bessarabia would cut her off from the Danube. Weeks became months and on 16th January 1856 the Prince wrote to Stockmar[74] 'Whether we shall have peace, and what kind of peace, or a continuation of the war and of what kind, is at this moment hard to say.'

The Allies were not aware how desperately the Tsar himself longed for peace. The drain on the Russian population through the casualties of the campaign was exhausting the country. Sometime before the death of Nicholas I Russian authorities estimated that 170,000 men had died; by the time of the Tsar Alexander II's accession another 85,000 deaths had occurred, and by the end of the war the total was half a million. It was Russia herself, the huge distances, the ferocious climate, which destroyed invader and defender impartially. 'Countless multitudes' of the Tsar's subjects perished transporting shells to Sevastopol, which must be carried 350 versts (230 miles) on the backs of bullocks, since railways did not exist. Of the armies which marched to the defence of Sevastopol in the Crimean campaign, in all probability only one man in ten arrived.[75] Ninety thousand men were said to have been buried on the north side of Sevastopol during the siege. The defence of Sevastopol had been as devastating to the strength of Russia as had been the advance on Moscow to the Grand Army of France.

In preparing for a renewal of their campaign the Allies held a Council of War in Paris in January 1856. On 16th January the Queen was informed—and by the King of Prussia to her surprise, 'the King of Prussia's ways are unfathomable!' observed the Prince[76]—that Russia had given way and was ready to discuss terms for peace.

The Queen expressed regret on 17th January that the last action to which the British army had been engaged should have been the defeat at the Redan, but Lord Palmerston writing back instantly told her 'Viscount Palmerston fully concurs in the sentiment of regret expressed by Your Majesty to Lord Clarendon, that the last action of the war should . . . have been the repulse at the Redan; but, however it may suit national jealousy, which will always be found to exist on the other side of the Channel, to dwell upon that check, yet Your Majesty may rely upon it, that Alma and Inkerman have left recollections which . . . will not be forgotten in the page of history.'[77]

The Peace Conference was to take place in Paris and one of the main difficulties—from the point of view of the Queen and the Prince the greatest difficulty—was the position of Prussia. Their personal links with Prussia were intimate, their eldest daughter was betrothed to the King of

Prussia's nephew and his father, the Prince of Prussia, was their close friend; yet the arguments against the admission of Prussia to the negotiations for peace were 'manifestly unanswerable'. It was only when the King of Prussia realised that negotiations for peace were about to begin that he became alarmed and anxious that Prussia should be included in the conference. He was met by a 'second refusal' in Paris and in London. King Leopold attempted to intercede but Prince Albert remained firm. In a letter which proves how closely he had identified himself with Britain he wrote 'Our position at the Conferences . . . will be one of extreme difficulty, for except the Emperor Napoleon we have no one on our side . . . his army is more intent on war against Germany than against Russia. . . . Austria is as selfish and as little to be relied on as ever. . . . Russia will not yield one hair's breadth more than she is *forced* to yield. . . . Russia is doing what she cannot help doing; and if she can shake off the compulsion which consists in the English and French Alliance and in the readiness of that Alliance to continue the war, she may suffer herself to be misled again into rejecting the conditions which we look on as necessary and indispensable. As for the special claims of Prussia . . . to take part in the negotiations, these have no sort of foundation. It is not revenge . . . which prevents us from admitting them, for this would be childish, but over and above the justifiable fear of increasing the number of our opponents in the approaching discussions, we are actuated by the conviction that it would be a most perilous precedent for the future to admit the principle, that a Power may take a part in the great game of politics, without having laid down their stake. . . . What right then, have others to interfere, who have taken no part in the conflict, and have constantly maintained that their interests are not touched by the matter in dispute and that therefore they would not take any part in the business?'[78]

Prince Albert's close friend the Prince of Prussia wrote to remonstrate and Prince Albert replied that no one wished more sincerely than he that Prussia should maintain her position as one of the Great Powers. Prince Albert always had in mind that Prussia and Britain were the two Protestant powers of Europe, and when a general treaty was signed, Prussia would be included. Until then 'nothing would create such serious obstacles as the infusion of the Berlin element (if I may so call it) into the transactions of the conference'.[79] What Prince Albert had predicted took place. On 18th March the Berlin plenipotentiaries were admitted and took part in the discussions which resulted in the General Treaty of Paris.

Only the Emperor Napoleon III discerned the Queen's personal difficulties. Writing to the Queen on 25th March 1856, Lord Clarendon remarked that the Emperor had said that England had 'much more interest in pleasing the King of Prussia than France. Lord Clarendon asked what that interest was. The Emperor answered, the marriage of the

Princess Royal, which must make the Queen anxious to be on good terms with Prussia.'[80] Lord Clarendon answered that the Emperor was greatly mistaken if he thought that the private feelings of the Queen ever interfered with what the Queen thought right for the honour or interests of England; long before the Emperor had made up his mind, Lord Clarendon knew the Queen had made no secret of the opinion that to admit Prussia to the negotiations for peace, 'after her conduct throughout the war had been condemned by Your Majesty's Government, would be degrading to England and a proof that she [the Queen] viewed political immorality with indifference'. The Emperor answered 'Do you know that is excellent to hear, and gives me great pleasure. I am much relieved that you have told me.'

On 16th March 1856 a salute of 101 guns announced that the Empress Eugénie, after a confinement of unusual severity, had given birth to Prince Eugène Louis Jean Joseph, later the Prince Imperial. Lord Clarendon reported 'The Emperor is enchanted with his son, dying for peace, does not care sixpence for the terms.'[81] His ambitions were centred on founding the Napoleonic dynasty which had long been his ambition.

On 30th March 1856, after infuriating and prolonged diplomatic difficulties, the formal treaty of peace was signed. The Crimean War was officially at an end. The two years of the war had changed Europe; the Protestant Germanic powers, Prussia and the German Federation, had not supported England but stood aloof. Within the Four Powers, England, France, Austria, Prussia, on whose agreement the peace of Europe was held to depend, a rift had appeared and England's principal ally was now, improbable as it might appear, France. It was a transformed Europe which confronted diplomatists in the late spring and early summer of 1856, and the old order was destined never to return.

Chapter Twelve

Prince Albert had never been robust. As a child he had had a delicate digestion and was easily exhausted. While still a youth he had trouble with his teeth and attacks of agonising toothache; above all he 'worried perpetually' over trifles as well as major matters. As long ago as 1844 Mr Anson had warned the Queen 'most seriously' that the Prince must adopt regular working hours, ending at a specified time each day, instead of 'endlessly harassing himself.[1] The Prince had not Lord Palmerston's gift of throwing off the cares of office. Jaunty and flippant Lord Palmerston might appear to be, but his energy, his daring, his power of taking decisions enabled him to be a successful Prime Minister at 80 years of age.

The Prince was often ill. From the beginning of 1850 onwards he suffered 'nerves'. At the end of October 1850, after a visit to York and a banquet in connection with the Great Exhibition, he had a gastric attack brought on by hurry, nervousness and the cooking of the celebrated chef M. Soyer, whose dishes were famous for their elaborate richness.[2]

An immense amount of work was done by the Prince in connection with the Great Exhibition and though the success was triumphant the Prince paid the penalty in 'one of those attacks to which his natural weakness of stomach made him liable'. In the autumn of 1851 the Prince and the Queen made a tour of the great industrial cities of England and the Queen wrote she was 'terrified for our Manchester visit'. From one o'clock in the morning the Prince was very unwell, 'sick and wretched';[3] by eight o'clock he had managed to pull himself together and the visit took place, but the Prince continued to feel unwell for some time.

In January 1854, the month before the Crimean War was declared, the Prince had catarrh. This was the period of the attacks on him in the Press and he wrote to Baron Stockmar that morally the New Year opened in 'a world of torment'. Writing again on 11th and 24th January, the Prince described his health as 'tolerable' but added he had rheumatic pains in his shoulder, as well as catarrh. It was inevitable that the attacks on him in the Press should distress both the Prince and the Queen and their digestions had suffered 'as they commonly do where the feelings are kept long upon the stretch'; he had been 'quite miserable' and that day he was unable to go out.[4] Next year, after the strain and depression of the disastrous winter of 1854-5, the stream of detailed memoranda and letters poured out by the Prince, the continuous overwork when the little green student's lamp from Bonn seemed never to go out, the Prince was seized with acute rheumatism in the right shoulder. 'I have endured frightful torture' he wrote in his diary; next day he was 'not much better' and continued to 'suffer terribly'. He wrote to Baron Stockmar explaining he had not been able to hold a pen which was the reason he had sent no letter for a week. He was better now, though still a 'cripple'; worse than all had been 'the long nights of sleeplessness and pain'.[5]

The peace, signed on 30th March 1856, brought no lightening of the Prince's labours. 'The things of all sorts that are laid on our shoulders, i.e. on *mine*, are not to be told.'[6] Stockmar, who was 'very much behind the scenes at more Courts than one', told the Prince '. . . Austria seems for the moment to think of nothing but of doing a good stroke of business for herself, with the *arrière pensée*, if things come to a rupture, of attaching herself again to Russia, and renewing in such an event the former Northern Alliance, rather than adhering to . . . the Western Powers. And at this moment this renewal is also the sole object of the Prussian policy, if there be anything there that deserves the name . . . the personal relations of Napoleon with England appear to be sincere and unwavering, but it is a wholly different question whether as much can be said for the French Government and people. This much I know for certain, that the dabblers in stocks in Paris are extremely sensitive to Russian intrigues. . . .'[7] Russia was anxious for Prussia to be kept out of the peace negotiations so that she might be alienated from England.

The 'Prussian Marriage', the most important single factor in Anglo-Prussian relations, was proceeding, though regarded in both countries with suspicion. On 20th March 1856 the Princess Royal was confirmed, after a preliminary examination on the previous afternoon, in the doctrines of the Church of England and the principles of Christianity by the Dean of Windsor in the presence of her parents, her grandmother, most of the Royal Family, the Ministers, great officers of state and members of the royal household. The Princess Royal, wrote the Prince to Stockmar, who could not be present because he was ill, answered 'very well and intelligently'.[8] The ceremony, which took place in the private chapel of Windsor Castle, was performed by the Archbishop of Canterbury. The Princess Royal was loved with special affection by Princess Feodora of Hohenlohe-Langenburg, Queen Victoria's half-sister. '. . . Dear Vicky . . . I must repeat,' Princess Feodora wrote,[9] 'is a great favourite with me, and all my children love *her* best of all your dear children. Let those rough manners and violent feelings be subdued by the excellent education she receives, and you will have when she is grown up, a firm, warm and amiable character, calculated to make those she loves happy, because she has a heart that *can* love.' The Princess Royal was still only 15, and the Queen and the Prince wished to make no public announcement of her intended marriage until three or four months before the event actually took place, though the news might be privately communicated to relations and friends.

This proposal conflicted with Prussian etiquette. '. . . According to their *established rule* in *Prussia*' wrote the Queen to Lord Palmerston on 24th March 1856[10] '*no* such *private family* agreement *can* take place, without being *officially announced* as a "*betrothal*" to the members of the Royal family, & published in the *Gazette* there. Now the difficulty arises—if this is done in Prussia, & it seems it *must be*—according to the customs of the country, wh. in the case of the *Heir Presumptive* to the Throne shd naturally not be omitted—*can* we *avoid* making an announcement *here*?— The only other alternative wld be to leave the thing unknown, wh. wld place us all in a very false position towards all our Relations, & wld deprive the young people of seeing each [other], wh. wld be very hard upon them, & wld moreover be an encouragement to the enemies of this marriage & throw (as many already do) *doubt* on its *reality* . . . Should not an announcement to the Privy Council be made informing it at the same time that the marriage wld not take place till the Prss. Royal had attained her 17th year?'

Lord Palmerston agreed with the Queen that the state of absolute secrecy concerning the betrothal should be put an end to. The Lord Chancellor, Lord Cranworth, had commented that people were inclined to remark that it was wrong that at so young an age the Princess should be bound to contract a marriage a year and a half hence, and ought to be left a free agent.

The Queen wrote she would like Lord Palmerston to inform Lord Cranworth that 'the Princess's choice altho' made with the sanction and approval of her Parents, has been one *entirely* of her *own heart*, & that she is as *solemnly* engaged by *her own free will* & *wish* to Prince Frederick William of Prussia,—as anyone *can be*, & that *before God*, she has pledged her word. Therefore, whether it be *publickly* announced or *not*, she could *not break* this solemn engagement. The Princess is confirmed & *old* enough to *know* her own feelings & wishes, tho' she may *not* yet be old enough to consummate the marriage & leave her Parents' roof.'[11]

The betrothal of the Princess Royal was announced on 29th April[12] but Count Bismarck was reported to be strongly against the match.

The Queen's letters to Lord Palmerston had changed their tone; hostility had disappeared. The difficulties with Prussia had helped to heal the breach between the Queen and her Minister and brought them together again. With her accustomed fairness of mind, the Queen recognised the Palmerstonian energy and ability which had been invaluable in bringing the Crimean War to a successful conclusion. On 11th April 1856 she bestowed the Order of the Garter on him.[13] Mutual confidence had been restored, and relations had become surprisingly cordial.

The Queen also proposed to raise Lord Clarendon a step in the peerage and award him a marquisate but he begged to be allowed to decline, writing to the Queen that he believed 'courtesy titles to his younger sons would be a positive injury to them in working for their bread, and he relies upon your Majesty's unvarying kindness for appreciating his reluctance to prefer himself to his children . . .'[14]

The Queen's concern for the Army did not slacken. Through her father, the Queen considered herself as identified with the Army by descent; she was 'a soldier's daughter' and military engagements became frequent and more binding than any others. She visited the military hospital at Chatham on 16th April 1856, and laid the foundation stones of the Royal Victoria Hospital at Netley on 19th May and of Wellington College, for the sons of Army officers, on 2nd June. She visited the new camp at Aldershot,[15] the first of many visits, spent the night in the Royal Pavilion and reviewed 18,000 troops, mounted on horseback and wearing the uniform of a Field Marshal, with the Garter.

Early in September 1856 she arranged to have a meeting with Miss Florence Nightingale. Sir James Clark, her old friend, was also an old friend of Miss Nightingale's and he wrote that the Queen wished to hear the story of Miss Nightingale's experiences with the army in the Crimea not only officially but privately. Miss Nightingale was to stay at Sir James Clark's house, Birk Hall, only a mile or two from Balmoral, and would be commanded to Balmoral for an official interview, and in addition the Queen proposed to drive over and have private conversations with her at Birk Hall.

On 19th September Miss Nightingale left Edinburgh for Birk Hall and on 21st September was commanded to Balmoral for an afternoon's talk with the Queen and the Prince Consort.

The meeting, an informal one, lasted for more than two hours and was a triumphant success. The Queen wrote to George Duke of Cambridge, who had become Commander-in-Chief in July on the resignation of Lord Hardinge, 'We are delighted . . . with her great gentleness, simplicity and wonderful clear . . . head. I wish we had her at the War Office.' 'She put before us' wrote the Prince in his diary that night 'all the defects of our present military hospital system, and the reforms that are needed. We are much pleased with her; she is extremely modest.'[16]

Miss Nightingale was commanded to Balmoral again and yet again. She conversed with the Prince Consort on metaphysics and religion and went with the royal party to church. On several occasions she dined informally. Most important of all, the Queen, as she had indicated, paid her private visits. One day she appeared suddenly quite alone, driving herself in a little pony carriage, and took Miss Nightingale off for a long walk. Another day she came over alone and unannounced, spent the afternoon, stayed to tea, and there was 'great talk'. Lord Clarendon said the Queen was 'enchanted with her'.

The outcome was the Royal Commission to examine the sanitary condition, administration and organisation of barracks and military hospitals, and the organisation, education and administration of the Army Medical Department. For the first time in history, the living conditions of the private soldier, his diet and treatment in health and sickness, in peace and war would be thoroughly investigated.[17]

*

Ever since their marriage in 1840 the Queen had been endeavouring to give the Prince the position she considered his due. 'Oh! if I only could make him King' the Queen had written.[18] This remained impossible, but the Prince had created for himself a position very different from the position he had occupied when as a dazzlingly handsome, penniless youth of 20 he came over to be inspected by the Queen in 1839.

The Queen wrote to Lord Palmerston on 5th June 1856[19] 'It is a strange omission in our Constitution that while the *wife* of a *King* has the highest rank and dignity in the realm after her husband assigned to her by law, the *husband* of a *Queen regnant* is entirely ignored by the law. This is the more extraordinary, as a husband has in this country such particular rights and such great power over his wife, and as the Queen is married just as every other woman is, and swears to obey her lord and master, as such, while by law he has no rank or defined position. This is a strange anomaly. No doubt, as is the case *now*—the Queen *can* give her husband the highest *place* by *placing* him *always near her person*, and the Nation would give it him as a *matter of course*. Still, when I first married, we had much difficulty on this subject; much bad feeling was shown, and several members of the Royal Family showed bad grace in giving precedence to the Prince, and the late King of Hanover positively resisted doing so. I gave the Prince precedence by issuing Letters Patent, but these give no rank in Parliament—or at the Council Board—and it would be far better to put this question beyond all doubt, and to secure its settlement for *all future Consorts of Queens*, and thus have this omission in the Constitution rectified. Naturally my own feeling would be to give the Prince the same title and rank as I have, but a Titular King, is a complete novelty in this country, and might be productive of more inconveniences than advantages to the individual who bears it. Therefore,

375

upon mature reflection, and after considering the question for nearly *sixteen years*, I have come to the conclusion that the title, which is now by universal consent given him of "Prince Consort" with the highest rank in and out of Parliament immediately after the Queen and before every other Prince of the Royal Family, should be the one assigned to the husband of the Queen Regnant *once and for all*. This ought to be done before our children grow up, and it seems particularly easy to do so *now* that none of the old branches of the Royal Family are still alive.

'The present position is this: that while every British subject, down to the Knight, Bachelor, Doctor and Esquire, has a rank and position by *Law*, the Queen's husband alone has one by *favour*—and by his wife's favour, who may grant it or not! When granted as in the present case, it does not extend to Parliament and the Council, and the children may deny the position which their mother has given to their father as a usurpation over them, having the law on their side; or if they waive their rights in his favour he will hold a position granted by the forbearance of *his* children. In both cases this is a position most derogatory to the Queen as well as to her husband, and most dangerous to the peace and well-being of her family. If the children resist, the Queen will have her husband pushed away from her side by her children and they will take precedence over the man whom she is bound to obey; if they are dutiful, she will owe her peace of mind to their continued generosity!

'With relation to Foreign Courts, the Queen's position is equally humiliating in this respect. *Some* Sovereigns (crowned heads) address her husband as "Brother", some as "Brother and Cousin", some merely as "Cousin" . . .

'The only legal position in Europe, according to international law, which the husband of the Queen of England enjoys, is that of a younger brother of the Duke of Saxe-Coburg, and this merely because the English law does not know of him. This is derogatory to the dignity of the Crown of England.

'But nationally also it is an injury to the position of the Crown that the Queen's husband should have no other title than that of Prince of Saxe-Coburg, and thus be perpetually represented to the country as a foreigner. "The Queen and her foreign husband, the Prince Albert of Saxe-Coburg and Gotha!"

'The Queen has a right to claim that her husband should be an Englishman, bearing an English title, and enjoying a legal position which she has not to defend with a wife's anxiety as a usurpation against her own children, her subjects and Foreign Courts.

'If properly explained to Parliament and the country, I cannot foresee the slightest difficulty in getting such a necessary measure passed, particularly if it be made quite clear to the House of Commons that it is in no way connected with a desire to obtain an increased grant for the Prince.'

Nevertheless the Bill had to be postponed. It was not, as the Queen's confidant, the popular Lord Aberdeen, warned her, that there was a danger the Prince might acquire the title of 'King Consort': his right to sit both in the House of Lords and in the Privy Council was questioned. Lord Derby pointed out[20] that owing to pressure of business some time might elapse before the Bill could be introduced and there might be an unfavourable campaign got up in the Press. Would it be better to mention it in the Queen's speech? The Queen had doubts about that being prudent.

When the Cabinet considered the Bill again in the spring of 1857, a new point was raised. According to the law and usage of England a woman receives her husband's rank, and not vice versa; the wife of a duke, though a commoner, becomes a duchess. If this fundamental principle were to be departed from and the husband of a Queen Regnant placed in a legal position analogous to that of the wife of a King, it would follow that the husband of a Queen Regnant ought to be constituted King Consort. Not only was there, throughout the nation, a strong objection to a King Consort, but should he survive his wife and marry again he would communicate his rank to his wife. Moreover the Bill would interpose him 'with great constitutional solemnity' between the Prince of Wales and the throne, and deprive the Prince of Wales of the constitutional priority which 'the Heir Apparent has hitherto enjoyed' in the Parliament chamber and at the council table.

On 15th March 1857 the Queen told Lord Palmerston that the Cabinet minutes she had just received caused her 'much surprise'; the arguments it contained must surely have occurred to the Queen's advisers before? 'But having now waited 17 years without approaching any nearer to the solution of what she considers a most important question to her and her Family . . . [she] is inclined to think it will be better for her, instead of attempting an Enactment by Parliament, with its attendant discussions, to do merely as much as her Prerogative will enable her . . . and to content herself by simply giving her husband by Letters Patent the title of "Prince Consort" which can injure no one while it will give him an *English title* consistent with his position, & avoid his being treated by Foreign Courts as a *junior Member* of the house of *Saxe Coburg*.'[21] After a short further delay this was done and on 25th June 1857 a Council was held at Buckingham Palace, at which 'Letters Patent were approved conferring upon his Royal Highness Prince Albert the title and Dignity of Prince Consort. . . . The words Prince Consort were inserted in the prayers instead of the words Prince Albert.'

The season of 1856 was one of exceptional gaiety. The excitement and relief of victory and peace, the touching affection of Prince Frederick William and the little Princess Royal, still only 15, were reflected in a series of balls and banquets. The Queen danced 'indefatigably' and was regarded as one of the most graceful performers of her day in minuets and country dances. Two years earlier, on 10th June 1854, at a ball in the Waterloo Gallery at Windsor she had danced every dance, finishing with a reel to the bagpipes. On 9th May 1856 the new ballroom and concert room at Buckingham Palace designed by Prince Albert was used for the first time for the coming-out ball of the Princess Royal. Two evenings earlier the Queen had given a 'dinner of reconciliation' at Buckingham Palace for Baron Brunnow, the Russian Ambassador, at which Tory ex-Ministers had wives of Whig Ministers for their partners, and Whig Ministers the wives of Tory ex-Ministers. Signs of discomfort made themselves apparent, especially in the case of Lady Clarendon, but ended in laughter.[22]

In the autumn of 1856 the Queen found she was again pregnant, but remained calm and when at 2 a.m. on 14th April 1857 Princess Beatrice was born she wrote 'I have felt better and stronger this time than I have ever done before'.[23] She had wished for a girl and Princess Beatrice was an unusually pretty baby, 'the flower of the flock'.

The Queen was happy and occupied with domestic concerns, beginning to choose items for the trousseau of the Princess Royal, whose intended marriage had been announced in the Prussian Official Gazette on 16th May and communicated to Parliament by a message from the Queen on 19th May. To Parliament, the Queen expressed her confidence in their assistance 'in enabling her to make such a provision for her eldest daughter, as may be suitable to the dignity of the Crown and the honour of the country'. The Prince wished that this opportunity should be used to settle once for all what financial provision should be made for the royal children. Hitherto the major part of the expense had been paid by the Queen out of her private income, and the Prince felt that frequent appeals to Parliament for money were degrading and might be unwelcome. The Ministry, however, hesitated and had some misgivings as to the feeling of the House in the case of the 'Prussian marriage'. Apprehension was unfounded. By a majority of 328 to 14 the House voted to settle a dowry of £40,000 and an annuity of £4,000 on the Princess Royal. 'The House' wrote the Prince[24] 'was *determined* to be *unanimous* out of respect for the Queen.'

The marriage was to take place in London and the Queen instructed Lord Clarendon, the Foreign Secretary, to direct the English Ambassador in Berlin 'not to *entertain* the *possibility* of such a question as the Princess Royal's marriage taking place at Berlin. The Queen *never* could consent to it . . . and the assumption of its being *too much* for a Prince Royal of Prussia to *come* over to marry *the Princess Royal of Great Britain* IN

England is too *absurd*, to say the least. The Queen must say there never was even the *shadow* of a *doubt* on *Prince Frederick William's* part as to *where*. . . . Whatever may be the usual practice of Prussian Princes, it is not *every* day that one marries the eldest daughter of the Queen of England. The question therefore must be considered as settled and closed. . . .'[25]

*

On the 26th June 1857 the first distribution of Victoria Crosses was held in Hyde Park. The institution of the Decoration in June 1856 was the result of the Queen's admiration of the heroism displayed by private soldiers in the Crimean campaign. The Victoria Cross was awarded to all ranks, irrespective of social position, to private soldiers, non-commissioned officers and commissioned ranks, to all ranks in the Navy as well as the Army. Inscribed 'For Valour', it was given only to men who had served in the presence of the enemy and performed some signal act of bravery or devotion. The Victoria Cross remains the most highly prized military and naval decoration. In 1857 it carried with it a pension of £10 a year.

A huge semicircle of seats to hold twelve thousand people had been erected; about four thousand troops were present and it was calculated over one hundred thousand people filled Hyde Park when the Queen, mounted, dressed in a black skirt and scarlet jacket, and accompanied by the Prince Consort, Prince Frederick William of Prussia and a suite in brilliant uniforms, decorated 62 holders of the Victoria Cross with her own hand. The men were brought up to her one by one; she bent from her horse and pinned the cross upon the breast of each man, and as each man withdrew the Prince bowed 'with a gesture of marked respect'.[26]

There was an atmosphere of rejoicing, of thanksgiving, for victory in the Crimean campaign throughout the country, though moderated by an uneasy feeling that the victory was not quite as glorious, or its fruits of such value as had once been expected. At least there was peace and it was into comparative tranquillity that the news exploded of the outbreak of the Indian Mutiny at Meerut, on 10th May 1857.

For some months past reports had been coming in that trouble was brewing in India, but Lord Palmerston was not in any degree panic-stricken.[27] It was not until the news of massacres and outrages committed on European women and children began to be known that horror seized the nation.

In 1857 the administration of India was divided between the East India Company, which maintained its own army, navy and system of tax collecting, and the Crown. It may broadly be stated that for thirty years before the Mutiny broke out a feeling had been growing stronger that the

379

military government of India ought to be transferred to the Crown. India had become more than the East India Company could manage.*

In February 1856 British military forces in India consisted of some 233,000 native troops and rather less than 40,000 European troops, including both East India Company and Crown forces.[28] A sepoy army was maintained in Bengal, another at Bombay and a third at Madras. A sepoy was an Indian soldier who had received the training of a European private, and an Indian sailor with a European training was (and is) called a lascar. It is important to keep clearly in mind that the Indian Mutiny was a military revolt of the Bengal sepoy army only. It was in no sense a national rising, though some discontented landholders joined in. A large number of annexations had been carried out by Lord Dalhousie in states where misgovernment had been scandalous, amongst them Oudh in Bengal, where the native ruler was deposed and pensioned off. He had no son and when he died his adopted son, the notorious Nana Sahib (later responsible for the massacre at Cawnpore), demanded that the pension should be continued to him. He was refused though he retained the rents from his predecessor's private landed estates. The Nana was resentful and began 'tampering with the sepoys'. A large number of professional soldiers had become redundant when Oudh was annexed, were thrown penniless upon the world, and became one of the causes of the Mutiny.

In addition the annexation of the Punjab by Sir John Strachey (uncle of Lytton Strachey) left a trained sepoy army idle and inflated with importance after the victory of Gujerat. Apparently trivial causes gave rise to serious consequences, since the caste system made discipline in the sepoy army almost impossible to enforce. Sir Charles Napier described how an officer of low caste might often be seen crouching submissively before the Brahman recruit he was supposed to command. The difficulty of taking baths in the cool climate of Afghanistan led to Hindus being forced to break religious rules; if Hindu troops crossed the sea, as they had to do to fight in the Chinese opium wars, their beliefs obliged them to pay fines and undergo purification to gain re-admission to their caste. The sepoys began to mutter, rumours spread; the Sikhs, the best infantry

* The dificulties of combining government with the necessities of a commercial undertaking were demonstrated in the two opium wars of 1840 and 1855, regarded as blots on British annals. Both wars were fought to force the Chinese to allow the importation of opium into China by the British. The Chinese authorities and a certain number of Indian rulers were engaged in a crusade to stamp out addiction to the drug. The opium trade, however, represented the most profitable part of the East India Company's commerce with China, and there were in addition questions of diplomatic status, loss of face, if the British allowed themselves to accept the dictation of the Chinese. Lord Palmerston decided on the use of force, but the gunboats used at his orders came from the East India Company's navy. The British were victorious and the opium trade continued.

in the world, were sought after by the recruiting sergeants, and now that it was being whispered that a Sikh army was to be raised to supersede the sepoys an old prophecy was revived that, in 1857, the centenary of the Battle of Plassey, European rule would be destroyed.

The story of the spark which set off the explosion is famous. At Dum-Dum in Bengal near Calcutta, early in January 1857, a lascar asked a Brahman sepoy to give him a drink of water from his cup. The Brahman refused, saying the lips of the low-caste lascar would contaminate the cup. The lascar retorted that the Brahman was going to lose his caste in any case because cartridges greased with the fat of pigs and cows were being manufactured by the government and every sepoy would be obliged to bite them before loading his rifle. To the Brahman the shock was devastating. Greased cartridges had been sent to India in 1853 and the Adjutant General of the Bengal army warned the authorities that none should be issued to sepoy troops until the grease had been proved to be inoffensive, but the warning was disregarded. The story spread like wildfire, it fell on soil all too ready to receive it; the agents of the Nana Sahib and the Brahmans of Calcutta expanded it, and the wildest whispers were believed. The sepoys were to be forced into using the cartridges and would lose their caste, the Russians were about to arrive in force and liberate all Mussulman sepoys. At Berhampore and Barrackpore the 19th and 34th Native Infantry took alarm and refused to receive percussion caps for use on parade. The official outbreak of the Mutiny occurred at Meerut, forty miles from Delhi, where two regiments of sepoy infantry and one of native cavalry were quartered, with a battalion of the 60th Rifles, a regiment of dragoons, a troop of horse artillery and a light field battery, the strongest British force at any station in Bengal. On 23rd April Colonel Smyth of the native cavalry ordered a parade of ninety-five skirmishers in order to give them a full explanation of the facts concerning the cartridges—which in fact they had long used. Only five men would touch them, the majority being influenced, as appeared on cross-examination, not by religious scruples but by fear of consequences from their comrades. The men were tried, by a native, not a British, court martial and sentenced to ten years' imprisonment, reduced by the commander of the division to five in the case of the younger men. On Saturday, 9th May 1857, the sentences were published in the presence of the whole brigade. As the men were led away they yelled curses at their officers and a native officer warned the senior officers that the men were determined to release the prisoners. An extraordinary and ominous stillness now descended on the sepoy quarters. Next day, when the British troops were assembling for evening church, some hundreds of sepoys broke open the jail, released the prisoners and joined by hordes of beggars, criminals and ne'er-do-wells, dispersed to plunder, slay and loot.

381

On Monday, 11th May, the native cavalry entered Delhi, released the prisoners in the jail, and within a few hours were joined by the sepoy infantry. Together they ranged through the city, murdering every European they met, setting fire to European houses and committing atrocities on European women and children. Hopelessly outnumbered, without a single company of British troops, the officer in charge of the magazine had no choice but to blow it up, collect the women and children and retreat—a retreat on which the sufferings, especially of the children, were ghastly and the number of survivors few. The supine behaviour of the British at the beginning of the Mutiny is explained by the faith of the British in the sepoys, especially the sepoys of the Bengal Army. Though India was ruled by the British as a conquest, a considerable proportion of the governors of India, men of noble character such as John Nicholson, the famous Lawrence brothers, John and Henry, and the Stracheys, loved and believed in India and Indians. Macaulay, who was closely connected with Indian administration, said 'We are trying to bring good government to people to whom we cannot give a free government.' In the now mutinous Bengal Army sepoy service was hereditary and the Bengal sepoys had been called by Lord Dalhousie a band of brothers.

The news of the outbreak at Meerut on 10th May was sent to the Queen by Lord Palmerston on 26th June 1857. Ashley, his biographer, states that the news did not reach Lord Palmerston until the middle of June, almost immediately followed by the news of the death of the commander-in-chief of the forces in India, General Anson.[29] The same night Lord Palmerston interviewed Sir Colin Campbell, who started for India to take command next day. The first vessel with troops for India sailed on 1st July and by the end of September about eighty ships with more than thirty thousand British troops were on their way.

On 1st July the Queen wrote in her Journal[30] there were 'such sad accounts from India, the mutiny among the native troops spreading, sad murders of Europeans at Meerut, still worse at Delhi . . . the Commander-in-Chief is marching on it.'

The series of atrocities and disasters for which the Indian Mutiny is infamous was now, however, about to begin with the massacre at Cawnpore at the orders of the Nana Sahib. The garrison at Cawnpore consisted of four sepoy regiments, two of whom, with the native cavalry, mutinied. Some four hundred British fighting men, of whom seventy were invalids, and several hundred women and children, with the faithful sepoys, took refuge in the magazine, a substantial building though largely disused, and for three weeks defended the women and children against continuous fire, suffering agonies from thirst, hunger and wounds in blazing heat, without medicines of any kind. The Nana Sahib then offered a safe passage to Allahabad to every member of the garrison who surrendered, and a ragged crowd of exhausted survivors tottered from the magazine and were embarked in barges thatched against the Indian midsummer sun. Almost at once the thatch of the barges was strewn with burning cinders and burst into flames, grapeshot and bullets were poured into the crowd from concealed positions, while troopers rode into the water and sabred the women and children. A hundred and twenty-five women and children who survived were dragged back to Cawnpore and imprisoned with a few survivors from one of the barges which had drifted ashore. The men were killed in the presence of the Nana Sahib, and the women and children, after the sepoys had refused to shoot them, hacked to death by criminals and ruffians. Cawnpore was followed by the famous siege of the Residency at Lucknow, the capital of Oudh, lasting from May to November 1857. On 17th May about 350 European men, 350 women and children, 120 sick and 300 faithful sepoys and other natives, took refuge in the Residency at Lucknow, which was nothing more than the private house of the resident with a few defences hastily thrown up. This tiny force was besieged by ten thousand disciplined troops and a number of irregulars, mainly from the private armies of local land owners. The scene within the Residency was one of terror and despair; weeping women clinging to their children prayed in their rooms while Indian labourers worked feverishly at unfinished fortifications.

On 7th July Major General Sir Henry Havelock began his famous march to recapture Cawnpore and relieve Lucknow. With about 1,000 troops and proceeding by forced marches, though it was now the hottest season of the year, he gained three victories and entered Cawnpore on 17th July, visiting the scene of the massacre where gore drenched the ground and blood-soaked women's dresses, children's curls and shreds of clothing testified to the horror which had taken place. Cholera and dysentery had attacked his troops, ammunition was short and though Havelock won yet another victory and was being urged to press on to Lucknow where the besieged were enduring torments from heat and water shortage and where disease was rampant, he decided he must return to Cawnpore for reinforcements. Three strong positions remained to be reduced.

The moral courage Havelock displayed in carrying out this painful decision is worthy of the highest praise. He turned back and re-entered Cawnpore to find he had so displeased the authorities that he was superseded by Sir James Outram. On 16th September 1857 Sir James Outram made his famous declaration of his intention to stand down and leave to Havelock, to whom it rightly belonged, the honour of relieving Lucknow. On 25th September Lucknow was stormed. But it was only too soon evident that all the relieving force could hope to do was reinforce the garrison of the Residency, which now consisted almost entirely of invalids, the women and children having suffered severely. Transport to carry away the sick was lacking. Sir Colin Campbell, the Commander-in-Chief, was raising fresh forces but seven more weeks had to be endured before, in the second week of November, Campbell, with his favourite regiment the 93rd Highlanders, came within sight of Lucknow. All Victorian children, and many later, were familiar with the story of how after months of dread, terror, water shortage and semi-starvation endured under a burning sun, the sound was heard far in the distance of the approach of the relieving force, the pipes of the 93rd Highlanders playing 'The Campbells are Coming', and as the final assault took place, through the smoke was to be seen the flag of Britain still fluttering from the Residency roof; during the siege it had never been hauled down.

Unhappily Havelock was attacked by cholera on 20th November and died on 24th November. In addition the experienced and humane Sir Henry Lawrence, Chief Commissioner of Oudh, had died during the siege from wounds caused by an exploding shell. It had been Lawrence's earnest wish that the outrages committed by mutineers and natives should not provoke reprisals. Severity of punishment was essential, but reprisals should be avoided. When, however, the rape and mutilation of women and children before their murder became known, reprisals became impossible to control. At Delhi, the mutineers, double the British forces in numbers, had occupied the Red Fort, while the British were encamped on the ridge overlooking the fort and the city. On 14th September 1857 the fort was stormed and by the 19th Delhi was once more in British hands. Against the advice of such long-time Indian administrators as John Nicholson and John Lawrence, Sir Henry's brother, an orgy of revenge followed. Mutineers were blown from cannon, hacked to pieces, hanged in hundreds. In one episode outside the walls of the fort, 400 mutineers were hanged simultaneously, while British officers seated beneath sipped whiskies and sodas and regimental bands played.[31] In rural districts suspect villages were razed to the ground, the inhabitants were driven out, their livestock slaughtered and their crops destroyed. Lord Canning, who succeeded Lord Dalhousie as Governor General, earned the name of Clemency Canning by issuing an appeal to the civil servants of the East India Company to refrain from unnecessary severity. It was widely held, however, that merciless punishment inflicted at an earlier stage would have stopped the Mutiny.

By the end of September the Mutiny was effectively quelled and the future government of India had to be considered. One of the difficulties was the understandable rage and vindictiveness felt in England, even more than in India itself, for the atrocities committed during the Mutiny. Yet it was impossible to hold and govern India without employing and trusting Indians.[32]

The language of the Queen herself during the Mutiny period was

384

balanced and devoid of hysteria. The news of the massacre at Cawnpore reached her when she was at Balmoral and she wrote to King Leopold 'We are in sad anxiety about India, which engrosses all our attention. Troops cannot be raised fast, or largely enough. And the horrors committed on the poor ladies—women and children—are unknown in these ages and make one's blood run cold. . . . I know you will feel much for us all. There is not a family hardly who is not in sorrow and anxiety about their children, and in all ranks—India being *the* place where everyone was anxious to place a son!'[33] Lord Clarendon wrote he was indignant to learn that the boy Maharajah Duleep Singh, who was being educated in England, had shown little or no regret for the atrocities which had been committed. The young Maharajah's father, one of the most harsh and cruel of Indian rulers, had been deposed by the British government and his son taken under British protection. The Queen pointed out that in spite of gentleness and amiability the Maharajah had an Eastern nature, and could hardly be expected as a deposed Eastern sovereign to be very fond of British rule or to like hearing the people of his country called fiends and monsters and that they were being brought by hundreds if not thousands to be executed. She advised Lord Clarendon to say nothing on the subject.

India had outgrown the East India Company. During the last twenty years mainly through annexations the territory ruled by the Company had doubled in size. Since 1853 the system of recruitment had changed, and this marked the beginning of the end of the old Company. Cadetships in the East India Company had previously been obtained by presentation, but since 1853 were awarded by competitive examination. Gradually the younger sons of upper-class families were replaced by intelligent young men of more middle-class origin. While the wisdom of this change was debated, it had become abundantly evident that the East India Company could no longer control the huge territories of India. Accordingly the Queen assumed the government, and the Act for the better government of India received the Royal Assent on 2nd August 1858. A month later the directors of the East India Company issued their final message, venturing to address the Queen herself: 'Let Her Majesty appreciate the gift—let Her take the vast country and the teeming millions of India under Her direct control: but let Her not forget the great corporation from which she has received them nor the lessons to be learned from its success.'[34] With these dignified words the East India Company took farewell.

The Queen assumed the government of India conscientiously and with a deep sense of responsibility. A proclamation setting forth the principles on which the government was to be conducted had now to be issued by the Queen in Council. The first draft was rejected by the Queen and the

Prince Consort, whose hand is evident throughout the matter. The Prince Consort wrote in his Journal 'It [the Proclamation] cannot possibly remain in its present shape.'[35] The points the Queen wished to be made were that she was 'a female sovereign who speaks to more than a hundred millions of Eastern people on assuming the direct government over them and after a bloody civil war, giving them pledges which her future reign is to redeem. . . . Such a document should breathe feelings of generosity, benevolence and religious toleration. . . .' The Queen strongly objected to a sentence in the draft which spoke of the power she possessed 'for the undermining of native religions and customs'. The Queen wished this sentence replaced by a declaration that 'the deep attachment which Her Majesty feels to her own religion and the comfort and happiness which she derives from its consolations will preclude her from any attempt to interfere with the native religions, and that her servants will be directed to act scrupulously in accordance with her directions'. General statements of the Queen's intention to 'relieve poverty' were to be replaced by 'a direct mention of railways, canals and telegraphs . . . with an assurance to those prejudiced populations that these works are the basis and will be the causes of their general and individual welfare'. The Queen terminated by expressing her wish that expression should be given 'to her feelings of horror and regret at the result of this bloody civil war . . . and Her Majesty thinks the Proclamation should terminate by an invocation to Providence for its blessing on a great work for a great and good end'.

It was in a spirit of conciliation, more marked than that displayed by her Ministers, that the Queen approached the enormous task of governing India with its vast new responsibilities, and it was a token of the importance she attached to her Indian Empire that from the time she assumed the government of India the Queen seldom appeared on public occasions without two Indian attendants in her suite.

*

During the last days of December 1857 a long-standing dispute over the Hanoverian Crown jewels, called by the Queen 'the diamond question',[36] was at last settled. On the death of William IV, his next living brother, the Duke of Cumberland, who was noted for his disagreeable behaviour, became King of Hanover and claimed a large quantity of superb jewels, at that time in the possession of the young Queen, partly on the grounds that they belonged to the Crown of Hanover and partly that they had been bequeathed to him under the will of Queen Charlotte. Exactly which the jewels were that he claimed on the latter ground proved difficult to identify.

The British government resisted the claim on behalf of the Queen.

For instance certain jewels worth £50,000 in 1761, a great sum at that time, had been bought by George III to be presented to Queen Charlotte. These were of a splendour unattainable by a small impoverished German state. They had been bought with English money and in the opinion of English people to call them the Hanoverian Crown jewels was ridiculous. Among the items in dispute[37] were five pearl necklaces, one of which had belonged to Queen Anne, while another was reputed to be the finest rope of pearls in Europe; two pairs of diamond earrings, one of which had cost £7,000, the other £5,600; a stomacher (a large ornament worn over the dress almost covering the chest) set with diamonds, one of which had been bought for £18,000, another for £5,800, and a 'George', part of the Garter insignia, set with nine brilliants which had cost £4,500. Numerous other pieces were equally splendid and included jewels presented to Queen Charlotte by the Nawab of Arcot.

The young Queen Victoria was fond of jewellery and, owing to the civil war in the reign of King Charles I, followed by other crises in succeeding reigns, the Crown of England was not outstandingly well furnished in this respect. She frequently wore a number of the Hanoverian pieces, being especially attached to the superb rope of pearls. What Greville described as 'a good deal of wrangling' followed, the King of Hanover still as surly and difficult in negotiation as he had been when Duke of Cumberland. The opinion of the Law Officers of the Crown was sought, a Commission was appointed, statements were taken and reports made. In 1846, after much delay, the Commission had reached a conclusion when one of its leading members, Lord Chief Justice Tindal, died and the Commission was broken up before a report could be made. The 'diamond question' then lapsed, but the King of Hanover died in 1851 and on his death the Hanoverian claims were renewed. Once more there was delay but in 1857 another Commission was appointed which after sittings of inordinate length decided on all points for Hanover and against the Queen, the award being published on 5th December 1857.[38]

The Queen and the Prince Consort were 'desperately annoyed' and considered the award unfair. Lord Clarendon told Greville the Prince Consort asked him 'whether Parliament could not be applied to to make good the jewels, which were the very ones the Q. had always worn; and that the dignity of the Crown required that she should be properly furnished with such ornaments. C. told him it was out of the question, that the Government could not make any such application to Parliament ... that her [the Queen's] popularity was in great measure owing to her own judicious conduct and abstinence from that extravagance which had marked the reign of George 4th; that nobody cared whether she was attired in fine Pearls or diamonds. . . .'[39]

While Hanover had voluntarily given up the claim to the pearls, which

Lord Lyndhurst had told Greville were worth about £150,000, on their side too the award came as a disappointment, large money compensation having been the hope. The jewels were delivered to the Hanoverian Ambassador, Count Kielmansegge, his receipt given and the claim was agreed to be fully discharged on 23rd January 1858.

*

The Princess Royal was 17 in November 1857, and her marriage to Prince Frederick William was to take place on 25th January 1858. For the Queen it was, she wrote in her Journal, 'The 2nd most eventful day in my life. . . . I felt almost as if it were I that was being married over again, only much more nervous.'[40] Vicky, to the Queen's relief, was 'composed, & in a fine, quiet disposition'. Her wedding dress was of white moiré antique, trimmed with three flounces of Honiton lace and wreaths and sprays of orange flowers and myrtle, with the veil and wreath to match. The Queen wore mauve and silver moiré antique, trimmed with Honiton lace, with a train of velvet, also trimmed with Honiton lace; she wore the royal diadem and the crown diamonds. Before the bridal party left the Princess Royal was daguerrotyped both alone and with her parents, but the Queen trembled so much with nervousness and excitement that the picture was indistinct.

The marriage ceremony was celebrated in the Chapel Royal, St James's, the Princess Royal walking between the Prince Consort and the King of the Belgians in the bride's procession, preceded by the elder three of her sisters, who were much moved—Princess Alice 'cried dreadfully'. The Archbishop of Canterbury, Dr John Bird Sumner, was evidently very nervous. But Vicky maintained her composure; both she and Prince Fritz gave the responses calmly and clearly and their confidence, wrote the Queen, removed her fear of breaking down. The Queen found the moment touching when the bride and bridegroom knelt before the altar, the Princess Royal with her young bridesmaids kneeling behind her. The Duchess of Kent looked handsome in purple velvet with ermine. The Princess Royal was in floods of tears when she said goodbye to her mother, but had recovered before she entered the carriage which was to take her and her husband to Windsor. Enthusiasm in London itself and all along the road was tremendous with cheers, shouting, pealing of bells and decorations. At Windsor the Eton boys took the horses out of the carriage and dragged it up to the castle with immense noise.

The Queen had had doubts about the temperament of the Princess of Prussia, Prince Fritz's mother. She had had a trying life, was cleverer and more far-sighted than Prince Fritz's father, the Prince of Prussia, with much more liberal feelings and sympathies, but she was nervous and excitable.[41] After the marriage of the Princess Royal and Prince Fritz, the Queen and the Princess of Prussia became more intimate. The Queen called her 'My dear kind friend' and relates how the Princess of Prussia came to see her on the afternoon of the wedding '. . . and we had a most *pleasant*, & satisfactory confidential talk about our dear Children. She is a great comfort & support to me.'

The Princess Royal and Prince Fritz wrote charming, happy letters but the Queen felt low and flat. One by one the guests left, the Prussians declaring themselves impressed and delighted, the Prince and Princess of Prussia becoming still more intimate and confiding to the Queen the difficulties of the Prince's position, but the Queen was '. . . quite depressed; all had been so brilliant, so satisfactory & now *all* was over, & our dear Child also gone!'

On 27th January the Court moved to Windsor. The Princess Royal and her husband met the Queen at Windsor station, so obviously happy that the Queen felt relieved and comforted. The marriage was a true union, and in all the vicissitudes which awaited them, their mutual affection provided a never-failing refuge. Next day Prince Fritz was invested with the Order of the Garter and a large dinner in the Waterloo Gallery followed. On 29th January the brief honeymoon ended and the Court moved back to Buckingham Palace. The Queen, the Prince Consort and the honeymoon couple drove to the station in an open phaeton and were almost mobbed by enthusiastic Eton boys.

There is a legend that the Queen did not care for her children, least of all for her eldest daughter. The legend is without foundation. The Queen did not care for young babies at what she called the 'frog stage'; many women do not. But when the children were older she loved them dearly, the Princess Royal especially, and with the exception of one accusation, written by the Prince Consort in one of his rare moments of rage, there is no indication that she resented the Princess Royal's adoration of her father or the Prince Consort's devotion to her. The Princess Royal was known to be his favourite child.

The volume of correspondence between the Queen and her daughter proves their affection. The number of letters preserved in the series from the Princess Royal, afterwards Crown Princess of Prussia and Empress Frederick, to the Queen is 4,161; the number from the Queen, now in the possession of the Landgraf of Hesse, in the Kronberg Archives, is 3,777. Both collections were counted by Count Corti in the course of his work on the life of the Princess Royal (grandmother of the present Landgraf) in the Archives at Windsor Castle and at Kronberg, entitled *The English Empress*.[42]

On 30th January 1858 the Queen gave a small party at Buckingham Palace for the Princess Royal's eight bridesmaids, their parents and some members of the household. Dinner was followed by a 'nice little dance' and the Princess said goodbye to her friends. The Princess Royal and Prince Fritz were to leave for Germany on 2nd February from Gravesend, crossing in the royal yacht *Victoria and Albert*. The Queen felt 'the dreadful separation hangs like a heavy cloud over us'.

The 2nd of February was a wretched day, dull, still, thick, and bitterly cold. The Prince Consort, the Prince of Wales, Prince Alfred and George Duke of Cambridge went with the young couple to Gravesend to see them embark. They were to be accompanied to Berlin by Lady Churchill and Lord Sydney. It began to snow as they set out and it snowed all day, but crowds had gathered to cheer the Princess in the streets and in spite of the weather, she used an open carriage. At Gravesend young girls with wreaths strewed flowers before her in the snow-covered streets. She was, reported the Prince of Wales, 'in a terrible state, when she took leave of her beloved Papa'.[43]

The Princess Royal said a final farewell to her father alone in her cabin and next day each wrote the other a letter.[44] In the privacy of her cabin the Princess had completely broken down and her father wrote 'My heart was very full when yesterday you leaned your forehead on my breast to give free vent to your tears. I am not of a demonstrative nature and therefore you can hardly know how dear you have always been to me, and what a void you have left behind in my heart. Yet not in my heart, for there assuredly you will abide henceforth, as till now you have done, but in my daily life which is evermore reminding the heart of your absence.'

From on board H.M.Y. *Victoria and Albert* on the Scheldt, the Princess Royal wrote 'My beloved Papa. The pain of parting from you yesterday was greater than I can describe:—I thought my heart was going to break when you shut the cabin door and were gone. . . . I miss you so dreadfully, dear Papa, more than I can say. . . . I meant to have said so much yesterday but my heart was too full for words. I should like to have thanked you for all that you have done for me and for all your kindness, all your love, wh. I shall most earnestly endeavour to deserve. . . . You know, dear Papa, how *entirely* you possess the deep confidence, reverence and affection of your child, who is proud to call herself such, and I may say of my husband too. . . . I feel that writing to you does me good, dear Papa. I feel that I am speaking to you.'

On 6th February 1858 the Queen and Prince Consort were delighted to hear from the British Ambassador in Berlin that the Princess Royal and Prince Fritz had safely arrived at the Palace of Potsdam and that the Princess had created a most favourable impression. She was at the moment in the height of her bloom, delightful in the childish prettiness of her looks, combined with a royal dignity. The Queen writes of 'Vicky's great success with high and low—her amiability, good nature, great dignity and kindness in speaking to everyone'.[45] Her success was 'quite a conquest, enchanting everyone'.

Her father wrote 'Thank God . . . you seem to gain "golden opinions" in your favour which naturally gives us extreme pleasure, but what gives us the most pleasure of all, was the letter so overflowing with affection which you wrote while yet on board the yacht. Poor child! . . . Well did I feel the bitterness of your sorrow, and would so fain have soothed it! But excepting my own sorrow I had nothing to give. . . .'[46]

The Princess Royal's heartbroken letter was written to her father, but her mother was given the letter to read, and there was no concealment.

On 11th February Prince Fritz telegraphed to his father-in-law reporting the Princess Royal's success at the Prussian Court; the Prince Consort commented, 'The Telegraph must have been amazed when it wrote: "The whole Royal Family is enchanted with my wife. F.W."'[47] In the following week the Prince Consort sounded a warning note. He was aware of the difficulties confronting the Princess Royal, more aware, now that Prince Fritz's father and mother were better known to him, than when the marriage was first thought of. 'Festival time is now over and the family which was all complaisance to the strangers and the feted may now be disposed to put you back in what they consider your place, and to resume theirs. But even this need occasion no estrangement. Your place is that of your husband's wife, and of your mother's daughter, you will desire nothing else, but you will also forgo nothing of that which you owe to your husband and your mother.'

On 10th March 1858 he wrote to congratulate her: '. . . You seem to have taken up your position in the difficult family with much tact.'[48] Nevertheless the outlook for the Princess Royal was cloudy and the goodwill which she herself possessed so abundantly was not felt towards her in the Prussian Court.

*

The Prince's health was not improving. He was, wrote the Queen, 'torn to pieces with business of every kind'[49]—the dangers and difficulties of the relationship between Prussia and Austria, the fragility of the British alliance with France, the prospects before his beloved daughter whom he sadly missed, were already combining to harass him; when out of a reasonably clear sky unexpected disaster brought Britain and France to the verge of war, causing Palmerston to fall.

On 10th January 1858, almost precisely a fortnight before the marriage of the Princess Royal, four Italian refugees arrived in Paris from London.[50] Their leader, Felix Orsini, had with him a number of bombs which had been manufactured in Birmingham. He travelled through Belgium and the English police informed the French authorities of his journey and its intention and gave a description of his appearance. Nevertheless on the evening of 14th January 1858 he contrived to be lying in wait for the Emperor Napoleon III and the Empress as they drove up the Rue Lepelletier to the Opera House. Orsini and his fellow conspirators hurled bombs, ten persons were killed and over one hundred and forty injured, but the Emperor and Empress were unharmed though spattered with the blood of the wounded. Orsini's intention was to supersede the French Empire by a social democratic republic, which would, he believed, transform Europe.

The Prince Consort's brother, Ernest, Duke of Saxe-Coburg and Gotha, was waiting in the Emperor's box when he heard an explosion. The Queen wrote 'He rushed down, the noise and cries were dreadful, as well as the rush of the crowd, many bleeding, who quite surrounded the Emperor and Empress. The Emperor's nose was grazed—and the Empress's dress splashed with blood from the wounded around her [she had also received a blow on the eye which affected it for some time]. . . . The Empress wonderfully composed and courageous, even more so than the Emperor. They remained through the whole Performance.'[51]

The rage of the French nation was intense. The Emperor had earlier protested to the Queen on the stream of assassins, trained and equipped in England to kill him, who were permitted by the British authorities to cross from England to France; and now Count Walewski, the French Foreign Minister, on 20th January 1858 sent a despatch to the French Ambassador in London, Count de Persigny, enumerating the recent attempts at assassination of the Emperor planned in England and declaring it was unthinkable that Britain should shelter, on British soil, men whose avowed intention was to murder the Emperor of the French.[52] French resentment was intensified by the violent language of certain French officers, 'the colonels', congratulating the Emperor and calling for the invasion of England as an infamous haunt in which infernal plots were laid and murderers and assassins protected.

The English were almost equally furious. Certainly the attempt by Orsini was greatly to be regretted and impossible to deny, the laws needed to be strengthened and as a result of Orsini's crime were in process of being strengthened; but according sanctuary to political refugees had for centuries been regarded as Britain's right. The English nation refused to allow their laws to be dictated to them by foreigners. Feeling, inflamed by 'the colonels' in England against France, as it had been in France against England, was outraged by the spectacle of one who, like the Emperor Napoleon III, had lived safely in England for many years as a refugee, attempting to interfere with English laws, and Persigny, who knew England well, despaired of the maintenance of the Franco-British alliance. Lord Derby declared there was no hope whatsoever of legislation against foreigners who had done nothing criminal in this country, while Granville observed 'The accounts from France are very bad. A war with France would not surprise me.'[53] Palmerston pointed out that it would be impossible to surrender Italian refugees to France and refuse to surrender them to Austria, while if London was closed to political refugees, they would find a new base in New York.

On 9th February Lord Palmerston brought in a Bill changing the law relating to conspiracy, from a mere misdemeanour to a felony, punishable by penal servitude for five years, hard labour for three years or transportation. 'The Bill will pass' wrote the Queen 'and Lord Derby has been useful about it.'[54]

The Bill did pass its first reading, by a majority of 299 to 99, another Palmerston triumph. But at its second reading—on 19th February, the week after Palmerston's Government of India Bill had also been successfully introduced—he received a surprising and signal defeat. Tempers had cooled. Walewski's despatch of 20th January had been published and was felt to have been dealt with inadequately. The government had been cowardly and deficient in dignity. The despatch ought to have been answered in a spirit worthy of the occasion; an important opportunity had been lost of asserting the great principles of English law. On the Emperor's side there was nothing he desired less than a rupture with England. His ministers rebuked the colonels and the newspapers which supported them, especially the *Moniteur*, for their outrageous language, and the crisis was over. But a hostile amendment aimed at Palmerston was brought forward in the House of Commons, regretting the defiance to France and censuring the government for failing to give more complete satisfaction. The Prince Consort wrote to Baron Stockmar[55] '. . . at this moment Lord Palmerston is the most unpopular of men . . . in the Lower House they would scarcely let him open his mouth. The motion, on which Radicals, Peelites and Tories were able to agree, was framed with extreme dexterity by Lord John [Russell], in concert with Sir James Graham, and given to Milner Gibson to fire off.'

Palmerston insisted on resigning, though urgently asked to remain by the Queen.* Though they were on greatly improved terms she did not completely trust Lord Palmerston. She had complete confidence, however, in Lord Clarendon, his Foreign Secretary, to whom she was attached, so feared finding herself once more left without friends. The Queen sent for Lord Derby who succeeded in forming a government, bringing with him Lord Malmesbury as Foreign Secretary.[56] Malmesbury, it will be remembered, was an old and close friend of Napoleon III, whom he had visited during the dark period of his imprisonment in

---

* Palmerston returned as Prime Minister in June 1859, with Lord John Russell as Foreign Secretary.

393

the fortress of Ham. The Emperor's desire for peace with England survived the acquittal of one of Orsini's chief fellow conspirators at the London Central Criminal Court—greeted by the anti-French London populace with shouts of exultation. Orsini himself was executed in Paris on 13th March 1858. It was one of Napoleon III's characteristics to be unwilling to sign death warrants and Orsini wrote the Emperor two letters, from the shadow of the scaffold, imploring him to become the liberator of Italy from Austrian tyranny. Napoleon III himself was a former sympathiser with the Carbonari (literally charcoal-burners), armed revolutionaries dedicated to the cause of Italian freedom and including many foreigners, amongst them Lord Byron who organised a successful revolt in Naples in 1820, and he was 'with some difficulty withheld from granting Orsini a pardon'.[57] The Emperor appointed General Pélissier, the distinguished Crimean veteran, Ambassador to London in 1858. Greville, whose grumpiness did not soften with advancing years, called him a 'military ruffian', nevertheless the appointment was popular and in August 1858 at Cherbourg in a series of dazzling festivities the French and English sovereigns met and cemented the *bonne entente* once more. Though the Emperor was at pains to emphasise the importance of the English alliance, the Prince Consort wrote in his diary 'I am conscious of a change in the Emperor.'[58] The display of French naval force at Cherbourg startled and alarmed observers, and the Prince was both anxious and angry. A difficult period in European politics was about to open, in which the most important issue was united Italy. The explanation of the change in the Emperor noted by the Prince Consort was that, as the result of Orsini's bombs, the Emperor now realised his life was and would continue to be in danger unless he took action on Italy. As an old member of the Carbonari and as a Bonaparte his own sentiments were naturally pro-Italian, but the powers were opposed to each other. Reduced to the simplest terms, Prussia and Russia would welcome the weakening of Austria by the loss of the Italian provinces, but they were not ready to take up arms against Austria on behalf of liberalism to which they were opposed. France and Britain were ready to forward the cause of liberalism but not that of nationalism, because Malta and Corsica, both at that time sympathetic to Italian unity, were vital to them as naval powers. Austria meanwhile, behaving with conspicuous lack of wisdom by the harshness, cruelty and tyranny of her rule, had forced unity on Italy. Only one national and liberal state was left in Italy, Sardinia, which included Piedmont, whose king was Victor Emanuel II and whose prime minister was Count Cavour, formerly the editor of *Il Risorgimento*. In 1857 a National Society was founded in Italy, with branches in every province, of which the aim was 'The Union of Italy one and indivisible, under Victor Emanuel as King'.[59]

Another reason for the change in the Emperor which the Prince Consort had noticed may have been that, just before the meeting at Cherbourg, Napoleon III had in fact taken preliminary steps to come to an understanding with Cavour and Victor Emanuel of which he did not think the Queen and Prince Consort would approve.

Within a few days the Prince developed a sick headache.[60] Prospects in Europe depressed him. Everywhere he looked he saw obstacles, impending difficulties, mountains of work piling up. The volume of the Prince Consort's correspondence preserved in the Royal Archives, the stream of memoranda he poured forth, is daunting. To take only a single issue, the Prince was harassed by the inadequacy of the defensive forces of Britain, an anxiety which the French display of naval force at Cherbourg did not allay, and concerned for the adequacy of the British army. The nation could not survive, as a first-rate European power, on the memory of Trafalgar and Waterloo.

Private affairs disturbed him. On 12th August 1858 news arrived of the death of Cart, the Prince Consort's valet, who had been with him since he was a small child and carried him up and downstairs before he could walk by himself. 'While I was dressing' wrote the Queen 'Albert came in, quite pale, with a telegram saying "My poor Cart is dead, he died quite suddenly" . . . I turn quite sick now writing it . . . I burst into tears. All day long the tears would rush every moment to my eyes. . . . Cart was invaluable, well educated, thoroughly trustworthy, devoted to the Prince. . . . He was the only link my loved one had about him which connected him with his childhood. . . . I cannot think of my dear husband without Cart . . . we had to choke our grief down all the day.'[61]

The death of Cart cast a shadow on the private visit which the Queen and the Prince Consort paid to the Princess Royal and her husband at the Palace of Potsdam in Berlin in August 1858. Both parents were anxious about the fate of the Princess Royal, with her 'child's heart and man's mind', and they were not reassured. It was 'sickeningly' hot and neither the Queen nor the Prince Consort felt well in heat; they were greeted with too much official friendliness, too many reviews took place in their honour, too many official visits were paid. The Prince longed for beloved Coburg, for the peace and shade of his old home, the Rosenau. Sir James Clark, who accompanied the Queen and Prince, noted '. . . the perpetual uniform . . . none of the Royal family, or princely class, ever appear out of the stiff military dress, the whole country seems occupied in playing at soldiers.'[62]

Especially disturbing was the state of the Royal Family of Prussia. The mind of King Frederick William IV, in spite of its brilliance, had always 'verged on the abnormal' and in 1857 the King had become so eccentric that his younger brother, William, father of Prince Fritz William, acted as his deputy. In 1858 the mind of Frederick William IV gave way completely, and his brother William became Regent with full powers. At first all was well. The reactionary ministry of Frederick William IV was dismissed and a new government, named 'the New Era', representing moderate liberal opinion, appointed. The Prince Consort was delighted.[63] '... The party of lawful progress does not have anything in common with the Democrats ... the people rely on the former and do not want to have anything to do with the latter.'

Unfortunately Prince Fritz William's father, though as Regent he had complete authority, did not arrange for his son to exercise any political functions. He was to be a soldier, a militarist, in tune with the new national aspirations, and to the regret of his father-in-law, the Prince Consort, he displayed indications that he was likely to prove an able soldier.[64]

The Queen had a nervous dread, almost a horror, of her daughter becoming pregnant. 'Though I quite admit' she wrote[65] 'the comfort and blessing good and amiable children are—though they are also an awful plague and anxiety for which they show one so little gratitude very often! What made me so miserable was—to have the two first years of my married life utterly spoilt by this occupation! I could enjoy nothing— not travel about or go about with dear Papa and if I had waited a year, as I hope you will, it would have been very different.'

Nevertheless shortly after marriage the Princess Royal did become pregnant. Her husband wrote a letter telling her father the news, which the Queen received badly. 'The horrid news contained in Fritz's letter to Papa upset us dreadfully' the Queen wrote to the Princess Royal on 26th May 1858,[66] adding mysteriously 'The more so as I feel certain almost it will all end in nothing.'

Though the Princess had a fall in September 1858 in the old Schloss in Berlin, 'to which I attribute all my misfortunes and baby's false position'—her foot caught in a chair and she 'fell with violence on the slippery parquet'—which she had not told 'dearest kindest Mamma' at the time because she did not want to make her anxious,[67] the Princess Royal's pregnancy ran its full course. The slight injury to her foot was made the excuse for her inability to meet her father in Coburg in May 1858, so he came to Berlin to see her instead. 'We tell everyone your foot is the cause of your not going to Coburg. ... I hope you do the same—and Fritz don't allow his own people and relations to enter into such subjects; it is so indelicate; Papa never allowed it and I should have been frantic.'

On 15th June 1858 the Queen again wrote of her shrinking from pregnancy. 'What you say of the pride of giving life to an immortal soul is very fine, dear, but I own I cannot enter into that; I think much more of our being like a cow or a dog at such moments; when our poor nature becomes so very animal and unecstatic.'[68]

In the inner circles of the Court the Queen was blamed for her behaviour towards the Princess Royal at this period and indeed for her behaviour generally towards all her children. Stockmar told Lord Clarendon that the Princess Royal—'this poor child here'—was worried and frightened to death because the Queen wished to exercise the same authority and control over her as she did before her marriage. Lord Clarendon, who considered the Queen was too severe with her children, told the Prince Consort that he and his wife had six children. 'Now we have never used severity in any shape or way, never in their lives had occasion to punish any of them, and we have found this mode of bringing them up entirely successful.' Stockmar is alleged to have described the Prince as 'completely cowed' and living in perpetual dread of bringing on the 'hereditary malady' in the Queen, the madness which was then thought to afflict her grandfather George III, now known to be the disease called porphyria. These allegations are made by Greville, not directly by Lord Clarendon himself, and are not accurate.[69] No one could read the voluminous correspondence between the Queen and the Princess Royal and doubt their devotion to each other. Admittedly the Queen was not an easy character, admittedly she was at times hysterical, but the Prince Consort was not 'completely cowed', and no 'hereditary malady' in the form of madness existed. The Queen possessed qualities of sincerity, generosity, loyalty and affection which compensated for her displays of emotionalism and which inspired devotion in almost everyone who came frequently into contact with her. On the morning of 27th January 1859, while the Queen was dressing she was agitated to receive a telegram that the Princess Royal 'had been some time indisposed', adding that the event was about to happen, and the baby was on the way. After luncheon a telegram from Sir James Clark announced the Princess Royal had a boy. 'All is happily over the Princess as well as can be & the young Prince also.'[70] Universal rejoicing followed and healths were drunk, by the domestic staff as well as the family and household.

It was not until two days later that the Queen had any inkling of the severity of the confinement, one of the worst recorded in obstetrical history. 'My precious darling, you suffered much more than I ever did' wrote the Queen '—and how I wish I could have lightened them for you! Poor dear Fritz—how he will have suffered for you! I think and feel much for him.'[71] Though the facts were softened to avoid upsetting the Queen and the sufferings and danger to the Princess Royal were not fully disclosed, the life of the baby Prince was admitted to have hung on a thread. Some uncertainty surrounds the condition of the little boy at his birth, the little boy destined to become the Emperor William II, 'the Kaiser'. William II had a withered arm, accepted as due to a birth injury; it was alleged that only after three to four days was this condition

397

observed, the doctors in attendance being absorbed in the Princess Royal, who hovered for days between life and death. In the Royal Archives is preserved a statement from Professor Dr August Martin, son of the accoucheur Dr Eduard Martin, denying that the injury could have fallen within his father's province. '. . . I cannot accept that my father, who was at that time the leading authority in his field, and Herr Schön-lein, could have failed to notice any injury to the bones or joints while examining and handling the child.'[72] It has been for centuries standard practice for a newly born infant to be examined by the doctor or doctors acting as accoucheur for any signs of physical imperfection, and in the case of a royal baby to be subsequently exhibited to state officials for inspection. In Professor August Martin's opinion the withering and lack of growth—the Emperor William II's left arm was shorter than his right—was the result of pressure on the nerve centre in the neck, pro-duced by the baby's pre-natal position and the severity of the confinement. He names the condition as a form of paralysis, not immediately apparent but which would become noticeable slightly later, and writes 'The treatment of the arm was entrusted to the relevant specialists and not to the accoucheur.' The Princess Royal's life was in danger for several days. She was too weak to be made aware of the disaster that had happened to her child. On 19th February 1859, Sir James Clark, who had a con-fidential interview with the Queen and gave her full details, told her he did not think 'she [the Princess Royal] will be able to walk for another month! . . . At first it was thought the baby was quite dead.'[73]

The Princess Royal herself was overjoyed to have a son.[74] 'I am *so* happy, *so* thankful he is a boy, I longed for one, more than I can ever describe, my whole heart was set upon a boy, and therefore I did not expect one. . . . You need not be afraid I shall be injudiciously fond of him, although I *do* worship him . . . and then I feel he is my *own* and he owes me so much, and has cost me so much.'

After the interview with Sir James Clark, the Queen knew of the defective arm and in a letter to the Princess Royal told her not to distress herself, and all would come right in the end, but there was no discussion until the Princess Royal came to see her mother alone at Osborne on 21st May 1859.[75] The meeting was ecstatic: 'It is hard indeed to be separated from one's own mother when one has only just learnt *what* one owes her' the Princess Royal had written immediately after Prince William's birth. '. . . Such happiness to be at last together again!' wrote the Queen '. . . Vicky only began to cry when she talked of her poor little boy's left arm being so weak, which it has been since his birth, having been injured in being brought into the world.'

*

It was at this moment, while the Prince was suffering tortures of anxiety over the sufferings and the danger of his beloved daughter, that the situation in Europe reached boiling point.

On 23rd April 1859 Austria sent a peremptory ultimatum to King Victor Emanuel at Turin demanding instant disarmament. Austria was determined to force the Italians to accept her rule. The ultimatum was ignored, Piedmont was invaded by Austria and the Austrians sustained the first of a series of important defeats at Montebello on 20th May. Here Napoleon III, still preserving the sympathies of an old Carbonaro, came to the assistance of Victor Emanuel. The Austrians were defeated again at the battle of Magenta on 4th June, followed by a third defeat at Solferino on the 24th. (The sufferings of the wounded at the bloody battle of Solferino were witnessed by a Swiss gentleman named Henri Dunant and resulted in the foundation of the Red Cross.)

Meanwhile a revolution had taken place in Florence. The Grand Duke, given the choice between abdication or declaring himself for Piedmont, fled. 'All Italy is now up' wrote Lord Malmesbury.[76] A Commissioner was appointed to manage the affairs of the Duchy, the appointment being made by King Victor Emanuel. In this apparently favourable situation Napoleon III, to universal astonishment and without consulting his allies, on 8th July 1859 concluded an armistice at Villafranca.

Prussia had mobilised with the intention of supporting Austria, a tragic disappointment to the Prince Consort. He agreed that Prussia should arm in order to be on a level with the international powers, but she was to remain neutral. He saw that a dangerous situation might develop in which Austria would be stubborn because she was sure that Germany and Prussia would draw the rage of France on themselves. But early in May Lord Malmesbury had an interview with the Prince Consort's brother, Ernest Duke of Saxe-Coburg and Gotha, who was 'red hot' against France. Duke Ernest had declared that Prussia had armed because it was impossible to resist the pressure of public opinion, and the Duke's aide de camp went so far as to hope that the Austrians would be defeated in the battle about to take place, as they were later at the battle of Montebello on 20th May. All Germany would then rise as one man and invade France.

The Prince Consort's hope of Prussia becoming a liberal constitutional monarchy in the midst of Europe under his old friend William Prince of Prussia, now Regent, was a dream, for the Regent was taking military measures, extending the period of conscription, reducing the 'Landwehr' (citizen army), and increasing the regular army. Reactionary and military influences were becoming dominant and the Regent was turning to the ideas of which the Prince Consort believed he had been cured in 1848, while the Prince himself laboured, to the edge of breakdown, to persuade him to adhere to constitutional methods.

Oppressed by personal anxiety for his beloved daughter, whose position as the Regent's daughter-in-law, apart from apprehension over her health, was extremely painful, and continuously harassed by affairs in Europe, the Prince Consort became ill, the first of a series of illnesses produced by mental fatigue, emotional disturbance and overstrain. He continued to work, driving himself mercilessly, but suffered from constant catarrh and described himself as getting on only 'tolerably well; much work and excitement, and constant east wind, lower the tone and keep the mucous membranes in a state of constant irritation'.[77]

Later in the year a new and agonising apprehension came to the Prince and the Queen when they learnt the Princess Royal, less than one year after her dangerous and terrible confinement, was once more pregnant. On this occasion everything was normal and a daughter, Charlotte, was born on 24th July 1860. 'What a joy! Thank God!' wrote the Queen.[78] The news reached her at Osborne in a telegram from Prince Fritz and the arrival of the new baby was celebrated in a festive supper, cooked by the children themselves in the miniature kitchen of their playhouse, the Swiss Cottage.

The Prince Consort's depression had been increased by the removal of his old friend and counsellor, Stockmar. Stockmar had brought him up politically and had been consulted by the Prince in every crisis; the quantity of memoranda exchanged between them, preserved in the Royal Archives, is prodigious. But Stockmar was now an old man, over seventy, his health was not good and he was inclined to be hypochondriacal. In 1856 he had left England and the Court of St James's for ever, and settled in retirement at Coburg, surrounded by his family.[79] No one had been able to take his place and the Prince Consort wished to visit him and discuss the Prussian German affairs which were causing him so much anxiety. He longed also to see his daughter and her eldest child William who was as yet a stranger to him. He had also an intense attachment to his childhood home and longed once more to see Coburg itself, the Festung (Fortress), the Rosenau, the country house where he had been born, and other scenes of his youth.

It was decided that the Queen and the Prince Consort should visit Coburg, and that the Princess Royal should meet her parents there with her little son. The party left Gravesend in the royal yacht on 22nd September 1860, reaching Coburg three days later. The Princess Royal was in deep German mourning for the death of Marie, Dowager Duchess of Saxe-Coburg and Gotha, only the day before. 'Could hardly speak I felt so touched . . .' wrote the Queen '. . . then our darling grandchild was brought in. Such a little love! He came walking in at Mrs Hobbs' [his nurse's] hand in a little white dress with black bows and was so good. He is a fine fat child, with a beautiful soft white skin. . . . He has Fritz's eyes and Vicky's mouth and very fair curly hair. We felt so happy to see him at last! . . . dear old Stockmar who remained some time, [looked] quite himself, though a little weak.'[80] The Prince says in his diary that he found him showing signs of age.

On 1st October 1860 the Queen began her Journal for the day 'Before proceeding, I must thank God for having preserved my adored one! I tremble now on thinking of it. . . . The escape is very wonderful, *most merciful!* God is indeed most gracious.'[81]

The Prince had gone out to shoot over a hill on which stands the castle called the Kalenberg, the Queen remaining at Coburg writing letters. Later, the Queen, with the Duchess of Saxe-Coburg and Gotha and the Princess Royal, met the Prince and his companions, lunched with them in the castle, and then the Queen and Princess Vicky began to sketch. Prince Albert now said he must go back to Coburg as he had people to see, leaving the Queen to follow. He was riding alone in a carriage with four horses, driven from the box, when about three miles from the castle the horses took fright, became uncontrollable and dashed off at full gallop. About a mile from Coburg the road crosses the railway at a level crossing. As the runaway carriage approached, the bar to prevent carriages crossing the line was drawn across the road and there was a wagon standing on the road just outside the bar. The Prince, seeing that a collision was inevitable, jumped from the carriage. Happily, though somewhat bruised and cut across the nose, the hands, arms and knees, he was not stunned and was able to go to the assistance of the coachman, who had been seriously hurt. One horse had been killed; the others had broken away from the carriage and rushed on to Coburg where they were seen by Colonel Ponsonby, the Prince's equerry, who at once drove to the scene of the accident. The Prince insisted on the doctors directing all their attention to the coachman and sent Colonel Ponsonby on to inform the Queen what had happened. The Queen and Vicky, carrying their sketches, had been walking down to the park gate, amused on the way by a pretty peasant woman telling Vicky how dirty her dress was getting by being trailed on the ground and advising her to pick it up, when they met a two-seated carriage with Colonel Ponsonby in it, who told them the Prince had sent him to say there had been an accident to the carriage but he had not been hurt, only scratched his nose; and that the doctor said it was of no consequence. 'This prevented my being startled or *much* frightened. That came later. . . . I went at once to my dearest Albert's rooms and found him lying quietly on Löhlein's [his valet's] bed with lint compresses on his nose, mouth and chin. He was quite cheerful, had not been in the least stunned, there had not been any injury and the features would not suffer. Oh! God! What did I not feel! I could only, and do only, allow the feelings of gratitude, not those of horror at what might have happened, to fill my mind . . . everyone in such distress and excitement, and such anxiety in Coburg . . . I sent off many telegrams to England, etc. . . .'

Next day, 2nd October 1860, the Prince was much better, rose at seven and when the Queen went down to his room she found him dressed and reading. It was, however, wrote the Prince Consort's brother, Ernest Duke of Saxe-Coburg and Gotha, 'only too evident on this occasion how greatly the Prince's nervous system is shaken. When Stockmar . . . observed his deep despondency and melancholy, he said to me: "God have mercy on us! If anything serious should ever happen to him, he will die." '82

On 10th October Ernest took Albert for the last walk of the visit. 'At one of the most beautiful spots, Albert stood still, and suddenly felt for his pocket handkerchief. . . . I went up to him and saw that tears were trickling down his cheeks . . . he persisted in declaring that he was well aware that he had been here for the last time in his life.'

From now on the Prince's health took a downward turn. He is constantly reported as suffering from headaches and digestive upsets. He was ill first for two days and then for two weeks at Balmoral, a more violent attack than ever before. On 5th December 1860 the Prince was 'seriously unwell' with violent sickness and shiverings, and though in the evening he was better the Queen wrote in her Journal he was 'very weak'. Later the attack was disclosed as more severe than the Prince cared to admit, but any illness of the Prince Consort's was always minimised to avoid alarming the Queen. It was 11th December 1860 before he was able to work again and he told the Princess Royal 'My attack was the real English cholera. . . .'83

Unwell and over-strained, he now had fresh cause for anxiety—an anxiety he was ill fitted to support—in the conduct of the Prince of Wales.

Chapter Thirteen

The Prince of Wales was a disappointment. He was not clever; some of his examination papers, done when he was 15 and preserved in the Royal Archives, are alarmingly backward. Far from being industrious, he refused to make any attempt to learn.

He was an affectionate child, with considerable charm, but from early childhood he had been subjected to a system calculated to bring out his worst qualities. Stockmar warned the Prince Consort that too much was expected; the Prince of Wales would either contract brain fever, or be sickened of books by the amount of knowledge pumped into him. In an atmosphere of affection, warmth, admiration, the Prince would have bloomed, but his good qualities were passed over. He never, for instance, received any credit for his love for the Princess Royal, who, as he was constantly reminded, was much more intelligent than he. His outbursts of rage and disobedience when he screamed, beat his head against the wall and kicked were produced by frustration, as was his behaviour when he plagued the footmen and deliberately made their clean uniforms dirty.

He was unfortunate in having a tutor whom he disliked in charge of him since he was eleven. Frederick Waymouth Gibbs, orphaned, as has already been described, after an unfortunate family history, was intelligent and gained a fellowship at Trinity College, Cambridge; he was conscientious, even devoted, in the execution of his duty, but unlovable. Colonel Lindsay, Gentleman in Waiting to the Prince of Wales's household at White Lodge, Richmond, wrote to Sir Charles Phipps, the Prince Consort's private secretary, that he considered 'a continuance of the present system will not be beneficial to the Prince. . . . Mr Gibbs has *no* influence. He and the Prince are so much out of sympathy with one another that a wish expressed by Mr Gibbs is sure to meet with opposition on the part of the Prince. . . . Mr Gibbs has devoted himself to the boy, but no affection is given him in return, nor do I wonder at it, for they are by nature thoroughly unsuited to one another. I confess I quite understand the Prince's feelings towards Mr Gibbs, for tho' I respect his uprightness and devotion, I could not give him sympathy, confidence or friendship.'[1]

In July 1858 it became obvious that the cramming system pursued by Mr Gibbs, with the approval and support of the Prince Consort and the Queen, had failed. If the Prince did not progress he was made to labour harder; increased hours of work were accompanied by rapping of knuckles, boxing of ears, deprivation of pleasures. None of these had produced the desired result. The Prince was not fit to attempt any examination in the autumn and it was clear that the system must be changed.[2] Mr Gibbs was to retire; Colonel the Hon. Robert Bruce, brother of Lord Elgin, was appointed the Prince's governor and Mr Tarver, who had worked under Mr Gibbs, but whom Colonel Lindsay had observed the Prince liked, was to be Director of Studies. Colonel Lindsay himself was marrying and retiring. The Prince was most anxious to enter the Army. 'Bertie spoke' wrote the Queen in her Journal (7th January 1857) '. . . of his great wish to serve in the Army, which as a *profession* I said he could not, though he might learn in it.' The Prince also expressed his anxiety to travel with more freedom and more extensively than the walking tours with selected companions which he had been allowed under the supervision of Mr Gibbs. The Prince of Wales, continued the Queen, 'spoke . . . of his wish *not* to enter the Navy',[3] which had never been contemplated by his parents. Prince Alfred was in the Navy already.

The Prince Consort writes in a summary which he kept of his son's activities of the Prince of Wales going to Rome for the winter after Christmas, and after his return attending Oxford University, following the 'University studies' but not living in College. He might perhaps enter the Army on his 17th birthday, 9th November 1858, but without examination, as an honorary Colonel (unattached), and his allowance was to be increased to £500 a year. In a memorandum the Prince Consort outlined the behaviour he wished the Prince of Wales to display, no lounging ways, no lolling in armchairs or on sofas, or 'placing himself in unbecoming attitudes, with his hands in his pockets', anything approaching a practical joke was unpermissible. Gossip, cards, billiards were not to be allowed, the Prince of Wales must be induced 'to devote . . . his leisure . . . to music, to the fine arts, either drawing, or looking over drawings, engravings, etc., to hearing poetry . . . or good plays read aloud. . . .'[4]

His parents did, however, on his 17th birthday, write him a kindly letter. They recognised he was growing up. Mr Gibbs had gone and the Queen admitted to the Princess Royal that 'Mr Gibbs certainly failed during the last 2 years entirely, incredibly'.[5] Henceforward the Prince was to be responsible directly to his parents. Colonel Bruce as his governor would continue to report but not as Mr Gibbs had done. The Prince was to learn to be responsible for himself. He must learn above all to follow

Christ's precept 'that you should love your neighbour as yourself, and do unto men as you would they should do unto you'. The Prince must train himself to become a good man and a thorough gentleman. 'Life is composed of duties, and in the due, punctual, and cheerful performance of them, the true Christian, true soldier and true gentleman is recognised.'[6]

This moderate degree of kindness and emancipation was so moving to the Prince that he showed the letter to Gerald Wellesley, the Dean of Windsor, in 'floods of tears'.[7] His emancipation, however, was not as complete as he imagined. The Queen and the Prince Consort had chosen three equerries of irreproachable character for his suite, two were V.C.'s, and they were required to make daily confidential reports on his behaviour.

The Prince was now gazetted a Lieutenant Colonel (unattached) in the Army, without any examination. He was disappointed, he had wanted to become a professional soldier, to work his way up by merit, as his brother-in-law Prince Fritz William was working his way, but his parents had no confidence in his ability. The Queen told the Princess Royal 'I feel very sad about him, he is so idle and so weak. God grant that he may take things more to heart and be more serious for the future, and get more power. The heart is good, warm and affectionate.'[8]

On 20th November 1858 the Prince was allowed to pay a visit of three weeks to Berlin where his sister, the Princess Royal, was awaiting the birth of her first child, destined to become the Emperor William II, 'the Kaiser'. On 17th November the Prince Consort cautioned his daughter[9] 'You will find Bertie grown up and improved. Do not miss any opportunity of urging him to work hard. . . . He takes no interest in anything but clothes and again clothes. Even when out shooting he is more occupied with his trousers than with the game! . . . I am particularly anxious that he should have mental occupation in Berlin. Perhaps you could let him share in some of yours, lectures, etc.'

Socially, the Prince of Wales's visit to Berlin was a brilliant success; though small, the Prince was good-looking and had an endearing charm. 'Dear little Wales' *Punch* called him.[10] He danced remarkably well, and possessed rare powers of enjoyment which he communicated to his companions. Even his father admitted 'Bertie has remarkable social talent'. But of works of art, statuary, pictures etc. he said nothing, unless pressed.[11]

From Rome, where he had a ten-minute audience with Pope Pius IX, he was recalled on 2nd May 1859 by the outbreak of war between France, Sardinia and Austria arising from the Italian revolution.

After three months' cramming at Edinburgh he went up to Oxford. Later the Prince said that his parents had made a mistake in taking a house for him—Frewin Hall in the Cornmarket—instead of allowing him to live in Christ Church, with the other undergraduates. A group of eminent intellectual authorities was gathered to instruct him and photographs of this period show the slim boyish figure of the Prince, then at the zenith of his good looks, looking childish, crushed and lonely among the solid, imposing, usually bearded, figures. The Prince's disposition was sweet and in spite of the past he invited his old tutor Mr Gibbs to stay with him in Oxford for a few days in October.

During the Long Vacation of 1860 an event took place which changed his life; the Prince, now almost 19, was sent to Canada to open the railway bridge over the St Lawrence at Montreal and to lay the foundation stone of the Federal Parliament building at Ottawa; he was then to proceed to Washington to visit the President, James Buchanan, who had been liked by the Queen and the Prince Consort when he was American Minister in London. The Prince scored an instant success in Canada, dancing until daylight at a huge ball, one of several given in Montreal. In Washington he was equally successful, winning all hearts and generating excitement wherever he went. On 11th October 1860 the Prince reached New York where the enthusiasm of his reception was, wrote Colonel (now General) Bruce, 'impossible to exaggerate'. The whole tour had been 'one continual triumph'.[12] Among a large collection of press cuttings preserved in the Royal Archives, the *New York Herald* reported the Prince surrounded by a large circle of eager lookers-on at a grand ball at Montreal on 27th August 1860. At first he appeared annoyed and 'blushed deeply at this perpetual observation, but afterwards became all gaiety and animation. . . . He enters into the pastime too, with all the zest and lightheartedness of an ardent temperament, and with a spirit truly democratic'. The *New York Herald* reporter commented that it looked as if the Prince was more pleased with a pretty girl than with 'all the State ceremonies and reception addresses of which he has been the honoured object'.

On 19th September 1860 at his last ball in Canada, at Hamilton, the *New York Herald* reported '. . . never has the Prince seemed more manly or in better spirits. He talked away to his partner . . . he whispered soft nothings to the ladies as he passed them in the dance, directed them how to go right, & shook his finger at those who missed the figures . . . in short was the life of the party. During the evening both he and the Duke of Newcastle inquired for a pretty American lady Miss B. of Natchez, whom they met at Niagara Falls and with whom the Prince wished to dance. His Royal Highness looks as if he might have a very susceptible nature, and has already yielded to several twinges in the region of his midriff.'

At a ball at Cincinnati on 29th September the *New York Times* printed an item, '. . . Miss Groesbeck, sister of the Hon. Mr Groesbeck, Ex-Member of Congress, was the belle of the evening. She laughed and chatted, danced and flirted with the Prince in the most bewitching manner, and completely bound him hand and foot for the brief hour of her triumph. . . .'

After the excitements of North America, and experience of savage storms in the winter Atlantic which delayed his cruiser *Hero* until 15th November 1860, halfway through the winter term, the Prince found Oxford dull and his learned instructors more tedious than ever. On 18th January 1861 he transferred to Cambridge, entering Trinity College, but once more living apart from the undergraduates with his suite, this time at Madingley Hall four miles outside the town. Here he was bored and unhappy as he had been at Oxford; photographs show the Prince of Wales looking small, crushed and miserable, in yet another circle of imposing learned dons. His success in North America intensified his frustration. He had found his vocation in life, to make business smooth, to make people gay, and through these qualities to influence international affairs. Scholarship, learning, depressed him and he never ceased to beg for a military career, or, if this was impossible, at least for a period of service with the Guards. General Bruce, having been in Canada and the United States with the Prince throughout the recent tour, was nervous. He had become convinced from observation that an early marriage for the Prince was desirable, otherwise the Prince's charm and love of pleasure made trouble inevitable. Arrangements were already being discussed for the Prince of Wales's marriage, with both the Queen and the Prince Consort regarding a bride from within the magic circle of Royalty as indispensable. The Queen, when about to marry the Prince Consort, then a penniless younger son of Saxe-Coburg and Gotha, a kingdom covering an area about the size of a small English county, had declared she could 'never marry a subject'. There must be a kingdom and royal rank even though the kingdom was the size of a pocket handkerchief. But when the Prince Consort began to make lists of suitable candidates he was taken aback to find how few Protestant princesses existed, and how plain were their looks. The Prince of Wales meanwhile vehemently declared he would marry only for love.[13] The Princess Royal was called in to help and produced photographs of the beautiful Princess Elizabeth of Wied, later to be Queen of Rumania and well known as the poetess Carmen Sylva, but the Prince was not attracted, and the Princess Royal was compelled to submit an 'outrageously beautiful' (*unverschämt hübsch*) schoolgirl, the Danish Princess Alexandra Caroline Marie Charlotte Louise Julie of Schleswig-Holstein-Sonderburg-Glucksburg.[14] Knowledge of her existence had been kept from the Prince of Wales because the match would involve political complications of the most undesirable nature. Some indication has already been given of the bitterness and complexity of the Schleswig Holstein question, and during the years following 1848 the rising tide of nationalism in Europe intensified bitterness. German nationalists burned with eagerness to seize the two Duchies of Schleswig and Holstein from Denmark by force and not only control the Baltic straits but build a canal through the duchies to connect the North Sea with the Baltic, thus giving Germany access to the Atlantic. Alexandra's father, Prince Christian, a distant relative of the King of Denmark, Frederick VII, had been appointed heir to the crown in 1853. He was a poor man, of irreproachable character, living on his pay as an officer in the Danish Guards, and his family had been brought up in a modest way, well suited to English democratic ideas. But the marriage was bound to be highly unpopular with the Prussian Court, to whom the Prince Consort would find himself in direct opposition. It was an open secret that on the death of Frederick VII, a drunken divorced reprobate, and the accession of Princess Alexandra's father to the throne, trouble on the Schleswig Holstein question would inevitably follow.

As a further complication, both the Queen and the Prince Consort disapproved on moral grounds of the Hesse-Cassel family to which Princess Alexandra's mother, Princess Louise, the future Queen of Denmark, belonged. She was the daughter of William, Landgrave of Hesse-Cassel. Gossip centred round the charming eighteenth-century castle of Rumpenheim near Frankfurt bequeathed jointly to his six children by the Landgrave's father in 1837 with instructions that the family should gather there as often as possible and amuse themselves. Dancing, singing and a certain amount of romping and practical joking went on and Rumpenheim was a centre of anti-Prussian feeling. Though the Queen and the Prince Consort were anxious to see their son safely married, their sympathies were with Prussia and Germany on the Schleswig Holstein question, and Princess Alexandra could hardly have been more unsuitable, except for her Protestantism and her beauty.

In the spring of 1861 disturbing news reached the Queen and Prince Consort. The Emperor Alexander of Russia had obtained photographs of Princess Alexandra and intended to show them to his heir and suggest the lovely Princess as a possible bride. This was formidable competition indeed. The rules of the Orthodox Church were not rigid and religious difficulties could be surmounted.

The Prince Consort was eager for the Prince of Wales to marry. The kind of success the Prince had enjoyed on his North American tour called up the shades of the Royal Dukes, and the Prince Consort told his son that if he were interested in Princess Alexandra all German objections would be overcome. When the Prince Consort viewed the selection of plain Protestant princesses offered to the Prince of Wales, his heart sank. Princess Alexandra was the single exception. 'It would be a thousand pities if you were to lose her' he told his son, and wrote to the Princess

Royal who was now Crown Princess of Prussia, Prince Fritz's father having succeeded to the throne of Prussia in January 1861: '. . . We dare not let her slip away.'[15]

In direct conflict with German nationalist sentiment the Crown Princess and her husband flung themselves into promoting the match. A protest from Ernest Duke of Saxe-Coburg and Gotha, the Prince Consort's brother, supported by Stockmar, was rebuked on 22nd July 1861 with a savagery rarely used by the Prince Consort.[16] 'What has that got to do with you ? . . . Vicky has racked her brains to help us find someone but in vain . . . it is of the utmost importance that this marriage should not appear to be a Danish trump against us and Prussia, but that it was started only through the mediation of our Prussian children quite without the knowledge of Denmark or any action by our Ministers.'

From 29th–31st May 1861 the Crown Princess and her husband had met Princess Alexandra privately with her parents at the Palace of the Grand Duchess of Mecklenburg-Strelitz, who was an English princess,[17] and their glowing accounts of Princess Alexandra's loveliness and charm circulated throughout Europe. The Crown Princess went further and arranged a meeting between Princess Alexandra and the Prince of Wales. The Prince came to Germany ostensibly to attend manoeuvres with Prince Fritz. Princess Alexandra left Copenhagen with her parents under cover of paying a visit to Rumpenheim and a rendezvous was selected in front of the altar of St Bernard in the cathedral at Speyer, for 24th September 1861. Next day Prince Fritz related that he walked away with the Bishop under the pretence of examining frescoes but kept an eye on the progress of his brother-in-law's conversation with the young Princess and that after some initial shyness 'the reverse of indifference on both sides' had been shown.[18] At this time Princess Alexandra was 16 and the Prince of Wales 19. The Prince of Wales went on next week to Balmoral and described the meeting to the Queen, who wrote in her Journal that he was 'decidedly pleased with Pss. Alix . . . her manners, her pretty face and figure'.[19] The Prince of Wales, however, could never do right in the Queen's eyes and on 1st October she wrote to the Crown Princess of Prussia 'Bertie is extremely pleased with her, but as for being in love, I don't think he can be or that he is capable of enthusiasm about anything in the world.'[20]

*

The Prince Consort was troubled and overworked. Since his serious illness in December 1860, with the exception of the welcome engagement of his second daughter Princess Alice, aged 17, to Prince Louis of Hesse-Darmstadt, nothing but bad news arrived. He told the Princess Royal on 6th December 1860 that on the previous day he had been 'too miserable

. . . to hold my pen' and write the weekly letter he was in the habit of sending her, though 'the great Alician event [the betrothal of Princess Alice] makes my heart as a father glad.' The young couple were 'as happy as mortals can be'.[21] But despite the warning symptoms of exhaustion, violent sickness and shiverings, the Prince continued to work as usual, rising daily at 7 a.m. Fresh demands piled up on every side. On 14th February 1861 he was suffering tortures from his old enemy toothache and compelled to 'shut himself up'. His 'indisposition had now taken the form of inflammation of the nerves of the upper part of the cheek'. He wrote in his diary on 17th February 1861 'My sufferings are frightful, and the swelling will not come to a proper head.'[22] Incision of the gum gave no relief. 'Sleepless nights and pain have pulled me down very much' he told Stockmar. 'This has been going on for nine days, and a second operation, which Mr Saunders has just performed, does not give me any assurance that he has reached the seat of the mischief.'[23]

A further stroke of misfortune was the death, on the night of 28th January in a railway accident at Wimbledon, of Dr William Baly, who had recently been appointed Royal Physician and was to take the place of Sir James Clark. Both the Queen and the Prince Consort had already become attached to him and the Prince was distressed and upset.[24] Dr William Jenner, a well-known doctor who had done experimental work on typhoid and typhus fevers, was appointed in his place. '. . . The name is classical,' remarked the Prince, alluding to the famous Dr Edward Jenner whose name is identified with vaccination.

The Prince's illness did not clear up until the end of the month; on the 14th, 15th and 16th of February he was still having painful sleepless nights, though he managed to work on. But after attending a meeting at Trinity House, the organisation in charge of lighthouses and lightships, he was 'exhausted . . . he ought not to have gone' wrote the Queen.[25] The pain in his 'poor face' continued, his glands were swollen. On 20th February 'Sir James Clark brought Dr Jenner, the successor to our poor excellent Dr Baly, who had been a great friend of Dr Baly's. He is a very able physician, and has a calm pleasant manner. Albert did not come to dinner.'

A fresh blow was almost at that moment falling. On 28th February 1861 during dinner the Queen and Prince Consort were 'deeply grieved' to hear that Sir George Couper, for twenty-one years Secretary and Comptroller of the Duchess of Kent's household, who had been ill for some days, had unexpectedly died about 6 o'clock that evening. 'He went out like a candle' wrote the Prince Consort.[26] Sir George Couper had taken the Duchess of Kent's affairs and finances out of the hands of Conroy and put them in order; she regarded him as her intimate friend and leant on him for advice and for help in every decision.

The Prince Consort feared the Duchess of Kent's health would be affected by the shock. Now aged 75, she was far from well, having suffered successive attacks of erysipelas since May 1859. At the time of Sir George Couper's death her right arm was so swollen and painful that on 9th March an operation had to be performed and the Duchess's arm opened. In spite of this painful treatment, a fresh gathering on her left arm and side was observed.[27] From this time onwards the Duchess's condition worsened. On 15th March 1861 the Prince Consort went to see her and returned in tears. The Queen went into her mother's room and found her lying on a sofa in a silk dressing-gown, breathing rather heavily but otherwise appearing normal, though taking no notice. One of the attendants said 'The end will be easy.' The Queen was overwhelmed. 'Oh!' she writes, 'what agony, what despair was this! ... I knelt before her, kissed her dear hand and placed it next my cheek; but, though she opened her eyes, she did not, I think, know me. She brushed my hand off, and the dreadful reality was before me, that for the first time she did not know the child she had ever received with such tender smiles! I went out to sob ... I asked the doctors if there was no hope. They said, they feared, none whatever.... As the night wore on into the morning I lay down on the sofa, at the foot of my bed ... I heard each hour strike. ... At four I went down again. All still—nothing to be heard but the heavy breathing, and the striking, at every quarter, of the old repeater, a large watch in a tortoiseshell case, which had belonged to my poor father, the sound of which brought back all the recollections of my childhood ... feeling faint and exhausted, I went upstairs again and lay down in silent misery. ...'

About half past seven the Queen returned to the Duchess's room, where the end was now visibly approaching. There was no return of consciousness. 'Albert took me out of the room for a short while, but I could not remain. ... I sat on a foot stool, holding her dear hand ... I felt the end was fast approaching, as Clark went out to call Albert.... Fainter and fainter grew the breathing. At last it ceased. ... The clock struck half-past nine at the very moment.'

The Queen was unacquainted with death, the solemnity of the moment when life departs, the marble majesty of human flesh in which life is extinct, and she was overwhelmed. She wrote in her diary 'The dreaded terrible calamity has befallen us, which seems like an awful dream ... Oh God! how awful! how mysterious! ... the constant crying was a comfort and relief ... but oh! the agony of it! ...'[28]

When the time came to leave Frogmore, where she and the Prince Consort had gone for the last phase of the Duchess's illness, the Queen gave way. 'It was a fearful moment.... I clung to the dear room [in which the Duchess had died and where the Queen and the Prince Consort were in the habit of going to pray], to the house, to all,—and the arriving at Windsor Castle was dreadful.'²⁹

Princess Helena and the Prince of Wales arrived from London and were taken by the Queen to see the 'beautiful peaceful remains, like a small statue', but the Prince of Wales found his mother's grief excessive.³⁰ Day after day her outpourings of grief continued. Its violence produced uneasiness in Court circles, many persons feeling with the Prince of Wales. For three weeks until 9th April the Queen took all her meals alone. 'It is *dreadful, dreadful* to think we shall never see that dear kind loving face again, never hear that dear voice again! . . . the talking of any ordinary things is *quite* unbearable to me . . . the outbursts of grief are fearful & at times unbearable. . . . One of my great comforts is to go to Frogmore, to sit in her dear room . . . dread as it is to feel the awful stillness of the house. Her life at last became one of great suffering, we could not wish it to be prolonged.'

'I had never been near a coffin before. . . . The *dreadful* thing as I told Albert yesterday is the certainty that the loss is irrevocable.'³¹

The Queen, when sorting her mother's papers, was moved: '. . . how very very much she and my beloved Father *loved* each other. *Such* love and affection. I hardly knew it was *to that extent*. Then her love for *me*— It is *too* touching; I have found little books with the accounts of my baby-hood, and they show *such* unbounded tenderness! Oh! I am wretched to think, how *for a time*, two people wickedly estranged us. It is *bad* shocking, how Lehzen could be so foolish—not to say more . . . to confound her (I believe) very right opposition to Sir John [Conroy] with my love and affection for my dearest Mama! . . . To miss a Mother's friendship, not to be able to have Her to confide in when a girl *most* needs it . . . drives me *wild* now. But thank God all that is passed *long long* ago and she . . . only thought of the last very happy years. . . .'³² After the reconciliation effected by the Prince Consort 'Every succeeding year seemed to draw beloved Mama nearer and nearer to me.'³³

The Duchess of Kent's death inflicted a load of additional work on the Prince Consort. All her property was left to the Queen, the Prince Consort being appointed sole executor. While Sir George Couper had rescued the Duchess's affairs and finances from their former confusion and put them in order, she had left behind an immense amount of correspondence, and Sir George had died only a fortnight before her. The Duchess's main support in her household had been Lady Augusta Bruce (sister of the Prince of Wales's governor, General Bruce), who had acted as her secretary. The Queen appointed Lady Augusta her resident bedchamber woman,³⁴ found her invaluable and became devoted to her, but the Prince received no such additional assistance and besides the burden of extra work arising from the Duchess of Kent's estate, the Queen's grief at her mother's death made it necessary to relieve her as far as possible from routine work. More labour at drafts and boxes, besides the daily communications with ministers, fell on the Prince Consort. The Crown Princess of Prussia came over for a visit of condolence to her mother but returned to Berlin on 2nd April 1861. 'By business I am well nigh overwhelmed' the Prince Consort wrote on 5th April 1861. In addition he was deprived for a considerable period of the services of Sir Charles Phipps whose wife had suffered a 'nervous seizure' the day after Sir George Couper's death.

On 3rd April 1861 the Prince Consort and the Queen went for a rest to Osborne. The Prince Consort reported to Stockmar that the Queen was well in body though terribly nervous and spent her time almost entirely alone, finding the children a disturbance.[35] The Prince Consort and the Queen remained at Osborne until 27th April, then returned to London for the Queen to make the announcement to the Privy Council of the marriage of Princess Alice with Prince Louis of Hesse-Darmstadt. On 18th May the Court returned to Osborne for a few days, including the Queen's birthday.

Unhappily Prince Louis developed measles, which, more seriously, he transmitted to Prince Leopold, now aged 8, who had to be left behind when the Court returned to London on 1st June, and was ill for three weeks.[36]

The birth of Prince Leopold in April 1853 had been normal and his general health was good, but on 2nd August 1859 Queen Victoria wrote to King Leopold 'Your poor little namesake is again laid up with a bad knee from a fall which appeared to be of no consequence. . . . I fear he will never be able to enter any active service. This unfortunate defect had nothing to do with his general health . . . and no remedy or medicine does it any good.'[37] It has already been noted that Prince Leopold was suffering from haemophilia, 'the bleeding disease', a constitutional, usually hereditary tendency to bleeding, from very slight injuries, or spontaneously—often with fatal results, accompanied by severe pain. In the early years of Prince Leopold's life the disease did not make itself so much felt; as he grew older and more active he suffered more, causing his parents constant and agonising anxiety.

Haemophilia is a mysterious disease, medically termed sex-linked recessive inheritance; it afflicts males only but is transmitted also by females. Some authorities hold that it can originate in a spontaneous mutation in the male genes and that this mutation must be traced to the Duke of Kent as no evidence of haemophilia exists in the Saxe-Coburg family.[38] Queen Victoria was a carrier, Prince Leopold was a haemophilic and Princess Alice and Princess Beatrice were carriers.

*

413

It was now being noticed that the Prince Consort looked ill. At the opening of the Royal Horticultural Show, now called the Chelsea Flower Show, on 5th June 1861, it was reported that he looked pallid and worn; the day was dark and showery, the Queen did not feel equal to attending, the royal children were in deep mourning, and the effect was depressing. It was in fact the last ceremonial in London at which the Prince appeared.[39] Yet though June 1861 was hot and oppressive, the Prince kept on the go and on the 16th the natural outcome was that he was 'upset by fatigue'. Ten days earlier, 6th June, at Turin, the Italian statesman Cavour had died of overwork, weakness and fever, described as 'typhoid being hastened by bleeding'. The Prince's symptoms of over-fatigue were similar and he wrote in his diary 'Am ill, feverish, with pains in my limbs, and feel very miserable.'[40] Though he was better next day and returned to his normal routine of toil, another 'sharp' attack followed on 26th July 1861 and similar bouts of illness recurred with alarming frequency.

While the Prince of Wales had returned to Madingley, at Cambridge, he 'often chafed against the fetters on his freedom which his father was indisposed to slacken and the Prince Consort paid Madingley many visits in order to . . . remind General Bruce of the need of enforcing the old restraints'.[41] The General had, however, changed his views on the evil influence of military society; the Prince's success on the North American tour was impossible to ignore and General Bruce had reached the conclusion that camp life was 'a good field for social instruction'. The Prince Consort was persuaded and after a meeting at Cambridge with General Bruce on 13th March 1861 it was agreed that the Prince of Wales should be permitted a ten weeks' course of training at the camp of the Curragh of Kildare, near Dublin, during the coming Long Vacation. The Prince of Wales was to be attached to the 1st Battalion of the Grenadier Guards, wear a Staff Colonel's uniform, but 'learn the duties of every grade from ensign upwards'. He was not to be detained at any one grade once he had thoroughly mastered it and it was considered that he could contrive to earn promotion every fortnight and 'with some exertion, arrive in the ten weeks before him, at the command of a battalion', and be made competent also to 'manoeuvre a Brigade in the Field'. This ambitious plan was made more difficult to fulfil by once again isolating the Prince from his young brother officers 'having regard to his position both as a Prince of the Blood and Heir to the Throne, as well as a Field Officer in the Army'. At the request of the Prince Consort the Prince of Wales moved into the quarters of Sir George Brown, General in Command Ireland; strict supervision was to be exercised, the Prince of Wales was to give dinner parties twice a week to senior officers, dine twice weekly in his own Regimental Mess, once a week as guest of honour of other regiments, and read and dine quietly in his own rooms on two evenings a week, one of which must be Sunday.[42]

On 29th June 1861 the Prince landed at Kingstown (Dun Laoghaire) and after a few days at the Castle went on to the Curragh. Though he was eager his progress was slow; the plan for rapid promotion laid down for him was beyond his abilities and General Bruce had to report on 15th August that there was no hope that he might be fit to command a battalion by the end of the month when the Queen and the Prince Consort were to visit the Curragh.

The Queen had not been to Ireland since 1849. Then her visit was to mark what had officially been decided as the end of the famine and to symbolise national reconciliation after the rising of 1848. Neither aim was achieved, though the Queen had enjoyed a personal triumph. Now anxiety for the Prince of Wales was uppermost in his parents' mind. Was he making progress? Was his moral behaviour all it should be? Though a review was to take place, there would be no attempt to rival the display of 1849, or the social festivities which had accompanied that visit.

The Prince's C.O., Colonel Percy, told the Prince 'You are too imperfect in your drill, Sir. Your word of command is indistinct. I will *not* try to make the Duke of Cambridge think you more advanced than you are.'[43] The Prince was upset but the Queen sent for Colonel Percy 'and thanked him for treating Bertie as he did just as any other officer. . . .'[44]

The Queen and the Prince Consort stayed at the Viceregal Lodge in the Phoenix Park; on 24th August they visited the Curragh, lunching at the Headquarters hut, and a review was held. 'Bertie marched past with his company and did not look at all so very small' she wrote to her uncle Leopold King of the Belgians.[45] The Prince of Wales stayed at the Curragh until 13th September, the result of his experience being to make him more impatient of the restrictions imposed on him and longing more than ever to be able to live as other young men.[46] On 15th October 1861, after a visit to his brother-in-law and sister in Berlin, he returned to Madingley. Before he left the Curragh, however, there had been a party, a wild guest-night mess party in the course of which his brother officers, amused at the sheltered life led by the Prince, had secretly conveyed into his quarters and into his bed, a young actress named Nellie Clifden, well known to them all and celebrated for her gaiety.[47] It was in the nature of a practical joke; there is no evidence that the Prince took it seriously, or that nothing of the kind had ever happened to him before, but he found Nellie Clifden amusing and when he went to Windsor, Nellie came too.[48] He did not show any eagerness in pursuing the possibility of his marriage with the lovely Princess Alexandra. He wanted freedom, he had tasted freedom and was in no hurry to assume a different set of fetters.

*

The Prince Consort continued worried and overworked. The attacks of toothache, neuralgia and shivering to which he had become subject, were pulling him down, and he had insomnia as well. Though at home the political situation was calm, Prussia and Italy were causing him misery. The Queen's enthusiasm, her absorbed interest in everything he thought, said and did, and on which he had come to rely, were for the moment withdrawn by her continued absorption in grief for the death of her mother.

A new series of blows now fell on the Prince when he was in no fit state to endure them. First typhoid fever broke out in Portugal, and a telegram from Lisbon on 6th November 1861 announcing that Prince Ferdinand had unexpectedly been a victim of the epidemic was followed by two further telegrams announcing the illness and death on the evening of 8th November of King Pedro V. The Queen wrote that she and the Prince were 'shocked and startled'.[49] The Queen and the Prince Consort had been attached to the Portuguese Royal Family for many years, they were Coburg connections. The Prince was particularly fond of King Pedro, who was not only a dear friend but a close relative, son of the Prince Ferdinand who had married Queen Maria of Portugal and whose visit to England on his way to Portugal had fluttered Princess Victoria's heart when she was a young girl of fourteen. (This Ferdinand in turn was the son of Ferdinand, sometimes called Coburg-Kohary because he had married the fabulously rich Kohary heiress, the uncle both of the Prince Consort and the Queen. The young King Pedro V had therefore been a first cousin once removed.)

At about the same time, through Lord Torrington, 'that arch gossip of all gossips',[50] the Prince Consort learned there was a story 'current in the clubs' that while at the Curragh the Prince of Wales had formed a liaison with an actress and had even brought her over to Windsor. 'A searching enquiry' confirmed the story and on 16th November 1861 the Prince Consort sent his son a long agonised letter written 'with a heavy heart upon a subject which has caused me the greatest pain I have yet felt in this life'.[51]

It is a curious letter. Surely there could not be occasion for surprise that the Prince of Wales should behave as the overwhelming majority of his companions, fashionable rich young officers in a 'crack' regiment of the Guards, were behaving? Provided the girl was healthy and not a blackmailer, and no evidence to the contrary appears to survive, the average aristocratic father would have felt it a good thing on the whole that his son should have some sexual experience before marriage. The average mother, after regrets, would have felt the same. But, on the subject of sex, the Prince Consort was unbalanced. Fraud or violence would have been more easily forgiven than 'intercourse'. He was unwell, in a nervous state, and he drew a frightening picture. The Prince of Wales had become the talk and ridicule of the idle and profligate; Nellie Clifden, who frequented the lowest dance halls in London, already went by the nickname of 'the Princess of Wales'. She would probably have a child, or get a child, of which the Prince of Wales would be the reputed father. 'If you were to try and deny it, she can drag you into a Court of Law to force you to own it & there with you (the Prince of Wales) in the witness box, she will be able to give before a greedy Multitude disgusting details of your profligacy for the sake of convincing the Jury, yourself cross-examined by a railing indecent attorney and hooted and yelled at by a Lawless Mob!! Oh horrible prospect, which this person has in her power, any day to realise! and to break your poor parents' hearts!'

The Prince of Wales was overwhelmed. The letter, which is immensely long, contains passages of embarrassing intimacy and would never have been written had his father been in his normal state of mind. Always haunted by a sense of his inadequacy and the knowledge that he was a disappointment to his parents, the Prince of Wales wrote his father a letter of misery and contrition which the Prince Consort agreed showed sincere repentance. An early marriage, he told his son, was the only hope for him but no forgiveness could restore him to the state of innocence and purity which he had lost, and he must hide himself from the sight of God.[52]

During the previous week, on 13th November 1861, the Prince Consort had related the story to the Queen, telling her she was not to know 'the disgusting details'. The Queen recoiled in horror '. . . Oh! that boy—much as I pity him I never can or shall look at him without a shudder as you can imagine.'[53] From 13th November onwards the Queen blamed the Prince of Wales for his father's fatal illness.

The effect on the Prince Consort was catastrophic. He was unable to sleep, he lost faith and hope for his son and heir and with them his interest in life. 'I do not cling to life' he told the Queen. 'You do: but I set no store by it . . . I am sure if I had a severe illness I should give up at once, I should not struggle for life. I have no tenacity of life.' In this frame of mind, the Prince Consort went to Sandhurst on 22nd November 1861 to inspect the buildings for the new Staff College and Royal Military Academy, in which he took a deep interest and which he had been, at least partially, responsible for erecting. It was a pouring wet day and he returned drenched and complaining of exhaustion and rheumatic pains.

From that day onwards the Prince's health took a sharp turn for the worse. The chill he contracted at Sandhurst was complicated by his insomnia; for two weeks he could get no sleep, distraught by his sorrow over the behaviour of the Prince of Wales. 'Albert has such nights since that great worry. It makes him weak and tired' wrote the Queen.

On 24th November 1861 the Prince wrote in his diary 'Am full of rheumatic pains and feel thoroughly unwell. Have scarcely closed my eyes at night for the last fortnight.'[54] Nevertheless he felt he must have a personal interview with his son and left by train at half past ten on 25th November 1861 to see the Prince of Wales at Madingley. The day was cold and stormy and the Prince Consort 'greatly out of sorts'. However, he took a long walk with his son, lengthened by the Prince of Wales's taking the wrong turning, and was back at Windsor by 1.30 p.m. next day, reassured, but feeling wretched, 'very suffering from neuralgic pains. He could not go out was . . . obliged to rest and very uncomfortable from the pains in his back and legs.' From the expedition to Madingley onwards the Prince's illness took another turn for the worse, for which the Prince of Wales was blamed. Next day he was no better and had not had at all a good night. He complained of weariness and weakness, frequently had to lie down and rest. Dr Jenner came and saw him before dinner and stayed the night.

In the second week of November 1861 the first news of a sudden and alarming international crisis was conveyed by Lord Palmerston, the Prime Minister, to the Queen.[55] The first shot in the American Civil War had been fired on 9th January 1861 in Charleston Harbour, South Carolina, when the Governor of South Carolina—which had formally seceded from the United States in December 1860—ordered the battery to open fire on a vessel sent by President Buchanan to reinforce Fort Sumter. Efforts at reconciliation between Southern slaveholders and Northern abolitionists failed; six Southern states seceded from the Union and with South Carolina set up the Confederate States of America. Abraham Lincoln, who took office as United States President in March 1861, determined that the Federal Union must be restored and war followed. During the opening period of the war British sympathies were with the Confederate side, largely on account of the cotton needed by Lancashire, and on 13th November Lord Palmerston informed the Queen there was reason to suspect that an American Federal steamer of war of eight guns which had lately arrived at Southampton, was intended to intercept the mail packet *Trent*, coming home with the West Indian mail, in order to take off Messrs Mason and Slidell, the two envoys from the Confederacy, supposed to be coming in her. Lord Palmerston had had a conference at the Treasury with the Chancellor, Dr Stephen Lushington, Judge of the Admiralty, the three Law Officers of the Crown, the Duke of Somerset, First Lord of the Admiralty, Sir George Grey and Mr Hammond, and as a result it was laid down that 'according to the law of nations as . . . practised and enforced by England in the war with France, the Northern Union being a Belligerent is entitled by its ships of war to stop and search any neutral merchantman, and the West India Packet [*Trent*] is such, and to search her if there is reasonable suspicion that she

418

is carrying enemy's despatches, and if such are found on board to take her to a Port of the Belligerent, and there to proceed against her for condemnation.' Such being ruled to be the law, the only thing to be done was to order the frigate *Phaeton* to drop down to Yarmouth Roads, 'and to watch the American steamer, and to see that she did not exercise this belligerent Right within the three-mile limit of British jurisdiction, and this was done.' Lord Palmerston also sent for Mr Adams,* the American Minister, and represented to him 'how unwise it would be to create irritation in this country merely for the sake of preventing the landing of Mr Slidell, whose presence here would have no more effect . . . than the presence of the three other Southern Deputies, who have been here for many months. . . .' Mr Adams in reply assured Lord Palmerston that the American steamer had orders 'not to meddle with any vessel under any foreign flag'.

However, on 28th November 1861, when he was ill and growing worse, the Prince wrote in his diary [Translation] '. . . An American warship holds up our mail packet *Trent* on the high seas and boards her, and removes by force four gentlemen from the Southern States, who were to have gone to London and Paris as envoys. They are carried off to New York. General indignation. The Law Officers declare the act a breach of international law.'[56]

The next day a despatch 'seen by Cabinet and Queen',[57] contained the statement 'It appears from the letter of Commander Williams [agent for mails on board the *Trent*] dated Royal Mail Contract Packet *Trent* at sea, November 9th, that the *Trent* left Havannah on the 7th instant with Her Majesty's Mails for England, having on board numerous passengers. Commander Williams states that shortly after noon on the 8th, a steamer having the appearance of a man-of-war, but not showing colours was observed ahead. On nearing her at 1.15 p.m. she fired a round shot from her pivot gun across the bows of the *Trent*, and showed American colours. While the *Trent* was approaching her slowly, the American vessel discharged a shell across the bows of the *Trent*, exploding half a cable's length ahead of her. The *Trent* then stopped and an officer with a large armed guard of marines boarded her. The officer demanded a list of the passengers, and compliance with the demand being refused, the officer said he had orders to arrest Messrs. Mason, Slidell, McFarlane and Eustis, and that he had sure information of their being passengers in the *Trent*. While some parley was going on upon this matter Mr Slidell stepped forward and told the American officer that the four persons he had named were then standing before him. The Commander of the *Trent*

---

* Charles Francis Adams (1807–1886) was an aristocrat from Boston, the son and grandson of two American Presidents. With him in London as his private secretary was his son Henry, the future historian.

and Commander Williams protested against the act of taking by force out of the *Trent* these four persons, then under the protection of the British flag. But the *San Jacinto* [the American warship] was at that time only two hundred yards from the *Trent*, her ship's company at quarters, her ports open, and tompions out. Resistance was therefore out of the question, and the four gentlemen before named were forcibly taken out of the ship. A further demand was made that the Commander of the *Trent* should proceed on board the *San Jacinto*, but he said he would not go unless forcibly compelled likewise, and this demand was not insisted upon.' Mr Mason was an envoy accredited by the Confederate States to the English Court, Mr Slidell to the French Court; the other two gentlemen were their secretaries. They had run the blockade from Charleston to Cardenas in Cuba in the Confederate steamer *Nashville*, escaping the vigilance of the Federal vessels who were on the look out for them.

Excitement and anger when the *Trent* arrived at Southampton and the facts became known, blazed through the country. 'Bear this, bear all' was the general cry, and war was demanded, the war America seemed determined to provoke. An abundance of inflammatory material existed between the two countries. The United States had defeated England and ceased to be English colonies in 1776; the English had burned Washington, the United States capital, in the war of 1812 against America; relationships of less importance—the behaviour of American Ministers, American business men, even American debutantes at Court—had been subjects of constant squabbles.

On 29th November 1861 Lord John Russell, British Foreign Secretary, wrote a memorandum, with enclosures to Lord Lyons, British Ambassador in Washington, in which he was instructed to make 'certain demands' of the government of the United States with regard to the *Trent* affair. In a further enclosure the British claims of the illegality of the acts of the United States vessel of war *San Jacinto* and her captain were fully set out. 'Should Mr Seward [William H. Seward, the U.S. Secretary of State] ask for delay in order that this grave and painful matter should be deliberately considered, you will consent to a delay not exceeding seven days. If at the end of that time no answer is given or if any other answer except that of a compliance with the demands of Her Majesty's government, your Lordship is instructed to leave Washington with all the members of your legation, bringing with you the Archives of the Legation, and to repair immediately to London. . . .' The British government demanded full reparation for an undoubted breach of international law and the restoration of the unfortunate passengers with a suitable apology.

The tone of the draft despatch, which dealt with the action of the *San Jacinto* at length, was, like the tone of the enclosure, bellicose and in addition Lord John Russell directed the Lords of the Admiralty to communicate with Vice Admiral Sir Alexander Milne: 'The act of wanton violence and outrage which has been committed, makes it not unlikely that other sudden acts of aggression may be attempted. Vice Admiral Sir Alexander Milne will take care not to place his ships in positions where they may be surprised or commanded by batteries on land of a superior force.' An expedition had been planned to Vera Cruz, for which Admiral Milne was instructed not to detail more than one line of battle ships and two frigates, and to dispose the rest of his fleet to protect the safety of Her Majesty's possessions in North America and the West Indies. 'Your Lordships [the Lords of the Admiralty] will no doubt be of opinion that Admiral Milne himself ought not to go to Vera Cruz, and in that case an officer acquainted with the Mexican coast' should be sent in his place.

This explosive material, the outcome of which, considering the delicate and prickly nature of the relations between the two countries, would almost certainly be war between Britain and the Northern states, reached Windsor in draft on Friday, 29th November 1861.

The Queen was by this time in an agony of apprehension, but hoping against hope, blaming the Prince's chill on his visit to Madingley, and his great mental depression on the Prince of Wales's conduct, which had caused his sleeplessness. Without these the feverish cold he had would have passed off easily. 'Dearest Albert was feeling weak but not worse. No fever.' Both the Prince Consort and the Queen dreaded the low fevers, bowel and gastric fevers, typhoid and typhus fevers which were responsible for so many deaths at the period. On Saturday, 30th November, he was worse. He had spent a bad night, and hardly slept after 3 a.m. 'My dear Albert felt very chilly and very uncomfortable and Dr Jenner found his stomach more uncomfortable. . . .' The Prince Consort was torn by anxiety. He realised the disastrous consequences which must follow from sending the despatches in their present form, but in his condition of health the effort involved in thinking and writing was almost insuperably painful and difficult.

In a letter to the Queen on 29th November 1861[58] Lord Palmerston had mentioned that Mrs and Miss Slidell, who were then in London, stated that the officer who boarded the *Trent* had said that he did so on his own responsibility and not on official instructions from Washington. On the other hand Lord Palmerston was informed from reliable sources that General Winfield Scott of the Northern army, who was in Paris, had stated that the seizure had been deliberately determined on by the Federal Cabinet, at the risk of provoking war with Britain, General Scott asserting that should war come he was commissioned to propose that France should join the Northern States against England, the consideration being the restoration of the Province of Canada to France. This was promptly contradicted by the Emperor Napoleon III; the French Government, as Palmerston observed, 'is probably thinking more about Cotton than about Canada'.

Nevertheless the Prince Consort made use of Mrs and Miss Slidell's statement. He was convinced that the Northern States, who had begun the war unsuccessfully and suffered a defeat at the first battle of Bull Run (21st July 1861), had no desire for another war—against the greatest maritime power in the world. His alterations were designed to give them a way out of the situation without offence to their sensitivity or sacrifice of their pride. On Sunday morning, 1st December 1861, though desperately ill, the Prince Consort forced himself to his desk at his usual hour of seven o'clock and drafted a memorandum for the Queen to copy suggesting alterations in the draft despatches.[59] 'The Queen returns these important drafts ... but she cannot help feeling that the main Draft, that for communication to the American Government, is somewhat meagre. She should have liked to have seen the expression of a hope, that the American captain, did not act under instructions, or, if he did that he misapprehended them, that the United States Government must be fully aware that the British Government could not allow its flag to be insulted, and the security of her mail communications to be placed in jeopardy; and Her Majesty's Government are unwilling to believe that the United States Government intended wantonly to put an insult upon this country, and to add to their many distressing complications by forcing a question of dispute upon us, and that we are therefore glad to believe that upon a full consideration of the circumstances, and of the undoubted breach of international law committed, they would spontaneously offer such redress as alone could satisfy this country, viz. the restoration of the unfortunate passengers with suitable apology'. In the margin is written in the Queen's handwriting 'This draft was the last the beloved Prince ever wrote, he was very unwell at the time & when he brought it to the Queen he said "I could hardly hold my pen" '. He could eat no breakfast and looked 'very wretched'. He insisted on walking on the Terrace for half an hour, attended Chapel with the Queen, looking pale and ill, knelt as usual, but could eat no luncheon. Sir James Clark and Dr Jenner came over to see him and were much disappointed. He ate no dinner, went to bed early, but could not sleep and was shivering with cold.

The amendments were universally accepted.[60] Lord Palmerston thought them excellent. Lord John Russell approved and the despatch was redrafted in accordance with the Prince's mild and conciliatory terms.

The importance of the Prince Consort's amendments cannot be exaggerated. England and the Northern States of America were hanging on the verge of war. Mr Seward told Lord Lyons of his relief in finding the despatch was courteous and friendly, not dictatorial nor menacing. The Prince's suggestions were adopted, Captain Wilkes of the *San Jacinto* was admitted to have acted without instructions and it was promised that the four persons taken from on board the *Trent* should 'be cheerfully liberated'.

*

The Queen was distressed by the brown colour and dryness of the Prince's tongue. Monday, 2nd December 1861, was a bad night; the Prince was sleepless and shivering and in great discomfort, though his tongue, the Queen was consoled to notice, seemed a little better. At 7 a.m. the Prince got up and sent for Dr Jenner; the Queen 'was terribly nervous and depressed. Dr Jenner said that there was no reason to be alarmed; but that one might fear its turning into a long feverish indisposition. . . . My dearest Albert did not dress, but lay on his sofa. . . . Sir James [Clark] came over & found him much in the same state . . . sometimes lying on his sofa in his dressing gown, & then sitting in an armchair in his sitting room . . . he kept saying, it was very well *he* had *no* fever, as he should not recover!—which we all told him was too foolish & he must never speak of it.—He took some soup with brown bread in it which unfortunately disagreed with him.'

Next day, 3rd December, the Queen wrote a snubbing letter to Lord Palmerston, who was anxious for the Prince to have additional medical advice.[61] 'The Queen is very much obliged to you for the kind interest displayed in your letter received this day. The Prince has had a feverish cold the last few days, which disturbed his rest at night, but Her Majesty has seen His Royal Highness before similarly affected and hopes that in a few days it will pass off. In addition to Sir James Clark, the Queen has had the advantage of the constant advice of Dr Jenner, a most skilful Physician, and Her Majesty would be very unwilling to cause unnecessary alarm, where no cause exists for it, by calling in a Medical Man who does not upon ordinary occasions attend at the Palace.'

In her Journal that day the Queen wrote 'Dreadfully annoyed at a letter from Lord Palmerston suggesting Dr Ferguson should be called in as he heard Albert could not sleep and eat. Very angry about it. In an agony of despair about my dearest Albert and crying much, for saw *no* improvement & my dearest Albert was so listless and took *so* little notice. Good kind old Sir James . . . reassured me and explained to Dr Jenner too that there was no cause whatever for alarm—either present or future. It was not likely to turn to a low fever. My Darling himself was in apprehension of a low fever. This they assured me he need not be. . . .' Dr Ferguson was not called in but two alarming nights followed when the Prince Consort was 'utterly restless', wandering about followed by the

423

Queen weeping in an agony of anxiety. Sir James Clark was summoned and gave the Prince some ether and Hoffman's drops, after which he slept soundly until 4.30 a.m.

On 6th December 1861 Sir Charles Phipps wrote to Lord Palmerston in a letter marked 'Confidential': 'The Prince is, I hope, decidedly better today—and has taken more food since last night than he had done before since Sunday. After your letter I thought it my duty to keep you informed, upon my own responsibility, of the state of H.M.'s health, but everything connected with the subject requires much management. The Prince himself, when ill, is extremely depressed and low, and the Queen becomes so nervous, and so easily alarmed, that the greatest caution is necessary. The suggestion that it could be desirable to call in another Medical Man would I think frighten the Queen *very much*, and the Prince already is annoyed with the visits of the *three* who attend him. Sir J. Clark is here daily, Dr Jenner remains here permanently, and Mr Brown the Windsor Apothecary, who knows the Prince's constitution better than anybody, also sees him. . . . If any further advice were sought, it would be necessary first to send for Sir Henry Holland. . . . You will easily believe with how much diffidence I hesitate to act on any suggestion of yours—but I sincerely believe that to ask to call another Doctor would do more harm than good. The mere suggestion the other night upset the Queen and agitated her dreadfully, and it is very essential to keep up the spirits both of Her and the Prince. H.R.H. has never kept his bed, and had several hours of sleep last night.'62

Next day the hopeful report was reversed. 'I am sure that you will be very much disappointed and grieved to hear that the Prince's illness is declared today to be a gastric fever' writes Sir Charles Phipps. 'The symptoms are all favourable . . . the illness however must have its course, and it always lasts a month. . . . The Queen is at present perfectly composed . . . but I must tell you, *most confidentially*, that it requires no little management to prevent her from breaking down altogether . . . what would particularly try her would be any public Alarm about the Prince, which coming back to her through the Public Prints would make Her fancy that the truth was concealed from her. . . . As cheerful a view as possible should be taken to her of the state of the Prince. I am waiting to see the Physicians with regard to calling in additional advice.'63

The 7th December was a day of suffering for the Queen. Though the Prince was up and dressed at 8 a.m., she saw the doctors thought him less well, '& I went to my room & cried dreadfully and felt oh! as if my heart must break—oh! such agony as exceeded *all* my grief this year. Oh, God! help and protect him!' The Queen remained in an agony of suspense in her dressing-room, Dr Jenner came in and explained 'in the kindest, clearest manner' that they had been suspecting fever all along

424

but it was only this morning that a light rash had appeared which was a certain indication. The case was now quite clear and Dr Jenner knew exactly how to treat it, but the fever must run its course. The Prince did not dress but passed the whole day in his dressing-gown. At luncheon 'Good Sir James', in whom both the Queen and the Prince had faith, came and reassured the Queen '*very much*, tho' he was surprised and disappointed . . . he [the Prince Consort] seemed getting on all right. Sir James assured me I need *not* be alarmed . . . but I seem to live in a dreadful dream. My angel lay on the bed in the bedroom & I sat by him watching him & the tears fell fast . . . saw Sir James and Dr Jenner talked over what could have caused this. Great worry and far too hard work for long! *That must* be stopped. Dear good Augusta Bruce arrived . . . I had sent for her, and she came directly.'

On Sunday 8th December 1861 the Prince had a fair but restless night, lying down first in one room, then another. Dr Jenner and the Prince's valet Löhlein sat up with him. He seemed pleased to see the Queen, calling her 'Weibchen' (little wife) which was his pet name for her. At 9 a.m. he drank a little coffee but complained it did not agree with him. He was very weak but could still walk. He became 'irritable and impatient, & extremely angry' at the thought that the Queen gave any orders; 'poor dear' commented the Queen. The diarrhoea which, wrote the Queen, 'always accompanies this complaint was but slight, the pulse not bad. The tongue still dreadful, dry and with a thick furred coat.' The day was so fine that the Prince wished to be moved into the large Blue Room, called the King's Room, in which William IV had died. The Prince asked for music so a piano was brought into the next room and Princess Alice played 'Eine feste Burg ist unser Gott' (A strong fortress is our God). That night Sir James Clark slept in the Castle. 'Took Ernest in for a moment after luncheon, who was surprised at finding him [the Prince] not looking more ill. Certainly he looks less ill than we expected. He wanders for moments a little, seldom smiles & is still very impatient . . . so impatient because I tried to help in explaining something to Dr Jenner and quite slapped my hand, poor dear darling . . . Went in again to see my dearest Albert at 20 m to 11. He was so pleased to see me—stroked my face & smiled & called me his "Fräuchen" [little woman, another pet name] . . . he was so dear and kind. Precious love!'

Sir Charles Phipps wrote to Lord Palmerston on 8th December[64] that Sir James Clark and Dr Jenner, not from any less favourable symptoms but from the rank and station of the patient, wished to call in further advice and next day Sir Henry Holland and Dr Watson would be asked to come to Windsor. Sir Henry Holland, as one of the physicians in ordinary to the Prince—he had been physician to the Queen since 1837 and to the Prince since 1840; his work is described as more fashionable than scientific—could not be passed over and Dr Watson, one of the physicians extraordinary to the Queen, had a very high reputation. Lord Clarendon remarked that he 'would not trust Sir James Clark and Sir Henry Holland to look after a sick cat'. Dr Jenner and Dr Watson he considered differently.

'This measure [sending for extra medical advice] has been made very difficult, first by the Queen being disinclined to it, and secondly by the fear of alarming the Prince himself' wrote Sir Charles Phipps. 'He is *extremely low* about himself—there is no doubt that the death of the King of Portugal not only grieved him very deeply, but would make him exceedingly nervous if he had any idea that his illness bore any similarity to that of which the King died. Any alarm or further depression might have a *very injurious* effect upon the Prince in his present state, and it will therefore require some tact and judgment to announce the arrival of fresh medical advice. The Medical Men themselves, as far as the treatment of the case is concerned, have no wish for assistance. Dr Jenner was for a long time Physician to the Fever Hospital, and his work upon the treatment of fever is a standard work throughout Europe. . . . The Queen's cheerfulness is beyond all praise. It seems quite impossible to see a person under circumstances which must cause anxiety maintain self-command, and act more reasonably. But if she were alarmed and broke down, I think the reaction would be very great.' In a separate note to Lord Palmerston enclosed in this letter Sir Charles Phipps wrote 'I think I should have done an injustice to the Medical Men who have been attending the Prince, if I conveyed to you the idea that they had been treating him for a Malady different from that with which he was really afflicted. A statement has today been sent out, for insertion in tomorrow's papers, which will inform the public that the Prince's illness is of a more serious nature than was at first anticipated, without, it is hoped creating unnecessary Alarm.'

That evening the Prince had given the Queen a fright by opening the door of her sitting-room just before dinner and walking into the room. Dr Jenner made him lie down at once and said he must not be left for a moment alone. Since then he had remained entirely in bed, not dressed. On 9th December the Queen wrote that she 'got into a great state . . . of agony' after luncheon at the idea of 'Albert's being frightened at seeing Dr Watson . . . & fear I distressed both Sir James & Dr Jenner. However . . . it went off quite well. . . . He wanders frequently & they say it is of no consequence tho' very distressing, for it is unlike my own Angel. He was so kind calling me "gutes Weibchen" (excellent little wife), & liking me to hold his dear hand. Oh! it is an anxious, anxious, time but God will help us thro' it.'

Dr Watson considered the Prince 'is *very ill* . . . the malady is very grave

426

and serious in itself—and that even the Prince's present weakness is very great—in short he says it is impossible not to be very anxious'.[65] Lord Palmerston on receiving this letter wished Dr Watson to remain entirely at the Castle, which annoyed the Queen intensely, and she sent Sir Charles Phipps to London to see Lord Palmerston about this 'most improper' interference. It was finally settled that Dr Watson was to stay the night of the 10th at the Castle but '*not* be in the way'.

For the remainder of the week there seemed to be an improvement. The bulletins were favourable and though the Prince was confused he was affectionate to the Queen, laying his head on her shoulder, while she kneeled by his side. On the 12th he had a fit of coughing and coughed up a large quantity of mucus, followed by shivering but his 'poor dear brown tongue' was a little better and Sir James Clark was satisfied with his progress, though there was a quickened breathing which caused anxiety. Nevertheless on Friday 13th December the Prince's condition was considered to be sufficiently favourable for the Queen to go for a short walk. Lady Augusta Bruce related what followed in a letter to her sister.[66] '. . . At about 4.30 p.m. Dr Jenner came to my room saying that such sinking had come on that he had feared the Prince would die in his arms then. Stimulants had been administered and taken with ease; the pulse had recovered and already there was a rally. The Queen was taking a turn at the time. Sir James, who was attending his poor wife dangerously ill at Bagshot and was going between the two, arrived soon after the Queen's return and decided it was necessary to break to her the alarming tidings of what had taken place in her short absence. He said she must know, if anything happened, the shock would be too terrible. Shortly after I came down unable to bear the anxiety and took courage to go into the Queen's room. . . . It was a terrible moment, a life of anguish and agony was concentrated in it. Oh darling what agony! . . . The idea of what might be, she could scarcely bear, but again with Sir James's warning in my ear neither could I bear to encourage hopes . . . I was alone with her and most touching it was. The words "The country, oh the country. I could perhaps bear my own misery, but the poor country" were constantly recurring. . . . The Prince of Wales had been telegraphed for . . . I waited to see Robert [General Bruce her brother, governor to the Prince of Wales]. They had no idea of danger. A letter from me had given them the only uneasiness. . . . The Prince [Consort] had quite rallied, they [the doctors] thought the crisis was come . . . the breathing was still bad, but if he could get over that day they thought he might recover. . . . He was quite calm, wandered very little, could always be recalled by a question, always knew her [the Queen] and showed her every mark of love and tenderness. She never gave way before him, was cheerful and helpful, and so happy to see him so easy and composed.'

427

Alone with Lady Augusta the Queen collapsed, and prayed and cried as if she should go mad. At 7 after a terrible outburst of grief to Sir Charles Phipps the Queen regained control of herself and went to sit by the Prince, 'Found him very quiet & comfortably warm, & so dear & kind, called me "gutes Fräuchen" & kissed me so affectionately & so completely like himself, & I held his dear hands between mine. . . . They gave him brandy every half-hour.' Sir James Clark told the Queen it would be necessary to give a rather unfavourable bulletin and Sir Charles Phipps telegraphed and also sent a special messenger to Lord Palmerston 'I deeply grieve to say the Prince's disease has taken a very unfavourable turn, and that the Doctors are in the *greatest anxiety*—they have even fears for the night.'[67] Sir Charles Phipps had telegraphed for the Prince of Wales, and he arrived during the night. At first he was not allowed into the room, fearing his presence might upset his father, but later he was allowed to come in.

The next morning, 14th December 1861, Sir Charles Phipps sent another messenger to Lord Palmerston with a note:[68] 'We are allowed again *a hope* . . . for the Prince has had a quiet night and all the symptoms are somewhat modified . . . except that there was quickness of breathing.' The Queen herself wrote in February 1872 that she had never before had the courage to attempt to describe this dreadful day but the terrible facts were imprinted on her mind as clearly as if they had occurred the day before; she had also the help of notes scrawled at the time.

At 1, 2, and 3 a.m. the Queen was brought good news. Dr Watson and Mr Brown were sitting up with the Prince. Mr Brown came in about 6 a.m. and reported the Prince was ' "better than he has been yet; I think there is ground to hope the crisis is over" '.

'Went over at 7 as I usually did' wrote the Queen. 'It was a bright morning; the sun just rising and shining brightly . . . never can I forget how beautiful my darling looked lying there with his face lit up by the rising sun, his eyes unusually bright gazing as it were on unseen objects and not taking notice of me . . . Sir James was very hopeful, so was Dr Jenner, & said it was a "decided rally",—but that they were all "very, very, anxious". Sir H. Holland was very anxious. All constantly there or in the next room & so was I.—More bulletins issued which were of course shown to me . . . I asked if I might go out for a breath of fresh air. The doctors answered "Yes, just close by, for half an hour!" . . . I went out on the Terrace with Alice. The military band was playing at a distance & I burst out crying and came home again. . . . Sir James was very hopeful, he had seen much worse cases. But the breathing was the alarming thing—*so* rapid, I think 60 respirations in a minute. . . .'

The Queen 'lay down on the sofa in dreadful agony not to be described. Miss Hildyard [the children's governess] came in & was most kind, also good Sir Charles Phipps, whose hand shook . . . I was crying in despair saying, how should and could I ever get on.' Sir Charles Phipps reported to Lord Palmerston 'Alas! the hopes of the morning are fading away. . . . A bulletin is about to be issued saying that the Prince Consort continues in "a very critical state". The Queen is wonderfully composed and says that she is prepared for the worst.'[69] Lady Augusta wrote that the children had been in the room, one after the other; he smiled to them but did not speak. 'He asked for Sir Charles [Phipps] and evidently knew him . . . but the lamp was sinking. Towards 9.30 the Queen had another burst of misery and asked for the Dean [the Hon. Gerald Wellesley, Dean of Windsor], who spoke beautifully, and she no less; so humble so meek so loving, so strong in the sense of duty. Princess Alice, the Prince and Princess of Leiningen, the Prince of Wales and Princess Helena were in the room, with Miss Hildyard and me, Robert [General Bruce] and others between the doors . . . Princess Alice whispered to me with great calm, "That is the death rattle" and went for her mother. Then in that darkened room they knelt; the Queen and her elder children . . . watching in agonised silence, the passing of that lofty and noble soul. Gentler than an infant slumber it was at last. . . . The poor Queen exclaimed "Oh yes, this is death".'

The Queen writes 'I bent over him & said to him "Es ist Kleines Fräuchen" (it is your little wife) & he bowed his head; I asked him if he would give me "ein Kuss" (a kiss) & he did so. He seemed half dozing, quite quiet. . . . I left the room for a moment and sat down on the floor in utter despair. Attempts at consolation from others only made me worse. . . . Alice told me to come in . . . and I took his dear left hand which was already cold, tho' the breathing was quite gentle and I knelt down by him. . . . Alice was on the other side, Bertie and Lenchen [Helena] . . . kneeling at the foot of the bed, Ernest Leiningen, the doctors and Löhlein, who was much overcome . . . Sir Charles Phipps, the Dean and General Bruce—who knelt almost opposite to me. . . . Two or three long but perfectly gentle breaths were drawn, the hand clasping mine and . . . *all, all*, was over. . . . I stood up, kissed his dear heavenly forehead & called out in a bitter and agonising cry "Oh! my dear Darling!" and then dropped on my knees in mute, distracted despair, unable to utter a word or shed a tear! Ernest Leiningen & Sir C. Phipps lifted me up, and Ernest led me out. . . . Then I laid down on the sofa in the Red Room, & all the gentlemen came in and knelt down & kissed my hand, & I said a word to each.' When Sir Howard Elphinstone, Prince Arthur's governor, was called he was taken aback. 'I expected to see the Prince's body. I saw instead the Queen lying on the sofa, at her side on the floor Princess Alice supporting her, behind her Princess Helena standing & sobbing violently. The Prince of Wales . . . stood at the foot of the sofa, deeply affected but quiet. I was so unprepared for this that I hesitated, almost retreated, until the voice of the Queen & her outstretched hand called me to my senses & I went forward, but unable to speak, at last, clutching my hand & with a violent effort she ejaculated "You will not desert me? You will all help me?"—I was deeply moved, & answered a few words from the very depths of my heart & retired.

'The Prince Consort was lying in the next room; his face calm, peaceful. He had gone without a struggle . . . Beautiful noble head it appeared. He died in the same room as King William IV.'[70]

Sir Charles Phipps wrote to Lord Palmerston in an undated letter 'The Prince is dead. I hope I had sufficiently prepared you for the dreadful event which took place at ten minutes before eleven this night. . . . The Queen though in an agony of grief, is perfectly collected, and shows a self control that is quite extraordinary. Alas! she has not realised her loss—and, when the full consciousness comes upon her—I tremble—but only for the depth of her grief. What will happen—where can She look for that support and assistance upon which She has leaned in the greatest and the least questions of her life?'[71]

Next day, 15th December 1861, Sir Charles Phipps wrote[72] of the Queen's calmness. . . . 'Except in the paroxysms of her grief she is perfectly composed. . . . She is determined to do Her duty to the Country.'

On 19th December Dr Jenner wrote to his friend Dr Edmund Parkes,* the eminent sanitarian, pioneer in the health of towns and friend of Miss Florence Nightingale.

'My dear Parkes' he wrote; 'The Prince of course had typhoid fever. . . .'

The drains of Windsor Castle, condemned years ago and never put in order, had proved more dangerous than a tropical jungle.

*

The widowed Queen was 42 years of age. She had ascended the throne when she was almost a child and already reigned for twenty-four years. What would now be her future, and what would happen to the government of the country?

Her love, her adoration, of her husband was already legendary; he had been the mainspring of her life. She depended on him in every detail of her existence, important and unimportant. He drafted her letters and despatches; she never chose a bonnet or a dress without his approval, after more than twenty years of marriage she grudged every hour they were apart. She trusted his judgment, in the crises which were shaking Europe, completely; she would always take his advice. And now he was gone for ever.

* A Parkes Sanitary Museum erected to his memory used to stand in the Buckingham Palace Road.

She was not an easy character, possessing remarkable qualities allied with emotions so intense as, at times, to reach violence. Without being in any degree intellectual—her education had been barely adequate—she had acquired in the school of experience, knowledge of the motives and behaviour of statesmen and politicians, kings and princes. She spoke and wrote several languages with considerable fluency. Physically she was strong; in twenty-one years of marriage she had borne nine children without losing one. She was obstinate—obstinacy was her chief failing—but she could be converted and when she gave way she did so with a good grace. Honesty, generosity, loyalty were her good qualities; she never bore malice and it was rare to come into close contact with her without being inspired with devotion.

The problem which confronted her was infinitely more complicated than when she ascended the throne. The British Empire had more than doubled in size, huge tracts—the vast subcontinent of India was only one—had come under British government. Exploration, railways, steamships and improved communications were opening up the world. There were few white patches left now denoting the unknown.

What would be the fate of the Queen?

Several disturbing possibilities suggested themselves but re-marriage was never one of them. Re-marriage was unthinkable. She had long since lost the flower-like prettiness of her extreme youth. She was stout, her hair had darkened, her complexion no longer had bloom, but her silvery voice, the charm of her manner, remained; she had gained dignity, a royal bearing and she was still the greatest match in the world.

She had been dominated by the Prince Consort; might she be dominated by some other man, or woman, in the same way? Or would she withdraw from the task of government, even abdicate? That was unlikely, having regard to her unfavourable feelings for the Prince of Wales. Might she come forward and be active in political affairs, especially foreign affairs, of which she knew a great deal and with which she had many links?

It was impossible for anyone even remotely acquainted with the Queen's character not to recognise it as formidable, a potential whose power was as yet unknown. A wave of national sympathy and affection rushed out to the bereaved Queen. Few members of the crowds who waited outside Buckingham Palace, regardless of the fact that the Prince Consort had died at Windsor, were concerned with the important issue—the effect of the Prince Consort's death on the government of the country. The words on all lips, the feelings in all hearts were: 'What is going to happen now to the poor Queen?'

431

APPENDIX 1

THE COBURG FAMILY

Queen Victoria's maternal grandfather was Francis (1750–1806), Duke of Saxe-Coburg and Saalfeld, whose family had ruled their principality since 1485, though its area had often been partitioned and re-partitioned. In 1826 Saalfeld was exchanged for Gotha, and the title then became Duke of Saxe-Coburg and Gotha.

Francis Duke of Coburg married in 1777 Augusta Reuss zu Ebersdorf (1757–1831), and the couple had nine children:

(1) Sophie, who married Emanuel Count von Mensdorff-Pouilly.
(2) Antoinette, who married Alexander Duke of Württemberg.
(3) Juliana, who married Constantine Grand Duke of Russia, younger brother of Tsar Alexander I and Tsar Nicholas I.
(4) Ernest I (1784–1844), Duke of Saxe-Coburg and Saalfeld (from 1826 Duke of Saxe-Coburg and Gotha). Ernest I married Luise of Saxe-Gotha in 1817, and the couple had two sons, Ernest II (1818–1893), Duke of Saxe-Coburg and Gotha, and Albert, later the Prince Consort.

   After the death of Duchess Luise in 1831, Ernest I married his niece Marie, the daughter of Antoinette Duchess of Württemberg.
(5) Ferdinand, who in 1816 became a Catholic and married Princess Antonie Kohary.
(6) Victoire, who married (1) Charles Emich Prince of Leiningen and (2) Edward Duke of Kent.
(7) Marianne (1788–94).
(8) Leopold King of the Belgians.
(9) Maximilian (1792–3).
Taken from Wilhelm Karl Prinz von Isenburg, *Stammtafeln zur Geschichte der Europäischen Staaten*, Berlin, 1966

APPENDIX 2

THE CONROY FAMILY

For practical purposes, the history of the Conroy family begins with the marriage of Feafeara Conry's son John to Elizabeth Foulke, daughter and sole heiress of Robert Foulke, member of a prosperous family of English settlers from Staffordshire. John Conry was 43, Elizabeth a beautiful girl of 18, and her father objected to the match, not only because John Conry had no money but because he was a Connaught man. The marriage nevertheless took place, and John Conry, who was a friend of the Bishop of Tuam, obtained a 'Bishop's Lease', a lease for ever at a nominal rent, of a small estate near Elphin in Roscommon. John Conry had social gifts and a condition of the lease was that he should build a house on the land to 'be company' for the Bishop. Feafeara also left a few acres in Roscommon, a remnant, according to Conroy tradition, of the ancient family estates, and John Conry set up as an Irish landlord. He rose in the world, became armigerous, that is was granted the right to use a heraldic family coat of arms, mixed with the best society in Dublin, became particularly intimate with the Ponsonbys, and added the O to the last syllable of his name which henceforward was spelt Conroy.

His son, John Ponsonby Conroy, father of Captain John Conroy, married Margaret Wilson, great-great-granddaughter of Verrion Wilson, a captain of horse in Cromwell's army, who had obtained large grants of land, in Longford and Leitrim, confiscated from Irish owners.

The circumstances and social standing of the Conroy family had thus been transformed since the days when objections had been made to Feafeara's son because he was a Connaught man.

The Conroy Papers were deposited in Balliol College Library by Sir John Conroy F.R.S. (Sir John Conroy's grandson); who went to Eton, took a first class in Natural Science at Christ Church, Oxford, became Science Tutor at Keble and from 1890 until his death in 1900 was Science Tutor and Fellow of Balliol.

APPENDIX 3

RA. Z. 485

THE ALLEGED PLOT OF THE DUKE OF CUMBERLAND AGAINST THE LIFE OF PRINCESS VICTORIA

(With comments by Queen Victoria)

In September 1878 the Queen received a letter from Mrs Henry Conroy, wife of Sir John Conroy's third son, Colonel Henry Conroy, Grenadier Guards, enclosing a small MSS volume.

The Greville Memoirs had recently appeared, and, though in the first incomplete edition, had caused a sensation. Mrs Conroy was anxious to defend her late father-in-law, Sir John Conroy, and the Duchess of Kent against Greville's assertions.

She declared that a 'danger' had existed 'so alarming that it was long withheld even from the knowledge of the Duchess of Kent . . . a conspiracy which aimed at the youthful life of Your Majesty. . . .' The author of this conspiracy—of high rank, unscrupulous character, and very great power—'was the Duke of Cumberland'.

'The early life of the Princess at Kensington Palace was' Mrs Conroy says 'idyllic; the first cloud was a rumour that the Princess had bad health, could hardly walk, was diseased in her feet and would never grow up. Sir John Conroy traced these statements to the Duke of Cumberland.' [Note by the Queen: 'It is well known that Sir John Conroy's daughter called Victoria was the cause of this.']

The Duke of Cumberland had gained ascendancy over the mind of King George IV and was heard to say 'one delicate life only stood between him and the Crown and notwithstanding all ideas to the contrary he should yet be King of England'. [Note by the Queen: 'Sir John C's invention.'] 'He was seized with the terrible temptation to remove the only life that then stood between him and the throne.' [Note by the Queen: 'He never showed the slightest symptom of this.']

'After months and months of these reports [of the Princess's illness] the Duke of Cumberland began to spread one of inconceivable wickedness . . . that the Duchess of Kent was too much attached to Sir John Conroy.' [Note by the Queen: 'Sir John's *own* authorship and invention.'] The Duke of Cumberland then urged George IV to remove the Princess Victoria from her mother's care, as owing to her relationship with Sir

434

John the Duchess was no longer the best guardian of her child. [Note by the Queen: 'All Sir John's invention and Pss. Sophia's fearful falseness.'] 'Sir John knew that the life of the Princess was at stake. An order had been given to remove her to the care of the King by a certain day—once there, the Duke of Cumberland would surround the Princess by persons in his own pay, and when, either by intentional neglect, or drugged or slowly poisoned, the Princess's declining state had ended in death, the people, accustomed to hear of the ill health of their Princess, would have thought it a very natural ending to a frail and delicate life.' [Note by the Queen: '*Utterly* false.']

'Sir John Conroy went to call on the Duke of Wellington and begged him to see the King and delay the separation [of the Princess from her mother]. The Duke of Wellington and Sir John Conroy felt their only course was to gain time and on each occasion the Duke of Cumberland urged the removal of the Princess they begged for delay.' [Note by the Queen: 'The Duke of Wellington disliked Sir John.']

'Thus time went on, from day to day, from month to month, without knowing whether their efforts might be in vain! . . . but in the midst of these difficulties . . . King George IV died. Even after the death of the King, Sir John Conroy still greatly feared the Duke of Cumberland. He thought some servant might be bribed to drug the food of the young Princess, inspected all the servants rigidly, and dismissed everyone who gave the faintest shadow of doubt *in any way*.' [Note by the Queen: 'Quite an invention.']

From this point the Duke of Cumberland's plot against Princess Victoria disappears and the remainder of the manuscript deals with Sir John Conroy's services and career, with the malign influence of Lehzen, the lack of good faith shown by William IV, the annoyances inflicted on the Duchess of Kent and the ingratitude shown to Sir John himself. Queen Victoria pronounced the volume to be 'a tissue of lies', and there is no doubt that she was correct. It is interesting only because it presents what the Conroy family, apart from Sir John Conroy, and many other persons believed was taking place.

APPENDIX 4

THE DESTRUCTION OF THE QUEEN'S DIARY

The most satisfactory account of the destruction of the Queen's Diary, is given in scholarly and elegant prose by Sir Philip Magnus on page 461 seq. of his admirable biography of King Edward VII. By generous permission of Sir Philip I am permitted to quote it *in toto*.

'King Edward's Will had directed that all his private and personal correspondences, including especially those with Queen Alexandra and with Queen Victoria, should be destroyed; and Lord Esher, who assisted Lord Knollys in that part of the task which could be accomplished within the Royal Archives, was amazed by the lack of system which he found. "No papers", he wrote, "were ever in more dire confusion"; and it is clear that only a limited amount of sifting was attempted, and that a vast number were burned.

'That lamentable combustion signalled the climax of a period of incendiary activity which started when Queen Victoria's diary passed in 1901 into the hands of her youngest child, Princess Beatrice. In fulfilment of a charge laid upon her by her mother, the Princess transcribed passages from that invaluable historical and personal record into a series of blue copybooks; and she destroyed Queen Victoria's manuscript by fire as she went along. That process of transcription and destruction, which was spread over a great number of years, distressed King George V and Queen Mary who were powerless to intervene; but no one could dispute Queen Victoria's absolute right to leave such directions as she thought proper about the disposal of her most intimate papers.

'About the method of that transcription and the extent of that destruction, a limited amount of evidence exists. It is possible, for example, to collate certain passages quoted by Sir Theodore Martin from the original diary, which he used while writing the Prince Consort's biography under Queen Victoria's personal supervision, with the Princess's subsequent transcriptions in the Windsor copybooks. It can be stated that Princess Beatrice felt constrained not merely to destroy, without transcribing,

436

substantial portions of her mother's diary, but also to alter substantially a great many other portions which she did transcribe and it must be added that posterity has suffered in consequence an incalculable and irreparable loss.

'In December, 1906, Lord Esher noted that a correspondence between Queen Victoria and Lord Granville, as well as many letters about Lady Flora Hastings, had been burned by King Edward's command. A worse act of what must be termed vandalism occurred in the following year when Esher discovered, as a result of editing Queen Victoria's letters, that the Queen's correspondence with Disraeli, as well as other confidential papers, were in the custody of Lord Rothschild as a trustee of the Hughenden property.

'At King Edward's request that material was despatched from New Court to Windsor Castle, where all private letters from the Queen about her family—Esher described them (16th November 1907) as "very Private" —and almost all letters written to Disraeli by King Edward as Prince of Wales were burned. Letters from Queen Victoria to Disraeli on political subjects were returned to Lord Rothschild, after other material from the same collection, including correspondence about Princess Frederick's marriage and letters addressed to Disraeli by other members of the royal family, had been destroyed. As late as 26th January 1913, Esther noted that King George V had ordered on that day the destruction of a mass of material relating to George IV in the royal archives.

'From his office at Buckingham Palace on 17th March 1913, Lord Knollys wrote laconically to King George V: "Sir, I have finished the papers and am vacating my room here today." He had been constrained to burn a substantial part of the social record of the nineteenth century, including much material which a biographer of King Edward VII would have wished to consult; and one deplorable later loss must also be recorded. Queen Alexandra died intestate on 20 November 1925; but her wish that all her papers should be burned after her death was executed with scrupulous fidelity by Lord Knollys' sister, the Hon. Charlotte Knollys, who had served the Queen as a Woman of the Bedchamber from 1870, and as confidante and intimate friend.'

REFERENCES

CHAPTER ONE

1. *George Duke of Cambridge, A Memoir of his private life*, based on his journals and correspondence, ed. Rev. Edgar Sheppard, 2 vols. 1907. Vol. I, p. 94.
2. Wilberforce, speaking in the House of Commons in April 1818 after Princess Charlotte's death. Hansard, *Parliamentary Debates*, Vol. 38, pp. 132–3.
3. *Creevey. A Selection of the Letters and Papers of Thomas Creevey*, ed. John Gore, John Murray, 1948, pp. 69, 167.
4. Lord Melbourne, as reported in RA Queen Victoria's Journal, 3 January 1840.
   The full title of the Royal Marriages Act, 1772, is 'An Act for the better regulating the future Marriages of the Royal Family', 12 George III, cap. 11. According to Halsbury's *Statutes*, if the heir to the throne marries a Catholic, he or she is automatically excluded from inheriting the Crown, by the joint effect of the Act of Settlement, 12 and 13 William III, cap. 2, and the Bill of Rights, 1 William and Mary, sess. 2, cap. 2.
   G. J. Renier, *The Ill-fated Princess*, Peter Davies, 1932, p. 16.
   G. T. Keppel, Earl of Albemarle, *Fifty Years of My Life*, 1877, p. 3.
5. Charles Greville, *The Greville Memoirs 1814–1860*, ed. Lytton Strachey and Roger Fulford, 8 vols., Macmillan, 1938. Vol. I, p. 59.
6. RA 48530–1, the Duke of Cambridge to George III, 12 January 1799.
7. Mrs Jordan to James Boaden, 1811, in *Mrs. Jordan and Her Family. Unpublished Correspondence of Mrs. Jordan and the Duke of Clarence later William IV*, ed. Arthur Aspinall, Arthur Barker 1951, p. 178.
8. Hansard, 16 April 1818, Vol. 38, p. 117 *seq.*
9. *Memoirs of Baron Stockmar*, ed. his son Baron E. Von Stockmar, trans. G.A.M., 2 vols., 1872. Vol. I, pp. 75–7.
10. Creevey, p. 172.
11. Philip Henry Stanhope, 5th Earl Stanhope, *Notes of Conversations with the Duke of Wellington, 1831–51*, World's Classics, Oxford University Press, 1938, pp. 128, 131, 322.
12. Greville, Vol. IV, pp. 244–5, Vol. V, p. 98.
13. E.g., RA 45284–6, 45288–9; RA M1/28–30, 32.
14. Rev. Erskine Neale, *Life of H.R.H. Edward Duke of Kent*, 1850, preface, p. xii, quoting a letter to the author from 'a man of high rank'.
15. William James Anderson, *Life of . . . Edward Duke of Kent*, Ottawa and Toronto, 1870, p. 22. RA 46643–5, Prince Edward of Kent to Mr Dobner, 4 October 1790.
16. RA Add. 7/1187, Certificate, 1816, by Lieut-Gen. F. A. Wetherall, relative to the loss of the Duke of Kent's baggage. RA PP 1/58, no. 38 (see note 20 below). Neale, pp. 42–4.

17. Anderson, pp. 14–15, and RA 46646, Prince Edward of Kent to Cox and Green-wood, 4 October 1790.
18. David Duff, *Edward of Kent*, the life story of Queen Victoria's father, Stanley Paul, 1938, pp. 84–7.
19. Neale, p. 78. RA 45288–9, Duke of Kent of Mrs Fitzherbert, 23 January 1812. BM Liverpool Papers, Addit. 38564, no. 136, memorial of Duke of Kent to [Prince Regent, January 1815], and Lord Liverpool to Duke of Kent, 23 February 1815.
20. RA PP 1/58, nos. 38, 41; M2/1; Y56/4, 5; Y57/1, 2, 5–8, 10, 11.
21. Creevey, pp. 162–4.
22. Sir Charles Webster, *The Foreign Policy of Castlereagh*, G. Bell, 1925, p. 11.
23. *Letters of Mrs. Fitzherbert and Collected Papers*, i.e. Vol. II of the *Life of Mrs. Fitzherbert* by Shane Leslie, Burns Oates, 1940, p. 150.
24. Her full Christian names are given as Mary Louisa Victoria by Sir Sidney Lee in *Queen Victoria, a biography*, revised edition, 1904, p. 6, and as Marie Luise Victoire in the *Almanach de Gotha*. At the end of her life, after a long residence in England, she signed her will 'Victoria Marie Louise'.
25. RA Add. 10/94, Princess Augusta to Earl of Arran, 7 July 1818. Stockmar, Vol. I, p. 77.
26. RA Y174, entitled 'The Wedding of H.R.H. The Duke of Kent with H.H. Princess Victoire zu Leiningen' [1861], trans. This is a MS. account by George Wagner, tutor to Princess Victoire's son and later the husband of Polyxene von Tubeuf.
27. RA Y71/65, King Leopold to Queen Victoria, 21 May 1845.
28. RA M2/2, 3, 8, letter of recommendation from Princess Charlotte, 19 August 1816; Duke of Kent's proposal, n.d.; Princess Charlotte to Princess Victoire, 10 October 1816, trans.
29. The Duke's rejection is clear from two subsequent letters he wrote to Princess Victoire, RA M2/4, 5, dated 1 and 3 October 1816, trans.
30. RA M2/23, 24, Duke of Kent to Duke of Saxe-Coburg and Saalfeld, 10 January 1818 and the latter's reply, 29 January 1818, trans. Cf. PRO F. O. 30/12, 13, 18, 21, correspondence of Castlereagh and Hon. F. Lamb on the guardianship of Princess Victoire's children.
31. RA M2/11, Duke of Kent to Prince Leopold, 30 November 1816, trans.
32. RA M2/14, Princess Victoire to Princess Charlotte, New Year, 1817, trans. Cf. RA M2/8, 16.
33. Lady Holland to Mrs Creevey, September 1817, in Creevey, p. 161.
34. RA M2/22, Prince Leopold to Duke of Kent, undated [after 6 November 1817], trans. RA M2/20, 21, Duke of Kent to Princess Victoire, two letters, one undated, the other 10 January 1818, trans.
35. RA Y174; P. P. Vic. 7522, 1 April 1870; Queen Victoria's Journal, 15 September 1848, 3 December 1856. R. Priesner, *Im Schimmer Früher Tage*, Coburg, 1965.
36. RA M2/29, 38, 47.
    RA M2/25, 28, Princess Victoire to Duke of Kent, 25 January, 1 March 1818, trans.
37. RA M2/43, Duke of Kent to Princess Victoire, [January 1818], trans.
38. RA M30, Diary of Augusta, Dowager Duchess of Coburg, 30 May 1818, trans. Extracts from her diary, 1806–21, were published as *In Napoleonic Days*, ed. H.R.H. Princess Beatrice, John Murray, 1941, pp. 190, 192.
39. Mollie Gillen, *The Prince and His Lady*, Sidgwick and Jackson, 1970.
40. Creevey, p. 163.
41. RA 46652–4, 46659, Prince Edward of Kent to Mdlle de St. Laurent and to M. Fontiny, 23 November 1790, trans.
42. Mary Ann Clarke, *The Rival Princes*, 1810.

439

43. RA 45315–6, Duke of Kent to Sir William Beechey, 26 August 1814.
44. RA 45340–1, Duke of Kent to Baron de Mallet, 26 January 1819.
45. RA 45361–2, Duke of Kent to Earl of Buchan, 6 September 1819.
46. Greville, Vol. I, pp. 53–4.
47. RA Y57/10–13, Duke of Kent to Thomas Coutts, 13, 15 May, 11, 17 July 1818. RA Add. 7/1345–9, Account of 'all unavoidable disbursements' by the Duke from 19 March to 31 December 1818, sent to Gen. Wetherall, 11 January 1819.
48. Hansard, 14, 16 April, 13, 25 May 1818, Vol. 38, pp. 46, 117, 630–1, 725–34.
49. Creevey, p. 167.
50. Creevey, p. 172.
51. Stockmar, Vol. I, p. 77.
52. Duff, p. 183.
53. RA Add. 7/1327, Duke of Kent to Sir Benjamin Bloomfield, 18 November 1818.
54. RA Add. 7/1340, Bloomfield to Duke of Kent, 17 December 1818.
55. Letters of George IV, 1812–1830, ed. A. Aspinall, 3 vols., Cambridge University, 1938, Vol. II, No. 745.
56. RA M3/1, Duke of Kent to Mr Putnam, 5 April 1819.
57. RA Add. 7/1341, Duke of Kent to Gen. Wetherall, 19 December 1818.
58. RA Add. 7/1345–9, 1457. See also Captain Hulme's claims in RA Add. O71/2–5, 16, 19, 22.
59. Harcourt Papers, Vol. VI, p. 222, Princess Augusta to Lady Harcourt, 25 January 1820.
60. RA M2/73, Duke to Duchess of Kent, 31 December 1818, trans. (except for last sentence quoted).
61. RA Add. 7/1344, 1386, Duke of Kent to Bloomfield, 28 December 1818, 15 March 1819.
62. See references in note 47 above, also RA Y57/16–19, 21, Duke of Kent to Mr Coutts, 29 September, 1 November 1818, 14, 31 January 1819; RA Y57/20, details of expenses and amount of loan required from Duke of Cambridge.
63. RA Add. 7/1355, Joseph Hume to Duke of Kent, 1 February 1819.
64. RA Add. 7/92, Lady Augusta Stanley to Queen Victoria 20 January 1869, reporting her conversation with Lord Chancellor Lord Hatherley, the son of Alderman Wood.
65. RA M1/27, Duke of Kent to Duke of Bedford, 15 March 1819.
66. RA Add. 7/1381, Lord Dundas to Duke of Kent, 5 March 1819.
67. RA 46607/8, Duke of Kent to Bloomfield, 15 March 1819.
68. RA Y57/22.
69. RA Add. 7/1390, Bloomfield to Duke of Kent, 6 April 1819.
70. In Napoleonic Days, p. 206, Dowager Duchess of Coburg's diary, 20, 24 March 1819.
71. Royal Kalendar 1819, p. 131. RA Add. 7/1375, Duke of Kent to Dr Davis, 28 February 1819. Also RA M3/1, Duke of Kent to Mr Putnam, 5 April 1819; RA Add. 7/1393–5, Duke of Kent to Gen. Wetherall, 13, 20 and 24 April 1819.
72. RA 45342–3, Duke of Kent to Baron de Mallet, 29 March 1819.
73. RA M3/1, Duke of Kent to Mr Putnam, 5 April 1819.
74. Kent County Archives Office, U 1186, C. 2/9, Duke of Kent to Gen. Knollys, 22 April 1819.
75. RA M3/2, Duke of Kent to Dowager Duchess of Coburg, 24 April 1819, trans.
76. PRO Works 1, Letter-books, Set 2, No. 4/1601, also Works 4, Minutes and Proceedings, Vol. 23, f. 389, Bloomfield to Col Stephenson, 5 April 1819.
77. PRO Lord Chamberlain's Books, Series 2, L.C. 1/41, p. 114, John Calvert to Rt. Hon. C. Arbuthnot, 10 April 1819.

78. RA Add. 7/1347, 1392, Duke of Kent to Gen. Wetherall, 5 January 1819; to Bloomfield, 13 April 1819. Cf. PRO Works 19. 16/1, Nos. 74, 79, 94: these are John Nash to the Surveyor-General of the Office of Works, 30 December 1816, 26 January 1818, and 16 October 1819. See also Works 1, Letter-books, Set 2, No. 3/1276, Duke of Kent to Stephenson, 17 February 1818.
79. PRO Works 19. 16/1, No. 163, memorial of W. Francis to Duchess of Kent, 1 December 1837; Nos. 297–320, inventory of goods supplied by the Lord Chamberlain, and account of furniture bought by the Duke from Elliot and Francis, and from Russell, May 1819. RA Add. Q1090, E. Snell to Col Couper, March 1840.
80. RA M3/3, Duke of Kent to Dowager Duchess of Coburg, 24 May 1819, trans.
81. PRO Works 19. 16/1, No. 310.
82. PRO Works 19. 16/1, No. 305 seq.
RA L5/108, memorandum by Sir Arthur Bigge, later Lord Stamfordham, 15 May 1899, in which he records that on a visit at that date to Kensington Palace Queen Victoria expressed her doubt that the room traditionally pointed out as where she had been born was in fact the right room.
83. PRO Works 1, Letter-books Set 2, No. 4/1608, Wetherall to Stephenson, 23 May 1819. See also Works 4, Vol. 23, f. 431.
84. RA Add. 7/1396, Duke of Kent to Wetherall, 23 May 1819.
85. RA Add. 7/1397, announcement of the birth, with list of official witnesses.
86. Stockmar, Vol. I, p. 78.
87. Robert Gittings, *John Keats*, Heinemann, 1968, Penguin, 1971, pp. 455, 471.
88. See 80 above.
89. Agnes Strickland, *From Birth to Bridal*, 1840. Copy in the Royal Library, Windsor, annotated by Queen Victoria.
90. RA M24/2, Dowager Duchess of Coburg to Duchess of Kent, 31 May 1819, trans.
91. RA M24/3, the same to the same, [27 August 1819], trans.
92. RA Y36/118, Princess Feodora to Queen Victoria, 7 January 1843.
RA Add. 7/1375, Duke of Kent to Dr Davis, 28 February 1819; RA M3/1, Duke of Kent to Mr Putnam, 5 April 1819.

CHAPTER TWO

1. RA Y69/26, King Leopold to Queen Victoria, 16 December 1842.
2. Stockmar, Vol. I, p. 78. A biographical sketch of Stockmar by his son is prefixed to this work, pp. xxxv–cx.
3. RA M3/4, Duke of Kent to Louis Philippe, Duke of Orleans, 8 June 1819.
RA 45288–9, Duke of Kent to Mrs Fitzherbert, 23 January 1819.
4. RA 43344–5, Duke of Kent to Baron de Mallet, 8 June 1819.
5. RA M3/6, Duchess of Kent to Dowager Duchess of Coburg, 22 and 23 June 1819 (original dated in error as May), trans.
RA M3/3, Duke of Kent to the same, 24 May 1819, trans.
6. RA M3/5, Bloomfield to Duke of Kent, 21 June 1819.
7. RA M4/26, Duchess of Kent to Earl Grey, 28 January 1831.
8. Greville, Vol. I, p. 84. Stanhope, *Wellington*, p. 297. Lee, p. 11.
9. RA Add. 7/1355, Joseph Hume to Duke of Kent, 1 February 1819.
10. RA Add. 7/1382, Duke of Kent to Wetherall, 7 March 1819.
11. Hansard, 2 July 1819, Vol. 40, pp. 1428, 1508–14.

12. RA M24/3, Dowager Duchess of Coburg to Duches of Kent, [27 August 1819], trans.
13. RA M5/94–105.
14. RA Add. 12/333, Princess Mary to the Prince Regent, 10 September 1819.
15. RA Add. 7/1408, memorandum of Duke of Kent, September 1819.
16. RA M3/17, 18, 19, Duke to Duchess of Kent, 25, 26, 27 October 1819.
17. RA M3/20, Duke of Kent to Duke of Coburg, 19 November 1819.
   RA 46616–17, Duke of Kent to Sir Alexander McKenzie, 1 November 1819.
18. RA M3/13, 14A, B, C, and 15, congratulatory letters and verses to the Duke of Kent on his birthday.
19. The numerous financial papers at this date include RA Add. 7/1408–1446, RA 45364–5, 46616–17.
20. RA Add. 7/1442, 1448, Duke of Kent to Wetherall, 25 and 31 December 1819.
21. See also Luke Howard, *Meteorological Observations*, 1833.
22. RA Add. U75, Conroy to George Cornish, 28 December 1819.
23. RA 45391–2, Duke of Kent to Admiral Donnelly, 6 January 1820.
24. The series of letters RA Z286 and Add. V1, Duchess of Kent to Polyxene von Tubeuf, 7 January to 18 February 1820, originals and trans. by Princess Beatrice, are quoted from often in this part of the text, along with RA M3/25, Duchess of Kent to her mother the Dowager Duchess of Coburg, 29 February and 1 March 1820.
25. RA 46624, bulletin on the Duke's condition, 20 January 1820.
   RA Y67/30, King Leopold to Queen Victoria, 22 January 1841.
26. RA 46628–9, Wetherall to Bloomfield, 22 January 1820.
27. Stockmar, Vol. I, pp, 78–9.
   RA 46631, Wetherall to Bloomfield, 23 January 1820.
28. John Wilson Croker, *The Croker Papers*, correspondence and diaries, ed. Lewis J. Jennings, 3 vols., 1884–5, Vol. I, p. 155.
29. Harcourt Papers, Vol. VI, p. 222, Princess Augusta to Lady Harcourt, 25 January 1820.
30. See 1 above and RA Y82/101, King Leopold to Queen Victoria, 7 January 1859.
31. RA Y203/79, Lehzen to the Queen, 6 September 1867. Cf. 7 above.
32. RA 46640 *seq.*, description of the funeral.
33. RA 46634, Prince Leopold to Bloomfield, 23 January 1820, trans.
34. RA Add. 12/359, 361, Princess Mary to the Prince Regent, 25, 27 January 1820.
35. Harcourt Papers, Vol. VI, p. 224, Princess Augusta to Lady Harcourt, 4 February 1820.
36. RA Y67/30, King Leopold to Queen Victoria, 22 January 1841.
37. RA Add. 7/1454, statement of the assets of the late Duke of Kent, February 1820.
38. RA Add. 12/365, Princess Mary to George IV, 2 February 1820.
39. RA Z481/2, 3; Z482/26, memoranda on the finances of the Duchess of Kent, April 1837.
40. RA Y82/101, King Leopold to Queen Victoria, 7 January 1859.
41. See note 19 above. RA Add. O71/2–5, 16, 19, 22, Capt. Hulme's claim, is also relevant.
42. Hansard, 3 July 1820, Vol. 2, p. 143 *seq.*
43. RA Z286, Duchess of Kent to Polyxene von Tubeuf, 1 February 1820.
44. RA 45372, Duke of Kent to Admiral Donnelly, 12 February 1819.
45. RA Y56/30, Louis Philippe, Duke of Orleans to Thomas Coutts, 3 February 1820.
46. RA M3/35, renunciation by Duchess of Kent, 16 March 1820.
   RA Y179/1, Duchess of Kent to Wetherall and Conroy, 11 February 1820.
47. Creevey, pp. 180, 217.

48. *Letters of Harriet Countess Granville, 1810–1845*, ed. Hon. F. Leveson Gower, 2 vols., 1894, Vol. I, p. 169.
49. See 1 above.
50. Conroy Papers, Balliol College Library, Oxford.
51. See Chapter Seven.
52. *Letters of George IV*, Vol. II, p. 418.
53. RA M3/36, bond for loan of £6,000 from Coutts to the Duchess of Kent, April 1821.
54. See 39 above.
55. RA Add. 10/94, Princess Augusta to Earl of Arran, 7 July 1818.
56. *Letters* of Countess Granville, pp. 196–7.
57. Creevey, p. 214.
58. Printed in *The Letters of Queen Victoria 1837–1861*, ed. A. C. Benson and Viscount Esher, 3 vols., 1907 (hereafter referred to as *Letters*) Vol. I, pp. 14–19.
59. RA Y36/132, Princess Feodora to Queen Victoria, 15 April 1843.
    RA Y198/69, is an affectionate note about 'Mrs Louis' written by the Queen in 1869.
60. *Letters*, Vol. I, p. 19.
61. RA Y34/101, Princess Feodora to Queen Victoria, 9 November 1837.
62. *Letters*, Vol. I, pp. 14–15.
63. RA Y203/79, 80, Lehzen to the Queen, 20 February, 6 September 1867.
64. Greville, Vol. IV, p. 218.
65. See 63 above.
66. RA Queen Victoria's Journal, 7 November 1838.
67. This is written by the Queen in the margin of RA Y203/81, a letter she had received from Lehzen dated 2 December 1867.
68. *Letters*, Vol. I, pp. 14–18, 24.
    RA Y36/128, Princess Feodora to Queen Victoria, 17 March 1843.
    Queen Victoria's Journal, March 1861, quoted Sir Theodore Martin, *The Life of H.R.H. The Prince Consort*, 5 vols., 6th edition, 1879, Vol. V, p. 317.
69. RA Y82/113, King Leopold to Queen Victoria, April 1861.
70. Conroy Papers, Balliol College Library, Oxford. Memorandum on Conroy's early career.
71. Conroy Papers. Duke of Kent to Sir George Beechwith, 20 November 1816.
72. Conroy Papers. Duke of Kent to Duke of Wellington, 4 December 1818.
73. See 39 above.
74. Hansard, 27 May 1825, Vol. 13, pp. 898, 909.
75. RA M3/37, Stockmar to Conroy, 20 May 1825.
76. RA M3/38, Conroy to Stockmar, 1 June 1825.
77. *Letters*, Vol. I, pp. 18–19.
78. RA Y179/4, Duchess of Kent to George IV, 18 September 1825.
79. *Letters*, Vol. I, p. 17.
80. Ibid., pp. 15–17.
81. RA M4/1, Conroy to Duchess of Kent, 14 July 1826.
82. Albemarle, p. 310.
83. Leigh Hunt, *The Old Court Suburb*: or, Memorials of Kensington, regal, critical, and anecdotical, 2 vols., 1902, Vol. II, p. 175.
84. RA Y54/89, memorandum by George Anson, 24 October 1841.
85. Greville, Vol. I, p. 272.
86. See 84 above.
87. Greville, Vol. II, p. 192.

88. RA M4/7-10, George IV to Duchess of Kent, 9, 19 December 1827, 17 January, 14 February 1828.
89. RA Y34/46, Princess Feodora to Princess Victoria, 4 March 1836.
90. See 68 above.

CHAPTER THREE

1. RA M7/67 and Add. V2, memorandum by Charles, Prince of Leiningen, 1840, trans.
2. Greville, Vol. II, p. 194.
3. Conroy Papers. Balliol College Library.
4. Karoline Bauer, *Memoirs*, trans., 1885, p. 44.
5. Stockmar, Vol. I, p. 80 seq.
   Count E. C. Corti, *Leopold I of Belgium*, trans. J. McCabe, Unwin, 1923.
   Dorothy Margaret Stuart, *The Mother of Victoria*, Macmillan, 1941, p. 110.
6. See 4 above.
7. See 5 above and Stockmar, Vol. I, p. 143 seq.
8. A note by Queen Victoria, attached to reminiscences of King Leopold written in 1862 and printed as App. A to Lieut.-General the Hon. Charles Grey, *The Early Years of H.R.H. The Prince Consort*, 1867.
9. Stockmar, Vol. I, pp. 163 seq., 293 seq.
10. Frances H. Low, *Queen Victoria's Dolls*, illus. Alan Wright, 1894.
    Leaves from the Diary of Henry Greville, ed. Viscountess Enfield, 1st series, 1883, pp. 8-9.
    Girlhood of Queen Victoria (see 50 below), Vol. I, p. 42.
    RA Queen Victoria's Journal, 5 March 1839.
11. Charles Knight, *Passages of a Working Life* during half a century; with a prelude of early reminiscences, 3 vols., [1863]-1865, 1873.
12. *The Journal of Mrs. Arbuthnot 1820-1832*, ed. Francis Bamford and the Duke of Wellington, Macmillan, 1930, Vol. II, p. 186. *The Lieven–Palmerston Correspondence 1828-1856*, trans. and ed. Lord Sudley, John Murray, 1943, pp. 11-12. *Correspondence of Princess Lieven and Earl Grey*, ed. G. LeStrange, 3 vols., 1890, Vol. I, p. 381.
13. Greville, Vol. II, p. 194 and see 15 below.
14. RA M4/19, memorandum by Princess Sophia to Conroy, 14 October [1829], trans.
15. Greville, Vol. IV, p. 199.
16. RA M4/16, Duchess of Clarence to Duchess of Kent, 12 January 1830, trans.
17. RA M5/7, Duchess of Kent to the Bishops of London and Lincoln, 1 March 1830.
18. *Letters*, Vol. I, p. 15.
    RA M5/1, 2, 3, list of books studied by Princess Victoria, a time-table of her lessons, and a report by Davys, March 1830.
    RA M5/29, Davys to Duchess of Kent, 5 January 1832.
19. RA M5/6, report by Grandineau, 3 March 1830.
20. RA M5/4, report by Barez, 2 March 1830.
    RA M5/59 is a later report from him, 3 July 1835.
21. See Chapter Six.
22. RA M5/5, report by Steward, 2 March 1830, and see 18 above.
23. RA M5/10, 14, report of the examination of the Princess by the Bishops, March 1830.

24. RA M5/8, memorandum of interview between the Duchess of Kent and the Bishop of London, 10 March 1830, with a later note by Prince Albert.
25. Ibid., and RA Y203/81, Lehzen to the Queen, 2 December 1867, with the Queen's notes in the margin.
26. RA M5/9 *seq.*, Duchess of Kent to Bishops of London and Lincoln, 13 March 1830, and to Archbishop of Canterbury, 27 March 1830, 3 April 1830.
    RA M5/14, Archbishop of Canterbury to Duchess of Kent, 13 May 1830.
27. Ida Macalpine and R. A. Hunter, *George III and the Mad-business*, Allen Lane, 1969.
28. Greville, Vol. I, pp. 293, 299.
29. Ibid., Vol. II, pp. 3–6. Lieven–Palmerston, p. 74.
30. RA Y203/81, Duchess of Clarence to Duchess of Kent, 1821, as reported by Lehzen to Queen Victoria, 2 December 1867.
    RA 37129, Duchess of Clarence to Princess Victoria, n.d. [May, 1821].
31. RA M4/20, Duchess of Kent to Duke of Wellington, 27 June 1830.
32. RA M4/21, the Duke's reply, 30 June 1830.
33. RA M4/22, 23, Duchess of Kent to Duke of Wellington, 1 July 1830 and his reply, 2 July. Greville, Vol. II, pp. 191, 195.
34. Hansard, 6 July, 15 November 1830, Vol. I, p. 500 *seq.*
35. RA Journal of Queen Adelaide.
36. Lieven–Grey, Vol. III, p. 88. Lieven–Palmerston, p. 74.
37. RA M4/24, memorandum by Conroy, 31 December 1830.
38. RA M4/25, memorandum by Conroy of the interview between the Duchess of Kent and Earl Grey, 24 December 1830.
39. RA M4/26, Duchess of Kent to Earl Grey, 28 January 1831.
40. RA M4/27, Earl Grey to Duchess of Kent, 30 January 1831.
41. RA M4/29, Duchess of Kent to Earl Grey, 23 April 1831.
42. RA M4/30, Archbishop of Canterbury to Duchess of Kent, 8 June 1831.
43. RA M4/32, 33, 35, Duchess of Kent to Earl Grey, 25 June 1831 and his reply the same day; William IV to Earl Grey, 26 June 1831.
44. Lee, pp. 30–1.
    Gabriele von Bülow (née von Humboldt), *A Memoir* compiled from family papers, trans. Clara Nordlinger, 1897, pp. 190–1.
45. RA M4/37, 39, memorandum of Duchess of Kent to Earl Grey, August 1831 and his reply, 9 August.
46. RA M4/40, Earl Grey to Duchess of Kent, 21 August 1831. Lee, p. 31.
47. Greville, Vol. II, p. 193.
48. *The First Lady Wharncliffe and Her Family*, ed. Caroline Grosvenor and Charles Beilby, Lord Stuart of Wortley, Heinemann, 1927, Vol. II, pp. 78–9.
49. Greville, Vol. II, p. 120.
50. Her diary will be referred to in these notes as RA Princess (or Queen) Victoria's Journal with the date—in this case 31 July 1832. (*The Girlhood of Queen Victoria*, 2 vols., a collection of extracts from the diary, was edited and published by Viscount Esher in 1912.).
51. RA Princess Victoria's Journal, 1 August to 9 November 1832, *passim*.
52. Lee, p. 36. Lady Catherine Jenkinson, eldest of three daughters of the Earl of Liverpool, first appears in the Royal Kalendar as Lady of the Bedchamber to the Duchess of Kent in 1830 and married Col Francis Vernon Harcourt in November 1837. She died in 1877.
53. Greville, Vol. II, pp. 190–3, 388.
54. RA Princess Victoria's Journal, 24 May 1833.

55. Greville, Vol. II, p. 388.
56. RA Princess Victoria's Journal, 16 June, 12 July 1833.
57. Ibid., May and June 1833, *passim*.
58. Ibid., 2 August 1833.
59. Ibid., August–September 1833.
60. RA Y61/12, 14, 25, 36, King Leopold to Princess Victoria, 13 December 1831, 23 January 1832, 11 March, 14 November 1834.
61. RA Princess Victoria's Journal, 14 April 1834.
62. Ibid., 5 June 1834.
63. RA Y33/3, Princess Feodora to Princess Victoria, 23 April 1828.
64. RA Y34/9, Princess Feodora to Princess Victoria, 2 October 1834.
65. RA Princess Victoria's Journal, 25, 26 July 1834.
66. RA Y34/11, Princess Feodora to Princess Victoria, 5 November 1834.
67. RA M7/42, Stockmar to the Duchess of Kent, 4 July 1834.
68. RA Princess Victoria's Journal, November–December 1834.
69. Ibid., 11 November 1834. See *Girlhood of Queen Victoria*, Vol. I, pp. 104, 355.
70. RA M7/43, Stockmar to the Duchess of Kent, 5 June 1834, trans.
71. RA Add. U72/15, Princess Feodora to Duchess of Northumberland, 25 March 1835.
72. See the next note.
73. RA Z492/31–38, correspondence between the Archbishop of Canterbury, the Bishop of London, Sir Herbert Taylor, and the Duchess of Kent, 30 June–17 July 1835.
74. Lee, p. 40.
75. RA M5/78, Duchess of Kent to Princess Victoria, 30 July 1835.
76. RA Princess Victoria's Journal, 12 December 1834.
77. *Letters*, Vol. I, p. 19. Lee, p. 20.
78. RA Princess Victoria's Journal, 2 August 1835.
79. Ibid., 17, 20, 21 August 1835.
80. Lee, p. 41.
81. RA M5/84, Duchess of Kent to Princess Victoria, 2 September 1835.
82. RA Princess Victoria's Journal, 3–25 September 1835.
83. RA Add. A11/22, Lehzen to King Leopold, n.d., trans.
84. RA Y34/1, Princess Feodora to Princess Victoria, 27–29 July 1834.
85. RA correspondence files, Belgian archives, letter of 3 January 1955.
86. RA Y61/22, King Leopold to Princess Victoria, 18 October 1833.
87. RA Princess Victoria's Journal, 29 September–7 October 1835.
88. Ibid., 4, 6 October 1835.
89. See 83 above.
90. Princess Victoria's Journal, 7 October 1835.
91. Ibid. The Princess made no entries in her Journal between 7 and 31 October 1835. The quotation in the text is from 5 November, and on 10 November she writes that this was the first day she was able to go downstairs.
92. Lee, p. 40. In December 1861 Queen Victoria told King Leopold (RA Y107/25) that her husband's symptoms were like hers had been at Ramsgate: 'Every day however is bringing us nearer to the end of this tiresome illness—wh. is much what I had at Ramsgate, only that I was much worse and was not well attended to.' The Queen, however, as her diaries and letters in 1861 show very clearly, was uncertain what illness the Prince was suffering from. See Chapter Thirteen.
93. RA M5/84–5, note by Prince Consort.
94. Hohenlohe-Langenburg Archives, Princess Victoria to Princess Feodora, 1 November 1835.

446

RA Y88/4, Princess Victoria to King Leopold, 3 November 1835, trans.
95. RA Princess Victoria's Journal, 14, 15 November 1835, 25 January 1836.
96. RA M5/86, memorandum by Dr Clark, 29 January 1836.
97. Hohenlohe-Langenburg Archives, Princess Victoria to Princess Feodora, 30 December 1835.
RA Princess Victoria's Journal, 12 January 1836.

CHAPTER FOUR

1. RA Princess Victoria's Journal, 13 January 1836.
Hohenlohe-Langenburg Archives, Princess Victoria to Princess Feodora, 15 November 1833.
2. Plan of state apartments. Plan No. 3. Proposed alternatives, initialled G W 26th July 1832. Royal Library, Windsor.
PRO Office of Works Papers.
3. RA Z192/5, Princess Victoria to Charles Prince of Leiningen, 12 August 1833.
4. RA L5/108, memorandum by Sir Arthur Bigge, 15 May 1899.
5. Greville, Vol. III, p. 309.
6. RA Princess Victoria's Journal, 25 January 1836 seq.
7. RA Y62/16, 18, King Leopold to Princess Victoria, 7, 22 January 1836.
8. RA Princess Victoria's Journal, 13 February 1836.
9. RA Y88/33, Princess Victoria to King Leopold, 14 March 1837.
10. RA Z58/18, the Princess Royal to the Queen, 30 July 1895.
Kronberg Archives, the Queen's reply, 4 August 1895.
11. RA Princess Victoria's Journal, 17 March 1836.
12. Ibid., 19 March 1836.
13. RA Y62/29, King Leopold to Princess Victoria, 25 March 1836.
14. RA Princess Victoria's Journal, 25 March–2 April 1836.
15. RA Y82/30, King Leopold to Princess Victoria, 11 April 1836.
16. RA Y34/52, Princess Feodora to Princess Victoria, 26 April 1836.
17. RA Princess Victoria's Journal, 19 April, 3 May 1836.
18. RA M4/57, memorandum by Charles Prince of Leiningen. This has a note in Prince Albert's hand.
19. Greville, Vol. III, p. 311.
20. RA M4/24.
21. RA M4/49, Duchess of Kent to Palmerston, 12, 14 May 1836.
22. RA M4/52, 54, Palmerston to Conroy, 13 May 1836.
23. RA Y62/37, King Leopold to Princess Victoria, 13 May 1836.
24. RA Princess Victoria's Journal, 13 May 1836.
25. RA Y88/11, Princess Victoria to King Leopold, 17 May 1836.
26. RA Princess Victoria's Journal, 18 May 1836.
27. RA Y34/51, Princess Feodora to Princess Victoria, 16 April 1836.
28. Lieut-General the Hon. Charles Grey, *The Early Years of the Prince Consort*, compiled under the direction of Queen Victoria, 1897, p. 96.
29. Ibid., p. 124.
30. RA Princess Victoria's Journal, 24 May 1836.
31. RA Y88/13, Princess Victoria to King Leopold, 26 May 1836.
32. RA Princess Victoria's Journal, 30 May 1836.
33. RA Y88/14, Princess Victoria to King Leopold, 31 May 1836.
34. RA Y62/28, King Leopold to Princess Victoria, 11 March 1836.

Early Years of the Prince, p. 209.

Letters of the Prince Consort, 1831–61, ed. Kurt Jagow, trans. E. T. S. Dugdale, John Murray, 1938, pp. 18, 20, Prince Albert to Prince William of Löwenstein, 26 October 1838, 25 February 1839.

35. RA Princess Victoria's Journal, 4–10 June 1836.
36. See 18 above.
37. RA 88/15, Princess Victoria to King Leopold, 7 June 1836.
38. *Early Years*, p. 216.
39. RA Add. A11/2, King Leopold to Lehzen, 1 May 1836.
40. See 37 above. RA Princess Victoria's Journal, 18 June, 4, 6 July 1836.
41. Ibid., 8, 20 April, 5, 7 May 1837.
42. Ibid., 10, 15 August 1836.
43. RA Y88/16, Princess Victoria to King Leopold, 22 June 1836.
44. RA M4/64, Duchess of Kent to Conyngham, 15 April 1837.
45. RA M4/65, Duchess of Kent to Conyngham, 2 May 1837.
46. Greville, Vol. III, p. 308.
47. Ibid., pp. 308–11.
48. RA Y88/22, Princess Victoria to King Leopold, 6 September 1836.
    RA Princess Victoria's Journal, 8–18 September 1836.
49. RA Y65/37, King Leopold to Queen Victoria, 12 March 1839.
50. RA Y82/112, 113, King Leopold to Queen Victoria, 8, 12 April 1861. Cf. RA Y62/3, King Leopold's letter of 13 October 1835.
51. RA Princess Victoria's Journal, 21 September 1836.
52. RA Y63/2, King Leopold to Princess Victoria, 22 September 1836.
53. RA Y63/6, King Leopold to Princess Victoria, 14 October 1836.
54. RA Princess Victoria's Journal, 6 October 1836.
55. Ibid., 6, 13 December 1836.
56. Ibid., 22–30 December 1836, 1, 5 June 1837.
57. RA Y88/30, Princess Victoria to King Leopold, 6 February 1837.
58. RA Y88/31, Princess Victoria to King Leopold, 22 February 1837.
59. RA Y88/32, Princess Victoria to King Leopold, 7 March 1837.
60. *Letters*, Vol. 1, p. 79.
61. RA Add. A1/11, Lehzen to King Leopold, 24 February, 11, 18 March 1837.
62. RA Add. A11/3, Stockmar to King Leopold, 24 February 1837.
63. PRO Granville Papers, 30/29, Box 423, Palmerston to Granville, 3 March 1837.
64. RA Add. A11/4, Stockmar to King Leopold, 3 April 1837.
65. RA M7/1, memorandum by Conroy, n.d. [early 1837]. RA M7 is a collection of papers on the events just before Queen Victoria's accession put together and arranged by the Prince Consort in 1861.
66. PRO Granville Papers, 30/29, Box 423, Palmerston to Granville, 18 May 1837.
67. RA Princess Victoria's Journal, 22, 23 May 1837.
68. PRO Granville Papers, 30/29, Box 423, Palmerston to Granville, 26 May, 30 May, 2 June 1837.
69. RA M7/12, 18, William IV to Princess Victoria and to Conyngham, 18 May 1837. The latter—which bears the sign manual—is an instruction to Conyngham to deliver the former to the Princess herself.
    RA M7/2–11, correspondence of Melbourne on the proposed grant, 17–19 May 1837.
70. RA M7/21, Duchess of Kent to Melbourne, 20 May 1837.
    RA M7/23, 24, Melbourne to Duchess of Kent and her reply, 21 May 1837.
71. RA M7/13, memorandum by Lehzen, written by Princess Victoria's request, 6 June 1837.

448

RA 7/14, 21, copies of the letter drafted [by Conroy and the Duchess of Kent] for the Princess to send to William IV, 20 May 1837, with a later note by the Prince Consort.

72. RA M7/15, memorandum by Lehzen, n.d.

73. RA Melbourne Papers, Russell and Taylor to Melbourne, 25 May 1837 (two letters).

74. RA M7/26, Melbourne to William IV, 21 May 1837.

75. RA M7/30, 38, Melbourne to Sir Herbert Taylor, 22 May 1837 and Taylor's reply the same day.

76. RA Princess Victoria's Journal, 24 May 1837.

77. See 72 above.

78. See 18 above.

79. See 71 above.

80. RA Princess Victoria's Journal, 1 June 1837.

81. Ibid., 9 June 1837.

82. RA Add. A11/12, Stockmar to King Leopold, 8–13 June 1837. On 12 June Princess Victoria wrote to her sister Princess Feodora: 'You know I suppose, that the King has been for some time very unwell, but he was so much worse on Thursday [8 June], that we were unable to go out on Saturday to the Opera & Mamma put off her *Ball* wh wld have taken place tonight . . .' Hohenlohe-Langenburg Archives.

83. RA Princess Victoria's Journal, 15 June 1837.
RA M7/56, memorandum by Princess Victoria, 15 June 1837.

84. PRO Granville Papers, 30/29, Box 423, Palmerston to Granville, 13 June 1837.
RA Add. A11/15, Stockmar to King Leopold, 16 June 1837.

85. See 18 above.

86. RA Princess Victoria's Journal, 18–19 June 1837.

87. Ibid., 20 June 1837.

CHAPTER FIVE

1. RA Queen Victoria's Journal, 20 June 1837. RA Y88/46, Queen Victoria to King Leopold, 20 June 1837 ('½p 8 A.M.') Hohenlohe–Langenburg Archives, Queen Victoria to Princess Feodora, 20 June 1837.

2. Greville, Vol. III, p. 372-3, 395. Croker, Vol. II, p. 359. Lee, p. 50 *seq*.

3. PRO 30/29, Granville Papers, Box 424, Holland to Granville, 30 June, 21 July, 15 September 1837. *Letters* of Countess Granville, Vol. II, p. 235.

4. RA Queen Victoria's Journal, 1 July 1837. RA M7/60, memorandum by the Queen, 20 June 1837, with a later note by the Prince Consort.

5. RA M7/68, private memorandum by Stockmar for the Queen, 1847 (date endorsed by the Prince Consort).
RA Melbourne Papers:
Conroy's memorandum, n.d., unfinished.
Conroy to Stockmar, 3 letters, the first of 30 June, two more of 23 June 1837.
Melbourne to Conroy, and Conroy's reply, 26 June 1837.
Stockmar to Conroy, 11 July 1837.
Duchess of Kent to Melbourne, 19 July, and Melbourne's reply, 20 July 1837.

6. RA M7/61, 62, Duchess of Kent to the Queen and the Queen's reply 20 June 1837.
RA M7/65, Duchess of Kent to the Queen, n.d.
RA Queen Victoria's Journal, 20 June 1837.

7. Greville, Vol. IV, p. 41.
8. Eric Hobsbawm and George Rudé, *Captain Swing*, Lawrence and Wishart, 1969.
9. PRO, Home Office, H.O. 119/9, S. M. Phillips for Lord Melbourne to G. Maule, 10 March 1834, requesting an opinion from the Law officers of the Crown.
10. W. M. Citrine and others, *Book of the Martyrs of Tolpuddle*, T.U.C. General Council, 1934. F. A. Carrington and J. Payne, *Reports of Cases . . . . . . 1833–35* B. M. pressmark 1243. d. 9.), pp. 596–601.
11. Hansard, 3rd series, Vol. 22, pp. 726–38, 859–63, 938–50; Vol. 23, pp. 114–27, 311–14.
12. Lord John Russell, *Early Correspondence*, Vol. II, pp. 132, 137–40, 142–6, especially Melbourne to Russell, 13 October 1835.
13. Letter·in *The Times* from Mr H. D. Jaques, 13 August 1971.
14. Greville, Vol. III, pp. 394–5.
    RA Queen Victoria's Journal, 14, 17, 19 July, 15, 17, 20 August, 20 October 1837.
    RA Z294, Duchess of Kent's Journal, [17] July 1837, trans.
    Memoir of Gabriele von Bülow, pp. 277–9.
15. Lieven–Palmerston, p. 137.
    RA Z294, Duchess of Kent's Journal, [17–22] August 1837, trans.
16. Ibid., and RA Queen Victoria's Journal, 23–29 August, 6 September 1837.
17. RA Queen Victoria's Journal, 8–19 September 1837.
18. Ibid., 28 September, 3 October 1837.
19. Ibid., 4 October 1837.
    Lieven–Palmerston, pp. 139–40.
20. RA Y154/33, Liverpool to Stockmar, 10 August 1837.
    RA Z482/12, the Queen to the Duchess of Kent. 17 August 1837.
21. RA Queen Victoria's Journal, 7, 17 November, 13–19 December 1837.
    RA Z482/35, the Duchess of Kent to the Queen, 6 November 1837.
    RA Z482/36, draft by Melbourne of the Queen's reply, 8 November 1837.
    RA Z481/1–3, Z482/25–8, memoranda on the history of the Duchess of Kent's finances, 1837.
    RA Z482/39–40, Duchess of Kent to Stockmar, 11 November 1837.
22. RA Queen Victoria's Journal, 22 December 1837.
    Relevant correspondence includes RA Z482/38–67 *passim*, especially 42, Melbourne to the Queen, 12 November 1837.
23. Lee, pp. 78–81.
24. RA Y154/36, Liverpool to Stockmar, 'most confidential', 8 January 1838.
25. RA Queen Victoria's Journal, 15 January, 18, 20, 26 February 1838.
26. Numerous examples are in RA A8/1–67, and the Palmerston Papers, Broadlands Archives.
27. PRO Lord Chamberlain's Records, L. C. 2/67, 68, reports and correspondence of the Keeper of the Regalia, April–June 1838. Major-General H. D. W. Sitwell, *The Crown Jewels* and other regalia in the Tower of London, ed. Clarence Winchester, Viscount Kemsley at the Dropmore Press, 1953. Information from Lieut-Colonel Stephen at the Jewel Office, April, 1972.
28. Greville, Vol. IV, pp. 69–73. Lee, pp. 87–91.
29. RA Queen Victoria's Journal, 27 June–2 July 1838.
30. Lawrence E. Tanner, *The History of the Coronation*, Pitkin, [1952], especially p. 78, where the pencil note made by the Sub-Dean is quoted. 'Form and Order of the Coronation Service of Queen Victoria', Royal Library, Windsor.
31. RA Queen Victoria's Journal, 4 July 1838.
32. Ibid., 10–16 July 1838.

33. Ibid., 23, 25 April 1838.
34. PRO Granville Papers, 30/29, Box 424, Holland to Granville, 22 August 1837, 16 November 1838.
35. RA Queen Victoria's Journal, 4–31 December 1838.
36. *Letters*, Vol. I, p. 254.
    RA Add. A11/69, 72, Stockmar to King Leopold, 19–23, 29 February 1838, trans.
37. RA Add. A11/81, Stockmar to King Leopold, 14 March 1838, trans.
    RA Y89/41, Queen Victoria to King Leopold, 15 July 1839.
38. RA Add. A14/66, Prince Albert to his father, Ernest I, Duke of Saxe-Coburg and Gotha, 6 March 1838, trans.
    RA Add. A6/6, Prince Albert to his tutor J. C. Florschutz, 28 July 1838, trans.
39. RA Add. A11/100, the Queen to Stockmar, August 1838.
40. RA Y65/40, King Leopold to Queen Victoria, 5 April 1839.
    RA A1/192, 212, Melbourne to the Queen, 26 August, 2 December 1838.
    RA A9/59, Palmerston to the Queen, 27 January 1839.
41. RA Add. A11/74, Stockmar to King Leopold, 1 March 1838.
42. RA A9/73, Palmerston to the Queen, 19 April 1839.
43. RA Queen Victoria's Journal, 2 February 1839.
44. Ibid., 14, 18 January 1839.
45. Statements by Lady Flora Hastings, as printed in *The Times*, 12 August, 16 September 1839.
46. RA Z486/2, statement by Lady Portman, 17 February 1839.
47. PRO Granville Papers, 30/29, Box 9, Holland to Granville, 1, 5 March 1839.
48. RA Z486/1, certificate by Drs Clark and Clarke, 17 February 1839.
49. Greville, Vol. IV, pp. 132–3.
50. RA Queen Victoria's Journal, especially 23 February, 7, 24 June 1839.
    RA Z486/3–38 includes further correspondence on the matter.
51. See 47 above.
52. RA Queen Victoria's Journal, 22 March 1839.
53. *The Times*, 12 August 1839, contains the letter of Lady Flora Hastings to Mr Hamilton FitzGerald, 8 March 1839, and a statement by FitzGerald dated 30 May 1839.
54. *Letters*, Vol. I, p. 194, Melbourne to the Queen, 7 May 1839.
55. RA Queen Victoria's Journal, 7 May 1839.
56. Ibid., 8 May 1839.
    RA C1/23, the Queen to Melbourne, 8 May 1839.
57. Greville, Vol. IV, p. 161.
58. *Letters*, Vol. I, p. 200.
    Sir Robert Peel from his private papers, ed. C. S. Parker, 3 vols. 1899, Vol. II, p. 389.
59. *Letters*, Vol. I, pp. 201–2, Melbourne to the Queen, 9 May 1839.
60. Ibid., pp. 204–5, the Queen to Melbourne, 9 May 1839.
    RA Queen Victoria's Journal, 9 May 1839.
61. Greville, Vol. IV, pp. 165–6.
62. RA Queen Victoria's Journal, 9 May 1839.
63. Greville, Vol. IV, pp. 163, 200–1.
64. Ibid., pp. 167–70 (The editors of Greville's text have put the words, 'are *sexual* though She does not know it, and', in square brackets, saying these words are struck through in the Greville MS.).
65. PRO Granville Papers, 30/29, Box 9, Holland to Granville, 20 May [1839].
66. RA Queen Victoria's Journal, 15–18 April 1839.
67. Ibid., 27–30 May 1839.

68. RA Z483/3, Abercromby to Conroy, 25 May 1839.
69. Greville, Vol. IV, pp. 177, 179, 196-9.
70. RA Queen Victoria's Journal, 18 March, 1-12 June 1839.
71. Ibid., 16-24 June 1839.
72. Conroy Papers, Balliol College Library.
73. RA Queen Victoria's Journal, 25-27 June 1839.
74. Ibid., 28 June-5 July 1839.
75. Greville, Vol. IV, p. 188.
76. Ibid., p. 181.
    RA Queen Victoria's Journal, 16 June, 5-7 July 1839.
    The Times, 6 October 1839, statement by Sir James Clark.
77. Greville, Vol. IV, p. 189.
78. RA L17/56, memorandum by Sir Arthur Bigge, 30 October 1897.
79. RA Queen Victoria's Journal, 17 July 1839.
80. Ibid., 30, 31 July 1839.
81. Ibid., 6 August 1839.
82. Ibid., 14 June 1839.
83. *Correspondence of Sarah Spencer, Lady Lyttelton 1787-1870* ed. Hon. Mrs Hugh Wyndham, 1912, p. 292.
84. RA Queen Victoria's Journal, 10 October 1839.

CHAPTER SIX

1. RA Queen Victoria's Journal, 11-14 October 1839.
2. RA Add. 14/84, 85, Prince Albert to his father, 12, 15 October 1839, trans.
3. RA Melbourne Papers, Melbourne to Russell, 13 October 1839.
4. RA Queen Victoria's Journal, 14-15 October 1839.
5. RA Y147/53, Prince Albert to Stockmar, 27 April 1841.
6. RA Y54/15, memorandum by George Anson, 16 February 1841, of a conversation with Stockmar.
7. RA Y86/8, King Leopold to Queen Victoria, 2 February 1864.
8. *Early Years of the Prince Consort*, p. 24.
9. RA Add. A6/9, Prince Albert to Florschütz, 1 January 1839, trans.
    Martin, *The Life of the Prince Consort*, Vol. I, pp. 26-7, King Leopold to Stockmar, March 1838, trans.
    RA Add. A6/6, Prince Albert to Florschütz, 28 July 1838.
10. RA Y89/41, Queen Victoria to King Leopold, 15 July 1839.
    Early Years, pp. 219-221.
    Letters of the Prince, p. 32, Prince Albert to Prince William of Löwenstein, trans.
11. RA Add. A6/25, Prince Albert to Florschütz, 5 November 1839, trans.
    Letters of the Prince, p. 25, Prince Albert to Duchess Caroline of Gotha, 11 November 1839, trans.
12. RA Queen Victoria's Journal, 12-22 October 1839.
13. *Letters of the Prince*, pp. 23-5, the Prince to Stockmar, 16 October, 8 November 1839, trans.
14. RA Y66/11, King Leopold to Queen Victoria, 24 October 1839.
    RA Queen Victoria's Journal, 27 October 1839.
15. Ibid., 20 November 1839.
    Stockmar, Vol. II, p. 25.

16. RA Queen Victoria's Journal, 1–4 November 1839.
17. See Chapter Five.
18. Greville, Vol. IV, p. 221.
19. RA Queen Victoria's Journal, 10–12 November 1839.
20. Ibid., 14–17 November 1839.
    Letters of the Prince, p. 26 *seq.*
21. RA Z490, the Queen to the Prince, 14 November 1839–31 January 1840, *passim*, especially 27–28 November 1839. (Portions of this correspondence are trans. from German).
22. RA Add. A14/87, Prince Albert to his father, 30 October 1839, trans.
    RA Z490, the Queen to the Prince, 15–19 November 1839.
23. Greville, Vol. IV, pp. 218-19.
    RA Queen Victoria's Journal, 23 November 1839.
    Peel Papers, Vol. II, p. 414, Arbuthnot to Peel, 12 December 1839.
24. *Early Years*, p. 275 *seq.*
25. Stockmar, Vol. II, p. 31. Martin, Vol. I, p. 60.
26. *Early Years*, p. 271 *seq.*
    RA Queen Victoria's Journal, especially 22, 29 November, 6 December 1839.
27. RA Y66/16, King Leopold to Queen Victoria, 22 November 1839.
    RA Queen Victoria's Journal, 19 December 1839, 27, 31 January, 2-6 February 1840.
    Hansard, Vol. 51, pp. 520 *seq.*, 539–42.
28. Greville, Vol. IV, pp. 232, 236, 238-9, 245.
    RA Queen Victoria's Journal, 5 February 1839.
29. RA Z490, the Queen to the Prince, 29 November 1839.
    Letters of the Prince, pp. 37–8.
    RA Queen Victoria's Journal, 28 December 1839.
30. RA Z490, the Queen to the Prince, 8, 23 December 1839, trans. (in part).
    Lady Lyttelton's Correspondence, p. 348.
    Letters of the Prince, pp. 40–2.
    RA Y89/63, Queen Victoria to King Leopold, 27 December 1839.
31. *Early Years*, p. 290 *seq.*
    Letters of the Prince, p. 55 *seq.*
32. PRO Admiralty Records, Adm. 2/1523.
33. RA Queen Victoria's Journal, 7–8 February 1840.
34. Ibid., 9–10 February 1840.
35. Copy of *Victoria from Birth to Bridal* in the Royal Library, Windsor.
36. Greville, Vol. IV, pp. 239–40.
37. Cecil Woodham-Smith, *Florence Nightingale*, Constable, 1951, p. 26.
38. Greville, Vol. IV, p. 240.
39. RA Queen Victoria's Journal, 10–12 February 1840.
    (The account of the wedding from *The Times*, 11 February 1840, is printed in *Early Years*, pp. 433–469.)
40. Greville, Vol. IV, pp. 240–1.
41. *Letters of the Prince*, pp. 54–5.
    RA Z490, the Queen to the Prince, 31 January 1840 (author's italics).
42. RA Queen Victoria's Journal, 13–16 February 1840.
43. H. Clifford Smith, *Buckingham Palace*, Country Life, 1931.
44. RA Melbourne Papers (Box 82), Murray to the Queen, 14 December 1838, with an account of the examination of Edward Cotton.
45. Ibid., Duncannon to Melbourne, 6 September 1838.

46. Ibid., report of Conyngham to Melbourne, September 1838.
47. RA Y54/89, memorandum by Anson, 24 October 1841.
48. RA Melbourne Papers, report by Hogg, 25 October 1838, and reports from Murray, 12 May, 29 November, 1 December 1838.
49. Ibid., Duncannon to Melbourne, December–January 1840.
    RA Queen Victoria's Journal, 10 January 1840.
50. *Early Years*, p. 319.
51. Palmerston Papers, Broadlands. Palmerston to Melbourne, June 1840.
52. *Letters of the Prince*, p. 69.
53. Martin, Vol. I, p. 71.
54. RA Y54/4, confidential memorandum by Anson, 28 May 1840.
55. PRO Granville Papers, 30/29 (Box 424), Holland to Granville, 21 February, 10 March, 12 May, 23 June 1840.
56. RA Y54/4, memorandum by Anson.
    Early Years, p. 341.
57. *Letters of the Prince*, pp. 70–1.
    Greville, Vol. IV, p. 266.
    RA Y54/5, memorandum by Anson, 11 June 1840.
    PRO Granville Papers, 30/29 (Box 424), Holland to Granville, 12, 18 June 1840.
    RA Queen Victoria's Journal, June 1840. (From early 1840 the references to Queen Victoria's Journal are to the abbreviated version as described in the quotation from Sir Philip Magnus printed in Appendix 4.)
58. Greville, Vol. IV, p. 268.
59. PRO Granville Papers, 30/29 (Box 424), Holland to Granville, 24 March 1840.
60. Greville, Vol. IV, p. 260.
61. RA Y54/6, memorandum by Anson, 21 June 1840.
62. *Early Years*, p. 351 *seq.*
    RA Y54/8, 10, memoranda by Anson, 15 August 1840 and undated.
63. PRO Granville Papers, 30/29 (Box 423), Clarendon to Granville, 24 November 1840.
    Early Years, pp. 365–6.
64. *The Times*, December 1840. RA Melbourne Papers, report on Jones's examination. PRO Admiralty Records.
65. RA Y54/11, memorandum by Anson, 20 December 1840.
66. RA Y54/16, 17, memoranda by Anson, 17, 19 February 1841.
67. Palmerston Papers, Broadlands, Palmerston to William Temple, 9 February 1841.
    Martin, Vol. I, pp. 100–1.
68. Ibid.
69. RA Y90/11, Queen Victoria to King Leopold, 5 January 1841.
    Kronberg Archives, Queen Victoria to the Princess Royal, 21 April 1858.
70. Lee, p. 127 *seq.*
71. RA Y54/24–6, memoranda by Anson, 4, 5 May 1841.
72. RA Y54/27–43, memoranda by Anson, 9–13 May 1841, *passim.*
73. RA Y54/45, 47, memoranda by Anson, 14 May, 11–12 June 1841.
74. Greville, Vol. IV, pp. 407–8.
75. RA Y54/66–71, memoranda by Anson, 29 August–3 September 1841.
76. Melbourne to the Queen, [4] September 1841, quoted in RA Y90/32, Queen Victoria to King Leopold, 8 September 1841.
77. RA Y200/7, 8, the Queen to Stockmar, 31 October 1841.
78. RA Queen Victoria's Journal, 2 December 1841.
79. Ibid.

CHAPTER SEVEN

1. RA Queen Victoria's Journal, 2 December 1841.
   RA M13/16, 21, Lady Lyttelton to the Queen, 3, 5 February 1842.
   RA Z294, Journal of Duchess of Kent, November 1841, trans.
   Lady Lyttelton's Correspondence, pp. 333–4.
2. Greville, Vol. V, p. 98, reporting an interview between Prince Albert and the Rev. Lord Wriothesley Russell.
   RA Y54/15, memorandum by Anson of conversations with Stockmar on 15 and 16 February 1841.
3. RA M12/1, 10, memorandum by the Prince, December 1841; Queen Victoria to Stockmar, 8 January 1842.
   RA Y54/100, memorandum by Anson, 26 December 1841.
   RA M12/16, 17, the Queen to Melbourne, 24 March 1842 and his reply the next day.
4. RA M12/32, Lady Lyttelton to Stockmar, 18 April 1842.
5. RA Y55/14, memorandum by Anson, 8 June 1843.
   Lady Lyttelton's Correspondence, pp. 327–9.
   RA M13/21, 27, Lady Lyttelton to the Queen, 5 February, 5 September 1842.
6. RA Y54/90, memorandum by Anson, 29 October 1841.
   Lady Lyttelton's Correspondence, pp. 319–22.
7. RA Z294, Journal of Duchess of Kent, January 1842.
   RA M13/14, 15, 17, 19, 20, 22, reports of Brown the apothecary, January–February 1842.
8. RA Y54/98, 100, memoranda by Anson, 28 November, 26 December 1841.
   RA Y169/59, Queen Victoria to Theodore Martin, n.d. Greville, Vol. VII, p. 69.
9. RA Add. U2/2, the Prince to Stockmar, 16 January 1842, trans.
10. RA Add. U2/1, 3, the Queen to Stockmar, 16, 17 January 1842.
11. RA Add. U2/4, the Prince to Stockmar, 18 January 1842, enclosing a note [for the Queen].
12. RA Add. U2/5, the Queen to Stockmar, 19 January 1842.
13. RA Add. U2/6, Stockmar to the Queen, [19 January 1842].
14. RA Add. U2/7, 8, the Queen to Stockmar, 19, 20 January 1842.
15. Greville, Vol. V, p. 39; Vol. VII, p. 69.
    RA Y152/18, Stockmar to the Queen, 8 August 1842.
    RA Z159/27, Lehzen to the Queen, 23 September [1842].
    RA Y169/57, 59, 60, correspondence of Queen Victoria and Mr Martin, November 1873.
    Martin, Vol. I, p. 297.
16. RA Y91/4, 9, Queen Victoria to King Leopold, 28 February, 9 May 1843.
17. RA Y55/19, memorandum by Anson, 29 June 1843.
18. RA Y54/16, 17, 77, 78, 91, 96, 97, memoranda by Anson, 17, 19 February, 9, 21 September, 3, 19, 23 November 1841.
19. RA A4, correspondence of Melbourne with the Queen, 1841 *seq*.
20. RA Y54/82–6, memoranda by Anson, 4–6 October 1841.
21. Hansard, House of Lords, 4 October 1841, Vol. 59, p. 1094.
22. RA Melbourne Papers, Anson to Melbourne, 7 October 1841, and Stockmar to Melbourne, 23 November 1841.
    RA Y54/100, memorandum by Anson, 26 December 1841.
23. *Lady Lyttelton's Correspondence*, pp. 285, 301, 332.

RA Queen Victoria's Journal, 7, 17 August, 25 September, 16 November, 16 December 1839, 30 January 1840.
24. *Lord Melbourne's Papers*, ed. Lloyd C. Sanders, 1889, pp. 527–8.
Lady Palmerston and Her Times, by Mabell, Countess of Airlie, 2 vols., Hodder and Stoughton, 1922, Vol. II, pp. 86–7.
Letters, Vol. I, p. 579.
RA Y55/4, 16, 41, 66, memoranda by Anson, 1843.
25. Lord David Cecil, *Lord M.* or the Later Life of Lord Melbourne, Constable, 1954, p. 518.
26. RA A4/153, 172, 174–7, letters and papers relating to Melbourne's finances, December 1847–February 1848.
27. See Martin, Vol. II, p. 156, who quotes from the Queen's Journal.
28. Greville, Vol. V, p. 129.
29. Martin, Vol. I, p. 165.
Lee, p. 148.
30. Greville, Vol. V, pp. 129, 257.
31. RA Y55/15, memorandum by Anson, 18 June 1843.
32. Lee, pp. 150–4.
33. RA A4/109, Melbourne to the Queen, 6 September 1843.
34. RA Y70/10, King Leopold to Queen Victoria, 8 September 1843.
35. Jean Duhamel, *Louis-Philippe et la Première Entente Cordiale*, Paris, [1951], p. 35, Queen Louise to Queen Marie Amélie, 9 April 1845, trans.
36. Martin, Vol. I, p. 174 *seq.*, using a memorandum by the Queen.
37. See 34 above.
38. Martin, Vol. I, p. 181.
39. Ibid., pp. 181–3, Prince Albert to Stockmar, 10 September 1843.
40. RA Y91/20, 21, Queen Victoria to King Leopold, 21, 26 September 1843.
41. RA Y55/48, memorandum by Anson, 29 November 1843.
42. RA Y55/59, memorandum by Anson, 6 December 1843.
RA Y91/32, Queen Victoria to King Leopold, 12 December 1843.
43. RA Y91/38, Queen Victoria to King Leopold, 6 February 1844.
44. Martin, Vol. I, p. 202, the Queen to Stockmar, 4 February 1844.
45. *Lady Lyttelton's Correspondence*, pp. 338–9.
46. Martin, Vol. I, p. 205, Prince Albert to Stockmar, 9 February 1844.
47. Lee, p. 158.
Lady Lyttelton's Correspondence, p. 342.
48. Francis d'Orléans, Prince de Joinville, *Note sur l'état des forces de la France*, Paris [1844]. The English translations had various titles, such as *The Condition of the French and English Navy*. The quotation in the text is taken from what is said on the title page to be the 4th edition, 1844 (BM press mark, 1397. f. 34 (II)).
49. RA Y91/50, Queen Victoria to King Leopold, 24 May 1844.
50. RA B8/110, the Queen to Aberdeen, 29 May 1844.
51. Lee, pp. 156–7.
Martin, Vol. I, pp. 213–25.
52. *Peel Papers*, Vol. III, pp. 394–5, Peel to Aberdeen, 12 August 1844.
53. Martin, Vol. I, pp. 228–9.
54. RA Y91/56, 59, Queen Victoria to King Leopold, 20 August, 15 September 1844.
55. RA Y92/1, 2, Queen Victoria to King Leopold, 8, 17 October 1844.
RA L25/1.
56. RA Y92/4, Queen Victoria to King Leopold, 29 October 1844.
57. *Peel Papers*, Vol. II, p. 584.

58. Lee, pp. 165–6.
   Greville, Vol. V, pp. 229–30.
59. Sir John Lytton Bulwer (Lord Dalling), *Life of Henry John Temple, Viscount Palmerston*, with selections from his correspondence, ed. Evelyn Ashley, 3 vols., 1874, Vol. III, p. 215.
   RA J47/3, Aberdeen to Peel, 8 September 1843.
60. Martin, Vol. I, p. 317 *seq.*
61. RA Y92/44, Queen Victoria to King Leopold, 7 July 1846.
62. Lee, p. 179.
63. Bulwer, *Life of Palmerston*, Vol. III, p. 228 *seq.*
   Martin, Vol. I, p. 348 *seq.*
   Letters, Vol. II, pp. 113–14, the Queen to Russell, 17 August 1846.
64. RA J44/43, Queen Marie Amélie to Queen Victoria, 8 September 1845, trans.
65. RA J44/44, Queen Victoria's reply, 10 September 1845, trans.
66. RA Y92/47, 48, 50, Queen Victoria to King Leopold, 7, 14, 29 September 1846.
67. *A Portion of the Journal kept by T. Raikes, Esq.*, 4 vols., 1856–7, Vol. IV, p. 441.
   Lee, pp. 180–1.
68. *Letters*, Vol. II, pp. 120–1, Palmerston to the Queen, 12 September 1846.
69. RA Y55/2, memorandum by Anson, 11 January 1843.
70. Conroy Papers, Balliol College Library.
   RA Y54/100, memorandum by Anson, 26 December 1841.
71. RA Queen Victoria's Journal, 16 November, 16 December 1839, 28 January 1840.
72. RA Z483/19–22, 24, Dunfermline to Duchess of Kent, December 1839.
73. RA Z483/28, 42, Couper to Duchess of Kent, 4 January 1840 and Duncannon to her, 9 January 1840.
   RA Queen Victoria's Journal, 7, 11, 23 January 1840.
74. RA Z483/37, Dunfermline to Duchess of Kent, 1 March 1840.
75. RA Z483/39, Dunfermline to Duchess of Kent, 21 April 1840.
   RA Z480/46, 47, Princess Augusta to the Queen, 29 January, 16 February 1838.
   RA Z294, Journal of Duchess of Kent, 15 April 1840, 21 April 1841, trans.
76. RA Z484/36, memorandum by Couper, n.d.
   RA Queen Victoria's Journal, 11, 28 January 1840.
77. RA Z484/19, Conroy to Russell, 17 October 1844.
78. RA Z483/44, Couper to Duchess of Kent, 15 May 1841.
79. RA Z483/36, Duchess of Kent to Couper, 15 February 1850.
80. RA Z484/36 includes the memorandum by Couper, 15 February 1850, his correspondence with the Duchess, 16 February, also his minute of 23 February.
81. Conroy Papers, Balliol College Library.
82. RA Z484/33, Parkinson to Conroy, 10 July 1848.
83. RA Z484/48, memorandum by Couper, 9 March 1854.
84. RA Z484/38, 39, Duchess of Kent to Couper, 2 March 1854.
85. RA Z484/41, the Queen to the Duchess of Kent, 2 March 1854.
86. RA Z484/42, the Duchess of Kent's reply, 3 March 1854.

CHAPTER EIGHT

1. Stockmar, Vol. II, pp. 116–26, memorandum by Stockmar, 'Observations on the present state of the Royal Household' [September 1841], trans.
2. Martin, Vol. I, pp. 154–5, the Prince to Stockmar, 27 December 1842, trans.

3. See 1 above.
4. Ibid.
5. Martin, Vol. I, pp. 158–9, Peel to the Prince, and the Prince's reply, 2 November 1841.
6. Vera Watson, *A Queen at Home* (written from the Lord Chamberlain's papers), W. H. Allen, 1952, p. 91.
7. Martin, Vol. I, p. 160.
8. RA M12/55, memorandum by the Queen and the Prince, 3 January 1847.
9. RA Y37/7, Princess Feodora to Queen Victoria, 10 December 1843.
10. RA M13/46, 67, 68, Lady Lyttelton to the Queen, 29 September 1843, 19–25 August 1845.
11. RA Y184 from M12/43, memorandum by Stockmar, 28 July 1846.
12. RA Y184 from M12/35, memorandum by the Queen and the Prince, 4 March 1844.
13. RA Y184 from M14/107, Dr George Combe to Sir James Clark, 22 June 1850.
14. RA M13/89, Lady Lyttelton to the Queen, 3 September 1847.
15. *Lady Lyttelton's Correspondence*, p. 329.
16. RA M13/70, Lady Lyttelton to the Queen, 26 August 1845.
17. RA M13/68, ibid., 22–25 August 1845.
18. RA M13/43, Lady Lyttelton to the Queen, 14 September 1843.
19. RA Y37/4, 15, Princess Feodora to Queen Victoria, 19 November 1843, 29 January 1844.
20. RA M13/87, Lady Lyttelton to the Queen, 18 August 1847.
21. RA M13/79, 95, ibid., 11 December 1845, 7 March 1849.
22. RA M13/85, 86, ibid., 6, 22 March 1847.
23. *Lady Lyttelton's Correspondence*, pp. 336, 339.
24. Greville, Vol. V, p. 229.
25. *Lady Lyttelton's Correspondence*, p. 354.
26. BM Add. 40, 439.
27. Ibid.
28. BM Add. 40, 441, the Prince to Peel, 9 June 1846 and Peel's reply, 10 June 1846.
29. BM Add. 40, 441, Peel to the Prince, 30 June 1846, and the Prince's reply, 1 July.
30. Blore's Report, 4 August 1846, in *Parliamentary Papers for 1846*, Vol. 26, pp. 784–5.
31. Hansard, House of Commons, 14 August 1846, Vol. 88, pp. 726–32.
32. H. Clifford Smith, *Buckingham Palace*, p. 54. (Christopher Hussey is the author of the part of this work on the building of the Palace.)
33. Ibid., pp. 33, 55.
34. Ibid., pp. 58–61.
35. Ibid., p. 56.
36. Clifford Musgrave, *The Royal Pavilion*, a study in the romantic, Bredon and Meginbotham, Brighton, 1951, p. 59.
37. RA Queen Victoria's Journal, 8 February 1845.
38. Musgrave, Chapter XIV.
39. BM Add. 40, 437, the Prince to Peel, 1 November 1843.
40. Ibid., Peel to the Prince, 20 March 1845, and the Prince's reply, 21 March 1845.
41. BM Add. 40, 440, Anson to Peel, 15 April 1845; Peel to the Queen, 17 April 1845.
42. *Letters*, Vol. II, p. 41, the Queen to Melbourne, 3 April 1845.
43. BM Add. 40, 440, the Queen to Peel, 22 June 1845.
44. John Charlton, *Osborne House*, Ministry of Works, 1970, p. 6.
45. Greville, Vol. V, pp. 229, 431.
46. Howard Colvin, *Royal Buildings*, Country Life Books, Hamlyn, 1968, p. 56.

47. Note by the Queen, quoted *Early Years*, p. 195.
48. *Lady Lyttelton's Correspondence*, pp. 364–5.
49. *Letters of the Prince*, p. 81, the Prince to his grandmother, Duchess Caroline of Gotha, 18 September 1842, trans.
50. Queen Victoria, *Leaves from the Journal of a Life in the Highlands*, 1868, p. 60 *seq*.
51. RA Y206, Sir James Clark's diary, 10 August 1849.
52. *Leaves from the Journal*, p. 101.
    Martin, Vol. II, pp. 108, 462 *seq*.
53. *Letters of the Prince*, p. 144, the Prince to his stepmother, Duchess Marie of Coburg, 11 September 1848, trans.
54. RA Y148/68, the Prince to Stockmar, 20 August 1848, trans. For details about Balmoral see Henry-Russell Hitchcock, *Early Victorian Architecture in Britain*, Architectural Press, 1954, pp. 9, 245 *seq*.; plates VIII 25–28, XV 54.
55. Sir William Henry St John Hope, *Windsor Castle, an Architectural History*, Country Life, 1913, p. 369.
56. Report by the Lord Chamberlain on Windsor Castle, 1848, quoted Watson, p. 96.

CHAPTER NINE

1. RA Y148/29, the Prince to Stockmar, 11 September 1847.
2. Hon. Evelyn Ashley, *The Life of Henry John Temple, Viscount Palmerston, 1846–1865*, with selections from his speeches and correspondence, 2 vols., 3rd edition, 1877. Vol. I, p. 191.
3. RA Y93/7, Queen Victoria to King Leopold, 7 September 1847.
4. Élie Halévy, *A History of the English People in the Nineteenth Century*, 6 vols., 1913–32, trans. E. I. Watkin and D. A. Barker, revised edition, Ernest Benn, 1949–52, Vol. III, p. 295, Vol. IV, p. 6 *seq*.
5. Clarendon Papers 1A, Russell to Clarendon, October 1847.
    Summary of Bank Return, 28 August, 30 October 1847, by courtesy of Sir George Bolton, K.C.M.G.
    Cf. Cecil Woodham-Smith, *The Great Hunger*, Hamish Hamilton 1962, chapter 15.
6. Clarendon Papers 3A, Wood to Clarendon, 15 August, 2, 11 September 1847.
7. Greville, Vol. VI, pp. 20–1.
8. RA Queen Victoria's Journal, 24 February 1848.
    RA Y15/53, Queen Louise of the Belgians to Queen Victoria, 27 February 1848.
9. *A Year of Revolution*, from a journal kept in Paris in 1848 by the Marquess of Normanby, K.G., 2 vols., 1857. Vol. I, p. 91 *seq*.
10. Ibid., Vol. I, p. 100.
11. Ibid.
12. RA Y93/23, Queen Victoria to King Leopold, 11 March 1848.
13. RA Queen Victoria's Journal, 26–28 February 1848.
14. Palmerston Papers, Broadlands. Report by Featherstonehaugh to Palmerston, 3 March 1848.
15. RA Queen Victoria's Journal, 4 March 1848.
    RA Y48/75, King Louis Philippe to Queen Victoria, 3 March 1848.
    RA J67/82, Russell to the Queen, 3 March 1848.
16. RA Y93/22, 24, Queen Victoria to King Leopold, 7, 14 March 1848.
17. RA Y93/25, 28, Queen Victoria to King Leopold, 16 March, 18 April 1848.

18. RA J70/100, 101, the Queen to Russell, 16 August 1848, and Russell's reply, 17 August.
19. Normanby, Vol. II, pp. 264–5.
   RA J69/171, Russell to the Queen, 26 November 1848.
20. Charles Gavan Duffy, *Four Years of Irish History*, 1883, p. 537.
   Martin, Vol. II, p. 12.
21. Thomas Frost, *Forty Years' Recollections*, 1880, pp. 127–8.
22. *First Report of the Commissioners for Inquiry into the State of Large Towns and Populous Districts. Parliamentary Papers*, 1844, Vol. XVII, Dr Southwood Smith's evidence.
   Friedrich Engels, *The Condition of the Working Class in England in 1844*, published 1845, new trans., Blackwell, Oxford, 1958.
23. RA Y148/61, the Prince to Stockmar, 5 June 1848.
24. Greville, Vol. VI, p. 51.
25. A. R. Schoyen, *The Chartist Challenge*, a portrait of George Julian Harney, Heinemann, 1958, p. 163.
26. RA C56/4, 5, Wood to Anson, 7 April 1848; Sir George Grey to Gen. Bowles, Master of the Household, 7 April 1848.
   RA Queen Victoria's Journal, 8 April 1848.
27. RA C56/11, Phipps to the Prince, 9 April 1848.
28. RA C56/18, Admiral Sir C. Ogle to Lieut-Col Seymour, Equerry in Waiting, 10 April 1848.
29. Donald Read and Eric Glasgow, *Feargus O'Connor: Irishman and Chartist*, Edward Arnold, 1961, p. 192.
30. RA C56/19, Russell on Mayne's behalf to the Queen, 10 April 1848.
31. See 28 above.
32. RA Y93/27, Queen Victoria to King Leopold, 11 April 1848.
33. RA Y148/61, the Prince to Stockmar, 5, 7 June 1848.
34. D. R. Gwynn, *Young Ireland and 1848*, Cork University Press, 1949.
   Ashley, *Life of Palmerston*, Vol. I, p. 95.
   The Times, 26 April 1848.
   Woodham-Smith, *The Great Hunger*, chapter 16.
35. *The Opening of an Era, 1848*, ed. F. Fejtö, English trans., Allan Wingate, 1948: Germany, by Dr Vermeil, p. 248 *seq.*
   H. A. L. Fisher, *A History of Europe*, Vol. III, *The Liberal Experiment*, Eyre and Spottiswoode, 1935, p. 926.
36. Martin, Vol. II, p. 57, the Prince to Stockmar, 30 March 1848.
   RA C56/29, Russell to the Queen, 11 April 1848.
37. *Opening of an Era*. Scandinavia, by L. Tissot, p. 171.
38. Martin, Vol. II, p. 314, the Prince to Stockmar, 25 August 1850.
39. Martin, Vol. II, p. 53.
40. Ibid., p. 50.
41. See 22 above.
42. RA Y94/7, Queen Victoria to King Leopold, 30 December 1848.
43. Woodham-Smith, *The Great Hunger*, chapter 18.
44. RA Y95/1, 2, Queen Victoria to King Leopold, 8, 29 January 1850.
45. RA Y95/35, Queen Victoria to King Leopold, 25 October 1850.
46. *Letters*, Vol. II, p. 318, King Leopold to Queen Victoria, 7 October 1850.
   RA Y95/38, Queen Victoria to King Leopold, 5 November 1850.
   RA Queen Victoria's Journal, 13 October 1850.
47. RA Queen Victoria's Journal, 4 October, 16 December 1839.

48. See Chapter Five.
49. Stockmar, Vol. II, p. 458.
50. Palmerston Papers, Broadlands. The Queen to Palmerston, 4 May 1841.
51. PRO Foreign Office Papers, F.O. 84/389.
52. Martin, Vol. II, p. 64, Russell to the Prince, 19 June 1849.
53. *Cambridge History of British Foreign Policy*, ed. Sir A. W. Ward and G. P. Gooch, Cambridge University Press, 1922–3, Vol. II, p. 298. Cf. p. 327.
54. Bulwer, *Life of Palmerston*, Vol. I, pp. 123, 130, 133.
55. Stockmar, Vol. II, p. 458.
56. RA Y55/38, Le Marchant to Anson, 13 October 1843.
57. RA Y93/27, Queen Victoria to King Leopold, 11 April 1848.
58. RA Y94/47, Queen Victoria to King Leopold, 16 October 1849.
    RA Queen Victoria's Journal, 16 October 1849.
59. Ibid., 15 October, 21 December 1849.
60. Martin, Vol. II, p. 308, memorandum by the Prince, 17 August 1850.
61. *Letters*, Vol. II, p. 288, the Prince to Russell, 18 May 1850.
62. RA C9/46, the Queen to Russell, 12 August 1850.
63. Ashley, *Life of Palmerston*, Vol. I, p. 329.
64. Ibid., pp. 211–27.
65. Ibid., p. 223.
66. Ibid., p. 226, Palmerston to William Temple, 8 July 1850.
67. Greville, Vol. VI, p. 243.
    RA Y95/20, Queen Victoria to King Leopold, 9 July 1850.
    Martin, Vol. II, p. 291, the Prince to the Duchess Dowager of Coburg, 9 July 1850, trans.
68. RA C9/42, the Queen to Russell, 28 July 1850.
69. Ashley, *Life of Palmerston*, Vol. I, p. 240, Palmerston to Sir George Grey, the Home Secretary, 1 October 1850.
70. Ibid., p. 239.
71. RA C9/53, the Queen to Russell, 11 October 1850.
72. RA A79/58, Palmerston to the Queen, 8 October 1850.
73. *Letters*, Vol. II, pp. 322, 324–5, the Queen to Palmerston, 12 October 1850, and to Russell, 19 October 1850.
74. RA A79/32, memorandum by the Prince for Russell, 8 July 1850.
75. RA A79/34, memorandum by the Prince for Russell, 11 July 1850.
    RA Y54/99, memorandum by Anson, 13 December 1841.
76. Spencer Walpole, *The Life of Lord John Russell*, 2 vols., 1889, Vol. II, p. 133.
77. *Cambridge History of British Foreign Policy*, Vol. II, p. 333.
    Letters, Vol. II, pp. 397–9, the Queen to Russell, 20 November 1851 and Russell's reply, 21 November.
78. H. A. L. Fisher, Vol. III, p. 911.
79. RA Y77/32, King Leopold to Queen Victoria, 5 December 1851.
80. Ashley, *Life of Palmerston*, Vol. I, p. 296, Normanby to Palmerston, 6 December 1851.
81. Greville, Vol. VI, p. 316.
82. RA C10/32, the Queen to Russell, 13 December 1851.
83. Ashley, *Life of Palmerston*, Vol. I, pp. 300–6, Palmerston to Russell, 16 December 1851.
84. Ibid., p. 307, Russell to Palmerston, 19 December 1851.
85. RA A79/131, Russell to the Queen, 19 December 1851.
86. Greville, Vol. VI, p. 315.

CHAPTER TEN

1. PRO Granville Papers, 30/29.
2. C. R. Fay, *Palace of Industry, 1851*, Cambridge University Press, 1951, p. 4.
3. *The Great Exhibition of 1851*, ed. C. H. Gibbs-Smith, HMSO, 1951, p. 6.
4. Martin, Vol. II, pp. 285-6, the Prince to Stockmar, 28 June 1850.
5. Hansard, Vol. 112, p. 903.
6. Martin, Vol. II, p. 290, the Prince to Stockmar, 2 July 1850.
7. Ibid., p. 296, the Queen to Stockmar, 23 July 1850.
8. Hansard, 4 July 1850, Vol. 112, pp. 933-4.
9. The Prince's diary, quoted Martin, Vol. II, p. 297.
10. Martin, Vol. II, p. 299, the Prince to Stockmar, 20 July 1850.
11. *The Times*, 27 June 1850, quoted Gibbs-Smith, p. 8.
12. Gibbs-Smith, p. 9.
13. 'Joseph Paxton and the Crystal Palace', *Industrial Archaeology*, Vol. 6, No. 2, p. 129.
14. Gibbs-Smith, p. 10.
15. G. M. Young, *Early Victorian England 1830-1865*, 2 vols., Oxford University Press, 1934. Vol. I, p. 212 *seq.*
16. Ibid., p. 214.
17. Martin, Vol. II, p. 359, the Prince to the Dowager Duchess of Coburg, 15 April 1851.
18. Sir Thomas Wemyss Reid, *Memoirs and Correspondence of Lyon (Lord) Playfair*, 1899, p. 119.
19. *The Times* quoted Gibbs-Smith, p. 11.
20. G. M. Young, Vol. I, p. 217.
21. RA Queen Victoria's Journal, 30 April 1851.
22. Lord Edmond Fitzmaurice, *Life of the Second Earl Granville 1815-1891*, 2 vols., 1905, Vol. I, p. 42.
23. RA Queen Victoria's Journal, 1 May 1851.
24. Wemyss Reid, p. 120.
25. G. M. Young, Vol. I, p. 219.
26. Charles Tomlinson, quoted G. M. Young, Vol. I, p. 220.
27. RA Queen Victoria's Journal, 17 June 1851.
28. Ibid., 18 July 1851.
29. RA F25/1, memorandum by the Prince, 10 August 1851.
30. RA F25/9, Cole to Phipps, 30 September 1851.
31. RA F25/3, 102-3, 124, 130, correspondence of Disraeli, Gladstone and others with the Prince, 1851-2.
32. RA F25/97, Col Grey to the Prince, 10 May 1852.
33. Fay, p. 118.
34. Queen Victoria's Journal, 10 October 1851, quoted Martin, Vol. II, p. 399.
35. Lord Kingsdown's unpublished recollections, quoted Martin, Vol. I, p. 119.
36. Greville, Vol. IV, p. 397; Vol. VI, p. 210.
37. RA Queen Victoria's Journal, 29 October 1850.
38. RA Y95/49, Queen Victoria to King Leopold, 24 December 1850.
   RA M12/45, the Queen to Stockmar, 26 November 1849.
39. Walpole, *Life of Russell*, Vol. II, pp. 120-1.
40. Greville, Vol. VI, pp. 257-8.
41. Martin, Vol. II, pp. 339-40, the Queen to the Duchess of Gloucester, [11] December 1850.

42. RA Queen Victoria's Journal, 4 February 1851.
   Lee, p. 218.
43. Greville, Vol. VI, p. 258.
44. Hansard, Vol. 114, p. 187 *seq.*
45. RA C19/1, 2, the Prince to Russell, 11, 12 January 1851.
46. Hansard, Vol. 118, pp. 239–42.
47. Lee, pp. 219–20.
   Martin, Vol. II, p. 350 *seq.*
48. RA Queen Victoria's Journal has several important passages on the death and funeral of Wellington, especially 16 September, 9, 18 November 1852.
49. Greville, Vol. VI, pp. 360–9, *passim.*
50. *The Times*, 18–19 November 1852.
51. RA Queen Victoria's Journal, 22 April 1853.
52. RA Z140/9–18, the Prince to the Queen, 9 May 1853 (a few lines are in German and trans.).
53. Ibid. /22–4, 9 February 1855.
54. Ibid. /27–8, 16 November 1855, trans.
55. Ibid. /29–31, 1 October 1856.
56. Ibid. /32–7, 5 November 1856, trans.
57. Ibid. /40–1, n.d.
58. Ibid. /43–5, n.d.
59. Ibid. /46–51, 12 March 1857.
60. Ibid. /58–9, 12 October 1856.
61. Ibid. /60–3 (two letters), n.d.
62. RA Y203/78 and Z491, the Queen's reminiscences, January 1862.
63. *Lady Lyttelton's Correspondence*, pp. 340–1.
   RA M13/68, Lady Lyttelton to the Queen, 23 August 1845.
64. RA M13/89, Lady Lyttelton to the Queen, 3 September 1847.
65. RA M14/58, memorandum by [the Prince], 15 December 1849.
66. RA M13/90, Lady Lyttelton to the Queen, 8 September 1847.
67. RA M14/22, 37, Dr Archdall to the Bishop of Chester, 14 July [1848], and a note by the Prince, 12 April 1849.
   RA M15/19, 47, 107, Birch to Stockmar, 24 November 1850, and memoranda by Birch, n.d. [February 1851] and 25 February 1852.
   Sir Philip Magnus, *King Edward the Seventh*, John Murray, 1964, p. 6 *seq.*
68. RA M15/36, Birch to the Prince, 24 December 1850.
69. RA M15/41, Birch to Stockmar, 23 January 1851.
70. RA M14/43, Birch to Stockmar, 1 July 1849.
71. See 67 above.
   RA M14/45, 58, the Queen to Stockmar, 26 November 1849; memorandum by the Queen, 15 December 1849.
72. RA M15/16, Birch to Stockmar, 20 November 1850.
73. RA M15/17, memorandum from the Prince to Stockmar, [November 1850].
74. Sir Sidney Lee, *King Edward VII, a biography*, 2 vols., Macmillan, 1925–7, Vol. I, pp. 29, 30.
75. Magnus, p. 8 *seq.*
76. Ibid.
77. RA M13/50, Lady Lyttelton to the Queen, 9 September 1844.

CHAPTER ELEVEN

1. James Howard Harris, Earl of Malmesbury, *Memoirs of an Ex-Minister*, 2nd edition, 2 vols., 1884, Vol. I, p. 402.
2. Ibid., p. 332.
   F. A. Simpson, *Louis Napoleon and the Recovery of France*, 3rd edition, Longmans Green, 1951, p. 223.
   Cambridge History of British Foreign Policy, Vol. II, p. 338.
3. Malmesbury, Vol. I, p. 317.
4. RA Y93/52, Y94/31, Queen Victoria to King Leopold, 13 December 1848, 19 June 1849.
5. RA Y97/3, Queen Victoria to King Leopold, 20 January 1852.
   Letters, Vol. III, p. 494, Queen Victoria to Napoleon III, 4 December 1852.
   Malmesbury, Vol. I, p. 372.
   Cambridge History of British Foreign Policy, Vol. II, p. 342.
6. Anthony Trollope, *Tales of All Countries*, 2nd series, 1863, p. 240.
   A. W. Kinglake, *The Invasion of the Crimea*, Edinburgh and London, 6th edition, 8 vols., 1877–92, Vol. I, p. 40 *seq.*
7. Kinglake, Vol. I, p. 53.
8. Sir Herbert Maxwell, *Life and Letters of George William Frederick Villiers, Earl of Clarendon*, 2 vols., 1913.
9. Kinglake, Vol. I, p. 147.
   Cambridge History of British Foreign Policy, Vol. II, p. 347 *seq.*
10. RA Queen Victoria's Journal, 16 October 1853.
11. Ibid., 12, 15 December 1853.
12. *Letters of the Prince*, pp. 203–4, the Prince to Stockmar, 24 January 1854, trans.
13. Hansard, 31 January 1854, Vol. 130.
14. Stockmar, Vol. II, p. 481.
15. Private information.
16. RA Y55/38, Le Marchant to Anson, 13 October 1843.
    RA Z171/13, the Queen to Anson, 12 February 1845.
17. Malmesbury, Vol. I, p. 393.
18. Simpson, pp. 208, 302.
19. RA Add. A19/1, 2, Malmesbury to the Queen, 13 December 1852; the Queen to Derby and to Melbourne, 14 December 1852.
20. Greville, Vol. VI, p. 402.
21. RA Add. A19/18, 26, Princess Feodora to Queen Victoria, 24, 30 December 1852.
22. RA Add. A19/35, Prince Ernest Hohenlohe to Walewski, n.d. [January 1853], trans.
23. RA Add. A19/37, Queen Victoria to Princess Feodora, 6 January 1853.
24. Simpson, p. 204 *seq.*
25. RA Add. A19/45, 50, Cowley to Russell, 17, 24 January 1853.
26. RA Add. A19/44, Russell to the Queen, 20 January 1853.
27. PRO Foreign Office papers, Cowley to Russell, 7 February 1853.
28. RA Queen Victoria's Journal, 20 February 1854.
29. RA J76/84, memorandum by the Prince on his visit to Napoleon III at Boulogne, dictated to Grey 12 September 1854.
30. RA Queen Victoria's Journal, 2–6 October 1854.
31. Report by the McNeill and Tulloch Commission into the supplies for the British army, p. xxxv.

32. E. Sheppard, *Duke of Cambridge*, Vol. I, chapter VI, 'The Crimean War'.
    RA Queen Victoria's Journal, 30 December 1854.
    RA G20/128.
33. RA G18/119.
    RA Add. A8/171–80.
    RA Queen Victoria's Journal, 31 January 1855.
34. RA Queen Victoria's Journal, 20, 22 February 1855.
35. Lee, p. 249 *seq.*
36. RA Queen Victoria's Journal, 31 January, 3, 5 February 1855.
37. Ashley, *Life of Palmerston*, Vol. II, pp. 76–7, Palmerston to Sir William Temple, 15 February 1855.
38. Charles Roux, quoted Simpson, p. 286.
39. Ibid., pp. 262–3.
40. Martin, Vol. III, p. 147.
    Ashley, *Life of Palmerston*, Vol. II, p. 98.
41. Martin, Vol. III, p. 228 *seq.*
42. Ibid., pp. 231–4, the Prince's account of the report by Clarendon, 6 March 1855.
43. RA Z263 contains the Queen's original notes, RA J76/91 (Y202/33) her memoranda, April–May 1855, on the visit of Napoleon III.
44. RA Queen Victoria's Journal, 16 April 1855 *seq.*; also her Journal as quoted by Martin, Vol. III, p. 239 *seq.*
    Simpson, p. 289 *seq.*
45. Malmesbury, Vol. I, pp. 392–3.
46. Greville, Vol. VII, p. 129.
47. See 43 and 44 above.
48. Simpson, p. 298.
49. General Sir E. B. Hamley, *The War in the Crimea*, 1891, p. 194.
50. Simpson, pp. 316–17.
51. RA Queen Victoria's Journal, 18 August 1855 *seq.*
    Martin, Vol. III, pp. 321–38 *passim.*
52. RA J76/92 (Y202/34), the Queen to Stockmar, 1 September 1855.
53. Greville, Vol. VII, p. 154.
54. Ibid., pp. 157–8.
55. Simpson, p. 318 *seq.*
56. *The Times*, 27 September 1855.
57. Simpson, p. 322.
58. Lieut-General Sir C. A. Windham, *Crimean Diary and Letters*, ed. Sir W. H. Russell, 1897, p. 205 *seq.*
59. RA Queen Victoria's Journal, 10 September 1855.
60. Count E. C. Corti, *The English Empress*, trans. E. M. Hodgson, Cassell, 1957, p. 16.
61. RA Add. A7/9, memorandum by the Queen, 29 September 1855.
62. *Cambridge History of British Foreign Policy*, Vol. II, p. 278.
63. Martin, Vol. III, pp. 11–12, Bloomfield to Clarendon, 28 February 1854.
64. Ibid., pp. 386–8, Prince Albert to Prince Fritz, 6 November 1855.
65. Ibid., p. 371, the Prince to Stockmar, 20 September 1855. *Leaves from the Journal*, p. 154.
    RA G38/71, the Prince to Clarendon, 28 September 1855.
66. Ashley, *Life of Palmerston*, Vol. II, pp. 100–1, Palmerston to Sir William Temple, 25 August 1855.
67. Simpson, p. 336 *seq.*
    Letters, Vol. III, p. 212, the Duke of Cambridge to the Queen, 20 January 1856.

68. Martin, Vol. III, p. 385, the Prince to Stockmar, 29 October 1855.
69. Ibid., p. 393, Palmerston to Walewski, 21 November 1855.
70. Ibid., p. 393, Napoleon III to Queen Victoria, 22 November 1855. See also ibid., p. 400.
71. Ibid., p. 397 *seq.*, Queen Victoria to Napoleon III, 26 November 1855.
72. PRO Foreign Office Papers, France, Cowley to Clarendon, 16 September 1855, quoted Simpson, p. 344.
73. Martin, Vol. III, p. 407, the Queen to Clarendon, 13 December 1855.
74. Ibid., p. 422 *seq.*
75. Simpson, p. 346.
76. Martin, Vol. III, p. 424, the Prince to Clarendon, 17 January 1856.
77. Ibid., p. 426, Palmerston to the Queen, 17 January 1856.
78. Ibid., p. 446 *seq.*, Prince Albert to King Leopold, 16 February 1856.
79. Ibid., p. 450.
80. Ibid., pp. 450–1, Clarendon to the Queen, 25 March 1856, partly a trans.
81. Fitzmaurice, *Life of Lord Granville*, Vol. I, p. 173.

CHAPTER TWELVE

1. RA Z171/5, Anson to the Queen, 12 March 1844.
2. Martin, Vol. II, p. 334, the Prince to Phipps, [November 1850].
3. Queen Victoria's Journal, 10 October 1851, quoted Martin, Vol. II, p. 399.
4. RA Y149/85–7, the Prince to Stockmar, 7, 11, 24 January 1854.
5. The Prince's diary, 22–25 September 1855, quoted Martin, Vol. III, p. 371.
   RA Y189/26, the Prince to Stockmar, 28 September 1855.
6. RA Y150/29, the Prince to Stockmar, 25 February 1856.
7. Martin, Vol. III, p. 458.
   RA Y153/151, Stockmar to the Prince, 21 February 1856.
8. Martin, Vol. III, p. 469, the Prince to Stockmar, 21 March 1856.
9. RA Y40/3, Princess Feodora to Queen Victoria, 26 November 1852.
10. Palmerston Papers, Broadlands Archives, the Queen to Palmerston, 24 March 1856.
11. Ibid., the Queen to Palmerston, 25 March 1856.
12. Lee, *Queen Victoria*, pp. 263, 268.
13. *Letters*, Vol. III, p. 237.
14. Maxwell, *Clarendon*, Vol. II, pp. 121–2.
15. Lee, *Queen Victoria*, p. 266.
16. Sheppard, *Duke of Cambridge*, Vol. I, p. 148, the Queen to the Duke of Cambridge, autumn 1856.
    The Prince's diary, 21 September 1856, quoted Martin, Vol. III, p. 503.
    Letters, Vol. III, p. 251n.
17. Woodham-Smith, *Florence Nightingale* pp. 263–4.
18. RA Queen Victoria's Journal, 18 February 1845.
19. Palmerston Papers, Broadlands Archives, the Queen to Palmerston, 5 June 1856, enclosing the memorandum printed in *Letters*, Vol. III, pp. 244–7.
20. *Letters*, Vol. III, pp. 249–51, Derby to the Queen, 28 June 1856.
21. Palmerston Papers, Broadlands Archives, the Queen to Palmerston, 15 March 1857, having received the Minute including a Draft Bill for the Prince Consort (the document which accompanies it in the file).
22. Malmesbury, Vol. II, p. 47.

23. RA Queen Victoria's Journal, 29 April 1857.
24. Martin, Vol. IV, pp. 42–4, the Prince to Stockmar, 28 May 1857.
25. *Letters*, Vol. III, p. 321, the Queen to Clarendon, 25 October 1857.
26. Martin, Vol. IV, pp. 64–5.
    RA Queen Victoria's Journal, 26 June 1857.
27. *Letters*, Vol. III, p. 297, note 2.
28. *Cambridge History of the British Empire*, Vol. V, p. 170 *seq.*
    Sir Patrick Cadell, *History of the Bombay Army*, p. 200.
29. Ashley, *Life of Palmerston*, Vol. II, p. 137.
30. RA Queen Victoria's Journal, 1 July 1857.
31. Private information.
32. *Letters*, Vol. III, p. 319, Canning to the Queen, 25 September 1857.
33. *Letters*, Vol. III, p. 313, Queen Victoria to King Leopold, 2 September 1857.
34. *Cambridge History of the British Empire*, Vol. V, p. 212.
35. Martin, Vol. IV, p. 284 *seq.*
36. RA Queen Victoria's Journal, 3 February 1845.
37. RA C58/24, memorandum by Lord Lyndhurst, October 1841.
38. RA C58/1, summary to events relating to the King of Hanover's claim.
39. Greville, Vol. VII, pp. 325–7.
40. RA Queen Victoria's Journal, 25 January–2 February 1858.
41. Ibid., 22 July 1856.
42. RA Z1/explanatory note.
43. RA Z294, Journal of the Duchess of Kent, 3 February 1858, trans.
44. RA Queen Victoria's Journal, 2 February 1858.
    Kronberg Archives, the Prince Consort to the Princess Royal, 3 February 1858, trans.
    RA Z1/3, the Princess Royal to her father, 3 February 1858.
45. RA Queen Victoria's Journal, 9, 13 February 1858.
46. Kronberg Archives, the Prince Consort to the Princess Royal, 6 February 1858.
47. Ibid., the Prince Consort to Prince Fritz, 11 February 1858.
48. Ibid., the Prince Consort to the Princess Royal, 17 February, 10 March 1858.
49. RA Queen Victoria's Journal, 4 May 1857.
50. *Cambridge History of British Foreign Policy*, Vol. II, p. 400.
    Martin, Vol. IV, p. 155.
51. RA Queen Victoria's Journal, 15 January 1858.
52. Martin, Vol. IV, p. 187.
53. Fitzmaurice, *Life of Granville*, Vol. I, p. 288.
54. RA Y103/3, Queen Victoria to King Leopold, 9 February 1858.
55. Martin, Vol. IV, pp. 191–3, the Prince Consort to Stockmar, 22 February 1858.
56. Lee, *Queen Victoria*, p. 282.
    Cambridge History of British Foreign Policy, Vol. II, p. 402.
57. Martin, Vol. IV, p. 213.
58. The Prince Consort's diary, quoted Martin, Vol. IV, p. 275.
59. *Cambridge History of British Foreign Policy*, Vol. II, p. 431.
60. Queen Victoria's Journal, 6 August 1858, quoted Martin, Vol. IV, p. 275.
61. RA Queen Victoria's Journal, 12 August 1858.
62. Clark's diary, [August 1858], quoted Martin, Vol. IV, p. 289n.
63. RA I31/30, the Prince Consort to the Prince of Prussia, 26 November 1858, trans., quoted Frank Eyck, *The Prince Consort, a political biography*, Chatto and Windus, 1959, p. 243.
64. Eyck, p. 244.

65. The Queen to the Princess Royal, 21 April 1858, quoted Roger Fulford, *Dearest Child*, Letters between Queen Victoria and the Princess Royal 1858–61, Evans Brothers, 1964, p. 94.
66. The Queen to the Princess Royal, 26 May 1858, quoted ibid., p. 108.
67. RA Z7/121, the Princess Royal to the Queen, 2 May 1859.
68. The Queen to the Princess Royal, 29 May, 15 June 1858, quoted Fulford, pp. 109, 115.
69. Greville, Vol. VII, p. 386.
70. RA Queen Victoria's Journal, 27, 29 January 1859.
71. The Queen to the Princess Royal, 29 January 1859, quoted Fulford, p. 159.
72. RA Add. U34/3, statement by Professor Dr August Martin, 28 April 1931.
73. RA Queen Victoria's Journal, 19 February 1859.
74. RA Z7/87, 96, the Princess Royal to the Queen, 28 February, 12 March 1859.
75. RA Queen Victoria's Journal, 21 May 1859.
76. Malmesbury, Vol. II, p. 175 *seq.*
    Kronberg Archives, the Prince Consort to the Princess Royal, 1 March 1859.
77. Martin, Vol. IV, pp. 449–50, the Prince Consort to Stockmar, 28 May 1859.
78. RA Queen Victoria's Journal, 24 July 1860.
79. Lee, *Queen Victoria*, p. 307.
80. RA Queen Victoria's Journal, 25–27 September 1860.
81. Queen Victoria's Journal, 1–2 October 1860, quoted Martin, Vol. V, pp. 202–4.
82. *Memoirs* of Ernest II, Duke of Saxe-Coburg and Gotha, 1888, Vol. IV, p. 55, trans.
83. Martin, Vol. IV, p. 500 *seq.*, Vol. V, pp. 255, 259.
    Kronberg Archives, the Prince Consort to the Princess Royal, 11 December 1860.

CHAPTER THIRTEEN

1. RA Z443/56, Col Lindsay to Sir Charles Phipps, 27 July 1858.
2. RA Z443, summary attached by the Prince Consort to the volume for July 1858 to June 1860.
3. RA Queen Victoria's Journal, 7 January 1857.
4. Viscount Esher, *The Influence of King Edward, and Essays on Other Subjects*, 1915, pp. 16–22.
5. Kronberg Archives, the Queen to the Princess Royal, 17 November 1858.
6. RA Z141/36, memorandum by the Queen and the Prince Consort, 9 November 1858.
   Esher, pp. 13–15.
   Lee, *Edward VII*, Vol. I, pp. 52–3.
7. Greville, Vol. VII, p. 383.
8. The Queen to the Princess Royal, 31 March 1858, quoted Corti, p. 45.
9. The Prince Consort to the Princess Royal, 17 November 1858, quoted Corti, p. 50.
10. *Punch*, 24 September 1859.
11. Kronberg Archives, the Queen to the Princess Royal, 22 December 1858.
12. RA Z172/47, Bruce to Phipps, 14 October 1860.
13. Magnus, p. 44.
14. The Princess Royal to the Queen, 17 December 1860, quoted Corti, p. 64.
15. RA Z141/81, 82, the Prince Consort to the Prince of Wales, 15 April, 10 June 1861.
    The Prince Consort to the Crown Princess of Prussia (the Princess Royal became Crown Princess of Prussia in January 1861), 12, 29 April, 8 May 1861, quoted Corti, p. 67.

16. The Prince Consort to Ernest Duke of Coburg, 22 July 1861, quoted Corti, p. 68.
17. Magnus, p. 46.
18. RA Z462/86, 87, the Crown Prince and Princess of Prussia to the Queen and the Prince Consort, 25, 26 September 1861.
19. RA Queen Victoria's Journal, 30 September 1861.
20. The Queen to the Crown Princess, 1 October 1861, quoted Corti, p. 72.
21. The Prince Consort to the Princess Royal (as she then was), 6 December 1860, quoted Martin, Vol. V, pp. 254-5.
22. The Prince Consort's diary, 17 February 1861, quoted Martin, Vol. V, p. 295.
23. The Prince Consort to Stockmar, 21 February 1861, quoted Martin, Vol. V, p. 296.
24. RA Queen Victoria's Journal, 29 January 1861.
25. Ibid., 19, 20 February 1861.
26. Ibid., 28 February 1861.
    Martin, Vol. V, p. 307, the Prince Consort to the Duchess of Kent, 1 March, and to Stockmar, 4 March 1861.
27. RA Queen Victoria's Journal, 1-9, 12 March 1861.
    Martin, Vol. V, p. 315.
28. Queen Victoria's Journal, 15 March 1851 *seq.*, quoted Martin, Vol. V, p. 315 *seq.*
29. Ibid., p. 321.
30. Magnus, p. 44.
31. RA Queen Victoria's Journal, 9 April 1861.
    RA Y106/9, 10, Queen Victoria to King Leopold, 20, 26 March 1861.
32. RA Y106/14, Queen Victoria to King Leopold, 9 April 1861.
33. RA Queen Victoria's Journal, 24 March 1861.
34. Martin, Vol. V, p. 336.
35. Ibid., pp. 335-6, the Prince Consort to Stockmar, 5 April 1861.
36. RA Queen Victoria's Journal, 24-27 May 1861.
37. RA Z104/26, Queen Victoria to King Leopold, 2 August 1859.
38. Private information.
39. Martin, Vol. V, p. 354.
40. The Prince Consort's diary, 16 June 1861, quoted Martin, Vol. V, p. 364; cf. p. 365.
41. Lee, *Edward VII*, Vol. I, p. 117.
42. RA Z446/13-15, memorandum of Bruce, 10 March 1861 and memoranda of the Prince Consort, 13 March 1861.
43. Magnus, p. 47.
44. RA Queen Victoria's Journal, 24 August 1861.
45. RA Y107/12, Queen Victoria to King Leopold, 26 August 1861.
46. Lee, *Edward VII*, Vol. I, p. 119.
47. Private information.
48. RA Z141/94, the Prince Consort to the Prince of Wales, 16 November 1861.
49. See 53 below.
50. RA Add. C10/44, Francis Seymour to his father Lord Hertford, 19 November 1861.
51. See note 48 above.
52. RA Z141/95, the Prince Consort to the Prince of Wales, 20 November 1861.
53. RA Z142 is a paper entitled by the Queen 'Account of my beloved Albert's last fatal illness from November 9 to December 14, 1861, written from my journal.' Up to 11 December the manuscript appears to be as she wrote it day by day; from the middle of that day (the 11th) she breaks off, and makes a note on 24th December to say that she had then written the part from mid-day on the 11th until Friday

evening, 13th December. She left the MS. there until 27 March 1862 when she recorded: 'Will strive to finish the dreadful account of what passed' and proceeded to finish her narrative of the events of 13th December but did not continue with Saturday 14th December until February 1872, 'with the help of notes scrawled down at the time.'

54. Kronberg Archives, the Queen to the Crown Princess, 27 December 1861.
   The Prince Consort's diary 24 November 1861, quoted Martin, Vol. V, p. 417.
55. *Letters*, Vol. III, pp. 593–5, Palmerston to the Queen, 13 November 1861.
   RA A29/126, Palmerston to the Queen, 10 November 1861.
   RA Q 9/7, the Law Officers to Russell, 12 November 1861.
56. RA Y161/1, the Prince Consort's diary, 28 November 1861 (extracts made for Martin), trans.
   RA Q 9/10, Russell to the Queen, 28 November 1861.
57. RA Q 9/15, Russell to the Queen, [29] November 1861, enclosing RA Q 9/16, 18, 20, 22, drafts of Russell to Lyons, 30 November 1861, a memorandum on the illegality of the action, and a draft or copy of Russell to the Lords of the Admiralty dated the same day.
58. *Letters*, Vol. III, pp. 595–6, Palmerston to the Queen, 29 November 1861. Cf. Martin, Vol. V, p. 418 *seq.*
59. *Letters*, Vol. III, pp. 597–8, the Queen to Russell, 1 December 1861.
60. RA Q 9/26, Granville to the Prince Consort, 2 December 1861.
   RA Q 9/47, 48, telegram and despatch from Lyons, 27 December 1861, 9 January 1862.
61. Palmerston Papers, Broadlands Archives, Phipps to Palmerston, 3 December 1861.
62. Ibid., Phipps to Palmerston, 6 December 1861.
63. Ibid., 7 December 1861.
64. Ibid., 8 December 1861.
65. Ibid., 9 December 1861.
66. RA Add. U55, Lady Augusta Bruce to her sister Lady Frances Baillie, 19 December 1861.
67. Palmerston Papers, Broadlands Archives, Phipps to Palmerston, 13 December 1861 (telegram and letter).
68. Ibid., 14 December 1861 (a.m.).
69. Ibid., 14 December 1861.
70. RA Add. A25/78–82, diary of Sir Howard Elphinstone, 14 December 1861.
71. Palmerston Papers, Broadlands Archives, Phipps to Palmerston, n.d. [14 December 1861].
72. Ibid., 15 December 1861.
73. RA Add. A7/142, Jenner to Parkes, 19 December 1861.

INDEX

In this index V = Queen Victoria and A = Prince Albert

Delhi, 382, 384, 385
Derby, Edward Stanley, 14th Earl of, 339, 344, 347, 354, 377, 392, 393
Dibdin, Thomas John, 1*n*
Disraeli, Benjamin, 157, 159, 319, 437
Donnelly, Admiral Sir Ross, 10, 41
Dover, George James Ellis, Lord, 86
Dublin, 295–6
Duffy, Charles Gavan, 286
Duleep Singh, Maharajah, 385
Dunant, Henri, 399
Duncannon, John Ponsonby, 1st Baron, 208, 209, 256
Dundas, Lord, 25
Dundas, Sir David, 42, 43
Dunfermline, James Abercromby, Lord, 177, 191, 255–6
Durham, John Lambton, Lord, 86, 255; Report on Canada, 153

East India Company, 379–80, 385
Ecclesiastical Titles Bill (1851), 324–5
Edward VII (as Prince of Wales), 228, 269, 292, 297, 315, 320, 359, 361, 390, 412, 427; birth, 224–5, 226; parents' early anxiety over, 226; education, 265–7, 334–7, 403–5; backwardness, 266–7, 334, 403; phrenologist's reports on, 267; inferiority complex, 267; fits of rage, 334, 336, 403; devotion to Princess Royal, 334, 403; 'dislike of chaff', 334, 335; 'positive and opinionated', 361; disappointment to parents, 403–5; in Army, 405, 414–15; successful visit to Berlin, 405; at Oxford and Cambridge, 405–6, 407, 414; North American tour, 406, 408, 414; question of marriage, 407–9; Princess Alexandra chosen for, 407–9; Curragh camp escapade, 415, 416–17; blamed for A's fatal illness, 417; A visits at Cambridge, 418; at A's deathbed, 428, 429; treatment of V's correspondence, 436, 437
Elizabeth, Princess (daughter of Duke of Clarence), 50, 51, 57
Elizabeth of Wied, Princess (later Queen of Rumania), 407
Ellis, John, 311
Elphinstone, Sir Howard, 429
Emerald (tender), 89, 90, 91

Engels, Friedrich, 294
Ernest Augustus of Hanover—*see* Cumberland, Duke of
Ernest Christian Charles, Prince of Hohenlohe-Langenburg, 60, 137, 347, 348; marriage to Feodora, 61–2; visits England, 93
Ernest of Leiningen, Prince, 425, 429
Ernst Württemberg, Prince, 91
Erroll, Lord, 216, 223
Esher, Lord, 436, 437
Eu, Château d', 239, 241, 242–4, 250–1
Eugénie, Empress, 370; marriage, 348–349; at Windsor, 357–8; Orsini attempt on, 392

Featherstonehaugh, G. W., 283–4
Feodora of Leiningen (later Hohenlohe-Langenburg), Princess, 12, 16, 23, 24, 26, 39, 53*n*, 58, 64, 72, 102, 115, 119, 139, 157, 268; at Sidmouth, 41, 42; V's closest friend, 52, 94; childhood with V, 53, 54–5; George IV's interest in, 59–60, 69; Conroy's plans for her marriage, 60; marriage to Ernest of Hohenlohe-Langenburg, 61–2; visits England (1834), 93–4; support for Lehzen, 97; children's education, 266; Napoleon III's marriage offer to daughter, 347–8; affection for Princess Royal, 372
Ferdinand II of Portugal (Ferdinand of Saxe-Coburg), 112–14, 115, 119, 251, 280, 416
Ferdinand VII of Spain, 241–2
Ferdinand II of Two Sicilies, 286
Ferdinand of Portugal, Prince, 416
Ferguson, Dr Robert, 423
Fisher, Dr John, Bishop of Salisbury, 39, 52, 56
Fisher, Major General (son of above), 56
FitzClarence, Lord Adolphus, 125–7
FitzGerald, Hamilton, 168, 169
Fitzherbert, Mrs, 8, 12, 33
Fitzwilliam, William Wentworth, 2nd Earl, 25
Fitzwilliam, Charles Wentworth, 3rd Earl, 295
Florschütz, Herr (A's tutor), 184, 185, 187
Francis Joseph, Emperor, 300

475

478

A Note on the Type

The text of this book has been set on the Monotype in a typeface called Ehrhardt. Though the first sizes of this type were cut as recently as 1937, it is actually a revival of a seventeenth-century Leipzig face. The typeface on which Janson is based was one of the earliest to manifest the characteristics now referred to as "Modern."

Printed and bound by Halliday Lithographers
West Hanover, Mass.

Title page and binding design by
Virginia Tan